ORLANDO FURIOSO

Ludovico Ariosto

ORLANDO FURIOSO

AN ENGLISH PROSE TRANSLATION BY

Guido Waldman

OXFORD UNIVERSITY PRESS

LONDON   OXFORD   NEW YORK

1974

Oxford University Press

OXFORD LONDON NEW YORK

GLASGOW TORONTO MELBOURNE WELLINGTON

CAPE TOWN IBADAN NAIROBI DAR ES SALAAM LUSAKA ADDIS ABABA

DELHI BOMBAY CALCUTTA MADRAS KARACHI LAHORE DACCA

KUALA LUMPUR SINGAPORE HONG KONG TOKYO

Paperback edition ISBN 0 19 281161 4
Cloth edition ISBN 0 19 212576 1

© Guido Waldman 1974

*First published as an Oxford University Press paperback, and
simultaneously in a clothbound edition, by Oxford University Press,
London, 1974*

*Printed in Great Britain by
Richard Clay (The Chaucer Press), Ltd.,
Bungay, Suffolk*

CONTENTS

But in a farther age shall rise along
   The banks of Po two greater still than he;
   The world which smiled on him shall do them wrong
Till they are ashes, and repose with me.
   The first will make an epoch with his lyre,
   And fill the earth with feats of chivalry:
His fancy like a rainbow, and his fire,
   Like that of Heaven, immortal, and his thought
   Borne onward with a wing that cannot tire;
Pleasure shall, like a butterfly new caught,
   Flutter her lovely pinions o'er his theme,
   And Art itself seem into Nature wrought
By the transparency of his bright dream.

          BYRON *Prophecy of Dante*, Canto Three

        (Dante prophesies the advent after
        Petrarch of Ariosto and Tasso)

INTRODUCTION

I. Ludovico Ariosto: The Poet and his Times

Niccolò Ariosto, a lesser nobleman in the service of the Estes of Ferrara, had ten children, in the eldest of whom (born at Reggio Emilia in 1474) he tried to instil a legal training: but Ludovico found greater pleasure in reading the Classics, and after a while was permitted to follow his bent. He studied Latin and Greek under the eminent humanist Gregory of Spoleto and, had his means allowed, would have become a cultured dilettante. But his father dying in 1500, Ludovico became head of the large family and had to provide for it. He therefore entered the service of Cardinal Hippolytus, whose brother Alfonso was shortly to become the reigning duke. Ludovico was already a competent poet in Latin and Italian, but Hippolytus, who was allotted his red hat at the age of fourteen, and not as a reward for piety, took a utilitarian attitude towards his retainers. Court poets had their virtues, no doubt, but they must earn their keep by more solid services than rhyming. Ludovico, tactful by discipline if not by nature, found himself regularly employed as Hippolytus' ambassador to the Holy See, either seeking a favour for his master, or averting the papal thunders from his head—and Julius II was no lamb. On one occasion the unfortunate envoy was refused audience and threatened with being dropped into the Tiber. For a man of independent spirit and a clear eye for human follies, the tasks imposed on him were bound to grate—especially as his one ambition was to write and write: already from about 1506 he was obsessed by his nascent *Orlando Furioso*. The break came after fourteen years, in 1517, when Hippolytus was to exercise a priestly duty in Hungary and Ludovico, summoned to accompany him, refused. Travel had its charms, Ariosto conceded, but a visit to Hungary was not on his programme. Better penury at home than wealth and station in alien lands.

Alfonso d'Este, the duke, was not averse, however, to taking a good court poet into his service—especially one with a growing reputation (the first edition of *Orlando Furioso* was already published, and he was solidly established as a comic playwright). The following year, 1518, therefore found the poet in the ducal household in Ferrara. Both brothers had a regrettably hard-headed notion of a court poet's duties; occasionally the singing had to stop and serious work to be undertaken. Ludovico found himself dispatched to the Garfagnana in 1522 as

Governor of that turbulent Este domain: turbulent because its rustic mountain-folk included a good proportion of bandits, and especially because the region was disputed by Ferrara, Lucca, and Florence, each of which maintained factions there ready to second a *coup* the moment there was any threat of redrawing the borders. Ludovico, a mild man by temper, was quite prepared to be steely on his lord's behalf, only to find, as he justly complained, that if he condemned, the villains had only to go behind his back to the duke to obtain an immediate reprieve. (Machiavelli was to advise his Prince, in the homonymous work already written but not yet published, to keep in his own hands the award of favours while leaving his lieutenants to incur the odium of harsh measures.) If Alfonso constantly undermined the work of his faithful governor, on whom he enjoined the utmost tact in dealing with his rustic subjects, he was clearly satisfied with his stewardship, for it was over three years before Ludovico could obtain his recall to Ferrara.

In 1525, however, he was back, and once more able to bask in the company of countless men (and women) of wit and learning who frequented the Este court. The additional attraction at Ferrara was Alessandra Benucci, his lady-love of twelve years' standing; now a widow, she had been wife of Tito Strozzi, a Florentine merchant residing at Ferrara. The relations between the poet and his mistress appear to have been serene and idyllic throughout (veiled allusions in the *Furioso* notwithstanding); if he did not cohabit with her it was to avoid losing the financial advantage accruing to him from an ecclesiastical benefice. Only at the end of his life did he make her his wife in a secret ceremony. His two children were by other women. In 1527 he had saved enough to build himself a modest house in Ferrara (still extant) with a little garden. Here he was permitted to devote the greater part of his time to his writing, notably to polishing and repolishing his great epic. But his health was failing when he accompanied his lord to the thermal spa at Abano: he had to leave the ducal retinue to be tended for fever by a friend at Padua in 1531. Recovered enough to resume his duties, he was entrusted with a mission to the military commander of Emperor Charles V, on whose power the Estes were now relying for their defence against papal incursions. Thus did Ariosto meet Alfonso d'Avalos, Marquis of Vasto, who proved to be not only a military leader of some talent but also a great admirer of the poet, on whom he conferred an annual pension of a hundred ducats and a selection of jewellery. Furthermore, the marquis commended him warmly to the emperor and effected their introduction at Mantua in November 1532. Great rewards and honours might now have accrued to the poet, but his last illness was already upon him.

If the spiritual scepticism he shared with his age prevented him from anticipating his future life with any strong convictions, he could take comfort in the past: the *Orlando Furioso*, on which he had laboured for wellnigh half his days, was now published in its third and definitive edition; he had an accessory reputation as an accomplished versifier in Italian and Latin lyrics; he had written four comedies which were frequently performed before titled audiences (stage sets for one Roman performance of *I Suppositi* were painted by Raphael, no less); he had written seven satires in *terza rima*, and left a fair volume of correspondence. Looking back now over his opus with a dispassionate eye, it must be confessed that his comedies—copybook exercises after Terence and Plautus—afford little pleasure; his occasional verses are skilful but forgettable. His satires, however, would have been the envy of Horace and Alexander Pope: in form utterly pleasing; in content, a most engaging self-portrait of a mild yet testy court retainer constantly having to kick against the goad, and gently self-derisive at his inability to live life the way he would wish. The seven satires: portrait of the poet as a middle-aged dog.

Mourned by a large circle of friends, Ariosto died in his house at Ferrara in July 1533. His tomb is, by courtesy of a Napoleonic general, in the great civic library of Ferrara.

The world into which Ariosto was born was not one in which the mediocre could make his way. The spirit of the Renaissance, the thirst to make new discoveries and apply the spiritual zeal of the Middle Ages to the challenges of a world of time and space, produced men of abundant vitality, men of keen mind and broad vision. The princely courts of Italy, insignificant in terms of political power, possessed for a while the lion's share of cultural wealth. The great artists and humanists of Ariosto's era are too numerous to list. In the race for the prize of artistic perfection there were many contenders, for the possibilities were now seen to exist of achieving in material form the most glorious visions of the imagination. Artists, writers, philosophers, and scientists looked about them and were not shy to build each on the others' foundations if only to raise the structure of human creativity higher towards the empyrean.

In this world of the Italian Renaissance the Este court enjoyed a position of eminence. The Estes ruled over a large tract of land in the Po valley between the Apennines and the Adriatic, including the cities of Reggio, Modena, and Ferrara. The family had risen to power in the thirteenth century and they were still at their apogee, unlike many other equally venerable dynasties in the peninsula. They were constantly squeezed, though, between the rival claims of the Venetian

Republic and the Papacy, who had lands adjoining to the north and south respectively. Each Italian state of this period, in order to preserve its independence, kept making alliances and new alliances as the political winds dictated, the smaller states shifting with every lurch of their larger neighbours. Five principal powers now dominated the peninsula: Sforza Milan, the Republic of Venice, Medicean Florence, the Papal States of Central Italy, and the Aragonese Kingdom of Naples. Allured by the treasures of Italy and incited by tenuous dynastic claims, three European princes turned covetous eyes across the Alps and awaited their chance—Charles VIII of France, Maximilian of Austria, and Ferdinand of Spain. When Ariosto was twenty, Charles VIII of France, invoked by the Sforza Duke, Ludovico il Moro, against the Neapolitans, crossed the Alps and, making a clean sweep of the peninsula, entered Naples unopposed. The next year (1495) a league including Venice, the slighted Sforzas (whose game Charles had refused to play), the Spaniards, and the Austrians ushered Charles back across the Alps.

However, his successor, Louis XII, found the prospect equally pleasing and made his entrance in 1499. He took Milan from the Sforzas (giving Cremona to helpful Venice), then reached an accommodation with his chief rival, Spain, whereby Lombardy went French, Naples Spanish. Each Italian state, meanwhile, tried to harness the alien horses to its own chariot. It took the choleric Pope Julius II to consolidate an opposition to the French, forming the Holy League with Maximilian, Ferdinand, and the Venetians; the French (with the help of Este artillery) defeated the League at Ravenna, 1512, but were ushered out nonetheless. The Venetians had, not four years previously, been the Public Enemy against whom Julius had leagued these same powers plus France in the League of Cambrai; to this league the Estes, fearful of Venetian encroachments, had willingly subscribed. But now, when Julius had bidden them join the new anti-French league with Venice for ally, the Estes had nervously declined, thus drawing down papal curses.

In 1515 Francis I was on the French throne and it was his turn for an Italian adventure. The fortunes of war ebbed and flowed across the peninsula—there were few winners and many losers—until young Charles of Hapsburg acceded to many thrones: those of his grandfather Maximilian's Austro-German Empire (with the Low Countries) and of his grandfather Ferdinand's Spain (with the Two Sicilies). Surrounded by the kingdoms of Charles V which stretched from the Rhine to the toe of Italy, Francis I sought in vain for allies in Italy; only after his defeat and capture by Charles at Pavia (1525), when he secured his release only by dint of diplomacy, did he succeed in fomenting a coalition including Pope Clement VII against the Emperor. Pavia, however, had spelt the end (for a few centuries) of the French presence in Italy: two years later the Imperial troops sacked Rome without hindrance. And the Estes? Their concern was purely to defend the integrity of their territory now against the Venetians, now against the Popes: whoever helped them, whether he spoke German, French, or Spanish, was their friend. And where arms failed, diplomacy or matrimonial alliances often served. Since the Estes were to govern Ferrara until the threshold of the seventeenth century, their politics must have been as well conceived as their artistic sponsorships.

II. Orlando Furioso and its Origins

In 778, as the Emperor Charlemagne withdrew across the Pyrenees after an expedition into Spain against the Saracens, his rearguard, led by his nephew Roland, was ambushed and cut to pieces at the Pass of Roncesvalles, as a result of traitor Ganelon's machinations. Legends of Charlemagne and his twelve paladins or peers were soon current, though three centuries and more elapsed before they were first synthesized in writing in the French poem *La Chanson de Roland*, the core of which is the tragedy of Roncesvalles where the flower of French chivalry perished. The notion was already prevalent—a product to some extent of the Crusades—that Charlemagne's warriors were noble of spirit, courteous, self-effacing, generous, merciful, courageous, gallant towards women, devout followers of Christ: they embodied the ideals of Christian knighthood. Turold's epic proved to be the first of a succession of tales spun round Charlemagne and Roland. The cast of characters was gradually augmented; the legends surrounding the Duke Aymon's four sons (of which Renaud was the most famous) and their steed Bayard were gradually interwoven with those of the emperor; as time went by, the heroes of King Arthur's Round Table became involved with their Carolingian counterparts and the chivalric cycle kept widening like a ripple on a pool. A hundred years after *La Chanson de Roland*, *Renaus* gave details of Renaud's ructions with Charlemagne, while *Aspremont* explained how the emperor withstood the African King Agolant's invasion of his Calabrian domains and how young Roland (Orlando) wrought wonders and captured the sword Durendal (the Italian Durindana). The twelfth-century French poet Chrétien de Troyes highlighted the romantic atmosphere in which Tristan loved Iseult, Lancelot loved Guinevere.

Originating in France, the legends soon conquered Italy, throwing up a host of storytellers ready to secure the loose threads to their spindles and continue spinning. A bastard language deemed suitable to the material, Franco-Lombard, was devised in which to relate

Introduction

L'Entrée en Espagne and *La Prise de Pampelune*, works of the four-teenth century. Europe was now familiar with Roland's (or Orlando's) exploits in the Levant, the wiles of Ganelon (or Gano) in setting Charlemagne and his paladins at odds. Charlemagne dwindles, in-cidentally, to a figure of fun, a weak, injudicious, quick-tempered monarch always convinced of his rectitude. In the early fifteenth century *I Reali di Francia* (The Kings of France), while embroidering on the familiar characters, Christian and Pagan, gave a new prominence to Roger (Ruggiero) and the evils wrought on his parents during the African invasion of Calabria by Agolant and his sons.

By the time Luigi Pulci set quill to paper every foible of every Christian knight, every Saracen warrior was well known: each had his sword, his steed, his measure of valour, his appetite for spoils and broils; the chivalric world was replete with magic and spells, hermits and necromancers; the redoubtable Archbishop Turpin of Rheims had his place of honour as chronicler (to whom, as to the ultimate authority on the implausible, Ariosto was frequently to turn with hilarious effect). What Pulci contributed with his *Morgante Maggiore* (1482) was a sardonic, educated Tuscan wit. He was a friend of Lorenzo de' Medici and, while fully capable of sustaining a cultivated role at court, chose to write in a plebeian style, injecting a rich vein of farce into his narrative. But behind the buffoonery lay a metaphysical depth, a perception of the meaning of chivalry, which the earlier narratives lacked.

The Estes had a passion for the chivalric romances and the lost world they portrayed—the panoply of which they tried to recapture by staging jousts on gala occasions. Taking the torch from Pulci, the Este vassal Matteo Maria Boiardo, Count of Scandiano, set to work on his own synthesis. He completed two parts of his *Orlando Innamorato* but died with Part III only started, in 1494, lamenting the French in-vasion of Italy. Boiardo, slighted by posterity for having written in an unacceptably provincial Italian, is a poet of enormous charm and humour with a flair for words and an inventive mind. Writing in octaves like his predecessor Pulci, he spun several tales simultaneously. Charlemagne holds a tournament at Paris to which thousands of Christian and Saracen champions come. Among the contenders are Gradasso, King of Sericana, with an army to capture Orlando's sword Durindana and Rinaldo's steed Bayard. Among the contenders, too, is Argalia, equipped with magic weapons and four giants, and accom-panied by his sister Angelica, Princess of Cathay. The pair have been sent by their father Galafron, Emperor of Cathay, to disrupt Charle-magne's court and lure his champions away, she promising herself to the man who defeats her brother. Like bees to the honey pot the knights flock to Angelica, who hastens back to the Orient with her retinue of suitors, Christian and Pagan. Only Rinaldo resists, having drunk from a well which made him loathe her. In Cathay, Angelica is besieged at Albracca by her slighted suitor, King Agrican of Tartary, while her other suitors perform mighty feats to defend her. Orlando kills Agrican. Rinaldo, drinking from another well, falls in love with Angelica who is turned frosty by a drink at the well of hate where first he had drunk. Angelica permits Orlando to escort her back to the West, where Rinaldo and Orlando, cousins but rivals for Angelica's hand, fall out and thus permit the Saracens to defeat Charlemagne at Bordeaux. Meanwhile Ruggiero and Bradamant are in love and destined to found the Este line. These and many other ingredients, served in the gently elegiac mould of Boiardo's verse, awaited the attention of Ludovico Ariosto.

Orlando Innamorato was published in 1495, the year after the poet's death. In about 1506 Ariosto, zealous to complete what Boiardo had initiated, set to work on his poem. *Orlando Furioso* was first published in forty cantos at Ferrara in 1516, dedicated to Cardinal Hippolytus (who playfully taxed the poet with frivolity). A second, revised edition, also in forty cantos, was published in 1521 and was several times reprinted. Another eleven years of assiduous work were to go into the poem before the final definitive third edition in forty-six cantos was published in Ferrara in 1532, in the autumn before Ariosto's death. He had taken Boiardo's engaging minuet and turned it into a splendid symphony. The same characters were all there with scarcely a single new one introduced. The framework was the same: the war between Christendom and the Saracens; Angelica and her lovers; Ruggiero and Bradamant. But the half-formed characters of tradition were all of a sudden endowed with sharp identity; they could excite passion in the reader; psychological depths were suddenly disclosed, vistas of violence, wrath and glory were opened by the poet—who would then reach out, chuck his listeners under the chin, and say of his characters: 'Don't fret—they're only made of cardboard!'

Three qualities mark the *Furioso* from all its predecessors. First, the skill of the poet as narrator, who can sustain his listeners' interest through a work of Homeric proportions, and never (with one general exception) permit them a moment's boredom. Secondly, the skill of the poet as versifier: all those years of polishing have produced an artefact of supreme beauty, stanza after stanza of musical verse which is a joy to the ear as to the imagination, which faithfully mirrors every passion the poet wishes to convey; Ariosto's genius expresses itself in his octaves as Leonardo's expresses itself on canvas, a perfect harmony of mind and hand. The third quality which marks the *Furioso* from its predecessors is the informing spirit of the poet: he holds together the diverse strands of his narrative with all the confidence of a genius, and enlivens the whole with his own sharp, tender, ironic, vital personality. If any flaws are to be discovered in the work (beyond the occasional lapse in psychology and neglect of dramatic possibilities), they are already adumbrated in the difficulties he met in matching his temperament to his courtier's role. To praise the Estes was no chore, for he could be justly proud of the dynasty and unfaltering in his loyalty to it. But the task of Laureate did not suit his creative vein and it is clear that a part of him goes to sleep whenever he fulfils his duty of homage—the passages in praise of his patrons may be skipped without regret. By extension, the hero and heroine, Ruggiero and Bradamant, are built up to prominence on the strength of their destiny as founders of the Este house, whereas their own personalities are relatively uninteresting. Ariosto seems to confess as much when, in the last canto, having rounded off his portrait of Ruggiero as a paragon of the knightly ideal, he says (with what I take to be a stifled yawn) that at jousting, wrestling, dancing, all the festive games at his wedding, he bore off the prize. Certainly in the course of the poem these two paragons, Ruggiero and Bradamant, come in for some sly digs from the poet, as though he were privately thumbing his nose at his much-applauded patrons while their attention is momentarily distracted.

The virtues of the poem, whose rich medley of plots and characters it would be superfluous to sketch here, are neatly underlined by one of Europe's most lucid thinkers who was also among Ariosto's greatest admirers; Voltaire, under the heading *Epopée* in his *Dictionnaire Philosophique*, comments on the *Furioso*: 'What has especially delighted me in this prodigious work is that its author, always in command of his material, treats it with gay badinage. He effortlessly gives voice to the sublimest things only to finish them with a twist of pleasantry which is neither out of place nor recherché. It is the *Iliad* and the *Odyssey* and *Don Quixote* all rolled into one—for his principal knight errant goes mad like the Spanish hero, and is infinitely more attractive. Furthermore Orlando captures one's interest while no one is interested in Don Quixote, whom Cervantes represents simply as a fool on whom japes are constantly practised.'

III. Orlando Furioso in English

Twelve versions of the poem had appeared in France before the first English translation saw the light in 1591—the version in 'English heroical verse' by Sir John Harington. The delay did not trouble cultured Englishmen who included a knowledge of Italian among their accomplishments. Edmund Spenser wrote his *Faerie Queene* at this time with the avowed intention of surpassing Ariosto, which suggests he must have been acquainted with one of the French versions, if not with the original. Posterity may well blame Spenser for espousing the octave—had he chosen a more English structure, he might today be more widely read. As for Harington, he incurred sharp censure from a later translator, William Stuart Rose (whose labours spanned eight years to 1831). Rose dismisses Harington's version as inaccurate, mercilessly condensed, pedestrian where the original was poetic, dreary where the original was witty. Rose is not much more indulgent to those who came between: J. Hoole, the Huggins/Croker partnership, H. Bent (*Ludovico Ariosto his Mad Orlando, Englished in Octaves*), all eighteenth-century translators. Rose himself, a man of wealth, leisure and culture, enjoyed the friendship of the exiled Ugo Foscolo, an Italian poet and critic of Byronic stature (and temper), and could therefore rely on the most authoritative help in construing the Italian. He was urged to his task by Sir Walter Scott—who knew a thing or two about writing romances. Scott was a zealous admirer of Ariosto's epic, and learned Italian in order to read it in the original. He notes in his *Journal* that he succeeded in scandalizing his Professor of Greek at Edinburgh by writing an essay in which he compared Homer unfavourably with Ariosto. The good professor would doubtless have been even more upset to hear Voltaire and, later, Byron make the same comparison and draw the same conclusion!

I follow in William Stuart Rose's steps, and, in the task of appraising his work, am glad to shelter behind a remark of Sir Walter's—who was, after all, his good friend: 'Sam made us merry with an account of some part of Rose's Ariosto; proposed that the Italian should be printed on the other side for the sake of assisting the indolent reader to understand English; and complained of his using more than once the phrase of a lady having "voided her saddle".' (*Journal*, October 19th, 1826.) True, alas—except that Rose favours the noun 'sell' as often as 'saddle'. His verse is, as its predecessors', in octaves; his language is wilfully archaic, as though conceived in gothic script. Where Harington presented the English reader with a pedestrian Orlando, Rose's, if more accurate, was merely whimsical.

Now what these translators had in common was their aspiration to be poets: Ariosto wrote in octaves, so they too would write in octaves. But the *ottava rima* in the hands of a craftsman of Ariosto's technical brilliance, an *ottava rima* which now floats, spins, ripples, now sparks and crackles, now hisses like blown spume, is not the 'Englished octave' presented to the British reader. For Ariosto art is all, and Ariosto is a genius. Moreover, the octave suits the fluidity of Italian with its sharp vowel sounds; it does not suit so well the more consonantal structure of English words. To say that Rose's octaves, and Bent's and Harington's, do no justice to Ariosto's art is to express my meaning mildly. Their octaves do not convey the magic, the excitement of his sounds and rhythms. And they do not convey the shades of his meaning: Ariosto was a poet of the most delicate nuances—in a few simple strokes he could convey an observation, an inflection of feeling: omit but one of those strokes and the delicate fabric disintegrates. How could any translator show fidelity to the original when he had to lay his version on the Procrustean bed of the 'Englished octave' and accept the tyrannous demands of its rhyme and metre, lopping off here, padding out there? The English version was necessarily a paraphrase—and to compare the two finished artefacts, the Italian and the English, is enough to make one weep.

Herein lies my apology for translating the epic into prose. It takes an Ariosto to match an Ariosto on his chosen ground. But his verve as a poet was largely matched by his skill as a *narrator*, and this, the narrative, I have striven to capture faithfully and whole. I could still attempt to salvage all I was able of the music and rhythm of the original, for prose is capable of an immense range. But above all I could try with a hard, sharp pencil to trace the original text in its every subtlest twist and angle. I could try to render the meaning in its lightest shadings, and sacrifice a shade of meaning only exceptionally when the demands of the ear had to take precedence over those of the intellect; Ariosto wrote to be heard rather than to be read, and the sound of words, needless to say, matters. (This will explain, if not excuse, the occasional inconsistencies in proper names where my ear expressed a bland subjective preference; for example, Alfonso, Ercole, but Hippolytus.) Ariosto permitted himself a vocabulary occasionally stilted by the standards of normal social conversation, and I too, while aiming on the whole for acceptable current English usage, have allowed myself certain words which survive only in *belles lettres*: 'damsel', for example in preference to 'girl'—there are various instances where the old-fashioned word seems better suited to my purpose than are those which have replaced it. As a rule, however, I have tried to avoid both the archaic and the modern idiom which is liable to date.

This prose translation, the outcome of five years' loving and concentrated effort, can only be regarded as a success if it achieves its goal: to awake the public to the attractions, to the pleasures of Ariosto's poem, a sublime work whose neglect in the English-speaking world can only be explained by the absence of a translation which conveys to us the living author. Several generations of Englishmen have been introduced to Homer not by Pope, not by Chapman, but by the late

E. V. Rieu, author of the immensely popular prose translations of the *Iliad* and the *Odyssey*. May the *Orlando Furioso*, a work on the same scale of grandeur, reach a wide audience at last in these pages.

I am glad to acknowledge my gratitude to many friends who encouraged me over the years; to Carol Buckroyd, as diligent and tactful an editor as one could wish for; and above all to my beloved Lalage, typist of three hundred thousand words and staunch supporter of my conviction that the *Orlando Furioso* was fun to read and deserved resurrecting.

GUIDO WALDMAN
Islington, October 1973

PUBLISHER'S NOTE

The Annotated Index at the end of the volume, and the summaries at the start of each canto relate to the stanza-numbers of the Italian original. The stanzas may be located individually by reference to the figures at the top of each page; an oblique stroke in the printed text marks the interval between each stanza.

FIRST CANTO

*1–4 Introductory. 5–9 The background. 10–32 Angelica flees
from Rinaldo and meets Ferrau. 33–81 Angelica flees from
Rinaldo and meets Sacripant.*

I SING of knights and ladies, of love and arms, of courtly chivalry,
of courageous deeds—all from the time when the Moors crossed the
sea from Africa and wrought havoc in France. I shall tell of the anger,
the fiery rage of young Agramant their king, whose boast it was that
he would avenge himself on Charles, Emperor of Rome, for King
Trojan's death. / I shall tell of Orlando, too, setting down what has
never before been recounted in prose or rhyme: of Orlando, driven
raving mad by love—and he a man who had been always esteemed for
his great prudence—if she, who has reduced me almost to a like
condition, and even now is eroding my last fragments of sanity, leaves
me yet with sufficient to complete what I have undertaken. / Seed of
Ercole, adornment and splendour of our age, Hippolytus, great of
heart, may it please you to accept this which your lowly servant would,
and alone is able to, give you. My debt to you I can in part repay with
words, with an outlay of ink; hold me not, though, a parsimonious
giver, for all I have to give, I give you. / Among the most illustrious
heroes to whose names I am about to pay honour you will hear mention
of Ruggiero, your forefather, the founder of your noble line. I shall tell
you of his pre-eminent valour, his splendid actions, if you will pay
heed to me and make room in your mind, busied with matters of
moment, for these my verses. /

Orlando, who had long been in love with the beautiful Angelica, and
who had for her sake left countless immortal trophies in India, in
Media, in Tartary, had now returned with her to the West, to where,
at the foot of the lofty Pyrenees, King Charlemagne and the hosts of
France and Germany were assembled in their tented camp to / force
Kings Agramant and Marsilius once more to lament their rash
stupidity—the one for leading from Africa as many men as could bear
lance and sword; the other for inciting Spain to visit destruction upon
the lovely realm of France. So Orlando arrived at a good moment; but
he was quick to regret his return, / for his lady was taken from him.
Such is the waywardness of human judgement! The damsel, whom he
had defended so constantly all the way from the Hesperides to the

shores of Sunrise, was taken from him now, now that he was surrounded by friends, in his own land, with not a blow struck. It was the wise emperor, anxious to extinguish a serious fire, who took her from him. / A quarrel had arisen a few days earlier between Count Orlando and his cousin Rinaldo, for both of them were aflame with love for this ravishing beauty. Charles, who could not abide this conflict, which rendered them questionable allies, gave this damsel, the cause of the quarrel, into the keeping of Namo, Duke of Bavaria; / and promised her as a prize to whichever of the two slaughtered the greater number of Infidels and wrought him the worthiest assistance in the vital conflict of that day. The outcome, however, was not in keeping with their prayers: the ranks of the baptized were put to flight, and among the many captives was the duke, whose tent was abandoned. /

Here the damsel was left who was to have been the victor's prize; she had mounted her horse before the crucial moment and, when that came, foreseeing that Fortune was that day to turn traitor to those of the Christian faith, she turned and fled. Entering a wood and following a narrow path she came upon a knight who was approaching on foot. / He wore a breastplate, and on his head a helmet; his sword hung by his side, and on his arm he bore his shield; and he came running through the forest more fleet of foot than the lightly-clad athlete sprinting for the red mantle at the village games. Never did a timid shepherd-girl start back more violently from a horrid snake than did Angelica, jerking on the reins the moment she saw the armed man approach on foot. / The man was none other than Rinaldo, son of Aymon, lord of Montauban, and a doughty paladin, whose charger, Bayard, had only a little earlier made off without him—a strange turn of affairs. When his eyes lit on the woman, he recognized her angel's countenance, even from a distance, and the lovely face which held him in amorous thraldom. / The damsel turned her palfrey's head and galloped off through the forest at full tilt. She made no attempt to choose the best and surest path, or to avoid the thickets and the underbrush: pale and trembling and quite unstrung, she left it to her horse to find his own way through. High and low, on and on through the deep, grim forest she coursed, until she came to a river. /

On the river-bank stood Ferraù, clothed in sweat and grime: a great need to slake his thirst and to rest had withdrawn him early from the battle. But here he was now forced to tarry, for in his greedy haste to drink he had dropped his helmet into the river, and was still trying to recover it. / The damsel, screaming with terror, came galloping in headlong flight. Hearing her voice, the Saracen leapt up the bank and peered at her face. As soon as she was close he recognized her: many a day though it was since he had last had news of her, and pale and distraught though she now appeared, she could be none other than the fair Angelica. / As he was chivalrous, and no less hot-headed than the two cousins, he hastened boldly to her rescue, reckless of his lost helmet. Drawing his sword, he ran full of menace towards Rinaldo, who feared him but little: many a time had they set eyes on each other, and indeed tested each other's valour at arms. / Both of them were on foot as they flung themselves upon each other with naked sword; no armour plate, no chain-mail could have resisted the blows they delivered—enough to split an anvil. Now, while the two warriors were hewing each other, the damsel's horse had perforce to pick his way with care, for as hard as she could dig her heels she spurred him faster and faster through the woods and fields. / For a long time the·two champions strove in vain each to gain the upper hand, but neither was less skilled than the other in the use of arms.

The lord of Montauban it was who first broke silence and addressed the Spanish knight, and spoke like one whose heart is all consumed with fire. / 'You are thinking', said he to the pagan, 'that you will be doing injury to me alone, and yet you will hurt yourself as well as me: if all this is because the brilliant rays of the new Sun have set your heart afire, what do you win by delaying me here? Even if you were to take my life or capture me, the beautiful lady will not be yours for all that—see, while we tarry here, she is slipping away. / You would do far better, if you still love her, to go and stand in her path, make her stop, detain her before she goes any further. Once we have her in our keeping, then let us make trial with our swords to see whose she should be. Otherwise, after a weary struggle, I can see that we shall both be the losers.' /

The pagan was not displeased with the proposal, and so they deferred their battle; indeed, the truce so drew them together, excluding from their thoughts both hatred and anger, that as they departed from the refreshing stream, the pagan would not suffer good Aymon's son to go on foot, but pressed him to come up and mount behind him; then they galloped away after Angelica. / Great was the goodness of the knights of old! Here they were, rivals, of different faiths, and they still ached all over from the cruel and vicious blows they had dealt each other; still, off they went together in mutual trust, through the dark woods and crooked paths. Goaded by four spurs, the charger came to a fork where the road divided. / Here, not knowing which path the damsel had taken (for in both there were fresh tracks which were not to be distinguished from each other), they left the decision to Fate: Rinaldo took the one path, the Saracen the other.

Ferrau thrust further and further through the wood, and in the end found himself at the place whence he had started. / Back he was by the river's side, at the point where his helmet had fallen in. With no further hope of finding the damsel, he went down to the water's edge to recover his helmet where it lay buried in the river; but it was sunk so deep in sand that he was to have much work to do ere he set hands on it. / He had fashioned a long pole out of the branch of a tree, shorn of its foliage, and with this he searched the river bed, prodding and poking every inch of it. While he was thus passing the time with ill-contained impatience, he noticed a knight of fierce countenance emerging chest-deep from the middle of the river. / He was fully armed except for his head, and in his right hand he bore a helmet: the very helmet for which Ferrau had so long been searching in vain. He addressed Ferrau with angry words and said: 'O vile deceiver, why take you so ill the loss of your helmet when you should long ago have surrendered it to me? / Remember, pagan, when you killed Angelica's brother (I am he): you promised me that after a few days you would throw the helmet into the river, after the other arms. If Fortune now carries my wishes into effect (which you were unwilling to do), be not dismayed. Or rather, be dismayed, if you must, but at your faithlessness. / But if you still crave for a fine helmet, find yourself another one, and acquire it with greater honour. Orlando the paladin has such a one, and Rinaldo too—perhaps his is even better; the one belonged once to Almont, the other to Mambrino. Bear off one of those two with your valour, for this you would do well to leave to me, as earlier you promised.' /

When the phantom surged up out of the water, the Saracen's hair stood on end and he paled, and his voice died in his throat. Then, hearing Argalia tax him with his broken pledge (Argalia was he called, whom he had slain here), he blazed inwardly with fury, and blushed for shame. / Having no time to invent an excuse, and well knowing that the phantom spoke true, he made no answer, but kept his lips sealed; his spirit, though, was so pierced with shame that he swore on Lanfusa's life to set his heart on no helmet other than the prize one that Orlando had wrested once from proud Almont's head in Aspromont. / This oath he observed more faithfully than that which he had earlier sworn. He set off, then, in such a bitter mood that many days later he still fretted and fumed. His only thought was to seek out the paladin, searching wherever he thought he might be. Rinaldo, following another route from Ferrau's, encountered different adventures. / He had not gone far before his fiery charger leapt into view. 'Stop, Bayard, oh stop! I cannot endure to be without you.' Deaf to his words, the steed would not approach, but drew away from him, faster and faster. Rinaldo followed, consumed with anger. But let us pursue Angelica in her flight. /

Through fearful dark woods she fled, through wild, desolate and deserted places. The stirring of a branch, of a green leaf of oak, elm or beech would make her swerve in fright; at each shadow she espied, whether by hill or dale, she imagined that Rinaldo was still close behind her. / Like a baby fawn or kid, who has watched through the leaves of the wood where he was born, and has seen the leopard's fangs close on his mother's throat, seen her flank and breast torn open; he flees through the thickets to escape the monster, trembling with terror and alarm; and every time he brushes against a twig he sees himself already in the cruel beast's jaws. / That day and night, and half the next day onward she pressed, and knew not whither. At last she came to a pleasant grove whose trees gently rustled in a delicious breeze; two limpid brooks murmured close by so that the grass was ever fresh and tender; the quiet waters, breaking as they flowed softly over the little pebbles, sounded musically. / Here she felt safe, and a thousand miles from Rinaldo, and she decided to rest a little from her weary journey and the summer's heat. She stepped down amid the flowers and, unbridling her horse, let him wander away to graze by the crystal waters whose verges were fresh with new grass. / Close by she noticed a beautiful thicket of flowering hawthorn and red roses mirrored in the limpid rippling water and sheltered from the sun by tall shady oaks. It was hollowed in the middle and offered a refreshing bower amid the deepest shade: the branches and leaves were so disposed that no sun—nor indeed any lesser observer—could peep in. / Soft young grass made an inviting bed for whoever ventured here. The lovely damsel stepped into the bower, lay down, and fell asleep. Not for long, however, for she thought she heard the trample of approaching feet. Silently she arose, and espied an armoured knight who had come to the water's edge. /

Whether he be friend or foe she could not tell; her doubting heart was assailed by hope and fear; as she waited to see how it would turn out, not so much as a sigh did she permit to escape her lips. The knight sat down on the bank of the stream and rested his cheek on his arm; so deeply did he lapse into thought that he might have been turned to unfeeling stone. / More than an hour, my Lord, the sorrowing knight sat, his head bowed in thought. Then he began to lament, a mournful, weary sound, and yet so sweet that out of compassion the very rocks would have split, and a cruel tigress would have turned gentle.

He sighed and wept; tears streamed down his cheeks. His heart was a furnace. / He spoke: 'You, thought, who set my heart afire and turn it to ice, and cause the pain which ever gnaws within me, what am I to do? For I have been late in coming, and another has been first to cull the fruit. Little has fallen to me but words and looks while another has gathered the best of the crop. If I am to be denied both fruit and blossom, why does my heart keep aching for her? / A virgin is like a rose: while she remains on the thorn whence she sprang, alone and safe in a lovely garden, no flock, no shepherd approaches. The gentle breeze and the dewy dawn, water, and earth pay her homage; amorous youths and loving maidens like to deck their brows with her, and their breasts. / But no sooner is she plucked from her mother-stalk, severed from her green stem, than she loses all, all the favour, grace, and beauty wherewith heaven and men endowed her. The virgin who suffers one to cull her flower—of which she should be more jealous than of her own fair eyes, than of her life—loses the esteem she once enjoyed in the hearts of all her other wooers. / Let her be abhorred by those others, and loved only by him to whom she gave herself so abundantly. O cruel enemy, Fortune! The others triumph and I die of need. What then: am I to find her no longer pleasing? Am I to relinquish my own heart's life? Ah, let this day be my last, let me live no longer if I am no longer to love her.' /

Should anyone ask me who it is who was shedding such copious tears into the brook, well, he was the King of Circassia, the love-lorn Sacripant. Love, let me add, was the prime and only cause for his cruel sorrow: he was, indeed, one of the lovers of this damsel, who at once recognized him. / For love of her he had come out of the East to where the sun sets, for in India he had learned, to his great sorrow, that she had followed Orlando to the West; then in France he had learned how the emperor had set her apart, promising her as the prize to whichever of the two yielded greater assistance to the Golden Lilies. / He had been in the field of battle, had witnessed the rout of King Charlemagne. He had gone in search of fair Angelica, but so far he had been unable to find her. This, then, was the sad tale, this the plight which weighed so heavy on his love-lorn heart, provoking his grief to utterance in words which might have made even the sun pause for pity./

While he was thus lamenting and shedding hot tears in copious streams, and uttering these words and many more which I think I need not relate, by a fortunate turn in his affairs, his words came to the ears of Angelica; and so in one hour he reached a point which otherwise he would never have reached, not in a thousand years. / The lovely woman paid the closest attention to the tears, the speech and behaviour of this man who was so assiduous a lover, even though this was not the first time she had heard him. Hard, though, and cold as a stone pillar, she would not stoop to pity: it would seem she disdained all human kind, and believed that no man was worthy of her. / And yet, seeing herself all alone amid those woods, she conceived the idea of taking him as a guide—for when the water is up to your neck you must be truly stubborn not to cry for help. If she let this occasion slip she would never again find so trusty an escort: she had already long experience of the king's rare fidelity in love. / She had no mind, however, to alleviate the misery which rent her lover, or to heal the wounds he had suffered by affording him the pleasure which all lovers crave. No, she would spin a tale, devise a subterfuge to maintain him in hope for so long as she had need of him; afterwards, she would revert to her accustomed hardness. /

Forth she stepped from the blind concealment of the thicket, and made so radiant and unlooked-for an appearance, she might have been Diana, or Venus issuing forth from a shady grove. Emerging, she said: 'Peace be with you. God protect you and my good name: pray, do not entertain so false an opinion of me—it goes against all reason.' / Never was such joy, such amazement to be seen in a mother's eyes when she lifted them to look on her son whom she had bewailed and lamented for dead as she heard the troops return without him: such, though, was the Saracen's joy, such his wonder on suddenly beholding her angel's face, her graceful movements, her overwhelming presence. / Brimful of gentle, loving thoughts he ran to his lady, his goddess, who threw her arms tightly about his neck—which she would perhaps not have done in her native Cathay. Now that she had his company, her thoughts turned to her father's kingdom, the cradle of her birth; hope suddenly revived in her of soon regaining her precious home. / She told him all that had befallen her since the day when she had sent him to the King of the Nabateans of Sericana to ask for help; and how Orlando had frequently saved her from death and outrage and all manner of evils; and how her virginal flower was still as intact as the day she had borne it from her mother's womb. / This may have been true, but scarcely plausible to anyone in his right mind; to him it seemed quite possible, however, lost as he was in a far deeper delusion. What a man sees, Love can make invisible—and what is invisible, that can Love make him see. This, then, was believed, for a poor wretch will readily believe whatever suits him. / 'If the knight of Anglant was so stupid as to neglect his opportunity, so much the worse for him: never again will Fortune offer him so rare a gift,' remarked Sacripant to himself. 'Far be it from me to imitate him, foregoing the offer of so great a good and then having only myself to blame. / I shall pluck the morning-fresh rose which I might lose were I to delay. Full well I know that there is nothing that a woman finds so delectable and pleasing, even when she pretends to resent it and will sometimes burst into tears. I shall not be put off by any repulse or show of anger, but shall carry into effect what I propose.' /

Thus spoke he. But while he was preparing for his gentle assault, a terrible din from the wood close by resounded in his ears, so that he regretfully had to give up his enterprise, and put on his helmet—for it was his habit to go about fully armed. He approached his charger, bridled him, climbed into the saddle and grasped his lance. / Out of the wood a knight appeared. Stalwart and proud was his mien. His raiment was white as snow, and a white plume crested his helmet. King Sacripant could not endure this importunate fellow's arrival, just in time to interfere with the pleasure which lay in store, and the look he darted at him was fraught with menace. / When the other drew near he challenged him to battle, confident that he would sweep him from the saddle. But the other, who did not deem himself a jot inferior, and was ready to prove it, cut short his haughty threats, setting spurs to his steed and lowering his lance. Sacripant was off, too, like a hurricane, and they charged straight at each other. / No lions in the tall scrub, no bulls charging each other full tilt ever met with the impact of those two knights: each ran his lance through the other's shield. The clash reverberated all about, from the grassy valleys even to the summits of the barren hills. Lucky it was that the warriors wore good, sound breastplates, for these defended their chests. / Neither steed swerved from his course, indeed they butted each other head on, like rams. The pagan warrior's died almost instantly; alive, he had proved himself a champion. The other's fell also, but no sooner did he feel the prick of the spurs in his side than he rose to his feet. But the horse of the Saracen king lay inert, his full weight resting upon his master. /

The unknown champion, who had remained in the saddle and seen the other overthrown, horse and rider, decided he had had enough of this skirmish and felt no need to carry it further. So he pulled away and rode off at a fast gallop along the path which ran straight through the forest; and before the pagan had extricated himself, the other was little short of a mile away. / Just as a ploughman, dazed and stunned, gets up when the lightning has passed, from where the shattering thunderburst has thrown him down beside his dead oxen; he gets up and beholds the pine standing bereft of its leaves and of its dignity, the very pine he was accustomed to see in the distance. So it was with the pagan when he regained his feet. Angelica had been witness of this dire event. / He sighed and groaned, not because his arm or foot may have been broken or sprained, but simply for shame: never in his life, before or since, was his face so red. This was not only because of his fall, but all the more so in that his lady it was who had pulled the heavy weight off him. He would have remained dumb, I am convinced, were it not that she restored him to speech. / 'Alas, good sir, take it not so hardly,' she said, 'for it was no fault of yours if you fell, but rather of the horse, who was less prepared for another fray than for rest and nourishment. Nor will this have added a jot to that warrior's glory, for he was quite clearly the loser: this is how I construe it, inasmuch as he was the first to leave the field.' /

While she was thus consoling the Saracen, who should arrive at a gallop but a messenger, mounted on a palfrey; he carried his horn and his pouch at his side, and looked tired and dispirited. When he drew near to Sacripant he asked him whether he had seen a warrior come this way through the forest, with a white shield and crested with a white plume. / 'As you see, he has overthrown me, and has only just departed,' replied Sacripant. 'Now tell me his name, so that I may know who it was who unseated me.' 'On that point', said the other, 'I can satisfy you at once. You must know that the rare valour which swept you from the saddle was that of a gentle damsel. / She is brave, but, more than that, she is beautiful. Her name is famous and I shall keep it from you no longer: it is Bradamant who has stripped you of all the honours you have won hitherto.'

With these words he galloped off, leaving the Saracen far from pleased: he knew not what to do or say, and blushed crimson with shame. / After long and useless reflection on what had taken place, coming back always to his defeat by a woman—the more he thought about it, the more it hurt—he mounted the other horse without a word; and without a word he drew Angelica up behind him, and reserved her for happier entertainment in more tranquil surroundings. /

They had not gone two miles when a terrific noise filled the forest all about and seemed to send a shiver through it from end to end. Shortly after, a great war-horse came into view, richly caparisoned in cloth-of-gold; he came bounding over streams, over briars, and splintered trees and whatever else stood in his path. / 'If the deep shade and the thickly meshed foliage do not impair my vision,' said the damsel, 'this charger forcing his boisterous passage through the choked wood is Bayard. Yes, this is certainly Bayard, I recognize him. Ah, how well he understands our need: one palfrey is quite unsuited to carry the two of us, and he is coming quickly to our assistance.' / The Circassian dismounted and approached the horse, meaning to grasp his reins. But the charger pivoted round quick as a flash and presented his hind-quarters; he did not reach the point, though, of unleashing a kick. A sad knight he would have been, had he been struck full on, for the horse had such power in his heels, he could have shattered a whole mountain of metal. / Then he meekly approached the damsel; he was almost human in his gesture of humility, like a dog dancing around his master who has just returned after a few days' absence. Bayard still remembered her, for she had tended him in Albracca in the days when she was so enamoured of Rinaldo, who was so cruel to her then, so unresponding to her love. / She took his reins in her left hand, and

9

with the other hand she caressed his neck and chest. The horse, who was of remarkable intelligence, submitted to her as meekly as a lamb. Sacripant meanwhile seized his opportunity: he mounted Bayard and spurred him and reined him in. Now that her own steed was lightened of his burden, the damsel moved from his hindquarters and resumed her place in the saddle. /

She happened then to look round, and her eyes fell upon a man of imposing stature advancing on foot, with much clanking of armour. She flared up with anger and vexation, for she recognized him as Rinaldo, Duke Aymon's son. He loved her, coveted her more than his life, but she loathed and avoided him, as a crane will flee from a falcon. Once upon a time it was he who hated her worse than death, while she loved him; now they had changed roles. / And the cause was to be found in two springs in the Ardennes, not far apart, whose waters produce diverging effects: the one inclines the heart to love, whereas love loses place in the heart of whoever drinks from the other; what first is fire turns to ice. Rinaldo had tasted the one, and love held him in thrall: Angelica the other, and she hated and shunned him. / The effect of that liquid blended with secret venom, transforming love into loathing, was to cast a pall over the damsel's limpid eyes the moment she had set them upon Rinaldo. With tremulous voice and anxious face she begged and entreated Sacripant not to wait for the warrior to approach any nearer, but to turn with her and flee. /

'Am I,' replied the Saracen, 'am I held in so little esteem by you, that you reckon me of no use, of no avail to defend you against him? Have you already forgotten the battles at Albracca, and the night when I alone stood as your shield and refuge against Agrican and all his men?' / She made no answer, and knew not what to do, for Rinaldo was now too close at hand: he arrived threatening the Saracen from a distance once he saw and recognized the horse, and recognized the angel-face which had kindled a furnace in his heart. What passed between these two champions I mean to defer to the next canto.

SECOND CANTO

*1–2 Introductory. 3–23 Rinaldo pursues Angelica. 24–30
Rinaldo sails for England. 30–62 Pinabello tells Bradamant of
the enchanted castle. 62–76 Pinabello plots against
Bradamant.*

LOVE, what makes you so unjust? Why can you never take heed of
our own desires? Whence comes it, treacherous Love, that you so
enjoy the sight of two hearts ill-assorted? Not for me the crossing
where the water is quiet and limpid: you needs must draw me in where
it is deep and murky. You call me away from any who would crave
my love, while she who hates me, she it is to whom you would have
me give my heart. / You make Angelica beautiful in Rinaldo's eyes
while she sees him as ugly and loathsome; when she it was who had
pined for him and seen in him the handsomest of men, he found her
frankly unendurable. Now he suffers agonies for her, but to no avail:
the old disparity has been reversed. She loathes him, and such is her
loathing that she would choose even death in preference to him. /

'Thief, get off my horse!' Rinaldo curtly commanded the Saracen.
'It is not my custom to allow what is mine to be taken from me: he
who wants it must pay, and I see to it that he pays dearly. The damsel
too—release her: to leave her to you would be a great mistake. It
seems to me ill fitting that so superb a charger and so noble a lady should
fall to the share of a thief.' / 'Call me a thief and you speak falsely,'
replied the Saracen no less haughtily. 'From what I hear, though, the
word could with some truth be applied to you. Which of the two of us
is more worthy of the lady and of the steed we shall presently discover.
As to the lady, I agree with what you have said: she is incomparable.' /

As two ferocious hounds, stung to rage by jealousy or other cause,
will approach each other baring their teeth, while their eyes light up
balefully, redder than hot coals; and they set to snapping at each other
savagely, bristling and snarling. Thus were Sacripant and Rinaldo
when, finished with hurling insults, they snatched out their swords. /
The one was on foot, the other mounted; what an advantage for the
Saracen, you will say. But no, he had none: mounted, he fared no
better than some novice page, for the horse instinctively avoided doing
any hurt to his master. With wrist and spur the Saracen might strive,
but the steed would move not a step to his bidding. / When he wanted

to urge him forward, the horse stood fast; if he would rein him in, he broke away at a trot or a canter; then he dropped his head and bucked violently, lashing out with his hind legs. Realizing that this was not the moment to tame the defiant beast, the Saracen grasped the pommel, stood up, and from the left side jumped to the ground. / Once the pagan had by a nimble leap severed his ties with Bayard and his rabid obstinacy, battle was engaged worthy of two knights as robust as these. Sword rang against sword, high and low: Vulcan's hammer rang not so brisk in the smoky cavern where he shaped Jove's thunderbolts on his anvil. / With full-bodied slashes at one moment, with feints and subtle jabs the next, they showed their mastery at this exercise. One moment you would see them towering, crouching the next; now shielded, now offering some opening; first looming up, then receding, parrying blows and often giving way before them; circling each other, and each stepping forward the moment his opponent had withdrawn his foot. /

But see how Rinaldo raised his sword high over Sacripant and brought it down with all his weight behind it. The other held out his shield, of bone laminated with good, tempered steel. It was stout enough, but Fusberta cleaved it apart. The whole forest groaned and echoed from the blow; steel and bone splintered like a slab of ice, and the Saracen was left with one arm benumbed. /

When the timorous damsel witnessed this savage blow and the havoc it wrought, her lovely face paled with fear, like that of a convict approaching the scaffold. There was, she decided, no time to lose if she was to avoid falling prey to Rinaldo, whom she detested as much as he, poor hapless man, loved her. / She turned her horse and plunged down a narrow rugged path into the thick of the forest, frequently casting terrified glances over her shoulder as she imagined Rinaldo hard behind her.

She had not gone far before she came upon a hermit in a valley; he had a long beard coming half-way down his chest and he looked devout and venerable. / Enfeebled by years and by fasting, he was approaching mounted on a donkey; he looked a man of the tenderest, most delicate conscience. When he set eyes on the exquisite face of the damsel who was drawing near, flabby and bloodless though he was, he felt in himself the stirrings of charity. / The damsel asked the good friar which way led to a sea-port, for she wished to leave France so as not to hear further mention of Rinaldo. The friar, skilled in the black arts, assiduously comforted the damsel, assuring her that in no time he would rescue her from danger; and he delved in one of his pockets. / Out he drew a book, and not without effect, for he had not finished reading the first page when he had conjured forth a spirit in the shape of a servant, to whom he enjoined his bidding. The servant, bound to obedience by the written words, betook himself to where the two knights confronted each other in the wood—and they were not relaxing. Boldly he stepped in between them. /

'Craving your pardon,' said he, 'could one of you please explain to me what you stand to gain even if you do slay the other? What benefit will accrue to your labours, when you have concluded your battle, if Count Orlando, without a blow struck, without so much as snapping a ring of his chain-mail, is on his way to Paris with the lady who has induced you to this dire affray? / I came upon Orlando a mile from here, on his way to Paris with Angelica; they were both laughing at you and at the way you are locked in so futile a battle. Perhaps your best plan would be to follow their traces now, while they are still close by; for if Orlando takes her to Paris, there will be no recovering her.' /

You should have seen how those knights were affected by the news, how stunned they were, and heart-struck, and cursed themselves for men without sight nor sense, for their rival had so abused them. But good Rinaldo stumbled away to his horse, sighing like a furnace, and swearing in his rage that if he caught Orlando he would tear out his heart. / He crossed to where Bayard stood waiting, leapt onto him and galloped away without even bidding farewell to the knight left standing in the glade, let alone inviting him to mount behind. Spurred on by his master, the fiery steed felled and splintered whatever stood in his path; no ditch or stream, no rock or briar could deflect the charger from his way. /

You must not be surprised, my Lord, if Rinaldo now remounted his horse with such ease after having pursued him in vain for several days without once being able to set hands on the reins. The horse had a human intelligence, and it was not out of malice that he led his master such a chase, but in order to lead him in pursuit of his lady whom he had heard so ardently invoked. / When she fled from the tent, the goodly steed saw her and marked her going; he happened to be light of saddle, for his rider had dismounted in order to engage in battle on an equal footing with a baron who was no less hardy a fighter than he. So the horse followed the damsel at a distance, anxious to deliver her into his master's keeping. / Anxious to lure him after her, he kept going before him through the great forest, never once permitting his master to mount, for fear that he would turn him away down some other path. Twice did he bring Rinaldo to where the damsel was, but all to no avail, for Ferrau interposed on the first occasion, and on the second, Sacripant, as you have heard. / Now, Bayard too had accepted the word of the spirit who had indicated to Rinaldo the false trail, so he answered readily to his master's commands. Afire with rage and love,

Rinaldo rode him full tilt towards Paris, his desires so outstripping him that not even the wind, let alone a charger, could keep up with them. /

Night brought only a slight interruption to his headlong rush to confront Orlando, lord of Anglant, such was the trust he had placed in the empty words of the canny magician's envoy. Morning and evening he rode until he saw before him the place whither King Charlemagne had withdrawn, broken and disarrayed, with the remnants of his army. / Expecting to be attacked and blockaded by the King of Africa, he was taking every care to bring in supplies and fresh troops, to dig trenches and repair battlements. He gathered in without delay whatever might prove useful for defence, and he planned to send to England for men to draft into a new army. / For he meant to sally forth and try again his fortunes in battle. Straightway he dispatched Rinaldo to Britain—or England, as it was later called. The paladin resented having to make this journey, not that he held anything against the country, but inasmuch as Charlemagne chose that moment to send him, without conceding him even one day's respite. /

Never had Rinaldo assumed a task more unwillingly, for it prevented his searching for the serene and lovely face which had stolen his heart from out of his breast. But, in obedience to the king, he set off without more ado and a few hours later he was at Calais; here he took ship the same day. / Such was his anxiety to make a quick return that, regardless of every boatman's wishes, he put forth when the sea was grim and hostile and showed signs of turning stormy. The Wind, irked at finding himself so little respected by the haughty knight, piled up the sea into a wicked tempest, and lashed it so furiously as to send its spray surging even to the crow's nest. / The wary mariners made haste to lower the mainsail and determined to put about and make for the harbour whence they had so untimely set sail. 'Not so,' said the Wind, 'for I'll not endure the licence you have taken;' and he blew, and he howled, and threatened shipwreck were they to set their course elsewhere than whither he drove them. / The cruel Wind took them by the stern, then by the bows, never abating, but rather increasing in violence. Hither and thither they drifted, sails reefed in, and scoured the open seas.

But as I have need of a number of warps and a variety of threads if I am to complete the whole of my tapestry, I shall leave Rinaldo and his pitching prow and return to the tale of his sister Bradamant. / I mean that remarkable maiden who swept King Sacripant to the ground; she was a worthy sister to the paladin, born of the same parents—Duke Aymon, that is, and Beatrice his wife. Her great strength and courage made her as popular with Charles and all the French as did the much-applauded valour of Rinaldo (and many, indeed, had been the occasions for comparison). / The lady was beloved by a knight who had crossed the sea from Africa with King Agramant; this knight, the seed of Ruggiero, was born of Agolant's luckless daughter. And the lady? She did not scorn such a lover, for she had not been bred from a bear or a savage lion. Fate, though, had denied them all but one occasion to see and to speak to each other. /

Bradamant, then, was riding in search of her lover, whose name was Ruggiero like his father's; she rode without companions, as self-assured as if she had a body-guard of a thousand squadrons. After knocking the Circassian king flat onto the face of Mother Earth, she traversed a wood and, beyond the wood, a hill, thus arriving at a pleasant spring. / The spring discoursed in a meadow decked with ancient trees and lovely shadows, and, murmuring, invited wayfarers to quench their thirst and tarry beside it. To the left a hillock, neatly tilled, afforded shelter from the noonday heat. Here, turning her eyes, the lady noticed the presence of a knight, / a knight who was sitting silent, pensive and alone in the shade of a thicket, on the bank—all green and yellow, white, and red—overlooking the limpid, crystal spring. His shield hung close by, and his helmet, from a beech-tree to which his horse was tethered; his eyes were downcast and tear-softened, and he looked weary and sorrowing. / The desire people commonly feel to enquire into other people's affairs led the damsel to ask the knight the reason for his sorrow.

Encouraged by the gentleness of her speech and by her noble mien, which at first glance suggested that of a gallant warrior, he made no secret of his sadness. /

And 'Sir,' he began, 'I was leading a troop of foot-soldiers and horse into the field where Charles was waiting for Marsilius, meaning to bar his way as he moved down from the mountains. With me I had a beautiful lady for love of whom my heart is aflame; and near Rodonna I came upon an armed man reining in a great winged steed. / No sooner had the thief—a mortal, or one of Hell's dread angels, I know not—no sooner had he seen my beloved than like a falcon dropping on his prey he was down and away in an instant, reaching out and grasping her as he went. Even before I was awake to the plight of my beloved, I heard her shrieks high above me. / Thus the rapacious kite will carry off a luckless chick from its mother's side, and she too late laments her inattention, and in vain runs crying and clucking after it. I could not pursue a man on the wing, shut in as I was amid hills, confined at the base of a steep crag; my horse was weary and could scarcely set one foot before the other down the rugged, arduous tracks strewn with boulders. / Now, as I would have cared less had I seen my heart ripped out of my breast, I left my men to continue their way without me, indeed without anyone to lead them. I set off as Love directed me, up through the craggy heights and where the ground rose less steeply, bending my steps to where I thought that harpy might have carried my peace, my consolation. /

'For six days I travelled, morning and evening, amid weird jagged crags and outcrops, with never a beaten path nor any sign of human traces. Then I came to a stark, grim valley hemmed in with cliffs and horrid caves and in the middle, on a rock, there rose a mighty castle, well seated and of remarkable beauty. / From a distance it seemed to blaze like fire, as though it were not built of brick nor of dressed stone; and as I drew closer to its shining walls, so did the castle appear more wonderful and splendid. Later I learned how industrious demons, evoked in the burning of incense and in magical incantations, had ringed the beautiful place in a wall of steel tempered in Hades' fires and in the waters of Styx. / Each tower gleams with this burnished metal which is proof against rust and stain. Day and night the guilty thief scours the country round, then to withdraw into his keep. Nothing that he covets can be protected from him—only vain curses and shrieks pursue him. Here it is that he is holding my lady, my very heart, and I may not hope to rescue her, never. /

'Alas, what can I do but look from afar at the keep in which my treasure is shut, like a fox who can hear his young one cry out from the eagle's nest, and circles beneath it, knowing not what to do, for he has no wings to fly up to it? Such is the castle, and so steep its crag that none can ascend to it unless he be a bird. /

'While I still tarried there, along came two knights with a dwarf to guide them, and they endued my desire with hope—but soon both desire and hope proved unavailing. Both were warriors of eminent valour: one was Gradasso, King of Sericana; the other, Ruggiero, a sturdy youth of highest standing in the African court. / "They have come", the dwarf explained, "to match their prowess against the lord of this castle who rides armed on the four-footed bird—a strange and remarkable feat." "Kind sirs," I begged of them, "take pity on me for the cruel and evil case which has befallen me! Should you be the victors, as I hope, please restore my lady to me." / And, weeping for sorrow, I told them how she had been taken from me.

'They showed kindness and offered me encouragement; then they descended the treacherous rocky slope. From a distance I watched the battle, praying God for their victory. Beneath the castle there was a stretch of plain as broad as could be spanned in two stone's throws. / As soon as they came to the foot of the high fortress, each of them wished to be the first into the fray; Gradasso it was who prevailed, whether by the drawing of lots, or because the precedence mattered less to Ruggiero. Gradasso set his horn to his lips; the rock re-echoed, and the castle which crowned it. Forth from the gate stepped the horseman; armed he was, and mounted on the winged steed. / Little by little it began to rise, like the migrant stork which starts by running, and then can be seen rising just a yard or two off the ground—and once its wings are fully spread it vigorously beats the air with them. To such a height did the magician wing his way that an eagle would scarcely reach so high. / Came the moment when he turned his steed, which folded its wings and hurtled downwards like a plummet, as a hunting falcon drops from the sky at the sight of a mallard rising, or a pigeon. Settling his lance, the rider cleaved the air which roared fearfully by; hardly was Gradasso aware of his descent than he felt the winged rider upon him, and the blow of his lance. /

'The magician broke his lance upon Gradasso, who struck at the wind and the empty air. The flying horse continued to beat his wings, however, and soared away, but the impact had knocked Gradasso's trusty steed onto his haunches on the green grass—and Gradasso was mounted on the best and most handsome charger that ever bore a saddle. / The flyer soared up to the stars, then turned and swooped again to earth, and struck Ruggiero all unsuspecting, Ruggiero whose mind was all intent upon Gradasso. Ruggiero winced at the heavy blow, and his horse recoiled several steps. But when he turned to strike back, he saw his enemy already far away, climbing the heavens. / Now he struck Gradasso, now Ruggiero, fetching blows at their heads, their chests, and backs; their own blows he avoided every time, for he is so swift he is well-nigh invisible. He sailed round in lazy circles, feinted at one, assaulted the other, and so bedazzled both of them that never could they descry whence he was coming. / The battle between the two earthbound and the one aerial warrior lasted until the hour which draws a dark veil over the earth and robs all things beautiful of their colour.

'It was as I say: not a jot have I added; I saw it, I know it, and even now have I scarcely the assurance to tell this to another, for this next wonder looks much more akin to falsehood than to truth. / The aerial horseman had covered the shield he bore on his arm with a fine silken cloth. Why he had suffered it to remain so long concealed in this cover, I have no idea; for the moment he displayed it openly, whoever looked upon it was dazzled perforce, and fell down as a slumped corpse. Then he was in the magician's power. / The shield flashed like a sparkling gem, more radiant by far than any other light. Such was its brightness, one could not but fall down blinded and senseless. Even at my distance, I too lost my senses and lay for a long while before I recovered them; and I saw no more sign of the warriors, nor of the dwarf—the field was deserted, the crag and the plain darkened. / I thought therefore that the sorcerer had caught them both at once and used his radiance to deprive them of their liberty, me of my hope. So with a last farewell I left that place where my heart was entrapped. Now judge you whether there is any sorrow caused by dire Love which can equal mine.' /

The knight lapsed once more into his doleful brooding now that he had explained the reason for it. He was Count Pinabello, son of Anselm of Altaripa, of the Maganza clan. Not for him, when all his tribe were evil, to stand out for fair-play and courtesy: no, he more than matched them in foul and ugly deeds—he overreached them all. / The beautiful lady listened in silence to the knight of Maganza, while her face constantly changed, for at the first mention of Ruggiero she lit up with gladness, but once she heard that he was held a prisoner she was overcome with tender compassion; many and many a time did she have the knight go back over his words. /

When at last the story seemed all clear in her mind, 'Take heart, sir,' she said, 'my coming may prove welcome to you, and this day a fortunate one. Let us go straightway to that hoarder's den, which conceals from us treasures so rich. Our efforts shall not have been wasted if Fate is not too unkind to me.' /

'You would have me return over the mountains, would you?' answered the knight, 'and show you the way? To lose so much labour matters little to me, having lost all else; but you, you are seeking to make your way over crags and shifting scree only to end a prisoner. So be it. You must hold me blameless, for I have warned you, and still you want to go thither.' / With these words he went to his horse and assumed the role of guide to the intrepid damsel who for Ruggiero's sake would run the risk of falling into the magician's hands and of being slain by him.

But who should come hastening up behind them at this point but a messenger, crying 'Stop! Stop!' with all his might; he was the very messenger from whom Sacripant learned who it was who had thrown him prostrate. / To Bradamant the messenger brought tidings that Montpellier and Narbonne had surrendered, raising the standards of Saracen Castille, and so too the entire coast of Aiguesmortes. Those of Marseilles were in distress for lack of her, she being the one appointed to protect them; their citizens had sent this courier to commend themselves to her and to entreat her aid and counsel. / This city, along with a great tract of coast stretching from the Var to the Rhône, was a gift from the emperor to Duke Aymon's daughter, in whom he placed both confidence and hope, for many a time had he beheld with wonder the prowess she displayed in the use of arms. As I say, then, this courier had arrived from Marseilles to seek her help. /

Bradamant was in two minds whether to return or not; she was pulled one way by her sense of honour and duty, and the other by the promptings of love's passion. Finally she decided to pursue what she had undertaken and deliver Ruggiero from the enchanted castle: should this prove beyond her powers, at least she would remain a prisoner in his company. / She made her excuse to such effect that the messenger seemed satisfied with it and remained silent. Then she turned her horse's head to make her journey with Pinabello, who now looked far from pleased, for he realized that she was of the family which in secret, and indeed openly, he detested, and he could imagine what would be in store for him were she to discover that he was one of the Maganzas. /

Between the houses of Maganza and Clairmont bitter hatred had long prevailed, and many times had they cracked each other's skulls and shed each other's blood most copiously. The wicked count secretly mused, therefore, on how to betray the imprudent damsel, or how, at the first convenient opportunity, to abandon her and take a different path. / His inbred hatred, his fear, and perplexity so filled his mind that unwittingly he took the wrong turning and found himself in a dark wood; in the middle of it there was an outcrop rising to a bare granite peak.

Duke Aymon's daughter kept steadily behind him and never abandoned him. / Finding himself in the wood, Pinabello thought about shaking free of the damsel. He said to her, 'Before it grows any darker it would be better for us to make our way to some dwelling. Down in the valley beyond that hill, if I recognize it aright, there is a stately castle. Wait for me here; I want to climb up to that bare peak to see for myself.' / So saying, he spurred his horse up to the summit of the lone hill, keeping an eye open for some way to shake her off his tracks. Now in the hillside he came upon a deep cleft dropping some hundred feet. Steps had been cut vertically into its side and at the bottom there was a door. / Yes, at the bottom a great wide door gave access to a more spacious chamber, from which a light shone, as though from a torch burning in the heart of the mountain cave. While the villain paused here in silence the damsel, who had followed him at a distance (for fear of losing him), came upon him at the cavern. /

Seeing his first plan come to nothing—that of losing her or of making away with her—the treacherous man lit upon a new and original approach. He went to meet her and brought her up as far as the cleft which hollowed the mountain; and he told her that he had seen at the bottom of it a damsel of gracious countenance / who must have been of no mean station to judge by her beauty and by the richness of her attire; sad was her look, though, and distressed beyond endurance, as though she were imprisoned there against her will. To learn something of her situation he had started his descent into the cleft when a man had come out from the inner chamber and driven her savagely in. / Courageous but imprudent, Bradamant accepted Pinabello's story, and in her anxiety to bring help to the maiden, she cast about for some way to get down to her. She looked round and her eyes lit upon the long branch of an elm tree in full leaf. With her sword she severed it, and lowered it into the chasm. / The severed end she entrusted to the hands of Pinabello; then, grasping it herself, she lowered her feet into the chasm and suspended herself from the branch. Pinabello smiled, and asked her how well she jumped; then he opened his hands, saying: 'Would that all your lot were with you here—thus could I put an end to the whole tribe of you.' /

The innocent damsel's fate, however, was not as Pinabello wished, for as she tumbled from rock to rock, not she but the good stout branch was the first to hit the bottom. There it snapped, but after affording her enough support to save her from death. She lay stunned awhile, as I shall go on to tell you in the next canto.

THIRD CANTO

1–4 Introductory. 4–19 Bradamant at Merlin's tomb. 20–62 Bradamant's posterity revealed by the Sorceress. 63–77 Bradamant prepares to encounter Brunello.

WHO will give me the voice and eloquence to do justice to so lofty a subject? Who will lend wings to my verses that they might soar up to the height of my theme? For now have I need of no ordinary breath to inspire my words, now that I must sing of my Lord, and of the forefathers whence he is sprung. / Behold, Phoebus, light of the world, look upon all the noblest lords ordained by Heaven to hold sway on earth; no family, not one is there of those you see more glorious than this in peace and war—nor one so age-old steeped in its nobility: and ever more shall it preserve its name (if I be not deceived in my prophetic sight), while the heavens shall yet circle the Pole. / Were I to give a full account of the honours of this House, no lyre would suffice, not mine, none, O Phoebus, but the very instrument on which you rendered thanks to the Lord of the Universe when he had felled the Titans. If ever you concede me finer tools, tempered to work on stone of such perfection, I shall devote all my skill, all my labour to carving these lovely images. / I shall for the moment take my ill-suited chisel to chipping free a first rough outline; later, perhaps, with more practice, I shall be able to reduce my work to perfection.

But let us return to one whose breast cannot be guarded by any shield or breastplate—Pinabello of Maganza, who nurtured the hope of slaying the damsel. / Imagining that she must have dropped sheer to her death, the treacherous man turned, ashen-faced, from that dismal cavity, now by him defiled, and hastened to remount his horse; and to compound his felonies (being wicked through and through), he made off with hers as well. / Let us leave him—while he plots against another's life, it is his own he forfeits—and return to the maiden who, by his betrayal, nearly met with death and burial all in one.

After striking the rocky floor she stood up, dazed, and went in through the door which gave access to the second, much larger chamber. / A square and spacious chamber it was, solemn and sacred as a church, its roof most gracefully supported on slender columns of alabaster. An altar was well situated in the middle, with a lamp burning before it; this, with its clear effulgence, illuminated the inner and the outer chamber. / Finding herself in a sacred and holy place, the damsel was touched with devout humility and, kneeling down, started to pray to God, from her heart as from her lips. Meanwhile a little door opposite grated and creaked open and a woman stepped forth; she was ungirded and bare-foot, and her hair fell loose about her shoulders.

She greeted the damsel by name, saying: / 'O Bradamant, great of heart, you are come here only by the will of God: some days ago Merlin's prophetic spirit warned me that you were to take an unusual path to come and visit his holy relics. And I have come here to reveal to you the dispositions that Heaven has made for you. / This grotto, ancient and memorable, is the work of Merlin, the wise magician of whom perhaps you have sometimes heard mention. Here it is that he was tricked by the Lady of the Lake. Down here is the tomb in which his body lies in corruption—the tomb into which, anxious to please his lady, he entered at her persuasion: there he laid himself down, a living man, there only to remain, dead. / His old corpse still shelters his living spirit until it hear the angel's trumpet sound to summon it to Heaven or drive it thence, according as he passes for dove or raven. His voice lives, and you shall be able to hear how clearly it sounds from the marble tomb, for never has he refused an answer to those who sought word from him on things past or future. / Many days ago it was that I came to this tomb from a far distant land to seek enlightenment from Merlin on a deep mystery of my craft. Now, as I wished to see you, I tarried here a month longer than I first intended, for Merlin, ever truthful in his predictions to me, set this day as the term for your arrival.' /

In bewildered silence Bradamant listened to her words; such was her amazement, she was not sure whether she were awake or dreaming. And, modest by nature, 'What is my worth', she asked with humble mien, 'that prophets should be foretelling my arrival?' / And, rejoicing to meet with so unusual an adventure, she straightway followed the sorceress, who led her to the tomb which held the bones and the spirit of Merlin. It was fashioned of hard polished stone, the colour of flame, and gleamed so that the sunless place was radiant with its light. / Whether it is the property of certain sorts of marble that they lighten the darkness like flaming torches, or whether it were the work of incense and incantations and the tracing of astrologers' signs (a more likely explanation to my mind), the radiance disclosed many beautiful works of sculpture and painting which embellished the sacred precincts. /

Scarcely had Bradamant set foot across the threshold than from the secret recess there issued, crystal clear, the voice of the spirit which haunted those mortal spoils: 'May Fortune prosper your every wish, chaste and most noble Lady; from your womb shall spring the fruitful issue destined to bring honour to Italy and to all mankind. / The blood deriving from ancient Troy, in its two most perfect streams, is to be blended in you to produce the ornament, the flower, the jewel of all dynasties that the sun has ever seen 'twixt the Indus, Tagus, Danube, and Nile, 'twixt all that lies between the Antarctic and the Bear. Marquises, dukes, and emperors will be in high honour among your posterity. / From you shall spring the captains and dauntless knights who, by their sword and wits, are to reclaim for Italy all the former honours of unvanquished arms. From you the just rulers will hold their sceptres, under whose mild and virtuous government, as under wise Augustus and Numa, the Golden Age will once again relive. / To give effect, therefore, to Heaven's will, which has from all time appointed you to be Ruggiero's wife, pursue your way with courage—for nothing shall intervene to upset this decree, nothing shall prevent your overthrowing at first impact the wicked robber who is secreting your prize.' /

Merlin said no more, but gave place to the enchantress, who was preparing to show Bradamant the likeness of each one of her descendants. She had selected a large number of spirits, whether summoned forth from hell or from some other place I know not, and had assembled them together, each one with different face and raiment. / Then she summoned the damsel to her in the pillared chamber, having first traced there on the ground a circle wide enough to encompass her if she lay down, and a palm wider still. And lest she be harmed by the spirits, she made a great pentacle to cover her. She told Bradamant to watch her in silence; then she opened her book and spoke to the demons. / A crowd began now to emerge from the outer chamber and gather round the magic circle, unable, however, to set foot in it, for their way was barred as surely as if it were girdled with walls or a trench. The demons passed into the beautiful vault which contained the great prophet's bones, proceeding first to make their three ritual turns. /

'If I were to tell you the names and deeds', said the sorceress to Bradamant, 'of all those who are appearing here, thanks to the enchanted spirits, before their birth, I cannot see when I should be able to let you go, for one night would not be long enough to reveal so much. I shall therefore pick out a few for you, as time and opportunity dictates. /

'See this first one, who resembles you in his handsome features and serene expression. He is to be the head of your family in Italy, conceived in you by Ruggiero's seed. I am expecting to see the earth dyed red by his hand with Pontieri blood, and the vengeance he shall wreak upon those who by foul treachery shall slay his father. / He shall despoil Desiderio, King of the Lombards, and in reward, he shall receive from the Empire the fine domains of Este and Calaon. Behind him is Uberto, your grandson, who shall bring honour to Italy and to the arts of war. Many a time shall he defend Holy Church against the barbarians. /

'Look, there is Alberto, the invincible captain who will adorn so many temples with his trophies. With him is Hugo, his son, who is to conquer Milan, and there unfurl his viper-emblems. That other one is Azzo, who shall succeed his brother in the lordship of Milan. Here is Albertazzo, whose shrewd counsel shall deliver Italy from Berengarius and his son; / he shall be deemed worthy to receive the hand of Alda from her father, the Emperor Otto. Look, another Hugo—behold how they succeed one another in excellence, faithful heirs to their father's valour! Justly shall it fall to him to reduce the Romans to humility and break their dire siege, delivering the third Otto and the Pontiff from their hands. / See Folco, now: he is to make over to his brother all his own possessions in Italy, and go far afield among the Germans to claim a great dukedom. He shall prop up the house of Saxony, one branch of which shall have fallen into disarray; heir to it through his mother's side, he shall restore it with his own posterity. /

'The one who now approaches is Azzo II, a man more inclined to courtesy than to war. Beside him are his two sons, Bertold and Albertazzo. The first will vanquish Henry II, and the sunny fields round Parma shall soak in German blood. The other is to marry the glorious, upright, and virtuous Countess Matilda. / His merits will make him worthy of such a match—and I hold it no small achievement at his age to have earned the hand of the First Henry's granddaughter, and with it a dowry of half the lands of Italy. This is Rinaldo, Bertold's cherished son; his shall be the honour of having delivered the Church from the hands of wicked Frederick Barbarossa. /

'Here is another Azzo; Verona shall be his, with its fair territory; and to him shall the Fourth Otto and Honorius II grant the title of Marquis of Ancona. It would take me all too long were I to show you every one of your descendants who shall be standard-bearer at the Consistory, or were I to relate every exploit accomplished by them for the Church of Rome. / See Obizzo and Folco, more Azzos, more Hugos, both Henrys—the son beside the father; two Guelphs, one of whom shall subdue Umbria and assume the dukedom of Spoleto. Here is one who shall staunch the blood and the cruel wounds of hapless Italy, turning tears into laughter: this is the one [she pointed to Azzo V] who shall crush Ezzelino, taking and slaying him. / Ezzelino, a most atrocious tyrant, shall be reputed the very son of Satan; he shall wreak such havoc, destroying his subjects and laying waste the lovely land of Italy that, next to him, Marius, Sulla, Nero, Antony, and Caligula shall pass for lambs. This same Azzo shall also be the one to overthrow Frederick II. / He with happier sway shall rule the beautiful land bathed by the river where Phoebus took his plangent lute and called after his son who had ill-driven the sun-chariot, when the fabled poplars wept amber, and Cygnus clad himself in white plumage. This land shall be a gift to him from the Holy See in boundless gratitude. /

'But what of Aldobrandino, his brother, and of the aid he shall bring to the Pontiff against Otto IV, when the Ghibelline host shall be encamped at the foot of the Capitol, having overrun all the lands nearby and imposed themselves on the Umbrians and Piceni? Unable to lend assistance for lack of gold, he shall request it from the Florentines; / and for lack of jewellery or better pledges, he shall hand over to them his brother as a hostage. He shall unfurl his victorious ensigns and defeat the German troops. He shall re-establish the Church on her throne, and mete out worthy punishment to the Counts of Celano. Cut off in the flower of his years, he shall end his life in the service of the Sovereign Pontiff. / And to his brother Azzo he shall leave the sovereignty over Ancona and Pesaro, and over every town lying between the Tronto and the Isauro, from the Apennines to the sea. Loyalty, too, and magnanimity he shall bequeath to him, and valour, which is greater treasure than gems or gold—for if Fortune has the disposal of every other good, yet over valour She has no power. /

'See Rinaldo, no less outstanding for his courage, were it not that Death or Fate is to be cruelly envious that the fair lineage should stand in such high exaltation. Even here the lamentations reach my ears, all the way from Naples where he is held hostage for his father. Here, now, is Obizzo who, still a young man, shall be appointed prince in his grandfather's place. / To his dominions he shall add bright Reggio and Modena the fierce—such will be his worth that of one accord their peoples will acclaim him Lord. See Azzo VI, one of his sons, a standard-bearer of the Holy Church: he shall obtain the dukedom of Andria with the hand of the daughter of Charles II, King of Sicily. / See the flower of illustrious princes grouped together in pleasing friendship: Obizzo, Aldobrandino, lame Niccolò, and Alberto, warm-hearted and mild. Lest I keep you too long I shall say nothing of how they shall add Faenza to their domains, and, with firmer hand, Adria, after which the wild salt sea is named; / and Rovigo, the city deriving its pleasant Greek name from its cultivation of roses; and Comacchio, the city set in the flood-lands of the Po, teeming in fish—fearful, though, of the river's twin mouths, where folk live whose calling is such that they welcome stormy seas and contrary winds. I shall say nothing of Argenta, of Lugo, of a host of other strongholds and thriving estates. /

'See Niccolò, still but a child when his people shall appoint him their lord; he shall bring to naught Tidaeus' plot to take arms against him. The sweat and strain of battle, the clash of steel will be his sport from childhood, and, marking the lessons of olden time, he shall learn to become the very flower of knighthood. / Those who take arms against him shall see their plans foiled and turned back against themselves; so well acquainted shall he be with stratagems that to outwit him will be no easy task. Too late shall Otto III recognize this—cruel tyrant of Reggio and Parma, he shall be stripped by Niccolò at once both of his power and of his evil life. / Never departing from the straight highway, the prosperous realm shall do naught but increase, refraining from injury to any but those from whom it has first suffered harm. For this reason the Great Mover is content that no bounds be set, but that the state continue to prosper ever more so long as the heavens continue in their gyres. /

'See Leonello, and see here the first duke, illustrious Borso, splendour of his age, presiding in peace, and compassing greater triumphs than any who have set foot upon another's lands. He shall confine Mars in a place of darkness, and tie the hands of Violence. His every purpose shall be that his people live content. /

'Here comes Ercole; his faltering steps and foot half burnt are a reproach to his neighbours, the Venetians, a reminder of the field at Budrio where he shall stop his fleeing troops and make them turn with him to face their foes. Nor does he thus to be rewarded by his friends with war—indeed, they drive him back as far as the Barco. Such is this lord's renown, I cannot rightly say whether it rests more upon his labours of war or of peace. / The folk of Apulia, Lucania, and Calabria shall long remember his deeds, when he shall fight the Catalonian king in single combat and bear away the glory. Not a few victories shall assure him a place among the unvanquished captains. After an interval of more than thirty years shall he, by his own power, re-establish the sovereignty of his line. / His realm shall be as indebted to him as any can be to its prince: not because he shall make fertile fields where first there were marshes; not because he shall make it more habitable for its citizens, by building walls and trenches, and adorning it with temples and palaces, piazzas and theatres and countless luxuries; / not because he shall protect it from the rapacious claws of the bold Winged Lion; nor because he alone shall continue at peace in his dominions and remain immune from threats or tribute when the French torch sets fire to the length and breadth of fair Italy; no, not for these and other benefactions shall his people stand indebted to Ercole, / so much as because he shall give them Alfonso the just and Hippolytus the good, his illustrious sons: no different shall they be from the sons of the Tyndarean swan-god, as the legend of old relates, who took it each in turn to forgo the light of day in order to draw the other free from the infected air. Each of them, too, shall show fortitude and readiness to lay down his life for the other's safety. /

'In the abounding love of these two shall their people rest more secure than if their city were girt with a double ring of steel from Vulcan's forge. To such a degree is wisdom and goodness united in Alfonso that future generations shall believe that Astrea is returned from Heaven to this earth, where heat and frost prevail. / He shall do well to show prudence, and, by his courage, to take after his father, for he shall find himself with but few forces hemmed in by the squadrons of Venice on one side, and on the other by one whom I know not whether to call mother or mere foster-parent: if mother, then she is scarcely kinder to him than were Medea or Procne to their children. / And as often as he sallies forth with his staunch followers, by night or day, so often shall he inflict defeat and memorable rout upon his enemies, both by sea and land. The folk of Romagna, worsted in battle against their neighbours and one-time friends, shall mark this well, staining with their blood all the land which lies between the streams of the Po, Santerno, and Zanniolo. / Within those very boundaries the Sovereign Shepherd's Spanish mercenary shall also learn his lesson, when, only a little later, he seizes the Bastia, and, after seizing it, puts to death its governor. For such a crime there shall remain not one, from humblest soldier to the very captain, to take the news to Rome that the citadel has been recaptured, its garrison slaughtered. / His shall be the honour, thanks to his shrewdness and his skill at arms, of delivering to the troops of France their signal victory over Julius and the Spaniards in the fields of Romagna; all over the battlefield horses shall wallow up to their bellies in human blood, and not all the Germans, Spaniards, Greeks, Italians, and French shall be sufficient to bury the dead. /

'The one who wears pontifical attire, and on his venerable head the purple hat, is the generous, sublime, great-hearted Hippolytus, Lord Cardinal of the Roman Church; in every tongue many enduring works shall be written for him in prose and verse: and the just heavens have seen fit that his own flowering era should have its Virgil, as Augustus had before him. / He shall embellish his fair posterity as the sun irradiates our world far better than the moon or any star, for every other light is always second to him. I see him setting grimly forth with but a handful of foot soldiers and even fewer mounted, only to return in jubilation, leading captive to his shores some fifteen galleys beside a thousand other craft. /

'See next the two Sigismondi, and here, Alfonso's five beloved sons —not mountains nor seas shall be able to prevent their renown from spreading throughout the world. One is Ercole II, wed to the daughter of the King of France; this other (to give you a complete account) is Hippolytus, who shall shine in his posterity with no less radiance than his uncle. / The third is Francesco; the other two are both called Alfonso. But, as I said before, were I to show you every one of your descendants whose virtues shall lend such glory to their tribe, light and darkness would have to succeed each other many times before I were finished. Now, with your permission, it is time that I dismiss the spirits and say no more.' /

The damsel consented, and the skilful enchantress closed her book; the spirits vanished all at once into the tomb where the bones were enclosed. Now Bradamant, once more conceded the power of speech, parted her lips to ask: 'Who were those two we saw so abject between Hippolytus and Alfonso? / They sighed as they came, listless and sad was the look in their downcast eyes, and their brothers, I saw, walked at a distance from them, as though seeking to avoid them.' At these words the enchantress' expression seemed to change, her eyes to moisten, and 'Wretches,' she cried, 'see to what punishment you are to be led by the constant urging of wicked men! / But, kindly children, worthy of virtuous Ercole, let not their faults overcome your goodness: they are, in truth, your own kindred—let justice give place to mercy.' Then, in softer voice, she added, 'I shall tell you no further about this; leave with a sweet taste in your mouth, and do not complain if I refuse to turn it to bitterness. /

'At first light you and I shall take the road which leads most directly to the gleaming, steel-girt castle, where Ruggiero lives in another's keeping. I shall be your companion and guide until you are out of the grim, evil forest; when we come to the sea, I shall point out your way so clearly that you shall be unable to mistake it.' / Here the dauntless maiden passed the night, spending a great part of it in conversation with Merlin, who urged her to hasten to the assistance of her Ruggiero.

When the sky brightened with fresh radiance, she left the underground dwelling by a path which continued a long way in blind darkness; with her came the lady of the spirits. / They emerged in a ravine hidden amid mountains impossible of access; and all day they climbed hillsides and crossed torrents, never stopping for rest. And, to relieve the monotony of their journey and attenuate the difficulties of their path, they engaged in pleasant conversation, broaching whatever subjects were most agreeable to them: / for the most part these consisted in the enchantress, well-versed in her science, instructing Bradamant in the stratagems and skills she would need if she were to recover her Ruggiero.

'Even if you were Pallas or Mars,' she explained, 'and had recruited a larger host than that of Charles or Agramant, you still would not last long against the magician; / for not only is the towering fortress impregnable behind its steel-girt walls; not only has he a steed which walks the air, and leaps and gallops through the sky; but also he has that lethal shield whose brightness, once it is disclosed, so dazzles the eye that it brings blindness—and so overwhelms the senses that the beholder must needs succumb as though to death. / You may think you can do battle with your eyes tight shut—but how will you tell when you are avoiding your adversary, and when you are hitting him? But I shall show you an antidote, and a swift one, to dispose of the blinding light and his other spells; there is none but this one in all the world. /

'Agramant, the African king, has given a ring, stolen in India from a queen, to one of his barons, Brunello, who is journeying a few miles ahead of us; such is its virtue that it renders all magic harmless to its wearer. Now Brunello is as well versed in thieving and duplicity as is Ruggiero's captor in the magic arts. / This Brunello, cunning and expert as I have told you, has been sent by his king to deliver Ruggiero, by his native wit and with the aid of the ring (already well proven in such enterprises) from the castle where he is held—such has been his boast, such the promise he has made to his lord, in whose affection Ruggiero stands higher than all others. / Now, so that Ruggiero should be beholden not to King Agramant but to you alone for his rescue from his enchanted cage, I shall explain the course open to you. For three days you shall journey along the sandy sea-shore, which will shortly be coming into view; on the third day the man who has the ring will stop at the same inn as you. /

'How will you recognize him? He is of medium build; his hair is black and curly; his skin is dark, but his face is pale and his beard most shaggy, as also his eyebrows. His eyes protrude and have a shifty look; his nose is flattened. To complete his picture, his dress is like that of a messenger, short and close-fitting. / Your conversation with him shall happen to turn to the subject of those strange spells. Show your desire to come to grips with the magician, which will be the simple truth; but do not let out that you have been told about that ring of his which disarms the power of magic. He will offer to show you the way to the castle and keep you company. / Go with him, and once the castle comes into view, kill him; let no pity stay your hand from putting my advice into effect. Do nothing which might betray your purpose to him, giving him time to seek concealment with the ring—for no sooner has he placed the magic ring in his mouth than he will vanish from sight.' /

With these words they came out by the sea where the Garonne flows into it near Bordeaux. Here the two women took leave of each other, not without tears. Aymon's daughter, who was tireless in her quest to deliver her beloved from captivity, journeyed on until one evening she came to an inn, where Brunello was. / She recognized Brunello on sight, for his description was etched in her memory. She asked him whence he had come, and whither bound, and he answered her, but lied in every particular. The damsel, forewarned, dissimulated just as well in her account of her nation, family, religion, name, and sex. And she darted frequent glances at his hands. / She kept glancing at his hands, wary of being robbed by him; indeed she took care not to let him draw too close, well acquainted as she now was with his disposition. They were together like this when their ears were deafened by a noise. What this was, my Lord, I shall tell you after allowing due pause in my song.

FOURTH CANTO

1–2 Introductory. 3–36 Bradamant gets rid of Brunello and overcomes the magician Atlas. 37–50 Bradamant finds and loses Ruggiero. 51–72 Rinaldo is blown ashore in Scotland and hears of a worthy exploit.

DECEIT is normally held in low esteem, pointing as it does to an evil disposition; there are, nonetheless, countless instances when it has reaped obvious benefits and deflected all manner of harm and ill report and mortal perils. For our conversation is not always with friends in this earthly life, dogged as it is by envy, and compounded of shadow far more than of light. / If it is so hard to discover a true friend, and that only after long probation, one to whom you can talk with complete freedom and disclose fully what lies in your mind—what is fair Bradamant to do with Brunello, who is neither open nor honest but false through and through, just as the enchantress had described him? /

She too dissimulated—perforce she had to with Brunello, the begetter of so many fictions. And, as I said, she looked frequently at his hands which were thievish and grasping. Suddenly a great din reached their ears. 'Glorious Mother!' cried the damsel, 'God in Heaven, what can this be?' And where the noise was, there, in a moment, was she. / Here she found the innkeeper with all his family and many others at their windows and yet more out in the street, all looking up at the sky as though there were a comet or eclipse. She witnessed a prodigious sight, one which would not be readily believed: a great winged horse was passing through the sky, with an armed man mounted upon him. / Broad were his wings and of unusual hue; and between them sat a horseman clad in bright polished armour. He was holding his course straight to the Westward, and sank away from view amid the mountains. He was a sorcerer, the innkeeper told them (and told them truly), who often passed this way, sometimes at a distance, sometimes close by. / His flight would carry him to the stars one moment, and almost graze the earth the next. And he would bear off every lovely woman he found in those parts—so that the luckless maidens who were blessed with comeliness (or imagined they were) dared not step out in full view of the sun, for he would snatch them up one and all. /

'He has a castle in the Pyrenees,' their host explained; 'it is built by magic, all of steel, and it is so resplendent that for sheer wonder there is nothing in the world to match it. Many a knight has made his way thither, but not one can claim to have returned—which leads me, sir, to fear that they must be captured or put to death.' / The damsel heard him out and exulted, for she was confident of proving the power of the magical ring to such effect—as she was bound to do—that the magician and his castle would be disposed of once for all. 'Let me have one of your men,' she asked the innkeeper, 'who knows the way better than I do. I cannot wait for the moment to do battle with this magician.' / 'You shall not lack for a guide,' put in Brunello, 'for I shall come with you. I have a note of the way, and also other things which will make you glad I came.' He meant the ring, but he did not show it or add any explanation, to avoid cause for regret. 'I should be glad of your company,' she replied—meaning that thus the ring would be hers. / What there was some use in saying, she said; what could harm her with the Saracen she kept to herself.

The innkeeper had a horse which took her fancy—a horse fit for riding and for battle. She bought him, and with the fair dawn of the following day she set out. She set out through a narrow valley; Brunello rode now ahead of her, now behind. / Across mountains and through forests they travelled until they came to the heights of the Pyrenees which command a view (if the air is not murky) of both France and Spain, and of two separate shores—just as from the saddle in the Apennines on the approach to Camaldoli, both the Slavonian and the Tuscan seas are to be viewed at once. Then they made their way down a steep and difficult slope into a deep valley. /

In the middle stood a rock whose exalted crown, raised so high into the heavens that it towered above all around it, was girt with a fine wall of steel. It would be idle for one who does not fly to contemplate visiting it, for his best effort would be totally wasted. Said Brunello, 'This is where the sorcerer holds knights and ladies in captivity.' / It rose up four-square, its corners cut flush and straight as a line scored out by a joiner; no sign was there of any path or stairway to make it accessible, and it was evident that the site was well adapted as nest or den to some winged beast.

Now was the time, the damsel saw, to take the ring and to dispatch Brunello. / But, to sully herself with the blood of an unarmed man, and a man of so little account, seemed to her too base a deed, and she was sure of gaining possession of the priceless ring without putting him to death. Brunello was quite off his guard, so she caught him and bound him fast to a lofty pine, taking care first to draw the ring from his finger. / Brunello wept and lamented, but she would not release him.

Slowly she picked her way down the mountainside and came into the plain at the foot of the crag. Here she had recourse to her horn in order to summon the magician to battle; and , after sounding it, she called him out into the field with ringing threats, and challenged him to fight. / It was not long before the magician . hearing the voice and the clarion call, issued forth from the gate. The winged steed bore him through the air charging against the seemingly warlike man. The damsel, however, was quickly reassured when she realized how little damage he was inflicting upon her—he carried neither lance nor sword nor mace to pierce her armour or break it open. / In his left hand he bore only his shield, which was draped in red silk; and in his right, a book, which he perused to miraculous effect: for at one moment he seemed to be charging, lance in rest (and many a man had blinked with amazement!), while at the next he appeared to strike with rapier, or mace—but he was far away and had made no contact at all. /

The horse was no figment—he was real, begotten by a gryphon out of a mare. He had his father's wings and feathers, his forefeet, his head and beak; in all else he took after his mother. He was known as a hippogryph—they are a rare breed, from the Rifean hills, way beyond the frozen seas. / Thence he abducted him by virtue of spells and, once possessed of him, devoted all his attention, all his skill and care to such effect that within a month he could ride him like a saddle-horse: he could make him wheel and turn obediently wherever he was, be it on the ground or in the air. No magical figment, this horse: unlike the rest, this was as real as could be. /

Everything else about the magician was sheer trickery; he could make yellow pass for red. Not that this troubled Bradamant, for, thanks to the ring, her eyes could not deceive her. Nonetheless, she struck out at the empty air and urged her steed this way and that, and fought and toiled just as she had beforehand been instructed to do. / After fighting awhile from horseback she decided to dismount, the better to carry out the instructions given to her by the canny sorceress. The magician now resorted to his ultimate spell against which there was, to his knowledge and belief, no antidote: he disclosed his shield, little doubting but that she would fall to the magic radiance. / He could of course have uncovered it at the outset instead of keeping the knights in suspense; but he derived pleasure from a few good passes with the lance, or some expert sword-play: sometimes one may see a cat, the wily creature, enjoying a little game with a mouse; and when he tires of it, with a snap of his jaws he will put an end to both. / In previous encounters the magician played the cat, the others the part of the mouse; but these roles no longer obtained once Bradamant came forward with her ring. She paid the closest attention to every move to ensure that the magician stole no advantage over her, and when she saw him uncovering his shield, she closed her eyes and fell to the ground. / This is not because she was struck, like all the rest, by the glint of the burnished metal; she did it to ensure that the vain enchanter dropped and dismounted beside her. All went exactly as planned, for no sooner had her head touched the earth than the flying horse beat his wings and, circling broadly, came to rest on the ground. /

Replacing the shield in its cover and leaving it slung from the saddle, he came on foot tô where the damsel lay like a wolf in the scrub, crouching in wait for the kid. The moment he was within reach she leapt up and grasped him tightly. As for the book on which the wretched man relied for all his fighting, he had left it on the ground, / and come running with his chain which he always carried for the same purpose—meaning to bind her fast just as he had bound others before her. But by now Bradamant had laid him on the ground, and if he offered no resistance, I cannot blame him: a weak old man could be no match for one of her vigour. / Quickly she raised her victorious arm, for she proposed to sever his head; but one look at his face and she held back, as though disdaining so cheap a vengeance. The man whom she had overpowered turned out to be a venerable elder with a doleful face; to judge by his wrinkled face and silver hair he must have been little short of seventy. /

'Take my life, then, young man, for God's sake!' cried the greybeard in petulant rage; but she was as reluctant to take it as he appeared eager to part with it. The damsel wanted to know who the sorcerer was, and to what end he had built his fortress in this desolate place and visited evil upon everybody. /

'Alas, I had no wicked intention', explained the old enchanter, weeping, 'when I built the handsome castle on the crag's top. And it is not avarice that has made me a robber: Love it was that moved me to rescue a gentle knight from extreme peril—for Heaven revealed to me that he is shortly to die a Christian, treacherously slain. / Between here and the Southern pole, nowhere does the sun behold a youth more excellent nor more fair than he; Ruggiero he is called and I, whose name is Atlas, have brought him up from his tenderest years. Thirst for honour and his own hard destiny have brought him to France in the following of Agramant the King; and I, who have ever loved him more than I would a son, I would withdraw him from France, and from danger. / I built this handsome castle all in order to detain him securely, once I had captured him—just as today I hoped to capture you. And I have brought in ladies and knights, as you shall see, and others of noble birth so that, if he cannot leave at will, these companions may serve to temper his regrets. / Save only when they ask to be let out, their every other pleasure is my business. Whatever good may be derived from any region of the earth, it is all to be found in this castle: music and song, fine raiment, pastimes, food and drink, whatever desire the heart can feel or lips can utter. Well had I sown, well reaped—but now you have come and all is disturbed. / Ah, but if your heart is not less gracious than your looks, do not obstruct this my honest scheme! Take the shield (I give it to you) and that horse which strides so swiftly through the air, but turn your thoughts from the castle; or bring out a friend or two, but leave the rest; or bring them all out, and I shall ask nothing of you except that you leave me my Ruggiero. / But if you are determined to take him from me, I pray you, then, before you conduct him back to France, release this afflicted soul of mine from its husk, rotting, now, and decayed.'

'Him I mean to set at liberty. You,' replied the damsel, 'keep croaking and babbling, now that you know. And don't offer me the gift of the shield or the horse, for they are mine now—they are no longer yours. / And even if you still had them in your gift, they would seem to me to make a poor exchange. You tell me that you are holding Ruggiero to ward off from him the evil influence of his fixed stars. Either you cannot know what the Heavens prescribed for him or, if you do know, you have no remedy. But if you are blind to the evil which immediately threatens you, must you not be blinder still to the evil in store for another? / Do not ask me to kill you, for you would ask in vain; if you really want to die—well, a man of fortitude can always make away with himself even if no one will consent to slay him. But before you dispatch your soul from your body, open the gates for all your prisoners.' Thus spoke the maiden, and urged the captive sorcerer towards the castle rock. /

Bound with his own chain Atlas set out, and Bradamant followed close behind him, for even thus she did not trust him far, for all that he looked quite chastened. They had proceeded thus only a few steps when they came upon a fissure at the foot of the crag, and the steps winding up the cliff in a spiral; they climbed up to the gate of the castle. / Atlas lifted a stone from the threshold, inscribed with strange characters and signs. Beneath it there were some vases, or urns; smoke constantly issued from these, and a hidden fire burned in them. The sorcerer smashed them, and at once the crag was empty, barren, and desolate; no sign remained of any wall or tower—as though a castle had never stood there at all. / Now the magician shook himself free of Bradamant, as the thrush will escape from a net. He disappeared and with him his castle, leaving his company at liberty. The knights and ladies found themselves outside, delivered from the majestic halls, and not a few of them were displeased to recover their liberty at the price of so much pleasure. /

Here was Gradasso and Sacripant, and Prasildo, the noble knight who came from the Levant with Rinaldo; and with him was Iroldo, his inseparable friend. Here at last fair Bradamant came upon her beloved Ruggiero, who, once he was sure who she was, gave her the heartiest welcome— / the sort of welcome he would extend to one whom he loved more than his eyes, more than his heart, more than his very life ever since the day she had removed her helmet for his sake, with the result that she was wounded. It would take too long to describe how and where they searched for each other night and day in that wild, deserted wood; never did they meet again until this moment. / Beholding her here, and well knowing that she alone had been the one to rescue him, his heart was so filled with joy that he counted himself blessed and uniquely fortunate. They went down from the crag into the valley where the damsel had won her victory.

Here they found the hippogryph; the shield, draped, hung at his side. / Bradamant went to take hold of his reins; he waited until she was close, then spread his wings and rose into the air, and settled a little further off on the hill slope. She followed him and, just as before, he rose into the air and settled yet a little further off—like a crow luring a dog after it hither and thither across the sandy scrub. / Ruggiero, Gradasso, Sacripant, and all the knights who had come down in a group all scattered; some of them went up, others down, according to where they expected the winged beast to land. He, after leading them on many a vain errand up to the topmost crests and down among the rocks of the damp valley floor, finally came to rest beside Ruggiero. / Now, all this was Atlas' doing; he was still bent on his compassionate plan to deliver Ruggiero from the great danger threatening him: this was his only thought, his only care. So he sent the hippogryph in his direction, meaning this way to contrive his removal from Europe. Ruggiero grasped the hippogryph, intended to lead him back, but the beast pulled away and refused to go with him. / So the impetuous knight dismounted from Frontino (as his own horse was named) and mounted the steed which trod the air, and with his spurs excited his proud spirit. The hippogryph trotted a few steps, then lifted his forefeet and rose into the sky, far lighter than the falcon, when its handler removes its hood and shows it the quarry. /

Seeing her Ruggiero swept up so high and in such danger, the beautiful damsel was utterly stunned, and remained for some while in a daze. She was much afraid that the fate of Ganymede, snatched up to the heavens, so she had been told, out of his father's keeping, might befall him too, for he was no less comely and well-favoured. / She gazed after him as long as she could see him, but when he faded from the distant sky, where her eyes could no longer follow him, she continued to pursue him with her heart. Meanwhile she sighed and wept, and her tears would not be appeased. When Ruggiero could no longer be descried, she turned her eyes to his steed, noble Frontino, / and determined not to leave him behind to be the prize of the first comer, but to take him with her and return him to his master's keeping—for she trusted to see him again.

The great bird soared and Ruggiero could not restrain him. He could look down at the mountain peaks, which lay so far below that he was unable to say where the land lay flat and where it rose into hills. / He ascended to such a height that to the eye of one watching from the ground he appeared but a speck in the sky, then set course to where the sun sets when its circle lies in Cancer. He clove the air like a well-pitched vessel riding the sea before a favouring wind. Let us leave him on his way, for he will make a good journey, and let us return to Rinaldo the paladin. /

Blown by the gale, which did not let up night or day, Rinaldo drifted one moment to the West, the next towards the Pole; day after day he beheld nothing but a great waste of water. Finally in Scotland he cast anchor, when the Caledonian forest came into view, where so often the clash of arms resounded amid the ancient shady oaks. / Through it travel knights errant renowned for their prowess from all over Britain, and from other lands near and far, from France, Norway, Germany. The man of little valour should not adventure there, for where he seeks honour he shall find death. Great deeds were accomplished here by Tristan, and Lancelot, Galahad, Arthur, and Gawain, / and other famous knights of the new Round Table, and of the old. Proud trophies and monuments to several of their feats still survive. Rinaldo had his arms and Bayard made ready, and quickly had himself set down on the shady shore, and commanded the captain to sail in haste for Berwick and there to await him. / Unattended by squire or retinue, the knight set out through the boundless forest, choosing whichever path seemed most likely to lead him to novel adventures. The first day he came to a well-appointed abbey which spent a good part of its substance on offering entertainment to the knights and ladies who passed that way. /

The abbot and monks gave Rinaldo a good welcome, and he asked them (once he had amply sated his body's hunger with choice fare), as knights often came upon adventure in this locality, how he could prove by some noteworthy feat whether he was deserving of praise or blame. / They told him that many and strange adventures were to be encountered by one wandering through those woods, but that more often than not there was little talk of them, for the deeds, like the woods themselves, were shadowy.

'Seek to go', they said, 'where you can be sure your actions will not remain buried, so that your toil and perils will be attended by Renown, who shall render a due account of them. / If you want to make trial of your valour, a most worthy enterprise awaits you, one which never, not even in times past, fell to the lot of a knight. The daughter of our king stands in need of help and protection against a baron called Lurcanio, who means to take away her reputation and her life. / This man Lurcanio has laid before her father an accusation (out of hatred more, perhaps, than for good reason) that he discovered her at dead of night fetching a lover up onto her balcony. By the laws of the kingdom she must be condemned to the pyre unless within a month, which is now drawing to an end, she find a champion who can expose the falsehood of her wicked accuser. / By the cruel and pitiless law of Scotland any woman, whatever her condition, who engages in union with a man, and is not his wife, must be put to death if an accusation is laid against her. And she has no recourse against death unless a mighty warrior come and undertake her defence, maintaining that she be innocent and not deserving of death. / Sorrowing for his daughter, fair Guinevere, the king has proclaimed throughout every town and castle that if any will take up her defence and stamp out the baneful calumny, that man (provided he be of noble birth) shall have her to wife, with an estate suitable as a dowry for a lady of her condition. / But if within a month no one has come to her defence, or has come but has not conquered, then she must be put to death.

'Here is an exploit you should undertake, rather than ranging through the forest as you are. Honour and renown shall be yours, for all time, and in addition the flower of womanhood, matchless among all the fairest who dwell between the Indus and Hercules' pillars; / wealth, too, shall be yours, and an estate which can ensure you a life of contentment; and you shall stand high in the king's favour, if he can owe to you the restoration of his honour, which now is almost spent. As a knight, too, are you not under oath to vindicate so great a wrong done to one who, by common consent, is the very model of chastity?' /

Rinaldo thought a while, then replied: 'Is a maiden to die, then, because she permitted her true love to discharge his passion in her loving arms? A curse on the man who imposed such a law, and a curse on the man who can suffer it! She who is without a heart deserves to die, not she who confers life upon her faithful lover. / Whether it be true or false that Guinevere received her lover, this is no concern of mine. Had she done so, I should blame her not at all, if she had only preserved her secret. Her defence is now my entire care; quick, then, give me a guide to lead me to her accuser, for, with God's help, I mean to deliver her. / It is not for me to vouch that she did not do it—I do not know, and could perhaps speak falsely. What I will say is that she

37

should incur no punishment for such an act, and that whoever devised these pernicious laws was unjust or downright mad: they should be repealed as evil, and new laws should be framed with greater wisdom. / If the same ardour, the same urge drives both sexes to love's gentle fulfilment, which to the mindless commoner seems so grave an excess, why is the woman to be punished or blamed for doing with one or several men the very thing a man does with as many women as he will, and receives not punishment but praise for it? / This unequal law does obvious injustice to women, and, by God, I hope to show how criminal it is that such a law should have survived so long!' They all agreed with Rinaldo that the ancients were unjust and careless when they consented to so bad a law, and that the king was at fault in that he could set it to rights but did not. /

When the new day broke above the horizon in a splendour of white and crimson, Rinaldo made ready his arms and his steed Bayard, and took a squire from the abbey; together they travelled many a mile through the dour, inhospitable forest towards where the duel over the damsel was to be fought. / They had left the main track to follow a short cut when they heard a tearful cry go up near at hand, which echoed through the forest. Rinaldo spurred Bayard, and the squire his mount towards a dell from which the cry had come; and they beheld two villainous men and between them a damsel who from a distance looked of surpassing beauty, / but as tearful and anguished as any woman or maiden, or indeed as any man, could look. The two men beside her had drawn their swords to dye the grass red with her blood, and she was seeking to put off her last moment a little, until they be moved to pity. Rinaldo came and, on sight of this, he charged in, roaring terrible threats. / The moment they saw help coming her way the villains turned and fled from sight into the depths of the valley. The paladin disdained to pursue them, but approached the damsel and sought to discover what grave fault had brought such punishment upon her. To avoid delay, he bade his squire take her up behind him on his horse, and they resumed their path. / As they rode, he saw better how beautiful she was and how graceful her manner, though she was still overcome with the shock of her encounter with death. Pressed to tell them who had brought her to this sorry pass, she began meekly telling them her story, which I shall keep for the next canto.

FIFTH CANTO

*1–3 Introductory. 4–74 Dalinda tells Rinaldo of Polynex's
plot against Guinevere. 75–92 Rinaldo discloses Polynex's
treachery and slays him.*

EVERY species of beast which dwells on this earth lives in peace among
its kind—and if fight it must, yet the male will never attack the female.
The mother-bear goes safely through the forest with her mate. The
lioness lays herself down beside the lion; the she-wolf lives secure in
her consort's company, and the heifer has no fear of the young bull. /
What scourge, though, what abomination has descended to wreak
disturbance in human breasts? Listen to husband and wife constantly
bandying insults, tearing each other's faces, striking each other black
and blue and leaving their wedding beds bathed in tears—and not only
tears, for sometimes brute anger has bathed them even in blood. / That
a man should bring himself to strike a fair maiden in the face or break
but a strand of her hair I take to be not merely a great wrong, but an
act wrought against nature, an act of rebellion against God; as for the
man who gives her poison, or who sunders soul from body with
steel blade or garotte, never shall I believe that such a one is truly a
man, but rather a fiend in human shape. /

Such must have been the two villains whom Rinaldo drove away
from the damsel, to judge by their behaviour in the dark valley, for that
was the last anyone heard of them. I left her preparing to disclose to the
paladin, who had proved so true a friend to her, the reasons for the
sorry pass to which she had come. Now to pursue our story: /

'You shall hear tell', the maiden began, 'of starker, more cold-
blooded cruelty than ever was known in Thebes or Argos, or Mycenae,
or any other place of worse renown. And if the Sun visits this region
less than others as he revolves his gleaming rays, I believe that he
approaches us reluctantly, for he would avoid sight of people so cruel. /
Now in every age we have examples of men dealing harshly with their
foes; but to slay the very one whose unique concern is your well-
being, is not this too foul and unjust? To give you a clearer notion of
why those men wanted, against all reason, to destroy me in the flower
of my youth I shall relate everything from the beginning. /

'You must know, sir, that when I was still only small, I entered the
service of the king's daughter, and grew up with her, and enjoyed a

good and honourable estate in the court. Cruel Love, though, envious of my lot, drew me into his own train, alas, and so devised it that of all the knights and pages at court the Duke of Albany should seem in my eyes the most handsome. / As he outdid the others in showing fondness for me, I felt moved to love him heart and soul; to listen to his words and watch his face was easy enough, but I could little judge what lay within his breast. I loved him, I trusted him, and I did not look back until I had brought him to bed with me—and little did it trouble me that this should happen in the palace, in the most secret of fair Guinevere's rooms: / the one in which she kept her most precious possessions and where she most often slept. This room could be entered from a balcony outside the window, and up to this balcony I would summon my lover, first lowering the rope-ladder to him with my own hands, whenever I wanted to have him with me. / Indeed, I would have him come as often as Guinevere gave me the opportunity: she tended to change beds in order to escape the sultry summer heat or the damp winter mists. No one ever saw him climb up, for that side of the palace gave onto some ruined houses, where no one ever went, day or night. /

'Our secret game of love lasted for days and months; my love but increased, and I was all a-fire within. And so blinded was I that I little realized how much he feigned, how little he loved, for all that his deceit should have been plain to me from a thousand obvious signs. /

'Came the day when he revealed himself in love with fair Guinevere; whether this was a new passion, or whether he had already been her suitor before our own love burgeoned, I know not. Judge you how he lorded it over me and ruled in my heart, for he disclosed to me his new devotion and blushed not to enlist my help in fostering it. / He assured me that the love he bore her was not the like of ours, was not even real—but that he hoped, by a pretence of passion, to obtain her for his lawful wife: whatever my lady's will in the matter, he should have no trouble winning the king's consent, for in all the land he was second only to the king in birth and station. / And he persuaded me that if I were a party to his becoming son-in-law to the king (and clearly this would raise him up as high as any man could be in the king's presence) he would not forget so great a favour, nor let it go unrewarded. He would prefer me to his wife, and to all others, he said; he would be my lover for all time. /

'Now to please him was all my care; I could not have found it in me to thwart him; those were days when I was only happy if I had earned his favour. So I took every occasion to speak of him and to sing his praises; I spared no pains to put my lover into the good graces of Guinevere. / God knows, I strove with all my heart to bring this to effect, but there was no winning her to my lord's suit. This was because she had set her heart on a gentle knight of pleasing manners and appearance, who had come to Scotland from a distant land. / He had come to the court from Italy with a younger brother, and here he achieved such rare skill at arms that there was no match for him anywhere in Britain. The king loved him well, so well, indeed, that he bestowed upon him castles, estates, preferments in abundance, and raised him to the eminence of his greatest barons. / This knight, then, whose name was Ariodant, was bound in gratitude to the king, but even more so to the princess; this was the result of his outstanding valour, but more, it was due to her knowing how he loved her: never did Vesuvius or Sicilian Etna, never did Troy blaze with such flames as those which, she was well aware, consumed Ariodant for love of her. /

'The love, then, the true, honest heart's love which she inspired in him resulted in my gaining no audience for my lord. Never did she give me an answer to breed hope—indeed, the more I pleaded for him and sought to move her to clemency, the more she scanted and scorned him, setting him at ever greater odds with her. / Many a time I urged my lover to abandon his empty dream, for he could never hope to gain a purchase in Guinevere's heart, totally dedicated as it was to another's love. I told him clearly that she was so inflamed with love of Ariodant that all the water in the sea could not extinguish a small part of the fire which raged within her. /

'When the duke, whose name was Polynex, had heard this from my lips all too often, and had been able to gauge for himself just how little his love was esteemed, he took the rebuff so ill—less for the pain of love unrequited than for the sting, proud man that he was, of seeing another preferred to him—that his fondness turned to spiteful hatred. / He planned, therefore, to set the princess and her lover at odds, and to sow harsh discord between them, and enmity past all hope of reconciliation. He would heap such shame upon her that, living or dead, there would be no vindicating her. This iniquitous plan he disclosed neither to me nor to any person. /

'Thus decided, "Dalinda," he said to me (for that is my name), "cut down a sapling again and again, but you will always see a fresh growth sprout from its roots. So it is with my ill-fated desire—cut off by failure after failure, it still produces fresh shoots, still hopes to reach fruition. / What matters to me is not my craving itself so much as the victory of achieving what I crave; and though I cannot compass it in reality I would be assuaged if I could bring it off in make-believe. In future, if ever you fetch me up to your balcony at a moment when Guinevere is lying a-bed naked, I would have you take up every garment she has put off and clothe yourself in them. / Be careful to copy the way she adorns herself and wears her hair, and try to imitate her as closely as you can. Then come out onto the balcony and lower the ladder; and I shall come to you imagining that you are the one whose clothes you are wearing. Deceiving myself thus, I hope soon to gain the mastery over my desire." /

'So said he; and I, being quite divorced from my true self, did not observe that this repeated request of his was a most obvious fraud. So I would often lower the ladder from the balcony, dressed in Guinevere's clothes, and he would come up; nor did I have any inkling of his deceit until after the damage had been done. /

'About this time the duke spoke to Ariodant—the two had been good friends before Guinevere made them rivals—in more or less these words: "Seeing that I have always loved and respected you among my equals, I am surprised that you reward me so ill. / I've no doubt but that you must be aware of the long-standing love between the princess and me; today I am going to my lord to ask her hand in marriage. Why, then, must you cross me? Why will you continue to set your heart so vainly on her? God knows I should respect your position if I were in your place and you in mine." / "Well, you surprise me even more," replied Ariodant. "I was in love with her before you had even set eyes on her. I know you are not ignorant of the love between her and myself—a love more passionate cannot exist. Her only desire is to become my wife; as for you, she loves you not at all—as you well know. / So why will you not respect our friendship as you say you expect me to do—and as indeed I would do if you stood higher than I did in her favour? No less than you I expect to have her to wife; you may be richer than I in this land, but I am held in no less regard by the king than you are, and, what is more, I am better loved than you are by his daughter." /

' "Ah, there", said the duke, "you are totally wrong, love-crazed as you are; you think you are the more beloved; I think likewise of myself; but by the fruits we shall be able to tell: show me what passes between you, and I shall disclose to you my secret in full. Then let whichever of us is seen to be the poorer yield place and make other provision for himself. / And I am ready, if you wish, to swear not to breathe a word of what you disclose to me; and I shall want your assurance that you will keep hidden what I shall tell you." So they agreed to this pact and swore an oath on the Gospels; and, having sworn each other to silence, Ariodant spoke first. / He told the duke fair and square how matters stood between himself and the princess: how she had given a spoken and written promise that she would never marry any man but he; and she had promised that, if the king refused him, she would eschew any subsequent offers of marriage, and would remain single for the rest of her days. / And, he said, thanks to the valour at arms he had demonstrated on more than one occasion, and expected yet to show to the praise, honour, and benefit of the king and his realm, he hoped to grow so much in the favour of his lord as to be deemed by him worthy of his daughter's hand in marriage, since that was also her pleasure. /

'"Thus far am I advanced," he continued, "and I do not believe that any rival can be close behind me. More than this I do not seek, nor do I crave for any more immediate token of her love. I would not wish for anything beyond that which God concedes in lawful wedlock— and it would be vain to press her, knowing as I do how far she out-strips all others in virtue." / When Ariodant had explained his case and the reward he was expecting for his toils, Polynex, who had already decided to set the princess and her lover at variance, answered in these terms:

'"You are nowhere near me, and I shall have you confess as much from your own lips; once you have looked at the very roots of my happiness, I shall have you admit that only I myself am blessed. / She is deceiving you; she neither esteems nor loves you, but is feeding you with hope, with words. When she talks with me about it, she always dismisses your love as mere folly. Me, I have more solid proof of how she cherishes me, beyond mere promises and prattle—and under seal of secrecy I shall tell you about it, though to keep silence might be more suitable. / Never a month goes by but I pass anything up to ten nights lying naked in her arms, and enjoying with her those pleasures which assuage an amorous desire. You can see, then, that the empty phrases you have met with are not to be compared with the pleasures I know. So yield to me, and make other provision for yourself, seeing how far below me you stand." /

'"I don't believe you," replied Ariodant; "without a doubt you are lying; you've fabricated all this to try scaring me away from my purpose. But you shall have to sustain what you have said, for your words do her an intolerable injury. I mean to show you up right away not only for a liar but also for a traitor." / "There would be no honour for us", returned the duke, "if we fell to fighting in this instance, when I can offer you the proof plain before your eyes the moment it suits you." Ariodant was shaken by these words, and a cold shiver ran up his spine. Indeed, had he fully believed the duke, he would have died of it there and then. / He felt stabbed to the heart, and with ashen face and in his mouth a taste of bitterness, he cried brokenly: "Once you have shown me this uncommon adventure of yours I promise to desert her traces, if in truth she has been so free with you, so mean to me. But don't imagine I'll believe what you have said unless first I see it with my own eyes." / "When the time comes I shall tell you," returned the duke, who then departed.

'I think that no more than two nights passed before he had arranged to come to me. To spring the trap, then, which he had laid so quietly, he went to his rival and told him to hide the following night among the houses where no one ever goes. / Here he indicated a place opposite the balcony up to which he always climbed. Ariodant suspected that the duke was trying to lure him to this spot with a view to setting an ambush here and having him killed; the bait would be his rival's offer to show him a side of Guinevere which he found unbelievable. / He decided to come, but not at a disadvantage in strength, so that if he were set upon, he would be in no fear of dying. Now he had a brother courageous and shrewd, the most renowned swordsman at court; his name was Lurcanio. In his company he felt more assured than had he had a bodyguard ten-strong. / He summoned his brother and told him to bring arms, and that night he brought him along, without disclosing his secret, though—he would not have told it to him nor to anyone. He posted him a stone's throw away and "if you hear me call", he said, "come; but otherwise, if you love me, do not move from this spot before I call you." / "You need not fear," said his brother. So Ariodant went silently and concealed himself in the solitary house which stood opposite my secret balcony. From the other direction came the wicked, deceitful man who was so happy to tarnish Guinevere's name. He made the usual sign to me—I was quite ignorant of his plot. /

'I was wearing a white dress trimmed with thread of gold, and on my head a gilded veil spangled with red, a costume which Guinevere alone, and no one else, was wont to wear. On hearing his signal, I came out onto the balcony which was so situated that I was exposed in front and on either side. / Lurcanio, meanwhile, anxious for his brother's safety, or out of common curiosity, had crept furtively after him, keeping well into the shadows, until he stood in the same building, not ten paces away from him. / In all ignorance I came out onto the balcony arrayed as I have said, just as I had come out to such good purpose on more than one occasion before. My raiment was extremely noticeable in the moonlight, and as I have Guinevere's build and am not unlike her in looks, it was easy to mistake our identities— / all the more so in that my balcony was at some distance from these abandoned houses. The duke, then, easily passed off his trick on the two brothers who were watching from the shadows. Imagine Ariodant's horror, his pain: Polynex grasped the ladder I lowered to him and climbed up onto the balcony. /

'As soon as he reached me, I threw my arms round his neck, never dreaming that I might be observed; I kissed him on the lips and all over his face, the way I normally did. He showed himself even more affectionate than usual, to perfect his deception. The rival, meanwhile, who had been brought along to witness the spectacle, stood abjectly in the background, and saw everything. / So overwhelmed was he with grief that he determined to take his life there and then; he set his sword into the ground by the pommel, meaning to fall against the tip of it. Lurcanio, who had looked on wide-eyed as the duke climbed up to join me, but with no idea of who was involved, noticed what his brother was doing, and stepped forward / and forestalled him before he pierced his breast by his own hand on a mad impulse. Had he been less quick, or at a slightly greater distance, he would have been too late, and would have moved to no avail.

' "Stay, wretched brother," he cried, "what has made you lose your wits? What! is a woman driving you to slay yourself—women, who can all drift away like mist before the wind! / Her death it is you must seek, for she deserves to die; conserve your own life until you can lay it down to your greater honour. She was to be loved, while her treachery was still a secret from you; now she is to be loathed with all your heart, now that you can see with your own eyes what sort of a whore she is. Keep this weapon which you would turn upon yourself, and brandish it to proclaim this base act before the king." / Ariodant, seeing his brother standing over him, desisted from his dire enterprise, but his intention abated not at all, for he had made up his mind to die. But he departed, bearing away a heart not merely wounded but pierced through and through with bitter anguish. He nonetheless pretended to his brother that his first mad impulse to self-destruction had now passed off. /

'The following morning, without a word to his brother or to any-body, he set out on a journey, impelled by his lethal despair. Many days passed before anyone had tidings of him—apart from his brother and the duke, nobody knew who it was who had driven him to leave; at the court, and indeed all over the kingdom, his action was widely dis-cussed. / After a week or more had passed a traveller arrived at court and came to Guinevere with woeful tidings: Ariodant had sunk to his death in the sea, and this through no fault of Boreas or other wind, but of his own free will. "From a rock which towered high above the sea, he leapt headfirst; / but before coming to this, he said to me—for I chanced to meet him on the way: 'Come with me,' he said, 'so that through you my end may be made known to Guinevere. And tell her that the end to which I am about to come, as you shall presently see, can be explained simply because I saw too much: happy would I be, had I lived sightless!' / We were standing on Low Head, as it happened, a cape reaching out towards Ireland. Now, with these

45

words, I saw him plunge from the summit of a rock and vanish head-first into the depths. I left him in the sea, and came with all haste to bring the news to you."

'Guinevere received the tidings in dazed horror. / Lord, what did she not say and do once she was alone in the safety of her bed! She beat her breast, she rent her clothes, she wrought havoc on her golden tresses. And she kept repeating Ariodant's last words, that the reason for his cruel and piteous state lay entirely in his having seen too much. / It was noised abroad that he had taken his life for sheer sorrow. There was not a dry eye, therefore, in all the court—neither the king, nor any knight nor lady could refrain from tears.

'Most sorrowful of all was the brother of Ariodant; indeed, he was so steeped in woe that he almost followed the dead man's example, turning his own hand against himself to go and join him in the grave. / He kept repeating to himself that it was Guinevere who had slain his brother, that it was only his brother's sight of that shameful act of hers that had driven him to his death. And he was seized with so blind an urge towards vengeance, he was so consumed with rage and anguish that he deemed it a small matter to forfeit the king's good graces and earn his hatred and that of all the people. / He went to the king, then, choosing a moment when the chamber was at its most crowded, and said: "Be it known, my lord, that only one person was to blame for driving my brother out of his wits, so that he took his life—your daughter. So pierced was he with grief on observing her unchaste in conduct, that he found death a better friend to him than life. / He loved her. Why should I hide this—his love for her was not dis-honourable: he hoped to deserve her hand from you in marriage, by virtue of his merits and of his faithful service. But while the poor unfortunate stood afar off sniffing the leaves, he saw another come and climb up into the forbidden tree, and rob him of all the fruit for which he craved." / Then he described how he had seen Guinevere come out onto the balcony and lower the ladder, and how a lover of hers had climbed up it—he could not identify him for, to avoid being recognized he had changed his dress and concealed his hair. He would resort to arms, he added, to prove the truth of his assertions. /

'You can imagine what pain her father felt on hearing his daughter thus accused. What he heard said of her was a thing he would never have imagined, and he was dumbstruck; he realized also that, if no knight undertook her defence and exposed Lurcanio as a liar, he would have to condemn her to death. / I believe you are not ignorant, sir, of our law which condemns to death any woman, old or young, proved to have made herself available to a man not her husband. She is put to death unless within a month she find a knight strong enough in her defence to be able to sustain her innocence in the face of the false accuser, and prove her undeserving of death. /

'The king, who believes that the charge must be false, in order to deliver her, has proclaimed that he will award her as wife, with an ample dowry, to whichever man will clear her of the infamous accusation. No warrior has yet spoken of stepping forward—indeed each is watching his fellows, for Lurcanio is so fierce a fighter that it seems he is feared by every single knight. / The worst is now expected, for Zerbin, her brother, has left the kingdom: for many months he has been travelling abroad, giving signal proof of his valour at arms. Were this valiant knight nearer at hand, or at least were he in some place where news of her might reach him in time, he would not fail to come to his sister's aid. / The king, meanwhile, is trying to discover by means other than arms whether the accusation is true or false, whether his daughter is rightly or wrongfully to die. He has arrested a number of ladies-in-waiting who ought to know if there is any truth in it; and I could see that if I were taken, the duke and I would be in all too dangerous a situation. /

'That very night I slipped away from court and betook myself to the duke, and showed him how vital it was to both of us that I should not be caught. He praised me for this, and told me to have no fear; and he persuaded me to accept the refuge of one of his castles not far from here, and I set out accompanied by two escorts he provided. /

'You have heard now, sir, of all that I have done to satisfy the duke of my love, so you must see clearly enough whether he for his part owed it to me to cherish me. Now listen and I'll tell you what was my reward, what bountiful gift to requite my deserts. Judge whether a woman who has loved greatly can hope to be loved in return. / For this treacherous, cruel, and thankless man has grown doubtful of my loyalty, and mistrustful of me, lest sooner or later I disclose his foxy deception. He has pretended, therefore, that he was sending me away to a castle of his as to a place of concealment until the king's anger had abated; but his purpose was to send me straight to my death. / He had given secret orders to my escort to slay me once they had brought me into these woods—a worthy requital for my fidelity. And his purpose would have been fulfilled had you not been within earshot of my cries. See how well Love treats those who follow him!' All this Dalinda related to the paladin as they pursued their way. /

Rinaldo blessed this piece of good fortune most of all, that he had come upon the damsel and had heard her unfold the entire tale of fair Guinevere's innocence. And if he had hoped to help her even assuming her to be justly accused, it was with all the greater assurance that he took it upon himself to prove her innocence, now that he found the accusation an evident calumny. / He pressed on with all speed towards Saint Andrews where the king was with his retinue, and where the singular battle was to take place to decide his daughter's case. When he was only a few miles from the city he came upon a page who had more recent news: / a knight had presented himself, a stranger, to take up Guinevere's defence; his emblem was unfamiliar, and he remained unknown, for he habitually chose concealment. Even now after his arrival, no one had yet had sight of his face; even his own squire would swear he had no idea who his master was. /

They rode on a little further and came to the walls of the city, and stood at the gates. Dalinda was afraid to go further, but she kept going, encouraged by Rinaldo. The gates were shut, and Rinaldo asked the porter what this meant. He was told that the entire city had gathered to watch the battle / now taking place at the other end of town in a broad, flat meadow between Lurcanio and an unknown knight. The duel, he was told, had already started. The gates were opened to Rinaldo and at once closed behind him. He passed through the deserted city, leaving the damsel at the first inn they reached. / He told her to stay here safely until he came back, which would not be long; then he hastened towards the field where the two warriors had already exchanged many a blow and were still fighting hard.

Here was Lurcanio whose heart was set in enmity against Guinevere; and here too was the other knight, valiantly sustaining her defence. / In addition there were six knights in the lists, all dismounted, and wearing breastplates, and Polynex, Duke of Albany, mounted on a powerful thoroughbred. As Lord High Constable, he was in charge of the lists. The sight of Guinevere in such peril filled his heart with joy, while his face remained proudly impassive. / Rinaldo thrust his way through the crowds, noble Bayard clearing a path as he went—indeed, those who heard his stormy approach jumped out of the way helter-skelter. In rode the paladin, a towering figure on horseback—he looked the very flower of champions. He drew rein before the king's tribune, and everyone drew close to hear what he had to ask. /

'Your Highness,' said he, 'let not this battle proceed further; whichever of these two dies, know that you will wrongly sanction his death. The first believes he is right, but he is in error, and speaks falsely, not knowing that he does so; for the self-same mistake which led his brother to slay himself has armed him for this fight. / The second knows not whether he is right or wrong, but purely out of courtesy and goodness of heart is he risking his life to save so rare a beauty from death. I come bringing safety to the innocent—and to him who perpetrates fraud I bring the reverse. Now for God's sake part these warriors, then listen to what I shall relate to you.' /

The king was so struck by the authoritative air of Rinaldo, who clearly must be a man of eminence, that he signalled for the battle to be suspended. To the king, then, and to the peers of the realm, and to the knights and all the vast crowd Rinaldo unfolded the story of the plot which Polynex had contrived against Guinevere; / after which he proposed to prove the truth of his assertions by arms. Polynex was called; he appeared, looking far from composed; nonetheless, he brazenly denied everything. 'Now,' said Rinaldo, 'now for the proof!' Each was armed, the field was ready, and they proceeded to battle without delay. / Oh, how much it meant to the king and to his people that Guinevere be proved innocent! They all hoped that God would give clear demonstration that she had been falsely taxed with un-chastity. Polynex was commonly reputed cruel, proud and mean, evil and false; few, therefore, would have been surprised if it turned out that he had contrived the whole deception. /

Glum, pale, and quaking, Polynex waited; at the third trumpet blast he set his lance in rest. Rinaldo, with an eye to a quick finish, hurtled towards his opponent, aiming to transfix him with his lance: in this he fully succeeded, for he thrust it into the other's breast till it had penetrated half-way up the shaft. / Thus transfixed he dragged him onto the ground a good six lengths from his horse. He leaped off Bayard, grasped his foe's helmet before he could raise himself and un-fastened it. But the other, scarcely in a fit state to continue the fight, humbly craved mercy and confessed to him, in the hearing of the king and the court, the treachery which had brought him to his death. / He did not reach the end of his confession, for half-way through a word both voice and life forsook him.

The king, who had seen his daughter saved from death and from dishonour, was as relieved and overjoyed as if, having lost his crown, he had just now seen it restored to him. He paid unique respect to Rinaldo, / whom he recognized as soon as the paladin took off his helmet, for he had seen him before; and he raised his hands to God who had afforded him such rare assistance. The other knight, the unknown warrior who had borne arms for Guinevere, to succour her in her evil plight, had stood aside to witness what had happened. / The king asked him to disclose his name, or at least to reveal his face, as he wished to reward him as he deserved for his good intention. The knight after many entreaties, took off his helmet, revealing beyond any doubt what I shall go on to tell you in the next canto, if you would like to hear about it.

SIXTH CANTO

1–3 Introductory. 3–16 Rinaldo's exploit happily concluded.
16–56 Ruggiero arrives on the island of Alcina and hears
Astolfo's story. 57–81 Ruggiero meets Alcina's minions.

UNHAPPY the man who works evil in the confidence that his misdeed
will remain concealed; though all others remain silent, the air will take
up the cry, and the very earth in which the deed lies buried. And often,
in God's providence, the sin leads on the sinner until, after some days'
indulgence, he inadvertently betrays himself though nobody has
challenged him. / The wretched Polynex had imagined that, with the
suppression of Dalinda, the only person who could divulge his secret,
he would obliterate all trace of his crime. But, heaping this second
extravagance upon the first, he hastened on the evil which he might have
deferred—he might have deferred and perhaps even have avoided it,
but instead he spurred himself on towards his death. / And he lost
his friends, his life and station all at once, as also his honour, which was
a far worse privation.

Now, as I was saying, the knight whose identity was still unknown,
after many entreaties, consented to remove his helmet; the face he
revealed was one much-beloved, one they had seen many a time: he
revealed himself as Ariodant, whose loss had been so bewailed throughout Scotland— / Ariodant, whose death Guinevere had bewailed, and
his own brother, and the king, too, and the court and all the people,
for he had been a paragon of courtesy and valour. It appeared, then,
that the traveller had given a false account of him; and yet it was
quite true that he had seen him plunge headfirst into the sea from the
cliff-top. / But a man at his wits' end will often enough court death
from a distance only to shun it on closer approach, so stark and grim
do its jaws appear. Thus it was with Ariodant who, once he found
himself in the sea, changed his mind about dying; and being strong,
bold, and agile, he set to swimming and regained the shore. / And,
dismissing his death-wish as a piece of sheer folly, he walked off,
soaking wet as he was, and came to the abode of a hermit. Here he
decided to tarry in secret, until such time as he learnt how Guinevere
had taken the news of his death—whether she had rejoiced at it,
or whether it had left her mournful and compassionate. / He heard,
first, of Guinevere's anguish, so acute that her very life was imperilled;

word of her sorrow had spread so wide that it was the talk of the whole island; indeed, she had been affected in quite the opposite way to what the false witness of his eyes had, to his great torment, led him to suppose.

Then he heard how Lurcanio had accused the princess before the king. / Anger towards his brother now enflamed his heart no less fiercely than his earlier love for Guinevere: Lurcanio's action seemed to him all too merciless and cruel, for all that it proceeded from brotherly affection. Not one knight, he learned, had stepped forward to defend her, for Lurcanio was so redoubtable a fighter that no one was in a hurry to oppose him; / and besides, those at all acquainted with him held him for a man of such discretion, wisdom, and prudence that he would never risk his life as he was doing, if what he said was untrue. This being so, it was generally felt wiser not to embrace what might be a bad cause. After much debate, Ariodant decided to counter his brother's accusation. /

'Alas,' said he to himself, 'I cannot hear of her perishing on my account—my death would be too bitter, too unkind, were I to see her die before me. She is still my lady, my goddess, still the light of my eyes: be it right or wrong, I must take up her defence, though I remain dead on the field. / I know I'm embracing a bad cause: so be it, and I shall die for it. None of this disturbs me except for the knowledge that my death shall entail the death of so lovely a maiden. In dying I shall find one sole consolation—that if her Polynex does in fact love her, she will be able to see for herself that he won't have lifted a finger to help her, / while I, whom she has so grievously wronged, I shall, as she will see, go to my death in an effort to save her. By the same act I shall wreak vengeance on my brother, who has set light to so great a fire: I shall make him smart when he discovers the final outcome of his cruel undertaking—he will imagine that he has avenged his brother when in fact he shall have slain him with his own hand.' / Thus minded, he equipped himself with new arms and a fresh horse; his apparel was black, and the shield he bore was black with a yellow-green motif. Happening upon a page who was a stranger to those parts, he hired him, and unrecognized (as I have related) he presented a challenge to his armed brother. / I have told you what happened then, and how Ariodant disclosed himself.

The king was overjoyed as much as he had been earlier, when his daughter was set at liberty. Never, he realized, could he hope to meet with a truer or a more faithful lover—one who, after being so wronged, had undertaken the princess's defence against his own brother. / In deference to his own inclination (for he loved Ariodant well), and to the prayers of the whole court and to those, most insistent, of Rinaldo, the king gave him his lovely daughter for a bride. And the Duchy of Albany, which reverted to the king on the death of Polynex, could not have fallen vacant at a better time, for he settled it upon her as a dowry. / Rinaldo besought pardon for Dalinda, and she was discharged of her guilt; now, sickened of living in the world, she turned her thoughts to God and paid her vows to Him; and, leaving Scotland without more ado, she went away to become a nun in Denmark.

But now it is time to return to Ruggiero, still coursing through the sky on the wind-borne beast. / Courageous man that he was, Ruggiero's face retained its normal hue; but I do believe that his heart within him was trembling like a leaf. He had left the European mainland far behind him, and had passed way out beyond the bounds which matchless Hercules had set for mariners. / That great and wondrous bird, the hippogryph, bore him away so fast in winged flight that he far outpaced the eagle when it guides the falling thunderbolt. No creature sweeps through the air at a speed to equal his—I doubt whether thunder and lightning are more swift when they dart from the heavens. / The winged steed, after flying straight as an arrow for many a league, never once deflecting from his course, finally, as though sated with the air, began in lazy gyres to descend upon an island. After long hiding from her lover and taxing his constancy, the virgin Arethusa came to just such an island by a dark, hollow passage beneath the sea. /

No lovelier, no happier land than this did he behold of any over which the steed had stretched his wings; were he to search the whole wide world, a more delightful land than this he would never find; here the great bird, after a broad circular sweep, descended with Ruggiero. Here were well-tilled plains and neat hills, limpid waters, shady banks, and soft meadows, / enticing thickets of cool laurel, of palms and loveliest myrtle, of cedar and orange-trees whose fruit and blossoms were disposed in sundry harmonious ways—these all afforded shade, with their thick spreading foliage, against the searing heat of the summer's day. And, safe amid their branches, flitted melodious nightingales. / Hares and rabbits were to be espied hopping among the deep-red roses and white lilies which a temperate breeze kept ever fresh; and deer, holding high their splendid heads, roamed about, stooping to crop the grass, quite unafraid that any might slay or capture them. Fawns and nimble goats skipped deftly—many was their number in these rustic parts. /

When the hippogryph was so close to the ground that to jump from his back would be less perilous, Ruggiero quickly slipped from the saddle and set foot on the green sward. He kept firm hold of the reins, though, lest the steed once more took wing, and tethered him to a green myrtle branch growing by the sea, by the water's edge, between a laurel and a pine. / And close by, where a spring bubbled up surrounded by cedars and fruitful palms, he set down his shield, drew off his helm and gauntlets, and turned his face now to the sea, now to the hills to capture the fresh vigorous breeze which, with a cheerful murmur, set the high tree-tops—the beeches and firs—a-rustling. / He dipped his parched lips in the fresh crystal pool and splashed himself to cool his veins, for he was overheated in his armour and little wonder if he found it burdensome, for not a solitary soul had presented himself for battle, and here he had travelled, all of three thousand miles at a stretch, armed to the teeth. /

While Ruggiero was here, his steed, which he had left in the cool shade of a dense thicket, shied away, frightened by I know not what he had descried in the tangled wood. He so tore apart the myrtle to which he was tethered that he became ensnared in the branches strewn underfoot; he tugged at the myrtle, bringing down a shower of leaves, but was unable to pull free. / If a log with but a soft core of pith is placed in the fire, it starts to whine, because the intense heat consumes the vaporous air inside it, and it sizzles noisily so long as the vapour forces a way out. Just so, the damaged myrtle moaned and hissed in vexation, and finally a sad, tearful voice / issued from an open pore, and framed words pronounced with utmost clarity: 'If you are good and kind, as your fair looks suggest, loose this animal from my branches. Let my own ill-fortune be sufficient torment without the addition of more evil, more pain inflicted upon me from without.' / At the first sound of this voice Ruggiero turned his face and jumped up; when he realized that it issued from the tree, he was no little astonished.

He hastened to untie the hippogryph and, blushing for shame, 'Whatever you are,' he said, 'whether human spirit or woodland goddess, pardon me. / If I deranged your fair branches and wrought damage to your living myrtle, it was through not knowing that a human spirit was hidden beneath your rough bark. But do not deny me an answer: tell me who you are, who live and speak, a rational being in a spiky, contorted body—so may heaven's hailstones ever spare you! / And if now or in the future I can do you some favour by way of amends, I promise you, by the fair woman in whose keeping lies the best part of me, that I shall so perform in word and action that you shall have just cause to thank me.' Thus spoke Ruggiero, and the myrtle quivered from head to foot. / Perspiration now beaded through the tree's bark, like a faggot green from the forest which feels the flame overwhelm it after vainly trying to resist the heat.

'Your courtesy so prevails upon me that I must tell you both who I was and who it is who has changed me into this myrtle by the soft sea-shore. / Astolfo was my name; I was a paladin, much feared in battle; Orlando and Rinaldo were my cousins, whose fame has broken all bounds. I was heir, after my father Otho, to the crown of England. Handsome I was, and graceful, so that I was beloved by not a few ladies—yet in the end I proved my own undoing. /

'I was returning from those distant isles washed on the East by the Indian Sea, where with Rinaldo and others I had been shut away in a darkened vault until Orlando there displayed his utmost strength. We were journeying Westward, then, along the dunes which endure the wrath of the North winds. / Hard, spiteful Fate traced our path which brought us out, one morning, onto a lovely beach on which stood a castle of the potent Alcina. She had come forth from it, and we found her standing alone at the edge of the sea: she was pulling ashore all the fishes she wanted, though she had neither net nor hook. / Swift-moving dolphins hastened to her, and ponderous tunny, open-mouthed; the sperm whales and the sea-lions were disturbed out of their indolent sleep; mullet and jelly-fish, salmon and black-fish came in shoals, as fast as they could swim; sea-wolves and cachalots, grampus and orcs rose out of the sea with their monstrous backs. / We descried a whale, the largest one ever to be seen in the ocean: its vast shoulders protruded eleven cubits and more above the briny waves. All of us fell into the same deception—we took it for an island, it lay so still with never even a ripple, and its two extremities were at so great a distance apart. / Alcina drew the fishes out of the water with simple words and magic charms. She and the witch Morgana were born of the same mother, but whether she was delivered first or last, or whether both at once I cannot say.

'Well, Alcina looked at me, and she liked what she saw, as was clear from her face; so she devised a crafty ruse to take me away from my companions; and here she succeeded. / With a cheerful smile she came to meet us, and showed easy courtesy as she addressed us: "Good sirs, if you would like to abide with me today, I shall show you every manner of fish among those I have caught: some with scales, some all pulpy, some fur-clad, and more abundant than the stars in the sky. / And should you wish to see a siren, who can still the waves with her sweet singing, go with me to this further beach where she always comes at this hour." She pointed to the vast whale which, as I said, looked like a small island. I, who have always (to my regret) been too impetuous, stepped onto that fish. / Rinaldo, and Dudone likewise, signalled to me not to go, but to no avail. Smiling, Alcina left them to themselves and stepped on behind me. The whale, faithful to its office, swam off through the salt waves. I was not long in regretting my folly, but by then I was too far from the shore. / Rinaldo flung himself into the sea to help me, but he almost sank, for a raging wind blew up from the

South, drawing a dark veil over sky and sea. I know not what became
of him. Alcina meanwhile addressed herself to reassuring me.

'All that day and through the night she kept me in the midst of the
sea on the monster's back, / until we came to this beautiful island.
Alcina owns a great part of it, having stolen a share from Logistilla,
a sister of hers who, as the only legitimate daughter, had been left the
whole of it by their father. Alcina and Morgana, as she fully avowed
to me, were both born of incest. / A wicked, pernicious pair they make,
surfeited with every sort of ugly infamy; not so Logistilla—she is one
who has steeped her heart in all that is virtuous, and lives in chastity.
The two have conspired against her, and have recruited more than one
army to drive her from the island; time and again they have seized
castles from her—over a hundred of them; / indeed, Logistilla would
be left with not so much as a parcel of land were it not that the island
is narrowed on one side by a creek, and on the other by a deserted
mountain—similar to the mountain and the firth which separate
England from Scotland. Not that this deters Alcina and Morgana
from trying to wrest from her what little is left. / The pair of them,
being vicious to the core, cannot endure her, because she is chaste and
good.

'But I was telling you how it came about that I was turned into a
tree: Alcina entertained me in luxury, all ablaze as she was with love
for me—and I burned for her no less ardently, seeing how beautiful
she was, and how indulgent. / In her delicate body I found all my
delight; every treasure was concentrated here, so it seemed to me, which
is normally shared out among human kind, some enjoying more,
others less, and no one having a large share. Lost in contemplation of
her looks, I quite forgot about France and all else—my every thought,
my every good design ended in her, and never went beyond. / I was
her beloved, too, as much as she was mine, or more. Alcina gave no
further thought to anyone else: she had abandoned all her other
lovers—for before me there had been a fair number. She made me her
counsellor, kept me at her side day and night, set all the others under
my command. Me she believed, to me she referred everything; night
and day she would never address another, only me. / Alas! Why must
I keep touching my wounds when I have no hope of a balm? Why
must I recollect the good that was, now that I am suffering the most
rigorous penitence? Whilst I counted myself happy, and whilst I
believed I stood highest in Alcina's love, she took back from me the
gift of her heart, and threw herself body and soul into a fresh infatuation. /

'I was late in discovering the fickleness of her nature, prone to falling
in and out of love all at once. I had reigned in her affection for but two

months when a new lover was assumed in my place. She drove me out
disdainfully, and withdrew her favour from me. Later I learnt that she
had meted similar treatment to a thousand lovers before me, and
always without cause. / And, to prevent their spreading about the
world the story of her wanton ways, she transforms them, every one,
planting them here and there in the fertile soil, changing one into a
fir-tree, another into an olive, another into a palm or cedar, or into the
guise in which you see me on this verdant bank; yet others the proud
enchantress changes into liquid springs, or into beasts, just as it suits
her. /

'Now you, sir, have reached this enchanted island by an unusual
way, and some lover shall, on your account, be turned into stone or
water or something of the sort. A sceptre shall be yours, from Alcina's
hand, and you shall reign, and you shall be the happiest of mortal
men: but make no mistake—your time will soon come to be changed
into a beast or a fountain, into wood or rock. / I have gladly given
you warning, not that I imagine it will be of any use to you; and yet it
is better that you should not go unprepared but rather knowing something of her ways. Perhaps, as faces differ, so do wit and skill, and you
will devise some way to forestall the worst—some way which a
thousand before you have not discovered.' /

Ruggiero had heard that Astolfo was cousin to his lady, Bradamant,
and he was deeply afflicted on seeing the change the knight had
undergone from his true self into a scrawny, sterile shrub. And for the
love he bore his lady, he would gladly have been of service to him (if
only he had known how); but all he could do was to offer him consolation. / This he did as best he could; then he asked him if there was
a way to reach the territory of Logistilla, whether by hill or by dale, so
as to avoid passing through that of Alcina. There was indeed, returned
the myrtle, a way studded with sheer rocks, if he went on a little
towards the right, and climbed the hill towards the craggy peak. / But
he was not to reckon on making much headway along that path, for
he would come upon a whole band of pugnacious roughs, who would
provide no easy passage. Alcina deployed them there to act as a wall or
dyke stopping whoever would seek to escape from her clutches.
Ruggiero thanked the myrtle for everything, then left him, duly
forewarned. /

He approached the hippogryph, untethered him, grasped his reins
and walked him away instead of mounting him, as he had done
before: he was not this time going to be carried off against his wishes.
He pondered how best to reach Logistilla's realm in safety; he was
firmly disposed to do whatever was necessary to avoid falling into
Alcina's power. / He considered mounting his steed and spurring him

on to a new flight through the air, but he feared this might prove a distinct mistake, seeing how little notice the beast took of the bridle. 'I shall force my way through, if I go the right way about it,' he told himself, but all in vain—he had not gone two miles from the shore when Alcina's splendid city came into view. / Off in the distance stood a wall which curved away, embracing a vast stretch of land; it was so high, its top seemed to merge with the heavens, and it looked as if it were solid gold from summit to foot. (There are some who part company with me here and maintain that it is an effect of alchemy; they may know better than I, but, again, they may be quite mistaken. To me it looks like gold, the way it gleams.) / When he was close to these walls whose splendour is unmatched by any others in the world, the doughty knight left the road, which ran broad and straight across the plain to the massive gates, and veered off to the right along the safer path leading up to the mountain heights.

Soon, however, his journey was disturbed and interrupted by the onslaught of the band of ruffians. / Never did you set eyes on a more fantastic throng, or see faces so monstrous and misshapen. Some of them were human from the neck down, but with the head of a monkey or of a cat; some stumped about on cloven hoofs; some were quick, agile centaurs. Some were young and pert, others old and stupid. Some were naked, others clad in strange pelts. / One galloped on an unbridled horse, another plodded along on a donkey or an ox, and yet another mounted a centaur; many rode on the backs of ostriches, eagles and cranes. Some set a horn to their lips, some their cup. They were male and female—some of them both at once. One carried a hook, the next a rope ladder, another a crowbar, yet another a stealthy file. / Their captain could be seen sitting astride a tortoise which shuffled stolidly along; he had a swollen paunch, the captain, and a fat face, and henchmen to support him on either side, as he was drunk and his head kept lolling forward. Some dabbed his forehead and chin while others flapped their garments to fan him. / A creature whose feet and belly were human, but whose neck, head, and ears were those of a dog, barked at Ruggiero to make him turn off towards the fair city which lay behind him. 'Not I,' retorted the knight, 'so long as I have strength to wield this'—and he flourished his sword, aiming its sharp point at the creature's face. /

The monster attacked him with a spear, but Ruggiero let fly at him and ran him through the paunch so that his sword stuck out through his back a palm's width. He grasped his shield and leapt in all directions, but the enemy thronged round him, pricking him here, clawing at him there. He whirled his sword and laid about him savagely, / splitting one open down to the jaw, the next right down to the chest, for this breed of scoundrels goes unarmoured (and besides, no helmet, shield, breastplate, or chain-mail can resist his sword). But he was so hemmed in on all sides that if he was to give himself room and hold this scum at bay, he would have needed more arms and hands than Briareus. / Had he thought of bringing out the shield of Atlas—the shield of the blinding light, which the magician had left suspended from the saddle—he would have overcome the ugly mob in a trice, and made them all fall down in a dazzle. It could be that he would not stoop to using it, preferring to rely on valour rather than on guile. / Be that as it may, he would sooner have died than fall a prisoner to so scurvy a crew.

Now who should sally forth from a gate in the walls (all gold and glitter, as I said), but two damsels. To judge by their bearing and apparel, they were clearly not of mean birth, brought up in poverty by shepherds, but reared amid the opulence of a royal palace. / They each rode on a unicorn whiter than the whitest ermine; both were of great beauty, and so exquisite in their dress and manners that a man would have needed the eyes of a god to look at their appearance and judge them for what they were. They could have passed for Beauty (had she a body) and Grace. / They both came to where Ruggiero was being hard pressed by the brutish throng. These all now melted away and the damsels held out their hand to the knight, who blushingly thanked them for their act of kindness. And, to do their pleasure, he was glad to go with them back to the golden gate. /

Above the gate, and jutting a little over it, the wall was ornamented, and there was not an inch but was encrusted in the rarest jewels from the Levant. Great columns made of solid diamond flanked the gate through the thickness of the walls. Whether they presented a true or false image to the eye, there was nothing like them for grace and felicity. / On the threshold and among the columns nymphs played and frolicked wantonly—their beauty might have been enhanced had they been more jealous of the respect which should have been their due as women. They were all dressed in green skirts and crowned with spring garlands. All smiles and charm, they welcomed Ruggiero into paradise. / The place could well be called by that name: I do believe it was the cradle of Love. Here it was all dancing and play-time, and the hours went by in one continuous festivity. Grey-headed Thought could not dwell here in a single heart, not even for a moment. There was no entrance here for Discomfort or Dearth, but Plenty was ever in attendance with her copious horn. / This was the abode of youths and maidens, here where soft April, presenting a serene and merry face, seemed constantly to smile. By a spring, some there were who sang in sweet, melodious voice; in the shade of a tree or a cliff others played and danced and indulged in honest fun. Another had gone apart, and was communing with his true-love. / Round the tops of the pines and laurels, of the tall beeches and shaggy fir-trees the little cupids flitted and swooped merrily. Some of them were gloating contentedly over their victories; some were carefully aiming their heart-piercing arrows; others were spreading nets. Down by a stream one was honing darts, while another was sharpening his against a smooth stone. / Here Ruggiero was presented with a majestic bay charger; sturdy and robust he was, and his trappings were spangled with precious stones and embroidered with thread of gold. The winged horse, the same which used to do the old Moorish wizard's bidding, was entrusted to a youth, who was to lead him after Ruggiero at a slower pace. /

The two lovesome maidens, the pretty pair who had protected Ruggiero from the band of knaves, the knaves who had forestalled him on the path he had taken off to the right, now addressed him: 'Your valorous deeds, sir, of which we have heard tell, embolden us to avail ourselves of your assistance. / We shall soon be coming to a bog which divides this plain in two. The bridge across it is held by a savage woman called Erifilla, who bullies and tricks and robs whoever would cross to the other side. She is built like a giant; her teeth are fangs and her bite venomous; her nails are pointed and she claws like a bear. / Not only does she keep molesting us on our path, which would be free of obstacle were it not for her, but also she often runs about the garden making a nuisance of herself in one way and another. Many of the murderous mob that attacked you outside the gate are spawn of hers— all of them are her followers, evil, like her, inhospitable and rapacious.' / Answered Ruggiero: 'For you I shall gladly fight not merely one battle but a hundred! Command my person as you will, to the limits of its resources—if I wear plastron and coat of mail, it is not to win myself land or silver, but simply to serve and prosper others, the more so when they are lovely ladies like yourselves.' /

The ladies replied with thanks as befitted a knight of his sort, and they continued in conversation until they came in sight of the bog and the bridge. Here they saw the insolent woman, armed—her arms were made of gold and adorned with emeralds and sapphires. The story of how Ruggiero risked her onslaught I shall defer to the next canto.

SEVENTH CANTO

1–2 Introductory. 2–32 Ruggiero seduced by the sorceress Alcina. 33–80 Bradamant sends the sorceress Melissa to rescue Ruggiero.

HE who travels far afield beholds things which lie beyond the bounds of belief; and when he returns to tell of them, he is not believed, but is dismissed as a liar, for the ignorant throng will refuse to accept his word, but needs must see with their own eyes, touch with their own hands. This being so, I realize that my words will gain scant credence where they outstrip the experience of my hearers. / Still, whatever degree of reliance is placed on my word, I shall not trouble myself about the ignorant and mindless rabble: I know that you, my sharp, clear-headed listeners will see the shining truth of my tale. To convince you, and you alone, is all that I wish to strive for, the only reward I seek.

I left off at the point where they came in sight of the bog and the bridge over it which was guarded by proud Erifilla. / Her armour was of the finest metal, encrusted with gems of various colours—red rubies, yellow topaz, green emeralds, and golden hyacinth. She was mounted, but not upon a horse: she had saddled a wolf, instead, with a saddle of unusual splendour, and this beast she was urging onto the bridge. / I doubt whether in Apulia there would be found one of his size—he bulked even larger than an ox. She had thrust no bit into his mouth to bring the foam to his lips—in fact I have no idea how she schooled him to her bidding. Her Pestilence wore a sand-coloured cape over her armour; apart from its colour, it was not unlike that which bishops and prelates wear at court. / On her shield and helmet she sported a bloated, poisonous toad. The damsels pointed her out to the knight: she had crossed to their side of the bridge to block his path, to joust with him and bring him to shame, as she was normally inclined to do. She shouted to Ruggiero to turn back, but he grasped a lance, and yelled defiance at her. / The massive Amazon did not hesitate: she straightway set spurs to her wolf, braced herself firmly in the saddle and charged, setting her lance in rest as she came; the ground shuddered. But, after the impact, she was left lying on the field— Ruggiero caught her under the helmet and tipped her from the saddle with such force, he carried her back some six lengths. / Now, drawing the sword he had buckled on, he was coming to sever her proud head from her shoulders, as well he could do, for Erifilla was lying prostrate amid the meadow-flowers. But the ladies called to him: 'She is over-thrown—that is enough: no need to wreak any starker vengeance upon her. Sheathe your sword, gentle knight; let us cross the bridge and continue on our way.' /

Their path led through a wood; it was somewhat rough and hard-going, for it was narrow and stony, and climbed steeply. When they reached the top of the hill, though, they came out into broad, open fields, and here they set eyes on the most splendid and delightful palace to be seen in the whole wide world. / From the outer gates stepped forth beauteous Alcina, and came to meet Ruggiero; and, surrounded by a handsome and dignified retinue, she extended to him a regal welcome. The whole court now paid such honour and respect to the valiant knight, they could not have done more had God himself come down from Heaven. / What was remarkable about the splendid palace was not its opulence (unrivalled though it was) so much as its inhabitants—the most attractive, courteous people in the world.

For youth and comeliness there was little to judge between them all; only Alcina outstripped them every one in beauty, as the sun is more radiant than any star. / She was so beautifully modelled, no painter, however much he applied himself, could have achieved anything more perfect. Her long blonde tresses were gathered in a knot: pure gold itself could have no finer lustre. Roses and white privet blooms lent their colours to suffuse her delicate cheeks. Her serene brow was like polished ivory, and in perfect proportion. / Beneath two of the thinnest black arches, two dark eyes—or rather, two bright suns; soft was their look, gentle their movement. Love seemed to flit, frolicsome, about them; indeed, Love from this vantage point would let fly his full quiver and openly steal away all hearts. Down the midst of the face, the nose— Envy herself could find no way of bettering it. / Below this, the mouth, set between two dimples; it was imbued with native cinnabar. Here a beautiful soft pair of lips opened to disclose a double row of choicest pearls. Here was the course of those winning words which could not but soften every heart, however rugged and uncouth. Here was formed the melodious laughter which made a paradise on earth. / Snow-white was her neck, milky her breast; the neck was round, the breast broad and full. A pair of apples, not yet ripe, fashioned in ivory, rose and fell like the sea-swell at times when a gentle breeze stirs the ocean. Argus himself could not see them entire, but you could easily judge that what lay hidden did not fall short of what was exposed to view. / Her arms were justly proportioned, and her lily-white hands were often to be glimpsed: they were slender and tapering, and quite without a knot or swelling vein. A pair of small, neat, rounded feet completes the picture of this august person. Her looks were angelic, heaven-sent —no veil could have concealed them. / Everything about her was an enticement, whether she spoke or laughed or sang, whether she but moved a step.

Little wonder that Ruggiero was ensnared, finding her, as he did, so entrancing. Little did it profit him to have been warned by the myrtle of her evil, treacherous nature—it did not seem to him possible for deceit and perfidy to keep company with so charming a smile. / On the contrary, he preferred to believe that if she had changed Astolfo into a myrtle by the sandy shore, it was because he had treated her with stark ingratitude, and so deserved his fate and worse. Everything he had been told about her he dismissed as false, deeming rather that the wretch was moved by spite and envy and was a shameless liar. / Intensely though he loved fair Bradamant, she was here and now wrested from his heart, for by magic Alcina erased all trace of the pangs with which up till now his soul was smitten. She alone became the unique burden of his love, she alone was now engraved upon his heart. Good Ruggiero must be forgiven, then, for this show of inconstancy. /

Around the festive board zithers, harps, and lyres set the air vibrating with delightful sounds, with soft harmony and tuneful notes. There was song, too, song of love's joys and ecstasies, and recitals of pleasing fantasies framed in verse of happiest inspiration. / Which of the splendid and sumptuous banquets arranged by any of those who sat upon King Ninus' throne, which of the many celebrated feasts offered by Cleopatra to the victorious Roman, which of these can compare to the banquet that the loving sorceress prepared for the paladin? No such feast, I am sure, was ever set out on Olympus when Ganymede ministered to imperial Jove. / When the food and the tables were cleared away, they all sat down in a circle to play a merry game which consisted in each whispering into his neighbour's ear to ask a secret—any secret. This gave the lovers ample occasion to disclose their passion without hindrance; the final outcome was an assignation for that very night. / This game was not continued for long—it was ended far sooner than was the normal custom.

The pages then led the way into the palace with torches, driving out the darkness with an abundance of light. Preceded and followed by elegant company, Ruggiero was escorted to his downy bed in a little bedroom: it was airy and pleasantly decorated, the first choice of all the rooms in the palace. / Once more he was pressed to partake of sweet delicacies and choice wines, after which the company bowed respectfully and withdrew to their own quarters. Ruggiero slipped between the perfumed sheets, which might well have been the handiwork of Arachne herself; he strained his ears now to listen for the approach of lovely Alcina. / At the slightest movement he heard, he would raise his head, hoping it was she; often he heard sounds when in fact there was nothing to hear—and then he would realize his mistake and sigh. Now and then he would jump out of bed, open the door, and look outside, but there was nothing to be seen. Endlessly he cursed weary time for moving so sluggishly. / Often he would tell himself: 'Now she has set out'—and he would start counting the steps which must separate Alcina's room from the one where he awaited her. These and other vain fancies occupied him in the interval before she came, and frequently he feared lest some obstacle be placed between his hand and the fruit. / Alcina all the while was steeping herself in precious perfumes; she put an end to these labours once all was at peace in the household and there was no need for further delay. Now she slipped out of her room and stole by a secret passage to where Ruggiero awaited her; in his heart all this time hope and fear had fought many a round. /

When Astolfo's successor looked up to see those joyful-twinkling stars, he felt as though hot sulphur were coursing through his veins, which threatened to start out from his skin. Now he was engulfed up to his eyes in sheer sweetness, in loveliness. He jumped out of bed and gathered her into his arms, quite unable to wait for her to undress — / for all that she was wearing neither gown nor petticoat: she had come in a light mantle which she had thrown over a white nightgown of gossamer texture. The mantle she abandoned to Ruggiero as he embraced her; this left only the insubstantial gossamer-gown which, before and behind, concealed no more than would a pane of glass placed before a spray of roses or lilies. / Ivy never clung so tightly to the stem round which it was entwined as did the two lovers cling to each other, drawing from each other's lips pollen so fragrant that it will be found on no flower which grows in the scented Indian or Arabian sands. As for describing their pleasure, better to leave this to them – the more so as they frequently had a second tongue in their mouth. / Such matters were kept a secret, or, if no secret, at least they were not spoken of: a seal on the lips often merits praise, seldom blame.

The whole court, astute company that it was, offered Ruggiero its service and a cheerful welcome; everybody reverenced him, deferred to him, for such was the will of love-struck Alcina. / There was not a pleasure which was overlooked, for the love-pavilion afforded every one of them. Two and three times a day they would change their costume depending on the pastime they next intended. Banqueting often, festival ever was the order of the day, with tourneys and trials of strength, with masques, and dances and bathing. Beside a spring, on a shady hillside they would read what was written of love in olden times; / or else they would course through the wooded valleys and over the glad hills, chasing the timid hare; or with their cunning hounds they would flush the frantic, flapping partridge from her cover amid the stubble and the underbrush; they would snare the thrush amid the scented juniper, using a running noose or a soothing lure. Or else they would bait their hooks or cast their nets to disturb the fish out of their contented secrecy. /

Thus did Ruggiero bask in every sort of pleasure, while toil was the lot of Charles the Emperor and of Agramant the King: I should not wish to forget their story, nor to leave aside Bradamant, who for many days bitterly lamented the loss of her lover whom she had seen borne off along so strange a path, she knew not whither. / Before taking up the kings' story, I shall take up hers: for many a day she scoured the country in vain, searching the shady forests and sunny fields, searching farmsteads and cities, hills and plains; but she could glean nothing about her dearest love who was so far, far away. Often she visited the Saracen host, but not a trace could she pick up of her Ruggiero. / Each day she would question over a hundred souls, but not one of them could give her news of him. She would go from one encampment to the next, seeking for him in every tent and pavilion. This was not difficult, for she could go among the mounted troops and those on foot thanks to the ring which, against all human experience, made her vanish when she put it in her mouth. / She could not, nor would she, seek him among the dead: the mighty downfall of a man so great would have made itself heard from the Indus to the lands of the setting sun. She could not tell, she could not imagine where his path lay, on or above the earth, and yet pitifully she kept searching for him, with sighs and tears and every kind of sorrow for companions. /

Eventually she thought of returning to the cave which sheltered the prophet Merlin's bones; she would scream so piercingly about his tomb that the cold marble would be moved to pity. And whether Ruggiero still lived, or whether Death—that ultimate necessity—had cut short his happy years, she would here discover. Then she would pursue whatever course was best proposed. /

Thus decided, she set off towards the forests neighbouring Ponthieu, where, in wild and hilly country, was concealed the tomb from which Merlin spoke. Now the enchantress who had ever followed Bradamant in her thoughts, I mean the one who had instructed her about her posterity in the gorgeous cavern— / the good and wise enchantress, who had always taken care of her, knowing her destiny as mother of unconquerable men, indeed of demi-gods—sought daily to know what she was doing, what saying, and daily cast spells to favour her. Ruggiero's delivery from Atlas, his abduction, where now he was in India, all this was known to her. / She had seen him mounted on that unbridled horse which he could not control, sailing out into the distance along so perilous and strange a path. Full well she knew how he was passing his time now in amusements, in dancing and feasting, in soft, pampered indolence, forgetful of his Liege, of his beloved, of his own renown. / And it might therefore have been the lot of so goodly a knight to pass the best years of his life in sustained idleness, only to lose his soul and body all at once. And that odour, which is all we leave behind once our frail carcass falls to dust, and saves us from the tomb and keeps us ever-living, that odour would be like a fragrant flower severed from its stem or plucked out from the grass. / But the kind sorceress, who took more care of him then he did of himself, thought how to bring him back to true virtue, despite himself, by a hard and rugged way—just like a skilled physician who treats a wound with iron and fire, and often with poison: even though at first he causes much pain, he ultimately does good, and receives thanks. /

She showed him no indulgence: a transcendent love made her so blind to all else that she had, like Atlas, set her heart upon restoring his life to him. Atlas, however, would have him enjoy long life bereft of honour and renown rather than forego one year of his carefree existence for all the praise the world could accord him. / He had sent Ruggiero to Alcina's island to make him, at her court, forget about arms. And, being a magician of consummate art, skilled in every kind of magic spell, he had bound that queen's heart to his in so strong a bond that there was no question of her breaking free, though Ruggiero were to grow as old as Nestor. /

But back to the enchantress who could see into the future: she set out and found the wandering Bradamant on her way to see her. Coming upon her friend the enchantress, Bradamant found new hope in place of the anguish which had hitherto been all her company. The prophetess disclosed the truth to her—that her Ruggiero had been carried off to Alcina. / The maiden was stunned to learn just how far away was her beloved—and worse, that without immediate and effective help, their very love for each other was imperilled. But the kind enchantress comforted her and was quick to apply a dressing to the throbbing wound: she gave her word that within a few days she would restore Ruggiero to her. /

'As you possess the ring', she said, 'which is proof against every magic spell, I have not the least doubt that if I take it with me to the place where Alcina is purloining your treasure, I shall foil her designs and bring back to you your only-beloved. I shall set out this evening with the gathering dusk, and as dawn breaks I shall be in India.' / She went on to explain to her the manner in which she intended to use the ring so as to rescue her loved one from the soft, womanly realm and bring him back to France. Bradamant drew the ring from her finger; not only this would she have handed over, but also her heart, her very life, if this might have procured help for her Ruggiero. / She gave her the ring, and commended herself to the enchantress; even more did she commend Ruggiero to her, bidding her convey to him all her fondest love. Then, by a different path, she set out towards Provence.

The enchantress went her own way, and, to put her plan into effect, she that evening conjured up a palfrey; he was black all over, except for a red foot. / I believe he must have been some spirit she had summoned in that shape from hell. Barefoot and ungirded, she mounted him; her hair , now hideously withered, fell loose about her. She took the ring off her finger lest it would inhibit her own magic. Then she left in such haste that the following morning found her on Alcina's island. / Here she underwent a remarkable transformation: she put on almost a foot in height, grew her limbs stouter, and ended up so proportioned that she passed for Atlas, the wizard who had brought up Ruggiero so dotingly. She clothed her chin in a long beard and induced wrinkles on her brow and all over. / In face, speech, and person she took him off so perfectly that she seemed none other than the sorcerer himself.

Then she concealed herself, and remained alert for the moment when at last Ruggiero did not have the love-sick Alcina at his side—this was a stroke of fortune, for, go or stay, she could not stand being parted from him for even an hour. / She found him all on his own, as she wanted, enjoying the freshness and peace of the morning beside a delightful stream which flowed down a hillside towards a pleasant, limpid lake. The delicious softness of his dress suggested sloth and sensuality; Alcina had woven the garment with her own hands in silk and gold, a subtle work. / A glittering, richly jewelled necklace fastened round his neck and hung to his chest, while his two arms, hitherto so virile, were now each clasped by a lustrous bangle. Each ear was pierced by a fine gold ring from which a fat pearl hung, such as no Arabian or Indian ever boasted. / His curly locks were saturated in perfumes, the most precious and aromatic that exist. His every gesture was mincing, as though he were accustomed to waiting on ladies in Valencia. All about him was sickly, all but his name; the rest was but corruption and decay. Thus was Ruggiero discovered, thus changed from his true self by sorcery. /

The enchantress, then, presented herself to Ruggiero in Atlas' likeness, with Atlas' grave, venerable face which had always commanded his respect; on his face he wore the look of angry menace which Ruggiero had feared from early childhood.

'Are these then the fruits', she exclaimed, 'for which I have toiled so long? / Early I fed you on the marrow of bears and lions; I accustomed you as a child to strangle snakes in grottoes and wild ravines, to disarm the clawing panthers and tigers and draw the tusks off live boars—was all this schooling to no better purpose than to make you play Adonis, or Atys, to Alcina? / Was this, then, the promise of your manhood, made to me when you were still but a child at the breast—this the promise of the stars I studied, and the sacral threads, the conjunctions, the dreams and auguries and omens which have been my all-too-assiduous study? It was in deeds of arms that you were to stand out, a matchless champion. / A goodly beginning, this, from which we can hope soon to see you become another Alexander, Scipio, or Caesar! Alas, who could ever have dreamed it possible that you of all people would become a bondsman to Alcina! To make this obvious to everyone, you wear about your neck and on your arms the chains with which she drags you to her bidding. /

'Though you care nothing for your own renown, and for the shining deeds for which Heaven has appointed you, why must you defraud your own posterity of all the good which I have a thousand times predicted to you? What of the womb in which—so Heaven has decreed—you're to conceive a glorious and god-like race, more radiant than the sun: why must you suffer it to remain eternally sealed? / The noblest spirits conceived in the Eternal Mind must at their appointed time take human form, springing from the stock rooted in you: prevent them not! Do not prevent the triumphant and victorious deeds whereby your children, and your children's children shall heal Italy of her dread afflictions and dire injuries, and restore her to her pristine glory. / Many and many a gracious soul, brilliant, illustrious, eminent, peerless, and holy is to be sprung as shoots from your fecund tree; even if all of these cannot weigh upon your decision, yet but one pair should be sufficient: Hippolytus and his brother, the likes of whom have seldom been encountered in the world to this day, for sheer eminence of virtue. / I used to speak to you more often of these two than of all the others put together, for, among them all, they shall enjoy the lion's share of pre-eminent qualities; also, when I spoke of them, I saw you pay closer attention than when I spoke of other of your seed—I saw you rejoice that such illustrious heroes were to be descended from you. /

'This woman you have made your queen, what has she to distinguish her from a thousand other whores? This woman, she's the whole world's concubine: judge for yourself whether she can really satisfy!

Now, that you may know who Alcina is, stripped of her artifices and deceits, put this ring on your finger and return to her, and you shall realize just how fair are her looks.' /

Ruggiero stood shamefaced and silent, staring at the ground, not knowing what to say. The enchantress put the ring on his little finger, and brought him back to reality. Coming to himself, Ruggiero was so overwhelmed with shame that he wished himself a thousand feet below ground, so that no one could look him in the face. / After these words, the enchantress switched back into her own likeness, as she had no further need to borrow Atlas', her effect once achieved. What I neglected to tell you earlier was her name: Melissa. She now gave Ruggiero a true account of herself and of her mission. / She had been sent, she explained, by one who loved him and ever longed for him, by one who could not be without him; she had come to deliver him from the shackles which had been forced upon him by sorcery. And in order the better to gain his confidence, she had assumed Atlas' form. But now that she had restored him to his senses, she would set all the facts before him. /

'A most worthy lady who loves you, and who would be deserving of your love—and, unless you are forgetful, you must realize how much you owed your liberty to the service she rendered you—this lady sends you this ring, proof against all magic. Her very heart she would have sent, had her heart possessed the same virtues as this ring to procure your safety.' / She went on to speak of the love which Bradamant bore him, and she commended her merits in terms which combined truth with warmth of feeling. Being a skilled messenger, she chose her words to the best advantage, and she implanted in Ruggiero an utter revulsion for Alcina, such as one would feel for any loathsome object. /

She made her an object of disgust to him, for all that he had loved her up till now; be not surprised, though—his love had been wrought out of enchantment, and, with the ring, the spell was broken. What else the ring showed up was that Alcina's beauty was in every detail an imposture: it was wholly fraudulent—nothing, from her soles up to her tresses, was natural to her. Her beauty evaporated, leaving nothing but dregs. / If a child sets aside a ripe fruit and then, forgetting where he put it, is brought to the very place many days later and happens upon his fruit, he is amazed to find it all rotten and putrid, and not at all as he had left it; and though he normally had a weakness for that sort of fruit, he throws this one away in loathing and revulsion— / so it was with Ruggiero: once Melissa had made him set eyes again upon Alcina, but this time wearing the ring that makes the wearer, while he has it on his finger, totally immune to magic, he was astonished to find that in place of the beauty he had just parted from, he was confronted with a woman so hideous that her equal for sheer ugliness and decrepitude could be found nowhere on earth. / She was whey-faced, wrinkled, and hollow-cheeked; her hair was white and sparse; she was not four feet high; the last tooth had dropped out of her jaw; she had lived longer than anyone on earth, longer than Hecuba or the Cumaean Sibyl. But she made such use of arts unknown in our day that she could pass for young and fair. / Young and fair she made herself by artifice, and deceived many as she deceived Ruggiero. But now, with the ring, he could read the cards aright and see the truth which for so many years had been kept hidden. Small wonder, then, if Ruggiero could no longer find in himself the slightest inclination to love Alcina, now that he was so equipped when he came upon her that her deceit could no longer serve her. /

But, as Melissa advised him, he betrayed no change in his face until he had resumed his armour, from head to foot, which for so many days he had neglected. And, so as to avert Alcina's suspicions, he pretended to try it on just to see how easily he could manage it—he pretended to see if he could still squeeze into it after so many days since he last wore it. / Then he buckled on his sword, which was called Balisard, and took up the miraculous shield, which not merely dazzles the eyes but so clouds the spirit that, to all appearances, it takes leave of the body. He took up the shield, then, still sheathed in its silken drape, and slung it from his shoulder. / Next, he went to the stables and had a horse saddled and bridled—a black horse, black as pitch, chosen on Melissa's instructions, for she knew that he could run like the wind. Those who knew him called him Rabican—he was the very horse which was borne on whale-back to this place, together with the knight who is now the sport of the breeze by the edge of the sea. / He might have taken the hippogryph, who was tethered next to Rabican, but Melissa had told him, 'Bear in mind that he is, as you know, too unruly.' And she gave him to hope that the next day she would take out the hippogryph and help Ruggiero to learn little by little how to control him and make him go anywhere. / Leaving him alone, too, Ruggiero would not arouse suspicions about the secret escape he was contriving. He did as Melissa directed—she kept, unseen, by his ear the whole time.

Thus feigning, he slipped out of the ancient harlot's palace, all soft sensuality, and came to a gate which gave onto the road leading to Logistilla's domain. / He drove into the sentinels, sword in hand, and caught them unawares; some he left wounded, others slain, and then charged out across the bridge. Before Alcina had an inkling of what had befallen, Ruggiero was already well away. In the next canto I shall tell you what path he took, and how he came to the realm of Logistilla.

EIGHTH CANTO

*1–2 Introductory. 3–21 Ruggiero escapes from Alcina. 21–28
Rinaldo's mission to Scotland and England. 29–68 Angelica
abducted by the pirates of Ebuda. 69–91 Orlando leaves Paris
in search of Angelica.*

SORCERERS and sorceresses, we may not know it but you thrive among
us! Artfully you disguise your faces and ensnare the hearts of the
opposite sex. You work your magic not by virtue of obedient sprites
nor by conning the stars for signs: by trickery, lies, and dissimulation
you bind the hearts of others with knots that cannot be untied. / Those
of us who possessed Angelica's ring—I mean the ring of Reason—
could descry each person's true face, undisguised by cunning artifice. A
man who passes for handsome and kind may well, beneath his veneer,
look like an ugly brute. Ruggiero, then, was most fortunate to have the
ring which disclosed to him the truth. /

As I said, Ruggiero feigned his way out and came to the gates, armed
and mounted on Rabican. He took the guards unawares and, as he
drove into them, he did not leave his sword in its sheath. Some he left
dead, others the worse for wear, before he rode out across the bridge
and smashed his way through the palisade. He set out towards the
woods, but after only a short way he came upon one of Alcina's
minions. / On his wrist the man was carrying some bird of prey which
he liked to take out with him daily into the fields or to a nearby pond
where there was always plenty of game to be caught. At his side trotted
his faithful hound, and he was riding a quite ordinary hack. Seeing how
fast Ruggiero was approaching, he judged that he must be a fugitive. /

The fellow made towards him and in an arrogant tone enquired:
'Why such haste?' Ruggiero did not see fit to reply, so the other, more
certain than ever that he was a fugitive, decided he must be stopped.
He extended his left hand and cried: 'What will you say if I stop you
in your tracks—you'll find no shelter from this bird of mine!' / The
huntsman released his bird, which winged away so fast that Rabican
could not outdistance it. Then he jumped off his horse and in a trice
had unbridled him: the horse became like an arrow shot from a bow
and arrived kicking and biting viciously. Right behind him came
the huntsman, as though borne on a lick of flame, or on the very
wind. / Now the hound did not wish to play the laggard, but was off

after Rabican like a hunting-cat after a hare. Ruggiero would have deemed it cowardly not to stand his ground, so he turned to face the man approaching at such a dashing stride. For all weapons the fellow carried only a small stick—the kind used to teach a dog obedience —so Ruggiero did not deign to draw his sword. / The huntsman reached him and landed him a powerful blow, while the hound sunk his teeth into his left foot. The unbridled horse meanwhile kicked out repeatedly with his back legs, which thudded against Ruggiero's right side. The bird wheeled and circled, every so often ripping at him with its talons, and so terrifying the charger with its shrieks that he scarce answered to spur or rein. / Finally Ruggiero's sword flashed out: if he was to stop their molesting him, there was no other way. Cut and thrust, he threatened the beasts and their master in turn, but his assailants only pinned him down the more: together they had closed the whole width of the path to him. Ruggiero foresaw the shame and evil he must incur if they delayed him further. / He knew that if he tarried there longer, any moment would bring into view Alcina and her minions. Already the valleys were ringing to the sound of bells, trumpets, and drums. He could see that against an unarmed groom with a dog his sword was not the answer: he would obtain better and faster results if he disclosed the shield which Atlas had made. / He stripped off the scarlet cloth which had covered the shield these many days, and the dazzle achieved its well-proved effect the moment it caught the eye of the beholders. The huntsman was left senseless; horse and hound collapsed all of a heap, and the bird's pinions fell inert, powerless to sustain it in flight. Ruggiero was glad to leave them all a prey to sleep. /

Alcina, meanwhile, had been told how Ruggiero had stormed the gates and killed several of the guard. She could almost have died for grief; she rent her garments and flayed her cheeks, cursing herself for an idiot and a fool. She raised the alarm at once and summoned her henchmen to her, every one. / She split them into two groups, sending one along the path Ruggiero had taken, and assembling the other at the harbour to board ship and put out from shore: in the shadow of the spreading sails the whole sea grew dark. Alcina embarked with these; such was her desperation, such her devouring lust for Ruggiero that she left her city unguarded. /

She left no one to guard her palace, which gave Melissa the opportunity for which she had been waiting, to steal into this sinister stronghold and liberate the unfortunates detained there. Here was her opportunity to find everything in its proper place and lay her hands on it—figurines to burn, seals to remove, knots, magic squares, and whorls to disarrange. / Then, hastening through the countryside in search of the discarded lovers whom Alcina had turned—a great host of them—into wood or stone, into springs or wild beasts, she restored them all to their proper selves. Finding themselves now able to move freely, they all set off in the footsteps of good Ruggiero, and so made their escape to Logistilla's kingdom, whence they returned each to his own land—Greece, Persia, Scythia, India. / Melissa sent them each back to his own land, laden with a debt of gratitude which could never be repaid.

The first to be restored to human form was Astolfo, the duke of the English, thanks to the kinship he enjoyed with Ruggiero, and to this knight's intercession for him; beside commending Astolfo to her, he gave Melissa the ring, the better to be able to help him. / At Ruggiero's behest, then, the paladin was restored to his true self. But Melissa felt she had accomplished nothing until she had restored to him his weapons and his golden lance which has only to touch a person to tip him from the saddle. This lance was Argalia's, but then fell to Astolfo; it brought high honour to both of them in France. / Melissa found the golden lance, which Alcina had put away in her palace, and all the rest of the duke's arms which had been taken from him in that haunt of evil. She mounted the charger which had belonged to Atlas, the Moorish wizard, and had Astolfo climb on behind; then, taking flight for Logistilla's, they arrived there an hour before Ruggiero. /

Ruggiero, meanwhile, was making his way to Logistilla, the kindly enchantress. His path lay amid hard boulders and bramble thickets, from one hill's crest to the next; one path he followed and another, ever steep and solitary, wild and inhospitable. Strained and weary, he came out upon a beach hemmed in between the mountains and the sea; it was in the heat of mid-afternoon, and the place was exposed to the South, arid and bare, sterile and desolate. / The blazing sun beat down upon the hill nearby, which reflected back a heat so intense that it set the air simmering, and the sand: it would have taken less heat to liquefy glass. Every bird sat silent in the soft shade; alone the cricket amid the thick, leafy shrubs shrilled his monotonous refrain, which filled, which deafened, the hills and valleys, the sea and sky. / Tedious and oppressive was the heat, the thirst and weariness which were all Ruggiero had for company as he pursued his sand-strewn way along the sun-drenched desert shore.

Now as I should do wrong to keep you ever attending to the same tale, I shall leave Ruggiero to bake and make off to Scotland to find Rinaldo. / Rinaldo was held in highest esteem by the king and the princess, and by all the citizens. And now, at leisure, he explained the reason for his visit: that he was come, in his liege's name, to seek help from the Kings of Scotland and of England. He went on to support Charlemagne's request with most justifiable reasons for honouring it. /

The king readily answered that the service and honour of Charlemagne and the Empire was ever dear to him, and he would help to the fullest extent of his powers. Within a few days he would marshal every available knight; and were it not for his advanced years, he added, he would place himself at the head of his forces. / Not that this consideration would, he felt, be sufficient excuse for his remaining behind: but he did have a son, a true stalwart and extremely clever, to whom he could entrust the command. At the moment he was abroad, but he expected him to return while the expedition was being prepared, so that he would find it ready-assembled on his arrival. / So he sent his bailiffs scouring the country to raise horses and men; he promptly had ships made ready, and munitions of war, provisions, and money. Rinaldo meanwhile departed for England, graciously accompanied as far as Berwick by the king, who was seen to weep at their leave-taking. /

With a fair, following wind, Rinaldo went aboard and bid everyone adieu; the helmsman unfurled the sails, they put out to sea, and came to the lovely Thames, where its flow is arrested by salt waves and its waters turn bitter. Borne in on the tide, the travellers made a safe passage, aided by sail and oars, upstream to London. / From Charlemagne, and from Otho, the English king who was besieged with him in Paris, Rinaldo had brought credentials and letters to the Prince of Wales requesting that every foot-soldier, every horse that could be mustered throughout the land should be assembled and conveyed to Calais, to go to the aid of Charles and the French. / This prince, then, who was occupying the throne in Otho's absence, paid such honour to Rinaldo, son of Aymon, as he would scarce have accorded to his own sovereign. He complied with his request, appointing a day on which all men fit for battle, whether in Britain or the surrounding islands, should assemble for the sea-crossing. /

But ought I not, my Lord, to do as the good musician playing his subtle instrument? He will select different strings, fresh harmonies, as he seeks effects, now muted, now strident. And I, intent on unfolding Rinaldo's story, have just remembered sweet Angelica: I left her fleeing from him, and falling in with a hermit. / I shall pursue her story a little. I told you how earnestly she enquired how she might reach the sea-coast, for she was so terrified of Rinaldo that she felt certain of dying if she did not cross the sea, imagining herself unsafe anywhere in Europe. But the hermit took his time, for he enjoyed her company. / Such rare beauty inflamed his heart and warmed the chill marrow in his bones. But, seeing that she took little notice of him, and indeed showed no disposition to bide with him, he mercilessly goaded and spurred his little mule, without being able to rouse him from his

73

lethargic gait; the mule would walk only a few paces, and quite refused to trot—as for a full canter, that was out of the question. /

Now, as he was dropping a long way behind, and in a while would completely lose her traces, the hermit had recourse to his dark cave, and summoned forth a host of demons. He selected one of them and told him what it was he wanted; after which, he bade him enter into Angelica's palfrey which was bearing away the lady—and his heart. / A cunning hound, well used to hunting the fox or the hare in the mountains, will see the prey going by one path, and will himself choose another, as though disdaining to follow the scent; but where the fugitive's path comes out, that is where he will station himself, and he will seize his prey in his jaws and rend open its flanks. Thus did the hermit, taking another path to come up with the damsel, whichever way she went. / What he planned to do is obvious to me, and I shall tell you—later on.

Angelica, all unsuspecting, rode on, covering unequal daily stages. But in her horse the demon lay concealed, as sometimes a fire is concealed only to blaze forth in a while so mightily that there is no putting it out, and to escape from it is difficult. / The damsel followed the path which lay beside the broad sea which washes the land of the Gascons; she rode close to the water's edge, picking her way where the ground was firmest. But her steed was drawn into the water by the powerful demon, and began to swim; the fearful maiden knew not what to do—she just clung tightly to the saddle. / She tugged and tugged on the reins, but could not turn her steed, who was swimming straight out into the deep. She drew up her skirts so as to keep them dry, and pulled her feet clear of the water. Her tresses hung loose about her shoulders, while the lascivious breeze caressed her. The great winds fell silent: perhaps they, like the sea, were arrested by so rare a vision of beauty. / In vain she turned her soft eyes towards the shore, and bathed her face and breast with tears; she saw the land ever receding and growing smaller and smaller. After swimming in a great arc, ever to the right, the beast carried her back to the shore, where it was all dark rocks and dreadful caverns.

Night was falling. / Finding herself alone in this desolate spot—the very look of the place was enough to inspire dread—at the hour when Phoebus sinks into the ocean, leaving a pall of darkness in the air and over the land, Angelica stood motionless: anyone descrying her there would have been in some doubt whether she was a real, sentient woman, or simply a rock tinted to look like one. / She stood paralysed in the shifting sand, her hair dishevelled, her hands clasped, her lips motionless; her languorous eyes were raised to heaven, as though accusing the Great Mover of having set all the Fates against her. She stood awhile as though in a trance, then tears came welling up and her tongue found utterance for her grief. /

'Fortune, what more have you to do', she said, 'before you are sated and replete with hounding me? What have I still left to give you, except for this wretched life of mine? But you do not want it, for you have been so prompt to save it from the sea where it might have found an end to its sorrows. You must have wanted to see me tormented still more before I die. / But I cannot see how you can hurt me more than you have done already. You have had me banished from my royal home, whither I have no hope of returning. I have lost my good name, which is worse: for though I have committed no fault, yet I give every-one the excuse to hold that, being a wanderer, I must be a loose woman. / Deprive a woman of her virtue, and what other blessing can she enjoy in this world? I suffer for being young, alas, and for being accounted, whether rightly or wrongly, beautiful. I cannot thank Heaven for this gift, as it is the source of all my sorrows. It was on this account that Argalia my brother died—little good did his enchanted weapons do him. / It was on this account that Agrican, King of Tartary, defeated my father Galafron, Great Khan of Cathay and the Indies, which led to my present sorry state, shifting my dwelling from day to day. Now that you have taken from me all my possessions, my honour and those dear to me, and done your worst to me, for what further misery are you preparing me? / If drowning me in the sea did not seem to you a cruel enough death, I'll not recoil if you send a wild beast to devour me and put an end to my torments, if only that will satisfy you. Send me any affliction, any at all and, as long as I die of it, I'll not be able to thank you enough.' Thus spoke the maiden through her tears. The next moment the hermit appeared. /

The hermit, from the top of a high rock had been observing Angelica who, all bewildered and forlorn, had been set ashore at the base of it. He had come six days before, borne hither by a demon who took an untrodden route. Now he approached her, with a show of piety as profound as that of Paul or Hilarion. / When the damsel noticed him, she took comfort, for she did not know him; her terror gradually abated, though her face still remained pale and drawn. When he was close by she said, 'Mercy, good father! I've come to a pitiful pass!' And, her voice choked with sobs, she explained to him what he already knew full well. / The hermit offered her good, devout words of comfort, and as he spoke, he boldly placed his hands now on her breast, now on her tear-stained cheeks. Then, gaining confidence, he tried to embrace her, but she angrily struck at his chest and pushed him away, her face suffused with a modest blush. / Out of his pocket the hermit now drew a phial of liquid and lightly sprayed a drop of it onto the maiden's eyes—eyes which sparkled with the most blazing brand in Cupid's armoury. The liquid drops put her to sleep: she lay supine on the sand, now a prey to the lustful old lecher. / He hugged her and felt her at his pleasure: she was asleep and could offer no resistance. He planted kisses on her lovely breast and on her lips; there was no one to see him in that wild, deserted spot. But when he came to the impact, his charger stumbled, for his wasted body would not answer to his desire— his was too elderly, unsuitable a jade, and the harder he forced him the worse his success. / He tried one way, then another, but could not get his flop-eared nag to jump; vainly he shook his reins and spurred him on, but there was no making him raise his head. Eventually he fell asleep beside the damsel, who was now to suffer a worse assault: when Fortune takes it into her head to make play with a mortal, she does nothing by halves. /

But, before I tell you what happened, I must make a slight digression. In the northern seas, over towards the setting sun, out beyond Ireland, there lies an island; its name is Ebuda. It has only a few inhabitants, the survivors of the destruction wrought upon it by the horrid orc and the other sea-beasts brought thither by Proteus, the vengeful god. /

An old legend, possibly true, relates that once upon a time a powerful king ruled the island; he had a daughter of such entrancing beauty that, when she walked on the briny beach, she could without effort leave Proteus burning even in the middle of his watery realm. And Proteus, coming upon her alone one day, caught her in an embrace and left her pregnant. / Her father, who was of exceedingly harsh and severe disposition, regarded the matter as an intolerable injury, so much so that no excuse, no pity would stay him from ordering her beheaded—passionate anger ruled him. Nor would he defer the execution of his cruel command in view of her pregnant condition. And the little grandson who had committed no fault: he had him slain even before he was born. / Proteus, the sea-god who pastures the proud flocks of Neptune, ruler of the Ocean, heard the dreadful torment of his lady and broke all bounds in his seething wrath. At once he sent on-shore his orcs and sea-lions and all his watery flock to ravage the sheep and cattle, yes, and the hamlets and farms and those who toiled there; / often, too, they surged up to the town walls and laid siege to them from all sides. The townsfolk had to stand armed guard day and night —a wearisome duty, and terrifying. Everyone had withdrawn from the open fields. Eventually, to find some remedy, they repaired to the oracle for a consultation, and this was its reply: / They must find a maiden as beautiful as the first and take her to the water's edge and offer her to the irate god to compensate for the one who was slain. If he was satisfied with her beauty he would keep her, and would harass them no further; but if he rejected her they must offer him another and yet another until he was content. / Thus among the comeliest of the fair sex a hard toll began to be exacted: each day one of them was offered to Proteus until one acceptable to him were found. The first met her death, and so did all who followed, for one and all were engulfed in the maw of a great orc who remained near the river's mouth after the rest of the terrible sea-herd was dispersed. /

Whether or not there is any truth in this story about Proteus, I really have no idea; at all events, a wicked, ancient law was there enforced against women, on the basis of such a story: the monstrous orc, who visits their shore every day, must be fed on their flesh. To be a woman is a hard enough lot at the best of times—but here particularly so. / Poor wretched damsels, borne by injurious Fate to so inclement a shore where the islanders keep watch upon the sea to make a wicked holocaust of alien women: for the more damsels from abroad who are sacrificed, the smaller the inroads they have to make among their own womenfolk. But as the wind does not always blow the prey in their direction, they go out scavenging along every other shore. / They scour every sea in their galleys and brigs and other vessels and from near and far they fetch in what they need to relieve their torment. Many women they carry off by force, a few they lure and entice, others they buy with gold; they keep gathering them in from all quarters and pack them into their prisons and keeps. /

As one of their galleys was passing close inshore, coasting along the deserted strand where poor Angelica lay asleep on the grass amid the underbrush, a number of sailors landed to refurbish their supplies of wood and fresh water. So they came upon this, the flower of feminine beauty and grace, lying clasped in the venerable father's arms. / Alas, too precious, too exalted a prey for men so base, so barbarous! Oh cruel Fortune, who would ever imagine that you could exercise such power over human affairs! You would feed a monster with the fairest of the fair, who stirred King Agrican to leave the Caucasian gates with half of Scythia in his train, and invade India, there to meet his death; / the fairest beauty, whom Sacripant preferred to his own honour and goodly kingdom; she who made Orlando, Duke of Anglant, besmirch his name and sully his lofty genius; she for whom, in massive disarray, the entire Orient stood to arms: now so abandoned is she, there is not one she can turn to for so much as a word of help. /

Oppressed by sleep, beautiful Angelica was shackled before she could rouse herself. With her they carried off the hermit in the ship already crowded with grieving humanity. The sail was hoisted to the masthead and drew the ship back to the grim island, where they shut the maiden in a dungeon until her turn arrived. / But her beauty produced such an effect upon those hardened folk that out of pity they postponed her sacrifice for many days, reserving her till the last possible moment. So long as there was another alien damsel to replace her, she was saved by her angelic countenance.

Finally, though, she was brought to the sea-monster, with the whole population following, weeping, in her train. / Who shall describe the sobs and shrieks and wails which mounted to the heavens? I am amazed that the shore did not gape open when she was exposed on the cold rock, to wait, chained and abandoned by all, for a stark, dreadful death. I shall not tell you more—it is too painful, and sorrow drives me to turn my rhymes in some other direction, / and find less harrowing verses until my weary spirit recovers: the baleful viper, the jealous tiger whipped up into a frenzy of rage, and whatever venomous species creep through the hot sands between the Atlantic and the Red Sea shore—they could none of them behold or contemplate without compassion the sight of Angelica tied to the bare rock. / Ah, if her Orlando had known—he had gone to Paris in search of her—or the two knights who were tricked by the wily old hermit who sent them his infernal messenger! They would have risked a thousand deaths to follow Angelica's traces and bring her aid. And yet, even had they known where to find her, what could they have done, seeing the distance that separated them from her? /

Paris meanwhile lay besieged by Agramant, King Trojan's famous son; and the day came when the city was reduced to such straits that it almost fell to the enemy. Were it not that God accepted the Christians' prayers and flooded the plain in a murky downpour, the Sacred Empire and the mighty name of France would that day have fallen to the African spears. / The Almighty Creator turned His eyes to the just lament of the old emperor, and dowsed the fires in a sudden rainstorm; probably no human ingenuity would have been able to master them. Wise is the man who always turns to God: for no one else can give him better assistance. The pious monarch well recognized this, owing his rescue to divine intervention. /

That night, Orlando imparted his fleeting thoughts to his restless bed. This way and that he drove them, and herded them all together, but could never pen them in. They were like the tremulous gleam which a limpid pool gives off under the rays of the sun or moon—high and low, to right and left it fans out, and leaps over the broad roof-tops. / His lady returned to haunt his mind—not that she had ever been absent from it—and stoked up to a new incandescence the fire which during the day seemed to have waned. She had come with him to the West from Cathay; and now, with Charles' defeat at Bordeaux, he had lost all trace of her. / Bitterly Orlando regretted this, and vainly brooded on his stupidity.

'What a coward's role I played, my love!' said he. 'Alas, how sickened I am to think that I could have had you with me night and day, for of your own goodness you did not deny me this, but I let you be handed over to Namo's keeping, and knew not how to forestall such an affront! / Did not I have reason to make a stand? Aye, and supposing Charles had stood his ground? Well, supposing he had—who could have forced my hand? Who was going to take you away in the teeth of my opposition? Could I not have fought, sword in hand, or made them first tear my heart out of my breast? Neither Charles nor all his henchmen together were capable of wresting you from me by force. / He might at least have left her well guarded in Paris or some / other stronghold. If he gave her into Namo's keeping, it must surely have been with a view to losing her. Who could have guarded her better than I? Who would have guarded her with his own life, more jealously than his own heart, his very eyes? I should and could have done so, but I did not. / Where are you now, my love, my pretty nursling, where are you without me? Are you not like the ewe lamb lost in the wood as the daylight wanes—hither and yon she wanders, bleating, and hopes the shepherd will hear her; it is the wolf, though, that hears from afar, and the poor shepherd weeps for his lamb in vain. / Where are you, hope of my heart? Are you still a-wandering all by yourself? Or have the wicked wolves found you unprotected by your faithful Orlando? And your flower, which could set me among the heavenly gods, the flower which I preserved for you intact, so as not to sadden your chaste heart, will they, alas, have plucked and despoiled it? / O, woe upon me, what would I but to die if they have plucked my pretty flower! Almighty God, afflict me with any sorrow, any, but not this! If this has truly come to pass, I must with my own hands take my life and damn my despairing soul.'

Thus cried Orlando, tormented knight, amid sighs and bitter tears. / Now was the time when every living creature concedes rest to his careworn spirit—some lying in feather-beds, others on hard stones or on the grass, or in the branches of beech and myrtle-trees. But you, Orlando, you scarcely shut your eyelids, pricked as you are by sharp and jagged thoughts, which leave you no peace to enjoy even the briefest snatch of slumber. / Orlando dreamed of a green bank all scattered with fragrant flowers, and there he saw a vision of ivory-white blent with a flush of crimson painted by Love's own hand, and a pair of limpid stars whose light nourished his soul, caught in Love's toils—I mean he saw the lovely eyes and face which had plucked his heart from his breast. / He enjoyed a wonderful sense of happiness and well-being, as deep as a man can feel who is happy in love. But a sudden storm blew up, which ravaged the flowers and threw down the trees—a storm the like of which you will not see when Aquilo, Auster, and Levanter meet and contend. He dreamed that he wandered through a wilderness in vain search of shelter. / Meanwhile the hapless lover somehow or other loses his lady in the failing light, and searches here and there through the woods and moors calling her name. And while in vain he cries, 'Woe is me! Who is it who has changed my solace into poison?' he hears his lady tearfully calling to him for help. / He runs to where he thinks the cries come from, and searches desperately high and low; imagine his searing grief when he can no longer descry his love's sweet radiance. Now he hears a voice from a different quarter, which cries: 'Look no more to have joy from her here below.'

At this dreadful cry he woke, to find himself bathed in tears. / Unmindful that the pictures must be false that fear or hope projects in the dreaming mind, Orlando was so wrought up about his lady, believing that some danger or disgrace must have overtaken her, that he leapt, fulminating, out of bed, clad himself in armour and chain-mail and all else he needed, then fetched Brigliador; but he dispensed with the services of a squire. / And to go anywhere at will without compromising his reputation, he wore not his distinguished emblem of red and white quarterings, but chose a black one—perhaps it was consonant with his sense of mourning. This sable emblem he had wrested from one Amostant whom he had slain a few years earlier. / He stole off in the depth of the night, greeting nobody and leaving no word for the emperor, his uncle; he did not bid farewell even to Brandimart, his boon companion whom he loved so well. But when the golden-haired Sun set forth from Tithonus' splendid halls and routed the dark shades of night, the emperor realized that the paladin was gone. / Charles was profoundly displeased to discover that his nephew had made off in the night, when he was most bound to stay with him and lend his assistance. And, unable to restrain his anger, he broke out in imprecations against him and heaped abuse upon him, uttering threats if he did not return, and promising to make him sorry for such a dereliction. /

Now Brandimart, who loved Orlando as much as his own self, was quick to act, whether in the hope of persuading the paladin to return, or simply from anger at hearing him the butt of such abuse and raillery. He scarcely waited for dusk to gather than he set out in his turn, without a word to his Fiordiligi for fear she try to oppose his decision. / She was a damsel he deeply loved, and he was seldom apart from her: she was comely, graceful, and of gentle manners; nor was she lacking in shrewdness and wisdom. If he did not take leave of her, it was because he planned to return to her within the day; but events so fell out that he was delayed beyond the expected time. / After vainly waiting for him, and finding him still not returned after nearly a month, her desire for him was so sharpened that she set off without guides or any company. She travelled through many lands searching for him, as at the proper time her story shall reveal.

But I shall not for the present say more about these two: I am more concerned about Orlando, the lord of Anglant. / Once he had altered the glorious emblem of Almont, he went to the gate and whispered into the ear of the captain of the guard, 'I am the count.' Immediately the drawbridge was lowered for him, and he took the road leading directly to the enemy camp. What followed you shall discover in the next canto.

NINTH CANTO

1–2 Introductory. 2–17 Orlando searches for Angelica. 18–56
Orlando meets Olympia, who tells him her sad tale. 57–94
Orlando takes up Olympia's cause, then resumes his search for
Angelica.

CRUEL, treacherous Love! See what it can do to a heart, once conquered! It can make Orlando forget the sovereign fealty that he owes his lord. Once upon a time he was a man of sound judgement, awake to his duty, a true defender of Holy Church. But now? Thanks to feckless Love, he pays no heed to his uncle, none to his self-respect, still less to God. / I can forgive him, though, with all my heart. Indeed, I am delighted to have such a partner in crime: for my own efforts at self-improvement are something short of zealous, but when it comes to harmful pursuits, I run with the foremost.

Off he went, dressed all in black, with no concern for the many friends he was forsaking, and passed amid the tented camp of the Africans and Spaniards: / or rather, not tented, for the rain had driven them to shelter under trees and roofs. There they were, then, bedded down in groups of ten, twenty, four, seven, eight, some further off, others closer in. They were all sleeping, haggard and exhausted, some spread-eagled on the ground, others with their heads pillowed on their hands. All asleep—and the count was free to slaughter all he wanted, but not once did he set his hand to Durindana. / For Orlando is great of heart, and would not stoop to striking men who sleep. Hither and thither he moved, intent on picking up the traces of his lady. And every time he came upon someone awake, with many a sigh he would give a description of her and of her apparel, and entreat the man out of kindness to tell him which way she went. / When the day dawned bright and clear he continued his search throughout the Moorish camp; this he could safely do, dressed as he was in Arab costume. He was also aided by the fact that French was not his only tongue: he spoke African with such fluency that he could have passed for a native of Tripoli. / Here he stopped, then, for three days, wholly intent on making a thorough search. After this he started to explore every town and village around; he not only visited those of the Ile-de-France, but also passed again through the Auvergne and Gascony, searching every last hamlet. From Provence to Brittany he searched, and from Picardy to the confines of Spain. /

It was the end of October and the onset of November, the season when the trees can be seen shedding their leafy raiment until they stand stripped and shivering in their nakedness, and the birds fly together in tight flocks. This was when Orlando began his amorous quest; all that winter he continued it, and still on into the following spring. / In the course of these wanderings from village to village he came one day to a river which separates the Normans from the Bretons and flows softly to the sea close by. It was swollen at present, and streaked with froth from the melting snows and the rains up in the mountains. And the current had demolished the bridge and swept it away so there was no crossing. / The paladin looked closely at each shore in turn to see how he was to reach the other side (inasmuch as he was neither bird nor fish). And what did he see but a boat coming towards him with a damsel sitting in the stern. She signed to him that she was coming, but stopped a little short of the bank. / She did not put into the shore, as though fearing lest the passenger come on board uninvited.

Orlando besought her to take him in her boat and land him on the other side, but 'No knight crosses here', she replied, 'who has not first given me his word that he will do battle at my request—the most just and honourable battle in the world. / If then, sir, you wish me to help you set foot on the other side, promise me that, before this next month is out, you will go to the King of Hibernia and join the fine host assembling there to destroy the island of Ebuda, the most sinister of any island set in the sea. / You must know that beyond Ireland there are many islands and one of them is Ebuda, which sends out its thievish people with orders to plunder. And any women they capture they give as food to a voracious beast which comes in daily to the shore and finds each time a new woman or maiden to devour. / For merchants and pirates go about bringing them in, and the more beautiful the better—and counting one a day, you can readily imagine how many women and maidens have died. But if you have room for pity, and are not entirely closed to Love, be glad to be numbered with this host who will be setting forth on so bounteous an errand.' /

Orlando could scarcely wait for the end of the story before he swore he would be the first at that enterprise, like a person who cannot endure to listen to an account of some wicked, loathsome deed. And he found himself thinking, then fearing, that those people had taken Angelica, for he had been seeking her high and low and still had found no trace of her. / This idea so perturbed him, quite sweeping out of his mind any previous plan, that without waiting a moment he decided to set sail for that evil land. And before the next day's sun had dipped into the sea, he found a ship at Saint Malo. He went on board, ordered the sails hoisted, and passed Mont Saint Michel in the night. / Leaving Saint Brieuc and Tréguier to port, he coasted along the broad Breton shore, then headed out towards the white beaches which give England its name of Albion. But the wind, which was from the South, dropped, then came up so strongly from the North-West that all the sails had to be hauled in and the ship left to run before it. / In one day the ship lost all the headway it had made in the last four. The good helmsman kept her well out to sea to avoid running ashore and splintering like glass. After blowing furiously for four days, on the fifth the wind changed and let them sail unhindered into the mouth of Antwerp's river. /

No sooner had the weary helmsman brought the damaged vessel into the river mouth and to shore than who should appear on the right bank and come down to the ship but an old man, well on in years to judge by his white hair. After exchanging greetings he politely turned to the count, judging that he must be the leader of the party. / And he besought him on behalf of a damsel to consent to come to her; he would find her not only beautiful but also surpassingly gentle and open. Or else, would he be prepared to wait, and she would come to the ship to see him. But would he please at least show no greater reluctance than the other knights errant who had passed this way: / for no knight, whether he arrived at this place by land or by sea, ever refused to see this damsel and counsel her in her terrible plight. On hearing this Orlando made haste to step ashore, and out of human kindness and courtesy set out with the old man. / The paladin was taken into a neighbouring mansion, and at the top of the stairs he came upon a woman in deep mourning, as was clear from her face and from the black drapes which covered everything in all the public and private rooms. She offered him a kind welcome, bade him sit down, and told him sadly: /

'I would have you know that I was the daughter of the Count of Holland, and he was so fond of me (for all that I was not his only child—I had two brothers) that no matter what I asked of him, he never refused me anything. This was the happy state of affairs when a duke happened to come onto the scene. / He was the Duke of Zeeland, the Danish isle, and was on his way to Biscay to fight the Moors. Handsome and young as he was, and ready as by then I was to offer my heart's love, he conquered me with scarcely a struggle—the more easily in that from all appearances he honestly loved me, and still loves me: so I believed and still believe, and I am sure I am right to do so. / In the course of those days, during which contrary winds kept him with us—"contrary" to the others, that is, not to me, for to the others those days extended to forty, while to me they were but a minute, so quickly did they go winging past—we spent much time talking together, and we exchanged vows that on his return we would be married with solemn ritual. / No sooner had Bireno left (for this is the name of my true love), than the King of Frisia (which lies just down the coast, across the river) decided that his only son, Arbante, should be my husband, and sent an embassy to my father in Holland, choosing his foremost dignitaries, to ask for my hand. /

'Unable to forswear the promise I gave to my beloved—and even had I been able to do so, I would not have been willing, for Love would not have let me be so fickle—I told my father, in order to put an end to the affair, which was well advanced and indeed almost concluded, that if I was to be wedded to the Frisian I would sooner be killed. / My dear father, whose only pleasure was my pleasure and who could not bear to see me unhappy, broke off the negotiations in order to comfort me and dry my tears. But the proud King of Frisia was so angry and outraged that he invaded Holland and started the war which sent all my kindred to the grave. / Not only is he powerfully built, and so strong that few men alive today could match him; and not only is he so wily in his evil way that no one else's strength, courage or cunning is of any use against him: but also he has a weapon quite unknown to our forefathers or indeed to any of our own generation, himself apart—an iron tube, two yards long, into which he thrusts powder and a ball. / At the back, the closed end, of the tube there is a little hole, almos invisible, to which he puts a flame, just the way a physician sets his finger on an open vein which needs to be staunched. Out shoots the ball with such a roar that it could be thunder and lightning, and its effect is no different from that of a thunderbolt: whatever it touches it fires, splits, cracks, and shatters. /

'He twice put our side to flight with this device, and killed my brothers: one in the first attack, with a ball which smashed his breastplate and penetrated his heart; the other he brought down in the second skirmish while he was fleeing in a crowd: he hit him in the back from a distance, and the ball came out through his chest. / Then one day while my father was seeing to the defences of the only castle left to him, for he had lost all the rest, he was brought down by the same trick: for while he was moving back and forth attending to the necessities of the situation he was hit between the eyes by the treacherous villain, who had taken aim at him from a distance. / With my brothers dead and my father, I was the only surviving heir to the isle of Holland; and the King of Frisia, who proposed to maintain his foothold in this territory, informed me, and my people, that he would grant me peace and respite were I to accept now what I had earlier rejected: his son Arbante for my husband. / Not so much out of the loathing, the execration in which I held him and his infamous family—for had he not murdered both my brothers and my father and sacked my homeland, leaving it scorched and in ruins?—as out of wanting to remain true to the promise I had made to my beloved, that no man would be my husband until he returned to me from Spain: / "I am ready", I replied, "to suffer my present plight a hundredfold, and to stake all that I have left: to be killed, burnt alive, to have my ashes scattered to the wind, rather than proceed with this."

'My people thought out ways to make me change my mind: some tried entreaties, others threatened to hand me and my realm over to him before my obstinacy brought doom upon us all. / And so, when it was clear that all protests and entreaties were in vain and that I was not to be moved, they made a pact with the Frisian and handed me and the walls over to him, as they promised. He treated me very correctly and assured me of my safety and my kingdom, provided that I came round to a less stubborn frame of mind and became the wife of his Arbante. / Seeing myself constrained in this way I looked to death as the only way to elude him; but to go without first avenging myself would have been far more bitter to me than all the hurt I had suffered. After much thought I reached the sad conclusion that my only hope lay in feigning. I feigned not simply acquiescence but a positive longing to be forgiven and to become his daughter-in-law. /

'Out of the many who had been in my father's service I chose two brothers, both of them courageous and of sound judgement, but above all loyal, having been raised with us in court from their tenderest years; and so much at one with me that they would think nothing of laying down their lives for my safety. / I imparted my plan to them; they promised to help me. One went to Flanders and had a ship made ready; the other I kept with me in Holland. Now, while the wedding invitations were going out to guests at home and abroad, news arrived that Bireno had assembled an army in Biscay to make an expedition against Holland. / For, after the first battle, in which one of my brothers was defeated and killed, I straightway sent a messenger to Biscay to bring the sad news to Bireno. While he was making his military preparations, the rest of the land was overrun by the King of Frisia, but Bireno, knowing nothing of this, had put to sea to come to our rescue. / On hearing this the King of Frisia left the care of the wedding to his son and put out to sea with his troops; he located the duke, scattered, fired, and smashed his fleet and, as Fortune willed, took him prisoner. This news, though, did not reach us at once.

'Meanwhile the young man married me and wanted to sink into bed with me, as the sun sinks to rest. / I had hidden my trusty servant behind the curtains, and he did not stir until he saw the bridegroom on his way to me; then, without waiting for him to get into bed, he lifted an axe and brought it down on the back of his head with such a mighty blow that he dispatched him before he could utter a word. I leapt at him and slit his throat. / Like an ox felled at the slaughter-house—so fell this young man of evil birth, thus spiting the king, the most wicked of men. Cimosco was the villain's name—Cimosco, the murderer of my two brothers and of my father, and the man who, the better to secure my country in bondage, wanted me for daughter-in-law; and one day he would perhaps have slain me too. / Making our escape while the going was good, we snatched up whatever was small and valuable, and with a rope my companion quickly lowered me from the window onto the deck of the boat which his brother had brought from Flanders and had waiting below in the sea. We spread the sails to the wind, dipped the oars into the sea and fled to safety, as God willed. /

'I know not whether the King of Frisia was more shattered by the death of his son, or enraged at me when he arrived the next day and found what had been done to him. Here he was, returning with his followers, the haughty conqueror, the captor of Bireno; and expecting to arrive for the wedding festivities he found instead nothing but gloom and doom. / His grief over his son and his hatred for me never leave him day or night. But since weeping has never restored the dead to life, and vengeance is a supreme way of working off hate, the part of his mind which should have been given over to grieving and anguish joined with his hatred in searching out the best way to lay hands on me and punish me. / All those whom he knew to be my friends, or who were indicated to him as such, all those who were supposed to have abetted me in my enterprise he killed, or set fire to their possessions, or pronounced them outlaws. And he would have killed Bireno to hurt me—for nothing else could cause me greater pain—but then it occurred to him that if he kept his prisoner alive, he had ready to hand a net with which to snare me. /

'But the condition he made is cruel and heartless: at the end of one year he would put him secretly to death unless before then he contrived, by force or by fraud, with the aid of his friends and kindred, using any means they can devise, to hand me over, a prisoner; so that only by my death can Bireno be saved. / Whatever could be done to assure his safety, short of sacrificing my life, I have done. I had six castles in Flanders and I have sold all of them; and however much or little I got for them I spent partly on trying to bribe his guards by means of astute intermediaries, and partly on inciting the English and Germans to mount an attack against the miscreant. / The intermediaries, whether proving powerless or simply falling short of their duty, have repaid me with words, not with help; and now that they have taken their fee, they scorn me. But the time is almost up, after which neither might nor wealth will any longer be able to save my beloved from torment and death. /

'I have lost my father and my brothers for his sake; for his sake I have been deprived of my realm; to release him from captivity I have parted with the one or two last possessions I still had to live on. Now there is nothing left for me but to give myself up to my cruel enemy, in order to secure his release. / If, then, there is nothing else for me to do, no way to ensure his safety other than to give my life for his, this my life will be a precious gift with which to ransom him. But there is one thing which troubles me: that I shall be unable to make a clear arrangement which will prevent the tyrant, once he has his hands on me, from tricking us both. / I suspect that once he has shut me away and done his worst to me, this will not mean that Bireno will go free and be able to thank me for his release; a man without honour and dominated by hatred, Cimosco may well not be satisfied simply with killing me, and whatever he does to me, he may do neither more nor less to poor Bireno. /

'Now the reason impelling me to explain my plight to you, and to as many knights and barons as come this way, is only this: I hope that by talking the question over with so many of you, one of you may be able to advise me how to ensure that, once I have been brought before the cruel king, he will not continue to hold Bireno, or decide that after killing me, he too should die. / I have asked warriors to come with me when I go to give myself up to the King of Frisia, and to give me their word that the exchange will be so conducted that my surrender and Bireno's release take place at the same moment; in this way, when I come to be killed, I shall die happy, as my death will have been instrumental in saving the live of my beloved. / I have not to this day found any man prepared to guarantee on his word of honour that he will not permit me to fall into the king's hands against my will, if I am brought before the king and he tries to seize me without releasing Bireno to me. Every one is afraid of that weapon of his; they fear it, for apparently there is no armour, however thick, which can give any protection against it. / But if your mighty, Herculean aspect is a true image of your valour, and if you believe that you can hand me over to him and still take me back from him if he dishonours the pact, please accept to come with me and surrender me to him—for if you stand by me I shall have no fear that, once I am dead, my lord may die.' /

Here the damsel finished her story, which she had frequently had to break off in order to sigh and weep. When she had finished Orlando, who had a ready propensity to doing good, made her only a brief answer, for he was a man of few words; but he promised her on his honour that he would do even more than she asked. / He did not intend to let her fall into her enemy's hands in order to save Bireno. It was both of them he would rescue, if he could rely upon his sword and his accustomed prowess. They put to sea that very day, as the wind set fair. The paladin was in a hurry, for he was anxious to reach the island of the sea-monster. / Holding course on one tack then on the other, the good helmsman steered the ship amid the deep lagoons. Island after island of Zeeland came into sight—as one appeared ahead, another would recede from view behind. On the third day Orlando disembarked in Holland, but not the lady who was at odds with the King of Frisia: Orlando wanted her to receive news of the villain's death before she set foot ashore. / The paladin armed, and stepped ashore mounted on a dapple-grey charger, born in Denmark and raised in Flanders, a great powerful beast but not particularly fleet-footed; for when he set sail he had left behind in Brittany his own steed, handsome, proud Brigliador, a horse second to none but Bayard. /

Orlando came to Dordrecht, where he found a large number of soldiers at the gates: all rulers have to be on their guard, but especially when their power is newly acquired; besides, news had just arrived that a cousin of the lord held captive here was on his way from Zeeland with an army and fleet. / Orlando asked one of them to go and tell the king that a knight errant wished to challenge him to battle with lance and sword, but first the stakes were to be agreed as follows: if the king overthrew his challenger, he should have the woman who killed Arbante, for the knight had her at hand nearby and could deliver her to him at any time; / but the king was to promise, for his part, that if he were defeated in the duel, he would release Bireno at once, and leave him free to go as he pleased. The soldier hastened to the king with the message. But the king, who had never found a use for the knightly virtues, immediately bent his mind to crafty, treacherous schemes. / It occurred to him that were he to lay his hands on the knight he would lay hold of the woman too, who had done him such injury, if it turned out that she really was in his keeping, and the soldier had understood the message aright. He sent thirty men off by a different route from the gate where the paladin was awaited; they took a long, hidden detour and came out behind him. / The treacherous man had him kept in play with words until he saw that his foot-soldiers and horsemen were in their allotted positions; then he sallied forth from the gate with as many more. Just as the experienced huntsman throws a cordon round a whole wood and the game therein, or just as the fisherman at Volana spreads a long net to scoop up the waters and the fish with them: / in the same way the King of Frisia made his dispositions to ensure that the knight did not escape. He wanted him alive, and not otherwise; and he expected to accomplish this so easily that he did not call for his artificial thunderbolt, with which he had dispatched so many people. Besides, he did not deem this instrument appropriate, his purpose being to capture, not to kill, him. /

A cunning bird-snarer, with an eye on a bigger catch, keeps alive the first birds he traps, using them as a lure to attract a larger quantity of birds: that is how King Cimosco saw himself acting here. Orlando, however, did not intend to let himself be caught in the first haul, and was quick to break out of the circle they had made. / The knight of Anglant lowered his lance and charged where the armed foe was thickest; and on his lance he impaled first one, then a second, then a third and fourth, as though they were made of dough; six he impaled, carrying them all on his lance; and the seventh, for lack of room, he did not impale—nevertheless he inflicted on him a wound from which he died. / Like frogs on the sandy verge of canals and ditches, whom the expert archer transfixes in the side or back, one after another: he does not slide them off his arrow until it is buried in them from tip to tail. Orlando tossed his heavy-laden lance from him and plunged into the fray, sword in hand. / His lance now broken, he clasped his sword which never missed its mark; cut or thrust, at every stroke he snuffed out another life—be it foot-soldier or horseman. Whatever it touched it dyed red, whether it had first been blue, green, white, black, or yellow. Cimosco bitterly regretted not having his tube and the flame to ignite it, just when he had most need of it. /

Bellowing curses, he commanded that these be brought to him, but he went unheeded: those who had withdrawn into the city were not prepared to come out again. Seeing everyone in full flight, the King of Frisia decided to run for safety himself; he made for the gate and wanted to raise the drawbridge, but the count was too quick for him. / The king turned his back and left Orlando in sole possession of the drawbridge and the succession of gates. He fled and overtook all the rest, for he had the swiftest horse. Orlando, however, wasted no time on the common throng: it was the villain whose life he was after, not theirs. But his steed was so sluggish that it seemed to be standing still while the fugitive's had wings. / Turning into one street, then another, he soon eluded the paladin; but then he waited a little before turning back with fresh weapons—for meanwhile he had sent for his hollow tube and his firing piece. Concealing himself round a corner he waited for him like a huntsman in ambush with his hounds in their spiked collars and his spear, waiting for the wild boar to come crashing towards him; / it snaps branches and sends the boulders spinning off, and wherever it raises its proud head one would imagine from the noise that the woods all about were shivering to splinters, and the whole mountain were being uprooted. Cimosco waited at his post: the bold count was not to pass without paying his penalty. As soon as he appeared the king applied the flame to the vent-hole and the explosion followed. / There was a flash from behind like lightning, and from the front a roar like thunder in the air. The walls shuddered, and the ground underfoot; the heavens echoed to the dreadful sound. The fiery bolt, which smashes and annihilates whatever it meets and spares no one, hissed and screeched. But, despite the wishes of the murderous villain, it did not reach its mark. / Whether it was too much haste that made him miss, or too great an anxiety to kill the baron; or whether his heart, trembling like a leaf, caused his arm and hands to shake as well; or perhaps it was the goodness of God who did not want his faithful champion to be so soon laid low—at all events, the shot was deflected onto the horse's belly. The horse fell prostrate, and never more arose. / Horse and rider hit the ground, the former heavily, the latter scarcely touching it, for he leapt up so sprightly and agile, he seemed to have found added strength and stamina. Like the Libyan Anteus who, after hitting the ground, used always to arise with renewed ferocity, so did Orlando appear on getting up, as though when he touched the earth his strength was redoubled. /

If you have ever seen fire fall from the sky, the fire that Jupiter unleashes with so fearful a sound, and seen it penetrate a closed magazine where charcoal is stored with sulphur and saltpetre; scarcely has it reached down to touch it than the whole sky, let alone the earth, seems to catch fire, walls split open, marble slabs are uprooted, and stones fly in the face of the stars; / that is how you should imagine the paladin, after he hit the ground: he moved forward with such an ugly look on his face that Mars himself would have quaked. The Frisian king jerked frantically on the rein and turned to flee, but Orlando was after him like an arrow shot from a bow, only faster: / and what he had been unable to do earlier on horseback he was now to accomplish on foot. He followed at such speed that, unless you had seen it, you would not believe it possible. In a few bounds he caught up with him, raised his sword above the king's helmet and brought it down with such might that he split his head right down to the neck and brought him toppling to the ground for his final spasms. /

A great tumult could now be heard, and the clash of swords: finding the gates open, Bireno's cousin had entered the city with the army he had led from his own country. Such was the terror the paladin had sown that Bireno's forces were able to enter without opposition. / The townsfolk fled without realizing who these troops were, nor stopping to ask; but little by little they came to notice by their dress and speech that they must be from Zeeland; they sued for peace, therefore, and offered their surrender, begging the leader to command them and assist them against the Frisians, for their duke was being held a prisoner. / The local people had always been hostile to the King of Frisia and his men, because he had killed their own lord, but more especially because he was unjust, wicked and rapacious. Orlando intervened, as friend of both sides, to bring peace between them. Thus united, they saw to it that every Frisian was slain or taken prisoner. / The prison gates were thrown down, nobody troubling to look first for the key. Bireno thanked the count and publicly acknowledged the debt he owed him. Then the whole party made its way to where Olympia was waiting on the ship—for this was the name of the woman to whom the lordship of the island belonged by right— / the woman who had brought Orlando here with no thought of his doing so much: for she would have felt fully satisfied if, she alone falling victim to the tyrant, her beloved had been delivered from his misfortune. The entire population paid her reverence.

It would take too long to describe how tenderly she and Bireno greeted each other, and how they both thanked the count. / The people re-established the damsel on her father's throne and swore fealty to her. She entrusted to Bireno, to whom she was tied forever by a strong bond of love, both herself and her realm. And he, having further business to attend to, left his cousin in charge of the whole island and its fortifications, / for he intended to return to Zeeland, taking his faithful bride with him: he said that he wanted to try out his chances in the kingdom of Frisia, for he had in his keeping a surety on which he placed great reliance—the king's daughter, whom he had discovered among the numerous captives. / He said that he wanted a younger brother of his to marry her.

At this point Orlando left, setting sail the same day as Bireno. He wanted no part in the spoils he had earned, except for one thing: that engine of war we have mentioned, which behaves not unlike a thunder-bolt. / He did not appropriate it out of any desire to use it in his defence; for he had always regarded it as cowardly to undertake any enterprise from a position of advantage. But he meant to jettison it somewhere in such a way that it could do no further harm; and he took the powder and the balls, too, and everything else connected with it. / And so, when he saw that they had left the shallows and reached deep water further out, at a point from which neither the left nor the right bank were any longer visible, he took hold of it and said: 'To ensure that no knight will ever again be intimidated by you, and that no villain will ever again boast himself the equal of a good man because of you, sink here. / O cursed, abominable device, constructed by the fiend Beelzebub in the forge of Hades when he planned to bring the world to ruin by you, back to hell from whence you came I consign you.' So saying, he threw it into the deep. The wind meanwhile pressed on the billowing sails and wafted the ship towards the cruel island. / So anxious was the paladin to discover whether his lady were there, whom he loved more than all the world—indeed, one hour without her was utter purgatory—that he was reluctant to set foot in Hibernia for fear he might be distracted by some new adventure; if so he would later find himself vainly lamenting, 'Alas! why did I not come more quickly!' / Therefore he put in nowhere along the coasts of England or Ireland, nor along those opposite.

But let us leave him to go where he is sent by the Naked Archer who has wounded him to the heart. Before I say any more about him, I want to return to Holland, and I invite you to return with me, for I know that you would be as sorry as I would if the wedding took place without us. / The wedding celebrations were sumptuous and splendid, though not as splendid nor as sumptuous as they say the celebrations will be in Zeeland. However, I do not suggest that you come to those, because new difficulties are going to arise to spoil the occasion: I shall tell you all about them in the next canto, if you will come to the next canto to listen to me.

TENTH CANTO

1–9 Introductory. 10–34 Bireno deserts Olympia. 35–64
Ruggiero safe with Logistilla, and Alcina discomfited. 65–92
Ruggiero at the parade of British troops. 92–115 Ruggiero
rescues Angelica from the orc.

AMONG all the lovers in the world who ever gave proof of constancy, through adverse times and in prosperity, however renowned they be, I should award the first place, yes, the first to Olympia. And if she be not the first, I shall still maintain that, in olden times as today, no one takes precedence over her as a lover. / Such are the many and signal proofs which she gave Bireno of her love that a woman could not carry greater conviction if she showed her heart open to view in her breast. And if souls as faithful and constant as hers merit a reciprocity of love, I declare that Bireno owes it to Olympia to love her not less but more than he loves himself; / and on no account ever to forsake her for another woman, not even for one of more resplendent beauty, not even were she the Grecian queen who set Europe and Asia at odds: no, no, rather than forsake her, he should forsake the light of the sun, his hearing, taste, and power of speech, his life and reputation, and whatever else more precious may be mentioned or conceived. / Now did Bireno love her as she loved him? Was he as faithful to her as she to him? Did he never once trim his sails to catch a wind other than that which drove him after her? Or did he misprize such fidelity and harden his heart against so great a love as hers? Well, I shall tell you—see if you don't compress your lips and arch your brows in disbelief! / When you have learnt, my ladies, what heartless conduct rewarded her for so much goodness, let none of you ever again believe a lover's word: to compass his desire, a lover, forgetful that God sees and hears all things, spins a web of promises and oaths all of which are in time scattered by a breath of wind. / Aye, a puff of wind scatters these lovers' promises and oaths the moment that they have slaked the avid thirst which goaded them. Let this be a warning to you, good ladies, to be less open to your lovers' prayers and tears: happy those who learn wisdom at another's expense! /

Beware of pretty young men in the flower of their years: their appetites are quickly sharpened and as quickly assuaged, like straw set ablaze. As a huntsman who pursues a hare in the cold as in the heat, over hill and dale, but no longer prizes it once he has it in the bag, and hastens off the moment he sights new quarry fleeing from him / —thus are these young men: so long as you treat them with hard indifference, they love you and court you as assiduously as a faithful suitor must. But the moment they can boast of victory, you cease to be women and become mere slaves. You will see them withdraw their false affections and offer them elsewhere. / Not that I am telling you to resist being loved—that would be quite wrong of me: without lovers you would be as vines growing wild in a vineyard, with no stakes or shrubs for their support. But I do urge you to avoid the downy-cheeked lad, flighty and inconstant, and to avoid plucking fruits which are bitter and unripe— though neither should they be overblown. /

I was telling you how they came upon a daughter of the King of Frisia, whom Bireno, from all accounts, intended to give as wife to his brother. But truth to tell, he fancied her for himself: she was too dainty a morsel, and he would have considered himself a fool to pass her up in order to give her to another. / The maiden had not yet turned fourteen; she was pretty and fresh as a new rosebud waiting to bloom with the rising day. Bireno fell in love with her: I tell you, never has dry timber flared up like this, nor ever have the golden ears of wheat fired by a jealous enemy, / the way he took fire, the way he burned right to the marrow when he discovered her grieving at her father's death, and saw her lovely face bathed in tears. Now just as that which is simmering on the stove goes off the boil if cold water is poured in, similarly the flame kindled in him by Olympia was simply snuffed out by this new love. / He was replete with Olympia; worse, he found her so tiresome he could scarcely bear the sight of her. And so urgent was his hunger for the little maiden that he would die of it should his satisfaction be too long deferred. But until the day appointed for his craving to be assuaged he held it in check, and feigned not merely love but adoration for Olympia, as though to do her pleasure was all he could desire. / And if he made much of the little maid, who could not prevent him from paying her undue attentions, nobody ascribed this to evil motives but to compassion, to goodness of heart: nobody was ever chided for succouring one who has been laid low by Fortune, or for comforting the afflicted—rather will he be applauded, especially when the unfortunate is an innocent little maiden. / Gracious Lord, how often is man's judgement clouded in dark mist: Bireno's heartless, evil deeds were reputed kind and virtuous!

The sailors set hands to their oars, and the ships put forth from the safety of the shore, merrily conveying Duke Bireno and his companions through the salt lagoons towards his Danish isle of Zeeland. / The shores of Holland had been left behind and lost from view, for they aimed to skirt the coast of Scotland on their port quarter so as to avoid Frisia, when they were overtaken by a gale and had to run before it on the high seas for three days; on the third day towards evening they put in to a deserted island. / They drew into a little creek and Olympia set foot ashore; all happy and unsuspecting, she enjoyed her supper with her faithless Bireno, then they both retired to bed, a tent having been set up on a pleasant spot. The rest of the company all returned to sleep on board their ships. / Seasickness and fear had for these last few days kept her sleepless; now she found herself safely on dry land, in the peaceful woodland, and she was free from all care and worry here with her lover beside her: for these reasons Olympia fell into so sound a sleep, she might have been a bear or a dormouse. / The false lover, awake to the possibility of contriving his mischief, softly crept out of bed once he sensed she was sleeping, and rather than dressing, tied his clothes into a bundle; he left the tent and rejoined his company in a trice, as though he had sprouted wings, and awoke them. Without a sound, he had them draw away from the shore and put out to sea. /

The shore was left behind; and poor Olympia, too, who slept on until Dawn of the golden rays scattered the ground with hoar frost, and the halcyons could be heard over the water lamenting their age-old sorrows. Neither waking nor asleep, Olympia reached out to embrace Bireno, but in vain. / She found nobody. She withdrew her hand. Again she tried: still nothing. She swept one arm this way, the other arm that; she reached out first with one leg then with the other: nothing. Fright banished sleep; she opened her eyes to look: no one to be seen. No longer did she snuggle warmly in her bereaved bed; she leapt up and was outside in a twinkling, / and ran down to the sea, tearing her cheeks, full of forebodings, indeed past all doubt. She tore her hair and beat her breast and strained her eyes, the moon still being up, to see whether anything could be made out beyond the shore—but she could see nothing, only the shore. She called 'Bireno', and at his name the sympathetic caves echoed 'Bireno'. / A rock rose by the water's edge, which the regular action of the waves had eaten away at the base so that it arched out over the sea. Olympia swiftly scaled it (for her agitation lent her strength) and she saw the billowing sails of her cruel lord receding into the distance: / she saw them in the distance, or thought she did—for it was still but first light. She dropped to the ground trembling; her face was whiter and colder than snow. But when she found the strength to stand again she cried out after the ships at the top of her voice, calling and calling the name of her cruel spouse. / And when her voice failed her, she vented her sorrow in tears, beating her palms together.

'Whither are you fleeing so fast, cruel one?' she cried. 'Your ship is not carrying the body that should accompany it: come back to fetch me—little extra burden is it to bear off my body as it has already embarked my soul.' Meanwhile she signalled with her arms and her garments to bring the ship back. / But the false young man stood far out to sea, and the wind that filled his sails dispersed the pleas and laments of hapless Olympia, and her sobs and cries. Three times, bent on her own destruction, she made to drown herself; but finally she stopped gazing at the water, rose and returned to where she had passed the night. /

She fell prone on the bed, bathing it in tears, and thus addressed it: 'Last night you gave welcome to two of us; why then were we not still two when we got up? O faithless Bireno! Oh cursed the day I was born! What shall I do? What can I do here all by myself? Who will help me, alas, who will comfort me? / I see no man here, nor any sign to show that men live here. No ship do I see which might offer me some hope of escape. I shall die of privation, and there shall be no one to close my eyes or give me burial, if the wolves that inhabit these forests do not first devour me. / O what fear! I seem already to see bears and lions coming out of these woods, and tigers and beasts armed by Nature with sharp fangs and claws to rend me. But what cruel beast could visit a worse death upon me than you have done, savage brute that you are! To slay me once will be enough for them, I know; but you—you are making me die a thousand deaths. / But what if a ship put in right now to show mercy and take me away, and I were saved from the wolves, the bears and lions that would rend me apart, or from starvation or other foul death? Would I be taken back to Holland, seeing that the ports and strongholds are in your keeping? Would I be taken back there to the land of my birth, seeing that you have falsely seized it from me? / Under pretext of kindred and friendship you have taken my realm from me. How quick you were to bring in your own men so as to gain full possession. Shall I return to Flanders? But I have sold everything off which I lived—little enough though this was—in order to aid you and deliver you from prison. Where am I to go? Alas, I know not! / Am I to go to Frisia, then, where I might have been queen, but for your sake chose not to be? This was the undoing of my father and my brothers, and spelled the end of all my fortune. I would not reproach you, thankless one, with all I have done for you, or use it against you—you know it all as well as I do. A fine reward you give me for it! / Ah, please heaven I be not taken by corsairs and sold into slavery! I would sooner than that welcome the wolf, lion, bear, tiger, any fierce beast to claw me open and break me in its jaws, and drag me dead to its lair.'

So saying, she buried her fingers in her golden tresses and tore at them lock by lock. / She set to running again along the edge of the beach, and her hair flowed about her as she kept turning her head. She seemed a prey to madness, as though not one but a dozen devils were after her—as though like Hecuba she had gone berserk at sight of her last son Polydorus' corpse. Now she stood on a rock and stared at the sea; and she herself, no less than the rock, seemed to have turned to stone. /

But let us leave her to her grieving until I return, for I want to take up Ruggiero's story: he was riding along the shore, weary and exhausted under the intense midday heat. The sun beat down on the hill and reverberated off it, while under foot the fine white sand smouldered. The armour he wore was well nigh glowing red-hot, as at its first making. / Thirst, the exhaustion of plodding through the deep sand, and the solitude of his journey kept him tedious, unwelcome company as he rode along the sun-blinded beach. After a while he came to an old tower which stood out of the water at the beach's edge, and in its shadow he discovered three ladies from Alcina's court: he recognized them by their dress and manner. / Reclining on Egyptian rugs, they were enjoying the fresh shade and a wide choice of wines in various jugs and all sorts of delicacies to eat. They had a little boat waiting off the beach; it was playing with the rippling waves until a helpful breeze should spring up and fill its sails, for at the moment the air was utterly still. / The ladies saw Ruggiero pursuing his way along the shifting dunes. They noticed how thirst had left its imprint on his lips, and how his worn face was bathed in sweat, and they invited him, bidding him not to be so set upon his journey, but to relent awhile and seek the fresh, sweet shade and give solace to his weary body. /

One of them approached his horse to hold his stirrup and invite him to dismount; another came with a crystal goblet of sparkling wine, which only excited his thirst. But Ruggiero was not going to dance to their tune: any delay would favour Alcina, giving her time to catch him up—she was now close behind him. / Imagine fine saltpetre and pure sulphur touched with a flame and igniting; or the sea boiling up when a dark whirlwind descends upon it. Far worse was the anger, the rage into which the third damsel flared when she saw Ruggiero calmly trudging on across the sand, ignoring them—and they fancied themselves as beauties! /

'A fine gentleman you are!' she shrieked at him. 'Those arms of yours—you stole them! And that horse would in no other wise be yours. I know what I'm talking about, which is why I'd like to see you properly punished—with death! You ought to be quartered, set on fire, hanged, you hideous thief, you scurvy, arrogant knave!' / The insolent woman heaped abuse on him, but Ruggiero answered her not a word, for he could expect little honour from so paltry a quarrel. With her sisters she straightway put out in the boat which awaited them on the water, and rowing frantically, they followed him along the shore, keeping him in view. / She kept intensifying her stream of abuse, ceaselessly inventive in finding new epithets.

Meanwhile Ruggiero came to the channel separating him from the land of Logistilla, the more engaging sorceress. Here he noticed an old boatman casting off from the further shore, as though he had already been told and was there ready waiting for Ruggiero's arrival. / On sight of him the boatman cast off and came gladly to fetch him over to a happier shore. If the face gives a true warrant for the heart, he was a kindly man, the soul of discretion. Ruggiero set foot upon the little skiff thanking God. He set forth across the tranquil reach, and enjoyed some conversation with the ferryman, a wise and experienced man, / who praised him for having contrived to tear himself free of Alcina in time, before she gave him the enchanted cup which she ultimately presented to all her lovers. And as he was conveying him to Logistilla's, where he would be able to witness virtuous behaviour, perennial beauty, and infinite grace, which / nourishes but never cloys the heart, 'At first sight,' he explained, 'wonder and reverence are the emotions that Logistilla excites; on further contemplation of her fathomless presence, all other good dwindles to little value. Her love is different to others': normally, hope or fear erodes the heart of a man in love. Now in her love, desire craves no more, but rests content on sight of her. / She will teach you more alluring preoccupations than music and dancing, perfumes, baths, and fine fare: rather, how your mind, better informed, can soar to the heights, loftier than the kite: and how the glory of the blessed can in part permeate the bodies of mortals.' As he spoke the boatman made great progress towards the safer shore. /

Now he noticed a fleet of ships out at sea all heading in their direction: they were bearing the slighted Alcina and the host she had assembled to bring ruin upon herself and her realm, or else to recapture her ravished treasure. Love played no small part in her motives, but an equal part was taken by injured pride. / Never since she was born had she been eaten by so intense an anger. She so urged the oars through the water that they threw up great plumes of spray to either side of the bows. So great was the noise, both sea and shore echoed with it.

'Bring out your shield, Ruggiero, now you must: else you are a dead man, or shamefully captured.' / So urged Logistilla's boatman; and, acting on his own words, he himself grasped the sheath, drew it off the shield and disclosed its light for all to see. The magic radiance it gave off so dazzled the eyes of the enemy that they were struck blind on the instant; some of them fell overboard from the stern, others from the bows. / A man keeping watch from the castle saw Alcina's fleet approaching and raised the alarm, hammering on the bell to summon the defenders to the harbour. The artillery rained missiles against the intruders who were contriving harm against good Ruggiero. So he received support from every side and was able to save his life and liberty. / Four ladies now came down to the beach, sent hither by Logistilla: stout-hearted Andronica, prudent Fronesia, Dicilla the just, and chaste Sophrosina who, having more to do here than the others, blazed and sparkled. And the army, which was unrivalled throughout the world, sallied forth from the castle and spread out along the shore. / Beneath the castle in the quiet estuary rode many a large vessel—a whole fleet of them—ready at the trumpet's shrill, ready day or night at a spoken command to issue forth to battle. Thus by the sea and land the battle was engaged, fierce and terrible; and because of it the realm which Alcina had earlier seized from her sister was thrown into turmoil. /

How many battles have ended in a way never predicted for them! Not only did Alcina fail to retrieve, as she expected, her fugitive lover; but her ships, which had been so numerous that the sea could barely find room for them all, were all consumed by the fires which broke out, till but one remained to her in which to make her sorry escape. /

Alcina fled, leaving her wretched followers in disarray, some burnt, others drowned or captured. Ruggiero's loss stung her far worse than any other of her afflictions. Night and day she would be given over to bitter lament and to abundant tears because of him, and often she regretted that she was unable to die and thus put an end to her cruel agony. / No fairy may ever die so long as the sun holds his course and the Heavens remain unchanged. Were it otherwise, Alcina's grief was such that Clotho might have spun out her life-thread faster: or she herself might, as Dido, have ended her misery with a dagger; she might have followed the majestic queen of the Nile into a mortal sleep. But fairies never can die. /

Let us return to Ruggiero, the knight worthy of eternal glory, and leave Alcina to her sorrow. He stepped out of the boat and onto the safer shore, thanking God for the happy outcome of his enterprise. Then, turning his back to the sea, he hastened across the dry land up to the castle. / Never before or since has mortal eye beheld a mightier nor a more beautiful castle. Its walls could not have been more precious had they been made of diamond or garnet. Jewels such as those to be found in it are never spoken of here below: whoever would hear tell of them needs must make the journey there himself—I don't believe that he would come across them anywhere else, except perhaps in Paradise. / What in particular gives these jewels their supremacy over every other is this: on looking at them, a man sees right into his own soul; he sees there reflected his vices and virtues, so that he no longer believes in the compliments he is paid, nor does he heed blame when he is charged unfairly. Looking into these bright mirrors, he discovers himself, and learns wisdom. / They give off a light, too, brilliant as the sun and so abundant that whoever possesses one of them may, wherever he be, make broad daylight at will, in spite of Phoebus. Nor are the walls remarkable only for their gems: the materials and the refinement of construction vie with each other, so that between the two there is no deciding which perfection is the greater. / Above the soaring arches, which looked as though they supported the very dome of Heaven, gardens extended which were so spacious and magnificent that even at ground-level they would be hard to lay out. Through the luminous crenellations could be seen the verdure of the fragrant trees, which were a delight in the summer, and in winter remained a mass of blossom and ripe fruit. / Trees as noble do not grow outside these lovely gardens, nor do such roses, violets and lilies, amarants and jasmine. You will observe, anywhere else, how all in one day a flower will be born, live out its term and die, drooping its head on its bereaved stalk, for it is subject to the changing seasons. / Here, though, every thing remained verdant green; the flowers bloomed in perpetual radiance, not through any beneficent working of Nature, but through the studious care of Logistilla: with no need to depend upon the climate (impossible though this would seem to anyone else), she maintained perennial spring in her garden. /

Logistilla was visibly pleased that so worthy a knight should have come to her, and she gave orders that everyone should make much of him and study to do him reverence. Astolfo had arrived some time earlier, and Ruggiero was delighted to see him. A few days later all the others arrived whom Melissa had restored to their proper selves. /

After a day or two in which to rest, Ruggiero went to the wise enchantress accompanied by Astolfo who, no less than he, was anxious to see the West again. Melissa spoke to her on behalf of them both, humbly entreating her to give them counsel and assistance in making good their return to whence they came. / 'I shall give the matter thought,' replied Logistilla, 'and two days hence I shall let you know what I have devised.' She took counsel with herself how best to help Ruggiero and, after him, the duke. Her conclusion was that the winged horse would have to return the former to the shores of Aquitania; but first the beast would have to be fitted with a special bridle wherewith Ruggiero could turn him in flight and rein him in. / She showed him what to do if he wanted the steed to climb, what to do to make him descend, how to make him wheel in a circle, or go fast, or simply hover. . And whatever the knight was accustomed to performing on a good earth-bound horse he soon became adept at achieving in the air on the feathered steed. / When Ruggiero was fully prepared he took leave of the kind enchantress, to whom he remained attached ever after by a strong bond of affection, and departed from that country. He set off, and first I shall tell of his adventures. Afterwards I shall relate how the English knight, on a longer and more arduous journey, made his way back to Charlemagne, and to the court where his friends were. /

Ruggiero departed, but did not retrace the path he had earlier taken against his will, when the hippogryph kept course out over the sea and he scarcely sighted land. This time, as he could make the beast fly hither and yon at his own whim, he chose to take a different way back, like the Wise Men when they avoided Herod. / Coming hither, he had left Spain behind and made a direct line for India, where it is washed by the Eastern Sea—where Alcina was entertaining a quarrel with her fellow-sorceress. This time he was disposed to see other lands than those where Aeolus incites the winds, and to complete the circle he had started, so as to girdle the earth, like the sun. / On his journey he saw Cathay to one side and to the other Mangiana, as he passed over great Quinsai. He flew over the Himavian range, and skirted Sericana to his right. From the hyperborean land of the Scythians, he turned in towards the Hyrcanian sea and reached Sarmatia; then, arriving at the point where Europe and Asia meet, he beheld the lands of the Russians and Prussians, and came to Pomerania. / For all his pressing desire to return to Bradamant, Ruggiero was unwilling to forgo the pleasure of discovering the world, but had perforce to pass by way of the Poles, Hungarians, and Germans and the rest of those bleak northern lands. Finally he arrived in far-off England. / You must not imagine, my Lord, that he was constantly on the wing; every evening he put up at some hostelry, avoiding poor accommodation as best he could. Days and months went by as he pursued his way, so eager was he to visit lands and seas. Then, arriving one morning at London, the hippogryph swooped down over the Thames. /

In the fields outside the city, he beheld armoured knights and foot-soldiers being marshalled, to the sound of trumpets and drums, in imposing ranks before Rinaldo, the flower of paladins. I told you, if you remember, how he had been sent hither by Charlemagne to seek help. / Ruggiero arrived just as the fine parade was proceeding outside the city; and to learn all about it, he asked a knight—after bringing his steed to earth. The knight was of friendly disposition and told him that the hosts here assembled under so many banners were those of Scotland, Ireland, England, and the outlying islands. / Once the parade was over, they would move to the coast, where ships awaited them in harbour, ready to plough across the sea. Relying on these troops who were coming to their rescue, the hard-pressed French were recovering heart.

'But for your fuller information, I shall point everyone out to you. / Look at that large ensign with the leopards and the fleurs-de-lys: it is held aloft by the great captain, and the other ensigns follow after it. His name is renowned in these parts: Lionet, Duke of Lancaster, the flower of valiant men, a brave and skilful warrior, nephew to the king. / After the royal standard, first comes that of Richard, Earl of Warwick; it shows three wings argent on a vert ground, and flutters upstream in the breeze. The ensign with the two antlers conjoined is that of the Duke of Gloucester. The flaming sconce is the Duke of Clarence's; the tree, the Duke of York's. / The lance broken in three is the emblem of the Duke of Norfolk; the lightning, that of the Earl of Kent; the gryphon, of the Earl of Pembroke; the scales, of the Duke of Suffolk. The sign of the yoke, there, wreathed with two serpents, is that of the Earl of Essex; and the garland on an azure ground is Northumberland's. /

The one displaying a boat sinking at sea is the Earl of Arundel; there goes the Marquis of Berkeley, and next, the Earls of March and of Richmond: the first displays argent, a cleft mountain, the second, a palm, the third, a pine in the water. Over there is the Earl of Dorset, and there, the Earl of Hampton, the former with the chariot, the latter with the crown. / The falcon drooping its wings over its nest is the emblem of Raymond, Earl of Devon; the or and sable emblem is Worcester's; the dog, Derby's; the bear, Oxford's. The crystal cross you see over there belongs to the wealthy Bishop of Bath. And the cloven chair on a grey ground are the arms of Harriman, Duke of Somerset. / The mounted troops, including archers, number forty-two thousand men; those proceeding to battle on foot are twice as many, give or take a hundred. Look over there at those ensigns; one is grey, one green, one yellow, and the last sable and azure striped—that is where Godfrey, Henry, Herman, and Edward are each leading their infantry after their standards. / The first is Duke of Buckingham; Henry is Earl of Salisbury; old Herman is Lord of Monmouth; Edward, there, is Earl of Shrewsbury. All these drawn up to the East are English.

'Now look to the West and you will see thirty thousand Scotsmen led by Zerbin, their king's son. / See the pair of unicorns, and between them the great lion with the silver sword in its paw: that is the standard of the Scottish king There you will find Zerbin, his son. For comeliness he is one in a million: Nature cast him, then broke the mould. Nor is there any like him for prowess, grace and strength. His is the dukedom of Ross. / The Earl of Athol's standard is azure, a bend Or. That other standard, showing a pent-up leopard, is the Duke of Moray's. See there the ensign of staunch Alcabrun, distinct with its many colours and many birds; in his wild domain he is neither duke, earl, nor marquis, but bears the title of chief. / The ensign with the bird staring at the sun is the Duke of Strafford's. Lurcanio, the Earl of Angus, has the bull flanked by two greyhounds. And there you see Ariodant, Duke of Albany, whose colours are argent and azure. That vulture attacking a green dragon is the emblem of the Earl of Buchan. Bold Herman, with the sable and argent emblem, is Lord of Forbes. / On his right is the Earl of Errol, with the torch on an emerald ground. Now turn to the Irish—they are drawn up on the plain in two squadrons. The Earl of Kildare leads the first, and the Earl of Desmond, from the rugged hills, the other. / The first has on his standard a flaming pine; the other, argent, a bend gules. England, Scotland and Ireland are not the only lands to furnish help to Charles: troops have arrived from Sweden and Norway, too, from Thule and even from distant Iceland—in fact from all those regions, where the people are by nature warlike. / They have come out from their forests and lairs, and they number sixteen thousand, or nearly. They are as hairy as beasts—their faces, chests, flanks, and backs, their arms and legs are covered in hair. The plain there has all the appearance of a forest where their spears cluster thickly round their white standard; Morath, their chief, carries it, waiting to dye it in Moorish blood.' /

While Ruggiero looked at the various standards of the fine host preparing to bring aid to France, and discussed them, and learned the names of the British barons, people started running towards him in amazement, one by one, to gaze at the unique, or rare, animal on which he was mounted. Soon he was the centre of a circle. / Now in order to heighten their astonishment and play upon it, good Ruggiero gave rein to his flying steed and touched spurs to his flanks; the hippogryph rose into the sky, leaving behind him a stupefied multitude. At once he shaped his course towards Ireland, for he had seen Englishmen from all parts. / He beheld fabled Hibernia, where Saint Patrick, as an old man, hollowed out the cave wherein such grace is—it seems—to be found, that the visitor there can cleanse himself of all his iniquity.

After this he turned his steed South towards the sea that washes the Breton coast, and looking down, he espied Angelica chained to the bare rock. / Chained to the bare rock, she was, on the Isle of Tears—for this was the name given to the island inhabited by those cruel savages, those barbarous folk who, as I related in a previous canto, went marauding along many a shore abducting every comely damsel in order to feed her infamously to a monster. / That very morning she was chained there for the huge sea-monster, the orc, to come and swallow her alive; for this, horrible to relate, was how he fed. I explained earlier that she was the prize of the corsairs who found her on the beach asleep beside the old hermit who had lured her there by magic. / The brutal, ruthless savages left the exquisitely beautiful damsel exposed on the shore to the cruel monster, and as naked as when Nature first fashioned her; not even a veil did she have to cover the lily-white, the rose-red, unfading in December as in July, which coloured her lustrous limbs. / Ruggiero would have taken her for a statue fashioned in alabaster or some lambent marble, and tethered thus to the rock by some diligent sculptor's artifice, were it not that he distinctly saw tears coursing down her rose-fresh, lily-white cheeks and bedewing her unripe apple-breasts, and her golden tresses flowing in the wind. /

As he looked into her lovely eyes Ruggiero was reminded of his Bradamant; he was pricked with compassion and love, and could scarcely refrain from weeping. Tenderly he addressed the maiden, after reining in his charger. 'Gentle lady, the only fetter you merit is that with which Love binds his votaries: / quite undeserving must you be of this plight or of any other. Who is the miscreant so perverted as to blemish the smooth ivory of your delicate hands with unwelcome bruising?' On hearing him speak she perforce became like white ivory sprinkled with carmine, seeing those parts of her exposed to view which, for all their beauty, modesty would conceal. / She would have covered her face with her hands were they not tied to the hard rock. But she bathed it in tears—this at least she was free to do—and tried to keep it bowed. After sobbing a little, she prepared to speak, in a sad, small voice; but the words did not come—they were thwarted by the loud noise now to be heard from the sea. /

The colossal monster now appeared, half submerged; like a long ship making port, driven before the wind from North or South, so was the terrible orc as it approached the morsel shown to it. Now the monster had almost reached her. The damsel was half-dead with fright —she was past comforting. / Ruggiero was holding his lance not in rest, but in free play, and he struck at the orc, a beast I can only describe as a great coiling, twisting mass, quite unlike an animal in shape, except for its head, with protruding eyes and teeth like a boar's. Ruggiero struck at it between the eyes, but he might as well have been striking at solid iron or stone. / His first thrust proving ineffectual, he returned to do better the second time. The orc, seeing the shadow cast by the spreading wings flitting here and there across the water, left its certain prey awaiting it on shore and started a furious chase, curving and coiling, after the elusive one instead. Ruggiero dropped down and struck many a blow, / like an eagle dropping from the sky when it has spotted a snake weaving through the grass, or lying on a bare stone in the sun, smoothing and titivating its golden scales: it does not attack so as to meet the hissing, venomous jaws head-on, but endeavours rather to sink its talons into the serpent's back, and aims its flight so as to avoid the snake's turning and biting it. / So Ruggiero wielded his sword and lance so as to avoid the monster's snout bristling with teeth, but aimed blows between its ears, on its back and at its tail.

If the beast turned, he swerved aside, choosing the right moment to descend and to gain height. But as what he struck was always adamantine he could not penetrate the rock-hard carapace. / Such a battle will be fought between an impudent fly and a mastiff in dusty August, or the months before and after—from the corn harvest to that of the grape. The fly will infest him and buzz around him, stinging him now on the eye, now on the snapping muzzle. And frequently the mastiff will snap his jaws shut on nothing—but the moment he catches the fly, that moment makes up for everything. / So powerfully did the orc thrash the water with its tail that the seas surged up to the skies, and Ruggiero could not tell whether his mount was beating the air with its wings or swimming in the waves. Many times he wished himself safely on dry land, fearing that if the hippogryph continued having to endure the flying spray, his wings would be so sodden that he would vainly wish for something floatable, be it only a cockle-shell. /

He hit on a new and better plan: to overcome the cruel monster with other weapons. He would dazzle it with the flash of the enchanted shield still in its cover. He flew to the shore and, as a precaution, took the ring which defied all magic and slipped it onto the little finger of the damsel chained to the bare rock. / This was the ring which Bradamant, to effect Ruggiero's release, had seized from Brunello, and subsequently sent to him in India by Melissa, to rescue him from wicked Alcina's hands. Melissa, as I described to you earlier, had used the ring to the advantage of many; then she had returned it to Ruggiero, who there-after had always worn it on his finger. / He gave it now to Angelica, lest she be harmed by the glint of the shield, and to protect her eyes, which had already ensnared him. The monstrous sea-beast was approaching the shore, his belly displacing half the ocean. Ruggiero took up his station and lifted the veil: and it was as though another sun had entered the sky. / The enchanted light struck the monster's eyes and wrought its wonted effect. As a trout or perch floats down a river made turbid with lime by some hill-dweller, thus was the monster, a ghastly sight as it lay upturned in the foaming sea. Ruggiero thrust at it all over but could find no way to penetrate its hide. /

All this while the beautiful damsel besought him not to continue his vain onslaught against the horny scales. 'Come back good sir, for God's sake,' she begged, weeping; 'unchain me before the orc revives. Take me with you, drown me in the depths of the sea, but let me not end in the belly of the ghastly fish.' Moved by this just entreaty, Ruggiero untied the damsel and carried her away from the shore. / Spurred, the steed thrust off the beach and launched into the air and galloped through the sky. On his back he carried the knight, with the damsel mounted right behind him. Thus did he deprive the monster of a feast which was far too dainty and delicious for it. He kept turning round, and in his breast, and in his lively eyes a thousand kisses were a-smoulder-ing. / Instead of circling Spain, as he had earlier planned, he put down at a neighbouring shore, where Brittany juts furthest out to sea.

By the shore there was a shady oak-wood, which forever resounded with Philomena's lament; in the middle was a grassy clearing with a spring, and to either side, a solitary hill. / Here the eager knight drew rein and set foot in the clearing; he had his charger fold his wings, (leaving at liberty, however, another steed, who had now spread his even wider). He dismounted, but could scarcely restrain himself from climbing onto a different mount; but his gear delayed him: it delayed

him, for he had to pull it off; it obstructed the impetus of his desire. /
With hasty fingers he fumbled confusedly at his armour, now this side,
now the other. Never before had it seemed such a long business—for
every thong unlaced, two seemed to become entangled. But this canto
has gone on too long, my Lord, and perhaps you are growing a-weary
with listening to it: I shall defer my story to another time when it may
prove more welcome.

ELEVENTH CANTO

*1 Introductory. 2–21 Angelica eludes Ruggiero, and so does
Bradamant. 21–28 An aside on fire-arms. 28–83 Orlando
slays the orc and rescues Olympia, then continues his search
for Angelica.*

A METTLESOME charger will often suffer himself to be reined in from
a full gallop, however gentle the hand on the rein. Seldom, however,
will the bridle of Reason check rabid Lust once it scents its quarry. It
is like a bear: there is no distracting him from the honey once he has
sniffed at it or tasted a drop left in the jar. /

What argument can there be to stop Ruggiero and change his mind
about taking his pleasure with lovely Angelica, whom he holds naked
there in the convenient solitude of the glade? Bradamant he has quite
forgotten, though she had always reigned in his heart. Or, if her memory
was indeed fresh as ever, well—he would still be a fool not to make the
most of the maiden present. / In this situation Xenocrates himself,
that austere paragon, would have yielded to lechery. Ruggiero had
thrown down his lance and shield and was feverishly pulling off his
armour. The damsel had modestly lowered her eyes to her exquisite
body when she noticed on her finger the precious ring which Brunello
had earlier stolen from her at Albracca. / This was the ring she took
with her to France the first time she made the journey with her brother,
who brought the lance which passed to the paladin Astolfo. With this
ring she neutralized the spells Maugis cast on her at Merlin's tomb.
With it she helped Orlando and others to escape one morning from
Dragontina; / with this ring she made herself invisible and escaped
from the dungeon where a wicked old man had imprisoned her. But
why should I enumerate all the instances when it has proved its
virtues? You know them as well as I do. Brunello found his way into
her castle and stole the ring from her, for Agramant wanted it. Ever

since that moment Fortune had frowned upon her until she lost her kingdom. /

Noticing the ring on her finger, as I said, she was so stunned with joy and amazement, she thought she must be dreaming, and could scarcely believe her eyes. She slipped it off her finger and straight into her mouth, and in less than a twinkling had vanished from Ruggiero's sight as completely as the sun behind a cloud. / Ruggiero looked in every direction and searched frantically all over the place, until he remembered the ring. He stopped, thunderstruck, thwarted. Cursing himself for his carelessness, he inveighed against Angelica for her discourtesy, her ingratitude—a fine way to thank him for his help! / 'Heartless damsel,' he complained, 'is this how you reward me? You would snatch the ring from me rather than allow me to offer it to you. Why will you not accept it from me? Not only the ring, but the shield, too, and the fleet-footed horse, and myself I would give to you, to use me as you will—only hide not your lovely face from me. I know, heartless one, that you hear me but will not answer.' / As he spoke, he went groping round the spring like a blind man; many a time he hugged the empty air, hoping to clasp the damsel in the same embrace.

She meanwhile was already well on her way, and kept on walking until she came to a spacious cave beneath a hill; here she found some food. / This was the abode of an old herdsman with a large herd of mares, which were browsing on the tender grass along the fresh streams down in the valley. On either side of the cave there were stables where they could take refuge from the midday sun. That day Angelica stopped here at leisure, unseen by anybody. / When evening came and she felt sufficiently restored, she dressed herself in rustic garments, all too different from her normal gay apparel, made after every conceivable fashion and hue—in shades of green, yellow, purple, blue, and red. Even so humble attire, however, could not disguise her natural beauty and nobility. / You who praise Phyllis, Neiera, Amaryllis, or elusive Galatea, be silent! For beauty none of them can touch Angelica—saving your presence, Tityrus, and yours, Meliboeus. The beautiful damsel selected from the herd of mares one which pleased her well, and the idea came to her there and then to make away back to the Orient. /

Ruggiero waited a long time to see if she would discover herself, but to no purpose; once it was clear to him that he was wasting his time and she was no longer there to listen to him, he turned back to remount the horse which was at home in the air as well as on the ground. But he saw that the hippogryph had worked free of the bit and was climbing unimpeded through the sky. / It was a sorry blow, coming on top of the last, to find himself deprived of the flying horse. The loss weighed heavily upon him, no less than the damsel's trick. But what hurt more than either was the loss of the precious ring—this grieved him most especially, less for its magical properties than for the fact that it had been a gift from his lady. / Utterly dejected, he put on his armour, slung his shield on his shoulder, turned his back to the sea and set off through the grassy glades towards a broad valley. Here, amid the deep shady woods he came upon a wider, more frequented path, which he pursued only a short way when to his right, where the forest was thicker, he heard a great din. /

A great din he heard, and the shock of arms, a terrifying sound. He hastened in amid the trees and came upon two antagonists hemmed in a narrow glade and locked in battle. I know not what their quarrel was, but they were exchanging savage blows without mercy. One of them was a fierce-looking giant; the other a bold, valiant knight. / The knight was defending himself with sword and shield, and side-stepping deftly to avoid being laid out by the club which the giant was wielding two-handed. The knight's steed lay dead on the path. Ruggiero stopped to watch the battle, and soon reached the conclusion that he would prefer to see the knight win, / though he did not interfere, but stood out of the way and continued to watch. Now the giant raised his massy club over the knight's helmet and brought it down with both hands. Under the impact the knight fell. The other saw him lying dazed and, in order to put an end to him, unloosed his helmet. This enabled Ruggiero to see the knight's face. / The face he set eyes on was that of sweet, lovely Bradamant, his heart's delight; and here was the wicked giant making ready to slay her. Ruggiero challenged him to battle and advanced with drawn sword, but the giant, not prepared for another combat, took the stunned woman in his arms, / and threw her over his shoulder and carried her off as a wolf seizes a lamb, or an eagle seizes in its hooked talons a dove or some such bird. Ruggiero could see how urgently his help was needed and ran after the giant as fast as he could; but the giant strode away so fast that Ruggiero could scarcely follow him with his eyes. / The giant ran off and Ruggiero pursued him down a path through the deep shade; the path gradually broadened out until it took them clear of the wood into a broad meadow.

But enough of these two for now: I am returning to Orlando; he had taken King Cimosco's thunder-machine and thrown it into the depths of the sea, so as to obliterate every last trace of it. / Little did that profit us, though: the Evil One, enemy of human kind, who invented the fire-arm, copying the action of the thunderbolt which splits the clouds and falls to earth—the Evil One, serving us almost as fatally as when he deceived Eve with the apple, saw to it that a sorcerer should recover the weapon in our grandfathers' time, or a little earlier. / The infernal contraption lay hidden for many a year under more than a hundred fathoms of water, until it was brought to the surface by magic and passed into the possession of the Germans; these tried one experiment after another, and the devil sharpened their wits until, to our detriment, they eventually rediscovered how to use it. /

Italy, France, every nation of the world came to learn the cruel science. Some hollow out the muzzle of the gun as they cast it in the furnace; others cast it solid and then pierce the muzzle; some make the muzzle small, others large, so that it weighs less or more; it goes by the name of bombard, or arquebus, small-bore cannon or large-bore; / mortar, it is called, or falcon or culverin, according to its inventor's fancy. It splits steel, smashes stone to pieces; wherever it goes nothing can resist it. Unhappy soldier, turn in your weapons to be melted down, even to your very sword: carry a musket on your shoulder or an arquebus—else you will go without wages! / Wicked, ugly invention, how did you find a place in human hearts? You have destroyed military glory, and dishonoured the profession of arms; valour and martial skill are now discredited, so that often the miscreant will appear a better man than the valiant. Because of you no longer may boldness and courage go into the field to match their strength. / Many a baron, many a knight now lies in earth, and so shall many more on your account, before this war is ended which has brought tears to all the world but most of all to Italy. I have said it, and I speak no lie: the man who invented such abominable contraptions was crueller by far than all the most evil of evil geniuses the world has known. / To his eternal punishment I believe that God must shut his cursed soul away in the blindest depths of hell, with Judas the accursed.

But let us go after Orlando who was so anxious to reach the island of Ebuda, where lovely, dainty maidens are given as food to a sea-monster. / The greater the paladin's haste, though, the less haste the wind displayed. Whether it blew from starboard or port, or from dead aft, it was always so slack that little progress was to be expected from its assistance. Sometimes it died away altogether; other times it turned so contrary that they were forced to put about or sail close-hauled. / God willed that he should not arrive ahead of the King of Hibernia— which left the field free for the deeds I shall describe to you a few pages hence. Drawing in to the island, Orlando said to the captain: 'Wait here and let me have the ship's boat: I mean to go unaccompanied to the rock. / I want the biggest chain and the biggest anchor you have on board: if I come into conflict with the monster I shall show you why I am taking them.'

He had the ship's boat put overboard and jumped into it, together with everything he needed for his enterprise. All his armour he left behind, taking only his sword; then he set out, unaccompanied, for the rock. / He pulled the oars in to his chest, sitting with his back towards his landing-place—like a sea-crab creeping out onto the shore from the surf or from the rock-pools. Fair Aurora had (much to jealous Tithonus' rage) just spread her golden tresses to the Sun, who remained half-hidden still, half-revealed. / He approached to within a stone's throw (well, a powerful stone's throw) of the bare rock, when he heard what may have been weeping—the sound was so faint and weak. He twisted round to his left and, searching the surface of the sea, espied a woman, naked as the day of her birth, bound to a tree-trunk, the water lapping her feet. / As she was some way off and kept her head bowed he was unable to make out who she was. He pulled urgently on his oars and drew nearer, anxious to discover more. Now it was that he heard the sea groan, the caves and forests boom; the waves swelled up and forth emerged the monster, breasting half the sea. /

As a vaporous cloud, swollen with rain and storm, rises from a dark valley and mantles the whole land, cloaking it in blackest night, and seems to eclipse the day; thus was the monster as it swam, so filling out the sea that it appeared to displace all of it. The waves shivered. Orlando collected himself; his demeanour was lofty—never a qualm in his heart or face. / Fully determined on the course to take, he moved at once; to shield the damsel and assail the monster directly, he positioned his skiff between her and the orc. He left his sword sheathed, but took up the anchor with the chain. Then, quite undaunted, he awaited the monster. / The orc came on and, seeing Orlando in his skiff only a short way off, opened its jaws so wide to swallow him that a man could have ridden in on horseback. Orlando drove forward right into its jaws, bringing the anchor and, if I am not mistaken, the boat as well. He wedged the anchor between its palate and its soft tongue / so that it could no longer bring its two fearsome jaws to shut together. Thus will a miner working at the rock face shore up the tunnel as he works forward, for fear that it cave in suddenly and engulf him while, all unwary, he is absorbed in his labour. The upper fluke of the anchor towered so high above the lower that Orlando could only reach it by jumping. /

Having secured his prop and ensured that the monster could no longer close its jaws, Orlando drew his sword and adventured through that dark cavern slashing and thrusting as he went. How was the orc to defend itself from the paladin at large in his throat? As well might one defend a castle once the enemy are within the walls. / Reeling with pain, the orc surged out of the water, exposing its flanks and scaly back, then plunged back in till its belly stirred up the sand on the bottom.

Feeling that there was now a surfeit of water, Orlando swam out. He left the anchor lodged in the beast's throat, but grasped the hawser to which it was attached. / With the cable in his hand he swam quickly to the rock, and once he had set foot ashore he hauled on the anchor, whose flukes were embedded in the ugly brute's throat. The orc could not help going with the cable, reeled in by Orlando's exceptional strength—the paladin could exert greater force in a single tug than could a capstan in ten. / As a wild bull, feeling a noose suddenly fall about its horns, jumps from side to side, twists, rolls to the ground and bounds up again, but can never free itself, so did the orc, dragged forcibly out from its native element, follow the hawser, endlessly thrashing and coiling, but quite unable to fight free. / The blood came belching forth from its mouth in such abundance that today this might have been called the Red Sea—and the beast so lashed the water that you could see the bottom where it was riven. The monster sent the water surging skyward even to blot out the clear sunlight.

At the din the woods, the hills, the distant shores resounded. / Forth from his grotto issued ancient Proteus, and came out onto the sea surface at the sound of such a rumpus; and when he saw Orlando go right into the orc and come out again, and haul so colossal a fish to shore, he fled for the ocean depths, heedless of his scattered flock; indeed, the clangour rose to such a pitch that Neptune harnessed his dolphins to his chariot and that day fled to Ethiopia. / Tearful Ino fled with Melicertes upon her shoulders; Nereids of the flowing tresses, Tritons, and other sea-sprites fled in all directions, seeking safety. Orlando hauled the horrid fish to land, but needed to waste no further effort upon it—the beast was dead, finished by its struggles and torments, before it was drawn out onto the beach. /

Not a few of the islanders had come out to watch this unusual conflict. Now these, inclined to empty superstition, decided that Orlando's heroic deed was a profanation: it would only draw Proteus' further enmity upon them, they argued, and rekindle his blind rage, and make him send his sea-flocks once more to invade their shores and re-open the ancient vendetta. / Better to crave peace of the offended deity, they felt, before worse befell them; this they would accomplish once they had taken the champion and thrown him into the sea to placate Proteus. As one torch sets the next one alight, and soon the whole place is aglow, thus from one heart to the next was the wrath enkindled whose object was to throw Orlando to the waves. / They came down to the shore, then, some with slings or bows, others with spears or with swords; they crowded in on him from every side, ring after ring of them, to mount a more powerful assault. The paladin was amazed at having to suffer so base an affront, such ingratitude: he had slain the monster and saw himself now being ill-treated, whereas he had hoped that honour and thanks would be his due. / Just as a bear led in a fairground by Russians or Lithuanians is scarcely disturbed, as it passes down the street, by the importunate yapping of little dogs, and does not even spare them a glance; similarly the paladin was not worried in the least by those rustics—why, he could have laid them all out at a single puff. / The moment he turned on them they all fell back, and he brandished Durindana. Those idiot folk had imagined, seeing him quite bereft of armour, without breastplate, without a shield upon his arm, that he would put up scant resistance. Little did they realize that from top to toe his skin was harder than diamond. / There was no stopping Orlando doing to his attackers what was beyond their power to do to him. Thirty of them he slew in ten sword-strokes, or barely more. Soon he had cleared the beach round him, and was already turning away to go and untie the maiden when fresh tumult and outcry was to be heard from another part of the shore. /

While the paladin had been keeping the savages in play, the Irish expedition had landed unopposed at several other points round the island, which they scoured from end to end, exacting pitiless reprisals against the inhabitants—whether justice or cruelty was their motive, they paid no regard to age or sex. / The islanders offered no resistance, or scarcely any; for one thing, they had been taken off guard, for another, the population was but scanty and at all events quite at a loss. Their goods were ransacked, their houses set on fire; they themselves were slaughtered; their walls all razed to the ground. Not a person was left alive. /

As though all this tumult, the screams, the general havoc, were no concern of his, Orlando approached the damsel who was to have been devoured on the bare rock by the sea-monster. As he looked at the damsel he thought he recognized her, and the conviction grew on him as he drew closer. Could she be Olympia? Yes, she was indeed Olympia, whose fidelity had been so basely requited. / Unhappy Olympia: after the shabby treatment she had received from Love, spiteful Fortune sent the pirates her way, and the same day she was carried off to the isle of Ebuda. She recognized Orlando on his approach to the rock, but as she was naked she bowed her head; she would not speak to him, indeed she dare not even raise her eyes to his face. / Orlando asked her what wicked fate had brought her to this island, for had he not left her as happy as could be in her bridegroom's company?

'I know not', she replied, 'whether I am to thank you for saving me from death, or to complain that, were it not for you, all my woes would today would have been ended. / I must thank you for saving me from a death which would have been too horrible—had I ended in the maw of that hideous brute. But I do not thank you for keeping me alive, for only death can release me from suffering. Let me see you give me that which can deliver me from every pain, and you shall have my thanks.' / And with many tears she described how she had been betrayed by her husband, who abandoned her sleeping on an island whence she was abducted by pirates. As she spoke, she turned away in the same pose in which Diana is captured in sculptures and paintings when she is bathing in the spring and throws water in Acteon's face: she concealed her breast and belly as best she could, / being more liberal with her sides and back. Orlando was anxious for his ship to come into port so that, having freed her from her chains, he could cover her in some raiment.

While he was intent upon this, Hubert supervened: Hubert, King of Hibernia, had heard that the sea-monster was lying prostrate on the strand, / and that a knight had swum in to plant an enormously heavy anchor in its throat, and had then dragged it to shore as a ship is dragged upstream. The king had come himself to see whether the man had spoken the truth who had related these things to him. Meanwhile his men were wreaking arson and destruction in every corner of the island. / For all that Orlando was quite disfigured, dripping wet and blood-smeared as he was from venturing right into the orc and re-emerging in the welter of gore he had drawn from the beast, the King of Hibernia nonetheless still recognized him for the Count of Anglant: in fact when he heard of the battle with the orc, he had at once concluded that no one but Orlando could have brought off such a feat. / He knew Orlando, having been a page of honour at the French court until the previous year when he had left in order to assume the crown on the death of his father. He had seen and spoken with Orlando any number of times. Removing his helmet, he cheerfully hastened up to greet the paladin and embrace him. / Orlando showed every bit as much pleasure at seeing Hubert as the latter at seeing him. They embraced once and then again, after which Orlando told the king about the way the damsel had been deserted, and who the traitor was: perfidious Bireno, of all men the one who had least call to act so. / He described the repeated proofs she had given of her love, and how her family and her possessions had all been made away with, and how in the end she was ready to lay down her life for Bireno; he himself, said Orlando, was a witness of much of this, and could render a full account of it.

As he spoke, the damsel's serene and beautiful eyes brimmed with tears. / Her lovely face was as the spring sky when, after a shower of rain, the sun bursts through to disperse the veil of cloud; and as the nightingale will then break into melody in the fresh green branches, so the Love-god bathes his plumage in the lovely teardrops and rejoices in the limpid light. / In the brazier of her splendid eyes the god heats his golden dart and anneals it in the trickling stream which flows between red and white blossoms. Thus tempered, he forcibly lets fly against the young king, who is protected by no shield, nor double coat of mail, nor tough hide: as he gazes at her eyes and tresses, he feels a stab at his heart, and knows not why. / Olympia's beauties were of a rare perfection: beauty resided not merely in her forehead, her eyes, cheeks, and hair, her nose and lips, shoulders and throat; but, to carry on down from her breasts, the parts normally concealed by a tunic were so excellently formed they could have been more perfect than any in the world. / They were whiter than virgin snow and to the touch smoother than ivory. The small rounded breasts were like beads of milk newly pressed from a reed. They were so set apart, they resembled two little hillocks and between them a pleasant shady dell in the season when winter snow still lies in the hollows. / The prominent hips, the flat belly, more limpid than a looking-glass, those white thighs, they all seemed the work of Phidias or of an even finer hand. Am I to describe to you those parts, too, which she was so vainly hoping to conceal? Suffice to say that from top to toe she was a very paragon of beauty. /

Had Paris, the Phrygian shepherd, set eyes upon her in the valley of Mount Ida, I cannot say how far Venus, though she surpassed those other goddesses, would have surpassed Olympia in beauty; nor perhaps would he have ventured to Sparta to violate the sacred laws of hospitality. Rather might he have said: 'Let Helen stay with Menelaus— this damsel is all I want.' / Had she been at Crotona when Zeuxis set to work on the portrait destined for the temple of Juno and assembled such a number of lovely nude women, meaning to borrow from each one a different part in order to compose one beauty to perfection, he would not have needed to look beyond Olympia, for in every part of her sheer perfection resided. / I do not believe Bireno ever saw that exquisite body naked, for I am convinced that otherwise he would never have behaved so cruelly or abandoned her in that desert place. The conclusion was that Hubert fell in love with her—there was no concealing the blaze in his heart.

He applied himself to comforting her, and to giving her hope that her present sorrow would be converted into gladness. / He promised to accompany her to Holland and swore that he would not rest until he had restored her to her realm and wrought just and memorable vengeance on the false traitor; all the strength of Ireland would be marshalled to this end, and he would not waste a moment setting this in train. Meanwhile he had the houses searched for feminine attire. / To find clothing for her there was no need to seek outside the island:

each day the store had been augmented by those of the women fed to the voracious monster. They had not searched long before they had collected a large and varied supply; Hubert had the damsel clothed—and much did he regret not being able to dress her the way he would have liked: / never, though, have Florentine weavers turned out silk or cloth of gold fine enough, never has embroiderer, given any amount of patience, diligence, and skill, wrought anything which to Hubert's mind would have passed for adequate (though Minerva herself or Vulcan had been the artisans) and worthy to clothe limbs so splendid—which perforce he kept recalling vividly to mind. / The paladin had many reasons for showing his approval of the king's new love; for one thing, Hubert would not let Bireno escape punishment for his dastardly betrayal; for another, he himself would be relieved of a considerable embarrassment, for it was not to aid Olympia that he had come, but to bring help to his own lady, if she were here. / That she was not here now could be quickly established; whether she had been here was impossible to discover, for every last man on the island had been killed—of the whole population not one survived.

The next day they put out from the harbour all together in a single expedition. The paladin accompanied them to Ireland, whence his course was to take him to France. / He stopped in Ireland scarcely a day in spite of entreaties—Love, who had sent him in search of his lady, would not concede him a longer sojourn. He left, first commending Olympia to the king and reminding him of his engagements—not that there was any need: the king was to effect far more than ever he had promised. / In a few days he assembled a host, and made an alliance with the Kings of England and of Scotland; this done, he seized Holland from Bireno, and the whole of Frisia too; then he fomented a rebellion in the miscreant's own country, Zeeland, and did not withdraw until he had slain Bireno—not that even this penalty was sufficient requital for the evil he had done. / Hubert made Olympia his wife, and raised her from countess to mighty queen.

But let us return to the paladin, who unfurled his sails and, after ploughing the sea night and day, refurled them in the same port whence he had earlier spread them to the sea-wind. Armed, he mounted Brigliador and turned his back on the winds and the salt waves. / The rest of that winter he wrought noteworthy feats, I believe, but they did not come to light even at the time, so I must not be blamed for not relating them. Orlando was more ready to perform good deeds than to talk of them after: none of his actions was ever divulged unless there were witnesses to hand. / He passed the rest of the winter so quietly that no true report of him was to be had. But when the Sun illuminated the sphere in the sign of the ram (the modest beast which carried Phryxus), and sweet, cheerful Zephyr returned bringing tender spring, the wonderful feats of Orlando came to light, sprouting up with the pretty flowers and fresh new grass. / Weary and sorrowing he went scouring plains and mountains, countryside and sea-shores. Then, as he entered a wood, a long-drawn cry, a piercing lament, struck his ear. He spurred his steed, drew his trusty sword, and sped in the direction of the sound: but I shall postpone to another time the account of what followed, if you wish to hear it.

TWELFTH CANTO

1–22 Orlando seeks Angelica in the enchanted palace.
23–65 Angelica misleads Orlando, Sacripant and Ferrau.
66–94 Orlando defeats a Saracen host, and comes to a cave.

WHEN Ceres, after visiting her mother on Mount Ida, sped back to the secluded valley where Mount Etna straddles the shoulders of Enceladus, the stricken giant, she did not find her daughter where she had left her, away from the trodden paths. After her cheeks and eyes, her hair and breast had borne the brunt of her grief, she uprooted two pines; / she lit them in Vulcan's fire, enduing them with a flame which could never be quenched; and taking one in each hand, she entered her chariot, drawn by a pair of dragons. Thus she set off to search woods, fields, hills and plains, valleys, streams, pools and torrents, the land and sea: when she had scoured all the daylight world, she plunged down into the infernal regions. / Had Orlando possessed not only the zeal but also the powers of the Eleusinian goddess, he would not have left a single wood, field, pond, stream, valley, hill, plain, land, or sea unsearched, nor even the heavens or the pit of eternal oblivion, in his quest for Angelica. But since he did not have the chariot with the dragons, he sought her as best he could. / He had sought her throughout France; now he was preparing to search for her through Italy and Germany, through new and old Castille, and thence across the Spanish sea to Libya.

While he was thus deciding, a voice came to his ear, and what sounded like weeping. He darted forward, and saw a knight approaching at a trot upon a great charger; / seated in front of him on the saddle and pinioned forcibly by his arm was a damsel in deepest distress. She wept and fought and gave evidence of utter sorrow, and she kept crying out, invoking the help of Orlando, the valiant Prince of Anglant; as his gaze rested upon the beautiful maiden, she looked just like the very one whom he had been seeking night and day through the length and breadth of France. / I do not say that she *was* sweet Angelica, his well-beloved—but she looked like her. Seeing his lady, his goddess being carried off in such a wretched, pitiful state, he was possessed by a frenzy of black rage, and with a terrible roar he hailed the knight; full of menace he hailed him, and drove Brigliador forward at full tilt. / The villain, wholly intent upon his prize, his booty, did not wait for him or answer, but shot away so swiftly through the trees that even the wind could scarcely have followed him. One fled, the other pursued, and a high lament could be heard sounding through the deep forest. They came galloping out into a broad meadow, in the middle of which stood a magnificent great palace. /

The stately edifice was built of many kinds of marble, a work of intricate design. In through the gate, wrought in gold, ran the knight with the lady in his arms, followed shortly after by Brigliador carrying fierce Orlando, fuming with indignation. Once inside, Orlando looked about him, but saw no sign of the knight nor of the damsel. / He jumped from his horse and stormed through into the living quarters. He dashed hither and thither, never stopping until he had looked into every room, every gallery; after vainly probing the secrets of all the ground-floor rooms, he climbed the stairs and wasted no less time and effort searching upstairs. / The beds, he noticed, were all adorned with silk and thread of gold; not a wall was to be seen, for they, and the floors were covered with tapestries and carpets. Upstairs and down-stairs and all over again Orlando hunted, but there was no joy for him: never did he set eyes upon Angelica or the thief who had wafted her sweet delicate face away from his sight. / And while vainly pursuing his quest hither and thither, full of care and anxiety, he came across Ferrau, Brandimart, King Gradasso, and King Sacripant and other knights who were also searching high and low, pursuing a quest as fruitless as his own. They all complained about the malicious invisible lord of that palace— / the invisible lord for whom they were all search-ing. All accused him of one theft or another; one was grieving over the loss of his horse, another was raging over the loss of his lady; others had other thefts to charge him with, and none of them could tear themselves away from this cage—some there were, the victims of his deception, who had been there for whole weeks and months. /

After combing through the weird palace five and six times, Orlando said to himself: 'I could stay here wasting time and effort to no purpose; the thief could have borne her out through another gate and now be far away.' Thus thinking, he sallied out into the green meadow in the middle of which the palace stood. / As he skirted the outside of

the woodland abode, his eyes fixed on the ground in case he caught
sight of fresh footprints to right or left, he heard his name called from
a window, and raised his eyes; and he imagined he heard that divine
voice, thought he beheld the very face which had so transformed him. /
He thought he heard Angelica addressing him in tearful entreaty: 'Help!
Help! I commend my virginity to you more than my soul, more
than my life. Am I to be ravished by this brigand in the presence of my
dearest Orlando? Rather slay me by your own hand than let me come
to so sorry a pass.' / These words set Orlando on a diligent search of
every room, over and over, in desperation but with hope renewed.
Now and then he would stop, and he would hear a voice which sounded
like Angelica's, begging for help. But wherever he was, it always came
from somewhere else and he could never locate it. /

But to go back to Ruggiero: I left him pursuing his lady, borne off
by a giant along a densely shaded path which emerged from the wood
into a broad meadow. He came to this very spot where Orlando
arrived earlier, if I recognize the place aright. The giant disappeared
in through the door with Ruggiero on his heels in tireless pursuit. /
As he set foot inside the threshold he looked round the great courtyard
and loggias, but could not espy the giant or the lady; in vain did he
turn his gaze this way and that; he looked upstairs and down many a
time but all to no avail—nor could he imagine where the villain could
so quickly have found a hiding-place with the damsel. / When he had
gone through the bedrooms, galleries, and public rooms, upstairs and
down four or five times, he searched yet again and did not give up
before searching even beneath the stairs. Finally, in the hope that they
might be in the neighbouring woods, he left; but a voice recalled him,
just as it had recalled Orlando, and made him, too, return inside the
palace. / The same voice, the same person whom Orlando took for
Angelica, Ruggiero took for Bradamant, on whose account he was
beside himself. Whether the voice spoke to Gradasso or to any other of
those wandering about the palace, each one identified it with the object
of his search. / This was a new and unusual piece of magic devised by
the wizard Atlas, who meant thus to keep Ruggiero so preoccupied
with this bitter–sweet love-quest of his that the evil influence would
pass him by—the influence appointing him to an early death. The
steel-girt castle had proved useless, so had Alcina; here he was, trying
something else. / It was not only Ruggiero whom Atlas plotted to
draw into this magic trap, but anyone else in France who enjoyed the
highest reputation for valour—these he lured in lest Ruggiero die at
their hands. And while he condemned them to this enforced residence,
he had left the palace so abundantly provided that knights and ladies
could dwell there in comfort and eat their fill. /

But let us return to Angelica; she was in possession of that remarkable ring which, placed in her mouth, made her disappear from sight, and on her finger, rendered her immune to magic. And after finding in the hillside-cave food, clothing, and a mare and whatever else she needed, she had decided to return to her lovely Asiatic kingdom. / She would have been glad of Orlando's company, or of Sacripant's, not that she held any preference for the one suitor over the other—she was equally unaccommodating to the desires of both—but as so many towns and strongholds lay on her path to the Orient, she needed a companion and guide, and these were the two most trustworthy. / She searched a long time for one of these two, within city walls and without, in the forest depths, all over the place, before she picked up a trace of them.

Fate eventually brought her to this place where Orlando was, and Ferrau and Sacripant, Ruggiero, Gradasso, and many others about whom Atlas had woven his strange toils. / In she went, for the magician could not see her, and hidden by her ring, she searched the palace and came upon both Orlando and love-struck Sacripant, who was also seeking her there in vain. She saw how grossly Atlas was deceiving them both, feigning her image. Which of the two to select she revolved in her mind for a long time without reaching a decision. / She could not decide which of the two was better for her purposes, Count Orlando or Sacripant, King of the fierce Circassians. In moments of danger Orlando would show greater valour and would be better able to save her. But if she took him for guide, she would make him her lord: she could not see how to demote him once she had had enough of him and wanted to reduce his hold or send him back to France. / Now the Circassian she could dismiss the moment she wished, even if she had raised him to the seventh heaven. For this reason alone she decided to appoint him her escort and to affect warmth and confidence towards him.

She took the ring from her mouth, therefore, and disclosed herself to Sacripant. She thought she was revealing herself to him alone, but Orlando and Ferrau happened just then upon the scene. / Ferrau and Orlando came upon her, for both were equally bent on searching upstairs and down, inside and outside the great palace for Angelica who was goddess to both of them. As one man they ran to her, for there was no spell to prevent them now that the damsel had the ring on her finger, thus thwarting Atlas' ambitions. / Two of these warriors of whom I sing wore breastplate and helmet; never from the moment they entered this palace had they taken them off, day or night—they wore them as naturally as any clothing, so accustomed were they to them. The third, Ferrau, also wore armour but he neither had nor wished for a helmet, / till such time as he gained possession of the helmet that

Orlando took from Almont, King Trojan's brother. It was while searching the river in vain for Argalia's fine helmet that he made this vow. And though he now had Orlando close at hand, Ferrau did not lay hands upon him: they were unable to recognize each other while they remained inside the palace. / Such was the magic of the enchanted palace that they were unable to recognize each other. Never, day or night, did they set aside breastplate, sword, or shield. Beside the entrance was a room with a constant supply of hay and barley; here their horses fed, still saddled and with their bridles dangling from the saddle-bows. /

Atlas' knowledge and skill was not up to preventing the knights from mounting their steeds and setting off in pursuit of the pink cheeks, golden tresses, and lovely dark eyes of the damsel spurring her mare in flight: she had no inclination to see her three suitors together though she might have disposed of them one at a time. / When she had drawn them away from the palace and no longer had to fear that perfidious magician and his pernicious deceptions, she took the ring which had saved her from more than one scrape and closed her rosy lips over it. At once she vanished from their sight, leaving them stupefied and bewildered. / Although her first proposal had been to desire Orlando or Sacripant to accompany her on her return to her father Galafron's kingdom in the far Orient, she quite suddenly took against both of them and changed her mind there and then. Without being indebted to either of them, her ring, she decided, could take the place of both. /

Thus derided, the hasty knights turned to peer foolishly here and there into the woods, like hounds after they have been cut off from the hare or fox they have been chasing, and the prey has suddenly darted into some narrow hole or thick shrubbery or ditch. Angelica laughed at them without indulgence as, cloaked in invisibility, she observed their movements. / There was only one path to be seen leading through the wood, and the knights assumed that the damsel must have gone up it ahead of them, for that was the only path available. Orlando dashed off; Ferrau was not slow to follow, while Sacripant, no less eager, spurred and egged on his steed. Angelica held in her mare, and set off after them at a gentler pace. / The knights kept up a gallop until the path ramified and petered out in the forest, whereupon they searched the grassy floor for signs of footprints.

Ferrau, who for cool arrogance could bear away the crown, turned on the other two scowling and shouted at them: 'What are you doing here? / Go back or clear off if you don't want to leave your corpses here. Let none imagine that there is room for others to pay court to my lady!' Orlando turned to Sacripant, the Circassian: 'What else could this fellow have said if he had taken us both for the humblest, meekest wenches as ever spun wool off a distaff?' / To Ferrau he said: 'You dumb brute, did I not recognize that you are without a helmet, I wouldn't waste another minute to show you whether you chose your words well or ill!' 'I care not a rap if I'm bareheaded,' replied the Spaniard, 'so why should this worry you? Bareheaded as I am, I can take you both on at once and make good my words.' /

'Listen, will you oblige me and lend this man your helmet,' Orlando asked Sacripant, 'just till I've sorted out his ideas for him, for never have I come across folly to match his.' 'Nor have I,' returned the king, 'but if you really hold to your request why not lend him yours—for I'm no less capable than you are of chastising an idiot.' / 'You dolts!' put in Ferrau, 'if I wanted to wear a helmet do you suppose I'd let you keep yours? I'd have taken yours from you willy nilly! If you want the truth of the matter, I am going without a helmet because I have sworn to remain bareheaded until I wear the beauty of a helmet now worn by Orlando the paladin.' / 'What?' exclaimed the paladin with a smile, 'do you think that, bareheaded as you are, you will be up to doing to Orlando what he did in Aspromont to the son of Agolant? No—if you saw him confronting you, I believe you'd quake from head to foot, and far from coveting his helmet, you'd hand over every bit of armour you're wearing, for sure.' / 'Many and many a time have I had Orlando so hard pressed', replied the Spanish braggart, 'that I could easily have taken from him all the armour he was wearing, let alone his helmet. If I did not do so it was because the thought did not cross my mind at the time: I had no desire for his helmet then: now I want it, and I trust I'll find it a simple task to take it.' /

Orlando now lost patience. 'You're lying, you dirty infidel!' he shouted. 'Where were you and when was it that you fought me and gained the upper hand? That paladin you're bragging over—I am he: you thought I was nowhere near. Now see if you're capable of taking my helmet from me, or whether I shan't take the rest of your armour off you. / And I don't want the slightest advantage over you.' So saying, he undid his helmet and hung it from the branch of a beech tree. Durindana was out in a flash, but Ferrau did not quail; he drew his own sword and took his stand so as to use this weapon and his raised shield to protect his bare head. / So the two warriors turned their horses and started circling each other, aiming their swords at the joints in each other's armour, or where the metal was weakest. Nowhere in the world would you find another pair better matched. They were equals in strength and daring, and they were both invulnerable. / I think you have heard, my Lord, of the spell which afforded Ferrau's body complete protection except for the part through which, as an unborn child, he took his nourishment; until the day when the cold mud of the tomb buried his face he always shielded this unsure part with soundly-tempered armour plating of seven thicknesses. / Similarly the Prince of Anglant was also protected by a spell, except in one place: he could be wounded on the soles of his feet—but took every care to protect them. For the rest, their frames were hard as adamant, if this story about them is true, and they each went about their business armed more for show than from necessity. /

The combat grew ever more savage and cruel, awesome and terrifying to behold. Ferrau cut and thrust—each stroke a telling blow. As for Orlando, every stroke made its effect on armour plating and chainmail: he thumped and smashed and split and ripped it all apart. Invisible, Angelica looked on, the only witness to so fearsome a spectacle. / Meanwhile the King of Circassia, imagining that Angelica must be riding only a little way ahead, had set off, once he saw that Ferrau and Orlando had come to blows, choosing the direction that he judged the damsel must have taken when she vanished from sight. The only witness to this combat, therefore, was Galafron's daughter. / She watched this dire, gruesome battle, then—and for each combatant it looked equally dangerous; after a while her impulse was to inject a new element into the proceedings, and she hit on the idea of making off with the helmet to see what the warriors would do once they noticed it was gone. She meant to keep it only for a little. / She meant, of course, to return it to Count Orlando, but only after having a little fun at his expense. So she lifted the helmet off the branch and held it in her lap awhile as she continued watching the knights. Then she left without a word to them and was already quite some way off before either of them noticed, so incensed were they against each other. /

But now Ferrau, the first to notice the loss, pulled clear of Orlando and said: 'Look what bungling fools he's made of us, that knight who was with us! What prize is left for the victor now that he has made off with the helmet?' Orlando drew back and turned his eyes to the branch; seeing the helmet gone, he flared up in a rage. / He agreed with Ferrau that the knight who had been with them earlier must have taken it, so he jerked round his steed's head and set spurs to him. Ferrau, seeing him gallop off, went after him; they came to where fresh footprints were to be seen in the grass, those made by the Circassian and the damsel; / the count took his way to the left, towards a valley, the path taken by the Circassian, while Ferrau kept towards the higher ground, following the path trodden by Angelica.

Angelica meanwhile had come to a delightful, shady spot with a spring; it invited all who passed that way to rest in its cool shade, and would suffer no one to leave without first drinking from it. / At the limpid water Angelica drew rein, little dreaming that anyone would come upon her there. Hidden by the magic ring, she had no fear of incurring misfortune. On reaching the grassy banks of the spring she left the helmet on a branch, then looked in the shrubberies for a good place to tether her mare and let it browse. / The Spanish knight who had followed her tracks came to the spring. The moment Angelica saw him she vanished from his sight and set spurs to her mare. She was unable to retrieve the helmet which had fallen onto the grass—she was too far from it. Noticing Angelica, the pagan galloped up to her delightedly. / She vanished, as I say, before his eyes, as a phantasm at the moment of waking. He searched amid the trees but there was not another glimpse of her to assuage his doleful eyes. Cursing Mahomet and Trivigant and their creed and every sage who taught it, Ferrau returned towards the spring; beside it in the grass lay the count's helmet. /

The moment he set eyes on it, he recognized it by what was inscribed in its rim: words indicating where Orlando won it and how and when, and who from. The pagan clad his head and neck with it, for his gloom did not prevent him from taking it—his gloom over the maiden who had vanished as nocturnal phantoms fade away. / After securing the goodly helmet on his head, all that he now felt he needed to complete his happiness was to find Angelica, who appeared and vanished in a twinkling. He searched the depths of the forest for her, and when he finally lost hope of ever coming across her traces, he turned back towards Paris and the Spanish camp, / assuaging the pain he felt in his heart at not having fulfilled his overriding desire, with the consolation of wearing what had been Orlando's helmet, as he had sworn. The count long sought for Ferrau when he was told the facts, but never was he to pull it off the pagan's head until the day when in the duel between two bridges he took his life. /

Solitary and invisible, Angelica went away; she looked dismayed, for she was sorry about the helmet which she had too hastily abandoned at the spring. 'It's because I had to go and do what I had no right to', she brooded, 'that I've deprived the count of his helmet; considering what I owe to him, this makes a fine reward, the first I have given him. / I took the helmet with the best intentions (God knows) even though the outcome was by no means fortunate: my only thought was to bring an end to the fighting, and certainly not that by my intervention that ugly Spaniard should today achieve his ambition.' So, as she went her way, she chided herself for having deprived Orlando of his helmet. / Vexed and displeased with herself, she took what seemed to be her best way, Eastwards. Often she went concealed, sometimes she revealed herself, as circumstances dictated. She saw many a stretch of land, until one day she came to a wood; here she came upon a young man cruelly wounded in the chest, between two dead companions. /

But I shall not continue Angelica's story here, for I have many things to relate first. Nor shall I devote any more rhymes to Sacripant or Ferrau for quite a while yet. The Prince of Anglant distracts me from them: he wants me to tell about him before I revert to the others, to narrate the trials and tribulations he underwent in pursuit of his great desire which he was never to satisfy. / At the first town he came to, being most concerned to remain incognito, he put on a new helmet with beaver. He did not trouble to ascertain how solid was its temper: little difference would that make to him, seeing what reliance he could place on the charm cast upon him. Thus concealed, he pursued his quest, never abandoning it night or day, rain, or shine. /

It was the hour when Phoebus was driving his horses out of the ocean, with dew-decked manes, and Aurora was scattering red and saffron blooms all over the heavens, and the stars had finished their dances and were putting on their veils to leave—when, passing close by Paris one day, Orlando gave mighty proof of his prowess. / He came upon two squadrons; one was led by Manilard, the grey-haired Saracen, King of Norizia, once upon a time a formidable warrior, now of greater value as a counsellor. The other followed the standard of the King of Tremisen, whom the Africans esteemed as a perfect knight. Those who knew him called him Alzirdo. / With the rest of the pagan host, these had spent the winter occupying the estates and strongholds in the vicinity of Paris; having wasted more than one day trying to take Paris by storm, King Agramant wanted to try besieging it as a last resort, unable as he was to capture the city otherwise. / To do this he had troops a-plenty, for beside his own army and the host from Spain who had followed King Marsilius' royal banner, he had recruited large numbers of the French: the whole land between Paris and the Rhône where it washes Arles, as well as part of Gascony (barring a fortress or two) was now subject to him. / Now when the frost-bound brooks began to melt in a shimmering flood, a warmer flow, and the meadows were clothed in fresh grass and the trees put forth tender shoots, King Agramant assembled all those who were following his fortunes; he intended to review his armies with a view to improving his dispositions. /

To this end the Kings of Tremisen and of Norizia were on their way to the appointed assembly where every squadron, whether strong or weak, could be passed in review. Orlando, as I said, happened upon this host while he was seeking—as usual—for the lady who held him confined in Love's prison. / The approach of Count Orlando, a man unmatched for valour, a man of so lofty a countenance, so imposing a demeanour that the very god of battle seemed but his second, attracted the notice of Alzirdo, who was fascinated by his remarkable build, his fierce eye, his wrathful countenance; he reckoned he must be a most mighty champion, but could not restrain himself from challenging him. / Alzirdo was young and arrogant; he was esteemed for his great strength and courage, and he spurred his steed forward to engage his opponent; he would have done better to stay with his men, for at the impact the Prince of Anglant pitched him to the ground, run through the heart. His steed fled in terror, for now he had no rider to check him. / A terrible roar filled the air the moment those squadrons saw the young man fall and his blood gush forth so copiously. The angry horde surged pell-mell towards the count, cutting and thrusting at him; to make matters worse, they rained a shower of feathered arrows on the flower of valiant knights. / Imagine the racket made by a herd of pigs running down the hillside or across the fields if a wolf slinking out of a hidden cave, or a bear venturing down from the mountain heights, has just seized a young porker which is grunting and shrieking in terror: such was the noise made by this brutish horde as it surged towards the knight, shouting: 'Kill! Kill!' /

Lances, arrows, sword-cuts rained down upon his breastplate, a thousand at a time, and as many upon his shield; one clubbed him from behind while others threatened him from the front and sides. But Orlando, who never once gave access to fear, was no more impressed by the menial horde and all their weapons than a wolf would be at the numbers of the sheep he found on penetrating into the fold at dusk. / He bared his lightning-sword which had sent so many Saracens to their grave; had someone tried to keep a count of how many fell, he would have had no easy task. The road was already running red with blood; there was scarcely room on it for so many dead, for there was no buckler nor helmet which could ward off the stroke where fateful Durindana fell, / nor cotton-wadded clothing, nor turbans wound in many folds about the head. The air was filled not only with groans and laments but also with flying arms and shoulders, and severed heads. Cruel Death, wearing many and various faces, all of them grisly, wandered through the field, remarking to himself: 'In Orlando's hand Durindana is worth a hundred of my sickles.' / The next blow did not wait upon the last.

Soon they all began to flee; and if at first, seeing that he was alone, they had rushed upon him, thinking to overwhelm him, there was nobody now ready to wait for his friend before pulling out of the mêlée, to make his escape with him. They fled in all directions, some on foot, others spurring their horses. None stopped to ask if the road was good enough. / Valour stalked about with a mirror which showed up every hidden wrinkle: a mirror into which nobody looked, except for an old man whose years had desiccated his blood, not his courage. He

saw how much better it was to die than to forfeit his honour by flight.
I speak of Manilard, King of Norizia. He therefore set his lance against
the French paladin— / only to snap it on the top ridge of the proud
count's shield. Orlando did not budge; sword at the ready, he struck
King Manilard as he passed, but Fortune assisted the king—the dire
sword in Orlando's hand glanced downwards. The king was beyond
reach of direct sword-thrusts, but none the less the blow hurled him
from his saddle. / The king fell stunned from his saddle, but Orlando
never turned to give him a second glance. He kept topping and lopping,
cleaving and felling; every Saracen felt that the knight was right after
him. They fled like a flock of birds who, after filling the whole sky,
vanish before the bold falcon. The host was now in utter disarray;
some fell, others ran, others dived for cover. / His bloody sword was
constantly brandished until the field was empty of living men. Orlando
hesitated before resuming his way, for all that he knew every inch of
the country. Whether he went right or left, his mind was far from the
path he took, for he was constantly anxious lest he sought Angelica
where she was not to be found, or took an opposite direction. / His
path took him sometimes through fields, sometimes through woods,
and often he enquired about her.

   Now he happened to stray from his path (just as he had strayed from
his true self), and came to the foot of a mountain where at night he saw
a distant light fluttering out from a rock-fissure. Orlando approached
the rock to see if it concealed Angelica. / As a man hunting the timid
hare in the stunted juniper thickets or out in the open stubble will
explore every bush, every bramble beside the cart-tracks and along the
sketchy paths in case he finds it concealed; so did Orlando take every
care in searching for his lady, wherever hope led him. / The count
hastened towards the light and came to the narrow cleft in the mountain
whence it issued. The mountain concealed a roomy cave here, but he
found himself confronted by a barrier of brambles and brushwood like
a wall and ditch to hide those in the cave from any who would do them
harm. / By day it would never be discovered, but the light betrayed it
by night. Orlando had an idea what the place must be, but he wanted
to make sure.

   He tethered Brigliador and silently approached the hidden cave; he
slipped through the thick foliage and penetrated the entrance without
calling up anyone to announce him. / The floor of this tomb in which
living people were immured was reached down a series of steps cut into
the bare wall. The place was not a little spacious, nor was it completely
deprived of daylight, for though little came in through the entrance,
the light flooded in through a window let into a fissure to the right. /
Beside a fire in the middle of the cave there was a damsel with an

entrancing face. She could not have been much over fifteen, or so the count judged at a glance. Such was her beauty, she made this inhospitable place look like a paradise, even though her eyes were tear-swollen, a clear sign of a sorrowing heart. / There was an old woman, too, and they were having an argument—as women often do—but when the count stepped down into the cave they broke it off and fell silent.

Orlando greeted them courteously—he was always courteous to women—and they at once stood up and amiably returned his greeting. / They did, in truth, show some dismay on hearing this unexpected voice and seeing so fierce a man come in armed from head to foot. Orlando asked who it was who was so unkind, barbarous, unjust, and cruel as to bury a maiden who looked so sweet and lovable in this cave. / The maiden answered haltingly; ardent sighs kept interrupting the flow of soft words which issued brokenly from her coral lips, which parted to disclose such precious pearls. Of lily and rose was the colour of her cheeks, down which her tears streamed until some were swallowed between her lips. May it please your Lordship to hear the rest of this story in the next canto, for it is time now to end this one.

THIRTEENTH CANTO

*1–31 Isabel tells her story. 32–44 Orlando rescues Isabel
from the brigands. 44–80 Melissa tells Bradamant of her
female posterity, and brings her to Atlas' enchanted palace.
81–83 Agramant prepares to review his army.*

THEY certainly had luck, the knights of old, as they looked in gloomy caves and wild woods, in ravines, in snake-burrows, dens of bears or lions, and came upon sights which today connoisseurs scarcely meet with in proud palaces—maidens in their prime, ravishing beauties. / I was just telling you how Orlando had found a damsel in the cave, and had asked her how she came to be there. Well, after giving vent to many a sob, she began in a soft melodious voice to explain her predicament to the count as briefly as she could. /

'Full well I know, sir, that I shall suffer for having spoken to you,' she said; 'this woman is bound to betray me to the man who has shut me up here. Still, I am ready to tell you my story, even if I pay for it with my life. What joy anyway am I to expect from him beyond his finally deciding to make away with me? / I am Isabel. I used to be the daughter of the luckless King of Galicia. I say I used to be—for now I am no longer his: I am daughter to grief, misery, and sadness. Love is to blame: I would not know whom else to complain of more than of spiteful Love—blandly approving at the start, only to weave a web of deceptions on the sly. / Mine used to be a happy life. I was well-born, young and beautiful, rich and esteemed. Now I am poor, wretched, and debased. There can be no sadder condition than mine. I would have you know the root cause of my present wretchedness, for though you bring me no help, your sympathy would be no little comfort to me. /

'My father held a tournament in Bayona, it must be some twelve months ago, and, on hearing of it, knights from many nations came to our land to take part. Now whether Love pointed him out to me or his own virtues were clear to see, Zerbin was the only man who won my esteem. He was the King of Scotland's son. / His gallantry in the field was quite prodigious. I saw it and fell in love with him—the point suddenly came when I realized I no longer belonged to myself. Still, though Love was my guiding light, I did clearly recognize where I had not placed my heart: not on a base object but on the worthiest and finest in all the world. / Zerbin was more handsome and braver far than all the other barons. He showed me love, and I believe he was truthful about it, and no less passionate than I was. We found a regular interpreter for our mutual love so that we remained one at heart even after we were separated from each other's sight— / for at the end of the tournament my Zerbin returned to Scotland.

'If you know what love is, you'll know my sadness as I thought of him night and day. And I knew that his own heart was seared by no less cruel a flame. He put no barriers to his desire but sought ways and means to bring me to him. / As we were of different faiths (he a Christian, I a Saracen), he could not ask my father for my hand, but had to resort to abducting me. Outside my father's opulent domain, which bordered on the sea and lay amid green meadows, I had a lovely garden by the shore, surrounded by hills and wide open to the sea. / This seemed to him a good place to carry out the purpose which our difference of religion prohibited, and he conveyed word to me of the plan he had made to secure our happiness. Near Santa Marta he had concealed a galley with armed men aboard, under the command of Odoric of Biscay, a skilled warrior by land and sea. / As he was unable to take a hand himself, for his old father had just obliged him to bring help to the French king, he was to send this Odoric in his place; he had picked him out as the closest and trustiest of all his close friends— and so he should have been if friendship can still be won by kindness. / He would come in a man-o'-war to fetch me there at the appointed time.

'So the great day arrived and I arranged to be found in my garden. That night Odoric, with a band of men adept both as sailors and swordsmen, sailed up a river to land near the city and came secretly into my garden / from where I was taken on board the well-pitched vessel before the townsfolk knew what had happened. My household were all naked and unarmed; some of them fled, others were slain or else captured and taken off with me. So I took leave of my country I cannot tell you with what joy, for I hoped soon to enjoy my Zerbin. /

'We had scarcely set course towards Mongia when a wind came up from port; it stirred up air and sea, and set the waves surging skywards. Up came the Mistral, blowing across our bows and gathering force by the hour till it gained such strength that it was useless trying to tack./ There was no use lowering the sails and securing the mast with extra stays, or lightening the superstructure—we could see we were being swept willy nilly onto the sharp rocks by La Rochelle. If a Higher Power did not assist us, the cruel storm would drive us ashore. The evil wind bore us along more swiftly than an arrow shot from a bow. / Odoric saw the danger and resorted to a measure which is not always successful: he took to the ship's boat. He dropped into it and had me lowered after him. Two more followed, and a whole score would have joined us had they been allowed to—but the first in held them off with their sword-points, cut the rope and we drifted away. / Those of us who took to the ship's boat were safely swept ashore; the battered vessel sank with all hands; the seas swallowed up every last piece of tackle. I stretched out my hands in thanksgiving to the eternal Goodness, the Infinite Love who would not have me prevented by the ocean's rage from seeing Zerbin again. / Even though I had left on board my clothes and jewels and cherished possessions I was quite content for the sea to have everything so long as it left me my hope of rejoining my beloved.

'Where we were cast ashore there were no beaten paths; no dwellings were anywhere to be seen—only a crag whose wooded summit was ever buffeted by the wind while the sea washed its base. / But now Love, the cruel tyrant whose promises never were to be trusted, and who always makes a point of frustrating and aborting any reasonable plans we might make, treacherously turned my comfort to anguish, my good into harm: the friend in whom Zerbin trusted grew warm in lust, cold in duty. / Perhaps he already lusted after me when we were at sea, but dared not betray himself, or maybe it was the tempting solitude of the shore which awoke his lust; at all events, he planned to satisfy his brutish appetite here and now. All he needed first was to remove one of the pair who escaped with us in the ship's boat. / One of them was a

Scotsman called Almon. He showed the greatest loyalty to Zerbin, who had commended him as an accomplished soldier when he entrusted him to Odoric. Now Odoric said to him that it would never do to take me to La Rochelle on foot; he asked him therefore to go on ahead and arrange for some palfrey to be sent our way. /

'Almon, all unsuspecting, at once set off towards the town which was hidden beyond the woods, not six miles distant. Then Odoric decided to confide his guilty desire to the other: he could not think how to get him out of the way, and anyway he trusted him absolutely. / The man I mean, who stayed behind with us, was called Coreb of Bilbao. They had been brought up together from babyhood, and Odoric persuaded himself that he could let him into his wicked secret, hoping that Coreb would embrace his friend's desire more readily than the dictates of honour. / Coreb, a true gentleman, was outraged at what he heard; he called the man a traitor and stood out against his vile plan, and not in words alone—lashing themselves into a rage, they both of them whipped out their swords. I was so terrified by this that I turned to flee into the deep dark woods. / Odoric was no mean swordsman; in a few strokes he gained the upper hand and, leaving Coreb for dead, he came after me. To catch up with me Love lent him wings (I'm convinced of this), and taught him many a wheedling word, many an entreaty to win me to his love and behest— / but all in vain, for I was fully determined to die rather than to yield to his wishes. As entreaties, subtle cajolery and threats availed him nothing, he resorted to brute strength. It was no use my pleading the trust which Zerbin had reposed in him and that I had thought myself safe in his hands. / I could see that my pleas were quite wasted on him and that there was no hope of outside help; he was coming at me like a famished bear, ever more ravenous and brutal. I used my hands and feet to defend myself, and even used my nails and teeth; I plucked at his chin, scratched his hide, and shrieked to the high heavens. /

'I know not whether it was chance, or whether it was my cries which could be heard a league off, or whether it was simply the lure of the beach where a ship has been wrecked, but I saw a mob appear above us on the hillside and move down towards us and the shore. On seeing them Odoric gave over, turned and fled. / Sir, this mob rescued me from the blackguard, but, to use the common saying, it was a case of out of the frying pan into the fire: true, they did not violate me—thus far at least I was fortunate, and they were not that evil-minded, not that any good was to be found in them, / but by keeping me a virgin they hoped to sell me for a far better price. Eight months have passed, and the ninth is beginning, since they buried me here alive. I have given up hope of being reunited to my beloved: from the odd phrase I have pieced together I understand that they have sold me to a merchant who is to take me to the Sultan in the East.' /

The gentle maiden spoke like an angel, her words punctuated with many a sob and sigh, enough to move asps and vipers to compassion. While she was thus reopening her wounds, or perhaps allaying her grief in the telling of it, some twenty men entered the cave, armed with sickles and spits. / Their leader, a mean-faced man, had only one eye, and a surly, mischievous look; his other eye had been blinded by a blow which had sliced his nose and chin. Seeing the knight sitting in the cave with the lovely damsel, he turned to his companions and cried: 'Here's a new bird landed in the net, though I never snared him!' / Then to the count he said: 'Never did I see the right man turn up at a more convenient moment. I don't know whether you guessed, or whether you know from what someone has told you, but I have been longing for armour as fine as yours, and that fetching dark cloak you're wearing. You have come at just the right time to fit me out with the very things I need!' /

Orlando had stood up. 'I shall sell you my armour', he observed with a sardonic smile, 'at a price that merchants don't normally reckon to pay.' From the fire next to him he snatched a flaming, smoky brand, flung it, and struck the brigand, as it happened, on the bridge of the nose. / Neither eye escaped the brand, but it did more damage to the left one: it deprived him of his last source of light, and, not content with blinding him, the savage blow dispatched him to join the spirits whom Chiron and his crew guard in the fiery swamps. /

In the cave there stood an enormous great table, thick as a man's arm; it rested on stout rough-hewn legs and was large enough for the whole band of brigands to sit at. As lightly as a supple Spaniard will throw a javelin Orlando picked up the table bodily and heaved it into the thick of the rabble. / One had his chest stove in, another his belly or his skull; others had fractured legs or arms; some were slain outright, others maimed; those with least injuries tried to escape. It was like when a heavy stone falls upon a knot of serpents sunning themselves in the late spring, and some have their backs crushed, others their heads shattered. / This can produce the strangest effects: one snake dies, another slips off without its tail, a third is paralysed all except for its tail which vainly coils and uncoils, while the next, born under a luckier star, slithers off through the grass to safety. All in all a spectacular blow, but not to be wondered at, seeing that it was the work of mighty Orlando. /

Those who escaped with little or no damage from the table (and Turpin specifically mentions seven survivors) took to their heels, but the paladin planted himself in the entrance, caught them without a struggle and, finding a handy rope in the cave, used it to bind their hands fast. / Then he dragged them out in front of the cave to where an ancient mountain-ash cast a spreading shadow. Orlando lopped the branches with his sword and hitched his captives up to be food for the crows. He had no need of any hooks or chains—the tree itself lent him the clefts he needed and he had but to hang them by their chins, purging the world of their pestilential presence. /

Seeing all her bandit-friends exterminated, the old woman fled, clutching her hair and weeping, into the depths of the wild wood. After weary, arduous wanderings, terror hastening her heavy steps, she came upon a warrior by the bank of a river; who he was I shall tell you later, / and go back now to the damsel imploring the paladin not to abandon her: she wanted to follow him wherever he went. Orlando gently consoled her, and when white Aurora, clad in violet and decked in a rose-garland, set out on her accustomed path, the paladin set out with Isabel. / They journeyed many days before anything happened worthy of mention; finally they met a knight who was being led captive.

Who he was I shall tell you by and by: just now I am being distracted by one whom you will be glad to hear about, I mean Aymon's daughter, Bradamant, whom I left languishing in Love's toils. / Vainly wishing for her Ruggiero to return to her, the lovely damsel was waiting at Marseilles, from where she visited vengeance almost daily on the pagan hordes, for these were at large in Languedoc and Provence, pillaging up hill and down dale. She proved herself a shrewd leader and a champion at arms. / Here she was biding, then; Ruggiero's return was very much overdue now, and as he still did not come she was obsessed by a thousand fears for his safety. One day while she was by herself and in tears, who should turn up but Melissa, the enchantress who had taken the magic ring to Ruggiero, thus providing the medicine to heal his heart, smitten with Alcina. / Noticing that the enchantress had returned, after so long an interval, without her beloved, Bradamant turned quite pale and faint and trembled so much she had scarcely the strength to stand. But the kind enchantress, on seeing her fear, went up to her all smiling and serene to bring her encouragement, just like a person bringing glad tidings. /

'Do not be anxious about Ruggiero,' she said. 'He is alive and well, and adores you as much as ever; only he has lost his freedom, for your enemy has robbed him of it once again. Now you must mount your steed and come with me straight away if you really want him: if you follow me I'll show you how you can set him at liberty.' / She went on to describe the sleight of magic which Atlas had devised: how he had counterfeited fair Bradamant's face and made her seem a prisoner before his eyes. 'All the ladies and knights who venture there', she added, 'he detains with this sort of deception. / Setting eyes on the magician, they all imagine they are espying the object of their quest, be it a lady, a page, a friend, or comrade—human desire differing in its objectives. So they search the palace through and through all to no avail; and yet so great is their hope and their desire to find what they are searching for that they are unable to tear themselves away. /

'When you reach the neighbourhood of the enchanted palace,' she explained, 'the magician will come out to you; he will pass himself off for Ruggiero, and use his evil craft to make it look as though your beloved is being overcome by one stronger than himself: you are supposed to go to his rescue and end up with all the others held captive. / If you are not to fall for the same deception which has trapped so many others, take heed; though your eyes will tell you that you are looking on the very face of Ruggiero and he is calling for help, just don't believe it; when he comes before you make away with his worthless life—and have no fear that you may be slaying Ruggiero: it will be not him but your very persecutor. / You'll find it no easy task, I know, to kill your Ruggiero—or so he will appear to you. But don't believe your eyes—the spell will bewitch them and conceal from them what is true. Resolve yourself now, therefore, before I bring you to the wood, lest you weaken at the last moment. You will never recover your beloved if you spare the magician's life through faintheartedness.' / Knowing how Melissa could be trusted, the valiant maiden was ready to take up arms and follow her, firmly resolved to slay the trickster, and the enchantress led her through farmlands and forests, many a long day's journey covered in haste; as they proceeded she tried to shorten the wearisome road with pleasant conversation. /

The pleasantest topic, to which she kept returning, was that of the eminent princes and glorious demigods which were to issue from her union with Ruggiero. As though all the secrets of the eternal gods were present to Melissa, she could predict everything that was to happen centuries later. / 'Tell me though, enlightened guide that you are,' the peerless maiden asked; 'just as you disclosed to me so many of my fair male issue years before their time, reassure me now about the women to be descended from me, if there are any who can pass for beautiful and virtuous.' And her gracious escort replied: / 'I can see among your issue chaste women, the mothers of emperors and kings, the solid pillars and restorers of illustrious houses and splendid realms. For all their feminine attire, they, no less than the knights in their armour, shall be endowed with eminent virtues—mercy, courage, prudence, matchless continence. / If I were to describe to you each one of your female descendants worthy of honour, it would be too much, for I

133

cannot see one whom I could pass over in silence. But out of a thousand I shall select one or two couples—this at least should be manageable. But why did you not ask me back in Merlin's cave, when I could have shown you what they looked like as well? / Your illustrious house shall give birth to that friend of glorious deeds and fair studies, liberal, great-hearted Isabel; I know not which to put first, her beauty and grace, or her sagacity and virtue. Day and night her city set by the Mincio—Mantua, which takes its name from Ocnus' mother—shall bask in her sunshine. / Here she will conduct an admirable, nay a dazzling contest with her most illustrious spouse to see which of them most prizes and cherishes excellence and opens widest the door to chivalry. If a man speak of the might he displayed on the Taro and in the Kingdom of Naples when he drove the French out of Italy, a woman will add: "Just by virtue of her chastity Penelope was no lesser mortal than Ulysses." / I shall sum up a great deal about this woman in a few words, foregoing the rest of what Merlin disclosed to me during my period of retreat at his tomb. Were I to embark upon her praises, I would be in for a far longer voyage than even Tiphys undertook in the Argo. In a word, then, all that is good shall be hers, both as to merits and as to natural gifts. /

'She will have a sister, too, called Beatrice—a most appropriate name, for not only shall she enjoy every lawful natural good so long as she lives, but she shall also know how to impart her happiness to her husband (a rich man among wealthy dukes); when she departs this life, she shall leave him in the depths of sadness. / While she lives, the viper-emblems of Lodovico the Moor, of Sforza and Visconti shall spread awe from the Northern snows to the Red Sea coasts, from the Indus to the mountains which rim your sea. Once she is dead, they and the Lombard realm shall be enslaved to the French, a grave misfortune to the whole of Italy. Without her, Lodovico's eminent prudence would have been deemed a mere accident. / There shall be others, born many years earlier, bearing the same name: one of them shall wear on her anointed head the crown of fertile Hungary; another, when she has laid aside her mortal spoils, shall in Italy be numbered with the saints; incense and votive images shall be offered her. /

'I shall mention no more: as I said, it would take too long to describe so many, even though each one of them is worthy to have her praises trumpeted in heroic, clarion tones. In silence I shall pass over the Biancas, the Constances, Lucretias, and the rest—they shall all of them be mothers and restorers to the illustrious Italian families over which they shall preside. / More than any before them, the families of your issue shall be fortunate in their womenfolk—in the perfect integrity of their wives as in that of their daughters. Perhaps because I was destined to repeat to you what Merlin told me, I have a strong urge to speak to you of them and give you more information about them. /

'First I shall tell you of Ricciarda, a paragon of constancy and rectitude. In Fortune's despite she shall be widowed young—as often befalls the just. Her sons shall be deprived of their father's realm and she shall see them exiled and delivered into the power of their enemies. But in the end she will be amply recompensed for her misfortunes. / I must not pass over the glorious queen from the noble house of ancient Aragon; never in any author of ancient Greece or Rome have I seen woman praised for greater wisdom or chastity. Never shall woman be so befriended by Fortune: God's Goodness shall appoint her to be mother to children such as Alfonso, Hippolytus, and Isabel. / Wise Eleonora is the name of this woman who will be grafted to your prosperous tree. What shall I say of her second daughter-in-law, the one who shall succeed her—Lucretia Borgia? She shall ever grow in beauty, merit, fortune, and good repute, just like a tender plant in soft earth. / As tin is to silver, copper to gold, the field poppy to the rose, the pallid willow to the evergreen laurel, tinted glass to a precious stone, so next to her, whom I honour though she is yet unborn, shall be every woman to this day who has been renowned for singular beauty, eminent prudence, and every other praiseworthy excellence. / Above all the other shining merits for which she shall be signalized during her lifetime and after her death, she shall be praised for having endowed Ercole and her other sons with royal bearing, and set them on the path to winning the high honours with which they shall be distinguished both at court and on the field of war. Transfer a perfume to a new jar and, whatever its quality, the aroma will nonetheless cling on for a while. / Nor must I omit to speak of her daughter-in-law Renée, daughter of King Louis XII of France and of Anne, eternal glory of Brittany. All the virtues ever to be found in woman, since fire first heated, water bathed, and the heavens revolved, have all assembled to adorn Renée. / It would take a long time to speak of Alda of Saxony, or the Countess of Celano, or Bianca Maria of Catalonia, or the King of Sicily's daughter, or fair Lippa of Bologna, and still others. Were I to give you a full account of their great merits I should sail far out into an ocean without shores.' /

After discoursing at leisure on the greater part of her progeny to come, Melissa reminded Bradamant again and again about the trick by which the magician had lured Ruggiero into his palace. When they came within reach of the old miscreant's lair, Melissa stopped; she thought it imprudent to go on lest he espied her. / For the thousandth time she repeated her instructions to the damsel, then left her. And Bradamant had not ridden on two miles along a narrow path when she saw a man looking like her Ruggiero; he was hemmed in by two cruel-looking giants, and was hard pressed by them—indeed they were on the point of killing him. / Seeing Ruggiero—or so he appeared to be—in such peril, the damsel's confidence turned into mistrust there and then, and her fine resolutions went clean out of her head. She imagined that Melissa must have a quarrel with Ruggiero over some recent injury, some unconfessed rancour, and that she was cunningly ordaining a plot to have him killed by the very one who so loved him. / 'Is he not Ruggiero,' she asked herself, 'who is ever present to my heart, and now even to my eyes? If it is not he whom I see and recognize now, am I ever to see or recognize anything? Why should I place the witness of my own eyes second to what I am told on trust? For even without my eyes, my heart can all by itself feel when he is far away or close at hand.' /

While she was thus musing, she heard what seemed Ruggiero's voice crying for help; and she saw him spurring his steed and giving him rein, while his two fierce adversaries galloped after him in hot pursuit. On impulse Bradamant dashed after them and came to the enchanted palace. / The moment she crossed the threshold she fell prey to the prevalent illusion. She searched for him up and down and in and out and round about; she did not give up day or night, such was the strength of the magic spell. And the magician had so arranged matters that Bradamant was constantly seeing and talking to Ruggiero, but neither he nor she recognized each other. / But let us leave Bradamant: be not dismayed to hear that she remains imprisoned in the spell—when the time is ripe for her to be released from it, I shall bring her away, and Ruggiero too. As varying the dishes quickens the appetite, so is it with my story: the more varied it is, the less likely it is to bore my listeners. / To complete the great tapestry on which I am working I feel the need for a great variety of strands.

Suffer me, then, to tell you about the Saracens assembling from their encampments to pass in review before King Agramant: a dire threat he poses to the Golden Lilies as he summons his troops to this latest review in order to assess their numbers. / Beside the great gaps in the ranks of the cavalry and infantry, there was a dearth of leaders, especially good ones, from Spain, Libya, and Ethiopia. The various squadrons, the corps under national flags, were wandering leaderless. To reorganize the troops and appoint new captains, the whole army was assembling in the field. / To replace the numbers slain in battle, he sent one chieftain to Spain, another to Africa where many troops were enrolled. He divided them all between their commands. With your permission, my Lord, I shall defer the account of the parade and reorganization to the next canto.

FOURTEENTH CANTO

IN the successive assaults and fierce skirmishes which had thrown the Africans and Spaniards against the French, countless men had been left dead, abandoned to the wolves and crows and rapacious eagles. And though the French had come off worse, for they had been driven from the field, it was the Saracens who were smarting most, on account of all those sheiks and emirs they had lost. / Their victories cost them so much blood that they were left with little cause for celebration. Now if today's events may stand comparison with those of yesterday, then the great and glorious victory fairly to be ascribed to your prowess, triumphant Alfonso, is similar to that of the Saracens—the victory which should now leave Ravenna permanently tear-stained. / When the French army, the troops from Picardy and the Scheldt, from Normandy and Aquitaine, began to give ground, you charged into the standards of the Spaniards, who were within an ace of victory, and your dashing young comrades followed in your steps, showing that day such valour, they well deserved to win their spurs from your hands. / Bold as you were, the moment you came within reach of danger you so shook Pope Julius' Golden Acorns and smashed his red and gold sceptre that you deserve the victor's laurel for saving the Lilies of France from being harmed. Yet another laurel should adorn your brow for having kept Fabrizio Colonna safe for Rome: / aye, to have captured and preserved unharmed the great Column of Rome's renown did you more honour than if by your own hand you had cut down all the fierce host which now fattens the fields of Ravenna, all those men of Aragon, Castille, and Navarre who fled without their banners, clearly finding no defence in their weapons and battle-waggons. /

That victory afforded us encouragement, but little rejoicing—for the sight of the leader of the expedition, the Captain of the French, Gaston of Foix, lying dead dampened our joy. And the storm which overwhelmed him carried off so many illustrious princes who had crossed the cold Alps in defence of their realms and of their allies. / All recognize that our safety, our very life has been secured by this victory which prevents the wintry tempests of wrathful Jove breaking over our heads. But we cannot rejoice or hold celebrations as we hear from all over France the bitter laments of tearful young widows in mourning. / King Louis will have to provide his battalions with new commanders whose duty it will be, for the honour of the Golden Lilies, to punish the thieving rascals who have violated wives, daughters, mothers, monks, and nuns—be they white, black, or grey— and thrown Christ in the Sacrament onto the floor to take from Him a silver tabernacle. / O hapless Ravenna, how much better had you not resisted the conqueror, had you but looked at the example of what befell Brescia, instead of serving as an example yourself to Rimini and Faenza! Send staunch old Trivulzio, Louis, to teach these troops of yours greater continence; and tell them how many men have died throughout Italy for having committed crimes such as these. /

Just as the King of France must now reorganize the command of his army, so then Marsilius and Agramant, the better to order their troops, wanted them to leave their winter quarters and assemble on parade: thus they would be able to appoint commanders to each squadron as the need became evident. / First Marsilius, then Agramant passed their battalions in review. In the lead marched the Catalans, following the banner of Doriphoebus. Next came the troops of Navarre, but without their King, Folvirant, who had died by Rinaldo's hand; the King of Spain had put Isoliero in command of them. / Balugant was in charge of the troops from Leon, Grandonio commanded those from Algarve. Marsilius' brother, Falsiron, led the army of Old Castille. The men of Malaga and Seville, and those from the green valley of the Guadalquivir between the Bay of Cadiz and fertile Cordova followed the ensign of Madarasso. / Stordilan, Tesira, and Baricondo followed in turn, each parading their men; Granada swore allegiance to the first, Portugal to the second, and Majorca to the last; (Tesira succeeded to the throne of Lisbon on the death of his kinsman Larbin). Then came the Galicians, led by Serpentine in lieu of Maricold. /

The men of Toledo, as also those of Calatrava (formerly led by Sinagon), and in addition all the men who wash in the Guadiana and drink its waters, all these were under the command of brave Matalista. Bianchardin led the troops of Astorga together with those from Salamanca and Plasencia, Avila, Palencia, and Zamora. / The Saragossans were under the orders of Ferrau, as also were King Marsilius' immediate entourage, a strong, well-armed contingent, among whom should be mentioned Malgarin, Balinverne, Malzarise, and Morgan, men all fated to live in exile: when they had lost their realms, Marsilius had welcomed them at his court. / Also at Marsilius' court were his bastard son, Follicon of Almeria, and Doricon, Bavarte, Largalifa and Analard, Archidant, Count of Saguntum, Amirant and doughty Langhiran; nimble-witted Malagur, too, and many others whose feats I propose to describe when the moment comes. /

After the Spanish armies had passed in splendid array before King Agramant, the King of Oran appeared on parade with his troops; he was well-nigh a giant. The Garamants were next on the field; they were lamenting the loss of Martasin, laid low by Bradamant. How painful it was for them that a woman could boast of having slain their king! / The third squadron to pass consisted of troops from Marmonda; they had been forsaken by Argosto, slain in Gascony. They needed a leader, as did the previous squadron, and the one now following. Though Agramant enjoyed no surplus of captains, he gave the problem careful thought, which resulted in new appointments, including Buraldo, Ormidà, and Arganio, whom he assigned to squadrons where the need existed. / To Arganio he entrusted the Libyans who were bewailing the death of their swarthy King Dudrinas. Gloomy and shame-faced, Brunello led his troops from Tangiers: after letting Bradamant rob him of the magic ring in the wood not far from Atlas' castle on the rock, he had fallen out of Agramant's favour; / and if Ferrau's brother, Isoliero, who had come upon him bound to the tree, had not testified before the king to the truth of his story, Brunello would by now have given his last twitch at the end of the hangman's rope. The king had already had the noose put round his neck, but changed his mind when many interceded for him; he had him set free, but swore to hang him the next time he caught him on the wrong foot. / Well might Brunello look glum, then, and hang his head.

Next came Farurant, followed by cavalry and infantry from Mauretania. After him came Libanio, the newly created King of Constantine, with his troops; Agramant had made over to him the crown and sceptre of the late Pinadoro. / Soridan led the Hesperian troops, Dorilon those from Ceuta; the Nasamons were under Pulian's command, while Agricalt marched in the men of Amon. Malabuferso led the men of Fez; the troops from the Canaries and Morocco were commanded by Finadurro. Balastro commanded the troops formerly led by King Tardocco. / The next two contingents were those from Mulga and Arzilla; while the latter still had its original leader, the former was leaderless, so Agramant allotted it to his boon companion, Corineo. Similarly he appointed Caico to rule the Almansillans in place of Tanfirion. The Gaetulians he committed to Rimedon. Next came Balinfron with the men from Cosca. / There followed the troops from Bolga; Mirabald was once their king, but now it was Clarindo.

Next came Baliverzo, the pick of the entire host for sheer knavery. The banner which followed was King Sobrino's; I doubt whether in the whole field you would find another banner unfurled over a contingent as well found as this, nor a Saracen warrior of sounder judgement. / The troops from Bellamarina, whom Gualciotto used to lead, were now being led by Rodomont, King of Algiers and Sarthia. He had returned only three days earlier, bringing fresh troops (mounted and on foot) from Africa—for Agramant had sent him thither while the sun was overcast in Sagittarius and spiky Capricorn. / In the entire African host there was not one Saracen stronger nor bolder than he; the gates of Paris had more to fear from him, and with better reason, than from Marsilius and Agramant with all the retinue which had followed them to France. And he, more than anyone else at this parade, was an enemy to our Faith. / Next came Prusion, King of the Alvaracks, followed by King Dardinel of Azumara. I know not whether some night-owl or raven or other such unwelcome, sinister bird had croaked from the roofs or tree-tops, predicting evil in store for both of them: the hour was already fixed in the stars when, the very next day, they were both to die in battle. /

There were no squadrons left to pass in review except for those of Tremisen and Norizia; their standards, however, were nowhere to be seen, nor was there any news of them. Agramant was at a loss what to say or think about their indolence, when at last one of the King of Tremisen's pages was brought before him, and told him what had befallen. / He told him how Alzirdo and Manilard lay prostrate on the field with a great number of their men. 'The stalwart knight who has slain our company, my Lord, would have slaughtered your whole army if it had been any slower at making off than I was—and I only escaped by the skin of my teeth. He treats horsemen and foot-soldiers the way a wolf sets about goats and ewes.' / Now a few days earlier a prince had come to the camp of the African sovereign. Search East and West, there was not a man stronger than he, nor more courageous. Agramant paid him full honours, for he was the son and heir to mighty Agrican, King of Tartary. His name: Mandricard the fierce. / He was renowned for many a dazzling exploit, and his fame was world-wide. But his greatest claim to glory was that of having won the gleaming breastplate which Trojan Hector had worn a thousand years before; this he achieved at the castle of the Syrian sorceress by dint of fearsome hazards too terrifying even to speak of. /

Now Mandricard, who was present at the page's narrative, boldly raised his chin and determined to go after that warrior there and then.

This decision, though, he kept to himself, either not esteeming anyone there as worthy of the confidence, or fearing lest someone else forestall him in the enterprise if he revealed his thought. / He had the page questioned as to how the knight was dressed, and was told: 'All in black, with a black shield, but no device on it.' And this, my Lord, was the truth, for Orlando had left off his insignia: his heart was in mourning, so he chose black for his outward trappings. / Marsilius had presented Mandricard with a glossy bay charger; his legs and mane were black, and he was the offspring of a Spanish sire and a Frisian dam. Ready armed, Mandricard leapt onto him and galloped off across the country, swearing not to return to the Saracen host unless he found the black knight. / He came upon many of the terrified fugitives routed by Orlando. Some bewailed the loss of a son, others of a brother whom they had seen expire before their very eyes. Abject cowardice was still imprinted on their wan features; such was their terror, they were still dumbstruck, dazed, and pallid. /

A little further on he came upon a cruel, brutal spectacle which bore witness to the astonishing feat described to the African king. Corpses here, corpses there. Mandricard picked his way among them, peering at them and anxious to gauge the wounds with his hands; he was peculiarly jealous of the knight who had slain all these people. / Imagine a wolf or mastiff that comes too late upon a dead ox abandoned by the peasants, and, finding nothing left but the horns, hoofs, and skeleton (for the birds and dogs have feasted on the rest), vainly inspects the dried-up skull; such was the savage barbarian as he stood there in the plain, cursing in frustration and livid with envy, having arrived too late at so rich a feast. / All that day and half the next he followed the uncertain traces of the black knight, making enquiries as he went.

Now he came to a shady meadow ringed by a deep river which left only a narrow tongue of land before it wound off in a different direction. Below Ocricoli there is a similar spot where the Tiber makes a loop like this. / At the point of access there was a large gathering of armoured knights. Mandricard asked who it was who had assembled so great a company here, and to what purpose. The captain replied, impressed by his lordly look and his costly caparison, trimmed with gold and jewels, which proclaimed him a warrior of some eminence. /

'We have been sent from Granada by our king', he explained, 'to escort his daughter whom he has betrothed to the King of Sarthia, though news of this has not yet been given out. When the cricket, which can now be heard on its own, falls silent towards evening, we shall bring her to her father who is with the Spanish host. Meanwhile she is sleeping.' / Now Mandricard, who scorned everybody, decided straight away to test these men and see how well they defended the woman committed to their charge. 'From what I hear, the lady is beautiful,' he observed. 'I should be pleased to see for myself. Conduct me to her or bring her here to me, for I must be on my way.' / 'You must be a fully-fledged idiot,' was all the captain would say. But the Tartar at once lowered his lance and ran the man through the chest, for his breastplate could not sustain the blow, and perforce he fell down dead. Mandricard withdrew his lance, for this was his only weapon. / He wielded neither sword nor mace, for when he acquired the arms which had once belonged to Trojan Hector, seeing that the sword was missing, he had had to swear (an oath not sworn in vain) that he would never hold a sword in his hand until he took Orlando's Durindana—a sword once greatly prized by Almont, now wielded by Orlando, but originally Hector's. /

The Tartar was indeed a bold man, to challenge those knights with the odds so much against him. Crying 'Who's going to bar my way?' he charged into them with his lance. Some lowered their lances, others drew their swords, and in a trice he was surrounded, but he dispatched a great number of them before his lance broke. / Seeing it snapped in two he grasped the stout shaft in both hands and caused such slaughter, a bloodier battle was never seen. Like Samson among the Philistines after he had picked up the ass's jawbone, Mandricard splintered shields and stove in helmets; often a single blow was enough to dispatch a steed along with its rider. / The poor wretches hurried, jostling each other, to their death, little deterred by the sight of their comrades falling before them: far more bitter to them than death itself was the manner of their dying—to be robbed of precious life by a mere broken spear-shaft, to meet death like so many snakes or frogs under a monstrous hail of blows is more than they could endure. / But once they had realized to their cost that death was evil however it came, the survivors started to flee—almost two thirds of their numbers being already dead. But the cruel Saracen, as though jealously guarding what was his own, could not suffer any of that bewildered throng to escape from him alive. / As the vibrant reed in a dried-out swamp cannot long survive, or the parched stubble in a field when the North Wind blows, fanning the fire lit there by the expert husbandmen: the fitful flames spread out everywhere, running along the furrows, hissing and crackling. The survivors now were just as defenceless against the Tartar's blazing onslaught. / Once he saw the way through, ill-guarded before, now totally unguarded, he followed the path detectable in the newly-trodden grass—and also the sound of wailing he could hear—and went to see the lady from Granada, to discover whether her reputation for beauty was well-founded. He stepped amid the corpses across the neck of land where the river looped back on itself. /

He espied Doralice (as she was called) in the middle of the meadow leaning against the ancient trunk of a rustic ash, weeping. Her tears welled up as though from a living spring and fell upon her lovely breast. Her pretty face was marked with sorrow inspired by the sufferings of her company and by fears for herself. / The sight of him coming, all disfigured with gore, and an ugly scowl on his face, only quickened her fear; her shrieks rent the air, so terrified was she for herself and her suite—for beside the armed escort, the lovely Infanta had guides in her train, men of maturer years, and a good number of matrons and maids-in-waiting, among the fairest in the kingdom of Granada. / When the Tartar set eyes on her face, unmatched for beauty in the whole of Spain, he knew not whether he was still in this world, or in paradise: tearful as she was, she had ensnared him in Love's inextricable toils, so how must she be when she smiled! His victory, then, brought him no reward except to surrender him, a prisoner, he knew not how, into the hands of his captive. /

His surrender, however, was not so complete that he allowed himself to be imposed upon by her tears, for all that she showed herself as heart-broken as ever a woman could be. But he hoped to turn her tears into radiant joy and proposed to take her off with him. He sat her upon a white pony and resumed his journey. / As for the ladies-in-waiting and the courtiers, young and old, who had accompanied her from Granada, he dismissed them one and all with his blessing. 'My company', said he, 'shall be more than enough for her; I shall be her tutor, guardian, and steward to meet all her needs. Ladies, gentlemen, adieu!' And there was nothing for them to do but to go their way, sighing and weeping, / and brooding as they went: 'Oh, how anguished will her father be; and her betrothed—imagine his fury, his pain when he hears! How terrible will be his vengeance! Alas, why is he not here now at such a pressing moment, to force this man to yield King Stordilan's illustrious daughter before he removes her to a greater distance!' /

So pleased was Mandricard with the rich prize afforded him by Fortune and his own valour, he now seemed in less haste than before to find the knight in black. Whereas before he had run, now he ambled, his mind preoccupied with finding some convenient lodging in which to unleash his pent-up amorous passion. / Meanwhile he comforted Doralice whose eyes and cheeks were damp with tears. He chose his words with considerable inventiveness and told her that on her reputation alone he had long been in love with her. He said that he had left his homeland, his prosperous kingdom which eclipsed all others in grandeur, not in order to visit Spain or France, but simply to contemplate her lovely features. /

'Must a man love, if he is to be beloved? Then I deserve your love, for I have loved you. Must he be well-born? Who is nobler than I, whose father was mighty Agrican? Must he be wealthy? Who enjoys greater estate than I? None but God has greater dominion. Must he be valiant? Then I have shown today, I believe, that I deserve to be loved.' / These words, and a host of others which Love put into the Tartar's mouth, served gently to soothe the terror-stricken heart of the damsel. Her dread was assuaged, and her pain solaced, which had all but rent her heart. She began to attend more patiently to her new lover and give him a kinder hearing. / Her attitude became gradually more accommodating and affable, and she no longer refused to look up, but allowed him to rest his eyes, lit with tenderness, upon her face. The pagan, who had on other occasions known the impact of Cupid's darts, derived from these signs not merely the hope but the certainty that the lovely damsel would not be invincibly opposed to his desire. / His mood was merry and blithe, such was the delight and satisfaction he found in her company.

Now the hour was approaching when chill night invited every creature to rest. Seeing the sun on the point of setting, he began to quicken his pace, until he came to where he caught the sound of flutes and pipes and saw smoke rising from peasant huts, / the abode of shepherds; this was the best accommodation available, scarcely elegant but convenient. The shepherd offered a courteous and respectful welcome to the warrior and the damsel, and they accounted themselves pleased with his entertainment; it is not only in cities and baronial halls that you will meet civility, but often also in barns and hovels. / What passed between Doralice and Mandricard in the dark I shall not hazard to describe; I leave it to the judgement of my listeners. One may readily believe that there was perfect harmony between them, for they rose on the morrow in an even happier frame of mind, and Doralice thanked the shepherd who had made them his honoured guests. / Thence they wandered from place to place until they came to the bank of a pleasant river which silently flowed to the sea, though it was hard to detect any movement in its water, which was so limpid and clear that, looking into it, one could see to the bottom without impediment. In the delicious cool shade of the bank they came upon two knights and a maiden. /

Now my soaring fantasy will not suffer me to tread always the selfsame path, but leads me hence, back to where the Moorish host deafens France with noise and clamour, from round the pavilion where Agramant, King Trojan's son, challenges the Holy Empire of

Rome, and bold Rodomont brags he will burn down Paris and raze sacred Rome to the ground. / It had been reported to Agramant that the troops had already crossed from England, so he summoned Marsilius and Sobrino, the old King of Garbo, and the other commanders. They all agreed on mustering their forces for a mighty assault on Paris, in the certainty that they would never succeed in storming it unless they did so before the reinforcements arrived. / To this end the king had already sent out into the neighbourhood to gather in ladders by the score, and planks and beams and wickerwork panels for which many uses would be found. Boats he assembled, too, and bridges. Most of all he attended to preparations for the first and second assault-wave, and went the rounds of the troops who were to mount the attack. /

The day before the eve of battle, the Emperor Charlemagne ordained that throughout Paris masses and offices were to be celebrated by priests and friars (white, black, and grey), and that everyone was to be shriven, so as to escape the hands of the infernal spirits, and then to receive communion—just as though they were all to die the next day. / With his barons and paladins, princes and prelates, he repaired to the cathedral and most devoutly participated in the sacred rites, setting an example to the rest. Joining his hands and raising his eyes to heaven, he prayed: 'Lord, though I am wicked and sinful, in your goodness suffer not your faithful people to be afflicted on account of my faults. / But if it is your will that they should suffer and that our waywardness be punished as it deserves, do but defer the retribution that it be not administered by the hand of your enemies: for if it fell to their lot to slay us, who are accounted your friends, the pagans will say that you are powerless, leaving your own followers to perish. / And throughout the world for each rebellious soul a hundred will rise against you, and the false law of Babel will drive out and suppress your religion. Defend your faithful, then; they are the ones who have cleansed your sepulchre and purged it of brutish dogs; many a time have they defended your holy Church and her vicars. / I acknowledge that our merits are not capable of satisfying our debt to you by so much as an ounce nor can we hope for your pardon when we consider the depravity of our lives. But if you throw on the scale the gift of your grace, our tribute is made up to the full amount. We cannot despair of your assistance when we remember your mercy.' /

Thus prayed the pious emperor, humble and contrite of heart; other prayers, too, he added, and a vow suitable to the magnitude of the need and the lofty splendour of his office. His urgent entreaties were not without effect, for his tutelary spirit, his angel, took his prayers and, shaping his flight heavenwards, bore them up to the

Saviour. / At that moment countless prayers were being borne up to God by other such messengers, for the saints, hearing his words, all turned their faces, suffused with compassion, to look at the Love Eternal and show Him their common desire—that the just entreaty of the Christian people calling for help should be granted. /

And the Ineffable Goodness, never besought in vain by trusting souls, raised his merciful eyes and summoned Michael the Archangel with a gesture. 'Go', he bade him, 'to the Christian army who have furled their sails off Picardy and so conduct them to the walls of Paris that the enemy do not hear their coming. / Fetch out Silence first and bid him from me to go with you on this enterprise; he will know exactly what to do to achieve what is required. This attended to, go straight away and seek out Discord; tell her to take her flint and tinder, and go to start fires in the Moorish camp; / have her breed so many quarrels among those accounted their champions that they fall to fighting each other, so that some are killed, some taken captive, some wounded, while others storm out of the camp in a rage, and their king will scarcely be able to count on their assistance.' The archangel made no answer but flew down from Heaven. / Wherever Michael bent his flight, the clouds scattered and the sky cleared; he was surrounded by a golden halo, bright as a lightning flash seen by night. As he went he thought where best to put down if he was to find that enemy of words to whom he meant to address his first commission. /

He went over in his mind all the places Silence tended to frequent, and ultimately his thoughts all arrived at the same conclusion: that the churches, the monasteries of friars and cloistered monks would be the place to find him. Here conversation was rigidly banned; Silence reigned where they intoned the psalter, where they slept, where they took their meals; Silence was posted up in every room. / Expecting to find Silence here he beat his gilded pinions with greater haste; he felt confident of finding here Peace and Quiet, too; and Charity. But he had only to land in the cloister to be cured of his delusion: Silence was not to be found there. 'He no longer lives here,' he was told, 'except in the signs up on the wall.' / Piety was not to be seen either, nor were Tranquillity or Meekness, Love or Peace. They used to be found here in days of old, but have since been driven out by Gluttony, Avarice and Wrath, Pride, Envy, Sloth and Cruelty. The angel was amazed at this turn of affairs; he looked here and there among this hideous throng and noticed that Discord was here too, / whom the Eternal Father had told him to find after Silence. He had expected to go down to Hades, imagining that she dwelt with the damned, but here he came upon her in this new inferno (who would have thought it!) amid the divine offices and the mass! It seemed odd to Michael to discover her here when he had anticipated a long journey in search of her. / He recognized her by her multi-coloured attire composed of countless uneven strips of material which gave her only periodic concealment, for they were in such tatters they kept falling open at every movement she made, at every puff of wind. Her hair was a mixture of silver and gold, black and grey, all at cross-purposes—part of it was plaited, part gathered in a ribbon, a great deal fell over her back, a little over her breast. / Stuffed down her bosom and clasped in her hands were sheaves of summonses and writs, cross-examinations and powers of attorney, and great piles of glosses, counsel's opinions and precedents— all of which tended to the greater insecurity of impoverished towns-folk. In front and behind her and on either side she was hemmed in by notaries, attorneys and barristers. /

Michael summoned her and bade her go down among the Saracen champions and cause memorable havoc with some bone of contention that would bring them all to blows. Then he enquired of her about Silence: she might well know where he was, for she was always on the move, sparking fires all over the place. / 'I cannot recall ever having set eyes on him anywhere,' replied Discord, 'though I've heard him mentioned often enough, and much commended for his slyness. But one of our company, Fraud, should be able to enlighten you, I think —she occasionally consorts with him. There she is,' she added, pointing a finger. / Fraud was pleasant-looking, soberly dressed; her eyes were meek, her bearing dignified, and she was so benign and simple in her speech she might have been the angel of the Annuncia-tion. For the rest, she was ugly and mis-shapen, though she contrived to conceal her deformities beneath a long and ample robe—which always concealed, in addition, a poisoned dagger. / Michael asked Fraud which road was most likely to lead him to Silence, and was told: 'He used to dwell exclusively among the virtues, with Benedict, and with the disciples of Elias the hermit, at the time when the monasteries were still in their infancy. Much of his time he spent in the schools back in the days of Pythagoras and Archites. / When there were no philosophers or holy men left to keep him on the straight and narrow path, he forsook his virtuous propensities and threw in his lot with the wicked. He began consorting with lovers at night, then with thieves; he was party to every sort of crime. Now he frequents Treachery a great deal, and I have seen him keep company with Murder. / He often slinks off into some dark hole in the company of forgers; as you see, then, he is constantly changing company and location and you'll be lucky to track him down. Still, there is a chance I can help you find him: if you make a point of reaching the house of Slumber at dead of night, you will find him without fail, for that is where he sleeps.' /

Although Fraud was a natural liar, her words had this time the ring of truth, and the angel believed her. So he flew out of the monastery at once, and so regulated his flight as to reach his journey's end at the home of Slumber—he knew its location—at the right moment to find Silence there. / In Arabia there is a pleasant valley quite remote from any village or town; it lies in the shadow of two peaks, and is planted with ancient firs and sturdy beeches. In vain the Sun tries to introduce bright daylight here—his rays can never penetrate the thick foliage concealing the entrance to an underground cave. / Beneath the dark wood a rock-cleft forms an ample, spacious cave; twisting strands of ivy cling to its brow. This is the place where heavy Slumber rests, flanked by plump, corpulent Sloth and by Laziness, sitting on the ground, unable to move and unsteady on his legs. / Scatterbrained Oblivion stands at the entrance; he lets no one enter, recognizes nobody; he hears no deputations, relays no messages, but holds everyone off impartially. Silence mounts guard, pacing about in felt slippers and a dark cloak, and from a distance he waves away all comers. /

Michael approached him and whispered into his ear: 'God would have you guide Rinaldo to Paris with the troops he has brought in to reinforce his sovereign. But you must do this so quietly that not a shout reaches the ears of the Saracens—who must be circumvented by these troops before Rumour can give notice of their arrival.' / For all reply Silence merely nodded assent and obediently followed him; they took wing and in one hop landed in Picardy. Here Michael moved the brave squadrons and so curtailed their route that a single day's journey brought them to Paris, without any of them realizing the miracle which had been wrought. / Silence was everywhere, spreading a thick veil of mist all about the army while elsewhere the day remained clear; this dense mist muffled every sound of trumpet and clarion. Then he went to the pagan camp bringing with him some singular property which made everyone deaf and blind. / While Rinaldo was on his way at such speed that it was evident that the archangel was leading him, and in such silence that not a murmur reached the Saracen camp, King Agramant had been deploying his infantry round the outskirts of Paris and along the moat beneath the threatened walls, in order that day to make one last supreme attempt. /

The man who can tell the numbers of the army moved against Charlemagne today by King Agramant would be able to count every shrub growing on the shady ridges of the wooded Apennines, every wave that breaks on the Mauretanian shore when the Atlantic is at its roughest, and every eye through which the heavens espy the furtive play of lovers at dead of night. / In Paris the bells could be heard ringing frantically; look in church after church and you would have seen hands raised to heaven and lips moving in prayer. If treasure seemed as beautiful to God as it does to our foolish way of thinking, this is the day when the faithful would have used pure gold for every statue dedicated to Him. / The venerable old men could be heard regretting that they had survived to bear such trials, and envying the sacred relics of those whose bodies had fallen to dust many a long year before. The younger men, however, were spirited and sturdy; they paid little heed to the dangers looming, scorned the talk of their elders, and ran hither and thither to man the walls. / There were barons here and paladins, kings, dukes, knights, marquises, and counts, soldiers from France and from other lands, all of them ready to die for the honour of Christ. They begged the emperor to lower the draw-bridges so that they could sally forth against the Saracens; he was heartened by their spirit, but was not disposed to let them out. / He deployed them in suitable places to stop the barbarians breaking in; here a handful of men was deemed sufficient, while there an entire company was not too many. Some were assigned to the fire-raising equipment, others to the engines, as the need dictated. Charles was everywhere at once, never still for a moment, assuring help and acting as a shield over all. /

Paris is set in a broad plain at the navel of France, or rather, at the heart. The river passes within its walls and flows out by another opening, but only after forming an island which constitutes one part (and the best) of the city; the other two parts (for the great city is divided into three) are bounded on the outside by the moat, on the inside by the river. / The city has a circumference of several miles, so it may be attacked from many points. But Agramant, reluctant to disperse his forces, proposed assaulting it from one side only, and withdrew across the river towards the West, to mount his attack from this quarter: thus to his rear he would have not a single town or region which was not under his rule, all the way to Spain. / Charlemagne had thrown up powerful fortifications all along the line of the walls, strengthening every embankment and building into them tunnels and arrow-slits. He threw colossal chains across the river at its point of entry into and exit from the city. But he made the most concentrated provisions for those points where the danger was greatest. / He had eyes like Argus' to foresee where Agramant would attack; indeed, the Saracen made no plan which had not already been forestalled.

Marsilius, assisted by Ferrau, Isoliero, Serpentine, Grandonio, Falsiron, and Balugant, remained in the rear with the troops he had led from Spain. / To his left, on the bank of the Seine, was Sobrino, with Pulian, Dardinel, son of Almont, and the King of Oran, who looked a giant, twelve foot from crown to sole. Alas, if only I were as quick with my pen as these men are with their weapons: look, Rodomont is bawling and cursing in a lather of rage—there's no holding him! / Imagine the importunate flies on a hot summer's day as, buzzing noisily, they swarm onto the remains of the sweets at an outdoor meal, or onto the dishes from which shepherds eat; or think of birds flocking in to pick off the ripe purple grapes clinging to their stakes. Thus were the Moors as, filling the sky with their shouts and clamour, they launched their attack. /

On the walls the Christians defended the city fearlessly, with sword, spear and battle-axe, stones and fire, little impressed by the barbarians' audacity. Where Death reaped one defender after the next, there was no one who through cowardice refused to fill the gap. The Saracens were driven back from the walls under a hail of blows and knocks. / Metal was not all they used, but great chunks of masonry and entire merlons from the battlements, and walls laboriously dismantled, roofing from towers and whole sections of parapet. The Moors found the scalding water thrown down upon them unendurably hot; this sort of rain was not easy to withstand, for it found its way into the men's helmets and clouded their vision— / indeed, it did almost more damage than the steel weapons. What then of the cloud of lime, the cauldrons of boiling oil and brimstone, pitch, and turpentine? Nor were Catherine wheels left behind in the arsenal; blazing with a ring of flame, these were hurled from every quarter, a shower of unwelcome garlands dropping on the Saracens. /

Meanwhile Rodomont, King of Sarthia, had thrown the second assault-wave against the walls; with him were Buraldo the Garamant and Ormida of Marmonda. At his side were Clarindo and Soridan, nor was the King of Ceuta lurking in the background. Behind them pressed the Kings of Morocco and of Cosca, each one eager to show off his prowess. / Rodomont's standard depicted a lion on a red ground; its fierce jaws were open as it submitted to being bridled by a lady. Rodomont identified himself with the lion; as for the lady who was checking him with a bridle, he modelled her on fair Doralice, daughter of King Stordilan of Granada. / She was the damsel whom (as I related) King Mandricard had abducted (I have described where and from whom). She it was whom Rodomont loved more than his kingdom, more than his very eyes. It was for her that he was now displaying gallantry and valour, little realizing that she was in another's power: had he known this, he would this very moment have done what he did later the same day. /

All at once a thousand ladders were set against the walls; on each rung of each ladder—no less than two Saracens. Hard pressed by those climbing up behind, each man urged on the man on the rung above. In some courage, in others fear was the motive force: there was no escape from entering the breach, for harsh Rodomont killed or wounded whoever hung back. / So each man strove to climb up onto the walls through the fire and missiles. All the other attackers, however, looked about in search of an easier opening. Rodomont alone scorned to make for any opening but where the hazards were greatest; and when the situation was getting out of hand, while the rest sent prayers up to the Almighty, he sent up curses. / He was armed with a tough, durable breastplate made from the scaly hide of a dragon. It once clad the chest and back of Nembrot, his ancestor who built the tower of Babel, thinking to hurl God out of His golden abode and wrest from Him the government of the stars. To this end he had his helmet and shield fashioned to perfection, as also his sword. / Rodomont was every whit as dauntless, proud and rabid as Nembrot, and if there were a path up to Heaven, he would not have waited for nightfall before taking it. This being so, he was not going to stand looking to see if the walls were solid or broken, or if the moat was fordable: he took the moat at a rush, indeed he flew at it, up to his neck in water and slime. / Mud-stained and soaked through, he plunged into the flames and stones, arrows and slings like a wild boar in the reedy plains of our Mallea, which uses its chest and snout and tusks to break passages wide open wherever it goes. Bearing high his shield, the Saracen advanced unshaken, scorning Heaven, let alone the wall. /

The moment Rodomont reached dry ground his arrival was felt on the catwalks which formed broad bridges behind the walls for the French troops. Now you would have seen many a head split open, many a friar's tonsure altered to the look of a bishop's cloven mitre, arms and heads fly off; a river of blood flowed from the walls into the moat. / The pagan threw down his shield, grasped his cruel sword two-handed and struck Arnulph, a duke whose home was where the Rhine flows into the salt sea. The poor wretch was as helpless before him as sulphur touched by fire. He fell, shuddered, and lay still, his head split down to his chest. / With a single, slanting blow he slew Anselm, Oldrade, Spineloccio, and Prando: the crush was so great in so confined a space that his sword proved quite devastating. Of these four the first two were lost to the Flemish, the last two to the Normans. Then he struck Orghetto of Maganza, cleaving him from crown to chest and still on down to his belly. / Andropono and Moschino he hurled into the moat from the battlements. The former was a priest. As for the latter, he worshipped only wine; many a hogshead had he drained at a draught. He shunned water like poison—to him it was viper's blood—yet here he was, dying in it: he took it most unkindly that water should prove the death of him. / Louis (from Provence) he cut in two; Arnold of Toulouse he ran through the chest; he made an end of Hubert, Claude, Hugo, and Denis (all men of Tours): their spirits gushed out with their warm blood. Beside these he killed four from Paris—Walter, Satallone, Odo, and Ambalde—and many others; I should never be able to give all their names and countries of origin. /

The Saracen host surged after Rodomont, and swarmed up ladders set against the walls at many points, but the Parisians no longer stood their ground here, seeing the futility of their initial resistance. Besides, they well knew that the enemy still had their main problem ahead of them, and this would prove no child's play: between the outer and the inner ramparts yawned a trench of awesome depth. / Our defenders showed great courage as they fought an enemy now above them; however, fresh defenders were brought into play, fighting from atop the steep inner ramparts, and showering spears and arrows onto the attackers swarming in—whose numbers would, I think, have been considerably sparser were it not for Rodomont. / Some he encouraged, others he rebuked; he drove them before him willy nilly; if any of them turned to flee, he pierced their breasts or split their skulls. Many he pushed and hustled, some he picked up by their arms, their hair, the scruff of their necks; and so many did he toss, head over heels down into the fosse that it was too narrow to contain them all. / While the barbarian horde was climbing down, or rather being sent crashing down, into the perilous trench from the floor of which they tried a different way of scaling the inner rampart, Rodomont, as though he had a wing attached to each limb, lifted his ponderous frame and cleared the trench at one leap—and he was in full armour. / It was a good thirty feet across, and he cleared it as deftly as a greyhound, hitting the ground as soundlessly as though he had landed on felt. Now he laid about him, reducing everyone's defences to shreds, as though their arms were made of soft pewter, nay, of mere bark, and not of iron—such was his sword and the power behind it. /

Meanwhile our side had laid a trap in the deep fosse: they had assembled a huge quantity of besoms and faggots well impregnated with pitch, but all well concealed from view, even though both walls of the fosse, from the dark bottom almost to the very top, were bristling with them; and they had concealed thousands of cauldrons / brimming with saltpetre, with oil, sulphur, and similar combustibles. Now, to bring a sorry outcome to the mad temerity of the Saracens down in the fosse who were expecting to scale the wall and reach the inner ramparts at several points, our side, on hearing the signal given from selected places, set a blaze going here and there. / The scattered flames united in one single conflagration, filling the entire trench from side to side and rising high enough to dry the damp breast of the moon. Dark, inky smoke spiralled upward, cloaking the sun and plunging the daylight into darkness. A close-linked chain of explosions could be heard, like a fearsome roll of thunder. / A ghastly concert of high-pitched shrieks, bellows, and yells arose from the poor wretches perishing in the fosse through the fault of their leader—a medley of sounds blending weirdly with the fierce crackle of the murderous blaze. Enough, my Lord, enough of this canto; I am quite hoarse and need to rest awhile.

FIFTEENTH CANTO

1–2 Introductory. 3–9 The battle for Paris. 9–37 Astolfo sails away from Alcina's island, and hears prophecies about Charles V. 38–90 Astolfo defeats Caligorant and slays Orrilo. 91–105 Astolfo on pilgrimage to Jerusalem with Grifon and Aquilant.

To achieve victory, whether by good fortune or good tactics, has always been commendable. True, if too much bloodshed is involved, the victorious captain may tarnish his reputation; conversely, the captain who drives the enemy from the field with no losses to his own side is marked out for divine honours and merits eternal glory. / Your victory, my Lord, was deservedly praised, that time when the Lion of St. Mark, so formidable on the water, had occupied both banks of the Po, from Francolino to the sea, and you dealt so effectively with it that even now if I should hear it roaring, I have but to look at you to be reassured. You showed how victory ought to be won: you killed our enemy and protected us. /

Such an achievement was beyond Rodomont who, in his boldness, overreached himself. He drove his troops into the fosse, where the sudden conflagration devoured the lot, sparing none. Indeed the great trench would not have been large enough to contain so many, but the flames reduced all the bodies to ashes, thus making room for them all. / Eleven thousand and twenty-eight finished up in the blazing pit into which they had reluctantly descended—but such was the will of their reckless leader. Here they now lay dead in a luminous blaze while the hungry flames still nibbled at their remains. And Rodomont, the cause of their ills, escaped these torments scot-free: / with a prodigious leap he had cleared the fosse to land amid the enemy on the inner rim—had he gone down into the fosse with the rest, this would indeed have been the last of his sallies. He looked back at the infernal trench, saw the flames reaching to the heights, heard his people's cries and shrieks, and bombarded Heaven with dreadful curses. /

Meanwhile Agramant had launched a savage attack against one of the gates, deeming that, while the cruel battle was raging here with the loss of so many men, the guard at the gate might be under strength, and could be overpowered. In his company were King Bambirago of Arzilla, King Baliverso the profligate, / King Corineo of Mulga, Prusion, wealthy King of the Fortunate Isles, and Malabuferso, King of Fez, where summer lasts the year round. There were many other lords with him too, and champions well armed and skilled in war; and still others who were without valour and naked—a thousand bucklers would not have steeled their hearts. / The King of the Saracens was proved quite wrong in his calculation: Charles the Emperor guarded the gate in person, supported by several of his paladins—Solomon was there, and Ogier the Dane, both Guidos, the two Angelinos, Namo, Duke of Bavaria, Ganelon, Avino, Avolio, Otho and Berenger; / also countless men of lesser degree, French, German, and Lombard, each one eager to shine in the presence of his liege.

Later I shall relate to you what happened; now I must turn my attention to a great duke who is calling and beckoning to me from a distance, entreating my pen to release him onto the page. / It is time for me to return to where I left Astolfo, the adventurous English duke, who was thoroughly sick by now of his long exile and longed to be back in his own country. Logistilla, who had defeated Alcina in battle, had raised his hopes, and was making it her business to send him home by the shortest and surest route. / So a galley was made ready, the finest ship that ever ploughed the sea. Now Logistilla, whose constant fear was that Alcina might interfere with his voyage, assigned Andronica and Sophrosina to accompany him with a strong fleet and bring him safely into the Arabian Sea or the Persian Gulf. / She instructed him to choose the route which skirted the lands of the Scythians, the far Indies and the realm of the Nabataeans, to arrive among the Persians and Eritreans by this more extended route, rather than choosing the passage through the Northern seas, always whipped by wicked winds, and in some seasons so starved of sunshine that for several months there is none at all. /

When Logistilla saw that all was ready, she gave the duke permission to leave, having first primed him with numerous admonishments and instructions which would take too long to tell. And to prevent his falling victim to magic spells a second time, she gave him a fine, useful book which he was to cherish and keep by him at all times. / This book she gave him listed all the antidotes to magic; it had an index guiding the reader back and forth through the pages to find the right passage. She gave him another present, too, of far greater use than any gift ever made: a horn which made such an appalling noise that it put to flight all who heard it. / The horn, I say, made such an appalling noise that whenever it was heard, it sent everyone fleeing; nowhere in the world was there to be found another horn with so irresistible an effect on its hearers: the sound of wind, earthquake, thunder was as nothing compared to this. Good Astolfo took leave of the enchantress after thanking her profusely. /

He left the harbour and calmer waters and a prosperous following breeze took him past the rich, populous cities of the aromatic Indies; on either hand a thousand scattered islands came into view. As he sailed on he sighted the land of Thomas the Apostle, when the helmsman altered course further Northwards. / Almost grazing the golden Chersonnese, the fine fleet breasted the ocean; as it coasted along the opulent shores, they saw the Ganges frothing into the sea; they sighted Ceylon and Cape Comorin, and the sea which foamed between the two coasts. A great step of their journey brought them to Cochin where they left behind them the boundaries of India. /

As he sailed the sea with his faithful, trusty escort, there was a question in the duke's mind, which he put to Andronica: did vessels hailing from the lands of the setting sun, whether driven by oars or sail, ever appear in the Eastern Seas? And was it possible to set sail from India and reach France or England without once making land? /

'You must know', Andronica replied, 'that the land is wholly ringed by the ocean, whose waters merge into each other both where they boil and where they freeze. But the extension of Ethiopia, the land ahead of us reaching far down to the South, has led certain people to maintain that Neptune cannot proceed beyond this point. / This being so, no ship sails for Europe from our oriental lands, nor does any vessel set out from Europe meaning to reach our shores: sailors approaching from either direction, and finding land ahead, feel inclined to turn back, for seeing the way it extends Southwards they imagine it must join up with the other hemisphere. / But with the passage of time I see new Argonauts, new Tiphyses hailing from the lands which lie furthest to the West, who shall open routes unknown to this day. Some of them shall round Africa, following the shores of the black peoples right on past the limits whence the sun returns to us after leaving Capricorn; / they shall discover the limit of the long stretch of land which makes us imagine two separate seas. They shall sail along every shore and past the neighbouring islands of the Indians,

Arabians, and Persians. Others shall leave to their left and right the Pillars established by Hercules, and, following the circuit of the sun, discover new lands, a new world. /

'I see the Holy Cross and the imperial standards set up on the verdant shore; some guard the storm-tossed ships, others are taking possession of the territory; they are picked men—I see ten of them routing a thousand, and kingdoms beyond the Indies being subjected to Aragon; and I see Charles V's captains sweeping all before them. / God willed that this route should in the past have remained concealed, and should so continue for still many a year: not before the sixth and seventh ages have elapsed shall it become known, for He has reserved its discovery until the day when He places the world under the monarchy of the wisest and most just emperor who ever lived or shall live, after Augustus. /

'I see the birth of a prince on the left bank of the Rhine; in his veins flows the blood of Austria and Aragon, and no valour ever mentioned in speech or writing can compare with his. I see Astrea restored to her throne by him, indeed restored from death to life; and the virtues, too, which the world banished when it banished her, shall return from exile by his power. / Because of such merits the Supreme Good has awarded him the crown of the great empire once ruled over by Augustus, Trajan, Marcus Aurelius, and Septimius Severus; not only this, but also that he should rule over every land East and West, however far flung, that sees the sun and the passage of the year. He wills that under this emperor there should be but one fold, one shepherd. / To give readier effect to the decrees written in Heaven from all time, Divine Providence assures him of invincible captains by land and sea. I see Hernando Cortez, who has subjected new cities to the imperial edicts, and Eastern realms so remote that we in India have never heard of them. / I see Prospero Colonna, and a Marquis of Pescara, and after them I see a young man from Vasto; these shall all make fair Italy costly for the Golden Lilies. Furthermore I see this third young man preparing to enter the field and outstrip the others in racing for the laurel crown—like a good athlete who sets out last only to catch up and overtake the rest. /

'I see in Alfonso (for this is his name) such valour, such dependability, that for all his extreme youth—he shall not have passed twenty-six years—the emperor shall entrust his army to him: thus safeguarding his army, he shall not merely save the day but, thanks to this commander, shall make the whole world subject to himself. / Just as with these commanders he shall extend his ancient empire as far as one may travel by land, so shall he be victorious in every campaign on the sea bounded on this side by sunny Africa, on the further side by Europe—for he shall secure the friendship of Andrea Doria, the same Doria who makes your sea everywhere safe from pirates. / Pompey, for all that he made a clean sweep of the pirates, was not as excellent as he; for Pompey's pirates had the most powerful empire of all time ranged against them, while this Doria shall purge the seas of their presence by his unaided strength and skill. From Gibraltar to the Nile I see every shore tremble at the mention of his name. /

'I see Charles acceding to the crown of Italy under the faithful escort of this captain of whom I speak, for he shall open the gates to the emperor. And I see that the captain does not keep for himself the reward he wins for his assistance, but has it made over to his own city, Genoa: at his instance, he obtains the liberation of his city, when others would perhaps have obtained its subjection to themselves. / This clemency he shows to his homeland merits greater honour than all the battles Caesar won in France, Spain, or your own country, in Africa or Thessaly; neither great Octavius nor Antony, his well-matched opponent, achieved greater honour for their exploits: by turning their swords against their own country they forfeited a part of their renown. / Let them blush, and whoever else presumes to enslave his homeland; let them not dare to raise their eyes when they hear Andrea Doria's name pronounced. I see Charles increasing his reward, for in addition to the freedom he shall enjoy in common with his fellow-citizens, the emperor shall give him the rich territory where the Normans are to establish the foundations of their greatness in Apulia. / Great-hearted Charles shall show esteem not only to this captain, but to all who shall have made free sacrifice of their blood in the service of the Holy Roman Empire. I see him deriving greater pleasure from awarding cities and even an entire province to a loyal retainer, and to all those who merit a reward, than from the acquisition of new empires and kingdoms.' /

Thus Andronica conversed with Duke Astolfo about the victories which, many years later, Charles V was to reap by his captains' hands. Meanwhile the fleet let out and reefed in the sails as they caught the East Wind, making adjustments to capture its every shift of quarter and change of strength. / They had now come in sight of the Persian Sea, looking like a broad flood, and after sailing across it for a few days they reached the gulf named by the Magi. Here the roving ships put into harbour and tied up stern to the quay; and here Astolfo, safe from Alcina's pursuit, went ashore to continue his journey. /

Many were the fields and woods he crossed, over many a mountain, through many a valley; often, by dusk and in broad daylight, he was confronted or pursued by robbers. He saw lions, venomous dragons, and other wild beasts cross his path—but the moment he set his horn to his lips, they all fled in a panic. / He came to Arabia Felix, as it is called, a land rich in myrrh and fragrant incense, in all the wide world the one spot chosen by the unique phoenix for its residence. Next he reached the sea which once avenged Israel when by divine consent it drowned Pharaoh and all his army. Then he came to the Land of the Heroes. / He rode beside Trajan's canal, mounted on a charger the like of which the world had never seen: he moved so lightly as to leave no traces in the dust. Never a footprint would he set on grass nor snow—he could have trodden the sea dry-shod—and at a flat-out gallop he outstripped wind, lightning, and the arrow. / This is the steed which was once Argalia's; he was conceived by wind out of fire, and he fed not on hay or oats but on pure air; Rabican was his name. The duke pursued his way till he came to where the canal joined the Nile.

Now before he reached the river's mouth, he saw a boat moving rapidly towards him. / At the stern he saw a hermit with a white beard which came half-way down his chest; the hermit hailed him from a distance, inviting him on board: 'My son, if your life is not hateful to you, and you would fain not meet your end today, pray cross to this further shore; the path you follow will lead you straight to your death. / You will not go more than six miles before you come to the gory lair of a horrible giant who towers eight feet above the tallest man. Let no knight or traveller hope to escape from him alive: he is a savage—with some, he slits their throats, with others, strips their skins, many he slashes in quarters, a few he swallows whole. / Amid such horrors he takes pleasure in a net of his, skilfully made: he sets it down not far from his den and so disguises it in the trodden dust that the unwary do not notice it, so fine is it, and so artfully disposed. He threatens travellers with such yells that he drives them terrified onto the net. / With bellows of mirth, he drags them, wrapped in the net, into his lair, showing no regard for knights nor damsels, whatever their dignity. He eats their flesh, sucks their brains and blood, and abandons their bones to the desert; and his house is hideously adorned with human skins hung all about. / Take this other road, then, my son; it will bring you safely to the sea.'

'I thank you, father, for your counsel,' the knight answered, unshaken, 'but in defence of my honour, which I value far more than my life, I discount every peril. You speak to me in vain of crossing the river; I shall keep straight on in order to find this cave. / By avoiding him I can save myself dishonourably; but such safety I abhor worse than death. If I go on, the worst that can befall me is to join many another in losing my life. But if God directs my arms, and the giant dies while I remain alive, I shall make the road safe for thousands: thus the advantages outweigh the drawbacks, / for I weigh one life against the safety of countless travellers.' 'Go in peace, my son,' replied the hermit: 'and may God send the archangel Michael from the highest Heaven to protect you.' And the simple hermit blessed him.

Astolfo continued along the bank of the Nile, placing greater reliance on his horn than on his sword. / Between the deep river and the swamp a little path ran along the sandy bank; this path was blocked by the lone house, a place devoid of humanity or normal human commerce. It was hung about with the skulls and bare limbs of the unfortunates who happened upon this spot; there was not a window, not a projection without at least one to be seen hanging from it. / In Alpine houses and castles the huntsman who has encountered great perils will often nail to the door the shaggy hides, grim paws, and great heads of bears; similarly the savage giant displayed the more powerful of the victims to cross his path. The bones of countless others could be seen scattered about, and every ditch was filled with human blood. / There he was on his threshold, this callous monster, who adorned his house with dead folk the way others deck theirs with purple and gold hangings. His name was Caligorant. Seeing the duke approaching from the distance, he could scarcely contain himself for joy: two months had elapsed, and the third was starting, since a knight last happened this way. / He hastened off towards the swamp which was thickly grown with dark green rushes, as his plan was to make a broad sweep and come out behind Astolfo's back; he hoped to drive him into the net concealed in the sand the way he had driven other travellers unfortunate enough to venture here. /

Seeing his approach the paladin reined in his steed, not a little uneasy that he might set foot on the net the hermit had warned him about. Now it was that he had recourse to his horn, which produced its usual effect when he sounded it: the giant was so terror-struck when he heard it that he turned back. / As Astolfo blew his horn, he remained on the alert lest he spring the giant's trap. But the villain fled in blind panic, and did not watch where he was going: such was his fright, he was quite unable to run clear of his own net—in he went and it closed about him, trussing him up and bringing him to the ground. / Feeling safe the moment he saw the giant crash to earth, Astolfo galloped up to him, dismounted, drew his sword, and made to avenge a thousand victims. But then he decided that to slay a foe thus netted would be deemed a cowardly rather than a valiant act, for Caligorant, he saw, had his arms, feet, and neck so pinioned that he could not move a muscle. /

Vulcan had made the net out of finest steel meshes but with such craft that to try snapping the weakest link would have been a wasted effort. This was the net with which he had bound Venus and Mars hand and foot—the jealous god had made it for no other purpose than to catch the pair of them in bed. / Then Mercury stole the net from the blacksmith-god; he wanted it to catch Cloris with, fair Cloris who flies after Aurora when the Sun rises, and scatters lilies, roses, and violets from her lap. Mercury lay in wait for this nymph until one day he netted her on the wing. / He caught the goddess in flight where the great river which rises in Ethiopia flows into the sea. After this the net was preserved for many centuries in the temple of Anubis at Canopus. Three thousand years later Caligorant stole it from the shrine: the impious robber stole it, and burnt down the city and plundered the temple. / He laid it here in the sand to such effect that whoever he pursued stumbled into it; then at the slightest touch it trussed them up, arms, neck, and feet. Astolfo removed a link from it and used it to fasten the robber's hands behind his back; he bound his arms and chest so tight he could not free himself; then he made him stand up. /

After freeing him of his other bonds, for the giant had become gentler than a maiden, he decided to take him along with him and exhibit him in the farms, towns, and castles he came to. He wanted also to keep the net: no finer artefact was ever fashioned with hammer and file. To the giant he assigned the task of carrying it as he led him away on a chain in triumphal pomp. / He also made the giant carry his helmet and shield as though he were his squire. Then he continued his journey, spreading happiness wherever he set foot, now that travellers could go that way in safety. He kept on until he saw the tombs of Memphis close at hand; Memphis was famous for its pyramids. Next he saw populous Cairo. / The crowds came running to have a look at the colossal giant. 'How in the world', they asked each other, 'did this little fellow manage to tie up that big one?' They so pressed Astolfo from every side that he could scarcely advance; and all of them admired and revered him for a thoroughly valiant knight. /

Cairo was not as large then as we are told it is today; today its population is too big even for its eighteen thousand principal streets: its houses are three stories high and even so thousands have to sleep in the road: the sultan lives in a castle remarkable for its size, beauty, and splendour; / and he has housed all under one roof fifteen thousand of his subjects, all of them renegade Christians, with their wives, families, and horses.

Astolfo wanted to visit the lower reaches of the Nile, and see how broad it was where it flowed into the salt sea at Damietta, for he had heard that whoever passed that way was killed or captured: / on the bank by the river mouth stands a tower, the lair of a brigand who goes about robbing everybody and terrorizes the villagers and way-farers as far afield as Cairo. No one can resist him, and rumour has it that there is no slaying him—he has received already a hundred thousand wounds, but to kill him has proved impossible. / To see if he could not snap the life-thread Fate allotted him, so that he might live no longer, Astolfo went in search of Orrilo (to give the brigand his name) and came to Damietta, beyond which, where the Nile entered the sea, he saw by the river bank the great tower which was home to this charmed creature, offspring of a gnome and a fairy. /

Here he found a savage battle in progress between Orrilo and two warriors. Orrilo was alone, but he was pressing his two opponents so hard it was all they could do to ward him off—and their prowess at arms was generally recognized, for they were none other than Grifon the White and Aquilant the Black, the sons of Oliver. / True, the sorcerer had a distinct advantage as he joined battle: he had brought with him a beast only to be met with in those parts—it lives on the river bank and in the water, and feeds on human flesh, the flesh of poor, incautious travellers and hapless sailors. / Now the beast lay dead in the sand near the port, slain by the two brothers; but if these now attacked Orrilo, two against one, at least they had not enjoyed an unfair advantage from the start. Several times they had dis-membered, but not killed, him—dismembering would not finish him off, for if he had a hand or leg cut off, he stuck it back on as though it were of wax. / Grifon would split his skull down to the teeth, Aquilant would cleave him down to the chest, but Orrilo only laughed at their blows, while the brothers grew increasingly furious, seeing them all wasted. Anyone who has seen quick-silver dropped from a height (or mercury as the alchemists call it), and noticed the way it fragments into particles which then reunite, would be reminded of this as he looked at Orrilo. / If they lop off his head, Orrilo stoops and gropes about for it; once he has found it he picks it up, this time by the hair, next time by the nose, and sticks it back on his neck, though Heaven knows how he makes it fast. Grifon may scoop it up and lob it into the river, but all to no purpose—Orrilo dives to the bottom like a fish only to clamber ashore with his head safe on his shoulders. /

Two comely ladies, soberly attired—the one dressed in white, the other in black, were watching the savage affray which they had insti-gated. They were good fairies who had brought up these two sons of Oliver; they had rescued them, when still babies, from the talons of two great birds / which had swept them away from their mother, Gismonda, and taken them far from their home. There is no need for me to rehearse the story, for it is familiar to everyone (though our author is mistaken over their father, ascribing the wrong one to them for some odd reason). So the two brothers waged the battle wished onto them by the two ladies. / The daylight, under this sky, had already faded (though in the Fortunate Isles the sun was still high in the heavens), and beneath the uncertain, nebulous moon the shadows reduced visibility when Orrilo retired to his lair—for the white fairy and her sister in black were pleased to defer the grim battle until the new sun showed above the horizon. /

Astolfo had almost from the outset recognized Grifon and Aquilant, by their vigorous sword-play even more than by their emblems, and without standing on ceremony he promptly greeted them. And they, noticing that this man leading the shackled giant was the lord of the leopards (for such were his arms at the English court) welcomed him no less cordially. / The ladies had a palace close by, and hither they brought the knights to take their rest. Handmaids and pages with flaming sconces came out to meet them half-way. The knights entrusted their steeds to grooms, and drew off their armour; then they went into a lovely garden where they found supper ready beside a clear, inviting spring. / The giant they left out in a field, secured with another thick chain to an oak—a good mature one which would not snap at a single jerk. Ten men were posted to guard him, lest he work free in the night and attack them and perhaps do them mischief while they were all unwary and defenceless. / The supper was sumptuous and abundant, but the fare was the least of their pleasures, for they were wrapped up in a discussion about Orrilo and his miraculous propensity for picking up his head or arm from the ground, if you'd thrown it down, and sticking it back on, only to return to the fight more savage than before. The whole thing seemed like a dream, if you thought about it. /

Now Astolfo had already read about Orrilo in his book (the book listing antidotes to magic spells) that there would be no severing soul from body so long as a certain enchanted hair remained on his scalp. Root out or sever that hair, and he must surely resign his spirit. That is what the book says—but nothing of how on such a head of hair to recognize the vital one. / Astolfo was exhilarated about his victory as though he had already won it: he expected to root out the hair, and the living soul, from the magician with a few strokes of the sword. So he promised to assume the entire burden of the enterprise himself and slay Orrilo, if the two brothers did not mind his entering the battle. / But they, convinced that he would spend his energy in vain, willingly relinquished the task to him.

The sky was already bright with the new dawn when Orrilo came down from his walls onto the plain. Battle was joined between him and the duke; Orrilo wielded a club while Astolfo, sword in hand, waited to deliver that one stroke in a thousand which would release the brigand's soul from his body. / Now Astolfo lopped off his hand clenched round the club; now he sliced away one arm or the other; now he split his breastplate right across, now he carved him into slivers—but Orrilo simply gathered his limbs up off the ground each time and became whole again. Had Astolfo chopped him into a hundred pieces, the knight would have seen him reassembled the next moment. / Finally that one in a thousand strokes caught him between the shoulders and the chin, and took off his head and helmet. Astolfo was off his horse as fast as Orrilo, twined his hand round the bloody locks and was up in the saddle in a trice; now he galloped towards the Nile with the head so that Orrilo could not recover it. / The poor fool hunted for his head in the dust, not realizing what had happened; but the moment he heard the horse galloping off, bearing his head away into the bush, he ran to his own steed, leapt into the saddle and was off in pursuit. He would have shouted 'Stop! Come back!' except that his mouth was now in the duke's hands. / At least he had not been deprived of his heels, so he spurred his horse in hot pursuit. Rabican, though, galloped like a dream and left him far behind, while Astolfo hastily searched the skull from nape to brow hoping to recognize the enchanted hair which gave Orrilo his immortality. /

In such a thick crop of hair there was none which grew longer or more curly than the rest; which one, then, was Astolfo to pick out and sever if he was to kill the miscreant? Better, he decided, to cut or pluck the lot; and for lack of a razor or scissors, he had recourse to his sword, whose razor-edge could shave. / Grasping the head by the nose, he shaved off the hair back and front, till he chanced upon the fated one among the rest; at once the face turned to a hideous pallor, the eyes showed white and the presence of death became clear from many signs. And the headless trunk which galloped in pursuit fell from the saddle and gave a final shudder. /

Astolfo returned to where he had left the ladies and the knights: in his hand he held the head which showed all the authentic signs of lifelessness, and he pointed away to the prostrate trunk. I am not sure how pleased they were to see it, though they put on a civil face for him—but the two brothers might have been eaten with envy at having the victory snatched from their hands. / And I doubt whether the two ladies were any better pleased at the outcome: they had contrived this battle between Orrilo and the brothers in the hope of delaying them here long enough to avoid the pernicious effects of a star which fated them to an early end in France. / As soon as the warden of

Damietta had established that Orrilo was dead, he released a dove with a letter tied beneath its wing. The dove flew to Cairo, where another dove was released for the next destination, as was the custom in those parts. Thus in a matter of hours Orrilo's death was known throughout Egypt. /

Having accomplished this exploit, the duke exhorted the noble youths to leave off fighting in the Orient and seek honour among their own people by coming to the defence of Holy Church and the Holy Roman Empire; the brothers required little prompting or encouragement, for their thoughts were already turned that way. / So Grifon and Aquilant each took leave of his lady, and the ladies, much though it grieved them, could not stand in their way. Leaving with Astolfo, they turned to their right, proposing to pay their respects to the holy places where God lived as man, before they made towards France. / They could have taken a road to the left, which was pleasanter and smoother going, and hugged the sea-coast, but they took the right-hand way, a weird, wild road which shortened the journey to the lofty city of Jerusalem by six days. Water and grass was to be found along the way, but it was totally lacking in all else. / So before they set out they assembled everything they needed for their journey and loaded their baggage and provisions onto the giant—who could still have carried a whole tower on his shoulders. At the end of the rough and rugged road, from a high mountain they set eyes on the holy land where the Supreme Love washed away our sins in His blood. /

As they entered the city they came upon an acquaintance, a nobleman in the flower of his youth, Samsonet of Mecca; he was wise beyond his years, highly chivalrous, renowned for his kindness and respected by the people. Orlando had converted him to our faith and even baptized him by his own hand. / They found him planning fortifications to resist the caliph of Egypt; he meant to enclose the hill of Calvary with a two-mile wall. The welcome he accorded them came from the heart, as was obvious from his face. He brought them in and lodged them most comfortably in his royal palace— / for he reigned over Jerusalem, holding just sway as regent for Charlemagne. Duke Astolfo made him a present of the great overgrown hulk who could replace ten beasts of burden, such was his strength. With the giant he gave him also the net which had put the giant at his mercy. / For his part, Samsonet gave the duke a fine, costly sword-belt, and a pair of spurs (each with a rowel and fastening of gold): these were supposed to have belonged to St. George, the knight who saved the damsel from the dragon. Samsonet had acquired them along with other booty when he had taken Jaffa. / They purged their sins in a monastery fragrant with the odour of good example, and, contemplating the mysteries of Christ's passion, they visited every shrine—Christian shrines now, to their eternal shame and degradation, usurped by the impious Moors. Europe is in arms and aches to do battle everywhere, except where battle is needed. /

While they were devoutly concentrating on penance and devotions, a pilgrim from Greece, an acquaintance of Grifon, brought him painful news which could not at all be reconciled with the accomplishment of his present intention, his long-made vow. The news so seared his heart that it drove out all thought of prayer. / The knight, poor fellow, loved a damsel called Orrigilla. A prettier face and comelier build you would not find in a thousand of her kind; but she had a wayward, fickle disposition the like of which you would not discover, I imagine, if you searched town and country, the mainland and the islands in the sea. / He had left her behind in Constantinople, where she had been prostrated by a severe bout of fever. Now while he had been hoping to go back and find her more beautiful than ever, and to enjoy her, he learned that she had gone to Antioch with a new lover: to continue sleeping on her own seemed to her pointless, for she was young and tender. /

From the moment he heard these sad tidings Grifon sighed night and day, and the pleasures which normally procure happiness and well-being only seemed to render him more disconsolate. (Let anyone who has felt the sting of Eros consider how well honed he keeps his darts!) The worst feature of his torment was that he was ashamed to confess it: / a thousand times his more judicious brother Aquilant had chided him for this infatuation and tried to root it out of his heart, deeming her the worst of worthless women. But Grifon would find excuses for her every time his brother spoke against her, and time and again he would knowingly deceive himself. / So, without a word to Aquilant, Grifon decided to go his own way to Antioch, to fetch away the damsel who had stolen his heart, and to find her seducer and wreak on him such vengeance that it would be talked of for ever after. In the next canto I shall describe how he carried out his plan and what resulted from it.

SIXTEENTH CANTO

1–4 Introductory. 5–16 Grifon meets Orrigilla and her lover
who fool him. 16–84 Outside the walls of Paris, Rinaldo and
the British engage the Moors in battle. 85–89 Within the
walls Charlemagne moves against Rodomont.

LOVE brings in his train heavy sorrows; I myself have tasted most of
them, indeed they have crowded so thick upon me that I can speak of
them as an expert. Now if I say—and have said before, sometimes in
spoken, sometimes in written words—that Love's pains vary, from the
trivial to the excruciating, believe me: I speak truly. / I say now as I
have said before and shall say till I die: the man who is captivated by a
worthy affection, though he see his lady shun him, though she be
totally rebellious to his inflamed desire, though Love treat him quite
without mercy after all the time and effort he has devoted to cultivate
him—so long as that man has placed his affections on a worthy object, though he languish and die, let him not weep. / Let him weep,
though, who has enslaved himself to a pair of alluring eyes, a pretty
head of hair, and, beneath it, a callous heart, compounded of little gold
and much dross. Such a man fain would escape, but, like a stricken
hart, carries the arrow embedded wherever he goes. He is ashamed
of himself and of his love, but dares not avow it, and vainly longs to be
healed. / Such is the case of young Grifon: he sees his error but cannot
mend it; he sees how abject is his love for Orrigilla, a despicable,
faithless woman; but evil habit has got the better of right reason;
judgement has yielded place to appetite. Be she never so fickle, thankless, and mean, he needs must seek her company. /

Now to resume our story: Grifon slipped secretly out of the city,
not hazarding a word to his brother, who had reproached him so often
in vain. He bore left down the hill towards Rama, taking the quicker,
more level road, and in six days reached Syrian Damascus, from where
he continued towards Antioch. / Near Damascus he came upon the
knight to whom Orrigilla had given her heart. The two of them
were as well assorted in their evil ways as are flowers and grass: they
both were false of heart, both treacherous and untrustworthy; and
they both disguised their faults—to the cost of others—behind an
outward charm of manner. / As I say, the knight was armed, in
splendid array, and mounted on a tall charger. With him rode base

Orrigilla; she was dressed in blue trimmed with gold. Two pages rode beside him to carry his helmet and shield, for he was on his way to a tournament at Damascus and wanted to mount a good display. / The King of Damascus had just announced a sumptuous celebration, which is what was bringing knights to the city in all the splendour they could muster.

The moment the trollop set eyes on Grifon she feared exposure to shame and insult, well knowing that her lover was not strong enough to survive Grifon's onslaught. / But, brazen and wily as could be, she set her face and mastered her voice so as to conceal all sign of fear— though inwardly she was quaking with fright. She had hit upon a stratagem in concert with her lover: she ran up to Grifon, therefore, feigning transports of joy, and spread her arms and flung them round his neck in a long, clinging embrace. / Then, matching affectionate gestures to honeyed words, 'My lord,' she cried tearfully, 'is this a well deserved reward to one who adores and worships you? A whole year have I been alone without you, and another is starting, and still you have not missed me. Had I gone on waiting for your return, I know not whether I should ever have seen the day. / After you had gone to Nicosia, to attend the great celebrations, and I was waiting for you to come back to me—had you not left me at death's door, prostrate with fever?—I learnt that you had gone on into Syria. This news came as such a grievous blow to me, as I knew not how to follow you there, that I nearly pierced my heart by my own hand. / But Fortune with a double gift has shown me that she, unlike you, has care of me: she sent my brother to me, in whose company I have travelled thus far without risk to my honour. Now she sends me this second blessing, which I prize above every happy accident: you. But she had been only just in time—had she waited, I should have died craving, my lord, for you.' / The artful woman, who could have outwitted a fox, embroidered her reproaches so astutely that she quite turned the tables on Grifon: she had him see in her lover not simply her kinsman but in very flesh and blood a second father to her. She could weave her yarn to such effect that Luke and John seemed less truthful by comparison. /

Not merely did Grifon not rebuke the woman, whose wickedness surpassed her beauty, for her perfidy; not merely did he not exact vengeance from the man who was now her lover: but if he defended himself when she loaded all the blame onto him, that was as much as he was prepared to do. And he was very cordial towards the other knight, as though they indeed were brothers-in-law. / Together they travelled towards the gates of Damascus, and as they journeyed, the knight told Grifon about the sumptuous tournament the wealthy

Syrian king was holding there. Everyone, he explained, regardless
of his condition, and whether Christian or not, was assured of safety
within the city and without for the duration of the festivities. /

In her day treacherous Orrigilla had betrayed not one but a thousand of her lovers. Hers is a story, however, which I can interrupt
long enough to return to the host two hundred thousand strong—
more numerous than the sparks flying up from the prodded fire—
which was sowing terror and destruction round the walls of Paris. / I
left off where Agramant was attacking a gate which he expected to
find undefended; at no point, however, were the fortifications better
safeguarded, for Charles in person commanded there, assisted by
champions at arms—the two Guidos, two Angelinos, Angeliero, Avino,
Avolio, Otho, and Berenger. / In the presence of Charles and Agramant each company strove to distinguish itself: highest praise and
abundant rewards were to be expected by those who stood to their
duty. The Moors, however, did not excel themselves sufficiently to
earn rewards on a par with their losses—several of them lost their
lives, an example to their fellows of bravery carried to the point of
folly. / The arrows discharged from the walls onto the attackers looked
for all the world like a hail-storm. Terrifying was the war-cry raised to
the heavens by the two opposing forces. But Charles and Agramant
will have to wait a while, for I must speak of that African war-god,
terrible Rodomont, who was scouring the city. /

I do not know, my Lord, whether you still remember this Saracen
of boundless temerity, who had left his men to be devoured between
the inner and the outer walls by the greedy flames—never was there a
ghastlier sight. I told how he leapt into the city across the fosse which
encircled it. / When news got about of the barbarous Saracen with the
weird arms and scaly hide, the elderly and those not given to fighting
—folk who strained their ears to every rumour—set up a loud wail,
wrung their hands in terror, and assailed the stars with high-pitched
shrieks. Those who could flee lost no time in locking themselves into
their homes or churches. / But the mighty Saracen, swinging his
wicked sword round his head, allowed but few to escape. Here he
lopped off a foot with half a leg, there he sent a head flying from its
shoulders; one man saw himself sliced across the middle, the next
was neatly split open from head to hip. Many were those he slew,
chased, and wounded, but not one of them received a scratch to his
face. /

As the tigress treats a peaceable herd in the fields of Hyrcania or
beside the Ganges; as the wolf treats the goats and ewes up on the
mountain which crushes Typheus; thus did the cruel pagan treat those
. . . cohorts, shall I call them? Phalanxes? No—that common rabble,

folk fit to die even before their birth. / Out of all those whom he slashed, stabbed, and slit there was not one who would turn to show his face. Fierce, terrible Rodomont charged down the street leading straight to St. Michael's Bridge; it was crowded with people, and he wheeled his bloody sword about him, making no distinction between master and servant, showing no greater mercy to the good than to the wicked. / To the priest his ministry was no safeguard; innocence availed nothing to the little child, nor did soft eyes and rosy cheeks to women and maids; the aged were herded and stricken down. Here the Saracen gave greater proof of cruelty than of valour, paying no regard to sex, rank, or age. / The impious king, master and chief of all the wicked, assuaged his wrath not only in human blood: he turned also against the houses, setting fire to the fair dwellings and desecrated shrines. In those days the houses were, from what we are told, nearly all of wood; this can be readily believed, for even today six out of ten houses are built in Paris thus. / Though everything was consumed by fire, it was evident that a rage as mighty as his could still not be sated. He took care so to grapple with his hands that at each tug he brought down another building. Believe me, my Lord, never did you see a cannon at Padua of sufficient calibre to bring a wall down in such sections as did Rodomont in a single jerk. /

If, while the fiend was wreaking his devastation with sword and fire, Agramant had broken through from outside, the whole city would have been taken that very day. But this was not to be, for an obstacle was provided by Rinaldo, the paladin who had arrived from England leading the troops of England and Scotland, escorted by Silence and the archangel Michael. / God willed that while Rodomont broke into the city and set it ablaze, Rinaldo, flower of the house of Clairmont, should reach the walls with the English host. Three leagues upstream he had thrown a bridge across the Seine and taken a roundabout path to the left, aiming to attack the Saracens without having the river across his path. / He had detached six thousand bowmen from the infantry under the exalted standard of Edward, and two thousand or more light horse under bold Harriman, and sent them on by the roads connecting Paris with the coast of Picardy, to enter the city by the gates of St. Martin and St. Denis and come to its relief. / With them he sent forward the waggons and baggage train. He himself set off upstream with the rest of the army on a flanking movement. They were equipped with boats, pontoons, and all that was needed to cross the Seine, which was not fordable. Once they were all across, and the bridges were destroyed, he marshalled the English and Scots into companies. /

But first, gathering the barons and commanders about him, and standing on a bank elevated above the level ground, so that they could all see and hear him, he spoke to them: 'Gentlemen, you have good cause to raise your hands to God who has brought you here so that, after expending only a little sweat, you may be distinguished by Him above every other nation. / Two princes will be saved by your hands, if you raise the siege laid to these gates: your king, whom you are bound to defend against bondage and death, and an emperor, one of the most highly praised of any who has held court in this world of ours; and with them, other kings, dukes and marquises, barons, and knights from many lands. / Saving this one city, it is not only the Parisians whom you shall put into your debt—and they are afflicted with terror and dismay not so much for their own sufferings as for those of their wives and children who must endure the same dangers, and for the holy virgins in the convents, lest their prayers today prove in vain— / saving this city, I say, it is not only the Parisians you'll oblige, but all the countries around. I am speaking not only of the neighbouring peoples: there is not a state in Christendom but has citizens within these walls—if you win, believe me, it will be not only France which owes you a debt. / If the men of old presented a wreath to the man who saved a citizen's life, what reward will be your due if you save a countless multitude? But if jealousy or cowardice obstructs so good and holy an enterprise, believe me, once these walls have fallen, neither Italy nor Germany shall be safe any longer, / nor any other region where He is worshipped who submitted to hang for us on the wood of the Cross. Do not rely on the Moors' keeping their distance, nor on your power at sea to keep your kingdom secure: if before now they have sallied out from Gibraltar and the Pillars of Hercules to make depredations along your shores, what will they stop at once they have overrun our territories? / Now even if no considerations of honour or advantage urged you to this task, it is still a common duty for those who march under the banner of the same Church to come to each other's assistance. Let no one doubt but that I shall deliver you a victory, routing the enemy with but little resistance: they seem to me an untrained host, timid, weak, and poorly-armed.' /

With these and better arguments, with swift eloquence, and ringing tones Rinaldo stirred up those brave barons, that fierce host; but here, as in the proverb, it was like spurring a mettlesome steed which was already at full gallop. He ended his harangue and ordered the companies to fall in quietly behind their ensigns. / Quite noiselessly he set the three-part army on the move. To Zerbin and his Scots he allotted the honour of advancing along the river and engaging the barbarians first; the Irish contingents he sent on a wide sweep through the deep country; the English horse and foot he held in the centre under the Duke of Lancaster. / When he had given them all their marching orders, Rinaldo rode out along the river bank and drew ahead of good Duke Zerbin and his troops; in a while therefore he came up against the King of Oran and King Sobrino with their army; they were stationed half a mile from the Spanish contingents and were keeping watch on this stretch of country. / The Christians, who had arrived under the faithful escort of Silence and the archangel, could no longer contain themselves in silence. Getting wind of the enemy, they raised a shout and their trumpets pealed out stridently; Heaven rang with the almighty din, and the Saracens' blood ran cold. /

Rinaldo spurred his horse ahead, settled his lance, and charged, leaving the Scots a good arrow's flight behind, so loath was he to delay engaging combat. Like a whirlwind heralding a dreadful tempest, such was the dashing knight as he spurred his charger Bayard out ahead of the ranks. / At the paladin's onset, the Moors showed signs of nervousness—lances trembled in the hand, feet in the stirrups, posteriors in the saddle. Only King Pulian did not change colour, for he did not realize this was Rinaldo. Little dreaming what obstacle he was up against, he made for him at a gallop, / setting his lance in rest and crouching into the saddle; he urged his steed with both spurs and dropped the reins on his neck. His adversary made no mere show of valour, but demonstrated in practical terms just what his renown rested upon, his smoothness and skill in mounted combat: Aymon's son might have been son of Mars. / In aiming their dire thrusts they were on a par, for each struck home at the other's head; but in strength and agility they were unevenly matched, for one drew away, the other fell dead. Clearer signs of prowess are needed than nimbly settling one's lance, though good luck is needed even more—for lack of it, prowess seldom if ever wins the day. /

Rinaldo withdrew his sturdy lance and charged at the King of Oran, a man of meagre courage though well endowed with flesh and bone. He fetched him a blow which can be accounted a master-stroke, though it struck the bottom of the king's shield; but if you must deny him praise for this, he has an excuse—he could not reach him any higher. / The king's shield could not oppose the lance-thrust, for all that it was made of palm-wood overlaid with steel. Out from his great belly his little, undersized soul made its escape. His steed, resigned to bearing so great a load on his back for the rest of the day, inwardly thanked Rinaldo: this one clash was to spare him a hot day's work. / His lance broken, he turned his steed—so light-footed he might have been winged—and drove full-tilt into the thick of the throng. He brandished bloody Fusberta before him, a sword to make all armour seem like brittle glass. No tempered steel could resist his cuts, but he must feel out living flesh at each stroke. / The sharp blade encountered little in the way of tempered metal, but rather bucklers of leather or wood, padded jerkins, winding turbans. No wonder, then, if Rinaldo floored, spiked, ripped, and sliced whomsoever he attacked—they could no more withstand his sword than can grass the scythe, standing corn the tempest. /

The first battalion had already been routed when Zerbin arrived with his advance guard; he rode ahead of his numerous host, his lance in rest, while his troops surged after his pennant with no less fierce a mien—they might have been a pack of wolves, or lions, going after lambs or goats. / As they drew close the mounted men each spurred his horse at the same moment: in a trice the brief space between the opposing forces dwindled to nothing. Now they led each other the unlikeliest dance: the Scots did all the striking, the pagans all the dying, as though they had been led to battle for no other purpose. / The pagans all seemed colder than ice, the Scots hotter than fire. The Moors imagined that every Christian must have an arm as heavy as Rinaldo's.

Now Sobrino launched his battalions into the fray without awaiting the herald's summons. His troops were superior to those others in leadership, weapons, and valour. / His were the least abject of the African troops, though even the best of them were pretty worthless. Dardinel now advanced his contingent, men untrained for battle and poorly armed, though he himself wore a shiny helmet and was clad in plate-armour and chain-mail. The fourth battalion, I think, was better, the one with which Isolier was bringing up the rear. /

Meanwhile Trason, the worthy Duke of Moray, delighted to take a hand in this noble venture, seeing and hearing Isolier commit his Navarrese to battle, threw the field open to his knights, bidding them join him in seeking glory. Then Ariodant, newly-created Duke of Albany, moved his men up. / The shrill screech of the sonorous trumpets, the din of drums, and barbarous instruments combined with the constant hum of arrows and shot, the rumble of siege-engines, wheels, mounted catapults, and the even higher pitched tumult of shrieks, groans, wails—all together produced an uproar not unlike the Nile cataracts, deafening the whole neighbourhood. / The whole vault of the sky was shadowed by the cloud of arrows shot from each side. The exhalation, the miasma of sweat, the dust, all seemed to infuse a dark fog into the air. Over here one host wheeled, there another; you might see a man pursuing one moment, escaping the next; you could see a man fall dead right on the spot (or close beside) where he had just slain an enemy. / Where one squadron was taken out to rest, another was at once sent forward in its place. Armed men clustered now here now there; here mounted troops were marshalled, infantry there. The ground beneath the clashing forces was red. The green had put on a bloody mantle, and where there had been blue and yellow flowers, now men and horses lay dead. / Zerbin wrought feats quite remarkable for a youth of his years; the pagan hordes flowed in from all sides but he hacked and hewed and utterly butchered them. Ariodant gave his new retainers a fair demonstration of his valour, and inculcated fear and wonder into the foe—troops from Castille and Navarre. /

Chelindo and Mosco, the two bastard sons of Calabrun, late King of Aragon, and Calamidor of Barcelona, who enjoyed a reputation as a fighter, had advanced ahead of the standards and, expecting to win glory and a crown by slaying Zerbin, they attacked him and stabbed his charger in the flanks. / Pierced by three lances the horse fell dead, but good Zerbin was on his feet at once and vengefully made for the trio who had so ill-treated his steed. His first victim was Mosco; the unwary youth stood over Zerbin, all set to take him prisoner, but the Scottish prince lunged and ran him through the side, pitching him from the saddle cold and pale. / Seeing his brother removed from the scene almost by stealth, Chelindo flew into a rage and rushed at the Scot meaning to bowl him over. But Zerbin grasped Chelindo's steed by the reins and jerked it to the ground, whence it never arose: never more was it to taste oats nor hay, for Zerbin put such power into his sword-stroke that he dispatched horse and rider at one blow. / Calamidor witnessed this stroke, and hastily turned his steed to make off, but Zerbin slashed at him savagely crying 'Wait, you villain!' The blow did not land where it was aimed, though it was not far off: it fell short of the rider, but caught the steed on the rump and laid it prostrate. / Abandoning his horse, Calamidor crawled away towards safety, but to no avail—Duke Trason happened by and rode right over him, crushing him under his weight. Ariodant and Lurcanio took their station where Zerbin was caught in the thick of the contenders; with them were other knights and barons all doing their best to procure the prince another mount. / Ariodant laid about him with his sword, as Artalic and Margan learned to their cost, though it was Etearch and Casimir who really sampled the strength of his arm: whereas the first two escaped with wounds, the last two were left dead on the field. Lurcanio showed the measure of his strength as he slashed, and clouted, flattened, and slaughtered. /

Do not imagine, my Lord, that the battle being fought further afield was less fierce than it was by the river, or that the troops led by the good Duke of Lancaster were hanging back. They attacked the Spanish standards, and the fortunes of the field were evenly balanced, for on both sides commanders and troops, mounted and on foot, were no mean fighters. / In front marched Oldrade, Duke of Gloucester and Fieramont, Duke of York; with them came Richard, Earl of Warwick, and bold Henry, Duke of Clarence. Confronting these were Matalista of Almeria, Follicon of Granada, and Baricondo of Majorca with their troops. / The fierce combat showed them evenly matched, and no advantage could be discerned to either side; now one side, now the other could be seen advancing, then withdrawing, like wheat in the gentle May breezes, or like the restless sea along the shore, washing in and out, never setting a constant course. After Fortune had played her game awhile, she ultimately turned hostile to the Moors. / All in a moment the Duke of Gloucester pitched Matalista out of his saddle, Fieramont overthrew Follicon, wounding him in the right shoulder, and, while both pagans were caught and taken prisoner by the English, the Duke of Clarence made an end of Baricondo. / This put such dread into the pagans, such ardour into the Faithful, that the former could do nothing but draw back, break ranks, and flee, while the latter kept pressing forward and gaining ground, harassing, and pursuing; had not help been at hand, the pagans on that quarter would have lost the field. / But Ferrau, who up to this point had never moved from the side of his sovereign, King Marsilius, on seeing the standard in full retreat and half his battalions destroyed, spurred his steed and urged him into the thick of the fighting.

As he arrived, he saw Olimpio da la Serra fall from his horse, his head split open. / Olimpio was a youth who could sing so sweetly to the accompaniment of the horn-shaped lyre that he boasted of softening even the flintiest of hearts. Happy he, had he known how to rest content with eminence such as this, and hold in disgust shield, bow and quiver, lance and scimitar which had brought him to an early death in France! / Ferrau loved him well and held him in high esteem; seeing him fall, then, he was far more distressed than at the sight of a thousand who had fallen earlier. He brought his sword down on Olimpio's slayer with such force that he cleft him from crown to chest, dividing his helmet, forehead, eyes, and face, and threw him dead to the ground. / Without pausing he went on whirling his sword about him, splitting helmets, slashing coats of mail, leaving his mark here on a forehead, there on a cheek, slicing off one man's head, another's arm, spilling out blood and life. He stabilized the battle on that front, where the quaking rabble had been fleeing in total disarray. / King Agramant now stepped into the fray, eager to show his mettle and join in the slaughter; with him were Baliverzo, Farurant, Prusion, Soridan, and Bambirago; as to the nameless folk whose blood they were to spill today—enough to fill a lake—they are so numerous that I should find it easier to count each fallen leaf when Autumn strips the trees. / Agramant withdrew a large contingent of horse and foot from the walls and sent them under the King of Fez to pass behind the tents and take up a position facing the Irish, whom he could see hastening in a broad flanking movement to sweep in and occupy the pagan camp. / The King of Fez quickly put this order into effect, for any delay would have been too costly.

Meanwhile Agramant called together his reserves, redeployed them, and sent them into battle. He himself set out for the river, for this is where he felt his presence was needed—a messenger had come hence from King Sobrino with a request for help. / With him Agramant brought more than half the entire host: just the noise they made was enough to make the Scots quail—such was their dismay, they broke ranks and sacrificed their honour. Zerbin, Lurcanio, and Ariodant alone stood fast against the onslaught, and Zerbin might well have perished, being on foot, but good Rinaldo spotted him in time. / The paladin had in the meantime routed a hundred standards; now, on hearing the grim tidings that Zerbin was in grave danger, alone, on foot, abandoned by his troops to the hosts of North Africa, he turned his horse and galloped to where the Scots were in full flight. / He arrived where he saw the Scots in hasty retreat, and cried out: 'Where are you off to? What is the meaning of this cowardice, abandoning the field to such a worthless foe? Look at them—there are the spoils I mean you to take home, to deck your churches with. What praise, what glory is yours, deserting your sovereign's son and leaving him alone and on foot!' /

Seizing a heavy lance from one of his squires, he espied Prusion, King of the Alvaracks, hard by, and closed in on him; he swept him from the saddle to lay him dead on the plain, then he slew Agricalt and overthrew Bambirago; next he inflicted a grave wound on Soridan, and would have finished him off like the others had his lance stood up to the task. / When his lance snapped, he drew Fusberta and scathed Serpentine da la Stella, who wore enchanted armour; nonetheless the blow was enough to stun him and topple him from the saddle. Thus Rinaldo cleared an ample space about the Scottish duke, who now had leisure to lay hands on one of the riderless steeds and mount it. / He was in the saddle none too soon; a moment's delay might have made him too late, for Agramant had arrived with Dardinel, Sobrino, and King Balastro. But Zerbin, once more ahorse, laid about him with his sword, dispatching one foe after the next down to Hades to bring news of conditions in the modern world. / Good Rinaldo made a point of laying low the most dangerous of the enemy, so he turned his sword against King Agramant, who seemed to him somewhat too fierce and bold: all alone he wrought more damage than a thousand, so the paladin rode at him on Bayard and struck him a slanting blow which knocked him and his mount onto their backs. /

While outside the walls cruel battle was raging as Hatred, Wrath, and Violence assailed each other, within Paris, Rodomont was slaughtering the citizens and setting fire to the churches and fair houses. Charlemagne, occupied in another quarter, saw nothing, and as yet knew nothing, of this. He welcomed Edward and Harriman into the city with their Englishmen. / A page approached him, ashen-faced and utterly breathless. 'Alas, my Lord, alas!' he exclaimed over and over before he could bring out anything else. 'Today the Roman Empire—today it is buried—today Christ has forsaken His people— today the devil has rained down from the sky to make this city unfit for man to dwell in. / Satan (it can be none but he) is bringing our poor city to wrack and ruin. Turn and look at the smoke spiralling up from the devouring blaze. Listen to the lamentations assailing the Heavens—they bear out what your servant says. He is but a single man who is ravaging our fair city with fire and the sword, and all flee before him.' / Imagine a man who hears a tumult and the frenzied clanging of church bells before he sees the fire which is no secret to any but himself, though he is the one most directly affected. Thus was Charlemagne when he heard of this remarkable incursion and then discovered it with his own eyes.

At once he directed the efforts of his best troops in the direction of the cries and uproar he could hear. / He summoned to his side a majority of his paladins and his champions, and had the standards borne towards the main square, for that was where the intruder had reached. He heard the tumult, and saw the grisly signs of the pagan's cruelty—human limbs scattered all over the place. No more for now: he who wishes to hear my pleasant tale, let him return another time.

SEVENTEENTH CANTO

_1-6 Introductory. 6-16 In Paris Charlemagne moves
against Rodomont. 17-24 Grifon arrives in Damascus for the
tournament, with Martano and Orrigilla. 25-68 The story
of King Norandin and monstrous Orcus. 69-135 The
tournament at Damascus, and the evil trick played on
Grifon by Martano and Orrigilla._

WHEN our sins have passed the bounds of forgiveness, God, in His
justice, to show equity on a par with His mercy, often gives power to
unspeakable tyrants, to utter monsters, and endows them with the
compulsion and the cunning to work evil. Thus He gave the world
Marius and Sulla, Tiberius and Nero, insane Caligula, / Domitian
and Heliogabalus, last of the Antonines; out of the common rabble
He called forth Maximinus and raised him to the imperial throne;
earlier, He had permitted the birth of Creon at Thebes; and to the
Etruscans He gave Mezentius, who nourished the soil with human
blood; in a less remote era He gave Italy in prey to the Huns, Goths,
and Lombards. / What shall I say of Attila? What of wicked Ezzellino
da Romano and a hundred like them, whom God inflicted upon us, to
plague and torment us, after we had strayed too long from the path of
virtue? Not only in ages past but in our own day we have clear
evidence of this, when to guard us, unprofitable and ill-born flock,
He has appointed vicious wolves for keepers: / men whose own hunger
evidently is not enough, nor their maws capacious enough to stomach
so much meat, but they needs must call in wolves with even greedier
appetites from the forests beyond the mountains to join in the feast.
The unburied bones of Trasimene, of Cannae and Trebbia seem but
trifling beside those which fertilize the fields and shores between
which the Adda, Mella, Ronco, and Taro flow. / Now God permits us
to be punished by peoples perhaps worse than ourselves, because of
our endless wickedness, our constant shameful ill-doing. The time will
come when we shall go to ravage their shores, if ever we grow better,
and their sins reach the point of moving the Eternal Goodness to
anger. / The Christians' excesses must have vexed the serene face of
the Almighty, for the Turks and Moors had overrun all their lands,
committing rape and murder, pillage and outrage.

But at no one's hands did they suffer worse than at those of rabid

Rodomont. I told how Charlemagne was brought news of him and set off for the main square to confront him. / On the way he saw his people cut to pieces, buildings burnt down, churches in ruins, much of the city laid waste; never was so cruel a sight to be seen. 'Whither are you fleeing in such panic, all you people? Is there not one among you to stop and size up the situation? What city, what refuge is left to you once you have so cravenly deserted this one? / Look at him: one man alone, trapped in your city, surrounded by walls, unable to escape: shall he leave without a blow attempted against him after he has slain every last one of you?' Thus exclaimed Charles in high rage, finding such cowardice insufferable.

He came to where he saw the pagan slaughtering his people, in front of his royal palace. / A large part of the crowd had flowed into the palace, hoping to find refuge here—the building had stout walls and was fortified to withstand sustained attack. Rodomont, beside himself with rage and scorn, had gained possession of the entire square. His hands disdained all men; with one he whirled his sword, with the other he scattered fire. / The great doors of the sublime lofty palace rang as he hammered at them. From the highest rooftops the people, believing their last hour was come, hurled down merlons and turrets; there were none to think twice about wrecking the roof: timber and stone, marble slabs and pillars all went the same way, as also the gilded beams prized by their fathers and grandfathers. / At the gate stood the Algerian king; his head and chest were clad in glistening steel. He was like a serpent issued forth into the light of day: after sloughing off his tarnished skin, he emerges resplendent in his newest scales, feeling fresh life and energy surge through him; his triple tongue vibrates, his eyes flash fire; wherever he moves every creature falls back. /

Stone, merlon, beam, bow, catapult—nothing that falls upon the Saracen from above could arrest his blood-stained right hand as it hacked and hewed and shook the great door. He had cut in it so wide a breach that he could clearly see and be seen through it by the faces crowded inside, all imprinted with the colour of death. / The lofty, spacious halls echoed with shrieks and women's wails: the afflicted women, beating their breasts, ran about the palace, pale and weeping; they clung to the doors and to the marriage beds which soon they must abandon to strangers. This was the perilous situation when the emperor arrived with his barons. / Charlemagne turned to his doughty retainers on whom at other times he had relied in desperate need.

'Are you not the men who were with me in Aspromont', he asked, 'to combat Agolant? And are you now all so bereft of strength that, though you slew him and Trojan and Almont with a hundred thousand others, you now fear a single man, one of the same blood, the same origin? / The might you displayed for me then, am I to see it impaired? Show this dog, this man-eating dog, what you can do. The brave thinks nought of death, whether it come early or late, if only he die well. But while you stand by me, I rely upon you, for you have ever brought me victory.' / This said, he lowered his lance, spurred his steed and charged at the Saracen. Ogier the paladin moved in at the same moment, and so did Namo and Oliver, Avino, Avolio, Otho, and Berenger, whom I can never see apart from each other. They all closed in to strike at Rodomont—aiming at his chest, his sides, his brow. /

But please let us speak no more of wrath, my Lord, nor of death; let this for now be enough about Rodomont, the Saracen whose cruelty matched his strength. It is time to return to Grifon, whom I left at the gates of Damascus with faithless Orrigilla and her would-be brother, in fact her lover. / Damascus is said to be one of the richest cities of the Levant, one of the most populous and splendid: it lies in a fertile, fruitful plain seven days' journey from Jerusalem; it is no less pleasing a spot in winter than in summer. A nearby hill conceals from it the first rays of the rising sun. / Two crystal streams flow through the city, coursing down many channels to irrigate the countless gardens which are always in leaf, always in flower. There is enough rose-water, they say, to turn mill-wheels, and whoever walks through the streets smells fragrant odours issuing from every house. / The principal street was carpeted in gay draperies of various hues; delicious herbs and leafy boughs decked the street and every wall. Every door, every window was hung with the finest draperies and rugs. Even lovelier were the beautiful women decked in costly jewels and gorgeous gowns. / In many houses festive dances could be seen in progress. In the streets the gentry offered a spectacle as they rode by on handsome, gaily caparisoned steeds. Even more splendid was the sight of the wealthy courtiers, the high nobility bedecked with gold and jewels and pearls from the coasts of India and Eritrea. /

Grifon and his companions made their way slowly, taking in everything on either side, until they were detained by a knight who invited them to dismount at a mansion of his, where he saw to it that they lacked for nothing—such being the custom of the place and his natural hospitality. He afforded them a bath, then jovially welcomed them to a sumptuous meal. / He told them how Norandin, King of Damascus and all Syria, had sent out invitations to all who belonged to the order of knighthood, be they citizens or strangers, bidding them to a tournament which was to be held the following morning in the public square. If any man were as valorous as he looked, here was his chance to give proof of it. / Although Grifon had not come for this purpose, he accepted the invitation—no occasion to prove his valour was to be eschewed. He questioned their host as to the occasion for this celebration, whether it was an annual rite or a new idea of the king's to try the mettle of his subjects. /

'The celebration is to be held every fourth moon,' their host replied. 'This one, though, is the first in the series—there has been none previous to this. It is to commemorate the day the king was saved by a rare stroke of fortune, after four months of constant grief and tears, with death ever in prospect. / Let me tell you the story:

'Norandin our king for many years was devoured with love for the graceful daughter of the King of Cyprus. She was of surpassing beauty. Finally he had her to wife and, accompanied by gentlemen-at-arms and ladies, he set out with her to return directly to Syria. / Once we were well out to sea and had been driven under full sail into the mischievous Carpathian channel, so wild a storm blew up that it alarmed even our veteran shipmaster. Three days and three nights we drifted off course amid the threatening seas until finally, exhausted and soaked through, we made land. Here we found fresh streams and green, shady hills. / We happily pitched our tents and strung up curtaining among the trees; fires were lit, cooking ranges prepared, and elsewhere tables were laid out on carpets. Meanwhile the king set off for the neighbouring valleys and vanished into the depths of the woods in search of game—goats, fawns, or stags. Two servants attended him to carry his bow. /

'While we were sitting there blithely waiting for our king to return from his hunting, we saw running towards us along the sea-shore a horrible monster: God preserve you, sir, from ever setting eyes on the hideous face of Orcus: better that you should hear of him by repute rather than approach him close enough to see him with your own eyes. / There was no gauging his height, he was so immeasurably huge. Instead of eyes he had two fungus-hued bones protruding from his forehead. He came towards us along the beach, as I said, like a mountain in motion. He had tusks sticking out like a boar's, and a long snout, and was dribbling disgustingly onto his breast. / He ran towards us, keeping his snout down like a bloodhound picking up a scent. On sight of him we all fled in terror, white as sheets: little comfort was to be gained from seeing him sightless, for he could tell more from sniffing the ground than others could with smell and sight to serve them. To escape him wings were needed. / We fled in all directions, but there was no escaping him, for he was swifter than the South Wind. Out of forty, barely ten of our number escaped by swimming to the ship. He bundled several of us under his arm, clasped more of us to his chest and stuffed yet more into a capacious pouch hung, like a shepherd's, from his side. / The blind monster carried us to his lair, quarried out of the rock by the sea's edge; its walls were of marble, as white as a page on which nothing has been written.

'Here dwelt also a matron whose face was stamped with suffering and sadness. With her were women and maidens of every age and condition, plain and fair. / Near the cave in which he lived, almost at the top of the hill, there was another cave of equal magnitude where he accommodated his flocks—they were numerous beyond telling, and he was their shepherd summer and winter. He let them out or penned them in as the mood took him, for his own pleasure rather than for any useful purpose; / human flesh was more to his liking, as he made clear before we reached his cave, for he took three of our young men and ate them alive; indeed he swallowed them whole. He came to the sheep-pen hollowed in the rock, pulled away a great boulder, drove out the flocks and shut us in there instead. Then he went off with his flocks to pasture them, playing on a set of pipes which dangled from his neck. /

'Meanwhile our king returned to the shore and took in his situation: he found a deep silence on every side, and the brush-huts, pavilions, and tents all deserted. He could not imagine who had thus despoiled him and, full of foreboding, went down to the beach. Here he saw his sailors standing off, hauling up the anchors and hoisting the sails. / The moment they saw him on the beach they sent in the ship's boat to take him off; but he no sooner heard about the monster and his depredations than he made up his mind without a moment's hesitation: he would follow the monster wherever he had gone—the loss of his bride Lucina so distressed him, he had no will to go on living unless he rescued her. / He picked up the monster's fresh traces in the sand and followed them hot-foot, impelled by his frenzied love, till he came to the cave I described, where, with the acutest terror ever experienced, we awaited Orcus' return; at every sound we thought we heard the hungry monster coming back to devour us. /

'As luck would have it, the king reached the cave when the monster was out, though his wife was in; on seeing him, "Get away!" she exclaimed; "Heaven help you if Orcus finds you here!" "Let him," replied the king. "Whether he does or not, whether I live or die will make no difference to my present state: the most miserable of men. I have not fetched up here by accident; I am here by my own wish to die beside my wife." / He went on to ask her for news of those whom Orcus captured by the sea-shore, but first of all he asked about fair Lucina, whether he had slain her or was holding her captive. The woman spoke kindly to him and gave him encouragement, saying that Lucina was alive and was in no danger of dying: Orcus never ate women. / "I myself and all these women here are evidence of this: Orcus has never raised a finger against me or any of us so long as we do not depart from this cave. Try to escape, and he'll exact a heavy penalty—there will be no respite for such a woman: he will bury her alive or chain her up, or expose her to the sun naked on the sand. / Today when he carried your folk up here he did not separate the women from the men, but thrust them all pell-mell into the sheep's cave just as he had found them. He will tell them apart by smell. Have no fear of the women being slain, but be assured that the men will, every one—he will cram his avid jaws with four or six of them a day. / I have no advice to give you on how to rescue her; be satisfied that her life is not in danger—she will stay here with us for better or for worse. But get away, child, be off with you for Heaven's sake, before the monster scents you and eats you up. The moment he comes he sniffs about—if there is so little as a mouse present he'll pick up its scent." / The king replied that he would not go until he had seen his Lucina; he would rather die with her than live without her. Seeing that there was nothing she could say to shift him from his resolution, the matron determined to help him and gave the problem all her thought and care. /

'Now the carcasses of several goats and sheep, male and female, were always kept hanging in the monster's lair; they provided food for her and the other women; several pelts also hung from the roof. The woman had the king take some of the fat from round the belly of a large ram and rub it all over himself, from top to toe, till it overpowered his own natural odour. / When she judged he was well impregnated with the fetid smell of the goat's-flesh, which was rank by now, she took its shaggy pelt and had him put it on—for it was fully big enough. Clothed in these strange trappings, she had him get down on his hands and knees and brought him to where a great boulder shut in his lady of the fairest face. / Norandin obeyed. He waited by the entrance to the cave in order to slip inside with the flock; he waited there on tenterhooks till evening. Evening came, and he heard the rustic pipes sound to call in the sheep from the dewy grass and return to their fold; the savage shepherd followed behind his flock. / I leave you to imagine if he quaked on hearing Orcus' return and on seeing his nightmarish face as it came close to the cave-mouth. But love got the better of fear; judge you whether his love was true or feigned! Orcus arrived, drew back the boulder to open the cave, and Norandin went in among the sheep and goats. / The monster drove in his flock, then came among us, after pulling the boulder to behind him. He sniffed us all and finally picked out two of our number, to feed on their raw flesh. Even now I break out in a sweat and tremble at the thought of those fearsome tusks. When he had gone, the king threw off the goat-skin and embraced his wife. /

'The sight of him there, which might have offered her solace and pleasure, only sharpened her misery. Here he was, where he must surely die, and yet there was nothing he could do to save her. "For all the misery of my plight," she told him, "it has been no little comfort to me, my lord, that you were not with us when I was taken here by the monster. / However acute my distress at the prospect of dying, my grief would, in the common order of things, have been purely on my own account. But now, whether it is sooner or later that you are slain, your death will cause me greater sadness than will my own." Thus she spoke, betraying far more distress at Norandin's fate than at her own. / "What brought me here", said the king, "was the hope of saving you and all our company. If I fail, I should sooner die than live in darkness without you, my ray of sun. As I came in, so may I leave—and you all with me if, like me, you do not recoil from enduing yourselves with this foul animal-smell." /

'He taught us the stratagem he had learnt from Orcus' wife to foil the monster's scent; and we were to dress in skins in case he felt us as we left the cave. When everyone had been persuaded of this plan, we killed as many goats as made up the number of men and women in our party; we chose the oldest goats, who smelt the rankest. / We rubbed our bodies with the greasiest fat from round the goats' bellies and clad ourselves in their shaggy hides. Meanwhile day issued from his gilded abode, and as the first ray of sun appeared Orcus returned to the cave; he blew his shrill pipes and called his flocks out from their pens. / To prevent our coming out with the flocks he blocked the cave-mouth with his hand, grasping us on the threshold; but the feel of goat-hair or fleece was enough for him to let us through. Men and women, we came out of the cavern this novel way, clothed in our shaggy hides. Not one of us did the monster detain until it was timorous Lucina's turn. /

'Whether it happened that Lucina refused, out of sheer repulsion, to grease herself as we had done; or that her gait was slower or smoother than that of the goat she was to imitate; or that her terror was heightened when the monster felt her rump and she let out a shriek; or perhaps that her hair fell loose—anyway, she was sniffed out: how, I cannot tell. / We were each so intent on our own escape that we had no eyes for anyone else. At her cry I looked round, to see that the monster had already stripped the shaggy pelt off her and thrust her back inside the hollow cave. The rest of us crept low with the flock in our disguises and followed the shepherd, who led us into a pleasant spot amid green hills. / Here we waited until the snouted monster laid down to sleep in the thick shade of a wood. Then we scattered, some of us to the sea-shore, others into the hills. Only Norandin would not come with us: he was so love-struck, he had to return to the cave with the flock, never to leave it this side of death, unless he left it with his faithful spouse. / When earlier, as they emerged from the cave, he had seen her left behind all by herself, his mind was so clouded by pain that he was all set to throw himself into the greedy monster's jaws. He ran right up to his snout and was not far from being crunched, but what detained him among the flock was the hope that he still might rescue her. /

'That evening Orcus drove his flock back to the cave, and his nose told him that we had escaped and he must go without dinner. He blamed it all on Lucina and condemned her to be chained perpetually on a prominent crag. Seeing her suffer through his own fault, the king wasted away but could not die. / Morning and evening the unhappy lover could look upon Lucina, tearful and woe-begone, for he was herded past her with the goats on their way back to the fold or out to pasture. She would sign to him, a look of entreaty on her afflicted face, for Heaven's sake not to stay there, as he was placing his life in jeopardy without being able to afford her any help. / Orcus' wife, too, begged him to be gone, but all in vain: he refused to leave without Lucina, and his constancy grew only firmer. It was a long time that he endured this servitude, bound thereto by Devotion and Love, until two travellers happened to pass this crag—Agrican's son Mandricard, and King Gradasso. / By a feat of daring they set fair Lucina free and hastened with her down to the sea to hand her over to her father who was here too. Good luck rather than skilled tactics enabled them to bring this off; they did it early one morning while King Norandin was penned in the mountain cavern, ruminating with the rest of the flock. /

'Now when day came and the cave was unblocked, the king discovered that his lady had departed: Orcus' wife gave him an exact account of what had happened. Norandin gave thanks to God and added this prayer: now that she had escaped her evil plight, let her be taken into such custody whence arms, entreaties, or treasure might redeem her. / Blithely he set forth to the green pastures with the rest of the flat-nosed flock, and here he waited until the monster dropped into the grass in the thick shade to sleep. Then he journeyed all day and far into the night until, safe from Orcus' clutches, he went on board a ship at Sataly. He has been back in Syria three months. / The king had searches made for fair Lucina in the cities and castles of Rhodes and Cyprus, of Africa, Egypt, and Turkey, but picked up no trace of her until but a few days ago. A few days ago he received news from her father that they had both arrived safely in Nicosia after a wicked contrary wind had stopped their vessel's progress for many days. / Overjoyed at these good tidings, our king has prepared a sumptuous festival, and means to have it celebrated the same way every fourth new moon, for it does him good to refresh his memory of the four months he endured in a shaggy hide in Orcus' flock, and the one day, such as tomorrow will be, that brought an end to his sufferings. / What I have told you I have in part witnessed, in part heard from one who lived it all—from the king, who was there from first to last, until his tears were changed to joy. Should you ever hear a different version, just you tell who propounds it that he has his facts wrong.' With these words their host told Grifon the solemn occasion for the celebration. /

Well into the night the knights discussed this topic, concluding that the king had given proof of outstanding love and devotion. Then they left the table and were shown to pleasant sleeping quarters. The next morning dawned bright and clear, and they awoke to the sound of revelry. / Drummers and trumpeters roamed the streets summoning one and all to the public square. With the streets echoing to the sound of horses and carriages and cries, Grifon put on his shining armour; this was of unusual make—for the white fairy had tempered it with her own hands, rendering it impenetrable and enchanted. / The knight from Antioch, Orrigilla's lover, a thoroughly paltry man, also donned his armour to accompany Grifon. Their kind host had set out for them a choice of lances, some light and sinewy, others great and hefty. Accompanied by some of his grander relatives, he came with them to the lists, and furnished them with pages, some mounted, some on foot, well trained in such services. / When they reached the lists, they did not go parading into them but preferred to draw aside, the better to view the fine warriors who were presenting themselves, singly, or in twos and threes, for the jousts. Some came with colours designed to convey their sense of bliss or sadness to their lady; others wore at their crest or depicted on their shield a symbol of love—love propitious or unkind, as appropriate. /

In those days the Syrians were accustomed to wear armour after the Western fashion; perhaps this was due to the vicinity of the French settled there as rulers of the holy places where Almighty God dwelt in human flesh. Nowadays to their shame, Christians, the arrogant wretches, leave these places in the hands of dogs. / They ought to be setting their lances for the greater spread of our Faith; instead, they are running each other through the breast or belly and wreaking destruction on the few who already belong to the Faith. You men of Spain, you Frenchmen, you Swiss and Germans, turn your steps elsewhere, make worthier conquests: what you covet here is already

Christ's. / If you wish to be called Most Christian, if you wish to be called Catholic, why do you kill Christ's men? Why despoil them of their possessions? Why do you not retake Jerusalem, seized from you by renegades? Why is Constantinople and the better part of the world occupied by unclean Turks? / Spain, have you not Africa for neighbour—Africa, who has done far worse to you than Italy? And yet to bring suffering on our wretched country you abandon the fine enterprise you started so well. And you, besotted Italy, fetid sink of all iniquities, are you asleep? Does it mean nothing to you that now this nation, now that lords it over you, when they were once your servants? / You Swiss, if it is fear of starving to death in your lairs which tempts you down to Lombardy, and if you come among us looking for someone to give you bread or else release you from famine by slaying you: the riches of the Turk are not far to seek—drive them out of Europe, or at least dislodge them from Greece. Thus you shall be able to escape hunger or at any rate meet a more meritorious end in those regions. /

What I say to you, I say also to your German neighbours: that is where the wealth is that Constantine brought from Rome—thither he took the best, giving away what remained: Pactolus and Hermus, rivers to be panned for pure gold, Mygdonia and Lydia, and all the country round, so widely praised for its virtues, extolled in so many histories—they are not too remote if you wish to travel there. / Great Leo, you shoulder the heavy burden of the keys of Heaven; if you hold Italy by the hair, do not leave her submerged in slumber. You are the shepherd: and if God gave you that staff to carry, and chose your proud name it was so that you should roar and stretch forth your hands to defend your flock from the wolves. /

But what with one thing and another we seem to have strayed right off our path; where was I? No, wait, I don't believe I've lost it beyond all recall—I was saying that in Syria they followed the same usage as the French in the matter of armour. Therefore the square at Damascus was a splendid sight with men armed in helmet and breastplate. / The lovely ladies threw red and yellow flowers from the tribunes down upon the jousters, who put their steeds through their paces, leaping and curvetting to the sound of brazen trumpets. Accomplished and poor ones alike wanted to show off, and spurred and drove their mounts—provoking cries of admiration, or of mockery and abuse as their performance warranted. / The prize offered for the tournament was a suit of armour which had been presented to the king a few days earlier by a merchant who chanced to find it on the road as he returned from Armenia. To the armour the king added a surcoat of most gorgeous weave and, in addition, pearls, gold, and precious stones enough to make the prize worth a considerable fortune. / Had the king recognized that armour, he would have treasured it above all others, and would certainly never have allotted it as the prize for the tournament, for all that he was open-handed and hospitable. It would take too long to explain who it was who had thus misprized and scorned it, abandoning it in the middle of the road to the first comer in either direction. / More about this anon; back now to Grifon.

When he reached the scene, more than one pair of lances had been broken, many a cut and thrust, he saw, had already been exchanged. Eight of the king's closest and most trusted champions had taken the field, banded together; they were young men skilled in arms and of great tenacity, all scions of noble families. / Here in the lists they took it in turns for a day to meet the challenge of all comers, first with the lance, then with sword or club, until the king was pleased to give the signal. Often breastplates were pierced: indeed, except that this was done in sport, they were just like foes fighting each other to the death—although the king could part the contenders at will. / The knight from Antioch, a man of little sense and a coward—his name was Martano—ventured boldly into the warlike lists, as though some of his comrade Grifon's spirit had been infused in him. He stood at the edge to await the end of a savage combat which had just been engaged between two knights. / The lord of Seleucia, one of the champions appointed to withstand all comers, was meeting the challenge of Ombruno, and with a sword-thrust which attained him full in the face, killed him. Everyone was dismayed at this, for Ombruno was generally regarded as a worthy gentleman as well as the kindest and most gallant in all the land. /

Martano saw this, and feared that the same thing might happen to him. Reverting to his normal nature, he began thinking how best to slip away, but Grifon, who stood beside him and was keeping an eye on him, thrust him forward, after all he had said and done, and directed him towards a noble champion coming in their direction, as one might drive a hound at a wolf: / the hound will take ten or twenty steps towards the wolf, then stop and bark, as he watches the wolf bare its menacing teeth, and the blazing glint in its eyes. Here, in the presence of princes, nobles, and warriors, timid Martano evaded the encounter, turning his horse's head and veering off to the right. / Shifting the blame on his mount might have been a way of excusing him; but with his sword, too, he put up such an abysmal performance that not even Demosthenes could have defended him. He might have been wearing paper, not steel, for armour, to see how he shied away from every blow. In the end he simply fled: this brought proceedings to a halt as the whole crowd broke into laughter. / As the populace hooted and clapped, Martano hastened away like a wolf making for its lair after being driven off.

Grifon stood firm, but he felt himself spattered and besmirched by his comrade's shame. He would sooner have stood in the midst of fire than right here where he was. / His heart burned, his face burned as if the shame had been all his own, for now the crowds would be expecting and hoping to see him put up a performance of the same dye. It was vital, then, that he display his prowess clearly for all to see: the bad impression would be magnified sixfold if he put a foot wrong, even if only by a fraction. / Grifon, who seldom missed his mark, lifted his lance off his hip, spurred his steed to a full gallop and shortly after brought his lance up for the strike; the impact was most painful for the baron of Sidon, who was sent sprawling. The whole crowd was on its feet in utter astonishment, for this was quite the reverse of what they expected. / Now Grifon came in a second time with the same lance, which he had recovered whole and entire, and broke it in three against the top of the shield of the baron of Laodicea, who was swept backwards onto his horse's rump and was on the point of falling three or four times; however he steadied himself, drew his sword, turned his steed and flew at Grifon. / Seeing his opponent still in the saddle, and that even so mighty a clash had not unhorsed him, Grifon remarked to himself, 'What my lance could not do, my sword will in five or six strokes.' And he fetched him such a blow on the temple, it might have been a bolt from Heaven; this he followed with another and another, till his opponent fell to the ground, stunned. /

Now came two brothers from Apamea, Tirse and Corimbo; in the lists they normally had the upper hand, but this time they were both spun out of the saddle by Oliver's son. One of them parted company with his horse at the lance-impact; the other survived until the swords were brought into play. By now it was generally considered that the prize would go to Grifon. / But Salintern had entered the lists. He was Lord Great Chamberlain and Master of the Horse to the king, and held sway over the whole kingdom. He was an outstanding champion, and it irked him that an alien warrior should carry off the prize. He grabbed a lance and hailed Grifon, challenging him with dire threats. / Grifon's reply, however, was to pick the best of ten lances he had, a really hefty one, and, to make doubly sure of his stroke, aimed full at the other's shield: the cruel point passed clean through shield, breastplate, and chest, cleared his ribs and emerged a palm's width from his back. The blow rejoiced everybody, except the king, for Salintern was mean and generally loathed. / Next, Grifon overthrew Hermophylus and Carmond, both from Damascus: the former was the king's commander-in-chief, the latter, his Lord High Admiral. The first impact sped Hermophylus straight out of the saddle, while it was Carmond's wretched steed who collapsed, unable to sustain Grifon's devastating blows, and fell on top of his rider. /

That still left the lord of Seleucia, the best of the eight champions, not only a mighty warrior, but with a steed and arms of matching excellence. As the contenders charged, each aimed his lance at the eye-slit in the other's helmet; Grifon got the better of the encounter, the pagan losing the footing in his left stirrup. / Throwing aside their spent shafts they drew their swords and fell upon each other savagely. Grifon landed the first blow, hard enough to have cleft an anvil. The pagan had selected his shield out of a thousand, but Grifon's sword laid bare the metal and the bone of it; had it not been of such quality and of double thickness, the blade would have sliced down onto his thigh. / The pagan at the same time caught Grifon a blow on the visor; had not this piece of armour, like all the rest, been enchanted, the blow would have cracked it open. But the pagan was wasting his time laying on with his sword: at all points Grifon's armour was rock-hard. Grifon, meanwhile, had smashed and pierced the other's armour at many points wreaking damage at every stroke. / Everyone could see how Grifon was gaining on the lord of Seleucia; unless the king parted them at once, the loser was likely to forfeit his life. So Norandin bade his guards go in and disengage the savage combat; each was led off in an opposite direction, and the king was praised for a deed well done. /

The eight who were supposed to hold the field against all comers but had not been able to resist the solitary challenger, had left the field one by one, having sustained their role so poorly. And all those who had come to challenge for the prize were left here with no one to fight, for Grifon all by himself had interrupted the challenge which all of them were supposed to mount against the eight. / So the tournament came to a premature end: it was all over in less than an hour. But Norandin meant to prolong the sport and keep it going until evening, so he came down from his tribune, had the field cleared, and divided the host of contenders into two; then he paired them off, according to their blood and their martial ability, to organize a fresh tourney. /

Meanwhile Grifon had returned to his lodgings in a seething temper: what excited him far more than the honour he had won was the disgrace Martano had incurred. But Martano was busily telling lies in order to shrug off the shame he had brought on himself; in this he was seconded by the sharp-witted, deceitful trollop of his—an expert at falsehoods. / Whether or not he fell for his excuses, Grifon thought it wiser to accept them; he favoured their slipping away there and then on the sly as the best course to take, fearing lest the people start a commotion if they set eyes on Martano. So they took a quick back way to the gate and out of the city. / Now whether it was Grifon or his steed who was weary, or whether it was that sleep weighed on his eyelids, he stopped at the first inn they came to, barely two miles outside the city. Here he drew off his helmet, stripped off his arms and had his steed unsaddled and unbridled; this done, he shut himself in his room and slipped naked into bed. / No sooner did his head touch the pillow than he closed his eyes in the soundest sleep: never did badger or dormouse sleep sounder.

Martano and Orrigilla meanwhile took a walk into a garden close by, where they hit upon as strange a trick as ever the human brain devised. / Martano's plan was to take the clothes and armour Grifon had stripped off, and also his horse, and present himself before the king as the knight who had wrought such deeds at the tournament. The thought was at once put into effect: Martano took the milk-white steed, the shield and plumed helmet, and donned the arms and surcoat, the emblems, everything Grifon wore. / Accompanied by his woman and his pages, he came into the public square, still thronged with onlookers. He arrived just as the contest with lance and sword was coming to an end. The king gave orders for the knight to be fetched in who wore a white crest and white apparel and rode a white charger: he was the victor, but his name was yet to be discovered. /

Arrayed in trappings which were not his own, like the proverbial ass in the lion's skin, Martano answered the expected summons and presented himself to the king in Grifon's place. The king stood up and greeted him chivalrously, with a kiss and embrace, and gave him a seat beside him; nor was he satisfied with giving him such tokens of honour and respect, but felt the need to broadcast his valour. / To the sound of trumpets he had him proclaimed the victor of that day's tournament. The word went out loud and clear to the people crowding the tribunes: the worthless name of Martano resounded on all sides. When the king set out on the return to his palace, he had the victor ride beside him on a footing of equality, and showed him such spectacular signs of favour, he might have been Hercules or Mars. / He allotted him fine, elegant quarters in his palace, and had equal honours paid to Orrigilla, to whom he assigned a train of noble gentlemen-in-waiting and knights from his own suite.

But it is time to return to Grifon, fast asleep and all unwary of any plot against him hatched by his companions or by whomsoever. Not till the evening did he reawake. / When he woke up and realized how late it was, he left his room at once and went through to where he had left his would-be brother-in-law and deceitful Orrigilla and the rest of their party. Not finding them, and noticing that his arms and clothes were missing, suspicion dawned on him—a suspicion which only deepened when he espied his comrade's emblems still there in place of his own. / The innkeeper appeared at this point and told him that his companion, arrayed in white arms, had some while since returned into the city accompanied by the lady and their suite. Little by little Grifon traced out the situation to which Love had blinded him until this moment: to his intense dismay he realized that Orrigilla's companion was her bed-mate, not her brother. /

It was vain for him to lament now over his obtuseness which, regardless of the truth divulged to him in Jerusalem by the pilgrim, had induced him to change his opinion in the light of words spoken to him by a woman who had already played him false so many times. He could have avenged himself then, but would not; and now that he would, his enemy had escaped him. And to make matters far worse, he was now constrained to settle for the coward's arms and horse. / He would have done better to go out wearing no armour at all, quite naked, rather than to put on that ignominious breastplate or wear on his arm the abhorrent shield, or on his head the helmet with the disparaged crest. But in his haste to catch the trollop and her lover, eagerness outstripped good sense.

He reached the city with about one hour of daylight still left. / To the left of the gate through which Grifon was to enter the city there stood a splendid castle; it was robustly built for war but, in addition, it boasted beautiful, sumptuous apartments. Here the king, lords, and nobility of Syria and the first ladies of the land had assembled, a noble gathering, on a pleasant balcony to partake of a joyous and right royal banquet. / The castle keep jutted out from the city wall, and so did the pleasant balcony, which commanded a view over the broad fields and many roads to a great distance. So when Grifon approached the gate wearing those arms marked with ignominy and shame, it was no surprise that he was spotted by the king and all his courtiers. / He was taken for the knight whose emblem he was wearing, and provoked the knights and ladies into fits of laughter. Base Martano, enjoying the height of favour, was sitting in the place of honour second only to the king; beside him sat the woman he deserved.

Now King Norandin turned to them with a smile, curious to discover who this coward was who had so little regard for his own dignity / that, after putting up so sorry a spectacle, he could brazenly show his face here again. 'I find it most remarkable', observed the king, 'that an accomplished and noble champion like yourself should associate with a fellow like him, a man so degraded that there cannot be another like him in all the Levant. Perhaps you do so to set off, by contrast, your own high valour. / Now I swear to you by the eternal gods, were it not for the esteem in which I hold you, I would make him a public laughing-stock, the way I treat others of his sort; I'd give him something by which to remember me as a sworn enemy to cowardice. But if he leaves here unpunished, the one he ought to thank is you, who brought him hither.' /

Martano, who had stomach for every vice, replied: 'Noble lord, I cannot tell you who this man is. I just happened upon him on my way from Antioch, and was persuaded by his outward mien that he would be worthy of my company. Until today's abject performance, I had heard nothing about him nor seen him show his mettle. / His showing today I found so painful that I very nearly took it upon myself to see that he never set hand to lance or sword again, to punish him for his extreme timidity. But considering where I was, and the respect I owe to your majesty, I restrained myself. Still, I have no wish that he should derive any profit from having been my companion for a day or two. / I feel quite contaminated by him, and if I see him leave here unmolested, this would be a slight to the profession of arms and would remain a weight on my mind for ever. Rather than let him alone, you could better please me if you had him hanged from the battlements: that would indeed be a meritorious act, worthy of your highness, for it would stand as a shining example to all cowards.' / With no prompting on his part, Orrigilla was quick to second his suggestion. 'His deed is not, in my opinion, so heinous', replied the king, 'that he should forfeit his head. In punishment for his grave misdemeanour, I will merely have him give the people further entertainment.' He summoned one of his barons and gave him the necessary instructions. /

The baron picked a good number of armed men and went down to the gate where he posted them in a silent ambush to await Grifon's arrival. As he entered, they pounced on him and easily caught him between the first and second bridge. Heaping mockery and insult upon him, they shut him into a dark cell until the next day. / The Sun had just raised his golden locks from the lap of his old nurse, Night, and was beginning to dispel the shadows on the mountain-sides and touch the peaks with his radiance, when base Martano, fearing that bold Grifon must eventually speak out and return the shaft against the man who flung it, took leave of the king and went his way; / to the king's invitation to attend the spectacle he had arranged, Martano invented some suitable excuse. The king, much taken with him, gave him many gifts on the merits of a victory he had not won, and extended to him ample privileges, conferring on him the highest honours. Well, let him be gone—you have my solemn word, he shall receive a reward in keeping with his deserts. /

Grifon was ignominiously brought into the public square, in which a vast crowd had assembled. His helmet and breastplate had been taken from him, which left him looking thoroughly abject in his doublet. They had placed him in a cart for all to see, as though he were being taken to his execution; the cart was drawn at a snail's pace by two gaunt, languid cows, all skin and bone. / The cart of infamy was driven, turn and turn about, by a succession of old fishwives and young slatterns all heaping abuse upon him; from the children he suffered even worse indignities, for besides insults, they pelted him with stones, and would have made an end of him had they not been restrained by wiser hands. / The arms, the cause of his present plight, and which had so falsified his true image, were being dragged through the mud behind the cart, a fate they well deserved. The cart came to a halt in front of a tribune; here a trumpet was sounded, and his shameful conduct (which was not his at all, judged as it was on the evidence of the eyes) was publicly proclaimed. / After this they hauled him off to exhibit him all over the city outside houses, workshops, and shrines—in the course of which he was called every name under the sun. Ultimately the mob ran him out of the city, determined to make him an outcast, to throw him out under a hail of blows, little realizing who he was. / The moment they unshackled his feet and untied his hands, he picked up the shield and grasped the sword which had ploughed a fair length of furrow. There were no lances or spears to oppose him, the mindless mob having come without any. The rest of the story I shall defer to the next canto, my Lord, as it is now time for this one to end.

EIGHTEENTH CANTO

1–2 Introductory. 3–7 Grifon savages the mob at Damascus. 8–37 Rodomont, driven out of Paris, learns of Doralice's fate. 38–58 The battle outside Paris. 59–70 Grifon and Norandin reconciled. 70–96 Aquilant brings Martano and Orrigilla, bound, to Damascus. 96–145 Adventures of Marfisa, Astolfo, and Samsonet at Damascus and at sea. 146–164 Rinaldo slays Dardinel, and the Moors retreat. 165–192 Cloridan and Medor rescue Dardinel's body.

MOST noble Lord, I have always applauded your every act, and with good reason, for all that my inept and clumsy style defrauds you of a great part of your glory. One virtue in you, though, I must single out for heartfelt praise: while everybody finds in you a ready listener, you are not over-hasty in your judgements. / Often, if a man is accused in his absence, I have heard you put forward excuse after excuse for him, or anyway listen with only half an ear until he is on hand to urge his own defence. Always, before you condemn, you would see him in person and listen to what he has to say; sooner than condemn him, you would postpone judgement for days, months, years. /

Had Norandin behaved likewise, he would not have treated Grifon the way he did. You have ever derived honour and advantage from your methods, while he merely blackened his reputation worse than pitch. Thanks to him his people suffered death, for Grifon went quite berserk: in ten slashes, ten rabid thrusts, he brought down thirty of them right beside the cart. / The rest fled hither and thither in utter panic, some dashing into the fields and down the roads while others, flocking back into the city, met in the gateway and fell all of a heap. Grifon uttered not a word, not a threat: eschewing all pity, he laid about him with his sword and avenged himself on the inert mob for all his humiliations. / Among those who were quickest to take to their heels and reach the gate, some there were, more concerned for their own than for their friends' safety, who hastened to raise the drawbridge; the rest of them simply kept running without a backward glance—some were weeping, others in a daze, and as they fanned out through the city they yelled and screamed and created an uproar. / Grifon, the brawny fellow, grabbed two men just as the bridge rose, alack for them! One of them he smacked against a hard stone, scattering his brains all over the place. The other he seized round the chest and swung up over the walls right into the city; the locals' blood ran cold as they watched this man tumble out of the sky. / There were many who were afraid that fierce Grifon had leapt up onto the battlements. There could not have been greater disarray if Damascus were under attack from the Sultan: everywhere arms and men were a-mustering, muezzin were wailing, the whole place was deafened by the noise of drums and clarions which echoed to the high heavens. /

But I want to continue this story another time, for I must pick up the traces of good King Charlemagne, who had hastened to confront Rodomont who was slaughtering all his people. I told you how the king was accompanied by the husky Dane Ogier, by Namo and Oliver together with Avino, Avolio, Otho, and Berenger. / The cruel Moor had sheathed his chest in a scaly dragon-hide which resisted eight mighty lance thrusts launched at it all at once by eight champions such as these. As a vessel will right itself once the helmsman has eased out the weather-side brace as he senses the Westerly strengthening, thus did Rodomont spring erect from an impact enough to overturn a mountain. / Guido, Ranier, Richard, Solomon, traitor Ganelon, faithful Turpin, Angeliero, Angelino, Hugh, Ivo, Mark, and Matthew from Mont Saint-Michel, and the eight I've just mentioned—these all crowded in upon the ferocious Saracen, as also did Harriman and Edward of England who had just come into the city. / A high-walled castle, solidly rooted on an Alpine crag, may shudder under the impact of North or West Wind when it rips up mountain ash and spruce —but it will be nothing to compare with the shudder of pride which shook Rodomont, afire with rage and thirsty for blood. Lightning and thunder united—such was his spiteful wrath. / He lashed out at the head of the man nearest, poor Hugh of Dordogne, and laid him flat, his skull cleft to the teeth despite the solid temper of his helmet. Meanwhile blows rained on his own person from all sides, but they were as ineffectual as needles against an anvil, so tough was the scaly dragon-hide he wore. /

The battlements were abandoned, the entire city was deserted, for Charles had assembled the whole populace in the square, where they were most needed. The crowds, who had fled to so little purpose, now ran to the square from every street: the king's presence so enkindled them that each man took heart and set hands to his weapons. / Sometimes folk will amuse themselves by shutting an untamed bull into the sturdy cage of an ageing battle-scarred lioness; her cubs, seeing the way the spirited beast bellows as he proudly paces the sand, and beholding horns such as they've never seen, back away, timid and abashed; / but if their mother leaps at the bull and fastens her cruel fangs into his ear, then they fly boldly to her assistance, for they too must steep their chops in blood; one sinks his teeth into the bull's back, the next into his belly. Thus it was with the pagan and the men of Paris: a dense shower of missiles rained down upon him from the roofs, windows, and closer vantage-points. / Men on horse and on foot crowded in so thick there was scarcely room for them all; like bees they were swarming in now from every street. Unarmed and naked they might be, and easier to harvest than a crop of cabbages or turnips— but even were they tied and stacked in a vast heap, Rodomont could never have come to the end of his reaping, not in twenty days. /

Now the pagan, unable to see the end of it in sight, was beginning to tire of this pastime. Staining the earth with the blood of a thousand or more did little to diminish the population. Meanwhile his breathing was becoming laboured, and he saw that if he did not disengage now while he was still fresh and while his body was still unscathed, when the time came to break out, he might not be able to. / He turned his baleful eyes and saw that every issue was blocked: then he would force a passage, then and there, and leave a trail of destruction. Goaded by brute rage, the devilish Saracen flourished his keen sword and fell upon the Britons freshly arrived under Edward and Harriman. / Imagine a wild bull pent up in a public square, goaded and struck all day long until, in a fit of rage, he breaks out into the eddying crowd which hems him in; the people flee in a panic as he tosses one after another on his horns. Thus, when he broke out, was the cruel African— / fifteen or twenty he cut in two, as many more he decapitated. One stroke up or down was enough for each—they might have been vines or willows he was pruning. All spattered in blood, the fierce pagan left a trail strewn with split skulls, severed arms, shoulders, legs, and other members wherever he went. Then he was gone. / In the manner of his departure he showed not a trace of fear, though he was in fact privately searching for the safest route of escape. He finally came to the Seine at the point below the island where it leaves the city. The soldiers and populace were emboldened now to press after and harass him. /

As some valiant beast, hunted through the woodlands of Numidia or African Massilia, displays its nobility even in retreat, and withdraws, slow and menacing, into the heart of the forest: thus was Rodomont— hemmed in by this weird, bristling forest of spears and swords and flying arrows, he did nothing to debase himself, but withdrew towards the river with long slow strides. / Yet three times anger spurred him to plunge into the fray from which he had retired, and steep his sword once more in blood, dispatching upward of a hundred souls. Finally, though, reason mastered passion, bidding him refrain before the Almighty grew disgusted. Wiser counsel prevailing, he threw himself from the bank into the river and escaped from peril. / In full armour, he breasted the water as though he were buoyed up with air-bladders. I tell you, Africa, though you may boast of Anteus and Hannibal, you never bore a man the like of Rodomont. Once ashore, he looked over his shoulder and grieved to see the city yet standing: he had scoured it all but not destroyed it, nor burnt it from end to end. / He was so eaten by rage and arrogance that he considered returning to the city; he groaned inwardly and sighed, reluctant as he was to leave before he had burnt down Paris and razed it to the ground. But as he stood fuming, he saw a figure approaching along the bank, one who was to quench his hatred and abate his wrath. Who it was you shall hear in a moment—but first I have something else to tell you. /

I must tell you of proud Discord, to whom Michael the archangel had committed the task of arousing Agramant's champions and pitting them against each other in flaming quarrels. That same evening she left the monastery, entrusting her office there to another: she left Fraud behind to keep dissensions rife until her return. / She also decided that she would be more effective if she brought Pride along with her; as they all lived under one roof, Pride was not far to seek. Pride came, then, but not before leaving a surrogate in the monastery:

for the few days she expected to be absent she appointed Hypocrisy in her place. / Ruthless Discord set out, then, accompanied by Pride, and on the road they fell in with Jealousy, the disconsolate misery, who was also on her way to the Saracen camp. With her came a little dwarf sent by fair Doralice to bring tidings of herself to Rodomont, King of Sarthia. / When she fell into the hands of Mandricard (how and where this happened I have already related), she secretly commissioned the dwarf to go and tell the king what had befallen. She hoped that consequences would follow from his learning the news, that wonderful feats would ensue when he set out to wreak vengeance and recapture her from the brigand who had intervened. / Jealousy had come upon the dwarf and, learning the object of his errand, she had fallen in beside him, for she felt that there was a place for her in this affair. Discord was pleased to happen upon Jealousy, the more so when she learnt what was afoot, for it could serve her own ends very suitably. / Here, she thought, was just what was needed to set Rodomont and Mandricard at loggerheads; to sow dissension among the others, other methods would serve—to ignite these two, here was the very thing.

She came, then, with the dwarf to Paris, which the fierce pagan had crushed in his talons, and they reached the river-bank just as the savage warrior was hauling himself out of the water. / The moment Rodomont discovered that the dwarf was sent to him by his lady, his rage evaporated, his brow cleared, and he felt his heart fairly tingling. The last thing he expected to be told was that someone had done her injury. He approached the dwarf and cheerfully questioned him: 'What news of our lady? Whence has she sent you?' /

'I should no longer call her my lady, nor yours, now that she is subject to another man,' replied the dwarf. 'Yesterday we met with a knight upon the road; he seized her and led her away.' At this news Jealousy, cold as an asp, stepped in and embraced the pagan. The dwarf went on to describe how one man single-handed had taken her and slain all her suite. / Discord now picked up her flint and steel and struck them together, while Pride reached in with the tinder: in a moment a fire was kindled which so enflamed the Saracen's heart, he could scarcely contain himself. He sighed and fumed and glowered so hideously that he threatened earth and heaven. / Imagine a tigress, when she has gone in vain into her empty lair and visited every corner of it, and finally realizes that her darling cubs have been taken from her: she will blaze up in such a passion, her anger will take her to such lengths that neither mountain nor river, neither night's darkness, nor hail-storm nor even distance can restrain the hatred which drives her in pursuit of the predator. / Thus was the Saracen, goaded to madness.

He turned to the dwarf and 'Be off back to her,' he told him. Then, without waiting for horse or carriage, without a word to anyone, he set off faster than a lizard that darts across a road under the blazing noon. He had no steed, but planned to take the first he came upon, whosoever it was. / Discord overheard his thought. With a smile she looked at Pride and said she would go and find him a horse which would land him in yet more quarrels; she would clear the entire road to ensure that only that one horse came his way—already she had decided where she would find it.

But I shall leave her and return to Charlemagne. / With Rodomont's departure, the perilous fires lit round the emperor burnt out, and he mustered his followers afresh. A few he left to man weak points; the rest he flung against the Saracens to check their impetus and win the day: he sent them out through every gate, from St. Germain's right round to St. Victor's. / He bade them assemble outside St. Marcel's gate, where there was a good stretch of level ground. Here they were to mass into a single host. Then, exhorting each one to wreak such slaughter that it would never be forgotten, he had the ensigns mustered in order of battle and signalled the troops to fall to. / King Agramant, meanwhile, had remounted his steed in spite of the Christians, and was engaged in a savage, perilous combat with Zerbin, Isabel's lover. Lurcanio and King Sobrino were hammering each other. Rinaldo had an entire host to contend with but, Fortune and his own prowess aiding him, he stopped, split, crushed them, and sent them running. / With the battle thus advanced, the emperor attacked the enemy's rearguard: Marsilius and the flower of the Spanish troops gathered round his standard. Charlemagne, grouping his cavalry outside his infantry, urged his brave people forward to such a din of trumpet and drum that the whole world seemed to shake with it. /

The Saracens were beginning to pull back; they were on the point of turning to flee, broken, and disarrayed beyond recall, when Grandonio and Falsiron appeared (men who had known tighter corners than this before), and Balugant and fierce Serpentine, and Ferrau who bellowed at them: / 'Soldiers! . . . comrades! . . . brothers! . . . hold fast! If we stick to our duty the enemy will be flimsy as a spider's web. Look at the high honours, the generous rewards which Fate has shown us today if we conquer. Look at the shame, the dire evil we shall suffer for all time if we are defeated.' / With these words he grasped a heavy lance and charged at Berenger, who was gaining ground upon Largalifa and had already split his helmet. Ferrau threw him to the ground and with his brutal sword felled a good eight Christians beside him. Practically each stroke brought down another knight. /

Elsewhere, Rinaldo had slain scores of pagans, more than I could number; the ranks confronting him were broken—everyone gave way before him. Zerbin and Lurcanio were no less zealous, each performing feats to be remembered by; the latter had run Balastro through, while the former had split Finadurro's helmet. / Balastro had commanded the troops of Djerba, led until recently by Tardocco. Finadurro had commanded the troops from the Barbary cities—Zamora, Safi, Morocco. 'Then is there not among the Africans one warrior capable of wielding lance or sword?' someone may ask. Ah, but let me continue: I shall not overlook any man worthy of renown. / Let us not forget Almont's son, noble Dardinel, King of Azumara: his lance accounted for Hubert of Mirford, Claude Wood, Eli, and Delphin Hill; his sword, for Anselm of Stanford, and two Londoners—Raymond and Pinamont: all were laid flat (and they were no weaklings), two of them stunned, one wounded, and four dead. / But for all the valour he displayed, he could not make his troops stand long enough to wait for our Christians, who were less numerous, but better fighters: they were superior at wielding sword and lance and at all the ploys of battle. The Mauretanians and Azumarans fled, and so did the Ceutans, Moroccans, and Canary Islanders. / The promptest fugitives, though, were the Djerbans; Dardinel stood in their way and, with pleas and threats, tried to restore their courage.

'If Almont deserved to live in your memories,' he cried, 'now let me see proof of it—let me see how ready you are to desert me, his son, in such a perilous pass. / Stand firm, I beg you for the sake of my green years in which you have placed such hopes. Allow yourselves to be cut down, and not one of our seed shall return to Africa—no, let that not be your choice! Everywhere the roads shall be closed to us if we do not hang together as one body; the mountains are too high a wall, the sea too broad a moat between us and our home-coming. / Far better is it to die here than to yield ourselves to the grim mercies of these dogs. Stand firm, for love of God, my loyal friends—we have no other choice. Our foes have no more lives than we have. They have but one soul, one pair of hands.' So saying, the young champion slew the Earl of Atholl. /

The memory of Almont put such fire into the hearts of the African fugitives that they thought better of turning their backs in flight; they lent their hands instead to rally to his name. William of Burnich, an Englishman, stood a head taller than his fellows; Dardinel cut him down to the uniform height. Then he lopped the head off Haramon of Cornwall, / who fell down dead; his brother ran to his aid, but Dardinel split him open from the shoulders to the crotch. After this he punctured the belly of Bogio da Vergalle, thus absolving him of his oath: he had promised his wife that if he lived he would return to her

within six months. / Nearby, Dardinel saw stout Lurcanio approaching.
Lurcanio had run Dorchin through the neck, leaving him prostrate,
and split Gardo from crown to jaw. Dardinel also saw his bosom-
friend Alteo trying to escape, but all too late: fierce Lurcanio caught
him a blow on the back of the neck which slew him outright. / To
avenge him, he seized a lance, swearing to Mahomet (if the Prophet
had ears) that if he hurled Lurcanio dead to the ground he would
deposit the Christian's untenanted armour in the mosque. Then,
galloping across the field, he struck him such a blow on the side that
his lance passed clean through him. He bade his followers strip the
corpse. /

There is no need to ask whether Ariodant wept over his brother,
whether he yearned to send his slayer down to join the damned. But
everybody, Infidel and baptized alike, joined in preventing his access.
He thirsted for vengeance, nonetheless, and carved himself a passage
with his sword. / Whoever stood in his path or opposed him he struck,
ripped, rammed, and floored, slashed and cleaved. And Dardinel, who
grasped his state of mind, was not unwilling to give him satisfaction,
but the pressing crowds stood in his way, too, and foiled his ambition.
If the one slew Moors, the other killed no less Scots, English, and
Frenchmen. / But Fate constantly barred their paths, and the whole
day elapsed without their coming to grips. To a more eminent hand she
reserved the pagan—seldom can a man escape his destiny. Rinaldo it
was who turned in his direction, and that spelt an end to the pagan's
immunity—Rinaldo came under Fate's guidance, to win himself
honour as Dardinel's slayer. /

But enough for now of the glorious deeds wrought in the West.
It is time to return to Grifon whom I left, blazing with wrath and
indignation, causing havoc among the flabbergasted Damascans who
had never been so frightened in their lives. At the rumpus King
Norandin with a troop a thousand strong hurried to the scene. / Seeing
the people in full flight, the king set out with his men-at-arms and
came to the gate, closed for battle, and had it opened. Grifon, meanwhile, who had driven off the foolish, feckless rabble, put on the
despised armour (such as it was) in order to defend himself. / He took
his station beside a shrine built as strong as a fortress and surrounded
by a deep moat; in this emplacement at the bridgehead he could guard
against being surrounded. With menacing cries the king's guard burst
out through the gate, but stalwart Grifon stood his ground and showed
little fear of them. / Seeing the guard advancing upon him, he went
out to meet them, and, after inflicting heavy casualties (for he wielded
his sword two-handed), he withdrew to the narrow bridgehead,
whence he could hold them at a slight distance. He would make con-

tinuous sallies which left terrible traces every time. / One edge of his blade then the other caught the enemy, mounted and on foot, hurling them to the ground. The pressure on him continually increased, though, as the people crowded in upon him, until he feared he would be submerged by the human flood building up. Already he was wounded in the shoulder and the left thigh; moreover he was out of breath. /

Now Valour, which often takes care of her own, procured him a remission from King Norandin. As the king hastened in perplexity towards the tumult, he noticed how many had already been slain, and saw wounds such as Hector himself might have inflicted: all this clearly attested how little justification he could have had in bringing shame upon a most worthy knight. / Drawing closer, he saw before him the man who had put so many of his people to death and raised a grisly mound of corpses in front of himself, sullying the moat and the water with blood; and he felt he was seeing Horatius holding that very bridge single-handed against the entire Etruscan host. To safeguard his honour, and because he regretted the turn of affairs, he recalled his soldiers—with little difficulty. /

He raised his bare hand, which held no weapon—the traditional sign of peaceful truce—and said to Grifon: 'Perhaps I should admit I am to blame and confess that I am sorry. My lack of judgement, and the instigation of others, led me astray: what I believed I was doing to the world's worst craven I did to the noblest champion alive. / And though the honour you have won yourself here sets off—no, in all truth, more than redeems—the insult, the shame done to you in ignorance today, I am ready to make amends to the limits of my capability once I know what I can give you in the way of gold, cities, or castles. / Ask me for half my kingdom: I am ready to give it to you today. Your supreme merits entitle you to this and more—to the gift of my heart: give me your hand, then, as a pledge of trust and of perpetual love.' With these words he dismounted and extended his right hand to Grifon. / As he saw the king approaching him graciously to throw his arms about his neck, Grifon laid aside his sword and his malevolence, and embraced his knees. The king noticed Grifon's two bleeding wounds and had them treated at once, after which he had the knight conveyed gently into the city and lodged in his palace. / Here he spent a few days nursing his wounds before he could resume his armour.

But I shall leave him and return to his brother Aquilant and to Astolfo in Palestine. When Grifon left the sacred walls, they searched for him many a day; they looked in all the holy shrines of Jerusalem and in many outside the city. / Neither of them possessed the clairvoyance to know what had become of Grifon; but the Greek pilgrim happened to give them a clue in the course of conversation, when he mentioned that Orrigilla had gone to Syrian Antioch, having developed a sudden infatuation for a new lover who hailed from there. / Aquilant asked him whether he had given this news to Grifon and, receiving an affirmative, he pieced together the rest—the cause, that is, of his brother's departure: he must have followed Orrigilla to Antioch with a view to snatching her from his rival and inflicting memorable vengeance upon him. / Now Aquilant could not brook the idea of his brother setting off alone without him on his mission, so he armed himself and went after him. But first he prayed Astolfo to defer his departure for France and his homeland until he himself was back from Antioch. Then he went to Jaffa and boarded ship, deeming the sea-route shorter and preferable. /

The South Wind was holding sway over the sea and so favoured him that he sighted Tyre the following day, and right after it, Saffet. He passed Beirut and Djebel and could sense that Cyprus was away off on his left. He made for Tartus, Laodicea and the Gulf of Alexandretta. / From here the helmsman turned the swift vessel's prow Eastward and, choosing his time, entered the mouth of the Orontes and there brought his ship to land. Aquilant had the gangplank lowered and rode ashore, armed, on his mettlesome steed. Making his way upstream, he eventually came to Antioch. / Here he made enquiries about his brother's rival, Martano, and learned that the man had left with Orrigilla for Damascus, where a solemn tournament was to take place at the king's invitation. So keen was Aquilant to go after his brother, in the certainty that he must have followed them thither, that he left Antioch that same day; this time, though, he preferred not to continue by sea. / His path took him towards Lydia and Larissa; rich, prosperous Aleppo lay ahead. Now God, to show that even here below He does not deny to virtue its reward, and to its opposite, punishment, induced Martano into encountering Aquilant about a league outside Mamuga.

Martano was preceded on his way by the joust-trophies, ostentatiously displayed. / On first catching sight of the paltry fellow, Aquilant imagined it must be his brother; the arms deceived him and the white array, whiter than virgin snow. 'Oh!' he exclaimed, the way one does under the prompting of gladness—but his face suddenly fell and he broke off, realizing on closer inspection that it was not he. / That woman with him, he suspected, had played some trick enabling him to kill Grifon.

'You!' he shouted at him, 'you two-faced thief by the look of you! How have you come by these arms? How come you to be mounted on

my brother's horse? Is my brother dead or alive? Tell me! How did
you take his arms and horse from him?' / On hearing this angry
voice, Orrigilla tugged her palfrey round in order to flee, but Aquilant
was too quick for her and made her stop willy-nilly. Martano, faced
with the savage menace of this knight who had caught him so unprepared, blanched and trembled like a leaf, quite at a loss as to what
to do or say. / In a livid rage Aquilant yelled at him and put his sword
to his throat, vowing with an oath to lop his and Orrigilla's heads off
their shoulders if they did not come out with the whole truth. Unhappy Martano swallowed a few times as he debated how best to
attenuate his heinous crime. Then he began: /

'This lady, sir, is my sister. She springs from good, honest stock,
but to her shame she has been condemned by Grifon to an infamous
existence. I could not endure this infamy, but as I did not feel strong
enough to take her by force from a man of his stature, I devised a plan
to rescue her by craft and stealth. / She, too, wanted to return to a
more deserving life and so I arranged for her to slip silently away from
him when he went to sleep. This she did; and to prevent his following
us and spoiling the plan we had contrived, we left him without armour
and on foot. And we have come thus far, as you see.' / Martano congratulated himself on being such an accomplished liar that Aquilant
would readily believe him and do nothing to him beyond retrieving the
armour, steed, and whatever else belonged to Grifon. He did not polish
his excuse to a point where it must be an outrageous falsehood. It all
held together except for the bit about the woman being his sister. / In
Antioch Aquilant had been told by several people that the woman was
his mistress. He flew into a rage, then, and 'You monstrous thief!' he
cried, 'you brazen liar!' He fetched him a punch which knocked two
teeth down his throat, after which, without further opposition, he
twisted his arms behind his back and tied them with a cord. / He did the
same to Orrigilla, though she had a great deal to say in her own excuse;
then he led them off through villages and towns, never leaving them a
moment until they reached Damascus. He would have dragged them
thousands of miles, through thick and thin, in order to find his brother
and dispose of them as his brother saw fit. /

Aquilant brought along their pages and baggage as well, and entered
Damascus. Here he found that Grifon's name was on every tongue:
everybody, young and old, knew the story of how he had shone in the
lists only to lose the honours of the tournament to his masquerading
companion. / The whole population, stirred up against base Martano,
pointed him out to each other, exclaiming, 'Is not this the scoundrel
who wins himself praise from others' merits, and—shame upon him—
disguises the courage of a man who lies asleep? And is not this the

odious woman who betrays the good and helps the wicked?' / 'A pretty pair they make,' people cried, 'marked with the same sign, two of a kind!' Some of them spat out curses at them, others railed at them. Cries of 'Hang! Burn! Tear them to pieces! Kill them!' filled the air. The crowds jostled and pushed to have a view of them, and ran ahead to the public square.

When the news reached the king, he showed greater pleasure than if he had received another kingdom. / He set out at once, just as he was, with only a small train to precede and follow him, and went to meet Aquilant who had avenged his brother Grifon. He showed him kindness and respect, bidding him home as his guest. With Aquilant's approval, he had the two prisoners lodged in a dungeon. / Together they went to see Grifon, who had not stirred from his bed since he had received his wounds. Grifon blushed on seeing his brother, assuming that he must have been told what had happened. Aquilant did tease him a little, but then they discussed how to mete out a just retribution to the pair who had fallen into their clutches. / Both Aquilant and the king wanted to do all manner of things to them, but Grifon insisted that they both be pardoned (this, because he dared not plead for Orrigilla alone). He spoke at length, with much close reasoning, and numerous objections were raised to what he said; ultimately it was decided that Martano should be handed over to be flogged, but not put to death. / They bound him then—and not in garland wreaths—and the following morning they flogged him up and down. Orrigilla was held until fair Lucina arrived—to whose discretion, whether for good or ill, they entrusted her fate. Aquilant remained enjoyably in Damascus until his brother was recovered and could resume his armour. /

King Norandin had learnt wisdom and temperance after the mistake he had made, and, needless to say, he was heartily sorry for the evil and humiliation he had inflicted upon a man who deserved honours and rewards. Day and night he pondered what to do to retrieve Grifon's goodwill. / And he proclaimed in the presence of all the citizens, who shared the guilt for such mischief, that he would restore to him the prize which the traitor had so cunningly intercepted; this he would do, conferring upon him the highest honours that a king could render to a perfect knight. To this end, he proclaimed a new tournament to take place a month hence. / The preparations were to be as sumptuous as lay within the means of a royal court.

Swift-winged Rumour spread the word throughout Syria and to Phoenicia and Palestine, so that it came to the ears of Astolfo: he and Samsonet, Viceroy of Jerusalem, decided that this tournament would not take place without them. / History claims that Samsonet was a valiant warrior and a man of eminent reputation. Orlando baptized him; Charlemagne (as I have said) appointed him Governor of the Holy Land. Samsonet and Astolfo, then, packed their bags and set out for Damascus, where, as by now no one could help knowing, the tournament was to be held. / They made their journey on horseback in short, easy stages so as to be fresh on the day of the tournament, once they had reached Damascus.

Now at a crossroads they came upon a person who looked like a man, to judge by attire and movements: she was a woman, however, and a remarkably fierce warrior. / She was the virgin Marfisa, a swordsman of such prowess that on several occasions she had brought the perspiration to the brow of Orlando, lord of Brava, and to that of Rinaldo of Montauban. Day and night she was always armed, always on the prowl, up hill and down dale, alert to measure herself against knights errant and foster her immortal fame. / Seeing Astolfo and Samsonet advancing, fully armed, and realizing at a glance that they must be no mean warriors—they were both of them tall and solidly built—she spurred her steed forward, enjoying the prospect of challenging them. On closer approach, though, she recognized Astolfo the paladin-duke. / She remembered him for a most agreeable knight, from the time when they had been together in Cathay; so she called him by name, and was quick to draw off her gauntlet and raise her visor. She went and flung her arms about him with delight, for all that she was by nature extremely haughty. As for the paladin, he was not backward in showing his regard for the excellent damsel. / They asked each other whither they were bound, and Astolfo, the first to reply, explained that they were on their way to Damascus, as the King of Syria had invited champions at arms to come and show off their prowess.'Well, I want to join you in this enterprise,' remarked Marfisa, ever eager to accept challenges. / Astolfo was highly pleased to have Marfisa for companion at arms, and so was Samsonet. They reached Damascus the day before the tournament and found lodgings outside the gates. Here, until the hour when old Tithonus roused his beloved Aurora from her slumbers, here they rested in greater comfort than if they had put up at the palace. /

When the new sun, gleaming bright, had scattered his brilliant rays in all directions, the fair damsel and the two warriors armed themselves; but first they dispatched messengers into the city, and these returned to tell them when King Norandin had arrived in the place appointed for the savage sport of splintering ash- and beech-lances. / Without further delay they left for the city and took the main street leading to the public square where warriors, scions of noble families, stood drawn up on either side, awaiting the royal signal.

The prize to be offered that day to the winner was a dagger and a mace, both richly ornamented, and a charger worthy to be awarded to so accomplished a gentleman. / In the firm conviction that today's prize, just like the previous one, and the honours of both tournaments, would go to Grifon the White, Norandin added the dagger, mace, and superb charger (the prize of the forthcoming jousts) to the prize-armour of the earlier tournament, in order to make a gift suitable to a man of valour and not scant his reward. / The arms already due to Grifon—those won in the previous tournament, but usurped by Martano, who profited little from trying to impersonate him—these the king had prominently displayed; the finely ornamented dagger he appended to them, while the mace he slung from the charger's saddle, so that Grifon could take possession of all the prizes at once. / Only, to safeguard his intention, the king warned off the spirited damsel who had just entered the lists with Astolfo and good Samsonet. For Marfisa, noticing the arms I have mentioned, recognized them instantly. They had been hers and were as precious to her as something exquisite and rare is bound to be— / for all that she had left them in the road, as they restricted her movements that time when she was chasing after that gallows-bird Brunello to retrieve her fine sword. This is a story I think I need not expand on, so I'll say no more about it. Suffice for me to have told you how Marfisa came to find her arms here. / I must also explain that, once she had recognized the arms by clear indications, nothing in the world would have persuaded her to wait even a day before putting them on. She could not stop to think which was the best way to set about recovering them; she simply advanced upon them, reached out and laid hold of them without so much as a by-your-leave. /

In her haste to grasp the arms a part of them scattered to the ground. The king was outraged at this and opened hostilities with a single glance. His people were no readier to swallow the insult; they snatched up lances and swords to wreak vengeance, quite forgetful of the sorry outcome which had recently resulted from interfering with a knight errant. / The eagerness of a young lover in springtime to be among the meadow-flowers, red, yellow, and blue; the eagerness of a fair maiden in festive attire to be at a ball was as nothing compared to the glee with which Marfisa, whose strength was astounding, welcomed the clash of arms and chargers, the flight of spears and square-tipped arrows, the shedding of blood, the commerce of death. / She spurred her steed, lowered her lance, and charged impetuously into the foolish rabble. One man she ran through the neck, another through the chest, and her impact flung several more to the ground. Then she drew her sword and hit out, lopping off one head, fracturing another, lunging through this man's side, leaving the next deprived of one or other arm. / Bold Astolfo and mighty Samsonet had joined her in donning breastplate and coat of mail. Now though they had not come here to this end, nonetheless, seeing battle thus engaged, they lowered their visors, rested their lances, and charged into the throng, where they hacked out a passage, laying about them with their slashing swords. /

The knights, who had arrived here from many lands to take part in the tournament, looked on at the sight of these weapons being plied with such savagery, and beheld the sport to which they had looked forward being turned into an occasion of dire sorrow (for not all of them knew why the populace was so outraged nor just what injury had been done to the king), and stood aside, puzzled and bewildered. / While some of them came to the assistance of the rabble to save them from last-minute regrets, others, no more partisan to the citizens than to the strangers, hurried in to separate the contenders; the rest of them, the wiser ones, held their horses and watched to see how it was going to turn out.

Among the first group were Grifon and Aquilant who moved forward to the defence of the trophies. / Noticing how blood-shot and dilated the king's eyes were with sheer venom, and learning from many sources the full story behind the rumpus, Grifon decided that he was as much the injured party as the king; this being so, he and Aquilant called for their lances and stormed away at a gallop to have their revenge. / Astolfo, for his part, had pulled well ahead, spurring Rabican forward and grasping his golden lance which, being enchanted, could overthrow every opponent on impact. He struck Grifon with it first, and left him prostrate on the ground; then he came to Aquilant and, barely glancing the rim of his shield, hurled him backwards into the dust. / Knights of highest attainment and experience quit their saddles on meeting Samsonet. The populace all sought the way out from the square, while the king fumed with rage and frustration.

As for Marfisa, seeing that the entire throng had taken to its heels, she picked up the original breastplate and the new one, and both helmets, and departed victoriously for her lodgings. / Astolfo and Samsonet were not slow to go after her and accompany her to the gate (for the mob made way for them) and they stopped at the palisade outside the gate. Aquilant and Grifon, smarting with humiliation at being unhorsed first time, hung their heads in shame and dared not go near the king. / They leapt onto their mounts and spurred away in hot pursuit of the enemy, while the king and a numerous retinue followed, all of them ready to be avenged or die. The foolish rabble yelled 'Kill! Kill!', but they kept their distance and awaited the outcome. Grifon came to where the three companions had turned against their pursuers; they were holding the bridge. / As he approached he recognized

Astolfo, who was wearing the same device, the same armour, and rode the same horse as on the day he slew Orrilo of the charmed life. In the lists he had charged against Astolfo without taking a close look at him; here he recognized him, though, and greeted him, then asked him about his companions / and why they had scattered the trophies and acted so disrespectfully towards the king. The English duke gave Grifon a true account of who his companions were; as for the arms which had sparked off the quarrel, he confessed he knew little about them: but, since he had come with Marfisa, he and Samsonet both felt inclined to second her. /

As Grifon was conversing with the paladin Aquilant arrived; he recognized Astolfo the moment he heard him talking with his brother, and this at once disarmed him. Many of Norandin's suite now approached, though they dared not come too close; seeing the opponents engaged in conversation they were all the more inclined to hold back and silently lend an ear. / One of them, hearing that Marfisa was here, Marfisa, renowned throughout the world for her strength, turned his horse and went to warn Norandin that he stood to lose his entire court today if he did not take steps to rescue them from Death and the Furies before they were all slain: it was Marfisa, no less, who had laid hold of the armour in the lists. / When King Norandin heard this name, which was so feared throughout the Levant that it made people's hair stand on end even when she was nowhere near, he was convinced that what his courtier said would surely happen if he did not take measures to prevent it; so he called his retinue, whose wrath had already turned into timidity, and pulled them back. /

On their side Grifon and Aquilant, Samsonet and Astolfo prevailed upon Marfisa to call off her quarrel. She advanced towards the king and addressed him haughtily: 'I know not, my lord, by what right you intend to award these arms, which are not yours, as a prize to the winner of your tournament. / They are mine, these arms; I left them one day in the middle of the road from Armenia, when I had to pursue on foot a thief who had done me grave injury. Let my emblem bear witness; here it is, if you are acquainted with it.' She pointed to it, etched on the breastplate—a crown riven in three. /

'You are right,' replied the king; 'they were given to me a few days ago by an Armenian merchant. Had you asked me for them, they would have become yours, whether or not they had been so before; although I had earlier awarded them to Grifon I have complete confidence that, in order to enable me to give them to you, he would have been equally ready to return my gift to me. / There is no need for you to call on the witness of your emblem to convince me that these are your arms; your word is sufficient, your own testimony being far more persuasive than any other's. That your arms are indeed yours is clear from the prowess you show, worthy of far greater prizes. Now take them, therefore, and let there be no further quarrel. Let Grifon accept from me a greater prize.' /

Grifon, who set little store by those arms, while his great concern was to do the king's pleasure, said to the king: 'I shall feel amply rewarded if you assure me that I am making you content.' And Marfisa, remarking to herself, 'My honour seems to be amply satisfied,' turned towards Grifon with a winning smile and requested the arms of him. It ended with her receiving them from his hands. / In peace and amity they returned into the city for an even more intense round of festivities. The tournament took place, and it was Samsonet who won the honours and the trophies: Astolfo and the twin brothers, and Marfisa, who could outclass them all, refrained from entering the lists, as they wanted their friend and comrade Samsonet to be the victor. /

They passed a good ten days in feasting and celebration with Norandin, after which they took their leave, for the lure of France was proving too much for them, and they had to go. Marfisa came with them, as she wanted to make the journey: she had long been wishing to match herself against the paladins / and see for herself whether their reputations were justified. Samsonet appointed a regent to rule over Jerusalem in his place, and the five of them, forming a select band with few rivals for strength anywhere in the world, took leave of King Norandin and went to Tripoli and to the sea nearby. / Here they found a galleon loading merchandise for the West; they reached agreement with her master, an old man from Luna, for the conveyance of themselves and their horses. The sky was clear all over and promised a smooth passage for many days to come. With the sky thus serene they cast off and a good wind bellied their every sail. /

As they approached the first port in Cyprus, the island sacred to the Love-goddess, they encountered a miasma which is not merely noxious to humans—it even blights metal. Life here is short. The reason for it is a marsh called Constantine—and surely Nature ought never to have been so perverse here at Famagusta, putting the putrid, malignant marsh on its doorstep, when she is so kind to the rest of the island. / The heavy vapours rising from the marsh precluded the ship's remaining long in port. So she spread her wings to a North-easter and swept round Cyprus to the right, putting in at Paphos, where she made fast; here the travellers stepped out onto the beautiful shore, some to pick up merchandise, others to visit this country full of love and pleasure. / From the sea there is a gentle incline running six or seven miles up a pleasant hill. On all sides there are myrtles and cedars, orange trees and laurel, and a thousand other fragrant trees. Thyme and marjoram, roses, lilies, and saffron scatter such sweetness over the aromatic ground that every breeze off the land carries the fragrance to travellers out at sea. / The entire hillside is bathed by an abundant rill flowing from a limpid spring. Well might one say that so happy a spot belongs to lovely Venus: every woman, every maiden here is better pleasing than any others in the world, and the goddess keeps them all smouldering with love, young and old, until their last hour. / Here they heard the same news of Lucina and Orcus that they had learnt in Syria, and how preparations were afoot in Nicosia to convey her back to her husband. Now the shipmaster, his business here concluded and the wind being favourable, weighed anchor and, bringing the ship onto a Westward heading, unfurled every sail. /

The ship beat to windward in a Nor'wester and made for the open sea. But then a Sou'wester, which seemed gentle when it got up and stayed gentle while the sun was high, freshened towards evening and whipped up the sea with such thunder and searing flashes of lightning that the sky seemed to split and catch fire from end to end. / The clouds spread a dark veil which shut out sun and stars. There was a constant roar from the sea beneath, the sky above them, and the wind on every side, and the storm flayed the wretched seafarers with darkest rain and hail. The night ever gained ground over the wrathful turbulent waves. / The sailors now showed the skills for which they were esteemed: one blowing on a whistle ran here and there signalling instructions to the rest; some made ready the spare anchors, some stood to the halyards or to the sheets; others stood to the tiller, secured the mast, or saw to clearing the decks. / The storm increased in violence all through the night, which was thicker and blacker than Hades. The shipmaster stood out to sea in the hope of finding less broken water there; and he kept turning the ship's head to meet the impact of the fearful breakers head on, not without hope that daylight would bring an end to the tempest. / But no end, no abatement to the storm, only a greater virulence marked the coming of day—if day you could call it, recognizable by the passage of the hours, not by the evidence of any light. Now with hope diminished and fear increased the poor shipmaster gave way to the wind and, turning the vessel's stern to the seas, drove across the cruel waters with all sails furled. /

While Fortune was harrying these travellers at sea, she was allowing no respite to the others on land—in France, I mean, where the Saracens and the English were at grips, hewing and slaughtering each other. Here Rinaldo attacked, broke open and scattered the enemy ranks and overthrew their banners. I told you how he had urged his steed Bayard against stout Dardinel. / Rinaldo saw the coat of arms of which Dardinel, son of Almont, was so proud; a man must be a true champion, he decided, to dare flaunt the same device as Count Orlando. On closer approach his assumption was borne out: Dardinel had raised mounds of dead men about him. 'Better root out and exterminate this evil shoot now,' he cried, 'before it grows any stronger.' / Wherever the paladin turned his face everyone cleared off and gave him a wide berth; the Faithful were as quick to pull back as were the Saracens, such was the respect in which the famous sword was held. Rinaldo, though, saw nobody but wretched Dardinel, and pursued him relentlessly. 'I tell you, boy,' he shouted, 'the man who left that shield to you left you a load of trouble. / I am coming to test you, if you wait for me, and see how well you defend your red and white quarterings: if you do not defend them now against me, you'll be even less able to defend them against Orlando.' 'Let me tell you', replied Dardinel, 'that if I bear this emblem I can defend it too, and win myself more honour than trouble from my father's red and white quarterings. / Just because I am a boy, don't think you can make me run away, or that I'll give you my shield; if you take my arms you'll take my life, but I hope in God that the reverse will happen. Whatever the outcome, no one shall ever be able to accuse me of being false to my ancestry.' With these words, sword in hand, he attacked the knight of Montauban. /

The Africans felt their blood run cold when they saw Rinaldo making for Dardinel with all the ferocity of a lion who has spotted in a field a bullock too young even for first love. The first blow struck was aimed by the Saracen, but it fell harmlessly against Rinaldo's helmet—the helmet of Mambrino. / Rinaldo scoffed: 'Now let's see if I'm better than you at finding the vein!' He spurred his steed, abandoned the reins, levelled his sword at his opponent's chest and lunged so powerfully that the blade came right out between his shoulders. Withdrawing the blade, he drew blood—and spirit, too: the body slumped from the saddle, cold and bloodless. / As a purple flower fades and dies if the ploughshare has severed it in passing; or as a poppy in a meadow hangs its head if it be weighed down with overmuch moisture: so, as all colour drained from Dardinel's face, he departed this life; his life ebbed out, and with it ebbed all the courage and strength of his followers. / Like waters which human contrivance will sometimes hold pent up: should the dam ever break, they gush forth and spread out with a great roar. Thus were the Africans: they could be held together while Dardinel was there to infuse courage into them—but now they scattered this way and that, now that they had seen him slip, dead, out of the saddle. / Rinaldo ignored those who would flee, attending rather to the rout of those who would stand firm. Saracens fell wherever

Ariodant passed—today he came very close to Rinaldo in valour. Lionet trounced many a man and so did Zerbin, each one bidding to outdo the other. Charles and Oliver, Turpin and Guido, Solomon and Ogier all did their duty. /

That day the Moors ran a grave risk that not one of their number would return to his homeland; but the prudent King of Spain bestirred himself and withdrew with his survivors. To survive defeat was, he held, wiser counsel than to lose his entire fortune and his shirt to boot; better to withdraw and save a number of his men than, by standing fast, expose them to perish one and all. / The ensigns, which had been in an enclosure protected by earthworks, he sent back to the camp with Stordilan and Madarasso, King of Andalusia, and the Portuguese King Tesira in one large host. He sent a message to Agramant, King of Barbary, to try to withdraw as best he could; if today he could save his person and their ground, he would have accomplished no small thing. / Agramant, who saw defeat looming on all fronts and never expected to see Bizerta again, for never had he known Fortune to show quite so horrible, so grisly a face, rejoiced that Marsilius had brought part of the army back into assured safety. He began his own withdrawal, recalling the ensigns and sounding the retreat. / Now most of the scattered troops would not listen to trumpet or drum or any signal; such was their panic, such their terror that many of them were to be seen drowning in the Seine.

King Agramant wanted to recall the host; with Sobrino he galloped to head them off, while all the commanders strove with their men to withdraw them into the shelter of the camp. / But it was all Agramant, Sobrino and the commanders could do, for all their pleas or threats, to rally even one third, let alone every one of their men to the ill-attended banners. Two men were dead or fled for every one who stayed, and even he was not uninjured—some were wounded behind, others in front, and every one of them was weary and woebegone. / In great dread they were pursued right in through the gates of their fortified camp. Now even here, for all the work they had done on its defences, they were not secure: Charlemagne knew how to grasp good Fortune by her locks when she turned her head. Dark night descended, though, interrupting the pursuit and bringing a lull—hastened on, perhaps, by the Creator, who had pity on his creatures. / Blood swamped the fields and flowed like a great river, flooding the roads. Eighty thousand was the number of the corpses which had that day been put to the sword. Countryfolk and wolves stole out from their lairs that night to strip and devour them. /

Charlemagne did not withdraw into the city but made camp outside, putting the enemy's tents under siege; bonfires blazed high in thick clusters all about. The pagans reacted by digging fosses and throwing up earth-works and bastions; they inspected the guard, keeping them on the alert, and remained in their armour all night. / Oppressed with anxiety, the pagans all night long were given over to tears, groans, and laments which they subdued and muffled as best they could. Some wept for friends and relatives who had died, others bewailed their own lot, wounded and in discomfort as they were; but most widespread of all was fear of worse to come. /

In the camp there were two Moors, natives of Ptolemais, humbly born; their story is worth relating—it is an example of true love. Cloridan and Medor were their names; in good fortune and ill they had always loved Dardinel, and with him had crossed the sea to France. / Cloridan, a hunter all his life, was robust and agile. Medor was born with lovely fair skin and pink cheeks: among all the host assembled on the expedition there was not a comelier or more pleasing face. He had dark eyes and a golden head of curls—he might have been an angel, indeed a seraph. / These two were among the many standing guard on the ramparts protecting the camp. Night had reached half her course and was watching the sky with drowsy eyes.

Medor could speak of nothing but his lord, Dardinel, son of Almont, and could not restrain his tears, to think of him lying dishonoured in the field. / He turned to his companion and said: 'O Cloridan, I cannot tell you how it grieves me that my lord has been left in the field, to be food—all too dainty, alas!—for wolves and crows. When I think how good he always was to me, I feel that even if I gave my life to serve his fame I could not repay him or discharge my immense debt to him. / I mean to go and find him, so that his body does not remain in the field unburied. God perhaps will have me go, concealed, into the silence of King Charles' camp. You stay here: if it is decreed in heaven that I must die, you can tell of me, so that, though Fate prevent so fair a deed, at least my good intention shall be known.' / Cloridan was amazed that such courage, such love, such fidelity should be found in a boy. Loving him as he did, he tried hard to dissuade him from his plan, but to no purpose, for a grief such as Medor's could never be alleviated nor assuaged. Medor was ready either to die or to give his lord burial. / Seeing that he could not dissuade him, 'Then I shall come too,' Cloridan said. 'I too want a part in a deed of such merit. I too crave for renown in death. What joy am I to find in anything if I am left without you, Medor? Far better to die with you under arms than to die later of sorrow, should you be taken from me.' /

Thus decided, they posted the relief-watch on their sector and away they went. They left behind them the ditches and palisades and in a while here they were among our unsuspecting Christians. The whole camp slept, every fire burnt out, for they little feared the Saracens. Steeped to the eyes in wine, in slumber, the Christians lay prostrate among their arms and waggons. / Cloridan stopped a moment and said: 'I'm not one to let an occasion slip by: Medor, shall I not kill off some of this host which stabbed my lord? You, keep a look-out with your eyes and ears so that no one creeps up on us. I shall take it upon myself to clear a wide path for you through the enemy.' / This said, he spoke no further, but slipped over to where learned Alpheus lay asleep. Alpheus, physician, wizard, and astrologer, had come the year before to Charlemagne's court, but little did his learning profit him this time, indeed it lied to him most brazenly: he had forecast his own death at a great age on his wife's bosom, / but now the stealthy Saracen had stuck the sword's point through his throat. He killed another four next to the astrologer before they had time to utter a word. Turpin makes no mention of their names, and time has obliterated their traces. After them he slew Palidon of Moncalieri who was sleeping snugly between two horses. /

Then he came to where poor old Grillo was sleeping, his head pillowed against a wine-cask. After draining the cask, he had looked forward to a peaceful, undisturbed slumber, but the adventurous Saracen cut off his head; blood and wine gurgled out together through the same spigot, for his body held many a hogshead. He was dreaming of drink till Cloridan came to sort him out. / After Grillo he snuffed out with two strokes a Greek and a German, Androponus and Conrad, who had long been enjoying the freshness of the night as they plied their cups and their dice. Happy would they have been had they known how to stay awake at their board until the sun rose across the Indus— but Fate would be powerless over men if everyone could foretell the future. /

Imagine a starving lion, lean and wizened from long fasting, in a crowded sheepfold; he kills, devours, and savages the feeble flock abandoned to his power. Similarly the cruel pagan shed the blood of our men in their sleep, wreaking slaughter on every side; nor did Medor's sword remain idle, though he scorned to slay the common herd. / He came to where the Duke of Albret was sleeping clasped in the arms of a lady-love; the couple were so tightly entwined that no air could have seeped between them. Medor sliced off both heads cleanly. Oh happy death! Oh sweet fortune! I do believe that their souls flew embracing, like their bodies, to their destination. / Malindo he killed and his brother Ardalic, sons of the Count of Flanders. Charlemagne had knighted them both, and given them the right to wear the Lilies on their emblem, because he saw them both return from a slaughter of the enemy, their daggers crimsoned. He had promised them lands in Frisia, too, and would have given them—but Medor prevented him. / The insidious weapons were close now to the tents erected by the paladins around the emperor's pavilion; the paladins were taking turns to stand guard.

At this point the Saracens held back and ceased their pitiless butchery; they turned aside, fearing that they were bound to come upon one man still awake in so vast a host. / And though they could have departed laden with booty, they deemed it gain enough if they could make good their escape. So Cloridan picked his way where the going seemed safest, with Medor close behind him. They came to the field littered with swords and bows, shields and lances; here poor men and rich, kings and vassals lay together in a crimson bog, men and horses all entangled. / With such a grisly tangle of corpses littering the field in all directions, the two friends' faithful task might have been thwarted until daybreak, had not the Moon, at Medor's prayer, put forth the tip of her crescent through the dark clouds. Medor devoutly raised his eyes to her in heaven and prayed: / 'Holy Goddess, rightly are you invoked under three names by our ancestors: in heaven, on earth, and in the underworld you reveal your supreme beauty under different guises, and in the forests you are a huntress chasing monsters and wild beasts! Show me where my king lies among so many dead: as he lived he was devoted to your sacred pursuits.' /

The Moon breached the clouds at his prayer (whether by chance or in answer to such faith) and disclosed herself, beautiful as the night when she gave herself naked into the arms of Endymion. In her radiance Paris was revealed, and both camps; hill and plain could be seen, and the two summits in the distance, Montmartre to the right, Montléry to the left. / Her radiance shone even more brightly on the spot where Almont's son lay dead. Weeping, Medor approached his dear lord, recognizing the red and white emblem, and his whole face was bathed in bitter tears (there was a stream under each eyelid). He lamented with such sweetness, he could have made the winds stop to listen, but he kept his voice low, almost inaudible, / not that he was anxious for his own life if he were overheard—he hated his life and would gladly have quit it—but he feared lest the pious duty which had brought him here might be impeded. After heaving the dead king onto their shoulders, sharing his weight equally, / they hastened their steps as well as they could under the load of their cherished burden.

Now the lord of day was already coming to take the stars from the sky and the shadows from the earth when Zerbin, who had the resource to drive sleep out of his breast when need arose, returned to the camp with the first light: he had hunted the Moors all night. / With him were some knights who espied the two friends from a distance; the group turned off in their direction, hoping for booty. 'My friend, we must throw down our burden', said Cloridan, 'and take to our heels: there would be little sense in two living men being lost to save one dead one.' / And he threw down his burden, assuming that his friend would do likewise; but poor Medor, who loved his lord more fondly, took the whole burden onto his own shoulders. Cloridan darted off, imagining that Medor was beside or right behind him: had he realized he was leaving him to his fate, he would have held back to await not one but a thousand deaths. / The knights, determined that the pair should surrender or die, spread out and blocked all their escape-routes. Their captain held back a little: he was even more anxious to catch them than the others were, for he was certain, from their terror, that they must come from the enemy camp. /

In those days there was an ancient wood there, thickly planted with shady trees and shrubs; it formed a labyrinth of narrow paths and was frequented only by wild beasts. The two pagans hoped it would be friendly to them and conceal them amid its branches. Those who are enjoying my story, I expect them to come and listen to it another time.

NINETEENTH CANTO

> *1–2 Introductory. 2–16 Cloridan and Medor fall prey to the Scots. 17–42 Angelica and Medor. 43–53 Marfisa, Astolfo, and their companions survive a storm at sea and reach the land of the killer-women. 54–108 Marfisa fights ten foes.*

A MAN riding high on Fortune's wheel cannot tell who really loves him, for his true and his spurious friends stand side by side and show him equal devotion. But should he fall upon hard times, his crowd of flatterers will slip away. Only the friend who loves from his heart will stand by his lord and love him when he is dead. / If the heart were open to view as is the face, certain men at court who are great and lord it over their fellows would change roles with certain others held in little account by their lord: the lowly one would become the man of eminence while the notable would melt into the anonymous throng.

But let us return to Medor, ever loyal and beholden to his lord, whom he loved dead as alive. / The unfortunate youth thrust his way through the most overgrown paths in search of escape, but the heavy burden he carried on his shoulders brought all his plans to nothing. The terrain was unfamiliar and he took a wrong turning which led him into impenetrable thorns. His friend Cloridan, lighter in the shoulder, had found safety at some distance from him. / Cloridan had withdrawn to a spot whence he could no longer hear the hullabaloo of his pursuers; but when he realized that Medor was not with him, he felt as though he had left his heart behind. 'How could I have been so mindless,' he cried, 'how could I so have forgotten myself as to hide in here, Medor, without you, without knowing when I left you or where!' / With these words he plunged back along the tortuous trail, through the labyrinthine wood and retraced his steps, following the tracks which led him towards his death. The sound of horses came to him, and shouts and the bellowed threats of the enemy, and then he caught Medor's voice and saw him alone on foot, surrounded by a host of mounted men. / They numbered a hundred and crowded in upon him. Zerbin, their leader, ordered that he be captured. Poor Medor kept turning like a lathe and held them off as best he could, slipping behind an oak, or an elm, a beech, or an ash-tree, but ever keeping close to his cherished burden, which he had now set down upon the grass as he could no longer carry it. He kept hovering about it / like a mother-bear attacked by a huntsman in her craggy mountain lair. She stands by her cubs, perplexed, and quivers with pity and rage at once: rage and her natural fierceness urge her to bare her claws and bloody her chops, but mother-love softens her and draws her back, in the midst of her wrath, to take care of her young ones. /

Cloridan did not know how to help him; he wanted to die beside him, but was not going to part with his life before he found means to dispatch more than one of the enemy. So he fitted one of his sharp arrows to his bow and from his concealment performed to such effect that one of the Scotsmen fell lifeless from the saddle, his brain pierced. / The rest all looked about them to see whence the murderous shaft had flown. Meanwhile Cloridan shot off another to claim a second victim next to the first: the second man was excitedly and loudly asking one fellow after another who had shot the arrow when the new one arrived —to penetrate his throat and cut him off in mid-sentence. / Now Zerbin, their captain, could stand this no longer. Fuming with rage he approached Medor and shouted: 'You shall pay for this!' He reached out and grasped his golden curls and tugged him forward petulantly— but when he laid eyes on the youth's handsome face he took pity on him and did not slay him. / Now the boy entreated Zerbin, saying, 'For the sake of your own God, sir knight, be not so cruel as to prevent my giving burial to the body of my king; further pity than this I do not crave nor would I have you think that I long to live. I care for my life only so far as it will enable me to bury my lord, no further. / But if you are a man possessed like Creon the Theban, and needs must fatten the beasts and birds, give them my corpse to feast upon, but let that of Almont's son receive burial.' Thus spoke Medor; his manner and his words could well have swayed a mountain. Zerbin was so touched by them, he blazed with love and pity. /

At this point a brutish knight, showing scant respect for his commander, swung his lance down at the suppliant's tender breast. This cruel, incongruous action upset Zerbin, all the more so as he saw the boy fall down stunned and dazed and to all appearances lifeless. / In his anger and grief, 'This shall not go unavenged!' he cried, and rounded menacingly upon the knight who had done this evil deed. But the knight forestalled him, stepping out of the way and making off. Seeing Medor prostrate, Cloridan leapt out from cover to engage battle; / seething with rage he tossed aside his bow and laid into the enemy with his sword, sooner to die than with any thought of wreaking vengeance adequate to his fury. He saw the sand turn red with his own blood, amid so many swords, and his end approaching. Now feeling his last strength gone, he dropped to the ground beside his friend. / The Scots followed their captain whose high rage drove him into the deep forest, leaving the two Moors, the one quite dead, the other barely living. For a long time young Medor lay there; blood flowed so copiously from his gaping wound that he would have reached his term had not help been forthcoming. /

Who came upon him was a damsel dressed in humble, pastoral attire; she had a royal presence, though, an exquisite face, a noble demeanour, and she displayed a studied modesty. It is so long now since I last spoke of her, you may scarcely be able to recognize her: in case you do not know, she is Angelica, the lofty daughter of the Great Khan of Cathay. / Once repossessed of her ring, which Brunello had taken from her, Angelica grew so haughty and supercilious she seemed to shun the whole of humanity. She kept her own company and would have disdained the companionship of the most renowned man alive: she was above remembering that one of her suitors was called Orlando, another, Sacripant. / The one mistake she regretted most of all was the warm feelings she had nurtured for Rinaldo: how immeasurably she had debased herself, she considered, turning her eyes so very far below her. Now this arrogance came to the attention of Cupid, who would brook it no longer; taking up his station where Medor lay, he fitted an arrow to his bow and waited. /

When Angelica saw the boy languishing, wounded, and very close to death, and grieving far more for his king who lay exposed than for his own hurt, an unaccustomed sense of pity stole into her breast by some unused door, softening her hard heart, the more so when he related his story to her. / And, recollecting the surgeon's art which she had acquired in India (where it appears that this skill is noble and worthy and highly esteemed, a skill transmitted from father to son rather than acquired by book-learning), she decided to treat him with the juices secreted by herbs, and allow him to attain to full maturity. / She remembered passing a pleasant slope and noticing a herb which grew there—it might have been dittany or panace or something of the sort: its effect was to staunch blood and allay every spasm and harmful hurt in the wicked wound. She found the herb nearby, gathered some and returned with it to where she had left Medor. / On her way back she met a herdsman riding through the wood in search of a heifer which had strayed from the herd two days since. She brought him to Medor whose strength was flowing out with the blood from his breast; the ground beneath him was by now so dyed with gore that the boy was close to expiring. / Angelica dismounted from her palfrey and had the herdsman dismount with her. Now she crushed the herb with a stone and took it between her white hands and pressed out the juice from it; this she applied to the wound, and spread it also on his chest and belly, down to his hips. Such was the virtue of this juice that the blood was staunched and his vigour returned, / giving him the strength to mount the horse led by the herdsman. But Medor would not leave before his lord had been laid to rest. He had Cloridan buried with the king; then he set out whither she would take him. Angelica stayed with him, out of compassion, in the humble cottage of the kind herdsman. /

Not until he was returned to health would she leave him, so much did he mean to her—for such was the tenderness which pity had evoked in her when she had first set eyes on the prostrate youth. And later, seeing how graceful he was, and how comely, she felt her heart being grazed as by some unseen file; she felt her heart abraded and little by little smoulder and ignite with love. / The herdsman lived with his wife and children in an extremely pleasant cottage hidden in the woods between two hills; his home was newly built. Here Medor's wound, thanks to the damsel, was soon restored to wholeness—but not before she began to notice a deeper wound than his in her own heart. / In her own heart she felt a far wider, deeper wound made by an unseen arrow shot by the Winged Archer from the dazzling eyes and golden curls of Medor. She felt herself on fire, devoured in flames, but it was Medor's plight she heeded, not her own. Her own she did not treat, and thought of nothing except to cure the very one who was wounding and tormenting her. / Her wound enlarged and festered in measure as his dwindled and healed. The boy grew better, she languished with a strange fever which made her hot and cold by turns. Day by day, beauty flowered in him, while the poor damsel wasted away, as a patch of snow out of season will waste when exposed on open ground to the sun. /

If she was not to die of longing, she would have to help herself without delay: it was clear to her that there was no time to wait until she was invited to take what she craved. So, snapping the reins of modesty, she spoke out as boldly with her tongue as with her eyes and asked for mercy there and then—which he, perhaps unknowingly, conceded to her. / O Count Orlando! O King of Circassia! Tell me just what good your eminent valour has gained you, what account has been taken of your honour and nobility, what reward your attentions have merited! Show me one single kindness the damsel ever did to you, at any time, to requite and reward you for all you have suffered for her sake! / O King Agrican, if you could return to life, how you would be pained, after the cruel, merciless way she rejected your advances! And Ferrau, and all you others I'll not mention, who have done great deeds without number for this thankless one, and all in vain—what a bitter blow it would be if you saw her now in this boy's arms! / Angelica let Medor pluck the first rose, hitherto untouched—no one had yet enjoyed the good fortune of setting foot in this garden.

To clothe what they had done in the trappings of virtue they were married with holy rites, Cupid standing sponsor to the bridegroom, the herdsman's wife, to the bride. / The nuptials were performed with all possible solemnity under that humble roof, and the tranquil lovers passed more than a month there in pleasurable enjoyment. The damsel could look no further than the youth. She could never have enough of him: though she clung constantly round his neck, her appetite for him never cloyed. / Whether she remained in the shade of the house or went out of doors, day and night she kept the comely youth beside her. Morning and evening she would wander hither and yon, exploring the bank of some stream or seeking some green meadow. At noontide a cave would shelter them, doubtless no less handy and hospitable than the one which offered Dido and Aeneas shelter from the rain and proved a trusty witness to their secrets. / Amid so many pleasures, whenever she saw a tree which afforded shade to a spring or limpid stream, she would hasten to carve it with a knife or pin; she did the same to any rock unless it was too hard. A thousand times out of doors, and another thousand indoors, all over the walls, Angelica's and Medor's names were inscribed, bound together in various ways with different knots. /

When she felt that they had tarried there all too long, she decided to return to Cathay in the Indies and place on Medor's head the crown of her fair kingdom. Now on her arm she wore a golden bracelet adorned with rich jewels, a token of the love which Count Orlando bore her;

she had long been wearing this bracelet, / which once upon a time
Morgana had given to Ziliant, the time when she was holding him concealed in the lake; Ziliant, restored to his father Monodant by Orlando's
valorous efforts, had given the golden trinket to his rescuer—but
Orlando would not wear it on his arm: being in love, he decided rather
to give it to his queen, about whom we are speaking. / If she prized this
bracelet more than it is possible to cherish an object of value, it was
not out of love for the paladin but simply because it was costly and
finely wrought. I cannot explain to you by what privilege she was able
to keep it on the isle of Ebuda, when she was exposed naked to the sea-
monster by the cruel, barbarous islanders. / Not having about her
anything else with which to reward the good herdsman who, with his
wife, had served her so faithfully ever since she had come under his
roof, she took the bracelet off her arm and gave it to him, asking him
kindly to accept it. Then they set out towards the mountains dividing
France from Spain. / They meant to stop at Valencia or Barcelona
for a few days until a suitable ship came to hand, one making ready to
sail for the Levant. As they came down from the mountains they
caught sight of the sea at Gerona, and, keeping the shore to their left,
they took the high-road in to Barcelona. / Before they arrived, though,
they came upon a madman; he was lying on the sandy beach, and was
smeared all over, back and front, with mud and slime, like a pig. He
rushed at them the way a dog will run at a stranger, and molested
them, and was on the point of doing them injury. But let us return to
Marfisa. /

Marfisa and Astolfo, Aquilant, Grifon, and the others were suffering
misery and the prospect of death on the seas against which they had
no protection. The storm kept swelling in pride and arrogance, in
menace and fury; already its wrath had endured three days and showed
no sign of abating. / Both the quarter-deck and the fore-deck were
smashed and shattered by the angry waves and ever rising wind;
anything left upright by the tempest the helmsman had cut down and
thrown into the sea. Bending over a crate, one seaman plotted the
ship's course by the light of a small lantern, while another was down in
the hold with a taper. / One man was stationed at the stern, another at
the bows, each with his sand-glass; every half-hour they checked their
course and the distance run, after which they both would meet at the
centre of the ship and, with their charts ready, would compare notes,
while the rest of the crew gathered round the shipmaster to hold
council. / 'We're standing into Limasol, into the sandbanks, by my
reckoning,' said one. 'We're at Tripoli, close to the sharp reefs where
the seas usually break up ships,' said another. 'We're lost off Sataly,'
asserted another, 'where many a helmsman has had reason to weep.'

Each man argued his own view, but all were equally oppressed by fear. /

On the third day the wind attacked with even greater savagery and the breakers seethed yet more viciously; the wind snapped the foremast and carried it off, while the seas swept away the helm and with it the helmsman. To remain fearless even now would have required a breast hard as marble, harder than steel. Marfisa, so undismayed up to this point, would not deny that today she knew fear. / Pilgrimages were vowed to Mount Sinai, to Compostella, Cyprus, Rome, the Holy Sepulchre, the Virgin of Ettinus—indeed to any and every site of renown. Meanwhile the shattered, afflicted vessel was tossed upon the sea and often into the lowering sky; and the shipmaster, to ease up, had had the mainmast cut down. / And parcels and crates and anything weighty he had thrown overboard from stem and stern and over the sides; the cabins and holds he had cleared, consigning the rich cargo to the greedy waves. Some stood to the pumps, to suck the unwelcome water from the ship and return the sea to the sea; others helped in the hold, wherever there were signs that the planks were parting. /

In hardship and misery they endured four whole days; they were totally defenceless, and the sea would have claimed a complete victory had she only held firm in her fury. But now Saint Elmo's fire appeared, which they had so longed for; it settled at the bows on a forestay, the masts and yards all being gone, and gave them hope of calmer airs. / On sight of the lovely flaming fire the seafarers all knelt down; with moist eyes and trembling voices they prayed for peace and a calm sea. The cruel storm, which until then had raged so tenaciously, now died down: the Nor'westerly and other contrary winds molested them no further, leaving the Sou'westerly in sole command of the sea. / The black-throated Sou'wester exerted his power over the turbulent sea— such power that as he breathed on the waters he set them flowing in so swift a stream that they bore away the vessel faster than the migrant falcon is borne by its wings; the helmsman was afraid lest their vessel be swept to the edge of the world, or wrecked or founder. / To remedy this, the good helmsman had makeshift sea-anchors thrown over the stern and the anchor-cable payed out, with a view to reducing their drift by two thirds. This expedient and, even more, the augury of the One who had kindled the flame at the bows, proved beneficial: it saved the ship, which might otherwise have perished, and allowed it to run safely before the seas. /

They found themselves making land in the Gulf of Alexandretta, towards Syria; they were heading for a large city, and indeed were so close inshore that the two forts flanking the harbour could be descried. Realizing the route they had taken, the shipmaster turned away,

deathly pale: this was not a place to land, but there was no standing out
to sea, no escape. / There was no standing out to sea, no escape, for the
masts and spars were gone and the ship's planks and timbers, pounded
by the seas, were all stove in, crushed or working loose. But to make
harbour there was to ask for death or for perpetual bondage: every
person whom accident or evil fate carries thither is either enslaved or
killed. / Furthermore the shipmaster had but to stop and hesitate and
he would incur a grave risk that people could arrive from the shore in
boats, arrayed for battle, and seize his vessel, which was in no state to
remain at sea, let alone to make war. While he was unable to reach a
decision, the English duke, Astolfo, asked him who could be keeping
him in such a quandary, and why he had not yet made harbour. /

The shipmaster explained to him that this entire coast was held by
the killer-women, whose traditional rule it was that all comers were to
be held in perpetual slavery or else killed. Only he could escape this
fate who achieved victory over ten men in combat, and the same night
in bed was able to pleasure ten damsels. / If he brings off the first test
but falls short in the second, he is put to death, and his companions are
set to work as ploughmen or cowherds. If he succeeds in both tests,
he can ask that his companions be set at liberty; for himself, he cannot
ask this but has to stay behind as husband to ten women, chosen
according to his fancy. / Astolfo could not help laughing as he discovered the strange practices of the natives. Samsonet now came up,
and Marfisa, then Aquilant and his brother, and the shipmaster informed them too of the reason which kept him outside the harbour. 'I
would sooner drown', he exclaimed, 'than undergo the yoke of slavery.' /

The sailors and the other passengers all shared the shipmaster's
feeling; Marfisa and her comrades, however, thought otherwise, for
they found the dry land safer than the waters: to them the sight of the
angry seas besetting them was far worse than the prospect of a hundred
thousand swords. This place, and any other where they could use their
weapons, inspired little fear in them. / The warriors were yearning to
step ashore, none of them with greater assurance than the English duke,
who knew that at the first blast of his horn the entire population would
clear off. One faction, then, favoured landing, the other was against it.
The issue was hotly argued until the stronger party so pressed the
shipmaster that, much against his will, he had the vessel brought into
harbour. / In fact hardly had they come close enough to be seen from
the shore than they had noticed a galley set out from the cruel city; it
carried a motley crew and expert helmsmen and made straight for their
luckless ship, which lay bemused by uncertain counsels. The high prow
of the one was secured to the low stern of the other, and they were towed
in from the pitiless sea. /

They entered harbour under tow, and by dint of rowing rather than with the aid of sail, for the galley had made a series of tacks which took it out of the wicked wind. Meanwhile the knights resumed their carapaces and grasped their trusty swords, all the time offering encouragement to the master and the other faint-hearts. / The harbour was in the shape of a crescent-moon, over four miles in circumference and six hundred yards across the entrance. On each tip of the crescent stood a fort. The harbour feared no assault from the storm-winds unless they came in from the South. The city encircled it like an amphitheatre, climbing up the hillside. / No sooner had the ship anchored in the harbour than six thousand women swarmed the quayside, all in martial array and armed with bows—for the word had spread throughout the city. And lest the captives had any illusions about flight, they were cut off from the open sea, the harbour-entrance being closed off by ships and chains always kept ready for this purpose. /

A woman ancient as Hector's mother, or as the Cumaean Sibyl, summoned the shipmaster and asked him whether his company wanted to forfeit their lives or whether they preferred to submit their necks to the yoke, according to the custom: they had to decide one way or the other, either to die or to remain prisoners. / 'It is true', she added, 'that if you can produce a man who has the spirit and the strength to do battle with ten of our men and slay them, and then to fulfil the husband's role with ten of our women in one night, why—he should become our prince, and you would be free to go on your way. / And you would be free to remain, all or some of you, if you so elected—but on condition that those of you who did elect to stay and keep your freedom would have to suffice as husband to ten women. But if your champion is overpowered by the ten adversaries whom he takes on all at once, or if he flags in the second test, slavery must be your will, death his.' /

If the old crone looked for signs of terror in the knights what she found was enthusiasm, for each of them was confident of being sufficient master of his weapon to be able to satisfy both requirements. Nor did Marfisa lose heart: she may have been ill equipped for the second performance, but where Nature left her unaided she was confident of making good with her sword. / The answer, concluded by a council of the knights, was committed to the shipmaster: from their number they would furnish forth one who could in all their names stand trial in the lists and in the bed-chamber. The challenge accepted, the helmsman approached and threw a rope for those on shore to grasp. The gangplank was lowered and the warriors stepped ashore, armed, leading their chargers. / They made their way from here into the city, where they found haughty damsels, their dresses tucked up, riding through the streets and tilting at each other in the public square like so many Amazons. Here no man was permitted to wear sword or spurs or any armour unless he went about in a band ten-strong, out of deference to the tradition I have explained. / The remaining menfolk were all busy at their shuttles and spindles, their reels, combs, and needles; they were dressed in feminine attire falling to their feet, which gave them a soft, languorous air. Some, though, were kept in chains to plough the land or watch the herds. They were few in number, the men, scarcely a hundred of them to a thousand women, in all the towns and countryside. /

Now the knights wished to draw lots as to which of them should take up their common defence by slaying the ten adversaries in the field, then impaling the next contenders in the other arena; but they did not include sturdy Marfisa, deeming that she would find an obstacle in the second joust, the night one, as she was not equipped to achieve a victory here. / But she insisted upon being included in the lottery and, as it happened, the lot fell upon her. 'I must venture my life', she told them, 'before you hazard your freedom. But I give you this sword as a pledge'—and she pointed to the sword girt upon her— 'that I'll put an end to your trammels the way Alexander disposed of the Gordian Knot. / It is my intention that travellers should never more, so long as this world endures, have cause to complain of this city.' This is what she said, and her comrades could not deprive her of that which Chance had allotted to her. Whether she lost for all of them, or won them all their liberty, they left everything in her hands. Armed with breastplate and coat of mail, she presented herself on the field of battle. /

High above the city there was an open space, circular, and surrounded by steps which served for seating. It was devoted exclusively to jousts and the like, to hunts, trials of strength, and to nothing else. It was closed off by four bronze gates. Hither the jostling throng of embattled women converged. Marfisa was summoned. / She rode in on a dapple-grey charger, all patches and speckles; he had a small head, spirited eyes, proud bearing, and fine build. Out of a thousand horses saddled and bridled in Damascus, this is the one King Norandin chose as the finest, most alluring, most mettlesome; he caparisoned him right royally and presented him to Marfisa. / Marfisa entered by the Austral Gate, the gate of the South Wind: hardly was she within than the pure, shrill blasts of the trumpet could be heard resounding through the closed arena. Then she saw her ten adversaries enter from the Northern quarter.

The first knight to appear looked as if by himself he could match all the rest. / He rode into the lists on a great charger, blacker than a raven all over except for his forehead and left hind foot; in these there was a touch of white. The rider wore the colours of the horse, to signify the proportion of joy to dark sorrow in him, as white to black in his steed. / The signal for battle was given and all at once nine of the antagonists lowered their lances; but the black knight scorned such an advantage and drew aside, and made no preparation to fight—he preferred to adhere to the rules of chivalry rather than to those of this kingdom. So he drew aside and waited to see how the one lance would fare against the nine. /

Marfisa's charger, silky smooth in his movements, bore the damsel swiftly into the fray; the lance she had in rest was so heavy that four men would have found it hard to lift—before disembarking she had singled out this one as being the most sturdy. The ferocious air with which she advanced caused a thousand cheeks to blanch, a thousand hearts to quail. / Such a hole did she make in the chest of her first opponent, it would have been considerable even had he been naked— but her lance penetrated his surcoat and breastplate, after first piercing a thick, well-plated shield, and stuck clean out of his back, visibly a good arm's length, such was the savage impact. Leaving him behind impaled on the lance, she rode on full tilt against the others. / The second and third she collided with so violently that they both quit their saddles and their lives at once, their spines fractured. What made the impact so heavy and sharp was that the adversaries were riding in a tight pack. I have seen bombards split ranks apart the way Marfisa tore through the enemy. / Several lances were broken upon her, but she might have been a stone wall struck by a leather ball for all the effect they had on her. The breastplate she wore was of such hard temper that the blows were powerless against her; it was magically wrought, smelted in the fires of Hades, and annealed in the waters of Avernus. /

Reaching the end of the field she drew rein, turned her steed, and stopped for a moment; then she was off again, charging into her adversaries, scattering them left and right and dipping her sword to the hilt in their gore. Here she lopped off a head, there an arm, while she caught one man such a swipe that he fell to the ground, bust, head, and arms, leaving his belly and legs still astride his mount. / She severed him, I say, straight across betwixt hips and ribs, which left him looking like a bust, like those sacred images made of silver, or more often of pure wax, which people both here and in remote parts of the world set up as a tribute of thanks, a votive offering, when they have obtained the answer to a pious prayer. / She spurred after one who was fleeing and caught up with him half-way across the arena, and parted his head from his neck in a way that no physician could ever rejoin them again.

One after another she killed, or so maimed them that their vigour drained out of them and she was confident that they would never again be able to get up to make war on her. /

The knight who had led his group into the arena remained on the sidelines all this while, deeming it an iniquitous shame to enjoy such an advantage of numbers over one solitary contender. Now, seeing the entire company put so promptly out of the fight by one opponent, to show that his reluctance was due to chivalry, not to fear, he moved forward, / and signalled with his hand to indicate that, before proceeding, he had a word to say. Now little realizing that so virile an exterior concealed a maiden, he thus addressed her: 'Sir knight, you must be weary now after having slain so many; and if I wished to tire you more than you are already, I should show you scant courtesy. / Let me concede you repose until tomorrow, to return then to the arena. It would do me no honour to stand against you today, spent and exhausted as you must be.'

'Labouring in arms is nothing new to me,' replied Marfisa, 'and I do not yield so readily to fatigue—as I trust I am about to teach you to your cost. / I thank you for your courteous offer, but I do not yet need to rest; and there is still so much of the day left it would be a shame to devote the rest of it to leisure.' 'Ah,' replied the black knight, 'would that I were as sated with every desire of my heart as I am ready to satisfy this one of yours: but look to it that the day be not further advanced than you think.' / With these words he promptly had two thick lances brought, two really hefty ones, and offered Marfisa the first choice, taking the other for himself. All was set; nothing further was needed but the shrill trumpet-peal to signal the start. The earth, the sky, and sea shuddered as they moved off at the first blast. /

You would not have seen a single one of the onlookers draw breath, move her lips, blink an eye, so intent were they all on following the contest to see which of the two champions would merit the palm. Marfisa aimed her lance with a view to pitching the black knight out of his saddle so he would never rise again; and the stalwart black knight was just as intent on putting Marfisa to death. / Their lances might have been of slender, dried out willow, not of thick, sappy oak, the way they splintered right to the butt. And the impact of the champions was so mighty that their horses both collapsed, just as if every sinew in their legs had been severed by one stroke of a scythe. But the warriors were quick to extricate themselves. / In her time Marfisa had unseated a thousand knights at first impact; never once had she been unhorsed—but on this occasion she was, as you have heard. This novel experience dismayed, indeed practically stunned, her.

The black knight, too, was no little surprised, for he was not readily unseated. /

. They scarcely touched the ground where they fell before they were on their feet, renewing the attack. One would lay on with a furious cut and thrust, the other would parry with shield or blade, or else leap aside. Whether a blow went wide or hit full on, the air hissed with it, the heavens re-echoed. Those helmets, those breastplates, those shields were demonstrably harder than anvils. / If the fiery damsel's arm was heavy, that of her opponent was not light—they had the measure of each other, each one receiving as he dealt. If it is a pair of fierce, dashing fighters you are seeking, you need look no further than these two, nor look for greater dexterity or strength: between the two of them they had these virtues to the limit. / The women, who had long been watching these awesome blows being exchanged, and no-ticing that the knights still showed no sign of labour or fatigue, praised them for the two finest warriors to be found within all the lands em-braced by the sea. It seemed to them that had the pair not been ex-cessively robust, they would be dead by now from sheer exhaustion. / 'It was lucky for me', remarked Marfisa to herself, 'that this man did not move earlier: had he taken his part with his comrades I may well have been killed by him, seeing that I can only just stand up to his blows as it is.' Meanwhile she kept laying about her with her sword. / 'It was lucky for me', the other brooded, 'that I did not let this man rest; I can scarcely hold him off now, while he is worn from his earlier fight. What would he have been like had he waited until tomorrow to regain his strength? How very fortunate that he would not accept my offer!' /

The combat lasted until evening, and it still was not clear who was gaining the upper hand. Neither of them would have been able to evade the other's blows once the light failed. When night came the courteous knight was the first to make a proposal: 'What shall we do,' he asked the illustrious damsel, 'seeing that we have achieved equal fortunes, and now importunate night has overtaken us? / It seems to me better that you prolong your life at least until the new dawn; I cannot extend your span by more than the length of a brief night; if that is as far as it will stretch, let the blame not rest on me but on the cruel law of the female sex which governs this land. / If I grieve for you and for your companions God knows, from whom nothing is hidden. Now you can come and lodge with me, you and your com-panions—with anyone else you will not be safe, for the people are plotting against you: many of them lost their husbands by your hand today, since each one of these men you have slain was husband to ten women. / For what you have done today ninety women seek vengeance, so if you do not come as my guest you must expect to be attacked in the night.' 'I accept your offer of hospitality', replied Marfisa, 'in the full assurance that you will prove as outstanding for your integrity and kindness as for your bravery and valour. / But as to being sorry that you must slay me, you may just as well rue the contrary: I don't believe that up till now you have found me an easier adversary than you are, or our battle mere child's-play. Whether you wish to continue the combat or to break it off; whether to pursue it under the one or the other luminary, I am ready at your bidding, as and whenever you wish.' /

So the contest was deferred until the new sun rose out of the Ganges, and no conclusion was reached as to which of the two warriors was the better. The hospitable knight approached Aquilant and Grifon and the others, and entreated them to be pleased to abide with him until the following day. / They accepted his invitation in complete trust, and, lighted on their path by flaming white torches, they made their way up to a regal dwelling which comported several delightful apartments.

The combatants were astounded when they took off their helmets and looked at each other: the black knight, to judge by appearances, was not yet eighteen. / The damsel was amazed that a youth should be so powerful a fighter. The other marvelled seeing, from Marfisa's tresses, whom it was he had been fighting. They each asked the other's name—a question they were both quick to answer. Now if you wish to discover what the youth was called I shall expect you in the next canto.

TWENTIETH CANTO

1–3 Introductory. 4–64 Guidone tells the story of the tribe of warlike women. 65–105 Astolfo procures his companions' escape from the warlike women. 106–144 Marfisa discomfits Pinabello and saddles Zerbin with an unwelcome companion.

IN feats of arms, as in the cultivation of the Muses, the women of old achieved distinction, and their splendid, glorious deeds irradiated the whole earth. Harpalice and Camilla achieved fame for their practised skill in battle; Sappho and Corinna shine, on account of their learning, with a radiance that night will never darken. / Women have proved their excellence in every art in which they have striven; in their chosen fields their renown is clearly apparent to anyone who studies the history books. If the world has long remained unaware of their achievements, this sad state of affairs is only transitory—perhaps Envy concealed the honours due to them, or perhaps the ignorance of historians. / In our own day I can clearly see such virtues evident among fair ladies that ink and paper is needed with which to record it all for posterity; this way, too, the calumnies of evil tongues may be drowned in perpetual shame. The praises of our womenfolk will then be such as to surpass those accorded to Marfisa. /

But, returning to this damsel, she did not mind revealing her identity to the chivalrous knight when he asked her who she was. Indeed she was quick to satisfy his curiosity, so eager was she to learn his own name. 'I am Marfisa,' she said—and this was quite sufficient, for her renown was world-wide. / When it was his turn, the knight gave an account of himself with a longer preamble.

'I imagine', he began, 'that my family name will be known to each one of you: not only France and Spain and their neighbours, but India, Ethiopia, and the chilly Pontus recognize Clairmont, the house which produced the knight who slew Almont, / as also the knight who dispatched Clariel and King Mambrino, and destroyed their kingdoms. From this blood am I sprung, born to my mother where the Danube flows by eight channels into the Black Sea, when my father, Duke Aymon arrived there on his travels. It is a year now since I left my mother to her sorrow, to go to France in search of my kinsmen. / But I could not finish my journey, for a gale from the South drove me ashore here, where I have been for ten months or more—I count the days and hours. My name is Guidone Selvaggio; I have little experience, little reputation so far. I slew Argilon of Melibea here with his ten knights. / I also passed the test of the damsels, so that I have ten to do my pleasure: these I have chosen as the pick of the realm for beauty and breeding. I rule them and all the others too, for they have conferred upon me their crown and sceptre. They will award as much to anyone who, with Fortune's favour, slays his ten opponents.' /

The knights asked him how it was that there were so few males in this land, and whether they were subject to their wives the way women are to their husbands elsewhere. 'Since I have been living here,' Guidone replied, 'I have often heard this explained. If you so wish, I shall tell you the story just as I have heard it. /

'When the Greeks returned home from Troy after twenty years—the siege lasted ten, and they spent a further ten wearisome years tossed on the seas and subject to contrary winds—they found that their womenfolk had resorted to a remedy against the itch caused by so long an absence: they had all chosen young lovers to avoid taking cold in their solitary beds. / Finding their homes full of children not their own, the husbands by common consent forgave their wives who, they realized, were unable to endure their deprivation; but the bastard children had to leave and seek their fortunes elsewhere, for the husbands would not tolerate these offspring being kept any longer at their expense. / Some of them were put outside to die, others were concealed by their mothers and so kept alive. Those who had grown up all split into groups and took their departures hither and yon: some followed the call of arms, some pursued the arts and sciences, while others tilled the soil, waited at court, herded the flocks—just as she appointed who ruled there. / One of those to leave was a young son of cruel Queen Clytemnestra; he was eighteen years old, fresh as a lily or rose newly plucked from its stem. He fitted out a ship and took to piracy, accompanied by a hundred youths chosen from all over Greece. /

'The Cretans at that time, having expelled barbarous Idomeneus from his throne, were recruiting armed men in order to strengthen their new state. They hired Phalantus (to give the youth his name) at a good wage and appointed him, along with his company, to garrison the city of Dictaea. / Among a hundred prosperous cities in Crete Dictaea was the richest and most attractive; with its beautiful, voluptuous women and its round of merriment from morning till night it was a happy spot. And as it had a long-standing tradition of hospitality towards strangers, it was not long before these Greeks were masters in their hosts' houses. / Being all of them young and most handsome (for Phalantus had chosen the pick of Greek youth), they attracted the hearts of the fair sex from the moment they arrived. And as, with all their good looks, the youths showed remarkable prowess in bed, they in a short time so captivated the ladies that they were loved above all else. / Eventually an end was put to the war for which Phalantus was engaged—and also to the military stipend; so, now that there was nothing further to be gained here, the young men wanted to leave. At this, the Cretan women were more distraught and shed more copious tears than if their fathers all lay dead before them. /

'The women earnestly pleaded with the youths, each with her own, not to go; but, meeting with refusal, they too left with them, deserting fathers, sons, and brothers; they absconded with rich jewels and plenty of gold taken from their families, for the whole affair was conducted in such secrecy that not a man on Crete got wind of their escape. / The hour chosen by Phalantus was so propitious and the wind so favourable that they were several miles out to sea before Crete woke up to its disaster. The fugitives came by chance upon this strand, which was then uninhabited; here they landed, and in safety they took closer stock of the fruits of their pillage. / This was the setting for ten days of amorous bliss. But as abundance in a young man's heart can so often lead to surfeit, the youths all decided to go without women and rid themselves of their importunity: no burden is heavier to bear than a woman of whom one is tired. / Eager as they were for gain and plunder, and little inclined to spending, they realized that it would take more than spears and bows to find the sustenance for so many concubines; so, loading up with the luckless women's jewels and gold, they abandoned them here and betook themselves to the shores of Apulia, where I hear that they founded the city of Taranto. /

'Realizing that they had been betrayed by their lovers, on whom they had placed too much reliance, the women were so aghast that for several days they could have passed for statues by the sea-shore. But once they recognized that nothing was to be gained from their shrieks and floods of tears, they turned their attention to finding some way out of their dreadful plight. / Various suggestions were discussed. Some of them favoured a return to Crete, preferring to submit themselves to the judgement of their stern fathers or slighted husbands, rather than to perish of hunger and privations on the desert shore or in the wild forests. Others maintained that a more honourable course would be to drown themselves in the sea. / They would do better, they argued, to roam the world as whores, as beggars, or slaves before they submitted themselves to the punishment their faults merited. These and similar conclusions were put forward, each one harsher and more oppressive, until Orontea stood up to speak. /

'Orontea traced her descent to King Minos. She was the youngest of them, also the fairest and shrewdest, and her sin was the lightest— she had been in love with Phalantus and had offered herself to him, still a maid, leaving her father for his sake. Her face and speech betrayed the wrath blazing in her noble heart; rejecting all the others' opinions, she announced her own, and carried it into effect. / She saw no reason to leave where they were: she knew the place was fertile, the air good, and that it was watered with limpid streams; the land was thickly wooded and for the most part flat. There were harbours and estuaries where travellers blown by an ill-wind would take refuge, bringing with them from Africa or from Egypt such various items as were necessary to sustain life. / Here she thought fit to settle, and wreak vengeance on the male sex which had so wronged them. Every ship which was forced by the wind to seek refuge in their havens was to be ransacked and set on fire, its occupants put to the sword; not a single life was to be spared.

'So much said, so much concluded: the enactment became law and was brought into effect. / Whenever they heard the wind rising, the women would take up arms and run down to the shore, led by the

implacable Orontea, who gave them their laws and ruled over them.
The vessels driven onto their coast were plundered and set afire, and
not a man escaped alive to tell the tale. / Thus they lived in solitude
for a number of years, sworn enemies to the male sex. Eventually,
though, they recognized that they would be heading for trouble unless
they changed their way of life: if they failed to reproduce themselves
their law would shortly become null and of no effect—it would fail
with the sterility of their clan, whereas their goal was to make it
eternal. /

'So they tempered the law's rigour a little and chose, over the course
of four full years, out of all those who happened their way, ten handsome and bold knights who had proved their durability in the love-
games. Matched, as they were, against a hundred women, it was
decided that to every ten women one husband was to be allotted. /
Before this, many were beheaded who had not measured up to the
challenge. But these ten, tried and true, were invited by the women to
share their beds and rule with them. They were made to promise,
though, that if other men were captured in their havens they were
every one to be put to the sword, all mercy stifled. / From conceiving
and giving birth the women began to fear lest so many males be born
that eventually their own sex would lose power to them and the régime
they so cherished would pass to male hands. So they took their precautions during their sons' unwarlike years to ensure that they would
never rebel. / To prevent the male sex from subduing them, a grim
law was enacted whereby each mother was to keep only one son: the
rest were to be smothered or taken out of the kingdom and bartered
or sold. Male children were sent away hither and yon, and their
mothers were instructed to exchange them for girls if they could, but
at all events not to return empty-handed. / Even then they would not
have raised one child to manhood had they been able to keep up their
own numbers without them; beyond this, the pernicious law extended no greater clemency to its own menfolk than it did to strangers,
who continued to be condemned uniformly to death. The only altera-
tion in the original code was that the women were no longer to slay
the strangers pell mell. / If ten or a score landed all at once, they were
thrown into prison, and one a day, not more, was picked out by lot
to perish in the horrible temple which Orontea had built; here she
had erected an altar to Vengeance, and given to one of the ten by lot
the cruel office of priest and executioner. /

'Many years after this, a young man was cast up on these murderous
shores; he was a descendant of Hercules, exceedingly valiant at arms,
and his name was Elbanio. Here he was captured before he knew it, for
he had landed all unsuspecting. Under heavy guard he was put into

close confinement and held with the rest for the barbarous rite. / In looks he was so handsome and agreeable, in manners and deportment so graceful, and in his speech so pleasant, so eloquent that an asp would have willingly lent an ear. An account of him, as of some rare species, soon came to the ears of Alexandra, daughter of Orontea who was still alive though well advanced in years. / Orontea still lived, while the remaining original settlers had all died. Meanwhile more than ten times their number had been born, and their increase enhanced their strength and standing. Still there was only one poker to ten furnaces—and these were kept shut most of the time. And still ten warriors were charged with giving a rude handling to all comers. /

'Alexandra, yearning to set eyes on the youth who was so highly praised, entreated her mother for this special favour and did contrive to see Elbanio and listen to him. Now when she made to go, she felt she was leaving her heart behind, to be gnawed and pricked. She felt herself ensnared and could not struggle free, and found herself in the end captured by her prisoner. / "If this land is still acquainted with pity," said Elbanio, "as is every other land where the journeying Sun brings light and colour, I would, for your sublime beauty which must captivate every gentle heart, risk asking you for the gift of my life, which then I should hold constantly at your service, to lay it down for you. / But if human hearts here are quite bereft of humanity, against all reason, I shall not ask you for my life, knowing how vain my entreaties would be. I would only ask that I be allowed to die, weapon in hand, as a warrior, whatever my merits as such, and not like a man condemned to death or a brute beast to be sacrificed." /

'Gentle Alexandra's eyes were moist with pity for the young man, and she replied, "Even if this land is more barbarous and evil than any other, I will not allow that every woman here is a Medea, as you imply—and even if all the others here were so, I nonetheless, alone of them all, mean to save you. / And though I have till now been as merciless and cruel as the others, I must confess that I have not before now seen reason to show pity. But I should be wilder than a tigress, and harder than a diamond if your comeliness, your valour, and courtesy had not quite softened me. / If only the law against strangers were less strict, I would not shrink from ransoming your life at the cost of my own more worthless one. But there is no one here who stands so high as to be able freely to help you. What you request, though it be little, will not easily be granted. / Still, I shall do what I can to obtain for you this satisfaction before you die—though I greatly fear that it will only procure you worse affliction, deferring your death." "Though I be confronted with ten men," replied Elbanio, "if I am armed, I shall feel such boldness that I trust to defend my life and slay them all, armed though they be." /

'Alexandra's only answer to this was to heave a great sigh; she left, taking with her a thousand amorous thorns embedded in her heart and beyond relief. She went to her mother and made her wish, that the knight be not left to die if he displayed such might as to slay ten adversaries single-handed. / Queen Orontea summoned her council and told them: "Our constant need is to discover the best men available to guard our harbours and beaches. Now to know whom to spare, whom to do away with, it is necessary to make trial of them as the occasion arises, so that we should not to our own detriment suffer the cowards to rule while the valiant are put to death. / I suggest, if you agree, that a further law be enacted whereby in future every knight driven by Fate onto our shores be offered the option, if he so wishes, before he die in the temple, of doing battle with ten adversaries. If he have the power to defeat them all, let him be guardian of the port, with others to assist him. / I say this because it appears we have a captive who offers to defeat ten men. If all alone he is a match for so many, then by Heaven he deserves to have his way. And if he turns out to be an idle braggart, he shall this way receive his deserts." Thus said Orontea, and one of the elders replied: /

' "The principal reason which induced us to have truck with men was not because we had the slightest need of their help to defend this kingdom: for this purpose we ourselves have all the courage, strength, and resource we need. Would that we could do without them, too, in the matter of propagating our race! / But as this is not possible without them, we have taken some of them into our company, always providing there be no more than one of them to ten of us, lest they gain the upper hand. This was done in order to conceive by them, not because we needed them to defend us. Their prowess only serves us to this one end—they may as well be unserviceable cowards in all other respects. / To keep among us a man so powerful goes totally against our main objective: if one man can, single-handed, put ten men to death, how many women will he dominate? If our ten picked men were of his calibre, they would seize power from us the very first day. This is no way to keep on top, putting weapons into the hands of those who can overcome us. / Bear in mind, too, that should Fortune so assist this man of yours that he does slay the ten, then a hundred women shall be widowed, and you shall hear their cries. If he wants to survive, let him suggest some way other than that of slaying ten men. Of course if he is up to supplying to a hundred women what they derived from ten men, he should be reprieved." / This was the opinion of cruel Artemia (to give the woman her name), and if Elbanio did not have his throat cut in the temple before the merciless gods, it was no thanks to her. But Orontea wanted to please her daughter, and, adducing a number of arguments in reply, so spoke that she prevailed upon the council to share her own view. /

'The fact that Elbanio was held to be the handsomest knight who ever lived so weighed in the estimation of the younger women in the assembly that the advice of their elders who, with Artemia, wanted to uphold the old order, was brushed aside. Elbanio was close to being quite simply reprieved as a favour. / The final decision was to spare him on condition that he slew the ten adversaries in battle, and then in a subsequent challenge could stand up to ten (not a hundred) women. The next day he was released from prison, given arms, and a steed of his choice, and confronted with the ten warriors, whom he slew, one after another, in the arena. / That night he was to show what he could do, alone and naked, with ten damsels; here he proved so gallant that he succeeded in sampling all ten of them.

'This success won him so high an opinion in Orontea's eyes that she welcomed him as her son and awarded to him Alexandra and the other nine damsels on whom he had carried out his nocturnal trial. / With fair Alexandra, after whom this land was subsequently named, she appointed him her heir, on the condition that he and all his successors preserved the law: whoever was unlucky enough to set his hapless foot on this soil was to choose between being sacrificed and taking on ten warriors single-handed. / If he succeed in slaying the ten men, he must contend that night with ten women; and if, here too, Fortune smile on him and he emerge victor, let him be ruler and leader of the tribe, and replace at his choice the ten vanquished men; thus let him reign until there arrive another who prove stronger than he and take his life. / For close on two thousand years the heinous tradition has been preserved, and still is today; few are the days when some unfortunate traveller does not die in the temple. If anyone requests, as Elbanio did, to take arms against the ten—it does sometimes happen—he will often lose his life at the first assault. Scarcely one in a thousand survives for the second test. / A few do survive, but they are so rare they can be counted on your fingers. One of these was Argilon, but he with his band of ten was only master for a while —contrary winds drove me ashore here, and I closed his eyes in eternal sleep.

'Would that I had died with him that day, rather than live to endure this shameful bondage. / The pleasures of love, the sport and gaiety which those of my age normally enjoy, the purple raiment, the jewels, the high estate—these bring but little joy to a man who is robbed of his liberty. Never more to be able to leave this land is an intolerable bondage. / I am constantly sad at heart, and have no taste for pleasures as I see how the best years of my life are being squandered in so debasing and effeminate a role. The fame of my clan is broadcast throughout the world and even to the heavens—perhaps I too would have my share in it were I with my brothers. / My destiny seems to have slighted me, appointing me to so abject an office. I am like a charger put out to grass because of some defect in eye or foot, some defect which renders him useless for war or other worthy service. As I have no hope of escaping from this base servitude except through death, it is death I crave.' /

Here Guidone's story ended as, in his bitterness, he cursed the day which had given him victory over the warriors and the women, and made over to him the realm. Astolfo listened, remaining in concealment until he had satisfied himself by various indications that this Guidone was, as he claimed, the son of his kinsman Aymon. / Then he spoke up: 'I am the English duke, your cousin Astolfo.' And he threw his arms around Guidone's neck and kissed him with much warmth and dignity, shedding not a few tears. 'Dear kinsman, your mother could not have hung a clearer sign about your neck—your valour at arms is quite enough to convince us that you are one of us.' / Guidone, who in other circumstances would have been overjoyed at finding so close a kinsman, greeted him now only mournfully, for the sight of him here made him sad: if he himself survived, then Astolfo would be enslaved, and that would be the very next day; if Astolfo were set free, it would be by his own death, so that the good of one of them must spell harm to the other. / He regretted, too, that if he won, the result would be perpetual bondage for the other knights as well. But were he to die in the conflict, he still would not be able to save them from slavery: if Marfisa came safely through the first morass only to be bogged down in the second, she will have defeated him to no advantage, for she still would be slain and her companions enslaved. / On their side, the tender years, the courtesy and courage of the young man had so touched Marfisa and her companions with love and pity that, if their freedom could be won only at the cost of his life, then they scarcely cherished their freedom. And if Marfisa had perforce to put him to death, she would as soon die too. /

She turned to Guidone: 'Come with us, we'll force our way out.' Guidone sighed: 'Leave all hope of ever escaping from here: you must lose to me or defeat me.' To which she replied: 'One thing I never fear is that I'll leave unfinished what I have begun. I know of no path safer than that along which my sword directs me. / Having sampled your valour in the lists, I am ready to undertake anything if you stand by me. Tomorrow, when the crowd throngs into the arena and takes its seat about the ring, let us set upon them and make them flee or defend themselves; let us leave their corpses to the wolves and vultures and their city in flames.' / 'I am ready to follow you', replied Guidone, 'and to die beside you. But let us not expect to survive—all we can hope is to avenge ourselves a little. Often I have counted ten thousand women up at the arena, and as many more standing guard over the harbour, the forts and walls; I know of no sure route of escape.' / 'Let them be more numerous than the men who followed Xerxes,' retorted Marfisa; 'let them outnumber the rebel angels who quit paradise to their perpetual disgrace—if you are with me, or at least if you do not side with the women, I mean to slay the lot of them inside one day!'

Here Guidone remarked, 'I know of no plan which could work, unless just this one: / just this one plan which has occurred to me, and which I'll explain to you, offers hope of success, if we bring it off. Apart from the women, no one is allowed to leave this city or set foot on the briny shore. Therefore I must rely upon one of my women, whose perfect love I have often put to severer tests than the one to which I shall put it now. / She is as eager as I am to obtain my freedom, provided she can come with me—hoping that, without her rivals' company, I shall live with her. She will have a galley or brigantine made ready in the harbour during the night hours, and your sailors will find it all prepared to set sail when they go on board. / Your knights, merchants, and sailors, who have favoured me by accepting my hospitality, must keep behind me in a tight group; if our path is blocked, we must force our way chest-first. In this way I hope that, with the help of our swords, I shall lead you out of this cruel city.' /

'You do as you please,' rejoined Marfisa; 'as for me, I know very well that I can leave this place. But it is easier for me to slaughter by my own hand the people dwelling within these walls than to be caught fleeing or showing any sign of fear. I mean to break out in broad day-light and by force of arms alone: any other way strikes me as shameful. / If I were recognized for a woman, I know that the women would honour and respect me; they would give me a ready welcome and per-haps a position of eminence in the tribe. But as I came here with these others, I do not want to enjoy greater privilege than they; it would never do for me to be free to stay or go while I abandoned these others to servitude.' / With these and other words Marfisa showed that only the concern she had for the risks facing her companions (should her own rashness make trouble for them) restrained her from attacking the whole tribe with lofty and memorable courage. In the event, she let Guidone pursue the plan which seemed to him to offer the surest advantage. / That night Guidone spoke to Aleria, as the most trusted of his wives was called; he did not have to press her much, for he found her already disposed to carry out his wishes. She commandeered a vessel, had it made ready, and brought on board her richest valuables, with the pretence that at daybreak she meant to take the ship out with her companions. / She had swords and lances, breastplates and shields brought into the palace, arms for the merchants and sailors who were half naked. Some of them slept, others kept awake, dividing between them both leisure and duties; often they looked out, ready armed, to see if the Eastern sky were yet reddening. /

The Sun had not yet drawn the dark veil from Earth's hard face, and Licaon's daughter had only just turned her plough along the furrows of the heavens when the tribe of women, eager to see the outcome of the battle, flowed into the arena, like a swarm of bees into their hive when the time has come for a change of queen. / Sky and earth resounded to the clarion shrill of trumpet, the rumble of drum as the people summoned their lord to conclude the battle he had started. Aquilant and Grifon were ready armed, as also were the English duke, Guidone, Marfisa, Samsonet, and all the others—all prepared, some mounted, others on foot. / To reach the sea and the harbour from the palace it was necessary to cross the arena—there was no other way, be it long or short, as Guidone explained to his company. After encouraging them to give of their best, he silently moved into the street and made his entrance into the packed arena, accompanied by his band over a hundred-strong. / Urging on his companions, he made quickly to leave by the further gate, but the numerous throng present, all armed and ready to strike, decided, on seeing him leading his group, that he was trying to escape. At once the women fell to their bows and arrows while a detachment moved to block their exit. / Guidone and the other gallant knights, especially mighty Marfisa, were not slow in setting to and striving to force a passage through the gates. But they were assailed by such a deluge of arrows, leaving many of their company wounded or dead, that in the end they feared they must have the worst of it. / The warriors all had sound breastplates— otherwise they would have had more to fear. Samsonet's charger was killed under him, and Marfisa's also dropped dead. Said Astolfo to himself: 'What am I waiting for? What better occasion than this to fall back on my horn? As our swords are getting us nowhere, let us see if I can't clear our path with my horn.' /

The horn, to which he always resorted in desperate situations, he now set to his lips; the earth, indeed the whole world, seemed to quake when the dreadful noise was unpent. So terrified was the populace that in their haste to flee they tumbled out of the arena aghast and stupefied; nor were any guards left on the gates. / Just as a startled family will risk death and throw itself out of windows and off great heights if they see the whole place ablaze with a fire which has spread little by little while drowsy slumber sat on their eyelids; thus, little prizing their safety, everyone fled from the appalling noise. / Hither and thither, up and down the dazed mob surged, seeking to escape. More than a thousand were piled up at each gate, blocking each other's way. Some lost their lives in the mêlée, others were smashed to pieces in their fall from terraces and windows. Many an arm was fractured, and many a skull—leaving their owners maimed or dead. / A confusion of cries and shrieks, chaos, and cataclysm assailed the sky. Wherever the sound of the horn penetrated, the panicking mob fled headlong.

You will not be surprised to hear that the common rabble showed a total lack of courage, for it is in the hare's nature always to take fright. / But what will you say of Marfisa or Guidone, normally so stout-hearted? Or of Grifon and Aquilant, Oliver's twin sons who had always been such a credit to their line? Hitherto they had reckoned a hundred thousand as zero, but here they were in craven flight like rabbits or timid doves startled by a loud noise close by. / The horn's magic power had the same dire effect on Astolfo's friends as on all the rest. Samsonet, Guidone, and the twins bolted away after terrified Marfisa. However far they ran, they could not put enough distance between themselves and the ear-splitting racket. Astolfo scoured the entire neighbourhood, blowing on his horn with ever-increasing vigour. / Some fled down to the sea, some up to the hills, others vanished into the woods. A few simply kept running, without a backward glance, and never stopped running for ten days. Some were in such a state as they sped out across the drawbridge that they never in all their life returned within the walls. The squares, houses, and temples were so cleared of people that the city remained almost deserted. /

Marfisa, Guidone, the two brothers, and Samsonet all fled, pale and quaking, down to the sea, closely followed by the sailors and merchants; here they found Aleria, who had a ship ready waiting for them between the twin forts. Collecting hastily on board, they dipped the oars into the water and unfurled every sail. / In and around the city the duke had ranged from the hills to the water's edge. Every street he had cleared, everybody fled from him, hid from him. Many women there were who in abject terror had flung themselves into privy, squalid recesses. Many others, not knowing where to go, had swum out to sea and drowned. / Astolfo reached the quayside, expecting to find his companions here, but he looked about him and scanned the empty beaches up and down—he could not see a soul. Raising his eyes, he descried them vanishing far out to sea, making full sail. He had to devise a new plan, then, for his journey, as the ship had sailed. / Well—let them go, and never mind that he has to make so great a journey all alone, through the lands of the barbarians and Infidels, where a man must be ever on his guard: there is no peril from which he cannot escape thanks to that horn of his, of proven effect.

Now let us attend to his companions who were fleeing across the sea, trembling with fright. / Under full sail they drove across the sea far from the cruel and bloody shore; when they were well beyond reach of the horrible noise and it could no longer frighten them, they were so stung with unwonted shame that their faces all blazed like fire. None dared look at another; they kept their eyes down, silent, and crestfallen. / Intent upon his passage, the shipmaster laid a course skirting Cyprus and Rhodes, then across the Aegean, where he saw a hundred islands, and perilous Cape Malea, recede from them. The favourable wind holding, he saw the Greek coast of Morea slip out of sight; rounding Sicily, he took the ship across the Tyrrhenian sea and hugged the pleasant shore of Italy, / until he put in at Luna, where he had left his family. Thanking God that he had sailed the deep without further harm, he stepped ashore on the familiar strand. Here the companions found a vessel preparing to sail for France; its master bade them come with him, so the same day they went on board, and soon they were at Marseilles. /

Bradamant, who held sway here, was then away; had she been on hand, she would have compelled them with kind words to accept her hospitality. They stepped ashore, then, and straight away Marfisa, bidding goodbye to the four knights and to Guidone's lady, set forth at a venture; / there was little merit, she explained, in so many knights travelling together: starlings and doves flock together, and so do hinds and deer and every timid creature—but the bold falcon, the proud eagle, placing no reliance upon the help of others, keep to themselves, as also do bears, tigers, and lions, fearless of being over-powered. / None of the others shared her view, so she was on her own. She set out on her wanderings, then, all by herself, taking unfamiliar paths through the woods. Grifon the White and Aquilant the Black chose the beaten track, with the other two, and the next day they arrived at a castle, where they received kind hospitality— / or so it seemed: but they quickly discovered that in effect it was the very reverse. The lord of the castle only feigned courtesy and benevolence in his welcome, but that night he had them captured as they lay, all unsuspecting, in their beds. Nor would he release them until he had made them swear to obsérve an evil practice. /

But before I tell more of this, my Lord, I want to follow the warlike damsel. She crossed the Durrance, the Rhône, and Saône and reached the foot of a mountain bathed in sunshine. Here, beside a swift stream, she saw an old woman coming towards her; she was dressed in black, and was weary and prostrated from a long journey, but even more from sheer gloom. / This is the old woman who had been in the service of the robbers in the mountain cave, until divine justice led Count Orlando thither to dispatch them all. She, fearing for her life for reasons you shall hear, had travelled for many a day by dark, concealed ways, avoiding anyone who might have recognized her. / Now judging by Marfisa's attire and trappings, the old woman reckoned her to be a visiting knight; she did not flee from her, then, as she tended to do from knights who were native to these parts. On the contrary, she stopped at the ford and waited with confidence and assurance for the approach of the distant knight. Thus it was that Marfisa came upon her at the ford, where the old woman approached and greeted her, / and asked to be carried across to the further bank mounted behind her. Marfisa, graciously inclined from her birth, took the old woman across the stream and willingly carried her a little beyond, to set her down where the road improved after a great stretch of bog. At the end of this road they saw a knight approaching. /

The knight, perched on a highly ornate saddle, and sporting fine raiment and lustrous arms, was riding towards the stream accompanied by a damsel and a single page. The damsel was most beautiful, but very haughty and cross-grained; the worthy knight, her escort, evoked in her sheer boredom and disdain. / The knight escorting her was Pinabello, one of the counts of Maganza, the very man who, a few months earlier, had dropped Bradamant into the hollow pit. The sighs, the impassioned sobs, and blinding tears he had been shedding at that time were all for the lady here present, who then had been in the power of Atlas the sorcerer. / But once the old sorcerer's enchanted castle vanished from the crag by virtue of Bradamant's heroic efforts, and those detained could go as they pleased, Pinabello's beloved, who had always been pliant to her lover's wishes, returned to him, and in his company was now wandering from castle to castle. /

Being ill-mannered and pert, the moment she saw Marfisa's old woman she could not refrain from laughing and jeering at her. Now lofty Marfisa, whose companions were not to be subject to insults of any kind, blazed up and angrily retorted to the damsel that the old woman was more beautiful than she was— / as she meant to prove against her knight: if she succeeded in unhorsing him, she would have the damsel's gown and her palfrey. Pinabello, who could never have afforded to acquiesce, was not sluggish in 'accepting the challenge. Seizing his shield and lance, he wheeled away, then came thundering down on Marfisa, / who set a mighty lance in rest and drove it at

Pinabello's visor; he hit the ground in such a daze that it was an hour before he could raise his head. As victor of the encounter, Marfisa had the damsel remove her gown and all her ornaments, and gave them to the old woman, / bidding the crone dress up in the youthful attire and all the trinkets. She also had her take the palfrey which the damsel had ridden hither. Then she resumed her journey with the old crone, whose adornments only served to enhance her ugliness. They travelled the long road for three days, during which time Marfisa did nothing worthy of mention. /

On the fourth day they met a solitary knight approaching at a frantic gallop. Should you wish to know who he is, well, he is that paragon of valour, handsome Zerbin, the king's son. He was seething with anger and vexation that he had been unable to wreak vengeance upon a man who had prevented his doing a great courtesy. / Vainly Zerbin had galloped through the wood after that henchman of his who had crossed him; the man had slipped away so promptly, and gained such an advantage in his flight, aided by the wood itself and by a mist which obscured the morning sun, that he got clean away from Zerbin until such time as his anger and outrage had abated. /

Fuming though he was, Zerbin simply had to laugh at the sight of the old crone—so glaring was the contrast between her youthful dress and her hideously senile face. To Marfisa, who rode beside her, he threw: 'You're a cunning one, sir knight, to escort a damsel the likes of her: you need fear no man's envy!' / The woman (if her horny hide was anything to judge by) was more ancient than the Sibyl and, tricked out as she was, she resembled a monkey that has been dressed up for a joke. Right now she looked uglier than ever, now as she glowered and looked daggers—you cannot insult a woman worse than by telling her she is old and ugly. / The excellent damsel pretended indignation in order to tease him. 'My lady's beauty is vastly superior to your courtesy,' she retorted, 'though I presume that you do not mean what you say. You pretend not to recognize her beauty so as to excuse your egregious poltroonery. / What other knight, finding this maiden in the forest, so young and beautiful, and so poorly attended, would not try to make her his own?' 'She suits you so well', observed Zerbin, 'that it would be a shame for anyone to take her from you; I for one would not be so indiscreet as ever to wrest her from you: enjoy her company! / Of course, if for some other reason you wish to cross swords with me, I'm ready to show you what I am worth; but do not so bedazzle me with this woman as to want to fight on her account. Be she ugly or fair, keep her—I refuse to interfere in so fine a friendship. You are well assorted—I would swear that your valour is on a par with her beauty!' / 'Like it or not,' rejoined Marfisa, 'you shall

have to try wresting her from me. It is intolerable that you should set
eyes on so pretty a woman and yet not seek to win her.' 'I do not see
why a man should expose himself to risk and exertions', replied
Zerbin, 'only to win a victory which serves the loser and merely
embarrasses the victor.' /

'If you do not like the stakes, I'll suggest another which you cannot
refuse,' proposed Marfisa. 'If I lose to you, she must stay with me;
but if I defeat you, I shall donate her to you willy nilly. Let us see,
then, which of us is to forego her. If you lose, you will have to be her
escort for good, wherever she feels like going.' / 'So be it,' replied
Zerbin, and at once he turned away to gain distance.

He raised himself in his stirrups, settled himself firmly in the saddle
and, to make sure of his mark, drove his lance at the centre of Marfisa's
shield—but he might have driven against a mound of metal. She, for
her part, caught him on the helmet with the result that he was spun
right out of the saddle in a daze. / Zerbin was none too happy at
having been unseated: such a thing had never before happened to
him—and he had unhorsed thousands himself. He felt he had incurred
perpetual ignominy. For a long while he lay speechless where he had
fallen; and he was all the more dismayed when he recalled his promise,
that he must now take the hideous crone under his wing. / The victor rode up to him and lightly observed: 'Here, I present her to you.
The more attractive and beautiful I find her, the happier I am that
she is yours. You are her champion now in my place. As to your
pledge—mind that the wind does not carry it off: you are to go as her
guide and escort (as you have promised) wherever she feels like
going.' / Without awaiting a reply, she spurred her steed and plunged
into the forest.

Zerbin, who assumed that Marfisa was a knight and a male, bade the
old woman tell him who the man was. The crone did not conceal the
truth from him, knowing how the disclosure would poison him and
make him blaze. 'The blow which pitched you out of your saddle was
delivered by a damsel. / If she usurps the knightly arms, the lance,
and shield, her valour entitles her to do so. She has just arrived from
the Orient to test herself against the French paladins.' At this, Zerbin
felt so humiliated that his cheeks burned red—and it would have been
small wonder had every piece of armour he wore blushed scarlet too. /
He mounted his horse, cursing himself for not having gripped better
with his thighs. The old woman sniggered to herself; she was looking
forward to needling him and making his life a misery. She reminded
him that he was to accompany her, and Zerbin, recognizing his
obligation, dropped his ears like a weary, defeated warhorse who feels
the bit in his jaws, the spur in his flanks. /

He sighed and 'Alas, grim Fortune!' he exclaimed, 'What sort of bargain is this? You have robbed me of a lady who was the fairest of the fair and who should have been mine. And you give me this woman —do you call that a fair replacement, an even exchange? To suffer a total loss was not as bad as to make so poor a bargain. / She, whose beauty and virtues were never equalled (and never could be) you have dashed against the sharp rocks and drowned, giving her body to the fishes and birds of the sea; and this crone here, who should long ago have been feeding the worms below ground, you have preserved some ten or twenty years longer than you should have, just to add to the burden of my sorrows.' / Thus spoke Zerbin. His words and countenance expressed a sadness no less acute at the thought of his odious new acquisition than at that of the loss he had suffered. Now the old hag, though she had never before set eyes on Zerbin, realized from his words that he must be the man of whom Isabel of Galicia had told her. /

If you remember what you were told earlier, the old woman had been on her way from the cave where Isabel, who had smitten Zerbin's heart, was held captive for many a day. Several times the damsel had told her the story of how she had left her father's shores only to suffer shipwreck in a storm and reach safety on the beach of La Rochelle. / So often had she heard Isabel describe Zerbin's handsome face and fine person that now, hearing him speak and raising her eyes to peer more closely at his face, she recognized that he was the very man on whose account Isabel was always repining in the mountain cave—she had complained more at no longer seeing him than at falling slave to the robbers. /

As she heard Zerbin giving vent to his anger and sorrow, she realized that he mistakenly believed that Isabel had been shipwrecked and drowned at sea. Now although she knew where matters actually stood, perversely unwilling to bring him comfort, she withheld the news that could have cheered him, and told him only what would cause him distress. / 'Listen to me,' she cried, 'haughty fellow that you are! Look at the way you scorn and sneer at me! If you knew that I had tidings of the woman whose death you bewail, what a fuss you would make of me! But I'd sooner let you strangle me or hack me to a thousand pieces before I told you a thing. Now had you been kinder to me, perhaps I should have let you into the secret.' / A mastiff rushing furiously to attack a thief will be subdued at once the moment the intruder offers him bread or cheese or binds him with some suitable spell. So it was with Zerbin, who was quick to change his tone and approach the old woman, dying to know more, now that she hinted at some private knowledge of the damsel whose death he had been lamenting. / He turned a friendlier face to her and begged her, craved and entreated her by God and men not to hide from him what she knew, be it good or ill. 'You'll hear nothing to your comfort,' the hag retorted, harsh and obstinate. 'Isabel is not dead, as you have thought: but her life is such that she envies the dead. / Only recently she fell into the hands of some twenty men, without your hearing of it; so even if you gain her back, don't count on still being able to cull her flower.' Oh, evil old woman, the way you deck out your tale, knowing well that you lie! Even though Isabel had fallen prey to twenty men, not one of them had violated her. / Zerbin asked her where she had seen the maiden, and when, but learnt nothing, for the obstinate old woman refused to add another word to what she had said. Zerbin first tried soft words on her, then threatened to slit her throat, but pleas and threats were equally useless—he could not make the ugly witch talk. /

In the end Zerbin saved his breath, as words had availed so little. What he had heard filled him with such jealousy that his heart could scarcely abide in his breast. He was so desperate to find Isabel, he would have passed through fire to see her—but he could go only where the hag wanted, such was his pact with Marfisa. / So Zerbin was led off the way it pleased her to go, by a lone, unfamiliar path. Whether they went up hill or down dale, they never looked each other in the face nor exchanged a word. But when the travelling Sun turned his back to the South, their silence was broken by a knight they met in the way. What happened now is revealed in the next canto.

TWENTY-FIRST CANTO

1–2 Introductory. 3–13 Zerbin defeats Hermonides. 13–66 Hermonides tells Zerbin the story of Gabrina's wickedness. 67–72 Zerbin and Gabrina journey on.

No cord, I verily believe, will ever truss a package, nor will a nail fasten a piece of wood as securely as a promise will bind a virtuous man with a tenacious, insoluble knot. It seems that in olden times men had only one way of portraying holy Fidelity: clad from head to foot in a white veil which one spot, one blemish could mar. / A pledge, whether sworn only to one or to a thousand, ought never to be broken. And in a wood or cave, far from towns and habitations, just as in the courts amid a throng of witnesses, amid documents and codicils, a promise should be enough on its own, without an oath or more specific token. /

Zerbin observed his pledge, as every pledge should be observed: he showed what value he placed upon his word when he left his chosen path in order to accompany the old woman, to whom he was as partial as to the pox or to death itself. But his promise prevailed over his inclination. / I described how, finding himself charged with her, he was so upset that he burned with resentment and spoke not a word. They proceeded on their way in utter silence. But this silence was broken, I added, when the Sun gave the world a last glimpse of his chariot-wheels: it was broken by a venturesome knight-errant who approached them down the middle of the road. / The old woman, recognizing the knight as Hermonides of Holland—his emblem was a crimson band on a sable ground—swallowed her pride on sight of his proud bearing, and meekly commended herself to Zerbin, reminding him of the promise he had made to Marfisa, who had entrusted her to his care. / The warrior approaching was hostile to her and to her family; he had slain her innocent father and her one and only brother; and the blackguard was still out to do to the rest of them as he had to these two. 'So long as you enjoy my protection', Zerbin told her, 'you're to fear nothing.' / As the stranger drew closer and scrutinized the face which he so detested, 'Either prepare to fight me,' he shouted in a tone of haughty menace, 'or leave the woman undefended and she shall die at my hand as she deserves. If you fight for her you shall perish—that is the fate of those who embrace evil causes.' /

Zerbin was civil in his reply: it was a mean, ignoble ambition, he said, and scarcely consonant with chivalry, to contrive the death of a woman. If it came to fighting, here he was—but let him first consider what it meant for a knight, gently-born as he was, to seek to daub his hand in a woman's blood. / These and other words he propounded in vain: action was required. They drew away to gain sufficient ground then turned and charged each other full tilt. Rockets sparked off during a festival do not travel as fast as did the two chargers bringing the knights into collision. / Hermonides aimed low, meaning to pierce his adversary's right side, but his puny lance went into splinters and scarcely grazed the Scottish knight—whose own thrust was by no means ineffectual: it broke the Dutchman's shield and drove a hole clean through his shoulder, sending him toppling to the ground. / Zerbin, believing that he had killed him, was quick to jump to the ground; moved with compassion, he lifted the helmet off the stunned face of the other warrior who, as though woken from sleep, looked at him, glassy-eyed and speechless. Finally he spoke: 'I am little

247

grieved at having been defeated by you, for you have the look of a true knight-errant; / but it sickens me that I should come to this pass on account of a treacherous woman—and I have no idea how you can be her champion, quite out of keeping with your worth. If you knew what has led me to seek vengeance upon her, you could never think about it without regretting that you have injured me in order to preserve her. / And if my spirit holds out long enough for me to tell the tale (though I fear it will not) I shall show you how utterly damnable this woman is in every way and beyond all limits.

'I had a brother who left our native Holland when still very young and enlisted as a knight in the service of Heraclion, Emperor of the Greeks. / Here he became boon companion to a chivalrous baron at court; this baron had a castle, pleasantly situated and strongly walled, on the Serbian border. His name was Argeus, and he was married to this evil woman, whom he loved so much that he overstepped the bounds of conduct which became a man of his merit. / But this woman was as flighty as an autumn leaf, when the season is at its driest and a cold wind strips the trees and furiously drives the leaves before it. Her husband had been enshrined in her heart awhile, but she was quick to tire of him, and turned her every thought, her every desire towards attaching my brother to herself as lover. / But the ill-famed cliffs of Acroceraunos do not stand so solid against the onslaught of the sea, nor does the pine, which has a hundred times renewed its needles and put down roots as deep below ground as its trunk shows above the Alpine crag—nor does even such a pine resist the North Wind as firmly as my brother resisted the entreaties of this nest of all unspeakable, wicked vices. / Now as frequently befalls an adventurous knight, who seeks challenges and often finds them, my brother was wounded in a combat hard by the castle of his friend. Often he would come to this castle without awaiting an invitation, whether he was in Argeus' company or not. He stopped here, then, to recuperate until his wound was healed. /

'While he lay here, it so happened that Argeus had to leave after some business of his own; at once the brazen woman made approaches to my brother, such being her inclination. But he, faithful soul, would not expose his flanks to so harmful a spur. To keep faith to the full he opted for what seemed to him the lesser of a choice of evils. / The choice he made was to forego his ancient friendship with Argeus and go far away, so that his name would altogether cease to be mentioned in the trollop's presence. Though this was a hard decision, it was more upright than to satisfy her depravity, or than to accuse the wife before her consort, who loved her with all his heart. / His wounds still unhealed, he put on his armour and left the castle, his mind made up never again to return there. But what was the use? Every defence he devised was nullified by Fate with some new stratagem.

'The husband returned home to find his wife in floods of tears, / all red-faced, and dishevelled. He asked her what was the matter. Before she would explain, she waited to be asked several times, revolving in her mind all the while ways to avenge herself on the man who had forsaken her—in a temper as fickle as hers it was natural that love should turn impulsively to hate. / Finally she spoke: "Alas, my lord, what is the use of concealing the fault I committed in your absence? Though I hide it from all the world, I cannot hide it from my conscience. A soul aware of its foul sin suffers an inner torment far worse than any form of physical punishment which could be meted out to me for my ill-doing— / if what is done under duress is indeed done ill. Be that as it may, let me tell you about it; then you can sever my pure white soul from my defiled body and dim my eyes for all eternity: that way at least I'll not need to hold them for ever downcast after such a scandal, and feel ashamed before every person I meet. / Your companion has destroyed my honour; the scoundrel has forced and violated this body, and, fearing that I tell you, he has just gone without taking his leave." With these words she brought down hatred upon one who till then was held in highest affection; Argeus believed her and without a moment's delay armed himself and hastened off to be avenged. /

'Familiar with the lie of the land, he caught up with my brother before he had gone far—my brother was weak and ailing, and was proceeding all unwary at a leisurely pace. In brief, reaching a deserted spot, Argeus laid hold on him to be avenged; my brother could produce no explanation which satisfied him—a battle had to be fought. / While Argeus was in good health and fired with fresh indignation, my brother was sick and showed his usual friendliness, and therefore had little defence against his friend who had turned against him. Unable to support the weight of so fierce an onslaught, Philander (this was the unlucky youth's name) was captured, little though he deserved such a fate. / "God forbid that my just anger and your wickedness should drive me to take the life of a man I used to love," cried Argeus. "And you loved me, too. Now, though in the end you have given me a poor token of it, I still want it to be plain to one and all that just as in the period of our harmony so now in our enmity I am superior to you. / I shall punish your crime in some way other than by steeping my hands further in your blood." With these words, he had a litter, made of green branches, prepared on the back of his horse, and on this he brought him back, more dead than alive, to shut him up in a dungeon of his castle, where the poor innocent was to be punished with perpetual incarceration. /

'Still, apart from the liberty he enjoyed before setting out, he was deprived of nothing else: in all other things he could command and give orders there just as though he were free. This evil woman, though, had still not tired of scheming how to have her way with him, and almost daily she visited him in his prison, for she had the keys and let herself in at her pleasure. / She kept assailing my brother, even more boldly than before. "What does this loyalty of yours profit you," she would say, "if everybody takes it for treachery? What glorious triumphs are yours, what proud spoils and rich booty, what merit is yours if everyone insults you as a traitor? / How well you might have served your profit and your honour had you given me what I wanted of you! Now I wish you joy of the fine reward you have earned for being so obstinate and unbending! You are in prison —and don't imagine you'll be let out until you soften your attitude; but if you do my pleasure I shall see to restoring your freedom and your reputation." / "Never!" cried Philander. "Never hope that my fidelity will prove false to itself. Though I endure such merciless treatment, quite at odds with my deserving, and everyone thinks the worse of me, it is enough for me that to the All-seeing One, who can revive me with eternal grace, my innocence is plainly evident. / If Argeus is not satisfied with holding me prisoner, let him also relieve me of my wearisome life. Perhaps Heaven will not deny me the reward for a good deed which here is so little appreciated. And perhaps Argeus, who regards himself as injured by me, will realize he has wronged me, once I am gone, and will mourn the death of his true companion." / Thus the brazen hussy several times made trial of Philander, but all to no avail. Still, in her blind lust she never slumbered in her efforts to assuage her guilty passion; she searched out her innate vices, probing for them far deeper than within her skirts, and looked them over carefully. She turned over one plan after another before setting her finger upon any one of them. /

'Six months went by without her setting foot inside the prison as she formerly did, and poor Philander was cherishing the hope that her feelings for him were changed. But Fate, prospering what was evil, gave this heinous woman the occasion to wreak notable mischief in the accomplishment of her blind and bestial craving. / Her husband had a long-standing feud with a baron called Morando the Handsome, who often made incursions by himself right into the castle when its lord was not there. If Argeus was there, Morando would forego the invitation and stay well clear of the place. Now to induce him to come, Argeus put it about that he was off to Jerusalem to fulfil a vow. / This he put about; and he made his departure in public and had the news spread abroad. His plan was known to nobody except his wife, in whom alone he confided. At dusk he would return home, but never, except at night time was he to be found there—at dawn, with changed emblems, he would always sally forth unseen. / He would range back and forth round about his castle, waiting to see if the gullible Morando would make his appearance according to habit. All day he would lurk in the forest, and when he saw the daylight fade into the sea, he would return home, where his unfaithful wife would let him in by a hidden door. /

'Except for his iniquitous wife, everyone believed that Argeus was miles away. So she took this opportunity and approached my brother with fresh mischief. She had a ready flow of tears, a flood of them streaming from her eyes onto her breast. "Where shall I find help", she cried, "to save my honour from being totally lost— / and my husband's along with mine? Were he here now I should not fear. You know Morando and how little he dreads gods and men when Argeus is not about. With threats and entreaties he is desperately trying to lure me to concede his wishes; not one of my household has he left unsuborned, and I don't know if I'll be able to save myself. / Having learnt that my husband has gone and will not be back for some time, he has had the effrontery to come into my house with no pretext or excuse other than this. If my lord were here, he would not dare to do this—indeed he would not dare approach within three miles of these walls. / And what hitherto he has sought through intermediaries he today asked me to my face, displaying such behaviour that I greatly feared I was about to incur dishonour and shame: had I not given him soft answers and pretended to be ready to oblige him, he would have seized by force that which, after my words, he expects to obtain peaceably. / I have made him a promise, which I do not intend to keep —it was extracted under threat and so is not binding; but my intention was to forestall his forcing me there and then. That is the position, and only you can help—otherwise this will spell the end of my honour, and of my Argeus', which causes you more concern, you have told me, than does your own. / If you deny me this I shall say that you do not possess the loyalty you boast of, but that every time you have spurned my suppliant tears you have done so out of cruelty, and not out of respect for Argeus, however much you have used him as an excuse. Our relationship would have remained concealed while from Morando I must expect patent dishonour." /

' "There is no need for all this preamble," replied Philander. "I am already on Argeus' side. Spin me what tale you will, such as I have been, such I propose ever to remain. And though I wrongly suffer for it, I have never imputed this sin to him. For him I am ready to go to my death, though the whole world and my fate stand against me." /

"Well, I want you to kill this man who is compassing our dishonour," she demanded. "Don't be afraid of any harm coming to you, for I shall show you a sure way to do it. He is to come back to me at the third hour, when night is at its darkest, and, on a signal I have apprised him of, I am to let him in undetected. / You will not mind waiting first in my bedroom in the dark: I shall see to stripping off his armour and delivering him to you practically naked.' In this way, it seems, the wife brought her husband into the fearful trap; I call her wife but she should rather be called a Fury from hell, cruel and malignant. /

'When baneful night descended, she fetched in my brother, armed, and held him in the darkened room until the unfortunate lord of the castle returned. Everything followed according to plan, for the counsels of evil seldom miscarry: Philander struck at good Argeus, mistaking him for Morando. / With one stroke he split his head and neck—in the absence of a helmet Argeus was unprotected—and without so much as a twitch he reached the bitter end of a wretched life. And the man who slew him never realized he had done so and would never have believed it possible. Oh strange accident that, meaning to help his friend, he treated him worse than he would have treated a foe! / With Argeus lying unrecognized on the ground, my brother returned the sword to Gabrina—this was the name of this woman who was born only to betray every man who fell into her clutches. Till then she had concealed the truth; now she wanted Philander to take a lamp and set eyes upon the man for whose death he was responsible. She showed him his friend Argeus, / and threatened to bring to light what he had done—which he could not deny—unless he satisfied her long-nurtured amorous craving. And she would have him put to death most ignominiously as a treacherous murderer. She reminded him, too, that he would do well not to make light of his reputation even if he had little love for life. /

'Philander was stunned with grief and dread when he realized his mistake. His first impulse was to slaughter this woman in sheer rage, and for a moment he toyed with the idea; having no other weapon upon him, he was ready to tear her apart with his teeth—until good sense prevailed, for he realized he was in his enemy's house. / As a ship on the high seas will sometimes be driven and buffeted by two contrary winds, and one wind will thrust it onwards until the opposing wind blows it back whence it came; and it is slewed round, stem and stern, by the winds until the stronger of the two prevails: so it was with Philander, driven one way and the other by two notions until he chose one as the lesser evil. / Reason pointed out to him the grave risk he ran, not merely of dying, but of meeting a nasty and degrading death if the murder became known in the castle. It was a thought he

252

could not bear to follow to the end. Like it or not, in the end he had to drink the bitter chalice: dread finally conquered obstinacy in his afflicted heart. / Fear of the gruesome, shameful punishment drove him to promise to do all that Gabrina wanted if, as he endlessly begged her, they could leave the place in safety. So the evil woman forcibly culled the fruit she had been craving, and then they left those castle walls.

'Thus it was that Philander made his return among us, leaving his disgrace and degradation behind in Greece. / He carried engraved in his heart the memory of his friend whom he had so senselessly killed —an odious triumph for the woman, barbarous as Procne or Medea, while for him, an utter disaster. Were it not for his solemn oath which restrained him, he would have slain her once he was out of harm's way. As it was, he loathed her with the deepest loathing. / From that day forth he was never seen to laugh. All his words were sad, and he was continually sighing. He had become a second Orestes who, after murdering his mother and the execrable Aegistus, was hounded by the avenging Furies. His grief was so persistent that it ultimately reduced him to a bed of sickness. / As for this trollop, brooding on how little my brother esteemed her, she transformed her hot infatuation into hatred and blazing wrath. She was no less incensed against my brother than she had been against Argeus, and decided to rid the world of her second husband as she had done with the first. /

'She unearthed a foxy physician, just the man for her purposes— he was more skilful at killing with poison than at curing with potions. She promised him rather more than his fee if he would first rid her of her lord with some lethal draught. / In my presence and that of many others the old reprobate arrived with the poison and proclaimed that it was a good potion to restore my brother to health. But before the patient had tasted the medicine, Gabrina, following a new plan (whether to be rid also of her accomplice or to avoid paying him what she had promised), grasped the physician's hand / just as he was holding out the cup with the hidden poison, and cried: "If I am concerned for the man I have so dearly loved, you have no right to demur. I want to be sure that you are not giving him some noxious draught, some poisonous juice. You are not to give the potion to him until you first taste it yourself." /

'Imagine, sir, how alarmed the old wretch must have been at this. In the heat of the moment he had no leisure to think what course to take. So, in order not to heighten suspicions, he chose to taste from the cup there and then—and the sick man, after such a show of confidence, drank up all the rest of what was given to him. / Imagine a hawk who holds a partridge in his talons and is about to devour it when his feast is interrupted and spoiled by the greedy hound whom he has regarded as a faithful companion; thus it was with the physician, intent on his evil gains: he was foiled by the very person on whom he relied for help. Mark this rare instance of overweaning boldness, and let this be the fate of every self-seeker. / His errand accomplished, the old man was about to set off home to take some antidote which might save him from the pernicious venom, but Gabrina prevented him. He was not to leave, she said, before the draught was digested and its potency proved. / He begged her in vain and offered her inducements to let him go. When it was clear to him that he must die and there was no escape, in desperation he revealed the whole story to those present—and there was little she could do to cover it up. So the worthy doctor ended by practising upon himself what so often he had practised upon others. / His soul set out on its journey in the footsteps of my brother's, who had gone on ahead. We who were there to hear what the old man had confessed, the plot which had left so few survivors, seized this odious beast, crueller than any that haunt the forest, and shut her in a dark cell to condemn her to the pyre as she deserved.' / This was Hermonides' account, which he would have continued, describing her escape from prison; but the pain from his wound was too much for him and he lay back, ashen-faced, in the grass. His two pages meanwhile fashioned a litter out of thick branches. On this Hermonides had himself laid, for otherwise he could not be carried hence. / Zerbin apologized to the knight and expressed his grief at having done him injury; but he had defended the woman he was escorting as knightly practice demanded—otherwise his pledge would have been meaningless, for when he had assumed charge of her he had promised to do his utmost to protect her from any who would molest her. / This aside, if there was any favour he could do him, he was at his entire disposal. The knight replied that he only wanted to urge him to be free of Gabrina before she put some scheme afoot against him and it became too late for regrets. Gabrina kept her eyes downcast all this while, because the truth is not readily refuted. /

Zerbin left now with the old hag to pursue the journey to which he was pledged. All day he cursed her silently for what she had made him do to that knight. Now that he was acquainted with who she really was, on the word of a man who knew the depths of her wickedness, if earlier he had found her tiresome and disagreeable, now he found her so loathsome he could not bear to look at her. / She was not unaware of Zerbin's feelings and she was not going to be outdone in malevolence; her loathing for him was not an ounce short of his for her— when it came to hating she gave even better than she got. Venom swelled her heart and showed on her countenance. In concord such as

I describe, then, they pursued their way through the age-old wood. /
Now as the day turned towards evening they heard cries and thuds
and crashes which indicated a fierce battle—and one close at hand,
to judge by the volume of sound. To see what was happening Zerbin
hastened towards the noise; Gabrina was not slow to follow. What
happened here I shall relate in the next canto.

TWENTY-SECOND CANTO

*1–3 Introductory. 3–4 Zerbin finds a dead knight. 5–30
Astolfo returns to France and destroys Atlas' enchanted
palace. 31–98 Ruggiero and Bradamant worst Pinabello
and his four champions.*

YOU ladies who are gracious and kind to your true loves, and contented with a single passion—and without doubt in this you must be
as one in a thousand—do not take amiss what I have been saying,
when I was carried away against Gabrina; nor at the verse or two of
censure I must still devote to the reprobate creature. / This is the
woman she was, and as I have been bidden by One who has power
over me, I am not evading the truth. But that does not tarnish the
high honour due to other women whose hearts are true. The apostle
who betrayed his master to the Jews for thirty pieces of silver brought
no disrepute upon John or Peter; nor is Hypermnestra's fame at all
clouded for being sister to so many guilty women. / For one woman
whom I make bold to denounce in my poem—my story must have it
thus—I am fully prepared to applaud a hundred others, and make
their virtues more radiant than the sun.

But now to return to the story which I am weaving from various
strands (and which many are deigning to enjoy), I was telling how
Zerbin, the Scottish knight, had heard a high shriek close by. / He
penetrated into a narrow defile between two hills; this is where the
shout came from. He had gone only a little way when he arrived in a
hollow, where he saw a dead knight. I shall tell you his name, but
first I want to turn my back on France and return to the Orient to
find Astolfo the paladin, who had set out for the West. /

I left him in the barbarous city from which he had driven out the
infidel population with the sound of his formidable horn. He had
delivered himself and his companions from a dire peril, and enabled
them to hoist sail and flee from those shores—to their utter shame. To

resume his tale, he left this land behind, taking the road to Armenia. /
In a few days he was in Anatolia and took the road to Bursia in
Bithynia, from where he continued on this side of the narrows and
arrived in Thrace. Following the Danube through Hungary, he
traversed the lands of the Moravians and Bohemians and crossed
Franconia and the Rhine in less than twenty days, as though his
steed had wings. / He crossed the forest of the Ardennes and came
to Aix-la-Chapelle; finally he reached Brabant and Flanders, where he
took ship. The breeze blew towards the West and so pressed on the
sail that at noon he saw England close by. He stepped ashore, leapt
upon his steed, and so spurred him that he reached London that same
evening. / Here he learnt that the aged King Otho had been in Paris
now for several months, and that practically every baron had lately
been following in his worthy footsteps. So Astolfo at once decided
to go to France. He returned to the harbour on the Thames, had the
sails set, and put forth, shaping a course for Calais. / A light breeze
on the bow had prompted the vessel to set sail; but this now began to
freshen until it proved too much for the helmsman, who was eventually
forced to run before it, to avoid being driven ashore. He kept the ship
straight down mid-channel, on a course different to their plan. / They
kept now on the port, now on the starboard tack, driven this way and
that by the gale until they made land near Rouen. As soon as he reached
the welcome shore, he had Rabican saddled, donned his armour, and
girded on his sword. Thus he set out, with that horn of his which was
worth a bodyguard one thousand strong. / He crossed a forest and
came to a clear spring at the foot of a hill; it was the time of day when
the sheep stopped browsing and were penned up in barns or mountain
caves. Overcome by the intense heat and beset with thirst, he drew off
his helmet, tethered his horse in a deep thicket, and approached the
fresh water to drink. /

He had not moistened his lips before a peasant, hidden close by,
stepped out from the shrubbery, jumped onto the horse and was away.
Astolfo heard this, and looked up; seeing what had befallen him, he
left the spring, his thirst sated without drinking, and dashed after
him as fast as he could. / The thief did not gallop flat out, in which
case he would have vanished in a trice: instead he would give rein,
then draw in, keeping to a canter or a fast trot. They emerged from
the wood after a great deal of this, and ultimately arrived at the place
where so many noble barons, without being in prison, suffered the
worst captivity. / The peasant fled into the palace with the steed who
could run like the wind. Hampered by his shield, helmet, and other
arms, Astolfo could only pursue him at a distance. Arrive he eventually
did, but here every trace he had been following vanished: there was

no further sign either of Rabican or of the thief; in vain he turned his eyes this way and that and darted about, / searching the galleries, the chambers, and public rooms, all to no avail—he could not find the knavish fellow. He could not tell where he had concealed his charger Rabican, swiftest of beasts. All that day he searched up and down, inside and out, all to no purpose. /

Now it came to Astolfo, weary and bewildered from all this searching, that the place must be enchanted. And he remembered the book he had always by him, the one which Logistilla had given him in India, so that he could help himself out of trouble when he fell under further spells. He looked in the index and quickly saw which page to turn to for the antidote. / About the enchanted palace a great deal was written in the book, including the methods to be used in order to confound the magician and loosen the bonds holding all those captives. Beneath the threshold a spirit was trapped, who wrought all these tricks and deceptions. Once he prised up the stone under which the spirit was buried, he would make the palace dissolve into smoke. / Eager to bring off so glorious a feat, the paladin was quick to reach down and try the weight of the heavy slab. Now Atlas, seeing those hands close to making nonsense of his magic art, assailed him with fresh spells, mistrustful of what might otherwise result. / He used his infernal phantoms to change Astolfo's appearance, so that in the eyes of some of the captives he appeared a giant, to others a peasant, to others an evil-looking knight—the captives saw the paladin under the various guises in which Atlas had appeared to them in the wood. To retrieve what the magician had stolen from them they all turned, then, on Astolfo. / Under this fresh illusion, Ruggiero, Gradasso, Iroldo, Bradamant, Brandimart, Prasildo, and other warriors rushed furiously upon the duke, to do away with him. But he remembered his horn in time and this cowed their lofty spirits. Had he not resorted to its noise of doom, that would have been the end of him, beyond recall. / But the moment he put the horn to his lips and made the horrifying sound heard all about, the knights all fled, like pigeons at the shot of a musket. The wizard himself was not exempt, but had to flee too—he bolted out of his lair, white with terror and alarm, and ran as far as he had to in order to be clear of the hideous din. /

The keeper fled along with his captives; and after them fled the horses—no mere rope could have tethered them. Several of them fled from their stalls, and followed their masters by various paths. Not a cat, not a mouse remained within, as though the noise were screaming for their blood. Rabican would have made off with the rest had he not run straight into the duke's arms. / Having expelled the magician, Astolfo lifted the heavy slab from the threshold; under it he found some images and other objects which I'll not describe. Eager to break the spells, he smashed everything the way the book instructed him. The palace dissolved into smoke and mist. / ·

Here he found Ruggiero's steed tethered with a golden chain: I mean the steed given him by this same Moorish magician to bear him away to Alcina; Logistilla had subsequently elaborated a bridle for this beast, and on him Ruggiero had returned to France, after skirting the entire right side of the globe, from the Indies to England. / I don't know if you remember how Ruggiero had secured the hippogryph to a tree by his bridle, that day when Galafron's daughter Angelica, had quite confounded him, vanishing, all naked, from his sight. As he looked on, amazed, the flying steed had made off back to his master, where he remained until today when the magic images were smashed. / No piece of fortune could have made Astolfo happier than this, for the hippogryph was the very thing for him if he wanted to explore land and sea as he did—those he had yet to visit—and girdle the earth in a few days. He well knew how ably the beast could carry him, for he had direct experience from previous occasions. / He had experienced riding him in India, that day when wise Melissa rescued him out of the hands of wicked Alcina, who had transmuted him into the semblance of a wild myrtle. Then he had taken good note how Logistilla had bridled the headstrong beast and how Ruggiero had been taught to make it go anywhere at his bidding. / Having decided to take the hippogryph, he saddled the creature—the saddle was right beside him, and he contrived, out of a number of bridles, one that would control him: the sturdy bridles of the horses which had fled were hung up there. Now all that stopped Astolfo from taking wing was the thought of Rabican. / He was right to cherish Rabican: there was not a better charger for jousting, and he had ridden him from the furthest Indies all the way to France. He brooded a long while, and finally concluded that he would sooner make a present of him to a friend than leave him here on the road, a prize for the first comer. / He kept a watch for any huntsman or peasant who might happen through the wood and might be induced to follow after him to some other place, leading Rabican. All that day, and until the dawn of the next he waited and watched in vain. In the morning, though, before it was light, he thought he saw a knight coming through the wood. /

But if I'm to tell you the rest of the story, I must first go after Ruggiero and Bradamant. When the horn fell silent and the handsome couple were well away from this place, Ruggiero was quick to recognize at a glance what Atlas had concealed from him: Atlas had seen to it that until this moment the pair had not recognized each other. /

Ruggiero looked at Bradamant and she at him in utter amazement, for their mind and vision had been clouded for so many days by the magic illusion. Ruggiero embraced his fair one who blushed redder than a rose; then he culled from her lips the first blooms of their blissful love. / A thousand times the two happy lovers renewed their embraces and hugged each other; they were so blissful, their breasts could scarcely contain their joy. They were grieved beyond measure that the magic spell had prevented their recognizing each other while they were in that restless palace, and so had made them lose so many days of happiness. / Bradamant was ready to concede all the pleasures that an honest virgin may give to a lover in order to keep him from sadness without hurting her own honour. Now she suggested to Ruggiero that if he was not to find her forever restive and stubborn about giving him the ultimate fruits, he should ask her father Aymon, in due form, for her hand—after accepting baptism. / Ruggiero would have submitted not merely to turning Christian for love of her (like her father and grandfather and all her noble house), but would there and then have given her what life remained to him, to please her. 'It would be a small thing', he told her, 'to place my head in fire, let alone in water, for love of you.' / To receive baptism, and then to have Bradamant to wife, Ruggiero set out to escort the damsel to Vallombrosa—a fair, rich monastery, devout and hospitable to all comers.

On emerging from the forest they came upon a woman whose face betrayed deep sorrow. / Ruggiero, kind and courteous with everyone, but especially with women, was moved at the sight of the lovely tears streaking her delicate face, and burned to know the cause of her grief. He turned to her and, after greeting her politely, enquired why her face was thus wet with tears. / She raised her beautiful, brimming eyes and answered him with good grace, giving him a full account of the reason for her sadness, as he had asked her: 'Gentle sir,' she said, 'these cheeks are thus tear-streaked out of pity for a young man who is to die in a castle here today. / He loves a beautiful maiden, gently born, daughter of Marsilius, the Spanish king; and, concealed beneath a white veil and in a woman's skirts, disguising his voice and countenance, without raising the suspicions of the household, every night he has been sleeping with her. But there is no secret but must eventually come to another's attention. / One man found out and told two others who related it to others still, until it came to the ears of the king. One of the king's henchmen came two days ago and had the pair seized in bed. They have both been shut in separate dungeon cells, and I don't believe that the young man will see today through before he dies under torture. / I have escaped to avoid witnessing such cruelty, for they will burn him alive; nothing can distress me more than the suffering to be inflicted upon so fine a young man. There is no pleasure so great but my enjoyment of it must turn at once to grief when I think of the cruel flames which have scorched those handsome and delicate limbs.' /

As Bradamant listened she appeared to be much disturbed by this story, and greatly upset; she seemed as concerned over the condemned man's fate as if he were a brother of hers—and her fear was not wholly unfounded, as I shall explain. She turned to Ruggiero and, 'It seems to me', she observed, 'that our arms should favour this man.' / And to the grieving woman she said: 'Take heart, and see to introducing us into the castle; if they have not yet slain the youth, they shall not, take my word!' Ruggiero, noticing his lady's kindly disposition, her pity and concern, was fired with eagerness to prevent the youth from dying. / And to the woman whose eyes were streaming with tears he cried: 'Come now! Here's a time to make yourself useful, not to weep! See to bringing us to this youth of yours. We shall wield a thousand lances, a thousand swords, we promise you, provided you take us to him quickly—but put your best foot forward, or help will come too late and meanwhile the flames will have devoured him.' / The bold words and proud bearing of this pair, remarkable for their spirit, succeeded in reviving hope whence it had ebbed. But more even than the distance to travel, the fear that their path might be obstructed, making their journey unavailing, kept the woman in two minds. /

Then she told them: 'If we took the path which leads straight and smooth to the castle, I believe we should arrive in time and that the fire would not yet be lit. But the one we have to take is so tortuous and bad that we should scarcely arrive inside a day; when we do arrive, I fear we shall find the young man already dead.' / 'Why do we not take the shorter?' asked Ruggiero. 'Because on that road stands a castle of the Counts of Ponthieu,' she explained; 'here only three days ago Pinabello, son of Count Anselm of Altaripa and the worst scoundrel that ever lived, imposed a harsh, iniquitous law on knights and ladies who happen by. / No knight or lady now passes that way without suffering insult and injury. They all have to continue thence on foot, the knight after forfeiting his arms, the lady her raiment. There is no abler jouster in France today, nor has there been for many a year, than the four champions who have sworn to uphold Pinabello's law at this castle. /

'How the custom (not three days old) started I shall relate to you, so you can grasp how fair and square was the occasion for laying the oath upon the four knights. Pinabello has a woman who is such an offensive beast that there is none to match her. She was travelling with him one day, I know not where, when they happened upon a knight who slighted her: / this was because she had laughed at the knight on account of an old crone mounted behind him. So the knight tilted at Pinabello—who was endowed with little strength and too much arrogance—and overthrew him. Then he made Pinabello's lady dismount in the meadow to see how she walked, whether bandy-legged or not. He left her on foot, after making her hand over her dress for the old crone to wear. / The damsel was left on foot; she was furious; she hungered and thirsted for vengeance, abetted by Pinabello, her faithfully ally whenever it came to doing harm. She could not rest, day or night, and claimed she would never smile again until he had unhorsed a thousand knights and a thousand ladies and deprived the one of their arms, the other of their gowns. /

'That same day four champions arrived at one of his castles by chance; they had just landed in these parts after coming from a far distant country. Their valour was such that four others as doughty in combat are not to be found in our day. They are Aquilant, Grifon, Samsonet, and a youth called Guidone Selvaggio. / Pinabello welcomed them at the castle I mentioned with every show of kindness; but that night he seized them all in bed, and would not release them until they swore on oath to remain here for a year and a month (this was the term he set) and despoil as many knights errant as passed this way. / The damsels escorted by the knights were to be made to dismount, and their garments were to be taken off them. This the four had to swear on oath; this pact they were constrained to observe, much to their grief and vexation. It seems that up till now not one man has been able to joust with them without being left on foot; scores have happened by, but they have all had to continue on foot and without their arms. / Their rule is that one of them, by lot, issues forth alone to engage the foe; but if he finds his opponent sturdy enough to keep his saddle while he himself is toppled, the other three are obliged to take up the challenge all in a band, a fight to the death. Seeing what champions each one of them is, you can imagine what they must be like acting in concert. /

'It scarcely fits the urgency of our mission, which can brook no delay, that you should even stop to offer combat (always supposing you win, as your proud bearing suggests you would); but it is not a thing to be achieved inside an hour, and there is every chance that the young man may be burnt to death if the entire day is lost in coming to his aid.' / 'Never mind about that,' Ruggiero retorted; 'what lies in our own power let us do, leaving the rest to Him who governs the heavens, or, if it is not His affair, then to Fate. Let this combat show you how able we are to help this youth who is to be burnt today for so feeble and slight a cause as the one you have explained.' / Without another word the damsel set out along the shorter road.

They had not gone three miles along it before they came to the draw-bridge and the gate where arms and skirts are forfeited, and life itself hangs in the balance. The moment they appeared, a man up on the keep sounded two strokes on the bell. / Out from the gate came an old man in a great hurry, trotting on a nag, and shouting: 'Wait! Wait! Stay where you are: there's a toll to pay here! If the custom has not been explained to you, I shall tell it you myself.' And he set about telling them of the law imposed by Pinabello. / Then he went on, meaning to give them advice as he had always done to previous knights: 'Strip the damsel of her raiment, leave your arms and your chargers here; do not expose yourselves to the risk of encountering four war-riors such as they. Clothing, arms, and steeds may be found any-where—only life is irreplaceable. /

'Enough of that!' cried Ruggiero. 'I know all about it, and I came here to prove myself and see if I am in fact as good as I have always accounted myself. Arms, clothing, steed I shall cede to no one if all I hear is vague threats—and I well know that my companion here won't be despoiled either just for mere words spoken. / But for God's sake see to it that I am quickly faced with those who would take my arms and horse: we still have that mountain to cross and cannot afford to linger here too long.' The ancient replied, 'Here's your man, just crossing the drawbridge,' and he spoke no lie: a knight had issued forth, wearing a crimson surcoat picked out with white flowers. / Bradamant entreated Ruggiero as a favour to leave it to her to un-horse the knight whose fine surcoat was picked out with flowers, but she could not sway him and had perforce to do as he wanted, that is, to leave the whole challenge to him while she looked on. /

Ruggiero asked the old man who it was who was coming out of the gate. 'That is Samsonet; I recognize his red garb with the white flowers.' The two contenders moved forward without a word and with but brief delay; they spurred their steeds and charged each other, their lances lowered. / Meanwhile who should issue forth from the castle but Pinabello and several men on foot ready and eager to remove the armour from the knights who were unseated. The bold warriors charged each other, their huge lances in rest—these lances were two palms' width thick, made of native oak, and practically like iron. / Samsonet had had a dozen such lances cut from their living stems in a wood nearby: and he had brought two of them to the joust. To escape their impact a shield and breastplace of adamant were needed. As he came out, he had one of the lances given to Ruggiero, and kept the other for himself. / With these lances, which would have passed through anvils, so solid were their metalled tips, the warriors clashed half-way, each one running against the other's shield. Ruggiero's shield, the sweated labour of naked demons, little feared the blow: it was the shield wrought by Atlas, and its properties I have earlier described to you. / I've already said that its magic radiance struck the eyes so mightily that to unveil it was to blind all sight and leave the onlooker stunned. So, if the need was not too pressing, it tended to remain covered with a veil. The shield must also have been impenetrable: at this impact it was quite unaffected. / The other's shield, less skilfully wrought, did not stand up to the ponderous blow; as though struck by a thunderbolt, it gave way to the lance-tip and split open—it gave way to the lance which found the arm behind it all too little protected. So Samsonet was wounded and flung, protesting, from the saddle. / This was the first of the companions who championed the wicked law who did not win the other's spoils, and the first to be unhorsed at the joust. The man who laughs must occasionally weep, occasionally find Fate rebellious. The watchman on the keep struck his bell as a signal to the other champions. /

Meanwhile Pinabello had approached Bradamant to discover who was the knight who with such valiant prowess had assailed the knight from his castle. Now divine justice, to give Pinabello his deserts, brought him to her mounted on the very horse which he had earlier stolen from her by a trick. / Just eight months had passed since the day when she had been on a journey with Pinabello, if you remember, and he had dropped her into Merlin's tomb; the tree-branch which fell with her saved her life—or rather it was her good destiny—but Pinabello left, taking her steed with him, for he believed she lay buried in the tomb. / Bradamant recognized her horse and, through him, the wicked count; and when she heard his voice and had scrutinized his face more closely, 'This is assuredly the scoundrel,' she cried, 'who tried to injure and humiliate me—and see if it isn't his sin which has brought him right to the spot where he shall be amply repaid!' / To threaten him, draw her sword, and attack him was the work of an instant; she took care, though, first to block his escape back to the castle. Deprived of the hope of finding safety like a fox going to earth, Pinabello fled into the depth of the forest, shrieking and never once turning to face her. / Pale with fright the wretch spurred away, placing his last hope in flight, but the spirited damsel kept her sword at his flanks and struck and pressed him. She kept up with him and never fell back. Great was the din—the whole wood groaned with it, though no one at the castle was aware of what was happening as they were all solely intent upon Ruggiero. /

The other three knights had meanwhile come out from the castle, accompanied by the ill-natured damsel who had imposed the evil custom. Each of these knights preferred death to a continued life of shame, and it brought blushes to their cheeks, pain to their hearts to have to join battle, three against one. / The cruel minx who had imposed this iniquitous practice reminded them of the pledge of vengeance they had given her. 'If I overthrow him for you with but this lance,' cried Guidone, 'why insist on other lances to go with me? If I lie, behead me—I'll not mind.' / Grifon and Aquilant said the same; each of them wanted to engage in single combat; they would rather be seized and killed sooner than outnumber a lone man. 'Why so many words to so little profit?' the woman replied. 'I brought you here to take this man's arms, not to make new rules, fresh bargains. / When I held you prisoners, that was the time to make these excuses, not now —now it's too late! You're to stand by the agreed pact, not give me vain and lying words.'

Ruggiero shouted at them: 'Here are the arms for you, here is the steed—his saddle and bards are new; and here is the lady's clothing. If you want them, what are you waiting for?' / Urged on one side by the woman, on the other by Ruggiero's cries and taunts, they perforce had to move into the affray, though they blushed for shame. The twin sons of the noble Marquis of Burgundy pulled ahead, while Guidone, whose steed was heavier, came close behind them. / Ruggiero rode in with the same lance that had felled Samsonet. He was protected by the shield which had been Atlas', up in the Pyrenees—the enchanted shield, that is, whose radiance no human eye could endure. Ruggiero fell back on it as a last resort in moments of extreme peril. / In fact there had been only three occasions when the peril was that dire: the first two were when he was escaping from the soft dominion of Alcina to return to a more praiseworthy life. The third occasion was when he left the orc in the foaming seas after snatching from its disappointed jaws the beautiful naked maiden who later proved so heartless to her rescuer. / Apart from these three times he had always kept the shield hidden under a veil in such a way that he could quickly lay it bare if he needed to. Now he advanced to the affray, as I said, in such dashing spirits that he feared his three opponents less than he would little children. /

Ruggiero's lance struck Grifon's shield at the top, where it merged with his visor; Grifon looked like toppling off one side or the other and finally did fall while his charger galloped on. He himself had pointed his lance at Ruggiero's shield but glanced it instead of hitting it dead on; as its surface was polished and smooth, his lance grazed it and produced the contrary effect: / he ripped the veil hiding the dreadful magic light which perforce makes people fall down in a dazzle. Aquilant, who rode with him neck and neck, ripped the veil even more and the shield flashed: the brightness struck the two brothers in the eyes, as also Guidone, who came galloping after them. / They hit the ground, one here, another there; the shield not merely dazzled their eyes but quite stunned their other senses. Ruggiero, unaware of the outcome, turned his horse, and as he did so, drew his sword which could cut and thrust to such sharp effect. He could see no one to oppose him, now, for the one clash had brought them all down. / The champions and also those who had come out on foot, the ladies, too, and even the horses, they all lay sprawled on their sides as though mortally wounded.

At first he could not understand; then he noticed that the veil was dangling from his left side—the silk veil which normally prevented the gleam which had produced the dire effect. / Quickly he turned his face to look for his beloved; he came to where he had left her at the start of the first duel. Not finding her there, he thought that she must have gone ahead to prevent the young man from dying, fearful perhaps lest he be burnt at the stake while they were delayed at the joust. / Among the fallen he saw the damsel who was their guide. He placed her, still unconscious, in front of him and rode away moodily. From a cloak she wore over her dress he fashioned a cover for the magic shield. As soon as he had concealed the noxious radiance, she returned to her senses. /

Off rode Ruggiero, red in the face and too ashamed to raise his eyes: he felt that everyone could reproach him for so inglorious a victory. 'What can I do to make up for such a disgrace?' he mused. 'If I won, people will say it was by virtue of magic, not by my own valour.' / While he rode on, brooding, he happened upon the very thing he was looking for: he came to a deep well dug in the middle of the road. Here the herds retired in the noon-day heat when they were replete with browsing. 'Now,' cried Ruggiero, addressing his shield, 'to ensure that you do not disgrace me a second time! / We shall part company: let this be the last time I am ever to suffer reproach on your account.' With these words he dismounted, took a large and heavy stone, tied it to the shield, and tipped both of them into the deep well to sink to the bottom. 'There remain buried,' he said; 'and with you let my shame forever lie hidden.' / The hollow well was full to the brim with water. The shield was heavy and so was the stone: they did not stop sinking until they lay on the bottom, the soft, light waters closing over them. Rumour, the vagrant, did not pass in silence over this splendid, noble deed, but promptly spread the word abroad, trumpeting the news until France, Spain, and the neighbouring lands were full of it. / As this remarkable event became known by word of mouth throughout the world, many warriors set out, near and far, in search of the shield. But none of them knew which was the forest with the well in which it was immersed—the woman who revealed the story would never divulge its location. /

When Ruggiero left the castle where he had won the battle with so little effort, leaving Pinabello's four champions looking like men of straw, he had only to remove the shield to remove the light which bedazzled eyes and spirits, and those who had fallen down as dead revived, full of wonderment. / All that day they spoke of nothing else but the strange thing that had befallen them, and how each one of them had been overcome by that horrible flash. As they discussed these things news reached them that Pinabello's star had set: they were told that Pinabello was dead, but not who had slain him. / Fearless Bradamant had meanwhile caught Pinabello in a narrow space, and a hundred times she had plunged her sword deep into his side and breast. When she had delivered the world of this putrid stench which had infected all the country round, she turned her back on the woods, her witnesses to the slaughter, and left with the steed the villain had stolen from her. / She meant to return to where she had left Ruggiero, but she could not find her way. Over hill and dale she wandered, searching almost everywhere in the vicinity, but her evil fortune never permitted her to find her way back to him. In the next canto I shall await those of you who are enjoying my story.

TWENTY-THIRD CANTO

*1-3 Introductory. 3-24 Astolfo entrusts Rabican to
Bradamant who takes the steed to Montauban. 25-38
Bradamant sends Frontino to Ruggiero but Rodomont
intercepts the steed. 38-52 Gabrina accuses Zerbin of
Pinabello's death and he is led to execution. 53-95 Orlando
rescues Zerbin, restores Isabel to him, and fights with
Mandricard. 95-136 Orlando learns of Angelica's marriage
to Medor, and goes mad.*

LET every man attend to the good of others, for seldom will a good deed go unrewarded—and if it does, at least it will never invite death, disaster, or ignominy. He who harms another sooner or later has to pay the penalty: it is not forgotten. Men will seek each other out, the proverb says, while mountains stand firm. / Now see what befell Pinabello

for his wicked behaviour; he finally came by his due chastisement—
the just deserts for his depravity. And God, who normally does not
abide seeing an innocent suffer wrongly, saved the maiden Bradamant;
and He will save whoever abstains from wrongdoing. / Pinabello
believed he had killed this damsel and left her buried in Merlin's
tomb; he never expected to set eyes on her again, let alone to see her
exacting from him the price of his misdeeds.

Little did it profit him to be in the midst of his father's domains—
here stood Altaripa, amid wild mountains, close to the territory of
Ponthieu. / Altaripa belonged to old Count Anselm, the father of this
scoundrel who found himself short of friends and allies in his flight
from Bradamant. At the foot of a hill she took the treacherous fellow's
worthless life; she had leisure for this—loud shrieks and pleas for
mercy were all the help he could summon. / Having slain the deceitful
knight who had meant to put her to death, she wanted to return to
where she had left Ruggiero, but her harsh fate would not permit this:
she was destined to stray off down a path which took her into the thick
of the forest, where it was at its most weird and lonely and intractable,
while the sun was abandoning the world to darkness. / Not knowing
where to find shelter for the night, she stopped where she was, beneath
the boughs, on the tender grass, and awaited the new day, now sleeping,
now gazing at Saturn or Jupiter, Venus or Mars, and the other heavenly bodies in their motion. Whether awake or asleep her mind was ever
fixed upon Ruggiero as though he were present. / Often she heaved
deep sighs of sorrow and regret that Wrath had overcome Love within
her. 'Wrath', she grieved, 'has sundered me from my beloved; would
that I had taken a little care, when I embarked upon this wretched
venture, to see I knew how to return the way I'd come. Where were
my eyes, my wits!' / These and other words she uttered, with many
more which she spoke within her heart. Her grief showed in a gale of
sighs, a downpour of tears. After her long vigil the light she yearned
for glimmered in the East; she fetched her grazing steed and rode
towards the daylight. /

She had not gone far before she found herself on the edge of the
wood, right where the palace had been, in which the malicious wizard
had for so many days mocked her with illusions. Here she came upon
Astolfo again; he had contrived a handy bridle for the hippogryph, and
now Rabican was his great concern, not knowing in whose hands to
leave him. / It happened that the paladin had his helmet off, so that
Bradamant recognized him for her cousin the moment she was out of
the wood. She greeted him from a distance and hastened joyfully to
embrace him; she spoke her name and raised her visor to make plain
who she was. / Astolfo could not have found a better person with

whom to leave his charger: Bradamant would take good care of him
and give him back on his master's return. Her arrival truly seemed to
him a godsend. He was always pleased to see her but now most
especially, with the need facing him. / Twice, three times they embraced in fraternal affection, and enquired most fondly after each other.
Then Astolfo remarked: 'If I'm to explore the realm of feathered
creatures, I am dallying too long.' As he disclosed his plans to the
maiden, he pointed out to her the flying steed. /

The sight of this horse spreading his wings caused her but scant
surprise—time was when she had seen Atlas the magician grasp his
reins as he rode against her; and her eyes had ached from gazing so
hard after the beast that day when Ruggiero was wafted far from her,
taking so long and strange a road. / Astolfo told her that he wanted to
give her Rabican, who ran so swiftly that if he moved at the shooting of
an arrow, he left it far behind. All his armour, too, he wanted to leave
with her, for her to keep at Montauban and give back to him on his
return, as he would not be needing it. / Aiming to fly through the air,
he had to make himself as light as possible. He kept his sword and the
horn, though in fact the horn alone should have been sufficient for all
eventualities. Bradamant also received the lance which had belonged to
Argalia, Galafron's son—the lance which tipped a man out of his saddle
on first impact. / Now he mounted the flying charger and had him
move very slowly through the air before setting spurs to him so that the
next instant the damsel lost them to sight. Thus will a sea-captain,
leaving port, have his vessel towed out if he fears the reefs and the
wind; when he has left the harbour and shore behind he spreads every
sail and runs before the breeze. /

When the duke was gone, Bradamant was left in a state of no little
distress: she did not see how she could bring her cousin's armour and
steed to Montauban when her heart was eaten up with a burning need
to see Ruggiero again—she expected to find him at Vallombrosa if not
sooner. / As she stood here undecided, she saw a peasant happen by;
she had him load the armour as best he could onto Rabican, then lead
the two horses after her (one of them laden): she had two horses already, what with the one she was riding when she relieved Pinabello of
his. / She decided to make for Vallombrosa, hoping to find her Ruggiero there; but she could not tell which was the best or quickest way,
and feared she might go astray—neither was the peasant all that familiar
with the area, so they were sure to lose their way together. However,
she set off at a venture, aiming at where she felt the monastery should
be. / She turned this way and that without meeting a soul to ask the
way. Shortly after noon she found her way out of the wood at a point
where a castle was to be seen close by, crowning the summit of a

hillock. She looked at it, and it looked to her like Montauban; and Montauban it was, where her mother was living and some of her brothers. /

When she recognized the place, she was filled with gloom beyond all telling: if she stopped there she would be discovered and she would not be allowed to leave again. But unless she did leave the flames of love would burn her to a cinder: they would be the death of her. She would not see Ruggiero again, nor go through with what they had planned to do at Vallombrosa. / She paused a while in thought, then decided to turn her back on Montauban. She set out for the monastery: from here she knew her way well enough. But, for better or worse, Fate saw to it that before she was out of the valley, she stumbled upon Alard, one of her brothers, before she had time to hide from him. / He was returning from allocating billets thereabouts to soldiers, mounted and on foot, having recruited fresh troops in the surrounding region at Charlemagne's request. They greeted each other warmly with fraternal embraces, then together made their way back to Montauban, talking of many things. / So the beautiful damsel entered the castle, where her mother Beatrice with tearful cheeks had long and vainly awaited her return, and had mounted a search for her throughout the length and breadth of France. But how tedious she found her mother's and brothers' kisses and handclasps after her affectionate exchanges with Ruggiero, which would be impressed forever in her mind. /

Unable to leave, she hit upon the idea of sending someone else straight off to Vallombrosa to explain to Ruggiero what was preventing her from going, and to beg him (if entreaties were needed) to have himself baptized there for love of her, and then to come on here to give effect to their plan and conclude their marriage. / By the same messenger she decided to send Ruggiero his own horse which he had always so cherished—and without question he was right to do so, for after Brigliador and Bayard there was no finer or more mettlesome steed to be found in all the Saracen lands, nor in those of the French king. / The day Ruggiero rashly mounted the hippogryph and rose into the sky, he left Frontino behind (to give the steed his name), and Bradamant sent him to Montauban, where she had him well tended and never ridden except for short distances at a gentle pace: this way he was now plumper and glossier than ever. / Her every gentlewoman, her every maiden she set to work helping her on an embroidery of finest gold on white and dark silk, a subtle piece of work. With this she covered and embellished the good steed's saddle and bridle. Then she picked one of their number, her nurse Callitrephia's daughter, the faithful confidante of all her secrets. / She had imparted to her a thousand times how deeply Ruggiero was graven upon her heart, and had extolled him to the highest heavens for his looks, his virtues, and manners.

Now she called the maiden and told her, 'I could not choose a better messenger for my purpose—I have no one to send who is more faithful or judicious, my Hippalca, than you are.' / (Hippalca was the maiden's name.) Bradamant sent her off after explaining where she was to go and giving her full instructions of what she was to say to her lord. She was to present her excuses for not having gone to the monastery, and explain that this was not to be imputed to deceitfulness but to Fate, which has more power over us than we over ourselves. / She gave her a cob to ride and handed her Frontino's sumptuous bridle. Were she to come upon anyone so mad—or so base—as to try stealing him from her, she had but to pronounce one word to restore the man to his senses: the name of the steed's owner—she knew of no knight so bold but he must quake at the mention of Ruggiero's name. / Bradamant plied the maiden with instructions about what she was to say to Ruggiero in her place; and when Hippalca had grasped it all, she set off without further delay. She rode for more than ten miles along roads, through fields and dense, dark woods without meeting anyone to molest her or even to ask her where she was going. /

About noon, as she was taking a difficult, narrow track down a hill, she happened upon Rodomont, who was armed and on foot, following a little dwarf. The Moor raised his proud head in her direction and cursed the Eternal Hierarchy, seeing that so fine, splendidly caparisoned a steed was not in a knight's keeping when he came upon him. / He had sworn to seize by force the first steed he came upon. Well, here was the first, and he could not have found a finer horse, one more to his measure—but he would have deemed it wrong to seize him from a damsel. And yet he longed to possess him, and was in two minds. He gazed at the steed, entranced, and kept murmuring: 'Oh why is his master not with him!' / 'If only he were here!' exclaimed Hippalca; 'perhaps he would make you think again: he who rides this horse is a far better man than you are—there is no champion alive to touch him.' 'Who is this man who so tramples upon the honour of the rest of us?' 'Ruggiero.' 'In that case,' Rodomont replied, 'I'll have the horse, since I am taking him from a champion of Ruggiero's calibre. / If he is really so stalwart as you make him out, and really does outclass all others, I shall have to restore to him not only his steed but also the price of the hire, leaving the choice of restitution to him. But tell him my name is Rodomont and if he wants to fight with me he shall find me: wherever I am, a radiance always betrays my presence. / Wherever I go, I leave my mark—the thunderbolt leaves no deeper one.' As he spoke he flicked the golden reins up over the charger's head and leapt into the saddle, leaving Hippalca in tears, stung by grief to hurling threats and insults at him. But he paid no heed. He started up the hill, / guided by the dwarf, in search of Mandricard and Doralice, while Hippalca followed them at a distance, still screaming curses and abuse.

What happened next is disclosed elsewhere. Turpin, however, who relates the whole of this story, makes a digression at this point and returns to the place where Pinabello of Maganza was slain. / Hardly had Bradamant turned her back and left this spot in her haste than Zerbin arrived by another path, accompanied by the deceitful crone. He saw a knight's corpse lying in the dell, but did not know whose it was. Now being chivalrous and merciful, he was moved to pity by this calamity. / Pinabello lay on the ground dead, bleeding from so many wounds that had he been attacked by more than a hundred swords at once they would have seemed excessive. The Scottish knight was not slow to pursue the still-fresh footprints in order to discover who had done this murder. / He told Gabrina to wait for him: he would be back in a minute. She planted herself by the corpse and looked it over carefully: if there was on it anything which took her fancy, why should it be wasted any further in adorning a dead man! Among her other faults, she was as greedy a woman as could be. / Had she had any hope of being able to steal them undetected, she would have taken his richly woven surcoat and his fine armour. What she could conveniently hide she took, while she smarted at having to leave the rest. Among her spoils was a handsome belt which she took off him and girt about her waist between two skirts. /

Zerbin was back soon afterwards, having followed Bradamant's traces in vain: the path, he found, twisted away into several offshoots leading upwards or down. As little daylight remained and he had no wish to stay among those crags in the dusk, he turned his back on the grim valley and went with the evil old woman in search of lodging. / In about two miles they came to a great castle called Altaripa; here they stopped for the night which was rapidly spreading across the sky. They had not been there long before bitter laments struck their ears from all sides, and they saw tears in every eye, as though the grief touched everybody. / Zerbin made enquiries and was told that news had been brought to Count Anselm that his son Pinabello lay slain on a narrow path between two hills. In order not to attract suspicion, Zerbin pretended surprise and dropped his gaze; but he thought that this must assuredly be the corpse he had found on his journey. / Soon the bier arrived, illuminated by sconces and torches; the wailing grew more intense, with handclaps loud enough to assail the stars, and the tears welled up more copiously from beneath eyelids to flood down cheeks.

The darkest, most clouded face of all was that of the wretched father. / While preparations were going forward to conduct the funeral according to the most solemn rites, in the traditional manner (though time corrupts tradition), a proclamation was published by the count, which interrupted the people's mourning: a great reward was promised to whoever informed him who it was who had slain his son. /

The proclamation was spread by word of mouth throughout the neighbourhood, until it came to the ears of the evil old woman. Being more rabid than any tigress or bear, she set out to finish Zerbin, out of hatred perhaps, or to be able to boast that she alone of human kind was bereft of all humanity, / or perhaps to gain the reward. She went to the grieving count and, after embarking on some likely preamble, announced to him that Zerbin was the culprit; with this, she slipped the handsome belt from her waist. The wretched father was quick to recognize it and to regard it as clear proof of the old crone's witness, of her sinister office. / Weeping, he lifted his hands to heaven and swore that his son would not go unavenged. The whole complement of the castle was alerted in haste and a cordon was thrown round the guest-quarters. So Zerbin, who imagined that his enemies were far away and never expected such ill-treatment, was seized in his first sleep by Count Anselm, who regarded himself as gravely wronged by his captive. / That same night he had Zerbin clapped into irons and chained in a dark cell. Before the Sun had scattered his rays, the unjust penalty was already ordained: he was to be quartered on the very spot where the crime imputed to him was committed. No further examination was conducted—the count believed him guilty and that was enough. / When fair Aurora, the next morning, tinged the soft air with colour, white, red, and saffron, the whole people assembled, crying 'Away with him!', to punish Zerbin for another's misdeed. The mindless rabble escorted him out, some mounted, some on foot—a disorderly procession—and the Scottish knight rode out, bound, and with head bent, on a little hack. /

But God, who often helps the innocent and never abandons those who trust in His goodness, had provided for his defence to such effect that there would be no slaying him today. Orlando arrived, and his arrival proved Zerbin's salvation. The paladin saw the folk down in the plain leading the dejected knight to his death. / With him was the damsel whom he had found in the cave in the wilds—the King of Galicia's daughter Isabel, who had fallen into the hands of brigands after abandoning the ship wrecked in the dire sea-storm. She it was who lay closer to Zerbin's heart than his own life. / Orlando had kept her company after rescuing her from the cave. When Isabel saw the throng in the distance she asked Orlando who they were. 'I don't know,' he said; and, leaving her on the hillside, he was off down to the plain.

One look at Zerbin told him that here was a most worthy baron. / He approached Zerbin and asked him where they were taking him, a prisoner, and why. The downcast knight raised his head, and once he had grasped the paladin's question, he told him how matters stood. He spoke to such good effect as to deserve the paladin's assistance. Indeed, Orlando realized from his words that he must be innocent and was dying without cause. / When he heard that Count Anselm of Altaripa was behind this, he was convinced that here was a flagrant injustice, for the scoundrel was capable of nothing else. Besides, the two were at daggers drawn owing to an age-old vendetta which simmered in the blood of Maganza and Clairmont, and which produced a succession of murders, outrages, and insults. /

'Untie the knight, vermin, or I'll slaughter the lot of you!' yelled Orlando at the villains. 'Who is this man who delivers such slashing blows?' asked one of them, who wished to appear the most zealous. 'If we were made of wax or straw, and he of fire, his shout would still be overdone.' And he made for the paladin, who lowered his lance against him. / Count Anselm's man had that night stolen Zerbin's shining armour and now was wearing it, but it did not protect him against the paladin's sharp onslaught. The lance caught him on the right cheek, and though it did not penetrate the helmet, which was finely wrought, it fetched him such a blow that it broke his neck and took his life. / Without arresting his charge or raising his lance, he drove clean through the next man's chest. Leaving the lance embedded, he quickly drew Durindana and drove into the thick of the mob. Here he split a crown in two, there he sliced a head off its shoulders; many a throat he punctured, and in no time he had slain or routed more than a hundred. / Over one third of them were already dead; the rest he harried, slashed, and sliced, skewered, speared, and lopped. One man threw down his shield, another his cumbersome helmet, others their spear or scythe. People dashed hither and thither across his path, dived for cover in the woods, hid in holes. Orlando, bereft of mercy today, meant to leave not one man alive if he could help it; / out of one hundred and twenty, at least eighty perished (these are Turpin's figures). Eventually Orlando returned to Zerbin, whose heart was all a-flutter—words cannot describe his elation on Orlando's return. He would have gone down on his knees to reverence his deliverer, but here he was, trussed up and mounted on a hack. / Orlando untied him and helped him into his armour, recovered from the captain of the posse who had put it on, to his undoing.

Zerbin meanwhile turned to look at Isabel, who had been waiting on the hillside and, now that she saw the affray ended, had brought her beauty to within closer range. / When Zerbin saw the damsel approaching—his beautiful and greatly beloved Isabel, whom a deceitful messenger had given him to believe was drowned, and whose death he had so often lamented—he felt himself freeze, as though a lump of ice had been placed in his breast, and he shivered a little; but soon the chill gave way to heat as he blazed up in flames of love. / What kept him from embracing her at once was his respect for the lord of Anglant: he thought, in fact he was convinced, that Orlando must be the damsel's suitor. So he fell into the depths of misery, and his impulse of joy was short-lived: to see her belonging to another was harder to endure than to hear of her death. / Much more did it pain him to find her in the keeping of the knight to whom he owed so much: it would not have been fair, it would not have been easy, to try taking her away from him. There was not another man whom he would have allowed to leave, taking this prize, without running riot—but his debt to the count necessitated his placing his neck beneath the other's foot. /

In silence they rode as far as a spring where they dismounted and stopped awhile. The tormented count drew off his helmet and had Zerbin do likewise. So it was that the damsel looked her beloved in the face and turned pale with sudden joy; then, as a flower drenched from heavy rain revives when the sun comes out, she revived, / and without hesitation or second thought, ran to her lover and threw her arms around his neck. She could not utter a word; tears bathed her breast and face. Orlando, watching this amorous display, required no further explanations: the evidence was clear to him that this man could be none other than Zerbin. / When Isabel had recovered her voice, while her moist cheeks were still damp, she could speak only of the great kindness done to her by the paladin. Zerbin, in whose scales the damsel weighed as much as his own life, threw himself at the count's feet and worshipped him as a man who within one hour had given him two lives. /

The conversation between the two knights would have been full of repeated thanks and promises, but they heard noises on the path through the dark, leafy trees. Quickly they clapped their helmets on their exposed heads and fetched their chargers; they were only just in the saddle when who should appear but a knight and a damsel. / This warrior was Mandricard, who had hastened away after Orlando to wreak vengeance upon him for Alzirdo and Manilard, whom the paladin had most valiantly assailed. Mandricard, however, was slowed in his pursuit once he had gained possession of Doralice: armed with but an oaken lance-haft, he had seized her from a hundred iron-clad soldiers. /

Now the Saracen did not know that the man he was pursuing was none other than Orlando; he did have clear evidence, though, that his quarry must be a prominent knight errant. It was on him, now, rather than on Zerbin that he fixed his gaze; he looked him quickly up and down and, seeing that he fitted the description, said: 'You are the man I'm looking for. / Ten days now I have been intent on tracking you down, spurred and goaded as I was by the rumours about you which came to our camp at Paris with the single survivor who staggered in, the last of over a thousand whom you dispatched to the Stygian shades. He it was who described the slaughter which the men of Norizia and of Tremisen suffered at your hands. / When I heard the account I was not slow to follow you, to set eyes on you and then to make trial of you. And as I acquainted myself with the device you wore on your surcoat, I know that you are the man. Even without this knowledge, even if you slipped in among a hundred others to hide from me, your fierce bearing would give you away to me.' /

'It cannot be said', replied Orlando, 'that you are a knight who lacks valour—I don't believe that so noble a wish could find room in a servile heart. If a desire to set eyes on me brings you here, I shall have you look within me as well as without: I shall take off my helmet so that your wish can be fully gratified. / But when you have looked me squarely in the face, there is still your other wish to attend to: you must still be satisfied on the score which sent you after me along this road. See whether my prowess is in keeping with this fierce bearing you so commend.' 'Let's come to that now,' cried the Saracen; 'I'm satisfied on the first count.' /

Orlando meanwhile kept looking the Saracen over from head to foot; he peered at both hips, then at his saddle—but on neither side was there a sign of any sword or club. He asked him what weapon he had for in case he missed his mark with the lance. 'Think nothing of it,' replied the other; 'I have scared many a man just as I am. / I have sworn not to wear a sword until I have wrested Durindana from Count Orlando; I am looking for him everywhere, as I have more than one score to settle with him. I swore this (if you care to know) the day I placed this helmet on my head; it, and all the rest of the armour I wear, belonged to Hector, who has been dead these thousand years. / Only the sword is missing from the fine suit of arms; how it was stolen I cannot say. Now the paladin has it, I understand, which explains what makes him so bold. If I can run up against him I'm confident that I'll make him restore his ill-gotten weapon. I seek him, too, as I would avenge illustrious Agrican, my father. / Orlando killed him by treachery—he could never have succeeded otherwise, I know.' The count now broke his silence and burst out: 'You lie, you and whoever else says this! But what you seek has fallen to your lot: I am Orlando, and I slew him justly; and this is the sword you are seeking—it shall be yours, if you earn it by your valour. / Mine though it is by right, let us stage a chivalrous duel for it; and let us hang it from a tree—I wouldn't have it be mine any more than yours during our combat. You are free to take it in the event that you slay or capture me.' This said, he took Durindana and hung it on a small tree in the middle of the field. /

They had drawn apart the length of half an arrow's flight; they had spurred their steeds, given them free rein; they were charging; now each had caught the other a sharp blow right on the visor. The lances shivered into a thousand splinters shooting skywards—they might have been made of ice. / Both lances had to break, for neither knight was pliable; it was with the surviving piece of shaft that they returned to the attack. The two warriors, inured to steel, now laid about each other savagely with their staffs, like a couple of bumpkins worked into a rage over water-rights or a field boundary. / Their cudgels did not stand up to four blows: the fury of the combat was too much for them. On either side tempers rose, though they had nothing left to fight with but their bare hands. Wherever these obtained a purchase, they prized loose armour plating, ripped chain-mail, tore at hip-sheathing tassets. Neither of them could have wished for a heavier hammer or stouter pliers to give them an advantage. / How was the Saracen to find a way to conclude the fierce challenge, salving his honour? It would have been madness to waste more time fighting as they were—inflicting more damage on the striker than on his victim. They grappled and in no time the pagan king had gripped Orlando tightly round the chest, meaning to do to him as Hercules had done to Anteus. / He seized him violently round the chest and jerked him back and forth; so immersed was he in his rage that he paid little heed to his bridle.

Now Orlando collected himself and, spying his advantage, closed in upon it, aspiring to victory: he placed a gingerly hand on the Saracen horse's head-stall and slipped off the bridle. / The Saracen exerted all his force in order to suffocate him or root him out of the saddle, but under the onslaught Orlando gripped so tightly with his knees that there was no forcing him one way or the other. The pagan tugged so hard, the girth worked loose beneath the count's horse: Orlando was on the ground before he knew it, his feet still in the stirrups, his knees still gripping the dislodged saddle. / With a noise like a dropped sackload of armour the count clattered as he hit the ground. Now the steed whose head was free of the bridle—the one whose bit had been slipped from his jaws—bolted in a blind panic, equally heedless of roads as of woodlands in his mad career, and carried Mandricard with him. /

Seeing her escort leave the field—and her side— Doralice felt insecure, and off she galloped after him on her cob. The pagan shouted furiously at his horse and belaboured him with his fists and feet, and threatened what he would do if he didn't stop (as though the steed were not a mere beast), and kept goading him all the more. / The beast was timid and cowardly, and simply kept running without watching his step. Already he had covered three miles, and would have gone further but for a ditch that thwarted him: in the bottom of the ditch there was neither feather-bed nor quilt, but here both horse and rider landed upside down. Mandricard struck the ground with a sharp thump, but he never winced nor broke a bone. / Here at last the charger stopped; but there was no steering him, for he had no rein. The Tartar clutched him by the mane, and fumed with rage. He was quite at a loss. 'Put my palfrey's bridle on him,' suggested Doralice; 'my mount is not very spirited, whether he's bridled or not.' / Now to have accepted the damsel's offer would have struck the Saracen as ungallant. But Fate, most propitious to his desires, saw to providing him with a bridle by another means—by sending that evil woman Gabrina his way.

After she had betrayed Zerbin she escaped, like a she-wolf who hears the pursuing huntsmen and hounds in the distance. / She was still wearing the dress and youthful ornaments which had been taken from Pinabello's pretentious damsel in order to clothe her. And she also had the damsel's palfrey—the very pick of this world's goods. The crone stumbled upon the Tartar before she realized he was there. / The sight of this woman, who looked like a monkey, a baboon, tricked out in this youthful raiment provoked Doralice and Mandricard to laughter. The Saracen decided to take her bridle for his own horse, and so he did. Having removed the bit, he menaced and yelled at the palfrey, and startled him into flight— / he fled through the woods, carrying off the crone, half-dead with fright; he carried her over hill and dale, down paths straight and crooked, through ditches, across hillsides, at random.

But I am not so taken up with her that I would scant the attention due to Orlando. Without hindrance, he repaired all the damage done to his saddle, / remounted his charger, and waited a while, watching for the Saracen's return; seeing no further sign of him, he decided to go after Mandricard himself. First, though, being a courteous man, before leaving, he bade farewell to the two lovers with kind and gentle words. / Zerbin was very sad at his leaving, while Isabel wept for tenderness; they both wanted to go with him, but the count did not wish for their company, pleasant and attractive though it was. The excuse he gave for leaving them was this: a warrior can incur no worse infamy than to go in search of an enemy taking with him a comrade to assist and defend him. / He asked them, in the event that Mandricard came across them first, to tell him that Orlando would remain in the vicinity for a further three days; after that he would be on his way back to the ensigns of the Golden Lilies, to be with Charlemagne's host; if Mandricard wanted him, it is from here that he would have to summon him. / They willingly promised to do this and anything he bade them. Then the knights took their separate ways, Zerbin hither, Count Orlando yonder. But before the count set out, he took his sword off the tree and once more buckled it on; then he set his steed moving in the direction in which he felt he was most likely to find Mandricard. /

The Saracen's steed had pursued so wild a course through the trackless wood that Orlando journeyed for two days to no avail: he found neither his quarry nor even a clue to where he was. He came to a stream which looked like crystal; a pleasant meadow bloomed on its banks, picked out with lovely pure colours and adorned with many beautiful trees. / A welcome breeze tempered the noontide for the rugged flock and naked shepherd, and Orlando felt no discomfort, for all that he was wearing breastplate, helmet, and shield. Here he stopped, then, to rest—but his welcome proved to be harsh and painful, indeed quite unspeakably cruel, on this unhappy, ill-starred day. / Looking about him, he saw inscriptions on many of the trees by the shady bank; he had only to look closely at the letters to be sure that they were formed by the hand of his goddess. This was one of the spots described earlier, to which the beautiful damsel, Queen of Cathay, often resorted with Medor, from the shepherd's house close by. / He saw 'Angelica' and 'Medor' in a hundred places, united by a hundred love-knots. The letters were so many nails with which Love pierced and wounded his heart. He searched in his mind for any number of excuses to reject what he could not help believing; he tried to persuade himself that it was some other Angelica who had written her name on the bark. / 'But I recognize these characters,' he told himself; 'I've seen and read so many just like them. Can she perhaps be inventing this Medor? Perhaps by this name she means me.' Thus deceiving himself with far-fetched notions, disconsolate Orlando clung to hopes which he knew he was stretching out to grasp. / But the more he tried to smother his dark suspicions the more they flared up with new vigour: he was like an unwary bird caught in a web or in birdlime—the more he beats his wings and tries to free himself, the worse ensnared he becomes.

Orlando came to where a bow-shaped curve in the hillside made a cave overlooking the clear spring. / Twisting on their stems, ivy and rambling vines adorned the entrance. Here during the heat of the day the two happy lovers used to lie in each other's arms. Their names figured here more than elsewhere; they were inscribed within and without, sometimes in charcoal, sometimes in chalk, or scratched with the point of a knife. / The dejected count approached on foot. At the entrance he saw many words which Medor had written in his own hand; they seem to have been freshly inscribed. The inscription was written in verse and spoke of the great pleasure he had enjoyed in this cave. I believe it was written in his native tongue; in ours this is how it reads: /

'Happy plants, verdant grass, limpid waters, dark, shadowy cave, pleasant and cool, where fair Angelica, born of Galafron, and loved in vain by many, often lay naked in my arms. I, poor Medor, cannot repay you for your indulgence otherwise than by ever praising you, / and by entreating every lover, knight, or maiden, every person, native or alien, who happens upon this spot by accident or by design, to say to the grass, the shadows, the cave, stream, and plants: "May sun and moon be kind to you, and the chorus of the nymphs, and may they see that shepherds never lead their flocks to you." ' / It was written in Arabic, which the count knew as well as he knew Latin. He knew many and many a tongue, but Arabic is one with which he was most familiar: his grasp of it had saved him on more than one occasion from injury and insult when he was among the Saracens. But he was not to boast if formerly his knowledge had helped him—the pain it now brought him quite discounted every former advantage. /

Five and six times the unfortunate man re-read the inscription, trying in vain to wish it away, but it was more plain and clear each time he read it. And each time, he felt a cold hand clutch his heart in his afflicted breast. Finally he fell to gazing fixedly at the stone—stone-like himself. / He was ready to go out of his mind, so complete was his surrender to grief. Believe one who has experienced it—this is a sorrow to surpass all others. His chin had dropped onto his chest, his head was bowed, his brow had lost its boldness. So possessed was he by sorrow that he had no voice for laments, no moisture for tears. / His impetuous grief, set upon erupting all too quickly, remained within. A broad-bellied, narrow-necked vase full of water has the same effect, as can be observed: when the vase is inverted, the liquid so surges to the neck that it blocks its own egress, and can scarcely do more than come out drop by drop. / Returning to himself a little, he considered how he might yet be mistaken about it: he hoped against hope that it might simply be someone trying to besmirch his lady's name this way, or to charge him with a burden of jealousy so unendurable that he would die of it; and that whoever it was who had done this had copied her hand most skilfully. / With such meagre, such puny hopes he roused his spirits and found a little courage.

He mounted Brigliador, now that the sun was giving place to his sister in the sky. Before he had gone far he saw smoke issuing from the housetops, and heard dogs barking and cows lowing; he came to a farmhouse and found lodging. / Listlessly he dismounted, and left Brigliador to the care of a discreet stable-boy. Others there were to help him off with his armour and his golden spurs, and to refurbish them. This was the house where Medor lay wounded, and met with his great good fortune. Orlando did not ask for supper but for a bed: he was replete with sadness, not with other fare. / The harder he sought for rest, the worse the misery and affliction he procured himself—every wall, every door, every window was covered with the hateful inscriptions. He wanted to make enquiries there, but chose to keep his lips sealed: he was afraid to establish too clearly the very question he wanted to cloud with mist so as to dull the pain. / Little good did it do him to deceive himself; somebody there was to speak of the matter unasked. The herdsman, who saw him so downcast and sad and wanted to cheer him up, embarked, without asking leave, upon the story of those two lovers: he knew it well, and often repeated it to those who would listen. There were many who enjoyed hearing it. / He told how at the prayer of beautiful Angelica he had brought Medor back to his house. Medor was gravely wounded, and she tended his wound, and in a few days had healed it—but Love inflicted upon her heart a wound far worse than his, and from a small spark kindled so blazing a fire that she was all aflame and quite beside herself; / and, forgetting that she was daughter of the greatest monarch of the East, driven by excessive passion, she chose to become wife to a poor simple soldier. The herdsman ended his story by having the bracelet brought in—the one Angelica had given him on her departure as a token of thanks for his hospitality. /

This evidence shown in conclusion proved to be the axe which took his head off his shoulders at one stroke, now that Love, that tormentor, was tired of raining blows upon him. Orlando tried to conceal his grief, but it so pressed him, he could not succeed: willy nilly the sighs and tears had to find a vent through his eyes and lips. / When he was free to give rein to his sorrow, once he was alone without others to consider, tears began to stream from his eyes and furrow his cheeks, running down onto his breast. He sighed and moaned, and made great circular sweeps of the bed with his arms: it felt harder than rock; it stung worse than a bed of nettles. / Amid such bitter anguish the thought occurred to him that on this very bed in which he was lying the thankless damsel must have lain down many a time with her lover. The downy bed sent a shudder through him and he leapt off it with all the alacrity of a yokel who has lain down in the grass for a nap and spies a snake close by. /

The bed, the house, the herdsman filled him on a sudden with such revulsion that, without waiting for moonrise, or for the first light preceding the new day, he fetched his arms and his steed and went out into the darkest, most tangled depths of the wood; when he felt he was quite alone, he gave vent to his grief with cries and howls. / There was no checking his cries and tears; night and day he allowed himself no respite. Towns and villages he avoided, and lay out in the open on the hard forest-floor. He wondered that his head could hold such an unquenchable source of water, and that he could sigh so much. Frequently as he wept he said to himself: / 'These are no longer tears that drop from my eyes so copiously. The tears were not enough for my grief: they came to an end before my grief was half expressed. Urged by fire, my vital spirit is now escaping by the ducts which lead to the eyes: this is what is now spilling out, and with it my sorrow and my life will flow out at its last hour. / These sighs, which are a token of my anguish, are not truly sighs: sighs are not like this—now and then they will cease, but never do I feel a relaxing of my pain as my breast exhales it. Love, which burns my heart, makes this wind, beating his wings about the flames. By what miracle, Love, do you keep my heart ever burning but never consumed by fire? / I am not who my face proclaims me; the man who was Orlando is dead and buried, slain by his most thankless lady who assailed him by her betrayal. I am his spirit sundered from him, and wandering tormented in its own hell, so that his shade, all that remains of him, should serve as an example to any who place hope in Love.' /

All night the count wandered in the wood; at sunrise, Fate brought him back to the spring where Medor had carved his inscription. To see his calamity written there in the hillside so inflamed him that he was drained of every drop that was not pure hate, fury, wrath, and violence. On impulse he drew his sword, / and slashed at the words and the rock-face, sending tiny splinters shooting skywards. Alas for the cave, and for every trunk on which the names of Medor and Angelica were written! They were left, that day, in such a state that never more would they afford cool shade to shepherd or flock. The spring, too, which had been so clear and pure, was scarcely safer from wrath such as his; / branches, stumps and boughs, stones and clods he kept hurling into the lovely waters until he so clouded them from surface to bottom that they were clear and pure never again. In the end, exhausted and sweat-soaked, his stamina given out and no longer answering to his deep, bitter hate, his burning wrath, he dropped onto the grass and sighed up at the heavens. / Weary and heart-stricken, he dropped onto the grass and gazed mutely up at the sky. Thus he remained, without food or sleep while the sun three times rose and set. His bitter agony grew and grew until it drove him out of his mind.

On the fourth day, worked into a great frenzy, he stripped off his armour and chain-mail. / The helmet landed here, the shield there, more pieces of armour further off, the breastplate further still: arms and armour all found their resting-place here and there about the wood. Then he tore off his clothes and exposed his hairy belly and all his chest and back.

Now began the great madness, so horrifying that none will ever know a worse instance. / He fell into a frenzy so violent that his every sense was darkened. He did not think to draw his sword, with which I expect he would have performed marvels. But in view of his colossal strength he had no need of it, nor of any hatchet or battle-axe. He now performed some truly astonishing feats: at one jerk he rooted up a tall pine, / after which he tore up several more as though they were so many celery-stalks. He did the same to oaks and ancient elms, to beech and ash-trees, to ilexes and firs. What a birdcatcher does when clearing the ground before he lays nets—rooting up rushes, brushwood, and nettles—Orlando did to oaks and other age-old timber. / The shepherds who heard the din left their flocks scattered through the woodland and hastened from all parts to this spot to see what was happening. But I have reached a point which I must not overstep for fear of boring you with my story; I should rather postpone it than annoy you by making it too long.

TWENTY-FOURTH CANTO

1–3 Introductory. 4–14 Orlando's madness. 15–45 Zerbin disposes of Odoric and Gabrina. 46–72 Zerbin piously collects Orlando's arms and fights Mandricard to try saving the sword Durindana. 73–93 Zerbin dies in Isabel's arms. 94–115 Mandricard and Rodomont fight over Doralice.

IF you have put your foot in the birdlime spread by Cupid, try to pull it out, and take care not to catch your wing in it too: love, in the universal opinion of wise men, is nothing but madness. Though not everyone goes raving mad like Orlando, Love's folly shows itself in other ways; what clearer sign of lunacy than to lose your own self through pining for another? / The effects vary, but the madness which promotes them is always the same. It is like a great forest into which those who venture must perforce lose their way: one here, another there, one and all go off the track. Let me tell you this, to conclude: whoever grows old in love ought, in addition to Cupid's torments, to be chained and fettered. / 'You, my friend, are preaching to others,' someone will tell me, 'but you overlook your own failing.' The answer is that now, in an interval of lucidity, I understand a great deal. And I am taking pains (with imminent success, I hope) to find peace and withdraw from the dance—though I cannot do so as quickly as I should wish, for the disease has eaten me to the bone. /

In the last canto I was telling you, my Lord, how Orlando, crazed and demented, had torn off arms and armour and scattered them everywhere, ripped his clothes, tossed away his sword, rooted up trees, and made the hollow caves and deep woods re-echo. And some shepherds were attracted to the noise, whether by their stars, or for some wicked misdeed of theirs. / When they had a closer sight of the madman's incredible feats and his prodigious strength, they turned to flee, but without direction, as people do when suddenly scared. The madman was after them at once; he grabbed one and took off his head with all the ease of a person plucking an apple from a tree or a dainty bloom from a briar. / He picked up the heavy carcass by one leg and used it to club the rest; he laid out two, leaving them in a sleep from which perhaps they would awake on Judgement Day. The others cleared off at once: they were quickfooted and had their wits about them. The madman would not have been slow to pursue them, but he had now turned upon their flocks. /

In the fields the labourers, wise from the shepherds' example, left their ploughs, hoes, and sickles and scrambled onto the housetops or onto the church roofs—there being no safety up elm or willow tree. From here they contemplated the fearsome frenzy unleashed upon horse and oxen: they were shattered, battered, and destroyed by dint of punches, thumps, and bites, kicks and scratches. It was a fast mover who could escape him. / Now you could have heard the neighbouring farms resound with shouts, the shrill of horns, and rustic trumpets and, most persistently, the peal of clarions; you could have seen a thousand men streaming down from the hills, armed with pikes and bows, spears, and slings; as many more came up from the plain, ready to wage a peasant war against the madman. / Imagine waves, driven by the South Wind which earlier had been playful, breaking on the shore; the second wave is higher than the first, the third follows with greater force; and, each time, the water builds up more and seethes more widely across the beach. Thus did the pitiless mob increase, coming down from the hills and out of the valleys against Orlando. / Out of that disorderly throng ten he killed who came within his reach, and then another ten. This experiment made it clear that it was far safer to stand well away. No one was able to draw blood from his body; steel was powerless to strike and wound it—the King of Heaven had given him this endowment so as to make him guardian of His holy faith. / Had he been capable of dying, his life would have been in danger; he might have learned what it was to throw aside his sword and, unarmed, to overreach himself.

Now having seen their every blow prove ineffective, the throng began to ebb. With no one left to confront him, Orlando made off and came to a hamlet. / Here he found not a soul, man or child, for everyone had abandoned the place in terror. There was plenty of food set out, humble fare of which shepherds partake. Spurred by hunger and frenzy, he made no distinction between bread and acorns but set to with his hands and teeth and devoured whatever came first within reach, whether raw or cooked. / After this he roamed about the countryside, preying upon men and wild beasts. He would range through the woods catching fleet-footed goats and nimble fawns. Often he would fight with bears and boars, wrestling them to the ground bare-handed; often he filled his ravenous belly with their meat, carcass and all. / He roamed across the length and breadth of France, until one day he came to a bridge. Beneath it a broad, full river flowed between steep, craggy banks. Beside it there stood a tower commanding a sweeping view in all directions. What he did here you shall learn later on: first I must continue Zerbin's story. /

Zerbin delayed a little after Orlando's departure, then took the path along which the paladin had preceded him; he rode at an ambling pace. I don't believe he had gone more than two miles before he saw a knight mounted on a little cob, bound and guarded on either side by two other armed knights. / He recognized the prisoner as soon as he was close, and so did Isabel. It was Odoric of Biscay, who had been the wolf picked to guard the lamb. He had been the first of all Zerbin's friends, the one to whose care the damsel had been entrusted, in the confidence that the trust placed upon him for all other purposes might also be placed on him for this. / Isabel was just in the middle of relating what had befallen her, how she had been saved in the ship's boat before the ship broke up in the waves, and how Odoric had tried to overpower her, and how she had been taken off to the cave. She had not reached the end of her story when they saw the villain led in, a prisoner. / The two flanking Odoric knew Isabel's story. Now they recognized that the man escorting her must be her suitor and their lord, especially as they could see the ancient symbol of his noble house depicted on his shield. A closer look at his face convinced them that they had recognized him aright. / They jumped down and ran open-armed to Zerbin; bareheaded and on bended knee they embraced him as one embraces one's master. Zerbin looked them both in the face and saw that one of them was Coreb of Bilbao while the other was Almon; he had sent them both with Odoric on the foray by sea. /

Said Almon: 'As it has pleased God in His mercy that Isabel should be with you, I can well understand, my lord, that I bring you nothing new if I tell you the reason why you find this scoundrel here with me, bound. From Isabel, who bore the brunt of his offence, you will have heard the whole story in detail. / You must know how I was hood-winked by the traitor, the way he rid himself of me; and how Coreb was wounded when he tried to defend this damsel. But what happened on my return she never saw or heard, so this she could not tell you. I shall explain to you what happened then. / From the city I hastily retraced my steps to the sea-coast; I had with me horses I had quickly obtained, and on my way I kept a sharp look-out for them, as I had left them far behind. I continued until I reached the sea-shore right at the spot where I had left them; I looked, but there was no sign of them, except for some fresh footprints in the sand. / These I followed, and they led me into the wild wood; hardly was I inside it than a sound assailing my ears brought me to where Coreb lay. I asked him what had become of the damsel and of Odoric, and who had attacked him. Learning what had happened, I set out to search the crags for the traitor. / I scoured the vicinity but could pick up no trace of him that day, so finally I returned to where Coreb was lying; he had stained the ground so red that had he been left there much longer, it was a grave he would have needed, and priests and friars to bury him, not a bed and doctors to cure him. / From the wood I had him carried to the city, and lodged him with an innkeeper, a friend of mine; here he was soon healed by the care and skill of an old surgeon.

'We obtained arms and horses and went in search of Odoric, whom we found at the court of King Alfonso of Biscay. There I challenged him to battle. / Aided by the king, who in his justice gave me freedom to fight my battle there, by right, and also by Fortune (who often allots victory according to her whim), I gained an advantage over the traitor. He became my prisoner, and the king, hearing of his guilt, allowed me to dispose of my captive as I wished. / I did not want to kill him, nor to let him be, but to bring him to you, as you see, in chains; I wanted the decision to be yours whether he should die or be reserved for punishment. What brought me here was the news that you were with Charlemagne, and my urge to find you. I thank God who has led me to come upon you in these parts, where I least expected to. / I thank Him also now that I see you have your Isabel with you, I know not how: I thought that, after the villain's work, you would hear no more of her.'

Zerbin listened in silence to Almon, and kept his gaze fixed upon Odoric—not out of hatred so much as out of regret that a friendship such as theirs should have come to so sorry an end. / When Almon had finished, for some while Zerbin was dismayed that the one man with the least cause to do so could have been so blatantly disloyal to him. After brooding for a long time he finally shook himself out of his trance with a sigh and asked the prisoner if the knight's account of him was true. / The traitor fell to his knees and said: 'My lord, everyone who lives on earth sins and errs: the only difference between the good and the wicked is that the latter are defeated in every battle fought against them by the slightest temptation, while the former run to arms and defend themselves—but if the enemy is strong, even they surrender. / Had you bidden me defend one of your castles, and had I, at the first assault, hoisted the enemy's flag without offering resistance, you might have cast in my teeth the charge of cowardice or, worse, of treachery. But had I been forced to yield, I am certain that thanks and praise, not blame, would have been mine. / The stronger the enemy, the better the loser's excuse. I had to defend my trust no differently from a fortress under siege. I made every effort to guard the fortress with all the wisdom and prudence I could muster, but in the end I was defeated by the irresistible onslaught and was driven out.' / Thus said Odoric. To tell the whole story, he added, would take a long time: it was a sharp goad, not a mild tingle which had provoked him. If ever entreaties had abated anger, if meek words had ever borne fruit, they must have done so now, for Odoric found what was needed to move a heart to softness. / Zerbin was in two minds as to whether or not to wreak stark vengeance for so grave a wrong. The thought of the wrong done stirred him to make an end of the villain; but the memory of the close friendship which had so long united them dowsed with the water of pity the fury blazing in his heart and moved him to clemency. /

While Zerbin was still deliberating whether to free Odoric or to hold him prisoner, whether to kill the traitor and thus be rid of him, or to keep him alive but under penalty, who should come galloping up but the palfrey, whose bridle Mandricard had taken; he was neighing and on his back was the old crone who had brought Zerbin to the brink of death. / The palfrey had heard them a long way off and come to join them, carrying on his back the old woman, who was vainly weeping and crying for help. When Zerbin saw her he raised his hands to Heaven which had been so good as to give into his power the only two people whom he had cause to hate. / Zerbin had the old witch held while he decided what to do with her. He thought of cutting off her nose and ears, to make her an example to wrongdoers; then he thought it would be far better to let the vultures make a meal of her.

In his mind he turned over various punishments. Here is what he finally decided. /

He turned to his companions and said: 'I am content to spare the traitor his life; if he does not altogether deserve pardon, neither does he deserve any punishment so cruel as death. Let him live; let him go free, since it seems that the blame rests with Love—any fault is excusable when Love lies at the bottom of it. / Love has often subverted steadier men than this one, and led people into excesses far worse than his, though he has done all of us injury. Let Odoric be forgiven; it is I who should be punished: I was blind to have entrusted the task to him without considering that fire readily burns straw.' / To Odoric he said: 'As penance for your crime I want you to escort this old woman for a year, during which you are not to leave her side. Night and day, wherever you are, wherever you go, you must never be a moment without her. You must defend her to the death against anyone who would do her harm. / You are to challenge any person at her bidding. During this period I place you under an obligation to visit every single region of France.' Thus said Zerbin.

As Odoric deserved to be dispatched below ground for what he had done, this punishment effectively placed him on the brink of a deep ditch: if he did not fall in, he would be very lucky. / So many women, so many men had the crone deceived, so many had she injured, that her escort would not be able to avoid challenges from knights errant. Thus they would both be punished together, she for the wrongs she had committed, he for wrongfully taking up her defence; it could not be long before he met his death. / Zerbin made Odoric swear a solemn oath to observe this pledge, on the understanding that if ever he broke faith, and if he fell once more into Zerbin's hands, there would be no more listening to entreaties: without mercy he would be put most cruelly to death. Then Zerbin bade Almon and Coreb release the prisoner. / So Coreb, with Almon's acquiescence, finally untied the traitor, but in no hurry: they both were sorry to be deprived of the revenge they had so longed for.

The faithless man went his way, then, taking with him the old witch. There is no mention in Turpin of what became of them, but I came upon another author who had more about them. / This author (his name does not matter) says that they had gone only one day's journey when Odoric broke his pledge, and rid himself of Gabrina's constraining presence by throwing a noose round her neck and leaving her dangling from an elm. A year later (my author does not say where), Almon played the very same trick upon Odoric. /

Zerbin, who had been following Orlando's traces and did not want to lose them, sent news of himself to his troops so that they should not remain perplexed for lack of it. He sent it by Almon, together with instructions which it would take too long to set out here. With him he sent Coreb; he kept with him no one but Isabel. / So great was Zerbin's love for the good paladin—and Isabel was no less devoted—and so intense was his desire to hear whether he had come upon Mandricard, the Saracen who had unhorsed him, saddle and all, that he was not going to return to his troops until three days had elapsed: / this was the interval mentioned by Orlando during which he would wait for the knight who still wore no sword. There was nowhere that the paladin went that Zerbin did not visit too.

So he arrived among the trees, a little off the path, carved with thankless Angelica's name; he found the trees all knocked to splinters, as also the cave close by, and the spring in a turmoil. / He saw something glinting in the distance: it turned out to be Orlando's breastplate. Then he found the helmet (not the famous one which had armed the head of the African Prince Almont). Hidden deeper in the wood was the steed; he heard him neigh, and raised his head at the sound to find Brigliador cropping the grass, the reins dangling from his saddle. / He searched the wood for Durindana and found it out of its scabbard. The surcoat he found, too, but in shreds which the poor count had scattered everywhere. Isabel and Zerbin looked glumly about them, not knowing what to make of it all. They could have hit upon every explanation save that Orlando was out of his mind. / Had they noticed a drop of blood they might have concluded that he had been killed. Meanwhile they saw a young shepherd, deathly pale, approaching along the bank of the stream. From the top of a crag he had witnessed the unhappy count's frenzy, seen him throw away his arms, rend his clothes, kill shepherds, and wreak havoc. / Questioned by Zerbin, he gave an exact account of what had happened, much to the amazement of the Scot, who could scarcely believe it: but the evidence was plain enough. At all events he dismounted and, with tears in his eyes and pity in his heart, gathered up the relics which had been scattered about. / Isabel dismounted too, and helped collect the arms and armour.

Now who should arrive but a damsel, in distress, by the look of her, and uttering frequent heartfelt moans. Should anyone ask me who she is, and what makes her so unhappy, my answer is that she is Fiordiligi, searching for some trace of her lover: / she had been left behind in Charlemagne's city, Paris, by Brandimart, who had slipped away without a' word to her. Here she had awaited his return for six to eight months, but seeing him still not returned, she set out in search of him from sea to sea, from the Alps to the Pyrenees. She sought him everywhere, except in the palace of Atlas the magician. / Had she passed that way, she would have seen him roaming about the palace with Gradasso, Ruggiero, Bradamant, Ferrau, and Orlando. Now once Astolfo drove out the magician with a horrible blast of his incredible horn, Brandimart set off towards Paris—but Fiordiligi was not to know this. / As I said, fair Fiordiligi chanced upon the two lovers, and recognized Orlando's arms and his steed Brigliador abandoned, the reins loose on his saddle. With her own eyes she took in the sorry situation, and with her ears she learned more about it— for the young shepherd told her, too, of how he had seen Orlando run amuck. / Zerbin collected the arms together and lodged them in a pine tree, like a fine trophy. And, meaning to forbid any knight, be he native or alien, from taking them, he made a brief inscription on the green trunk: 'The arms of Orlando the paladin'—as much as to say, 'Let no one remove them who cannot stand up to Orlando.' /

His praiseworthy task completed, he was just remounting his horse when Mandricard appeared. He saw the pine tree proudly bearing its trophy and asked Zerbin to explain it, so Zerbin told him what he himself had learnt. At this the pagan king, reckless and exultant, went up to the tree and pulled out the sword, saying: / 'No one can rebuke me for this! It was before today that I won it: I can justly take possession of it anywhere, wherever it happens to be. Orlando was afraid to defend it, so he has feigned madness and thrown it away; but even if he finds such an excuse for his cowardice, he cannot prevent my asserting my rights.' / 'Do not touch it!' cried Zerbin. 'At least don't imagine you'll have it unopposed. If you take Hector's weapon thus, it will be sheer thievery rather than of right.'

Without further words they fell upon each other; each was the other's match for courage and valour. Already a hundred blows had echoed forth and battle was not yet fully joined. / Wherever Durindana fell, Zerbin was not there: he moved quick as a flame. He had his steed leaping this way and that like a doe, wherever the footing was best. And how right he was not to forfeit the best ground, for if that blade caught him a blow, he would have gone to join the dead lovers who people the forest of shady myrtles! / As a nimble hound, attacking a pig seen wandering in the fields away from the herd, will circle round it and jump this way and that, waiting for it to stumble, thus Zerbin watched each move of the sword, up or down, and took care to avoid it. He looked to protect at once his life and his honour. He would strike and withdraw in the nick of time. /

As for the Saracen, every swipe of his vicious sword, hit or miss, left the impression of a March gust between two Alpine peaks, shaking a leafy wood, now bending the tree-tops to the very ground, now flinging the snapped branches in the whirling air. Though Zerbin evaded many a stroke, eventually one came which caught him— / a down-slash he could not avoid, which caught him on the chest, between sword and shield. His cuirass was robust, and so was his plate-armour, and the tasses over his belly were flawless, but they could not withstand the sword: they all gave access to the cruel blade which sliced through whatever it met, from breastplate to saddle-bow to cuisses. / Had not the blow fallen a little short, it would have sliced him down the middle like a cleft stick. Instead, it penetrated his flesh just sufficiently to wound his skin; the shallow cut was not a hand's span in length. A red rivulet of warm blood flowed down his shining armour to his feet. / I have seen a cloth of silver divided this way with a handsome purple stripe, the work of the lily-white hands of one by whom I often feel my heart split in two. Little did it profit Zerbin to be a champion warrior, or to have strength and courage a-plenty—he was no match for the Tartar king in finesse of swordplay nor in main force. / This blow of Mandricard was more severe in appearance than in effect, and Isabel felt her heart split in her frozen breast.

Zerbin blazed up with rage and vexation and, in an access of boldness, grasped his sword two-handed and brought it down with all his might on the Tartar's helmet. / The savage blow knocked the proud Saracen forward practically onto his charger's neck; had his helmet not been enchanted, his skull would have been cracked in two. But he was prompt to avenge himself—no question for him of 'You wait till next time': he raised his sword over the other's helmet hoping to split it down to the chest. / Zerbin, whose eye was as quick as his brain, jerked his steed sharply to the right, but not fast enough to avoid the keen sword, which struck his shield. The blow sheared it from top to bottom into two equal parts; it snapped the arm-brace at the bottom, wounded him in the arm, split his hip-tasset, and landed on his thigh. / Zerbin tried one attack and another, but all to no avail: the armour he struck at remained totally unscathed. The Tartar meanwhile was gaining the upper hand: he had inflicted on the Scot seven or eight wounds, deprived him of his shield, and half mangled his helmet. / Zerbin kept losing blood. His strength was failing, though he seemed unaware of it: his robust heart did not falter—it had the vigour to sustain his failing body.

His lady, meanwhile, whom fear had drained of colour, approached Doralice and begged her for God's sake to intervene in the savage, wicked affray. / Doralice was as gracious as she was beautiful, and she willingly did as Isabel asked—besides, she was not sure how the battle would end. So she disposed her lover towards peace. Similarly, at Isabel's prayer, the avenging wrath in Zerbin's heart seeped out and dispersed. He set out as she directed him, leaving his battle for the sword unfinished. /

Fiordiligi silently deplored the sight of the poor count's trusty sword being so ill-defended; it grieved her so much she wept for rage and struck her forehead. She wished that Brandimart had been there for this exploit; if ever she found him and told him what had happened, she did not believe that Mandricard would be flaunting that sword for very long. / She continued her vain quest for Brandimart, morning, noon, and night: her path took her far from him, for he had already returned to Paris. She travelled on over hill and dale until at a river-crossing she saw and recognized wretched Orlando. But let us pursue Zerbin's story. /

He felt an enormous guilt for having abandoned Durindana—it troubled him more than any other ill, even though he could scarcely keep his saddle for all the blood he had lost and kept losing. When in a little while his wrath abated and, with it, his excitement, the pain of his wounds increased—it increased so violently that he felt his life ebbing away. / Too weak to continue, he stopped by a spring. The kindly damsel did not know what to do or say in order to help him. She could see him dying of neglect, for here they were too far from any town where she might have found a doctor to assist him, out of pity or for a fee. / She could only grieve in vain and call Fate and Heaven cruel and pitiless. 'Alas, why did you not drown me', she cried, 'when I set sail across the ocean?' Zerbin had turned his languorous eyes upon her and felt more sorrow at her laments than over the obstinate rage which had now brought him to the brink of death. / 'Love me still after I am dead, my beloved,' he said to her, 'for if I grieve now it is not because I am dying but only for leaving you here without a guide. Had it fallen to my lot to end my life's last hour in a place of safety, I should die happy and content and fully satisfied, dying upon your breast. / But as it is my hard, evil fate to abandon you into unknown hands, by your lips, by your eyes, by your tresses which first ensnared me I promise you that I go despairing into the deep darkness of Hades, where the thought of having left you thus will be a far worse torment than any other I shall find.' /

At this, Isabel in the throes of grief lowered her tearful face and put her lips against those of Zerbin; she was drooping like a rose left on the bush beyond its time and turning pale on the shady border. 'Do not imagine, my love,' she cried, 'that you shall make this last journey without me. / Never fear: I mean to follow you, to heaven or to hell. Our two spirits must set forth together, and stay together in eternity. The moment I see you close your eyes my grief will finish me; if it cannot do so, I promise you with this sword I shall today pierce my breast. / My hope is that our bodies will fare better dead than ever they did alive. Perhaps someone will chance this way and, moved to pity, will give them burial together.' So saying, she sorrowfully gathered with her lips the last of his vital spirit which death was stealing, so long as the slightest breath of it subsisted. / Now Zerbin forced his failing voice to say: 'By the love you showed me when for my sake you abandoned your father's shores, I beg and entreat you, my goddess, and if I can command, then I command you: for so long as it pleases God, remain alive; and never forget that I have loved you as much as it is possible to love. / God will perhaps see to helping you and keeping you safe from all evil, as He did when he rescued you from the cave, sending Orlando your way. Thus in His mercy he saved you from the sea, and from Odoric's abuse. Should it later come to pass that you must die, then choose death as a lesser evil.' / I don't believe that he could utter these last words in an audible voice; he ended like a feeble flame dying for lack of wax or whatever it feeds upon. Who can fully express how the maiden grieved when she saw her dearest Zerbin lying in her arms pale and limp and cold as ice? /

She abandoned herself to grief over the bleeding corpse and bathed it in copious tears. She shrieked so loud that the woods and country-side for miles around echoed with it. She did not spare her cheeks or breast but beat and tore at them—and how wrong she was to tear even her golden curls, ever vainly calling her beloved's name! / Her grief had plunged her into so passionate a frenzy that she might easily have turned the sword against herself, little heeding her lover's wish, had not a hermit arrived to hinder her impulse—his cell was close by and often he came to the clear fresh waters of this spring. / The holy man, in whom deep goodness was wedded to innate prudence, a man brimming with charity, an exemplary man gifted with eloquence, persuaded the grieving damsel, with effective arguments, to be patient. He set before her, as a mirror, women from the Old and New Testaments. / He had her see that there was no true happiness except in God, and that all human hopes were transient and mutable and of little moment. He spoke to such effect that he persuaded her to abandon her cruel, obstinate intention and instilled in her a desire to dedicate the rest of her life to the service of God. / Not that she would ever forgo either her deep love for her lord, or the possession of his mortal remains; wherever she went, wherever she tarried, his corpse had to accompany her and be with her night and day.

So with the aid of the hermit, who was as strong and robust as his age permitted, they placed Zerbin on his mournful steed and travelled for many days through those woods. / The old man would have thought it imprudent to bring the fair young maiden back with him, just the two of them, to his solitary cell concealed in a bare cavern close by. It was dangerous, he told himself, to carry flame and tinder in the same hand. He did not place sufficient reliance upon his years and prudence to put himself to such a test. / So he decided to take her to Provence, to a town not far from Marseilles where there was a sumptuous convent for holy women, a beautiful edifice. In order to carry the dead knight they laid him in a coffin made for them in a castle on their way; it was long and roomy, and well sealed with pitch. / Travelling for many a day, they covered a great tract of ground, always avoiding inhabited areas: as the war was omnipresent they wanted to keep as well hidden as possible. Finally their way was barred by a knight who reviled and insulted them most scurrilously. I shall tell you about him when the time comes, but now I am returning to Mandricard, the Tartar king. /

With the battle ending as I described, the young man withdrew to the cool shade and crystal-clear waters; he freed his horse of saddle and bridle and let him browse at will on the tender grass of the meadow. But he was not there long before he saw in the distance a knight descending to the plain from the hills. / The moment she raised her eyes Doralice recognized him and pointed him out to Mandricard. 'Here comes proud Rodomont, if my eyes do not deceive me at this distance,' she told him. 'He is coming down the hill to fight with you— now your might should serve you well. He is gravely offended at losing me, betrothed as I was to him, and is coming for vengeance.' /

Imagine a keen hawk which sees a duck or woodcock, partridge, pigeon, or other such bird approaching in the distance, and draws himself up, looking eager and spirited: thus was Mandricard. He was confident he would make short work of Rodomont as, gleeful and cocksure, he went to his horse. He slipped his feet into the stirrups and grasped the reins. / When they were close enough to hear each other's boasts, Rodomont began to shout menaces, gesturing with his hands and head. 'I shall make you rue your temerity,' he cried. 'You have taken your presumptuous pleasure, and in so doing, you have not avoided the risk of provoking me: now here I am, about to wreak memorable vengeance upon you.' / 'There is no use trying to scare me with threats,' retorted Mandricard. 'That's a way to frighten women and children and people who know nothing of arms—but not me: why, combat is more to my liking than repose. Here I am, ready for action, on foot or mounted, armed or unarmed, in the open field or in the lists.' /

Now they bandied insults; they bellowed with rage; swords were drawn; cruel steel clashed upon steel—like a breeze which at first is but a breath, then rises enough to shake the oak and ash; it sends dark dust whirling skywards, then rips up trees, flattens houses, sinks ships at sea, and raises a fearsome tempest which destroys the flocks scattered through the woods. / The two pagans, paragons of strength and courage, displayed their warlike talents in an exchange of blows consistent with the traditional ferocity of their lineage. The ghastly din of their clashing swords made the earth quiver; their weapons sent sparks, or rather flashes by the thousand, shooting skywards. / The two kings fought a hard, stubborn battle, never pausing to rest or draw breath; one way and another each kept trying to wrench open the other's metal sheathing, to penetrate the other's chain-mail. They neither lost nor gained ground; as if a fosse or wall encircled them, as if an inch of ground cost them too much, neither budged from a tight, narrow circle. / One blow in a thousand delivered two-handed by Mandricard caught Rodomont on the forehead, making his head spin as he saw every star in the firmament. Sapped of all his strength, he fell back until his head touched his horse's crupper; he lost his footing and, in the presence of his beloved Doralice, almost left the saddle. /

Now imagine a sturdy crossbow, well constructed with a good weight of high-grade steel; the more it is tensed, the more powerful its charge, and the more force exerted upon it by winches and levers, the greater thrust with which it will snap back once released, its impact exceeding the pressure under which it has been placed: so it was with Rodomont, who shot upright and lashed out at his enemy, two blows for one. / He landed his first right where he himself had been struck; the blow could not damage the Tartar's brow thanks to the protection of Hector's armour, but it so stunned him that for a while he could not tell if it were morning or night. Rodomont followed straight through with a second furious blow, again aimed at the other's crown, / but the Tartar's horse, recoiling from the sword hissing down from above, saved his master to his own detriment: to evade the sword he sprang back, and the blade, which was destined for his master, not for himself, cleaved him through the head. The poor beast, unlike his master, was not wearing the Trojan helmet: hence he had to die. / The steed fell, but Mandricard bounced to his feet, shaken to his senses, and whirled Durindana. Seeing his horse dead provoked him inwardly, which he showed in a terrible conflagration of rage. Rodomont drove his charger at him, but Mandricard recoiled no more than a rock from the surf; the steed it was who fell, while the Tartar remained standing. / Rodomont, feeling his steed give way, quit his stirrups, vaulted from the saddle and dextrously freed himself to land on his feet. The two could now confront each other on an equal footing, and the combat flared up hotter than ever; the hatred, anger, and pride boiled over and they were about to lay into each other when who should hasten up but a messenger, who separated them. /

It was a messenger from the Saracen host, one of many dispatched throughout France to recall to their standards the commanders and the knights of lesser nobility. The Emperor of the Golden Lilies had laid siege to their camp, and if help were not quickly forthcoming, they could see destruction staring them in the face. / The messenger recognized the knights not only by their emblems and surcoats, but by the way they brandished their swords and by the savage blows which no hands but theirs could have delivered. He dared not step between them, though, not even in the assurance that being the king's messenger would afford him safety amid such wrath. Not even the knowledge that ambassadors are exempt from punishment could raise his courage. / So he went up to Doralice and told her that Agramant, Marsilius, and Stordilan with a small contingent were being besieged by the Christians inside insecure defences. This said, he begged her to explain the situation to the two warriors and make peace between them and bring them back to the camp to save the Saracen host. /

The damsel stepped boldly in between the knights and said: 'I command you, by the love I know you bear me: save your swords for a better use and come at once to the aid of our Saracen host, beleaguered in their tents; they expect urgent help or utter ruin.' / To this the messenger added an account of the Saracens' dire peril, and told them just how matters stood; he gave letters to Rodomont from Agramant, King Trojan's son. Their eventual decision was for the two warriors to lay aside all venom and make a pact until the day the siege was raised; / then, once they had relieved their people, without further delay they would eschew each other's company and resume cruel war and burning enmity until they had established by armed might which of them was worthy to possess the damsel. The oath was sworn on her hand, and she stood guarantor for both of them. / Now hasty Discord was present, enemy to peace, to any kind of truce, and Pride, too, who would not stand for such a pact or consent to it. But Love also was present, and he was more than a match for them—bravely he held them both off with his quiverful of arrows. /

A truce, then, was concluded between them, as it pleased Love, who had them in his power. One of them was without a horse—the Tartar's lay dead—so Brigliador, browsing on the fresh grass by the stream, happened upon them most opportunely. But I see that I have reached the end of the canto, so with your permission I shall make a stop.

TWENTY-FIFTH CANTO

*1–4 Rodomont and Mandricard leave for Paris. 4–70
Ruggiero rescues Richardet, who tells how he won Fiordispina's
love. 71–97 They join Aldiger to go to the rescue of Maugis
and Vivian.*

OH what conflict there can be in a young man's mind between a thirst
for glory and the impulses of Love! There is no telling which of the
two motives is the stronger when now one, now the other predominates.
In both champions duty and honour weighed heavily, so they broke off
their love-duel until they had saved their camp. / Love, though,
weighed more heavily still; were it not for the bidding of their lady,
they would never have relinquished their fierce battle before one of
them had won the victor's laurels, and Agramant would have waited in
vain with his troops for help from these two. Therefore Cupid does not
always wreak mischief; if he often does harm, he sometimes does good. /
So the two pagan warriors deferred their quarrel and set off for Paris
with Doralice to rescue the African host. With them went the little
dwarf who had followed Mandricard's traces to lead jealous Rodomont
to a confrontation. / They came to a meadow where some knights
were taking their ease by a brook; two of them were unarmed, two wore
helmets, and with them was a woman of comely face. Who they were I
shall explain elsewhere, not here: first I must speak of Ruggiero.

I have described how he threw the magic shield down the well. / He
had not travelled a mile beyond the well before he saw a messenger
approaching at a gallop; he was one of those sent by Agramant to the
warriors from whom he was expecting help. He learnt that the Saracens
were in such danger from Charlemagne's blockade that, short of
immediate assistance, degradation or even death would be their lot. /
Ruggiero was perplexed by many thoughts which all assailed him at
once; but this was not the time or the place to decide on his best
course. He let the messenger go, then turned his steed to follow the
damsel who was guiding him; he kept urging her to hasten, as there
was no time to lose. / They continued along their way until, as the sun
was setting, they came to a stronghold of Marsilius in the middle of
France, one which he had seized from Charlemagne in the course of
the war. They did not stop at the drawbridge nor at the gate—nobody
blocked or obstructed their entry, even though the palisade and fosse

were thronged with armed men. / As the damsel accompanying him was recognized by the bystanders, they were allowed through unhindered without even being asked from where they had come. They reached the square which they found aglow with flames and teeming with a malicious throng.

In the middle he saw the young man condemned to death. His face was white; / it was tearful and downcast, and when Ruggiero looked up at it he imagined he was looking at Bradamant, so closely did the youth resemble her. The more he gazed at his face and figure the more the likeness struck him. 'Either this is Bradamant,' he told himself, 'or else I'm no longer Ruggiero. / Perhaps she was over-hasty in taking up the condemned boy's defence: her intervention must have miscarried and she has been captured, as I see. Oh why such haste, why could I not have been with her on this venture? But I have arrived, thank God, and there's still time for me to save her.' / And without further delay he grasped his sword—he had broken his lance at Pinabello's castle—and drove his steed into the unarmed throng, assailing them in the chest, sides, and belly. He whirled his sword, catching one man on the brow, the next at the throat, another on the cheek. The rabble fled screaming: the entire throng was left maimed, if not with cracked skulls. / Imagine a flock of birds by a lake, flitting about confidently as they grub for food, when suddenly a hawk plummets down upon them from the sky and strikes or snatches one of their number; the rest scatter, each deserting his companion to attend to his own escape. Thus you would have seen the crowd behave the moment Ruggiero drove into them. / Some half dozen who were slow in leaving had their heads lopped off clean; as many more he split down to the chest, while a countless number were cleft down to the eyes or the jaw.

I'll grant you that they were not wearing helmets, but merely head-pieces of shining metal; had they been properly helmeted, though, he would have slashed them with almost as much ease. / No knight of the present day could match him for sheer strength—nor could any bear or lion or more ferocious beast, whether native or foreign to our shores. An earthquake might have equalled him, or the mighty Devil: not the one in hell—it's my Lord's Devil I mean, the one which spits fire and forces its way everywhere, by land, sea, and air. / At every stroke at least one man fell, and more often two; he killed four and even five at a stroke, which soon brought the total to a hundred. The sword he had unsheathed could cut through steel as though it were soft whey. Falerina the sorceress had made this cruel sword in the garden of Orgagna, for the purpose of slaying Orlando; / much did she regret having made it when she saw it used to destroy her garden. Imagine, then, the havoc and devastation wrought by it in the hands of a champion such as Ruggiero! If ever he manifested his rage, his strength, his supreme valour it was here and now as he strove to rescue his lady. /

The mob stood up to him as well as a hare to unleashed hounds. A good number were killed; those who fled were legion. Meanwhile the damsel guiding Ruggiero had released the youth from the bonds tying his wrists, and procured him arms as best she could, a sword for his hand, a shield to sling from his neck. / He now did his utmost to avenge himself on these folk who had done him grievous wrong; he laid about him to such effect that he left a reputation for prowess and valour. The sun had dipped his golden rays into the Western sea when victorious Ruggiero and the young man set out from the castle. /

When the youth was outside the gates with Ruggiero, he thanked him profusely and most gracefully: his benefactor had, after all, risked his life to save him without knowing who he was. He asked Ruggiero to divulge his name, as he wanted to know who it was to whom he owed such a debt of gratitude. / 'I am looking at the comely face and beautiful figure of my Bradamant,' Ruggiero mused, 'but I do not hear the dulcet tones of her voice. And her words are not appropriate to thanking a faithful lover. If she really is Bradamant, how is it that she has so soon forgotten my name?' / To establish who it was, Ruggiero employed subtlety. 'I have seen you somewhere before,' he remarked, 'but though I have pondered and racked my brains I cannot remember where it was. Will you remind me, then, if you can recollect? And do me the pleasure of telling me your name, so that I may know who it was whom I saved today from the pyre.' /

'It could be that you have seen me before,' replied the other, 'but I cannot say where or when. I too wander about the world seeking high adventure. Perhaps it was a sister of mine you saw, one who wears armour and carries a sword at her side; we are twins from birth and look so alike that even our family cannot tell us apart. / You are not the first, nor the second, nor even the fourth to have mistaken us; neither our father, nor our brothers, nor even our mother who bore us at one birth is able to tell us apart. True, our hair used to mark a sharp difference between us when I wore my hair short and loose in the male fashion, while she wore hers long and coiled in a plait. / But one day she was wounded in the head (it would take too long to tell the story) and to heal her a servant of God cut her hair till it only half covered her ears. After that there was nothing to distinguish us beyond our sex and name: mine is Richardet, hers is Bradamant; we are brother and sister to Rinaldo. / And if it would not bore you to listen, I would tell you a story to amuse you—something that happened to me on account of my resemblance to her: at first it was rapture, but it ended in agony.' Ruggiero, in whose ears no song was sweeter, no story dearer than one in which his lady featured, begged him to tell his story. /

'My sister had been wounded by a party of Saracens who had come upon her without a helmet, so she had been obliged to cut her long tresses if her dangerous head-wound was to heal. Now recently she happened to be travelling through these woods, her head shorn as I have said. / On her way she came to a shady spring and, being weary and dejected, she dismounted, took off her helmet and fell asleep in the tender grass. (I don't believe there can be a story more beautiful than this one.) Who should come upon her but the Spanish Princess Fiordispina, who had come into the woods to hunt. / When she saw my sister clad in armour all except for her face, and with a sword in place of a distaff, she imagined she was looking at a knight. After gazing awhile at her face and her manly build she felt her heart stolen. So she invited my sister to join the hunt, and ended by eluding her retinue and disappearing with her among the shady boughs. /

'Once she had brought her into a solitary place where she felt unlikely to be disturbed, little by little, by words and gestures she revealed that she was love-struck. With burning looks and fiery sighs she showed how consumed she was with desire. She paled and blushed and, summoning her courage, gave her a kiss. / It was clear to my sister that the damsel had illusions about her; my sister could never have satisfied her need and was quite perplexed as to what to do. "My best course is to undeceive her," she decided, "and to reveal myself as a member of the gentle sex rather than to have myself reckoned an ignoble man." / And she was right. It would have been a sheer disgrace, the conduct of a man made of plaster, if he had kept up a conversation with a damsel as fair as Fiordispina, sweet as nectar, who had set her cap at him, while like a cuckoo, he just trailed his wings. So Bradamant tactfully had her know that she was a maiden. / She was in quest of glory at arms, like Hippolyta and Camilla of old. Born in Africa, in the seaside city of Arzilla, she was accustomed from childhood to the use of lance and shield. These revelations did not abate love-struck Fiordispina's passion one jot; Cupid had thrust in his dart to make so deep a gash that this remedy was now too late. / To Fiordispina my sister's face seemed no less beautiful for this, her eyes, her movements no less graceful; she did not on this account retrieve mastery over her heart, which had gone out to Bradamant to bask in her adorable eyes. Seeing her accoutred as a man, she had imagined that there would be no need for her passion to remain unassuaged; but now the thought that her beloved was also a woman made her sigh and weep and betray boundless sorrow. /

'Anyone who heard her tears and grieving that day would have wept with her. "Never was any torment so cruel", she lamented, "but mine is crueller. Were it a question of any other love, evil or virtuous, I could hope to see it consummated, and I should know how to cull the rose from the briar. My desire alone can have no fulfilment. / If you wanted to torment me, Love, because my happy state offended you, why could you not rest content with those torments which other lovers experience? Neither among humans nor among beasts have I ever come across a woman loving a woman; to a woman another woman does not seem beautiful, nor does a hind to a hind, a ewe to a ewe. / By land, sea, and air I alone suffer thus cruelly at your hands—you have done this to make an example of my aberration, the ultimate one in your power. King Ninus' wife was evil and profane in her love for her son; so was Mirra, in love with her father, and Pasiphae with the bull. But my love is greater folly than any of theirs. / These females made designs upon the males and achieved the desired consummation, so I am told. Pasiphae went inside the wooden cow, the others achieved their end by other means. But even if Daedalus came flying to me with every artifice at his command, he would be unable to untie the knot made by that all-too-diligent Maker, Nature, who is all-powerful." /

'Thus the fair damsel grieved and fretted and would not be assuaged. She struck her face and tore her hair and sought to vent her feelings against her own person. My sister wept for pity and felt embarrassed as she listened to her grieving. She tried to deflect her from this insane and profitless craving, but her words were in vain and to no effect. / It was help, not consolation, that she required and her grief only continued to increase. The day was now drawing to a close and the sun was reddening in the West; rather than spending the night in the woods it was time now to withdraw to some lodging. So the damsel invited Bradamant to this castle of hers not far away. / My sister was unable to refuse, so they came to the very spot where the wicked mob would have burned me to death had you not appeared. Here Fiordispina made much of my sister; she dressed her once more in feminine attire and made it plain to one and all that her guest was a woman. / Realizing how little benefit she derived from Bradamant's apparent masculinity, Fiordispina did not want any blame to attach to herself on her guest's account. In addition, she nurtured the hope that the sickness already implanted in her as a result of Bradamant's male aspect might be dispelled by a dose of femininity to show how matters really stood. /

'That night they shared a bed but they did not rest equally well. The one slept, the other wept and moaned, her desire ever mounting. And if sleep did occasionally press upon her eyelids, it was but a brief sleep charged with dreams in which it seemed to her that Heaven had allotted to her a Bradamant transformed into a preferable sex. / If a thirst-tormented invalid goes to sleep craving for water, in his turbid, fitful rest he calls to mind every drop of water he ever saw. Likewise her dreaming mind threw up images to requite her desires. Then she would wake and reach out, only to find that what she had seen was but an empty dream. / How many prayers and vows did she not offer that night to Mahomet and all the gods, asking them to change Bradamant's sex for the better by a clear and self-evident miracle! But she saw that all her prayers were vain; perhaps Heaven even mocked her. The night ended and Phoebus lifted his fair head out of the sea and gave light to the world. / With the new day they left their bed, and Fiordispina's pain was aggravated when Bradamant, anxious to be clear of her predicament, mentioned that she was leaving. As a parting gift, Fiordispina presented her with an excellent jennet, caparisoned in gold; also with a costly surcoat woven by her own hand. / Fiordispina accompanied her a step of the way then returned, weeping, to her castle, while my sister pressed on so hastily that she reached Montauban the same day. Our poor mother and we, her brothers, crowded round her, rejoicing—for lack of news of her, we had been gravely anxious for fear she were dead. /

'When she removed her helmet we all stared at her cropped hair which previously had fallen about her neck; and the new surcoat she was wearing also caught our attention. And she told us all that had befallen her, from start to finish just as I've told you: how after she was wounded in the wood she cut off her fair tresses in order to be healed; / and how the beautiful huntress came upon her as she was by the spring; and how she took to her deceptive appearance and segregated her from her party. She did not pass in silence over Fiordispina's grief, and we were all filled with pity at it. She described how she lodged with her, and all she did until her return to our castle. /

'Now I had heard a great deal about Fiordispina, whom I had seen in Saragossa and in France. I had been much allured by her lovely eyes and smooth cheeks, but had not let my thoughts dwell upon her: to love without hope is idle dreaming. But, brought again so fully to the fore, she reawakened my passion at once. / Out of this hope, Love prepared bonds for me, having no other cord with which to capture me. He showed me how to set about obtaining what I wanted of this damsel. A little deception would procure an easy success: the similarity between my sister and myself had often deceived others, so perhaps it would deceive her too. / Shall I, shan't I? My conclusion was that it is always good to go in pursuit of one's pleasure. I did not divulge my thought to a soul, nor seek anyone's advice on the matter. When it was night, I went to where my sister had left her armour; I put it on and away I went on her horse without waiting for dawn to break. / I set off by night, with Cupid for guide, to be with lovely Fiordispina, and I arrived before the Sun had hidden his radiance in the sea. Happy the man who outstripped his fellows in bringing the news to the princess: as bearer of good tidings he could expect thanks and a reward from her. /

'They all of them took me for Bradamant—just as you did—the more so in that I had both the attire and the horse with which she had left the previous day. Fiordispina lost no time in coming out to meet me; she was so jubilant and affectionate, she could not possibly have shown greater pleasure and joy. / Throwing her graceful arms around my neck, she softly hugged me and kissed me on the lips. You can imagine after this how Love guided his dart to pierce me at the heart of my heart! She took me by the hand and quickly led me into her bedroom; here she would suffer none but herself to undo my armour, from helmet to spurs; no one else was to take a hand. / Next she sent for a dress of hers, richly ornate, which she herself spread out and put on me as though I were a woman; and she caught my hair in a golden net. I studied modesty in my glances, and none of my gestures betrayed my not being a woman. My voice might have betrayed me, but I controlled it so well that it aroused no suspicions. / Then we went into a hall crowded with knights and ladies who received us with the sort of honour paid to queens and great ladies. Here several times I was amused when certain men, unaware that my skirts concealed something sturdy and robust, kept making eyes at me. / When the evening was further advanced and the meal had been over for some while— the fare had been an excellent choice of what was then in season— Fiordispina did not wait for me to ask the favour which was the object of my visit, but invited me hospitably to share her bed for the night. /

'When the waiting-women and maidens, the pages, and attendants had withdrawn, and we were both changed and in bed, while the flaming sconces left the room bright as day, I said to her: "Do not be surprised, my lady, at my returning to you so soon—perhaps you thought that you would not see me again for God knows how long. / First I shall tell you why I left, then why I have returned. Had I been able to abate your ardour by staying, I should have wanted to live and die in your service, and never for an hour be without you. But seeing how much pain my presence occasioned you, as I could do you no better service, I chose to leave. / Fate drew me off my path into the thick of a tangled wood, where I heard a cry sound close by, as of a damsel calling for help. I came running and found myself at the edge of a crystal lake where a faun had hooked a naked maiden in the water

and was cruelly preparing to eat her raw. / I went over, sword in hand
—only this way could I help her—and slew the boorish fisherman.
Straight away she dived into the water and said: 'It is not for nothing
that you have saved me. You shall be richly rewarded and given as
much as you ask for: I am a nymph and I live in this limpid lake. / I
have the power to perform miracles, to coerce nature and the elements.
Ask to the limits of my capabilities, then just leave it to me: at my
singing the moon comes down from the sky, fire turns to ice, the air
turns brittle, and with mere words I have moved the earth and
stopped the sun.' /

' "I did not ask her for a hoard of treasure, or for power over nations,
or for greater valour or might, or for honourable victory in every war.
My only request was that she would show me some way I could fulfil
your desire; I did not ask to achieve this in one way or in another, but
left the method up to her own discretion. / Scarcely had I disclosed
my wish than I saw her dive a second time, and for all reply to my
request she splashed the enchanted water at me. The moment it
touched my face I was quite transformed, I know not how. I could see,
I could feel—though I could scarcely believe my senses—that I was
changing from woman to man. / You would never believe me, except
that now, right away, you shall be able to see for yourself. In my new
sex as in my old, my desire is to give you ready service. Command my
faculties, then, and you shall find them now and ever more alert and
bestirred for you." Thus I spoke to her, and I guided her hand to test
the truth for herself. /

'Imagine the case of a person who has given up hope of having
something for which he craves; the more he bemoans his deprivation,
the more he works himself into a state of despair; and if later he
acquires it, he is so vexed over the time wasted sowing seed in the sand,
and despair has so eroded him that he is dumbfounded and cannot
believe his luck. / So it was with Fiordispina: she saw and touched the
object she had so craved for, but she could not believe her eyes or her
fingers or herself, and kept wondering whether she were awake or
asleep. She needed solid proof to convince her that she was actually
feeling what she thought she felt. "O God, if this is a dream," she
cried, "keep me asleep for good, and never wake me again!" /

'There was no roll of drums, no peal of trumpets to herald the
amorous assault: but caresses like those of billing doves gave the signal
to advance or to stand firm. We used arms other than arrows and
slingstones; and I, without a ladder, leapt onto the battlements and
planted my standard there at one jab, and thrust my enemy beneath
me. / If on the previous night that bed had been laden with heavy
sighs and laments, this night made up for it with as much laughter and

merriment, pleasure and gentle playfulness. Never did twisting acanthus entwine pillars and beams with more knots than those which
bound us together, our necks and sides, our arms, legs, and breasts in a
close embrace. / It remained a secret between us, so our pleasure continued for a few months. But eventually someone found us out, so the
matter became known to the king—to my undoing. You, who rescued
me from his people who had lit the pyre in the square, you can understand the rest: but God knows what an ache I am left with.' /

Thus Richardet told his story to Ruggiero, and allayed the tedium
of their night journey. They were climbing towards a precipitous knoll
pock-marked with caves. A steep, stony, narrow track offered difficult
access to the top, where stood a castle, Agrismont. It was in the keeping
of Aldiger of Clairmont, / bastard son of Buovo and brother of Maugis
and Vivian. The claim that he was legitimate son to Gerard is fool-
hardy and unfounded; but be that as it may, he was robust, prudent,
generous, chivalrous, and kind, and he took good care of his brothers'
defences night and day. / He gave his cousin Richardet, whom he
loved like a brother, the courteous welcome due to him, and, out of
regard for him, was equally affable to Ruggiero. But he did not go out
to meet him in his normally cheerful frame of mind, but in a state of
gloom, because today he had received news which cast a pall over his
heart and face. /

Returning Richardet's greetings he told him: 'I have bad news for
you, brother. I have learnt today from a reliable messenger that
Bertolai of Bayonne, the scoundrel, has made a pact with spiteful
Lanfusa whereby he is to give her precious booty in exchange for our
brothers, good Maugis and Vivian. / Ever since Ferrau gave them into
her charge she has confined them in some horrible dark place until the
conclusion of her ugly, shabby deal with this man I speak of. Tomorrow
she is to send them to Bertolai at a place between Bayonne and a castle
of his. He will come in person to pay her the gratuity which will buy
him the best blood in all France. / I have just sent warning to Rinaldo:
I sent the messenger off at a gallop, but I think he is bound to arrive too
late, given the distance to travel. I have no men with whom to mount
an expedition: I am zealous in spirit but crippled in resources. If that
villain gains possession of our brothers he will kill them, so I don't
know what to do or say.' /

This hard news came as a blow to Richardet; and as it hurt him, so it
hurt Ruggiero who, seeing the two of them fall to meditating but
deriving no profit therefrom, spoke up boldly: 'No need to worry: I
want this enterprise all for myself. To restore your brothers' freedom
my sword will be a match for a thousand swords. / I want no men to
help me—I believe I can cope with this single-handed. All I ask is for a

man to guide me to the place where this bargain is to be effected. I shall see to it that the screams of those present at the vile transaction carry all the way to your ears.' These were his words; they came as no surprise to one of his listeners, who had seen proof of his abilities. / The other paid no more attention to his words than he would to a big talker of small judgement. But Richardet drew him aside and told him how Ruggiero had rescued him from the pyre, and how certain he was that, when the time came, his friend's achievement would clearly outstrip even his boast. After this, Aldiger took greater notice of him and respected him and held him in high regard. / At table, where abundance reigned, he honoured him as his lord. Here it was concluded that they could go unassisted to the aid of the two brothers.

Meanwhile indolent Sleep came to close the eyes of masters and servants, all but those of Ruggiero: a disturbing thought pricked his heart and kept him wakeful. / The siege endured by Agramant, of which the messenger had just apprised him, weighed on his conscience. It was clear to him that the slightest delay in coming to his liege's aid would redound to his own discredit. And what would be his infamy, his shame, if he kept company with his lord's enemies! If he accepted baptism he would be deemed a rogue and a coward. / At any other time he might have been credited with truly religious motives. Now, though, when Agramant needed his help to raise the siege, people would tend to believe that he acted out of fear and cowardice rather than out of religious conviction. These considerations lacerated Ruggiero's heart. / He was also distressed at having to go without taking leave of Bradamant. This thought and the other kept his mind in a state of uncertainty. His expectation of finding her at Fiordispina's castle had proved totally wrong although, as I explained earlier, he was supposed to be going there with her to come to Richardet's aid. / Then he remembered that he had promised to meet her at Vallombrosa; she must have gone there, he thought, and now must be wondering why he had never arrived. If only he could at least send a letter or messenger to set her mind at rest, for not only had he obeyed her but poorly—he had also left without a word to her. /

After turning various thoughts over in his mind, he finally decided to write and tell her what had happened. Though he did not know how to send a letter so that she would be sure to receive it, this did not deter him—he might well find a reliable messenger along the road. Without further delay he jumped out of bed and called for paper, pen, ink, and light. / The servants, discreet and circumspect, brought him the things he required, and he began to write. He started, as usual, with some lines of greeting. Then he told her of the message he had received from his liege, requesting help, and how, if he did not go promptly, his king would meet his death or be taken by the enemy. / A decision had to be made, he went on to say, now that he had been approached for help; she could see the endless blame that would attach to him if he denied his help at this juncture. Also, as he was to become her husband, he had to keep his name unsullied: as Bradamant was honest through and through, he explained, nothing base would be suitable for her. / And if ever he had sought a good reputation by his conduct, and, having acquired one, had sought to cherish and foster it, now he was truly jealous for his good name, now that he was to share it with her: as his wife, she was to be totally one with him in spirit, though their bodies were two. / And what he had told her orally he repeated here in writing: when his period of fealty to his liege was over, if he did not die first, he would become a Christian formally, just as by intention he was already. And he would ask her father, and Rinaldo her brother and her other kinsmen for her hand in marriage. /

'I should like, with your permission, to go to my lord's relief, so as to silence the ignorant rabble, who would otherwise heap scorn upon me, maintaining that I never abandoned the king night or day in his prosperity, but that, with Fortune favouring Charlemagne, I am flying my ensigns on the victor's side. / I need fifteen or twenty days, the time to visit the African camp and see to raising the dire siege. Meanwhile I shall look for a suitable and just excuse to return to you. This is all I ask of you for my honour's sake; the rest of my life is at your entire disposal.' / Ruggiero dilated in words such as these, which I cannot fully set forth, and with many more words besides; he did not finish until he saw that the whole page was full. Then he folded the letter, closed, and sealed it and thrust it next to his breast, in the hope that the next day he would come upon someone to convey it secretly to his lady. / After closing the letter, he also closed his eyes in bed and found peace, for Sleep came and sprinkled his tired body with a branch dipped in the waters of Lethe. His rest continued until a cloud of scattered pink and white blossom brightened the lands of the radiant East, and from his gilded abode the Day newly arose. /

When the birds in the green branches began to greet the new light, Aldiger was the first one up: he wanted to guide Ruggiero and Richardet and lead them to where his two brothers were to be surrendered to cruel Bertolai. Hearing him up and about, the other two left their beds. / Once they were dressed and well armed, Ruggiero set out with the two cousins, having vainly begged them to leave the exploit all to him. But, anxious as they were for their brothers, and also feeling that it would be ungallant to leave everything to him, they were immovable as rock in denying him his wish: they simply would not consent to his going alone. / They arrived on the day when Maugis and Vivian were to be bartered for treasure by the waggon-load. The place was in broad, open country exposed to the glare of the sun. No laurel or myrtle was to be seen, nor cypress, ash, or beech—nothing but bare gravel and dwarf scrub never touched by ploughshare or hoe. / The three bold warriors stopped where a road crossed the plain. Here they saw a knight arrive; his armour was adorned with gold, and his emblem was the phoenix—the rare and beautiful bird who outlives a century—on a verdant ground. Enough, my Lord: I see I am at the end of this canto and beg leave to rest.

TWENTY-SIXTH CANTO

1–2 Introductory. 3–29 Ruggiero and Marfisa help defeat the Maganza machinations. 29–53 The allegory of the beast on Merlin's fountain. 54–137 Ruggiero and Marfisa at grips with Rodomont and Mandricard.

In days of old there used to be gentle ladies who prized virtue above wealth. In our own day it is hard to find a woman for whom gain is of second importance. But those who, out of true goodness, avoid the common propensity to greed, it is they who deserve to enjoy happiness in their lifetime and immortal glory after their death. / Bradamant is worthy of eternal praise: she did not set her heart upon wealth or power but simply upon Ruggiero—on his martial valour, his eminence of heart and breeding. She merited so valiant a knight for her suitor; she merited the exploits he performed to please her—exploits later deemed miraculous. /

As I was saying, Ruggiero was on his way with Aldiger and Richardet of Clairmont to rescue the two captive brothers. And I described how they saw a knight approaching, whose demeanour was proud, and whose emblem was the phoenix—the bird which constantly renews itself and is unique in the world. / When the knight saw this group who were on their way to strike their enemy, he decided he wanted to make trial of them, to see if they were as valiant as they looked. 'Is one of you inclined to match himself with me,' he asked, 'to bandy blows with lance or sword till one of us falls while the other keeps his seat?' / 'I should fight with you,' replied Aldiger, 'whether you chose to swipe with your sword or tilt with your lance. But another enterprise, which you could witness if you stayed, so far precludes this that there is scarcely time to talk with you, let alone to joust. We expect to fall in

with six hundred men or more, whom today we have to challenge. /
Pity and love have brought us here to rescue from them two of our
kinsmen whom they will drag here as captives.' He went on to explain
how they came to be here, armed. 'Your excuse is so just', observed
the warrior, 'that I cannot dispute it. And I can tell for certain that you
are three knights with but few peers. / I asked to exchange a pass or
two so as to find the measure of your valour; but since you mean to
show it off at the expense of others, that is enough for me—I will not
joust with you. I pray you, though, let this helmet of mine and this
shield be added to your arms: if I join you, I trust I shall show that I
am not unworthy of your company.' / It looks to me as if some of you
would like to know the name of this man who was offering to join
Ruggiero and his comrades-in-arms at this perilous juncture. Well, this
woman (man let her no longer be called) was Marfisa, who had saddled
poor Zerbin with that evil-minded crone, Gabrina. / The two Clair-
monts and good Ruggiero gladly welcomed her into their company,
assuming that she was a knight, not a damsel, not the person she really
was.

Shortly after this, Aldiger noticed and pointed out to his companions a banner fluttering in the breeze; a crowd was gathered round
it. / When they had drawn closer and could better make out their
attire, which was Moorish, they recognized that these must be Saracens; in their midst they descried the prisoners, tied and mounted on
little cobs, ready to be given over to the Maganzas in exchange for gold.
Marfisa addressed the others: 'Now that they are here, what is to stop
us from joining in the fun?' / 'The guests are not all here yet,' explained Ruggiero; 'a good number are still missing. It's a grand ball
we have in preparation—let us take care to make it as splendid as
possible. It won't be long before they come.' As he spoke they saw the
traitors of the house of Maganza on the point of arriving, so they were
almost ready to open the dance. / From one side arrived Maganzas,
leading mules laden with gold, articles of clothing, and other objects of
luxury. From the other side, in a cluster of lances, swords, and bows
glumly came the two captive brothers, who could see that they were
expected. Bertolai, too, their spiteful enemy, could be heard talking
with the Moorish captain. / Neither Aldiger nor Richardet could
restrain themselves once they caught sight of Bertolai; they both set
their lances in rest and attacked the villain. The first drove clean
through his saddle-pommel into his belly, the other speared him full in
the face. Would that all evil men might go the way Bertolai went under
these thrusts. /

At this signal, Marfisa moved in with Ruggiero, awaiting no second
trumpet; she set her lance in rest and before she broke it she had un-

horsed three men in succession. The Moorish commander was a worthy target for Ruggiero's lance, which sent him scuttling to the nether world—him and two more for company. / This gave rise to an illusion among those assaulted—an illusion which ultimately spelt their doom: the Maganza side imagined they had been hoodwinked by the Saracens, while the hard-pressed Saracens accused the other party of murder. A violent battle broke out between them—bows were drawn, lances and swords brandished. / Ruggiero leapt now into the one contingent, now into the other, making away with ten or a score, while as many more on either side were dispatched and expunged by Marfisa. None was touched by their razor-swords but fell dead from the saddle—helmets and breastplates gave way to them like dry tinder in a brush-fire. / If you remember ever having seen (or have had described to you) what happens when bees fall to quarrelling and fighting among themselves, and a swallow flies greedily into the swarm and kills and maims and eats several of them—then you can imagine the effect of Ruggiero and Marfisa upon these folk. /

Richardet and his cousin Aldiger did not change partners in the dance the way their comrades did: they had left the Saracens to attend exclusively to the Maganzas. Richardet had great strength and courage, and these were sharpened by the hatred he nursed against the Maganza tribe. / This same incentive turned Aldiger into a ferocious lion; he split every helmet with his sword, cracking them like so many egg-shells. What man, though, would not have been courageous, would not have passed for another Hector, with comrades-in-arms such as Marfisa and Ruggiero, the very flower of champions? /

As Marfisa fought she often turned to look at her companions; seeing their prowess put to the test, she praised them all admiringly. Ruggiero's valour, though, seemed to her quite astounding, in-comparable; she was inclined to believe that he was Mars in person, descended here from the Fifth Heaven. / She observed the terrifying blows he delivered and saw that they never missed their mark: against the sword Balisard, iron might have been cardboard, not a hard metal. He split helmets and stout breastplates and sliced mounted men right down to their horses so that they toppled to the ground, in two equal halves, one to each side. / The stroke, carrying through, would slay the horse along with the rider. He sent heads spinning off shoulders by the cluster, and many a time he severed bust from hip. Sometimes he sliced five and six like this at a blow. Were I not anxious lest truth, wearing the mask of falsehood, be denied belief, I would go further—but I had better understate the facts. / Our worthy Turpin, who knew he told the truth but let men believe what they would, attributes marvels to Ruggiero, though you might call him a liar if you heard him. Confronted with Marfisa, every warrior seemed as ice to a flaming brand. She attracted Ruggiero's eyes no less than he did hers to watch his mighty valour. / And if she thought him Mars, he would perhaps have taken her for Bellona, had he recognized her, contrary to her appearance, for a woman. A rivalry may have sprung up between them which brought no joy to the poor wretches against whose flesh and blood, sinew and bone they exerted themselves to see who was the stronger. /

Four of their spirit and courage were enough to rout both sides. The fugitives now had no weapons they liked better than those which reached the ground: happy the man whose steed was a racer—amblers and trotters were little prized—while those without a horse were brought to realize how wretched is the calling of arms for the man who goes on foot. / The booty and the field were left to the victors, for not a soldier, not a muleteer remained behind. The clan of Maganza fled one way, the Saracens the other: the latter abandoned their prisoners, the former their chattels. The victors, with joy in their faces and even more in their hearts, were quick to untie Maugis and Vivian, while the pages were no less diligent in untying the baggage and lifting it all to the ground. / Beside silver a-plenty in the shape of goblets of different kinds, and the most ornate and beautifully formed feminine attire, there were tapestries fit for royal apartments, made in Flanders out of silk and gold thread, and an abundance of other luxuries; they found flasks of wine, too, and bread and other victuals. /

On removing their helmets they all saw that it was a damsel who had helped them—they could tell by her golden curls and by the delicate beauty of her face. They paid her every respect and begged her not to conceal her name, so deserving of glory. And Marfisa, always affable among friends, was not reluctant to give an account of herself. / They could not have enough of gazing at her, after the way they had seen her doing battle. But she had eyes only for Ruggiero; only to him would she talk—the others she did not esteem, she found them all wanting.

Meanwhile the pages came to invite her and her companions to enjoy the fare which they had laid out beside a spring sheltered by a hill from the summer heat. / This spring was one of Merlin's, one of the four he had created in France. It was enclosed with fine, polished marble, lustrous and whiter than milk. Here Merlin had carved reliefs with godlike artistry: you would have said that his figures were breathing and, but for their muteness, alive. /

Here was depicted a beast emerging from the forest. A grisly beast he looked, cruel and hideous, with ass's ears, the head and teeth of a wolf (all wizened with famine) and lion's claws; for the rest he was all fox, and he was shown scouring the whole of France and Italy, Spain and England, Europe and Asia, and ultimately the entire world. / Everywhere he had wounded people and slain them, both the common throng and the most exalted rulers—indeed he seemed to have caused far worse havoc among kings and barons, princes and satraps. He did still worse to the court of Rome, where he had slain cardinals and popes, and he had sullied the fair See of Peter, bringing scandal to the Faith. / Before this fearsome beast every wall, every rampart was shown crumbling. Not a town was to be seen defending itself; castles and forts opened to him. He was even shown acceding to divine honours and being worshipped by the mindless rabble; he arrogated to himself the custody of the keys to heaven and hell. /

Then a knight was shown sallying forth, his hair encircled with imperial laurels; with him came three young men, whose royal dress was woven with the symbol of the Golden Lilies. A lion, too, with emblems similar to theirs, was shown coming forth against the monster. Their names were inscribed above their heads or on the hem of their garments. / One of them, who had plunged his sword up to the hilt in the evil monster's belly, had the name of Francis I of France inscribed above him; with him was Maximilian of Austria; the Emperor Charles V had driven his lance through the beast's throat, while the fourth, who had pierced his chest with an arrow, was Henry VIII of England. / The Lion, who had the figure X written across his back, had sunk his teeth into the ugly brute's ears and so worried and shaken him that several others came now to his support—the world seemed to have shed all fear of the beast. To make amends for past failings noble spirits hastened up—not many, at that—and with their aid the monster's life was taken. / Marfisa and the knights wanted to know whose hands these were that had killed the beast who had brought sorrow and gloom to so many places. Although the names were inscribed on the marble, they were meaningless to them. So they turned to each other with the request that if one of them knew the story, he should tell it to the rest. / Vivian looked towards Maugis, who was listening without uttering a word, and said: 'You are the one to explain this story; it seems to me that you must be well acquainted with it. Who are these men who have slain the beast with arrows, swords, and lances?'

'It is not a story', remarked Maugis, 'which any historian has so far related. / You see, the men whose names are inscribed on this marble have never existed: but seven hundred years from now they shall be living to the great honour of a century to come. Merlin, the skilled British magician, had the fountain built in the time of King Arthur, setting good sculptors to portray on it events yet to come. / This cruel beast issued forth from the depths of hell at the time when lands were assigned boundaries, when weights and measures were established, and agreements written. At first he did not roam all over the world—many countries he left inviolate. In our own time he brings distress to many parts of the world, but it is the commoners, the lowly rabble whom he attacks. / From his advent to our own day he has kept growing, and he shall continue to grow until he shall eventually be the greatest monster that ever lived, and the most dreadful. Pytho, who has come down to us in written accounts as so awesome and horrifying, was not half so hideous or detestable as this monster. / He shall wreak cruel slaughter, and no place on earth shall escape his effects—ruin and contamination. What the reliefs show is only a fraction of his odious handiwork.

'Now these men—we have read their names, which shall shine with more sparkle than garnets—shall come to the rescue of mankind, hoarse with crying for mercy, in its greatest need. / No one shall outdo Francis, King of France, in harrying the cruel beast, and it is fitting that he outstrip many in this, with no one to surpass, and few to equal him: regal in splendour, a paragon of every virtue, he shall expose the shortcomings of many who had seemed perfect—just as every light is diminished the moment the sun appears. / The first year of his prosperous reign, his crown not yet firm upon his brow, he shall cross the Alps and smash the ambitions of one who shall have invaded the mountains from the other side. Righteous and noble anger shall be his spur, for the humiliation of the French army shall still be unavenged—the shame endured from the wrath of peasants in pastures and sheepfolds. / From here he shall descend to the rich Lombard plain with the flower of France about him, and so devastate the Swiss that never again shall they think to overreach themselves. And to the great shame and ignominy of the Church, the Spaniards, and the Florentines, he shall capture the castle which till then shall have been deemed impregnable. / To take it, one weapon will be worth far more to him than any other: his honoured sword, with which he shall earlier have taken the life of the all-corrupting monster. Before this sword every standard must turn to flee or else fall prostrate; no fosse, bastion, or thick rampart can keep a city safe from it. / Every excellence that is the due of a happy ruler shall be his; he shall have the courage of great Caesar, judgement such as Hannibal showed at Trasimene and Trebbia, and the fortune of Alexander, without which every scheme must be but smoke and mist. He shall be so magnanimous that as I contemplate him I can see that he has no equal.' /

So said Maugis, leaving the knights with a desire to know the names of some of the others who were to kill that infernal beast so inclined to carnage. Here the name Bernard was to be read among the first, written boldly to show Merlin's esteem for him. 'Bibbiena shall be renowned because of him,' Maugis explained, 'as also the neighbouring cities, Florence and Siena.' / Not a person there set a foot ahead of Sigismondo Gonzaga, Giovanni Salviati, or Louis of Aragon, who all were bitter foes to the hideous monster. Here too was Francesco Gonzaga, with his son Frederick following in his traces; with him was his brother-in-law of Ferrara and his son-in-law of Urbino. / One of these had a son, Guidobaldo, who would let no one outstrip him—not his father nor anyone else; there was Ottobono of Fieschi, and Sinibaldo, both running neck and neck in pursuit of the beast. Luigi da Gazzolo had planted the hot tip of an arrow in its neck, shot from the bow Phoebus gave him, when Mars, too, placed his own sword on his hip. / From the house of Este two Ercoles, two Ippolitos, with yet another Ercole and Ippolito—of Gonzaga the one, of Medici the other—follow the monster's traces and tire it by their pursuit. Giuliano is not seen lagging behind his son, nor Ferrante behind his brother. Andrea Doria is no less eager. And Francesco Sforza lets no man overtake him. / There are two from the splendid, glorious, magnificent house of Avalos; their emblem is the rock shown crushing wicked Typheus from his head to his snake-feet. No one forestalls these two in draining the horrible monster of his blood; one of them is the ininvincible Francesco di Pescara, the other has Alfonso del Vasto written at his feet. / But where have I left Consalvo Ferrante, the pride of Spain? He was held in such high esteem, and was so praised by Maugis that there were few in that company to match him. William of Monferrato could also be seen with those who had slain the brute. All these were but a handful, though, compared with the countless number that the monster had slain or wounded. /

When they had eaten, they passed the heat of the day in innocent games and cheerful conversation, lying on finest rugs amid the bushes that embellished the spring. To let the others rest more easily, Maugis and Vivian kept armed guard. Now they saw a woman, without company, coming rapidly towards them. / It was Hippalca, from whom Rodomont had wrested Ruggiero's steed Frontino. She had followed him a long time the previous day, beseeching him one moment, cursing him the next. As this proved unavailing, she had made her way to Agrismont to find Ruggiero; on her way, though, she was told, I don't know how, that she would find him here with Richardet. / Knowing the place well, for she had been here on other occasions, she made straight for the spring and found Ruggiero in the manner I have described. But, being a good, practised messenger, able to go beyond her brief, she pretended not to recognize Ruggiero when she saw him in the company of Bradamant's brother. / She made Richardet her sole concern, as though it were to him that she had come; and he, recognizing her, went to meet her and asked her whither she was bound. Her eyes were still red with weeping; she sighed and told him—but spoke loud enough for Ruggiero, who was nearby, to overhear. /

'At your sister's command, I was leading by the bridle a handsome steed, a remarkably good horse whom she dotes upon and calls Frontino. I had led him over thirty miles towards Marseilles, where she expects to be in a few days, and where she had told me to await her. / I was so confident in my belief that no one would have the audacity to steal him from me when I told him that he belonged to Rinaldo's sister. But this turned out to be an illusion yesterday when a brute of a Saracen took him from me, and could not be induced to give him back even when I told him to whom the horse belonged. / All yesterday and today I entreated him until, seeing my prayers and threats fall on deaf ears, I cursed him soundly and left him not far from here—he and his horse were hard driven as he defended himself as best he could, weapon in hand, against a warrior who was pressing him so hard that I hope he may prove my avenger.' / As she spoke, Ruggiero stood up, for he had not been able to catch every word, and begged Richardet, in consideration and reward for the service he had rendered, to let him go all by himself with this damsel, to have her point out to him the Saracen who had taken the good steed from her. This he besought most earnestly. / Though Richardet felt that it might seem all too unchivalrous to let another man accomplish a task with which he himself was faced, yet he bowed to Ruggiero's wish. So Ruggiero took leave of the company and set off with Hippalca, leaving the others filled with admiration, indeed with awe, at his valour. /

When Hippalca had led him off a little away, she explained that she was sent to him by the lady in whose heart his valour was so deeply etched. And, dropping all further pretence, she went on to discharge the commission with which her mistress had sent her on her way. If earlier she had spoken otherwise, she explained, that was because of Richardet's presence. / She told him that the man who had taken the steed from her had also remarked with great insolence: 'Now I know that this horse is Ruggiero's, I take him from you all the more gladly. If he is minded to get him back, tell him—I shan't hide it from him— that I am Rodomont, and my valour dazzles the whole wide world.' / As he listened, Ruggiero showed in his face how his heart blazed with anger, considering how dearly he cherished Frontino, and by whose hands the steed was entrusted to him. Furthermore, the theft struck him as a personal insult: it would be to his shame and discredit if he did not hasten to retrieve him from Rodomont and wreak suitable vengeance upon the thief. / The damsel guided Ruggiero and did not dally, for she was in a hurry to confront him with the pagan. They came to a fork in the road, one branch going down into the valley, the other, up the hill; both branches ended up in the valley where she had left Rodomont. The hill-road was hard-going but short, the other was far longer, but gentle and easy. / Hippalca, driven by her urge to retrieve Frontino and have her revenge, chose the hill-road to shorten the journey considerably.

Meanwhile Rodomont and Mandricard with the others I have mentioned were taking the valley road; they kept to this easier road and so did not encounter Ruggiero. / They had deferred settling their difference, as you know, until they had brought help to Agramant; and in their company they had the very cause of their quarrel, Doralice. Now listen while I resume their story. Their path brought them straight to the fountain where Aldiger, Marfisa, Richardet, Maugis, and Vivian were taking their ease. / Marfisa, at her companions' request, had put on female apparel and adornments, some of those which treacherous Bertolai had destined for Lanfusa. And though she was seldom to be seen without her breastplate and other sturdy armour, today she left them off, and let herself be seen dressed as a woman as she had been asked. /

As soon as Mandricard laid eyes on Marfisa, on the assumption that he could capture her, he decided he would make a gift of her to Rodomont in compensation and a fair return for Doralice—as though Love could be thus ruled, as though a lover could sell or swap his lady, as though he had no reason to be glum if, on losing one lady, he acquired another! / To provide Rodomont with a damsel, then, in order to keep Doralice for himself, he decided to present him with Marfisa, and challenged all the knights he saw in her company: Marfisa struck him as graceful and beautiful, a woman worthy of any knight, one who would at once take Rodomont's fancy, just as Doralice had done. / Maugis and Vivian were armed, as they were standing guard for the rest, so they left the spot where they were sitting, both of them all set to do battle. They expected to grapple with both adversaries, but Rodomont had not come for this and made no sign or motion of any kind. The joust, then, was two against one. /

Vivian moved first in a spirited charge, lowering a hefty lance as he came, but Mandricard, the pagan king renowned for his exploits, charged with even greater impetus. Each aimed his lance to achieve the sharpest impact. In vain did Vivian strike at the pagan's helmet—his foe did not even sway, let alone fall. / Mandricard carried a firmer lance and shivered Vivian's shield as though it were ice; he pitched him out of the saddle to land in the soft embrace of meadow-grass and flowers. Up came Maugis, now, to wreak prompt vengeance for his brother, but he was so hasty in his closing that he afforded Vivian company sooner than revenge. / The third brother, Aldiger, was armed and mounted before his cousin; he challenged the Saracen and boldly charged at him full tilt. His lance caught Mandricard a resounding blow on his fine helmet, a finger's-breadth below the visor, which sent his own weapon flying heavenwards, snapped into four pieces, while leaving the Saracen totally unmoved. / Mandricard struck him on his left side, and it was so powerful a blow that his shield offered little resistance, his breastplate still less—they split like bark. The cruel metal passed through his white shoulder, and he swayed to leeward and windward until he found himself prostrate amid the meadow-grass and flowers, with crimson on his armour and pallor in his cheeks. / After him came Richardet, charging with great boldness and lowering so heavy a lance that he clearly showed, as he had shown on frequent occasions, how worthy he was to be a French paladin. He would have given the pagan sound proof of this had they been on an equal footing —but he was spun head over heels, for his steed fell: it was not his own fault. /

As no further knight presented himself to take up the pagan's challenge, he thought he had secured the lady over whom he had fought, and approached her by the fountain. 'My lady,' he said, 'you are ours if there is no one else to take the saddle in your defence. You cannot refuse or excuse yourself—the custom of war must be observed.' / Marfisa looked at him haughtily and observed: 'You are badly mistaken. I allow that you would be correct about my being yours by custom of war if one of these men you have overthrown were my lord or my champion. But I am none of theirs; I belong to nobody, only to myself: who wants me must first reckon with me. / I too know how to wield a lance and shield, and more than one knight have I overthrown. Give me arms and my horse,' she told her pages, who obeyed promptly. She took off her dress and appeared in a doublet; her handsome, well-proportioned body, all but her face, took on a likeness to Mars. / When she was armed, she girt on her sword, leapt nimbly into the saddle and urged her steed this way and that three times or more, then set him galloping in broad sweeps.

After this she challenged the Saracen, settled her stout lance and engaged battle. Thus must Pentesilea have been at Troy when she took the field against Achilles the Thessalian. / At the mighty impact the lances shivered like glass right to the heel, but those who tilted them did not give an inch, so it appeared. Marfisa, who wanted to know clearly whether at closer quarters the same measure of resistance would serve her against the fierce pagan, made for him, sword in hand. / The ruthless pagan cursed heaven and the elements, seeing her still in the saddle, while she decried heaven no less bitterly, for she expected his shield to shatter. Swords drawn, each now hammered the other's magic armour—both were equipped with enchanted armour, and never did they need it more than today. / Now their armour-plating and chain-mail were of such quality that neither lance nor sword could cut or pierce them: the savage battle might well have continued all that day and the next one too. But Rodomont now threw himself between them and rebuked his rival for this delay.

'If you must do battle,' he protested, 'let us finish the one we began today. / We made a pact, as you know, pledging ourselves to bring help to our forces. Until we had done so, we were not to start another battle or joust.' Then he turned respectfully to Marfisa and pointed out to her the messenger, explaining how he had come from Agramant with a request for help. / And he asked her if she would agree not only to breaking off or deferring her combat but also to coming with them to the assistance of King Agramant. In this way she would cause her fame to rise to higher spheres on firmer pinions than she would do by thwarting so great a design all for a trivial quarrel. / Now Marfisa had always been eager to make trial of Charlemagne's paladins with sword or lance: indeed it was precisely this which had led her to come from so distant a land to France—to ascertain whether their reputation was genuine or spurious. The moment she heard of Agramant's dire need she decided to go with them. /

Ruggiero meanwhile had followed Hippalca along the mountain road in vain; finding, on arrival at their destination, that Rodomont had left by a different road, he thought that he could not have gone far. In the belief that the road must lead straight to the fountain, he left at a fast trot in pursuit of the still-fresh tracks leading from there. / He bade Hippalca return to Montauban, a day's journey from here: if she came with him to the fountain she would be taken too far out of her way. He told her not to worry—he would recover Frontino and soon have news to send her at Montauban or wherever she happened to be. / And he gave her the letter he had written at Agrismont and stuffed into his breast. Also he gave her many messages by word of mouth and begged her to present his fullest excuses to Bradamant. The good messenger committed everything to memory, took her leave, turned away on her palfrey, and did not stop riding until she reached Montauban that evening. / Ruggiero quickly followed the traces left by the Saracen on the level road, but he did not come up with him until he saw him by the fountain with Mandricard. The two of them had promised not to do each other mischief along the way, nor until they had brought help to the host which Charlemagne was on the point of forcing to its knees. /

Reaching the fountain, Ruggiero recognized Frontino, and through him he recognized the man who rode him. Hunching his shoulder against the heel of his lance, he challenged the African in ringing tones. But today Rodomont surpassed Job: curbing his ferocity and arrogance, he refused battle—and he the most persistent seeker after broils! / This was the first, and last, occasion on which the Algerian King ever refused a fight. But so deserving did he find his ambition to join in helping his liege that even had he been confident of holding Ruggiero in his claws more firmly than a swift, nimble leopard with a hare, he still would not have taken the time to exchange so few as two strokes of the sword. / Add to this that he knew it was Ruggiero who was challenging him over Frontino: this was Ruggiero, whose renown surpassed that of all other knights; this was the champion whose mettle he had longed to test by direct experience. And still he would not accept the challenge, so much did the blockade of his liege weigh upon him. / He would have travelled three hundred—nay, a thousand—miles, were it not for this, to purchase such a fight, but today if Achilles in person had challenged him, he would have done no more than you have heard, so well had he dowsed the flames of his wrathful temper to a mere glow.

He told Ruggiero why he was refusing battle, and besought him to lend a hand in their enterprise. / This way, he explained, he would be doing what a knight loyal to his sovereign ought to do. The moment the siege was lifted, they would have ample time to settle their own quarrels. To this Ruggiero answered: 'It will be a small matter for me to defer this battle until Agramant has been rescued from Charlemagne—provided that first you give me back my Frontino. / If you want me to postpone till we reach court the duel to prove that you have acted infamously and behaved in a manner unworthy of a strong man, stealing my horse from a woman, let go of Frontino and give him into my keeping. Do not imagine otherwise that I'll forgo our combat here and now or give you so much as an hour's respite.' /

While Ruggiero was demanding either Frontino or battle on the instant, and the African was hedging on both requests, neither to surrender the steed nor to delay, Mandricard advanced from his own side and broached another quarrel: he noticed that Ruggiero was wearing as his emblem the bird who reigns over his kind. / On an azure ground he sported the white eagle, the beautiful emblem of the Trojans: he traced his origins back to mighty Hector, so this was his device—but Mandricard did not know this, and would not suffer it, and called it a grievous slight that another should wear on his shield the white eagle of renowned Hector. / Mandricard likewise wore the bird which seized Ganymede on Mount Ida. I believe you are familiar with the story, among others, of how he won it as a reward for victory the day of his triumph at the hazardous castle, and how the enchantress gave it to him together with all the fine arms that Vulcan had once presented to the Trojan warrior. / On another occasion Mandricard and Ruggiero had done battle, and solely for this; how they came to break it off you already know, so I shall not recall it. After that they had never clashed again until now, when Mandricard, seeing the shield, proudly yelled defiance: 'I challenge you,' he shouted at Ruggiero. / 'How dare you wear my emblem! This is not the first time I have warned you. Idiot, do you expect indulgence a second time just because I let you off once? But as neither threats nor blandishments can cure you of your folly, I shall show you how much better you would have done to obey me straight away.' /

As a piece of dry tinder, warmed through, will catch fire at the slightest puff, so Ruggiero's fury blazed up at the first word he heard from Mandricard. 'Do you reckon to check me,' he asked, 'just because this other is also contending with me? Well, I am quite able to take Frontino off him and Hector's shield off you—just you watch! / Once before I did battle with you over this, not so long ago; I forbore to slay you then as you had no sword at your side. That time we only made passes, this time we shall have action, and you shall rue that white bird of yours: it is the ancient emblem of my house—you usurp it, I wear it by right.' / 'No, it is you who usurp my emblem,' retorted Mandricard, and drew his sword, the one which a little earlier Orlando had in his madness thrown away in the wood. Good Ruggiero, who could never forget the laws of chivalry, seeing that the pagan had drawn his sword, dropped his lance on the road, / grasping his good sword Balisard at the same time and getting a firmer grip on his shield. But Rodomont drove his steed promptly in between them, and Marfisa with him, and while he pushed back one contender, she pushed back the other, both beseeching them to refrain. It irked Rodomont that the Tartar had twice broken the pledge they had made: / first, thinking to acquire Marfisa, he had stopped to engage in more than one passage at arms; and now, to wrest an emblem from Ruggiero, he was showing scant concern for King Agramant.

'If you must behave this way,' he said, 'let us first settle our own quarrel; it is right and far more just than any of these others you are pursuing. / This was the condition on which we made our truce, this was the agreement between us. Now when I've finished my fight with you, I shall answer him for his steed. As for you, if yóu stay alive, you can go on to finish your duel over the shield—but you'll have your hands so full with me, I trust, that there will be little left for Ruggiero to do.' / 'You won't have the portion you're expecting,' retorted Mandricard. 'I shall give you more than you bargained for; I'll make you sweat from top to toe and, like a spring that never runs dry, I still have all that it takes to settle accounts with Ruggiero and a thousand with him and every last man who wants to pick a fight with me.' /

Tempers rose, insults volleyed from side to side. Mandricard, fuming, wanted to settle scores with Rodomont and Ruggiero both at once, while Ruggiero, who was not accustomed to swallowing insults, would tolerate no truce: brawl and broil is what he wanted. Marfisa went from one to another to repair the damage, but alone she could do little. / When a river overspills its high banks and seeks a new bed, the peasant hastens to block one leak, then the next, to prevent the water from drowning his green pastures and unharvested grain, but he is balked, for while he shores up the bank here, he sees it softly yielding there, and the water gushes through in several streams. / Thus, while Ruggiero, Mandricard, and Rodomont were all at sixes and sevens, each one intent upon proving himself the toughest and overreaching his companions, Marfisa tried to calm them—for this she strove, spending her time and effort in vain: she would take one of them and pull him away only to see the other two flare up angrily. / In her urge to restore peace, 'Good sirs,' she proposed, 'listen to my advice! It is as well to defer all quarrelling until Agramant is out of danger. But if you must all be so self-assertive, then I will take issue again with Mandricard: I want to see whether he has it in him to win me by force of arms, as he has boasted. / But if the object is to rescue Agramant, then let him be rescued, and let there be no strife among us.' 'Me, I'm quite ready to go', observed Ruggiero, 'the moment I have my horse back. The long and the short of it is: either my steed is returned, or he must be held by force; either I shall stay here, dead, or I shall return to the camp on my own horse.' / 'You'll not find the second as easy to achieve as the first,' observed Rodomont. 'And I protest that if our liege comes to harm it will be your fault—as for me, I'm not dragging my feet over doing in time what needs to be done.'

Ruggiero paid little heed to his protest, but, choking with rage, grasped his sword. / Like a boar he hurled himself at Rodomont and drove into him so hard with shield and shoulder that he dislodged him him and made him lose his footing in one stirrup. But Mandricard shouted: 'Either postpone your battle, Ruggiero, or fight with me!' so saying, he struck Ruggiero on the helmet—as cruel and foul a deed as ever there was. / Ruggiero drooped to his horse's neck, and when he tried to straighten up he could not, for he was caught a heavy-handed blow by Rodomont; had his helmet not been of adamantine temper it would have split right down his face. Stunned, Ruggiero released his grip on sword and rein which both fell from his hands. / His steed bore him off across country; Balisard stayed behind on the ground. Marfisa, who that day had become his comrade-in-arms, visibly flared up and caught fire, now that she was alone among the two Saracens. Being courageous and bold, she faced up to Mandricard and, summoning all her strength, brought her sword down on his head. / Meanwhile Rodomont pursued Ruggiero; one more blow like this last, and Frontino was his. But now Richardet drew in with Vivian and placed himself between Ruggiero and the Saracen. He blocked Rodomont and forced him back, parting him from his quarry. Vivian meanwhile handed his sword to Ruggiero, who had returned to his senses. /

As soon as good Ruggiero came to himself and Vivian had given him his sword, he lost no time in avenging himself on Rodomont, and flew at him—like a lion who has been tossed by a bull but does not feel the pain, so much does impulsive rage spur and lash him on to vengeance. / He rained blows on the Saracen's helmet; had he recovered his own sword which, as I say, was knocked from his hands at the outset by foul play, I doubt whether Rodomont's helmet would have given his head much protection—and this was the helmet made to the order of the King of Babel when he planned war upon the heavens. / Now Discord, confident that it would all be scrapping and tussling here from now on, and that no room was left for peace and conciliation, told her sister, Pride, that she could safely return with her now to their little friends the monks. Let them be off while we remain behind. /

Ruggiero had struck Rodomont on the brow. Such was the force behind the blow that Rodomont fell over backwards till his helmet, and the tough hide covering his back, touched Frontino's crupper; three and four times he swayed from side to side, ready to fall limply from the saddle, headfirst; he would have lost his sword, too, had it not been tied to his wrist. / Marfisa meanwhile had brought the sweat out on Mandricard's brow, face, and chest, and he had done as much to her; but so perfect were both their breastplates that they could never find a flaw anywhere, and up till now they had achieved equal fortune— until Marfisa's steed made a turn, at which point she needed help from Ruggiero: / making a tight turn where the ground was soft, Marfisa's horse slipped and could not save himself from falling on his right flank. As he struggled quickly to his feet he was knocked sideways by Brigliador, on whom the ungallant pagan rode in. Down he fell again willy nilly. / Seeing the damsel fallen and in distress Ruggiero lost no time in coming to her aid, now that he had the leisure, for his foe had been carried far off in a daze. So he struck the Tartar on the helmet, a blow enough to have split his head open like a cabbage-stalk, had he had Balisard, or had Mandricard been wearing a different helmet. / Meanwhile Rodomont came to, looked round and espied Richardet

—and remembered what a nuisance he had proved earlier when he came to Ruggiero's help. So he turned upon him and would have been quick to give him brusque thanks for his good turn had not Maugis stopped him in time with great skill and novel magic. / Maugis equalled the best sorcerers in his knowledge of spells, and although he did not have his book with which he had power to stop the sun, he did recollect his formula for commanding demons. Quickly he constrained one to enter Doralice's palfrey and goad him into a frenzy. / Into the gentle hack on whom Doralice was mounted Maugis, simply with words, introduced an angel of Minos. And the hack, which hitherto had never moved except in obedience to his rider's hand, suddenly leapt sixteen feet into the air to land thirty feet off. / It was a huge leap, but not one to jolt a rider out of the saddle. When the damsel saw herself up in the air she let out a shriek, convinced that her last hour had come. After his leap the nag, as though borne by the devil, tore off with her as she yelled for help, and galloped so fast that no arrow would have caught him. / At the sound of that voice Rodomont abandoned the combat and galloped away after the frenzied palfrey to rescue the damsel. Mandricard did likewise, and gave no further trouble to Ruggiero and Marfisa: he was off in pursuit of Rodomont and Doralice without asking for a truce. /

Marfisa had meanwhile got up from the ground, burning with rage and resentment and all prepared for vengeance—an idle thought, however, seeing the distance her enemy had travelled. Ruggiero saw how the battle had ended, and if he sighed he roared, too, like a lion: they well realized that they could never catch up with Frontino and Brigliador on the steeds they rode. / Ruggiero was not going to call off his battle with Rodomont before he had decided the issue of Frontino; and Marfisa did not mean to leave Mandricard in peace yet, because she had not made trial of him to her satisfaction. To both of them it would have seemed unpardonable to abandon the combat in this fashion. So they agreed on a decision to follow the traces of the two who had wronged them. / They would find them with the Saracen host, should they fail to find them before, as they would have gone to raise the blockade before the King of France overran them all. So they made straight for the place where they expected to have them within their grasp. Ruggiero did not set off just like that, but first told his companions of his plan. / He returned to find the brother of his fair lady apart from the rest, and protested his friendship in all circumstances, whether things went well or ill. Then he deftly requested him to greet his sister in his name—he chose his words so subtly that neither Richardet nor the others suspected anything. /

He said goodbye to him, to Vivian and Maugis and wounded

Aldiger, and they for their part professed themselves his most obliged servants always and everywhere. Marfisa, however, was so bent upon reaching Paris that she had forgotten to take leave of her friends; but Maugis and Vivian went after her to call a greeting from a distance. / And so did Richardet; but Aldiger was prostrate and had perforce to stay where he lay. The two Saracens had taken the road to Paris, and now Ruggiero and Marfisa were on the same road. In the next canto I hope to tell you, my Lord, of the miraculous and superhuman feats performed to the detriment of Charlemagne's men by the two pairs of whom I speak.

TWENTY-SEVENTH CANTO

1–4 Introductory. 5–33 The Saracen champions blockade Charlemagne in Paris. 34–101 The Saracen champions fall to quarrelling among themselves. 102–140 Rodomont loses Doralice to Mandricard and leaves in high dudgeon.

WOMEN have often made better decisions on impulse than on reflection, for among the countless faculties bestowed on them by Heaven this one is peculiar to them. Men's decisions, however, will seldom be good unless aided by mature deliberation and after the outlay of time and thoughtful rumination. / Maugis' plan seemed a good one, but it was not (even though, as I said, it delivered his cousin Richardet from dire peril): in constraining the demon to draw off Mandricard and Rodomont, he never reckoned with their simply being carried to the very place where they would prove the undoing of the Christians. / Now had he had leisure to reflect, it is likely that he could have rescued his cousin equally well without harm to the Christians: he might have commanded the demon to take the damsel so far on her way East or West that no more would have been heard of her in France. / Thus her lovers would have followed her anywhere else just as they followed her to Paris; but Maugis, for lack of heed, did not think of this precaution. And, in the absence of a path prescribed by the sorcerer, the Scourge banished from Heaven, who ever craves blood, carnage, and fire, took the path which resulted in greater damage to Charlemagne. /

The palfrey, egged on by the demon, bore off the terrified Doralice —and no river could stop her, still less any ditch, wood, marsh, rise, or dip—until she had passed through the English and French camp and all the host championing Christ's ensigns, to be reconsigned to her father Stordilan, King of Granada. / The first day, Rodomont and Mandricard followed her awhile from afar, seeing her back; but finally they lost sight of her and followed her traces like a hound accustomed to tracking the hare or roebuck. They did not stop until news reached them that she was back with her father. / Watch out, Charles, for such savagery is to fall upon you that I can see no escape for you: not only this pair, but King Gradasso too, and Sacripant have moved against your camp. And Fate, to gnaw you to the bone, has deprived you at one time of both the lights you had beside you— radiant with strength and wisdom—and you, left in darkness, are blind. /

I mean Orlando and Rinaldo: the one is completely crazed and demented, scouring hills and plains, naked, in rain and shine, in the cold and the heat. The other, whose senses are scarcely more stable, has made off in your moment of need, for, not finding Angelica in Paris, he has left in search of her. / A fraudulent old magician had him believe, by some monstrous deception (as related near the beginning), that Angelica was in Orlando's company; so, heartstruck with jealousy as sharp as ever a lover felt, he went to Paris, but when he appeared at court, the mission to Britain fell to his lot. / Now after the battle of Paris, in which his was the credit for blockading Agramant, he returned into the city and searched every convent, house, and fortress —unless she were immured inside a pillar the diligent lover would have found her. In the end, seeing that neither she nor Orlando was there, he set off eagerly in search of them. / He thought that Orlando must be making merry with her in his domain at Anglant or Brava, so he kept visiting them in turn, but in neither place could he find her. Back he would go to Paris, believing that the paladin must soon turn up there, for his absence from the city was no light matter. / Rinaldo would stop in Paris a day or two; then, as Orlando did not appear, he would return to Anglant or Brava in search of news of him. By night and by day, in the dawn freshness and the noonday heat, there he would be out riding; by sunlight and by moonlight he must have made this journey not once but a hundred times. /

But the old Adversary, who made Eve lift her hand to the forbidden apple, cast his baleful eye upon Charlemagne one day when good Rinaldo was far away. And, seeing the rout which could now be inflicted upon the Christian host, he assembled here the very pick of the Saracen champions. / He influenced King Gradasso and King Sacripant, companions ever since leaving Atlas' palace of illusions, to go to the help of Agramant and his besieged host, and to the destruction of the Emperor Charles. He guided them through the unfamiliar country and smoothed their path. / He entrusted one of his minions with urging Rodomont and Mandricard in the steps of Doralice, whom another demon was spurring ahead. Still another he dispatched to prevent Marfisa and bold Ruggiero from taking their ease. The demon escorting this last pair, however, held back somewhat and did not arrive with the rest. / Marfisa and Ruggiero arrived half an hour behindhand: the black angel, meaning to give the Christians a sound beating, astutely saw to it that the quarrel over the steed Frontino should not crop up to interfere—it would have broken out again had Ruggiero and Rodomont arrived together. / The first four met in sight of the camps of the besieged and the besiegers, where all the flags could be seen fluttering in the breeze. After some debate their ultimate conclusion was to bring help to King Agramant and rescue him from the blockade in spite of Charlemagne. /

They drew together, and as they thrust into the heart of the Christian camp they kept up the cry 'Africa!' 'Spain!', and revealed themselves for Saracens. 'To arms! To arms!' The cry was heard all over the camp, but not before the sound of scuffles—and a whole troop from the rearguard was not merely attacked but routed. / The Christian army was set by the ears, not knowing what was happening—some thought it must be those Swiss or Gascons having another riot. But as most of them were in ignorance of the facts, each nation at once gathered to its standards, some to the sound of drums, others to clarion calls: great was the noise which echoed to the very heavens. / The emperor, clad in armour (all but his head) and accompanied by his paladins, went to enquire what it was that had put his squadrons into disarray. Uttering threats, he stopped one group after another. He could see many coming away with gashes to their face or chest, others with bloodied head or throat, with severed arm or hand. / He went further and came upon many lying on the ground, or rather in a scarlet pool, immersed in their own blood—a ghastly sight—and beyond the help of doctor or magician. He saw heads parted from trunks, and severed arms and legs, cruel to behold. From the first to the last line of tents he saw dead men on all sides. / Where the little group had passed they had left a long gash as a mark of their passage that the world would never forget: truly they merited eternal splendour and renown. But Charlemagne gazed upon the cruel slaughter, dumbfounded and seized with rage and indignation, like a man whose house has been struck by lightning and who traces the path of its destruction. /

This first rescue-party had not yet reached the outworks of the African camp before brave Ruggiero arrived with Marfisa from a different side. The illustrious pair looked the place over a couple of times and, after determining which was the shortest route to rescue their besieged lord, they were quick to move. / When a powder-trail in a mine is set alight, the impetuous flame burns its way along the ridge of black powder so fast, the eye can scarcely keep up; then a great roar is heard, and the hard rock or thick wall crumbles: thus were Ruggiero and Marfisa—their coming was like the flame, their effect in the battle like the blast. / They set to slashing heads, down and across, and to lopping arms and shoulders, for the rabble was not spry enough at clearing out of their path. Those who have seen the way a storm will strike one side of a mountain or valley and leave the other side alone can imagine the path taken by these two through the host. / Many who had escaped from the wrath of Rodomont and the first assailants thanked God for giving them such limber legs, such nimble feet; but when they were balked by running headlong into Marfisa and Ruggiero, they saw that a man, whether he stands or flees, cannot argue with his allotted fate. / Those who fled one peril only succumbed to another, and paid with their flesh and bone. Thus will a timid vixen, bent on escape, fall with her young into the jaws of the hound when man, her neighbour who deals her blow upon blow, drives her from her familiar lair, cunningly smoking her out from her place of safety. /

Marfisa and Ruggiero safely reached the Saracen camp, where everyone raised their eyes to heaven and thanked God for this stroke of fortune. Now nobody feared the paladins any more—the most abject pagan would have challenged a hundred of them—and it was decided to issue forth without respite to make the field bloody. / Saracen trumpets, clarions, drums filled the air with formidable clangour; in the fresh breeze the banners and ensigns could be seen fluttering. On the other side, Charlemagne's captains assembled the troops of France, Italy and England along with the Germans and Britons, and fell to in a savage, bloody battle. / What with the force of Rodomont the Terrible, of rabid Mandricard and of Ruggiero, fountain of strength, of King Gradasso the world-renowned, of dauntless-browed Marfisa, and of Sacripant, the Circassian king, second to none, the King of France had perforce to invoke Saints John and Denis and retire into Paris. / The dauntless courage, the astonishing strength of these champions and of Marfisa cannot be imagined, my Lord, still less described; add to them Ferrau and many another famous Saracen, and reckon up how many were slain that day, and what a cruel blow Charlemagne suffered. / Many of the fugitives drowned in the Seine in their haste, for the bridge could not hold so many; how they wished for wings like Icarus, for death lay behind and before them! The paladins were captured, every one of them except for Ogier and Oliver, Marquis of Vienne; he returned, wounded

beneath the right shoulder, while Ogier's skull was cracked. / And
had Brandimart abandoned the game as Rinaldo and Orlando had
done, Charles would have been driven from Paris—if he escaped alive
from such a conflagration. Brandimart did what he could, after which
he gave way to the onslaught. So Fortune smiled on Agramant, who
once more laid siege to Charlemagne. /

The shrieks and wails of widows and little orphans and bereaved
old folk ascended from this murky air to where Michael sat in serene
eternity; they showed him how the faithful were prey to wolves and
crows—how the dead of France, England, and Germany lay covering
the whole field. / The holy angel blushed, for it seemed to him that he
had ill obeyed the Creator; he reckoned himself deceived and betrayed
by faithless Discord, to whom he had entrusted the duty of sparking
quarrels among the pagans: she had done this task poorly—indeed, if
he looked at his intended goal, she seemed to have done the very
opposite of what he designed. / A faithful servant, whose memory
falls short of his devotion and who realizes that he has overlooked
something which should have been as close to his heart as his life and
soul, quickly attends to retrieving his mistake and does not want his
master to discover it first. So it was with Michael, who would not
ascend to God without first discharging his duty. / He winged his
way to the monastery where he had found Discord on previous occasions; he discovered her sitting in the chapter-house at the new
elections to monastic offices. She was enjoying the sight of the monks
flinging their breviaries at each other's heads. He put his fingers in
Discord's hair and thumped and kicked her without end; / then he
belaboured her head, arms, and back with a crucifix till he broke the
stock. 'Mercy!' wretched Discord shrieked, embracing the divine
messenger's knees. But Michael did not release her until he had hustled her swiftly into the camp of the African king. 'Expect worse to
befall you', he warned her, 'if I see you once more outside this camp.' /
With her back and arms all shattered, and afraid of being yet again
subjected to those heavy blows, that terrible wrath, Discord ran at
once to collect her bellows. She added fuel to the fires already burning
and started fresh ones, kindling in many hearts a mighty conflagration
of anger. /

And she so inflamed Rodomont, Mandricard, and Ruggiero that
she made them all go before Agramant, now that Charlemagne was not
pressing the pagans—indeed the advantage was on their side. The
champions explained their differences and the seed out of which they
grew, leaving it to the king to decide which of them should be first
into the field. / Marfisa spoke up for herself, too: she wanted to finish
the duel already started with the Tartar, Mandricard, she said, for she

had been provoked into it by him. She refused to give way to the others or to defer the battle by so much as an hour, let alone a day— her battle with the Tartar must come first, she insisted. / Rodomont was no less determined to have the field first to settle matters with his rival—their duel had been suspended till now in order to bring help to the Africans. Ruggiero put in his own claim, saying that Rodomont's holding onto his steed was more than he could stomach: the first combat must be his with Rodomont. / To make matters worse, Mandricard stepped in: on no account was Ruggiero to keep the eagle of the white wings. He was so beside himself with rage that he wanted to settle all three quarrels at once (if the other three were game; and the trio would indeed have met his challenge had the king consented). /

With entreaties and gentle reminders King Agramant did all he could to achieve a peaceful settlement; but when he saw that they were all deaf and refused to consider any truce, he pondered how best at least to obtain some agreement on the order of their battles. Finally he decided that the best solution was for each of them to draw lots for the field. / He prepared four slips of paper: on the first were written the names Mandricard and Rodomont; the others said Ruggiero and Mandricard, Rodomont and Ruggiero, Marfisa and Mandricard. These he had drawn out at the whim of the capricious Goddess. The first to come out was Rodomont with Mandricard; / Mandricard and Ruggiero came second, Ruggiero and Rodomont third; last came Marfisa and Mandricard—which left the damsel looking petulant, though Ruggiero seemed no better pleased: he knew that the first two contenders had it in them to put an end to all their quarrels, leaving nothing for himself or Marfisa. /

Not far from Paris there was a stretch of ground with a circuit of almost a mile, enclosed by a bank of no mean height, ready-made as a theatre. There had formerly been a castle here, but the walls and roof had fallen to ruin from fire and the sword. (A similar one can be seen on the road from Parma to Borgo San Donnino.) / Here the lists were made ready, enclosed by a low picket fence, squared off to the right measure as the purpose demanded, and with two wide gates, as was customary. Come the day when the king saw fit to hold the combats between the knights who had no interest in apologies, the pavilions were erected on either side up against the pickets. / In the pavilion to the West bold Ferrau and Sacripant helped Rodomont, the giant-limbed Algerian, to put on his dragon's hide. King Gradasso and stout Falsiron were in the pavilion to the East, helping Mandricard, King Agrican's heir, into his Trojan armour. / On a large, elevated tribune sat the King of Africa, and with him the King of Spain; here too sat Stordilan and the other leaders whom the pagan troops revered.

Happy the man who found a place up on the bank or in the tree-tops, to give him elevation. The throng was enormous; it eddied about the whole perimeter of the lists. / To accompany the Queen of Castille there were queens, princesses, and noblewomen from Aragon, Granada, Seville, and the lands towards the Pillars of Hercules. Among these was Stordilan's daughter, Doralice; two fabrics contributed to her rich attire, one red, the other green—but the red was poorly dyed and fading. / Marfisa wore her dress belted at the waist, as appropriate to a maiden-warrior: this perhaps is the way Hippolyta and her Amazons looked by the River Thermodont. The herald, in a coat of arms with the emblem of King Agramant, had come into the field to publish the rules and prohibit any outside participation in the combats, whether by deed or word. / The massive throng was waiting eagerly for the start of the battle, frequently complaining at the delay of the two famous knights in coming forth.

Now from Mandricard's tent a mighty uproar could be heard which grew ever louder. My Lord, it was brave Gradasso, King of Sericana, and the powerful Tartar who were behind the tumult and shouts which could be heard. / Gradasso had finished arming Mandricard with his own hand; he was just about to buckle on the illustrious sword, which had been Orlando's, when he noticed on the pommel the name Durindana and the quarterings which had once been hapless Almont's, until they were wrested from him at a spring in Aspromont by Orlando as a young man. / When Gradasso saw it he was certain it must be Orlando's famous sword, to obtain which he had raised a great army, the finest ever to leave the Levant, and some years previously had subjugated the kingdom of Castille and made conquests in France. But he could not conceive how it had come into Mandricard's possession. / He asked the Tartar whether he had acquired the sword from the count by force or by treaty, and where and when. Mandricard told him of the great battle he had fought over it with Orlando and how the count had subsequently feigned madness: 'He hoped in this way to disguise his fear of having to fight me continuously so long as the good sword was in his possession.' / The count had imitated the beaver, he explained, who rips off his genitals if he sees the huntsman closing in, well knowing that these are all he is after.

Gradasso did not wait for him to finish but broke in: 'I shan't give it to you nor to anyone: I've expended so much gold, so much sweat, so many men on it that it is mine by right. / Go provide yourself with another sword—I want this one, as may not surprise you. Orlando may be mad or sane, but I mean to have this sword wherever I find it. You usurped it without witness along the way. I challenge you for it: my scimitar shall speak my cause, and we shall go to judgement in the lists. / Before you use it against Rodomont prepare to win the sword. It is an old tradition for a knight to purchase his weapon before he goes in to battle.' 'No sound is more delightful to my ears', replied the Tartar, raising his head, 'than an invitation to battle. But first obtain Rodomont's consent: / obtain precedence for your battle, deferring his to second place. Don't imagine I shan't meet your challenge—yours and any other's.'

At this Ruggiero broke in: 'I won't have the pact broken or the lots confounded. Either Rodomont enters the field first, or his battle must come after mine. / If Gradasso prevails with his notion of first winning the weapon with which to fight, then you are not to use my white-winged eagle until you have wrested it from me. However, what I have willed I don't mean to retract: the second combat shall be mine if the first is Rodomont's. / But if you upset the order in part, I shall upset it completely—I do not intend to leave you my escutcheon unless you fight me for it here and now.' 'If each one of you were Mars, you'd neither of you keep me from possessing the good sword or the noble arms,' retorted Mandricard in a rage, / and, stung to fury, he laid into Gradasso with his fist and landed him such a blow on the right hand as to make him drop the sword: Gradasso never imagined that Mandricard could be so insanely reckless and, taken off guard, found he had lost hold of Durindana. / Thus humiliated, he blushed, with shame and anger; what made it all the more painful was that the incident took place so publicly. Craving for vengeance, he stepped back a pace to draw his scimitar.

The Tartar meanwhile, all self-assurance, was challenging Ruggiero. / 'Come on, then, both of you together, and Rodomont too, and Africa, and Spain and the whole human race—I'm ready for the lot of you!' With these words Mandricard, who feared nothing, flourished the sword of Almont; savage and scornful, he clutched his shield to fight Gradasso and good Ruggiero. / 'Leave him to me,' shouted Gradasso; 'I'll cure him of his madness.' 'By God you shan't,' yelled Ruggiero; 'this is my battle.' 'Stand back!' 'Stand back yourself!' they shouted, neither yielding a step.

So a third battle was engaged, and a bizarre outcome this would have had / were it not for several who intervened in their quarrel, somewhat ill-advisedly—they almost learned to their cost what it means to try risking one's own neck to save another's. Nobody there would have composed the quarrel had not the lieges, Marsilius and Agramant, come onto the scene—in their regard everyone showed reverence and deep respect. / Agramant had the cause for this heated new quarrel explained to him, then was at pains to direct that, for this day only,

Gradasso should be kind enough to yield the sword of Hector to Mandricard, so that his bitter feud with Rodomont might be brought to a conclusion. /

While Agramant was striving to calm them, addressing himself now to one, now to another of them, the other pavilion was resounding with another quarrel, between Sacripant and Rodomont. The Circassian, as has been said, was attending upon Rodomont. With Ferrau he had helped the Algerian into the arms of his forbear Nembrot, / and now they had come out to where the charger, champing on the bit, was flecking the rich bridle with foam: Frontino, I mean, on whose account Ruggiero was in such a fury. It was up to Sacripant to send his champion mounted into the lists, so he made a careful inspection to see that the steed was well shod, well harnessed, and duly prepared in every way. / Now on a closer inspection of the steed's distinguishing marks, built as he was for speed, he recognized him beyond any doubt for his own Frontalact whom he had so cherished, and who had caused him such tears: for some time after his charger was stolen, he missed him so much that he would go everywhere on foot. / Brunello had stolen the horse from under him before Albracca, the same day that he had stolen the ring from Angelica, the horn and sword Balisard from Orlando, and the sword from Marfisa. Returning to Africa, the thief had presented Balisard and the steed to Ruggiero, who had re-named him Frontino. /

Once he was sure that he was not mistaken, Sacripant said to Rodomont: 'I'll have you know, sir, this is my horse: he was stolen from me at Albracca. There are witnesses to prove it, but as they are far away, if anyone contradicts me, I shall maintain the truth of my words, sword in hand. / I am prepared, however, in view of our comradeship of these past days, to lend the steed to you today, for clearly you cannot do without him. My condition is, though, that you recognize that he is mine and on loan to you from me. Otherwise do not imagine that you'll have him unless you first fight me for him.' /

Now in the whole profession of arms there was no man with greater pride than Rodomont, no man, to my knowledge, in olden times who could have equalled him for strength and courage. 'Sacripant,' he replied, 'had it been anyone but you who dared to speak to me in this way, he would quickly have learned to his cost how much better for him had he been born dumb. / But for the sake of our recent comradeship which you have mentioned, I am content to favour you with a simple warning: defer your business until you have seen the outcome of the combat about to flare up between myself and the Tartar. There I expect to set before you an example which will make you glad to say: "Do keep the horse!" ' / 'To play the boor is your form of courtesy,' remarked Sacripant, exasperated. 'I tell you now quite flatly, keep your hands off that horse: I shall stop you as long as I can grasp this avenging sword—and if I can't defend him from you otherwise, I'll fight with tooth and nail.' / From words they passed to growls, to shouts, to threats, to blows—for in their towering rage they blazed up and came to grips faster than ever straw caught fire. Rodomont was wearing breastplate and full armour; Sacripant wore neither armour nor chain-mail, but he was so deft at parrying that he seemed wholly covered by his sword. / There were no limits to Rodomont's strength and ferocity, but they did not exceed the foresight and dexterity which Sacripant commanded. Never was a wheel quicker at turning the millstone to grind corn than was Sacripant's motion of hand or foot as he saw the need. / But Ferrau and Serpentine bravely drew their swords and leapt between them, followed by King Grandonio and Isolier and many other Saracen chiefs.

This, then, was the rumpus overheard from the other pavilion by those who had gone vainly to patch the quarrel between Mandricard, Ruggiero, and Gradasso. / A message was brought in clearest terms to King Agramant that Sacripant had started a ferocious battle with Rodomont over the steed. The king, thoroughly nonplussed by all these discords, told Marsilius: 'You see to it that matters don't become worse between these warriors while I attend to the other commotion.' / Rodomont, on sight of his liege, checked his pride and drew back, while the Circassian withdrew no less respectfully. With regal countenance and solemn, deep intonation, the monarch asked them the cause of such fury. When he had grasped it fully, he tried to reconcile them, but all to no avail. / Sacripant refused to leave his steed to Rodomont a moment longer unless the latter chose meek words to entreat the loan of him. Rodomont, his usual disdainful self, retorted: 'Neither heaven nor you could make me beholden to any but myself for what I can obtain by my own force.' / Sacripant, asked by Agramant what his claim was to the steed and how he was stolen, gave a full account of the story and blushed as he told it, when he came to how the stealthy thief, catching him in a reverie, had propped the saddle on four stakes and walked the horse out naked from under them. /

Marfisa was among those attracted by the noise. As soon as she heard of the theft of the steed her brow darkened, for she was reminded that she had lost her sword that day. And she recognized here the horse which seemed to have wings as he fled from her. She recognized good King Sacripant, too, whom she had not recognized before. / The other bystanders, who had often heard Brunello boasting about this, began turning towards him and making open signs that he was the culprit. Marfisa, grown suspicious, started questioning one man and the next who stood near her until she came to discover that the man who had stolen her sword was Brunello. / And she learnt how this theft, which should have earned him a running noose round the neck, had brought him the kingdom of Tangiers as a gift from Agramant: a fine sort of example! Reviving her ancient resentment, Marfisa decided upon immediate vengeance, to punish him for all the jibes and insults to which he had subjected her along the way because of the stolen sword. / She had her page fasten her helmet—she was otherwise fully armed. (I can discover scarcely ten occasions in her life when she was seen without breastplate from the day she accustomed herself to wearing one: she was incredibly dauntless.) Helmeted, she went to where Brunello was sitting among the foremost on the high bank. / On reaching him she grasped him in the chest and lifted him clean off the ground, the way a rapacious eagle will lift a chicken in its hooked talons. And she carried him to where the quarrel was going on before King Agramant. Brunello, seeing himself fallen into evil hands, cried and cried and begged for mercy. / Above the confusion of cries and shouts which pervaded the camp from end to end Brunello could be heard so clearly yelling now for mercy, now for help, that at the sound of his wails and shrieks the whole assembly came running.

Marfisa, arriving before the King of Africa, drew herself up and spoke as follows: / 'I want to hang this thieving vassal of yours by the neck with my own hands, because the same day that he took this man's horse he stole my sword. But if anyone wants to maintain that I do wrong, let him come forward and have his say, for in your presence I mean to insist that he lies and that I am doing my duty. / But since it might be objected that to do this I have waited for all these quarrels, while these more famous champions are all engaged in other disputes, I shall delay three days before hanging him. In that time let anyone come to his defence or send someone thereto, for after that, if there is no one to stop me, I shall rejoice a thousand carrion-birds with him. / Three leagues from here a tower stands before a little copse; there I shall betake myself with but a handmaid and a page for all company. Should anyone make bold to come and wrest the thief from me, there let him come, for I shall await him.' This said, she at once set out for the place she had indicated, without awaiting a reply. / She placed Brunello in front of her astride the horse's withers, keeping hold of him by the hair, while the wretch wept and cried out, calling by name the people on whom he counted.

These complications left Agramant so bewildered, he did not see how he could resolve them. What struck him worst of all was Marfisa's taking Brunello from him like this, / not that he esteemed him or cherished him: he had loathed him intensely now for many a day and had often considered hanging him after the ring had been taken from him. But he saw his own honour flouted by this act, and he blushed for shame. He wanted to hasten after her himself and be avenged with all his might. / But King Sobrino, who was present, strongly urged him against this course: it ill befitted the dignity of his majesty, he said, even if he had firm hopes, nay, utter certainty of coming off the winner. It would redound to his discredit, not to his honour if it were said that he had exerted himself to defeat a woman. / There was little honour but much danger in any battle he joined with her. He would be better advised to leave Brunello to the gallows. Even if he believed that he had but to cock an eyebrow to save him from the noose, he should do no such thing—he should not inhibit the execution of justice. / 'You could send someone after Marfisa', he added, 'to ask her to let you be the judge in this matter, with the promise that she could have the satisfaction of securing the noose about the thief's neck. Should she be obstinate and refuse, let her keep him and do exactly as she pleases—let her hang Brunello and every other thief so long as there is no rift between you.' / King Agramant willingly abided by the advice of prudent, wise Sobrino. He let Marfisa go and did not pursue her to harm her, nor did he suffer anyone else to do so. Nor, again, did he send an entreaty after her, but endured the slight, God knows with what fortitude, in order to subdue greater quarrels and rid his camp of all this commotion. /

Crazy Discord laughed at this: from this moment she little feared peace and harmony; she scurried all over the place, beside herself with glee. Pride was with her, leaping and capering and piling more tinder onto the flames, and shouting so loud that she sent the signal of victory right up to Michael in the higher kingdom. / At the shrill, terrible cry Paris trembled, the Seine eddied. The noise of it resounded even in the Ardennes forests, driving all the beasts from their lairs. The Alps heard it and Mont Genèvre and the three shores of France, the shores of Arles, Blaye, and Rouen. The Rhône and the Saône heard it, as did the Garonne and the Rhine. Mothers clutched their children to their breasts. / Now there were five knights all bent upon obtaining precedence for their own quarrel; and each quarrel was so involved with the next that Apollo himself would never have sorted them out.

Agramant started to untie the knot of the first quarrel explained to him, the one between Mandricard and Rodomont over King Stordilan's daughter. / The monarch went several times from the one to the other in order to settle their difference; he appealed several times to each as a just sovereign and faithful brother. But, finding them both equally deaf, obdurate, and recalcitrant, neither one prepared to forgo the damsel over whom they were quarrelling, / he finally decided, as the best plan to satisfy both suitors, that the one to be her husband should be the one she herself preferred: once she had made her choice, they were to abide by it. Both of them were pleased with this compromise, each one trusting to be the favoured suitor. / Rodomont reckoned that the vital pronouncement which could make him happy would be to his advantage: he loved Doralice long before Mandricard did, and she had shown him the highest favours consistent with her chastity. He was not alone in this opinion—the entire Saracen host shared it. / What he had achieved for her in jousts, tournaments, and in battle was common knowledge. Mandricard, it was considered, must be out of his mind to abide by such a compromise. But the Tartar, who had many and many a time lain with her after the sun had set and knew exactly what he could count on, simply laughed at the vanity of public opinion. /

The two renowned suitors ratified their agreement on their sovereign's hand, then went to the damsel. And she, bashfully lowering her eyes, said that she preferred the Tartar. Everyone was astonished at this, and Rodomont was so dumbfounded and dismayed that he dared not raise his eyes. / But once his natural choler dispelled the shame which had brought blushes to his cheek, he called the judgement fallacious and unjust. His sword was buckled on; he grasped it and proclaimed, in the hearing of the king and the others, that it must be his sword that should either lose him or win him his cause, and not the arbitration of a flighty woman whose inclinations always went against her duty. / Mandricard rose to this: 'Please yourself,' he said, so that before his ship came into port there would yet have been a fair expanse of sea to plough, were it not that King Agrimant rebuked Rodomont: he was not to call out Mandricard again on this question. This took the wind out of his sails. / Now Rodomont, seeing the finger of scorn pointed at him in the presence of the barons, twice in one day—once by his liege, to whom he yielded out of respect, and once by his lady—would not stay a moment longer; taking with him only two attendants from the throng surrounding him, he left the Moorish camp. /

As a bull who has yielded the heifer to the victor goes away heartsore from the herd in search of the remotest wood or shore or sandwaste, where he bellows ceaselessly night and day without assuaging his love-pangs; thus did the Algerian king depart, rejected by his lady and befuddled with great sorrow. / Ruggiero was going after him to recover his good steed—this is why he had armed himself—when he remembered Mandricard, to whom he was committed for the next combat. So he did not pursue Rodomont but returned to enter the lists with the Tartar king before Gradasso forestalled him to settle his own quarrel over Durindana. / To see Frontino ridden away before his very eyes and to be unable to prevent it was past enduring; but once he had settled his business with Mandricard he firmly intended to recover the steed. Sacripant, however, did hasten off in Rodomont's footsteps: unlike Ruggiero, he had no other quarrel to divert him, nothing but this to attend to. / He would soon have overtaken him were it not for a strange adventure he encountered on the way which delayed him till evening and made him lose the traces he was following: he came upon a woman who had fallen into the Seine and would have perished had he not arrived in time to save her. He leapt into the water and drew her to the bank. / Then, when he tried to remount his steed, the beast would not wait for him but led him a chase until evening and did not allow himself to be caught easily. He did catch him finally, but now could no longer find his way back to the point where he had left his path. Two hundred miles he wandered over hill and dale before he came up with Rodomont. /

Where he found him and how the battle was fought to the serious disadvantage of Sacripant, and how he lost the horse and was himself captured I shall not relate here; first I have to tell of the fury, the blazing rage against the damsel and against King Agramant with which Rodomont left camp, and what he said as he inveighed against them both. / Wherever he went the grieving Saracen scorched the air with burning sighs. Often Echo, out of pity for him, answered from the hollow caves.

'O feminine mind,' he said, 'how easily you turn and change; you are the very opposite of constancy. Oh unhappy the man who trusts in you! / Neither long service nor the great love which was made clear to you in a thousand ways had power enough to secure your heart or at least to keep it from changing so promptly. It is not because I appear to you inferior to Mandricard that I am deprived of you. I can find no reason for my situation other than this: you are a woman. / I believe that Nature and God brought you into the world to be a burden, you evil sex, a heavy penalty for men who without you would be happy, just as they produced the foul snake, the wolf, the bear, and made the air teem with wasps and horseflies, and sowed tares and vetches among the wheat. / Why has not fair Nature arranged for men to be born without you, just as human skill can graft one pear or sorb or apple-tree onto another? But Nature cannot always do things properly—indeed, only consider the name: Nature can do nothing

perfect for she is herself a woman. / Do not preen and puff yourself
up, women, with asserting that men are your children: roses are born
on briars; the lily springs from a fetid weed. Troublesome, arrogant,
spiteful, unloving, faithless, foolish, brazen, cruel, wicked, thankless,
you are born into the world for a perpetual plague.' / With these
complaints and a thousand more besides, Rodomont went his way,
now muttering to himself, now bawling to be heard far off, railing
against the female sex.

Of course he was not being reasonable: for every one or two women
to be held at fault we must believe that a hundred are to be accounted
virtuous. / Even though among all the women I have ever loved I
have yet to find a single constant one, I would not say that they are all
faithless and thankless—I'd merely blame my own cruel fate. There
are many women, and there have been many more, who have not
given men grounds for complaint; but if there is only one bad woman
in a hundred, it has always been my fate to fall prey to her. / Still,
I mean to go on searching before I die, indeed before my hair grows
any whiter, and perhaps one day I shall say that for me too there is a
woman who has not broken faith. Should this happen (and I have not
given up hope), I shall glorify her untiringly, with all the power of
tongue and pen, in verse and prose. /

The Saracen was no less incensed against his sovereign than against
the damsel. He broke all bounds of reason, inveighing against him as
against her, and wishing to see such a tempest of disaster fall upon his
kingdom that every house in Africa fall to ruin, and no stone be left
upon a stone; / and that Agramant, driven from his kingdom, live
in sorrow and mourning, a miserable beggar; and that he, Rodomont,
should be the one to restore his fortunes and replace him on his
ancestral throne, and reap the fruit of his loyalty, and make him
see that a true friend ought to be favoured, right or wrong, even were
the whole world against him. /

Thus, reflecting bitterly now against his lady, now against the king,
Rodomont rode a long day's journey, never sleeping and allowing but
little rest to Frontino. The next day or the one after he found himself
by the Saône, for he had taken the road towards the sea of Provence,
meaning to sail back to his African kingdom. / The river was filled
from shore to shore with barges and slender galleys which had been
carrying provisions for the army from many parts—all the country
between Paris and the pleasant coast of Aiguesmortes, and all that
lay to the right, looking towards Spain, had fallen into Moorish hands. /
The provisions were taken off the boats and loaded onto carts and pack-
horses to be conveyed under escort to places inaccessible by water.
The river-banks were crowded with fat herds brought hither from

different regions, and their drovers spent the night in various houses along the shore. /

With the approach of night, when darkness fell, the Algerian king accepted the invitation of a local innkeeper to stop with him. He saw to his steed, then a varied choice of dishes was set before him, with wine from Corsica and Greece—Rodomont was Moorish in all things else, but his drinking habits were French. / The innkeeper studied to honour his guest with a fine dinner and every attention, for he could tell from his bearing that he must be a man of eminence and of high valour. But Rodomont, who was not himself that evening and lacked his normal self-possession (for his thoughts had in spite of himself reverted to his lady), said never a word. / The good innkeeper was one of the most diligent of his trade ever recorded in France—he had secured his inn and his goods even among the enemy strangers. Now he had called in some of his relatives to serve the Saracen (they were kept on hand for this purpose): but none of them dared open his mouth, seeing their guest all silent and brooding. /

In total abstraction Rodomont pursued his train of thought; he kept his eyes lowered and never raised them to look anyone in the face. After a long silence he sighed, as though just awoken from a deep sleep, shook himself, raised his eyes and took in the host and his family. / Then he broke silence and, looking a little mellower, less overwrought, he asked the innkeeper and the other bystanders whether any of them had a wife. He was told that the innkeeper and all of them did have wives. So he asked each one what he thought of his wife's fidelity. / Except for the innkeeper, they all asserted their belief that their wives were chaste and virtuous. Exclaimed the innkeeper: 'Believe what you will, I know that you're all mistaken! Fools, your credulity earns you my opinion that you're all brainless—and this gentleman must think so too, if he is not to say that black is white. / Just as the phoenix is unique and there is never more than one living at a time, so there is never more than one who can call himself safe from betrayal by his wife. Each man believes himself to be that fortunate one, to be the only one who achieves this distinction. But how is it possible for everyone to achieve it if there can never be more than one living at a time? /

'I once shared your present delusion that there could be more than one chaste woman; but a gentleman from Venice whom good fortune brought to my door, was able, with true instances of his own, to draw me out of my ignorance. I have never forgotten his name: Gian Francesco Valerio. / He was familiar in every detail with the tricks normally practised by wives and mistresses; on this score he could reel off stories of today and of long ago and experiences of his own to show me that the chaste woman, whether poor or well-to-do, never did exist—and if one appeared more chaste than the rest, she was simply more adept at concealment. / He told me so many stories that I cannot remember a third of them. But one of them so etched itself on my mind that never was anything more firmly inscribed on marble. And anyone who heard it would be bound to see these mischievous women as I saw, and still see, them. Now if you do not mind hearing it, sir, I shall tell this story against them.' /

'How can you please or delight me better now', the Saracen replied, 'than by telling me a story whose moral chimes in with my own view? The better to listen to you while you narrate it, come and sit opposite me so that I can see your face.' But it will be in the next canto that I shall tell you what the innkeeper related to Rodomont.

TWENTY-EIGHTH CANTO

1–3 Introductory. 4–85 The innkeeper tells Rodomont a story in dispraise of women, and is corrected. 86–102 Rodomont continues to Provence and meets Isabel.

LADIES (and ladies' devotees), by all means disregard this tale which the innkeeper is preparing to relate to the disparagement, to the ignominy and censure of your sex—not that a tongue as common as his can either sully or embellish your image. The ignorant herd will always carp at everything; the deeper their ignorance, the more they will talk. / Skip this canto: it is not essential—my story is no less clear without it. As Turpin included it, so have I, but in no spirit of malevolence or provocation. That I dote upon you my tongue has confessed—it has never stinted your praises—and I have proved it, furthermore, in a thousand ways; I have demonstrated to you that I am, and can only be, yours. / Those who wish, then, may skip three or four pages without reading a line of them; those who prefer to read them must regard the story in the same light as legends and fables. But, as we were saying, when he saw that everyone was ready to listen to his words and room was made for him facing Rodomont, the innkeeper began his story as follows: /

'Astolfo, the King of the Lombards who was left his kingdom by his monastic brother, was so handsome in his youth that seldom had anyone matched him for beauty. No Apelles, no Zeuxis, no one even superior to these could have painted a more handsome man. Yes, he was handsome, and everyone recognized it, but he was far and away his own greatest admirer for this. / He valued less the eminence of his station, which set him over everybody else; or the magnitude of his wealth and nation which made him greater than all the neighbouring kings; what he valued most of all was the pre-eminence he enjoyed throughout the world for his beautiful physique: nothing gave greater delight to his ears than to hear himself praised on this account. / Among his courtiers one he especially cherished was a Roman knight called Fausto Latini. In his company the king often flattered himself, one moment on his beautiful face, the next, on his exquisite hand. One day he asked Fausto whether he had ever, anywhere, set eyes on a man as well built as himself. Now the reply he received was not what he expected. / "Judging by what I see and by what I hear people say, you have few peers in the world for beauty—in fact I should reduce these to one only: that is, one of my brothers, Jocondo. Apart from him, I readily believe that you leave everyone far behind—he alone equals and surpasses you." /

'To the king it seemed an impossible thing to hear, for he assumed that he still held the palm. He was seized with the most ardent wish to meet a youth praised in these terms. He therefore prevailed upon Fausto and extracted from him a promise to go and fetch his brother —though it would be hard to persuade him to come, and Fausto explained why: / his brother had never set foot outside Rome in all his life. He was nurtured in serene tranquillity on the wealth which Fortune had allotted him. The inheritance bequeathed him by his father had neither grown nor shrunk in value. To him Pavia would seem further afield than would the River Don to any other man. / What would prove even more difficult would be to part him from his wife, to whom he was attached by such a bond of love that he could not wish for anything she did not wish for. But, to obey his liege, Fausto agreed to go to Rome and do his utmost. The king, beyond entreaties, proffered other inducements and gifts that left no room for refusal. / So he set out and a few days later reached Rome and the family domain. Here he pleaded so hard with his brother that he persuaded him to come. He also induced his sister-in-law (hard though it was) to acquiesce, setting before her the good that would result from the visit as well as the perpetual obligation he would owe her. /

'Jocondo fixed the day of departure; meanwhile he engaged horses and attendants, and ordered new clothing, to make his appearance suitably dressed—for a handsome cloak will enhance a man's looks. As she shared his bed by night and his company by day, her eyes ever swollen with tears, his wife told him that she did not know how she would endure his being so far away and not die of it: / she felt her heart rooted out of her left side at the mere thought of it. "Come, don't weep, my love," he would say to her, though inwardly he wept no less than she; "may this journey prosper me as surely as I shall return within two months at the most. Were he to give me half his realm, the king could not make me stay a single day longer." / This did not console her. He would be gone too long, she said, and if he did not find her dead on his return it would be a miracle. Her grief attended her day and night and did not suffer her to taste food or close her eyes in sleep; often Jocondo out of pity regretted the promise he had made to his brother. / She wore a necklace from which hung a cross encrusted with jewels and holy relics collected in many places by a pilgrim from Bohemia. Her father had brought it home when he returned, a sick man, from Jerusalem; at his death he bequeathed it to her. This she now slipped off and gave to her husband, / begging him to wear it around his neck for love of her, as a perpetual memento. Jocondo was delighted with the gift and accepted it, not that he needed anything to remind him of her: neither time nor absence, neither good nor evil fortune could shake the memory of her which he held fast and would retain even in death. / The night before the dawn of his departure, Jocondo's wife, who was about to be deprived of him, seemed to die in his arms. She did not sleep a wink. An hour before daybreak her husband took his last leave of her, mounted his horse and was off. She climbed back into bed. /

'Jocondo had not gone two miles before he remembered his cross: he had put it under his pillow the night before and forgotten it there. "Heavens," he muttered to himself, "what excuse can I make that she will accept? She is sure to think that I don't appreciate her boundless love." / He thought of an excuse, but then it occurred to him that, whether he sent it by his servants or by anyone else, it would not do: he would have to deliver it in person. So he stopped and said to his brother: "You go on slowly to the first inn at Baccano. I have to return to Rome, but I expect to catch up with you on your way. / No one else can attend to this for me, but don't worry—I'll soon be with you." He turned his mount, said goodbye and trotted off without taking any of his servants. As he re-crossed the river the sun was beginning to disperse the night darkness. At his house he dismounted and went to the bed, where he found his wife fast asleep. / He lifted the curtains without a word—and was no little surprised by what he saw: his chaste and loyal wife under the covers in a young man's arms! He recognized the adulterer at once—the acquaintance was of long standing: it was a page from his household, a boy of humble stock whom he had raised. / Was he dumbstruck and dismayed? You had better take another's word for this than undergo the experience at first hand, as did Jocondo to his great chagrin. In a fit of fury he made to draw his sword and slay the pair of them; what stopped him was the love which despite himself he bore his thankless wife. / Indeed, Cupid (the rascal) had such a hold over him that he would not even suffer him to wake her, lest he pain her with being caught in so great a lapse. So he crept out of the room as silently as he could, descended the stairs, mounted his horse and, pricked as he was by Love, so pricked his steed that he caught up with his brother before reaching the inn. /

'Everyone noticed the change that had come over his face, the gloom he was in, but none of them could go far towards penetrating his secret. They imagined he had left them to go back to Rome, but he had gone to Cuckoldsville. Everyone realized that love was at the root of his trouble, but no one could say exactly how. / His brother assumed that he was dejected at having left his wife all alone—while on the contrary he was fretting and fuming that he had left her all too well cared for. With knitted brow and pouting lips the poor man gazed down at the ground. His brother tried every way to console him but to little effect, not realizing the matter. / He kept applying the wrong salve to the wound, increasing the pain where he should have removed it, widening the gash where he should have closed it—all this by talking to him of his wife. Jocondo had no rest day or night; sleep and appetite shunned him past recalling, and his face, once so handsome, changed beyond recognition. / His eyes seemed to have sunk into his head, his nose seemed bigger on his gaunt face; so little remained of his good looks that there was no further point in matching him with others. Grief brought on a fever so bad that he had to stop at Siena and again at Florence. If he had retained any of his beauty, he was soon like a plucked rose wilting in the sun. / Fausto was distressed to see his brother so far reduced; but what distressed him much more was that his king would take him for an utter liar: he had sung his brother's praises and promised to show him for the handsomest man alive, but he would be producing the ugliest.

'Still, he pressed on until he brought his brother into Pavia. / As he did not want the king to see his brother unprepared, for fear he himself should look a fool, he warned him by letter that his brother had arrived more dead than alive; a canker at the heart, accompanied by a wicked fever, had so blighted his handsome face that he no longer looked the man he once was. / Jocondo's arrival delighted the king as much as the forming of a friendship; he had no dearer wish in the world than to set eyes on him, and he was not sorry to find the visitor come second to him, yielding precedence in comeliness, even though he realized that, were it not for his disease, Jocondo would be his own equal or superior. / He lodged his guest in his palace, visited him daily, conversed with him all the time; he saw to his every comfort, and to pay him attentions was his constant care and delight. But Jocondo, gnawed as he was by the cruel memory of his wayward spouse, just languished. He could attend games, listen to music, but nothing would lessen his pain by a drop. /

'His apartments were on the attic floor, and were approached through an old ante-chamber where he often withdrew by himself— for every pleasure, all company was hateful to him; here he would subject his heart to the burden of ever more disquieting thoughts. But (who would have believed it?) here it was that he found the cure for his pernicious wound. / At one end of the room, which was in darkness, for the windows were never opened, he noticed a gap between the wall and floor which admitted a ray of light. He put his eye to the chink—and what he saw would scarcely be credible on hearsay alone: but this was not something he heard from others—he saw it for himself, and even then he could not believe his eyes. /

'He had a complete view of the most secret and most beautiful of the queen's rooms, to which none but her closest intimates were admitted. What he saw here was the queen and a dwarf entwined together in a sort of wrestling match; the little man was so expert at this that he had thrust the queen beneath him. / Dumbfounded and stupefied, Jocondo just watched; he thought he must be dreaming; but when he was sure that he was seeing for real and not in a dream, he believed his eyes. "So she submits to a misshapen hunchback," he mused, "when she has the world's greatest king for a husband, the most handsome and chivalrous of men! What an appetite!" / He thought of his own wife, whom he had kept reviling as the worst of women, for she had taken the page-boy to her bed; but her deed now seemed quite excusable: it was not her fault so much as that of her sex, which could never be satisfied with a single man. If all of them were stained with the same ink, at least she had not taken up with a freak. /

'The next day at the same time he returned to his post and saw the queen and the dwarf still playing the same trick on the king. The game was repeated on the following day, he saw, and again on the next— indeed they had no rest-day. And the queen, much to his perplexity, kept complaining that the dwarf did not love her enough. / One day he noticed that she was upset and quite out of sorts, for she had had her maid call the dwarf twice and still he had not come. She sent for him a third time, but the maid returned to say: "The rascal is clowning, Madam, and refuses to come to you for fear of losing his gratuity." / So strange a sight smoothed Jocondo's brow and cleared his eyes. He became more jocund, as his name implied, and his glumness turned to gaiety. He became happy again, filled out, took on colour, looked once more like a cherub from paradise—a transformation which astonished his brother and the king and the entire household. /

'If the king was eager to learn from Jocondo what had caused his sudden recovery, Jocondo was no less eager to tell the king and apprise him of the mischief. But he did not want the king to punish his wife any more than himself for this crime; so, in order to tell him without harming her, he first made the king swear on the Sacred Host. / He made him swear that, whatever he was told or shown that offended him, even though he saw that his majesty was directly affronted, he would never exact vengeance, neither now nor later. Further, he swore him to silence so that the culprit should never realize from any action or word that the king knew of it. / The king, who could have believed anything but this, promised all he asked. Jocondo then explained to him the reason for the melancholy which had come over him for so long—how he had found his shameless wife in the arms of one of his lowly menials, and how his pain would have been the death of him had consolation been further delayed. / But in his majesty's palace he had witnessed something which greatly diminished his sadness: for even if he himself had incurred shame, at least he knew that he was not alone. As he spoke they had come to the chink in the wall, and he revealed the grotesque little dwarf: he was mounted on another's filly, spurring her as his back jerked up and down. /

'That this struck the king as outrageous you will accept without my having to swear to it. He was ready to explode, to run amuck; he was ready to ram his head against every wall, to scream; he was ready to break his oath. But in the end he had perforce to plug his mouth and swallow his acrid, bitter rage, having so sworn upon the Sacred Host. / "What am I to do? What do you advise," he asked, "as you forbid me to satisfy my most just wrath with condign and brutal vengeance?" "Let us leave these heartless women," suggested Jocondo, "and try all the rest to see if they are equally pliant: let us do to other men's wives as they have done to ours. / We're both young and would not readily meet our match for beauty. What woman will rebuff us when they are defenceless against even the ugly? If neither good looks nor youth will serve us, at least our riches will help. I do not mean to return before despoiling a thousand men's wives of their prime treasure. / The long absence, the sights to be seen, the frequenting of women from other lands all, it seems, tend to assuage and lull the heart's amorous passion." The king approved this idea and wanted to leave at once. An hour or two later he set out, attended by two pages, with Jocondo. /

'In disguise they scoured Italy, France, Flanders, and England, and as many fair-cheeked ladies as they saw, they found responsive to their prayers. They would give money, and they would receive pay-ments—indeed often they recovered their disbursements. Many ladies received their addresses, and as many more made advances to them. / They would spend one month here, two months there, proving to their satisfaction that if faith and chastity were not to be found in their own wives, no more were they to be found in those of others.

'After a while they both began to tire of ever seeking new adventures: they could not enter strangers' houses without the risk of being killed. / Better to find one woman whose face and manner pleased both of them; one who gave them both satisfaction and over whom they would never be jealous. "Why", exclaimed the king, "should I object to sharing a woman with you more than with another? I know well enough that in the whole tribe of women there is not one who will rest content with a single man. / One between us, then: without overworking ourselves, but just as our natural urge invites us, we shall enjoy pleasant sport with her—and never a quarrel over her. And I don't believe that she will have cause for complaint: if every woman had two husbands she would be more faithful to the pair of them than to one alone, and perhaps one would hear fewer grumbles." /

'The young Roman seemed quite content with the king's proposal, so, thus resolved, they scoured many a mountain and plain until at last they found what they were looking for: the daughter of a Spaniard who kept an inn on the waterfront at Valencia. She was well-mannered and beautiful. / She was very young, indeed her springtime was still but in the bud. Her father was burdened with many children and poverty was his mortal enemy, so that he made no difficulty about giving her into their keeping, to take her wherever they chose, for they had promised to treat her kindly. / So they left with the damsel and took their pleasure with her in turns, in peace and charity, like two bellows each blowing alternately upon the furnace. They intended to visit the whole of Spain before crossing to Africa. The day they left Valencia they put up in an inn at Jativa. / While they went out to visit the town, its palaces, shrines, and public buildings (for this was their practice every time they came to a new city), the damsel stayed with the serving boys: some were making the beds, others grooming the horses while others saw to supper being ready on their masters' return. /

'Now one of the boys at the inn had once worked at the maiden's house, in her father's employment. He had loved her from the first, and had enjoyed her love. They exchanged glances now, but not openly, both of them fearing to be discovered. But as soon as their masters and the rest of the household left them the chance, their glances became more pointed. / The page asked her where she was bound for and to which of the two gentlemen she was attached. Fiammetta explained the situation to the Greek (for by these names they were known). "Alas," sighed the boy, "when I hoped the time was coming to live with you, my own Fiammetta, you go away and I don't know how I'll ever see you again. / My dreams turn from sweetness to gall now that you belong to others and are to go so far from me. I dreamt, once I had saved up some money by the sweat of my brow—money saved from my wages and from the tips of many guests—I would return to Valencia and ask your father for your hand in marriage." /

'The maid shrugged her shoulders: "You've left it a little late." The boy sighed and wept and put on an act: "Would you leave me to die in this condition? At least clasp me in your arms and let me discharge so great a passion. Before you leave, every moment I spend with you will help me to die happy." / "Believe me," replied the tender creature, "I want this no less than you do: but I cannot see where we'll find the time or place here among so many eyes." "Well, I'm convinced", returned the Greek, "that if you loved me with only a third of my love for you, at least tonight you'd find some way for us to have a little fun together." / "How can I", she asked, "if I always sleep between the two of them? There's always one or the other making love to me—I'm always in the arms of one of them." "That should be no problem," rejoined the Greek; "if you really wanted to, you would find a way readily enough to slip out from between them. And you ought to want to if you really care for me." /

'She thought awhile, then told him to come when he was sure that everyone was asleep. She clearly explained how he was to come in and how to leave the room. And the boy, following her instructions, listened till the whole household was fast asleep, then came to her door and pushed on it: it gave, and he stepped in very softly and felt his way carefully with his feet. / He took long strides, always holding his weight back on his lagging foot while his leading one advanced as though fearful of knocking into a glass pane, as though it were not solid floor but egg-shells he had to walk on. He reached out in front of him in the same mind, and groped his way till he found the bed— into which, at the point where the sleepers had their feet, he quietly intruded head first. / He slipped between the legs of Fiammetta, who was lying on her back, and slid up her until they were face to face, when he hugged her tightly. He straddled her till daybreak: indeed he rode her hard, without once changing horses, for he found no need to—this one, he thought, trotted so nicely that he did not want to dis-

mount her once all night. / Jocondo and the king had felt the motion
which kept jolting the bed but, each of them victim of the same
illusion, ascribed it to his companion. When the Greek had ridden his
course, he left the way he had come.

'The sun was darting his rays over the horizon when Fiammetta got
up and summoned the pages. / Said the king teasingly to his friend:
"You must have ridden quite a distance; it's high time you rested, for
you've been on horseback the entire night." Jocondo returned the remark. "You've taken the words out of my mouth," he said; "you're
the one who needs to rest, it will do you good—you've been riding to
hounds all night long." / "I too", pursued the king, "would certainly
have let my hound off the leash for a while if you'd lent me the horse
long enough to satisfy my purposes." "I am your vassal," Jocondo
replied, "and you can make or break pacts with me as you please.
You need not have been so subtle with me, then—you could simply
have said, 'Give over'." / One accused, the other retorted and a
serious quarrel blew up between them; from bantering they passed to
stinging remarks, for each was concerned not to be made a fool of.
They summoned Fiammetta, who was close at hand and fearful lest
her deception be discovered. Each wanted her to say to the other's
face that which made each of them, by denying it, appear to be lying. /
"Tell me," the king bade her severely, "and have no fear either of me
or him: who was the doughty fellow who enjoyed you all night long
without giving a share to anyone else?" Each expecting to hear the
other proved a liar, they both awaited her reply.

'Fiammetta threw herself at their feet, fearing her end had come
now that she was discovered, / and asked their pardon. Moved by
the love she had long nurtured for a young man, she explained, and
conquered by pity for a tormented heart which had suffered so much
for her, she had that night committed her error. She went on, without inventing anything, to explain how she had behaved between
them in the hope that each would think it was his companion. / The
king and Jocondo stared at each other in utter amazement: never had
they heard of anyone being tricked in quite this way. Then they burst
into fits of laughter, their mouths open and their eyes shut till, practically breathless, they fell backwards onto the bed. / When they had
laughed so much that their ribs ached and their eyes streamed, they
said to each other: "What precautions can we take against being
fooled by our wives when it's even useless hemming this maid between
the two of us so closely that we both touch her? If a husband had
more eyes than hairs he could not prevent his being betrayed. / We
have sampled a thousand women, all of them beautiful, and not one
of them yet has resisted us. Were we to try more, they would be just

the same, but for a conclusive proof this little maid is enough. We can accept that our wives are neither more wicked nor less chaste than the rest. And if they are just like all the rest, why, let's return and make the most of them." / Thus decided, they bade Fiammetta summon her lover, whereupon they publicly gave her to him in marriage, with a sufficient dowry. Then they took horse and, instead of continuing Westward, they turned East and returned to their wives, who never occasioned them another moment's distress.' /

Here the innkeeper ended his tale, which had been followed with the closest attention; Rodomont did not interrupt him once from start to finish. Now he remarked: 'I do believe there is no limit to woman's wiles; not all the books in the world could record a fraction of them.' / Now there was present an old man—a man of shrewdness and courage, and more right-minded than the others. He would not allow that all womankind should be thus ill-considered, so he turned to the story-teller and told him: 'We hear scores of things which don't hold a grain of truth—your tale is one of them. / I don't believe the man who told it to you, even if he spoke Gospel truth in all else: opinion, not his own experience of women, made him speak this way. He may have borne a grudge against one or two women which made him excessively hostile and captious about all the rest; but let his anger subside and I warrant you would hear him heaping far more praise on them now than blame earlier. /

'Now had he wanted to praise them, he would have found far greater scope to do so than ever he did when he condemned them: for one to be chided there are a hundred to be honoured. They should not be damned one and all, then, without making an exception for the virtues of infinite women. And if this Valerio of yours said otherwise, he spoke in anger, and did not express his true feelings. / Now tell me: is there one among you who has kept faith with his wife, or denies ever going after another man's wife, given the opportunity, and even giving her presents? Do you believe you'll find one such man in all the world? Who says yes lies; who believes it is a fool. You, have you ever found a woman soliciting you?—and I don't mean streetwalkers. / Do you know any man who would not leave his wife, however beautiful she was, to follow another woman, if he had hopes of a quick and easy conquest? And what would he do if a woman or young girl paid court to him or offered him presents? To please some woman or other I believe that every one of us would forfeit our own skins. /

'The women who have left their husbands, more often than not they've had good cause: they find their men tired of them at home and gone out eager for other men's wives. But men, when they love, ought to wish their love returned, to receive in measure as they give. If it fell to me to make and suspend laws, I would enact a law to which no man could object: / every woman caught in adultery would be put to death unless she could prove that her husband had once done so too. If she could prove it, she would be absolved—she would need fear neither her husband nor the court. Christ left us among his precepts: Do not do to others what you would not endure yourself. / Unchastity is the worst vice that can be imputed to women, and not to the whole sex at that. But in this respect who has a worse record than we do? Not a single chaste man is to be found. And we have all the greater cause to blush, considering that swearing, theft, fraud, usury, murder, and worse, if worse there be, is rare except among men.' / To illustrate his remarks, the old man, just and forthright as he was, adduced instances of women who never damaged their chastity whether by thought or deed. But Rodomont, who shunned the truth, gave him such a bleak, threatening look that he frightened him into silence—but not into revising his ideas. /

The pagan king put an end to the arguments and altercations and left the table. He lay down in bed to sleep until the dense darkness of night had cleared, but it was in sighing over his lady's offences, more than in sleeping, that he passed the night. At daybreak he left the inn, planning to continue his journey by boat: / having all proper respect for his steed as a good knight should—and his was the fine charger which he possessed in spite of Sacripant and Ruggiero—he realized that he had pressed on harder these last two days than he should have done on so fine a horse.

So he boarded ship to berth him there and restore him and pursue his way more quickly. / Without delay he had the boatman launch off and set to rowing from the shore. The boat, small and lightly laden, went readily down the Saône. Rodomont could not escape his cares, though, nor shake them off either by land or by water; he found them in the bows and in the stern, and if he was on horseback, he carried them mounted behind him. / That is to say, they rode in his head or in his heart, driving out and excluding all consolation. The poor wretch could see no defence since the enemy was within the citadel: he knew not from whom to expect mercy if his own household warred against him. Night and day, he was forever being attacked by the cruel one who should have been helping him. / That day and the night following he sailed down river, his heart heavy with sorrow; he could not put out of his mind the wrong he had suffered at the hands of his lady and of his liege. And he felt the same pain and grief in the boat as he had done on horseback; though he was on the water, he could not extinguish the flames; though he changed his location, he could not change his state of mind. / A sick man, exhausted and prostrate from a raging fever, will toss and turn; he hopes by turning on one side or the other to feel some relief; but he cannot rest on his right side, nor on his left—either way he is equally tormented. So it was with Rodomont, who found no relief from the ill that afflicted him, whether he was on land or on the water. /

Tiring of the boat journey, Rodomont had himself set ashore. He passed through Vienne and Valence and saw Avignon with its gorgeous bridge: all these cities between the Rhône and the Pyrenees fell to Agramant and Marsilius the day these kings won the field from Charlemagne. / He bore right, towards Aiguesmortes, intending to cross quickly to Algiers, when he came to a village on a river; it was favoured by Bacchus and Ceres, but, owing to the constant depredations it had suffered from the troops, it had been deserted. To one side he saw the wide sea, to the other, the blond corn undulating in the sunny valleys. / Here he came upon a chapel recently built on a knoll; the priests had abandoned it when the wars had overrun the neighbourhood. Rodomont set up his quarters here: he favoured the site, which was remote from the battle-front, with which he wanted nothing to do. So he settled for this instead of for Algiers. / He decided against going to Africa, so agreeable and convenient did this place seem to him. He had his servants, his baggage, and his charger all accommodated with him in the same building. The riverside village was only a few leagues from Montpellier and one or two other well-favoured villages, so that he could obtain every commodity. /

One day when the Saracen was brooding, as now he usually did, he saw a delectable-looking damsel crossing a grassy meadow by a narrow track; with her came a bearded monk, and they were leading a great charger burdened with an object draped in black. / Who the damsel and the monk were, and whom they were bringing with them should be clear to you: it was of course Isabel, in charge of the corpse of her beloved Zerbin. I left her on her way to Provence, escorted by the eminent old man who had persuaded her to dedicate to God all the rest of her meritorious life. / Even though she looked pale and distraught and her hair was awry, and hot sighs kept issuing from her breast, and her eyes were two springs, and there were other clear signs that her life was sad and wearisome, she still possessed enough beauty to give refuge to Cupid and the Graces. /

The moment the Saracen set eyes on the beautiful damsel he suppressed his constant inclination to loathe and revile the gentle sex which cannot but embellish the world. Isabel seemed to him fully worthy an object for his second love, enough to quench his first love completely, the way one nail drives out another. / He approached her and, with the gentlest tones he could muster, and the kindliest face, he asked her about herself. She explained to him exactly what she had in mind: to leave the mad world and win God's friendship with holy works. The haughty pagan laughed at this—an unbeliever, he was hostile to every law, to every faith— / and he called her intention wrong and light-headed, and claimed that of course she was making a dreadful mistake. She was no less guilty, he said, than the miser who buries his riches: he derives no benefit from them himself and withholds them from others' use. Lions, bears, and snakes should be shut away, but not what is fair and innocent. / Now the monk was listening, and to save the unguarded damsel from being drawn back onto the old road, he sat at the helm like a seasoned sailor. He was quick to set out a sumptuous, opulent feast of spiritual nourishment—but the Saracen, who was born without a palate, did not sample it, for he disdained it. / After vainly interrupting the monk, whom he could never silence, he lost his temper and seized hold of him in a rage. But you might find me too prolix if I were to continue, so I shall end this canto: let what happened to the old man for talking too much be a lesson to me!

TWENTY-NINTH CANTO

1–2 Introductory. 3–30 Isabel eludes Rodomont by guile.
30–49 Rodomont's self-imposed penance, and his fight with
Orlando. 49–74 Orlando's excesses and Angelica's narrow
escape from him.

OH the weak, inconstant minds of men! How ready we are to vacillate, how ready to change our ideas, especially those born of lovers' spite. I had just seen Rodomont so incensed against women that he broke all bounds: I could never imagine him cooling his passion, let alone quenching it. / Gentle ladies, I am so offended by what he said against you without cause that until I have shown him, to his chagrin, just how wrong he has been I shall not forgive him. I shall so exert myself, with pen and ink, that it will be plain to everyone how much better he would have done to have remained silent, even to have bitten his tongue sooner than slander you. /

Now experience clearly reveals the crass ignorance of his speech. He brandished the dagger of his wrath against the whole sex indiscriminately: then one glance of Isabel's so touched him that he changed his mind on the spot—he wanted her, now, instead of Doralice, though he had scarcely set eyes on her and did not yet know who she was. / Hot and tingling with this new love, he reasoned with her (to little purpose) to break her total, steadfast dedication to the Creator of all things. But the hermit acted as her buckler, her plate-armour; lest her chaste decision be destroyed, he shielded her as best he could with the surest, most valid arguments. / After enduring a great deal of tedious discourse from the valiant monk and vainly inviting him to take himself off to his desert without the damsel, and after seeing himself brazenly flouted by the uncompromising fellow, the Saracen angrily grasped him by the beard and pulled out a whole fistful of hair. / Then, his rage redoubled, he closed his fingers round the other's neck like pincers and, whirling him about a couple of times, tossed him up into the sky, towards the sea. What became of the monk I cannot tell—I do not know. Various and conflicting stories exist: one claims that he was so shattered against a rock that there was no telling his head from his foot; / another, that he landed in the sea, three miles away, and died for not being able to swim, having vainly offered up many a prayer and supplication; another, that a saint came to his aid, carrying him ashore with visible hand. One of these may be the truth—at any rate my story says no more about him. /

Once rid of the garrulous monk, cruel Rodomont turned back to the distressed, bewildered damsel with greater composure and, using the terms employed between lovers, told her that she was his heart, his life, his consolation, his dearest hope, and all the rest of it. / He behaved towards her most gallantly, without the slightest display of force: her gentle look which captured his heart quenched and stifled his customary arrogance. And although he might simply have seized the fruit, he chose not to attack the bark, deeming that the fruit could not be good unless he received it from her as a gift. / In this way he expected little by little to win Isabel to do his pleasure. But she, finding herself in this strange, solitary place, like a mouse at the feet of a cat, would sooner have found herself in the midst of a fire. She kept pondering what to do, what path to take in order to escape unblemished and intact. / She was resolved to slay herself before the cruel savage had his way with her and forced her to so grave a sin against Zerbin, the knight whom harsh and pitiless Fate had allowed to expire in her arms: to him she had privately vowed her chastity for all time. / She saw the pagan king's blind appetite ever growing and could not think what to do, well realizing that his ultimate aim was the squalid act to which her opposition would have scant effect. But as she considered one thing and another, she hit upon a way to protect herself and save her chastity, as I shall relate to her enduring fame. /

As the evil Saracen was now accosting her with language and actions quite devoid of the courtesy he had originally shown, 'If you leave my honour safe,' she told him, 'and I need not fear for it in your company, I, for my part, shall give you something of far greater value to you than the depriving me of it. / Do not despise a lasting contentment, a true joy second to none, for the sake of a trifling pleasure so easily available the world over: you can find a hundred, a thousand comely women any time, but no one in the world, or very few, can give you what I can. / I know of a herb—I've seen it on my way here and know where to find it—which, boiled with ivy and rue over a fire of cypress-wood, and then pressed out between innocent hands, produces a juice: and whoever bathes himself with this juice three times so hardens his body that he becomes proof against fire and steel. / Truly, whoever applies the liquid three times is invulnerable for a month—every month it must be re-applied, for its virtue lasts no longer. I know how to make it and today I shall do so, and today you shall feel its effect: and, if I am not mistaken, you will be better pleased than by the conquest this day of all Europe. / In reward for this, here is what I ask of you: swear on your honour neither in word nor deed ever more to threaten my chastity.'

With these words she recalled Rodomont to his honour, for he conceived such a craving to be invulnerable that he promised her even more than she asked. / He would keep his oath until he had tried the remarkable juice for himself; meanwhile he would refrain from any act or show of violence. Later, he decided, he would not keep his word, for he neither feared nor respected God and the saints—when it came to breaking faith, the whole of deceitful Africa yielded to him. / Rodomont swore a thousand oaths to Isabel not to molest her provided that she prepared the juice that could render him invulnerable as Cygnus and Achilles.

Up cliffs and down dark ravines, remote from towns and villages, she went gathering herbs; the Saracen never left her side but stayed close to her. / After gathering here and there as many herbs (with and without roots) as were needed, they returned home late; here Isabel, that paragon of chastity, spent the rest of the night boiling the herbs most expertly. Throughout the whole mysterious operation Rodomont was present. / Now as he passed the night in games with his few attendants, the heat from the fire in that confined place produced in him such a thirst that, with a sip here, a gulp there, he emptied two whole casks of Greek wine which a day or two earlier his pages had taken from some travellers. / But Rodomont was unaccustomed to wine, which Moslem law forbids and condemns. And it tasted to him like the liquor of the gods, better than nectar or manna; so, repudiating Saracen custom, he drank it by the bumper-full, flasks at a time. The excellent wine was passed round many a time till all their heads were spinning like lathes. /

Meanwhile the damsel took off the boil the cauldron in which the herbs were cooking and said to Rodomont: 'Lest you should think my words are just air, I shall give you what it takes to distinguish truth from deceit and convince the dullest mind—I shall give you proof, here and now, and on my own person, not upon another's. / I want to be the first to try the potency of the benignant juice in case you imagine it contains a deadly poison. I shall bathe myself with it from the crown of my head down my neck and over my breast. Then turn your might and your sword upon me to try the juice's power, the sword's sharpness.' / She bathed herself as she said, then joyfully offered her bare neck to the unwary pagan: he was all unwary and perhaps befuddled by the wine, against which helmet and shield are unavailing. The brute believed her and used his hand and his cruel sword to such effect that he lopped her fair head, once the abode of love, clean from her shoulders. /

Her head bounced thrice: from it a voice could be clearly heard pronouncing the name of Zerbin, to follow whom she had found so novel a way to escape from the Saracen. Depart in peace, then, beautiful, blessed spirit, who preferred fidelity and a name for chastity (virtually alien and unknown in our day) to your life, your green years! / If only my verses had the power, how hard I should work to the limit of my poet's art, which so refines and enhances speech, so that for a thousand years and more the world would have knowledge of your illustrious name. Go in peace to the supernal seat, and leave to other women an example of your faith. / At this incomparable, this amazing act, the Creator looked down from Heaven and said: 'I commend you more than Lucretia, whose death deprived Tarquin of his realm. For this cause I mean to make a law, one such that time may never dissolve, and I swear by the inviolable waters of Styx that no future age shall alter it: / in future every woman bearing your name shall be sublime of spirit, beautiful, noble, kind, and wise; she shall achieve the mark of true virtue, and afford writers cause to celebrate the praiseworthy, illustrious name, so that Parnassus, Pindus, and Helicon shall ever ring with the name of Isabel.' / God spoke thus, and made the air serener, the sea calmer than ever before. The chaste soul returned to the third heaven, back into the arms of her Zerbin.

Shamed and flouted, merciless Rodomont, a second Brehus, remained on earth. Once he had digested his excess of wine, he cursed his mistake and regretted it, / and considered how to placate or in part to satisfy Isabel's blessed soul: though he had slain her body, at least he could give life to her memory. To this end he converted the chapel in which he was living—the site of her death—into a tomb for her. This is how he did it. / He assembled masons from the whole vicinity, some with blandishments, others with threats; when he had a good six thousand men, he alleviated the neighbouring hills of many a heavy rock and had these compacted as a great mound, ninety yards from top to bottom, which encased the chapel containing the pair of lovers. / It almost copied the imposing mound thrown up by Hadrian on the Tiber's bank. Beside the tomb he had a tall tower built in which he planned to live awhile.

Over the nearby river he built a narrow bridge, but two yards wide. The bridge was long, but so narrow that it scarcely allowed room for two horses, / whether approaching it abreast or arriving from opposite ends. The bridge had no parapet of any kind: it was possible to fall off either side. He meant to exact a high toll from every knight who crossed the bridge, whether pagan or Christian—he promised their spoils as trophies for the couple's tomb. /

In less than ten days the bridge across the river was completed. The tomb was not so quickly built, nor was the tower yet carried to its summit, though it was raised high enough for a sentry to take up his post on it and alert Rodomont with his horn each time a knight approached the bridge. / Rodomont would arm and go to challenge him from whichever bank served his purpose—if the passing knight arrived from the tower-side, Rodomont would cross to the further bank. The bridge was the jousting-place, and any charger veering at all off centre would fall into the river, which was deep—there was no danger in the world to match it. / The Saracen imagined that by frequently incurring the risk of falling from the bridge headfirst into the river, where he would be bound to drink a great deal of water, he would be cleansed of the fault to which he was induced by too much wine—as though the water would dilute not merely the wine he had drunk but also the evil which the wine had made his hand or tongue commit. / Many knights passed this way within a few days. Some arrived in the course of their journey, for this was the most frequented road leading to Italy and Spain. Others were attracted hither by adventure and by honour (dearer than life itself) to try their mettle. One and all, confident of winning the palm, forfeited their arms and many their life as well. / If those he overthrew were pagans, he contented himself with despoiling them and taking their arms on which, before hanging them on the marble of the tomb, he clearly inscribed the name of their erstwhile owner. The Christians he held prisoner, and I believe he later sent them all to Algiers. The building-work was not yet completed when who should arrive but mad Orlando. /

The raving count chanced to arrive at the wide river where Rodomont, as I've said, was urgently building the tower and the tomb; these were still unfinished, and the bridge barely completed. Except for his visor the pagan was fully armed at the moment when Orlando came to the river and the bridge. / Impelled by his madness, Orlando jumped over the barrier and ran onto the bridge. Rodomont glowered as he waited on foot in front of the great tower, and yelled threats at him from a distance: he would not deign to use his sword against him. 'Stop, you rash, reckless peasant, you impudent, meddlesome oaf: / this bridge is for lords and knights, not for the like of you!' Now Orlando, who was in a day-dream, did not listen but simply kept on. 'I'll have to punish the idiot,' thought the pagan and, nothing loth, made to hurl him into the water, never imagining he would meet resistance. / At this point a gentle maiden arrived at the bridge to cross the river. She was dainty in her dress, her face comely and her manner studiedly modest. She was Fiordiligi, the damsel (you may remember, my Lord) who was looking for the traces of her lover Brandimart, in every place except where he actually was, in Paris. / She reached the bridge at the moment when Orlando came to grips with Rodomont, who wanted to throw him into the river.

Now she was well acquainted with the count and recognized him at once. She was astonished at the folly that possessed him to go about naked. / She stopped to see what would result from the fury of two men as strong as these. Each was intent on putting all his might into heaving the other off the bridge. 'How can a madman be so strong?' the pagan muttered between his teeth as he twisted and turned this way and that, full of bile, contempt, and rage. / He tried out new holds with either hand, looking for the best grip, and skilfully advanced his right foot or his left, now between the other's legs, now outside them. Rodomont at grips with Orlando looked like a sturdy bear expecting to uproot the tree out of which he has fallen—as though the tree were wholly to blame and he were furious with it. / Orlando, whose wits had foundered, I know not where, and who was relying solely on his brawn (which few, if any, could match), dropped backwards off the bridge still clasping the pagan. They fell into the river with a mighty splash and sank to the bottom together, while the banks groaned. / The water parted them at once. Orlando, who was naked and swam like a fish, struck out with his arms and legs and reached the bank; as soon as he was out of the river he ran off without waiting to consider whether what he had done redounded to his credit or not. The pagan, however, was hampered by his armour and made a slower, more laboured return to the shore. / Meanwhile Fiordiligi, having safely crossed the bridge and the river, explored the tomb in search of her

Brandimart's insignia; finding here neither his arms nor his surcoat, she hoped to find him elsewhere.

But let us return to Orlando, who left the tower, river, and bridge behind him. / I should be mad if I undertook to relate each and every folly of Orlando, for they were so many, I wouldn't know when I should finish. But I shall select a few important ones, fit to be sung in verse and appropriate to my story. And I shall not pass in silence over his prodigious feat in the Pyrenees above Toulouse. / He had travelled a long way, prompted by his dire insanity; eventually he came up into the mountains which divide France from Spain. As he proceeded in the direction of the setting sun he came onto a narrow path over-hanging a deep valley. / Here two young woodcutters found him on their path. They were driving before them a donkey laden with wood; one look at him told them that there were no brains in his head, so they shouted at him threateningly to go back or move aside and clear out of their way. / For all reply Orlando gave the donkey a petulant kick in the chest: there was nothing like it for sheer drive, and the beast rose into the air, so that to an observer he looked like a little bird on the wing, and landed on the top of a hill rearing up across the valley a mile or so away. Then he fell upon the two young men. /

One of them had better luck than sense: in a panic he hurled him-self into the precipice which fell away twice a hundred feet. Half-way down he hit a soft, pliant, leafy bush, which, apart from some scratches to his face from its thorns, let him go safe and sound. / The other grasped a spur jutting from the rockface to scramble up it; he hoped, if he gained the top, to find safety from the madman—who did not, however, intend that he survive: he grabbed the fugitive by the feet as he was trying to climb up, and, extending his hands to arm's length, tore him in two, / the way one may see a man tear a heron or chicken apart to feed its warm entrails to a falcon or goshawk. How fortunate it was that the one who risked breaking his neck was not killed! He related this prodigy to others so that Turpin came to hear of it and wrote it down for us. / This and many other fantastic feats he accomplished as he crossed the mountains.

After much wandering he finally descended Southwards towards Spain. He took his way along the sea-shore in the region of Tarragona and, as his compelling madness dictated, he chose to make his home on the beach; / to afford himself some protection from the sun he dug into the fine, dry sand. While he was here, fair Angelica and her husband chanced upon him. (As I told you earlier, they had come down to the Spanish shore from the mountains.) Now she came within an arm's length of him, not having yet noticed his presence. / It never crossed her mind that he might be Orlando: he had changed too much.

From the moment he was possessed by madness he had always gone naked, in the shade as in the sun. Had he been born in sunny Assuan or where the Libyan Garamants worship Ammon, or in the mountains at the source of the Nile his skin could not have been more deeply tanned. / His eyes were almost hidden in his face, which was lean and wizened; his hair was a matted, bristling mass, his bushy beard looked appalling and hideous. Angelica had no sooner set eyes on him than she turned back, quaking; quaking, she filled heaven with shrieks and turned to her escort for help. / When crazed Orlando noticed her he started to his feet to grab her—he took a liking to her delicate face and immediately wanted her. That he had once so loved and worshipped her was a memory now totally destroyed in him. He ran after her the way a hound pursues game. / Young Medor, seeing the madman in pursuit of his lady, charged at him on horseback and struck at him, finding his back turned. He expected to strike the head off his shoulders but found his skin as hard as bone, indeed harder than steel— Orlando was born under a spell of invulnerability. /

As he felt himself struck from behind, Orlando turned, clenching his fist, and, with a force beyond measure, punched the Saracen's horse. The blow landed on the steed's head, smashing it like glass, and killing him. On the instant, he turned away and chased after the fleeing Angelica, / who was frantically whipping and spurring on her mare—even had she flown faster than an arrow from a bow, the beast would have seemed slow for her present need. Then she remembered the ring on her finger: this could save her, and she thrust it into her mouth. The ring, which had not lost its virtue, made her vanish like a flame puffed out. / Whether it was fright, or that she lost her seat while transferring the ring, or that the mare stumbled—I cannot say which was the reason—the moment that she put the ring into her mouth and hid her lovely face she pitched out of the saddle and landed on her back in the sand. / Had her fall landed her two inches closer, she would have collided with the madman and been slain by the impact alone. Great good fortune helped her at this point: as to the horse, she needs would have to help herself to another horse as she had done before—she was never to recover this one who was trampling the beach ahead of the paladin. / Do not fear: she will secure another.

Let us follow Orlando now, whose frenzied impetus was no whit dispelled with the vanishing of Angelica. He followed the steed across the bare sand, constantly gaining on her; now he could touch her . . . he had her by the mane . . . now by the bridle . . . at last he held her. / He seized her as gleefully as another man would a maiden. He adjusted the reins and headstall then gained the saddle in one leap, only to

drive her many a mile at a gallop restlessly hither and yon, never un-
harnessing her, never letting her taste grass or hay. / Wanting to
jump a ditch, he landed in it upside down with the mare. He was unscathed—never felt a jolt—but the wretched beast threw out her
shoulder. Seeing no way of pulling her out, he finally loaded her onto
his shoulder, climbed out of the ditch and walked with his burden
the length of three arrows' flights and more. / When she grew too
heavy he set her down in order to lead her; she limped slowly after
him. 'Come on,' he urged her, but he urged in vain: had the mare
followed him at a gallop she would not have satisfied his crazy whim.
In the end he slipped the halter from her head and tied it above her
right hind hoof. / Thus he dragged her along, assuring her that this
way she would be able to follow him more comfortably. The road
was rough: one stone tore at her coat, the next at her skin, and
finally the ill-used beast died from her lacerations and sufferings.
Orlando spared her not a glance, not a thought: he pressed on at a
run. /

Even when she was dead he did not stop dragging her as he continued his way Westward, sacking farms and houses as he went,
whenever he felt the need for food. He seized fruit, meat, and bread
which he guzzled, and overpowered everybody: some he left dead,
others, maimed; he tarried little and kept pressing onwards. / He
would have dealt scarcely more tenderly with his lady had she not
hidden herself: he could not tell black from white and believed that his
inflictions were a kindness.

A curse upon the ring, and upon the knight who gave it her—were
it not for that, Orlando would at a stroke have been avenged on his
own and on many another's account! / Would that not she alone but
the whole surviving sex had fallen into Orlando's hands: they're a
nasty tribe and not an ounce of good is to be found in any of them!
But before my slackened strings produce a discordant note in this
canto, I should do well to continue it later, lest it prove irksome to my
listeners.

THIRTIETH CANTO

1–4 Introductory. 4–17 Orlando commits more devastation and swims to Africa. 17–75 Ruggiero slays Mandricard in a duel. 75–95 Bradamant fretfully awaits Ruggiero's return.

ALLOW your reason to be mastered by sheer pique, put up no defence against it, leave blind rage to force your hand (or tongue) into offending your friends: then well may you weep for it—the wrong is not so easily righted! Alas, in vain I regret and curse myself for what I said in anger at the end of the last canto. / But I am like a sick man who has endured all too much pain and, at the end of his tether, gives way to passion and starts to curse. This relieves the pain, and with it the impulse which has allowed his tongue such freedom. Then he comes to his senses and regrets his impulse: but what has been said cannot be unsaid. / I crave pardon, ladies, which I hope your kindness shall afford me. You must excuse me if, overwhelmed as I am by a strong passion, I babble deliriously. Blame it on my enemy—a lady who has reduced me to the most abject condition, making me say things I regret. That she's at fault, God knows: that I love her, she knows. / I am no less divorced from myself than was Orlando. I have no worse an excuse than he does, as he wanders over hill and over dale, scouring great tracts of Marsilius' kingdom.

For many a day he dragged the dead mare after him without let or hindrance, until he came to where a broad river flowed into the sea: here he had to abandon the carcass. / As he swam like an otter, he entered the river and emerged on the further shore, where he met a shepherd riding his horse down to the river to water him. The shepherd did not avoid Orlando as he approached, seeing that he was naked and alone. 'I should like to swap my mare for that jade of yours,' the madman told him. / 'I'll point her out from here, if you like: there she is, lying dead on the other shore. You can have her seen to by a doctor—that apart, I find no fault in her. Let's have your nag, then, with some makeweight. Come now, dismount please: I want him.' The shepherd laughed and, without a word, drew away and made for the ford. / 'Hey, can't you hear? I want your horse!' cried Orlando, going after him in a temper. Now the shepherd had a staff with good solid knots to it, which he used against the paladin, sending him into a blind fury—more savage than he had ever looked before. He let fly with a punch at the shepherd's head, smashing his skull and knocking him dead to the ground. / He jumped onto the hack and dashed off at a venture, robbing many a man. The horse never tasted hay nor oats, so in a few days he collapsed. Did Orlando continue on foot? No—he meant to have horses a-plenty: as many as he found he purloined to his own use, after slaying their owners. /

Finally he came to Malaga, where he wrought greater havoc than anywhere previously. Not only did the fearsome lunatic rob everybody, leaving them in such straits that neither this year nor next would they have made up for their losses, but also he killed so many people and razed and burned so many houses that he laid waste more than a third of the city. / After this he came to a town called Algeciras, on the straits of Gibraltar (or Hibraltar as it is also called). Here he noticed a boat casting off. It was full of merrymakers setting off across the glassy-smooth waters for a pleasant sail in the morning breeze. / The madman started yelling: 'Stop!' for he had a sudden urge to ride in a boat. But his shouts and yells were all in vain, for he was not a cargo they were ready to embark. Their vessel drove through the water as swiftly as a migrant swallow through the air. Orlando beat and belaboured his mount and forced him into the water with his crop, / until the beast had no choice but to plunge in, for all his efforts to resist were in vain. He went in up to his knees, to his belly and rump, so far that barely his head emerged from the water. He could not hope to turn back, for the crop kept drumming him between the ears. Poor wretch, he would have to make the crossing to Africa or else drown on the way. /

The boat that had put out from dry land was meanwhile lost to view: Orlando could not descry its hull from any angle—it was too far off and the billowing waves concealed it from his low vantage-point. He kept urging the horse through the waves, his mind made up on crossing the sea, until the steed, waterlogged and breathless, reached the end of his swim—and of his life: / he sank to the bottom, and would have taken his burden with him, but Orlando used his arms to stay afloat. He bestirred his legs and the palms of his hands as he blew the water from his face. The day was serene, the water calm; and he certainly needed the fairest weather, for with any sea running, he would have been left dead in the water. / But Fortune, who takes care of the insane, pulled him from the sea onto a beach at Ceuta, about two arrows' flights from the town walls. For many days he pursued his course at a venture, hastening Eastwards along the shore, until he came upon a countless horde of black soldiers camped by the sea. / Now let us leave the paladin to his travels: we shall revert to him when the time comes. As to what became of Angelica, my Lord, after her narrow escape from the madman, and how she found a good ship and better weather to return to her own country, and how she gave Medor the sceptre of the Indies: perhaps another will sing to a better accompaniment. / I have so many things I want to relate that I do not care to pursue her adventures any further.

Let our pleasant discourse now attend to Mandricard, the Tartar who had ousted his rival and was happily enjoying Doralice, a beauty matchless throughout Europe now that Angelica had left and chaste Isabel had gone to heaven. / Proud Mandricard could not enjoy to the full the preference accorded to him by the beautiful woman, for others had a bone to pick with him: young Ruggiero was not going to yield him the white eagle-emblem; renowned Gradasso, King of Sericana, claimed his sword, Durindana. / Try as he might, Agramant was quite unable to unravel the tangle, and so was Marsilius. Far from prevailing on them to make friends, he could not even induce Ruggiero to let Mandricard have the ancient Trojan's shield, or Gradasso the sword just long enough for him to settle one issue or the other. / Ruggiero would not suffer Mandricard to take his shield into any other combat; Gradasso would not let him use against any but himself the sword which famed Orlando used to wear. 'Well then, let us see on whom the lot falls,' proposed Agramant, 'and let there be no more discussion. Let us see what Fortune decides: and let preference go to whomsoever she prefers. / If you wish to please me and put me into your debt, you will decide by lot which of you is to fight, on the understanding that the man on whom the lot first falls shall be entrusted with both your quarrels: if he wins on his own account, he wins for his fellow; if he loses, he loses for both. / There is little or no difference between Gradasso and Ruggiero as champions, I believe: whichever of them wins the lottery will, for sure, excel at arms. Let victory go then to whichever side Providence dictates: the knight shall be no whit to blame—all will be imputed to Fortune.' /

Ruggiero and Gradasso remained silent at Agramant's words. They agreed that whichever of them won the lottery would take upon himself both quarrels. Two identical slips were therefore prepared with their names, placed inside an urn, and thoroughly shaken together. / A simple boy put his hand into the urn and extracted a slip: it chanced that Ruggiero's name was to be read on it, Gradasso's remaining behind. Ruggiero's joy, seeing his name come out of the urn, is impossible to describe—or Gradasso's woe: but what Heaven sends needs must be accepted. / Gradasso turned all his care and attention now to fostering Ruggiero to ensure his victory. He reviewed one by one every trick with which he was familiar and which could favour his colleague: how to parry now with sword, now with shield, which thrusts would miscarry, which were unfailing, when to incur, when to avoid, risks. / The pact and the lottery achieved, the rest of the day was spent in the customary fashion by each of the two contenders' receiving their friends' recommendations. The populace, eager to see the fight, jostled each other to fill the arena; many of them, not content with arriving before dawn, waited up there all night. /

The idiot throng, unable to see further or grasp more than what lay before its eyes, avidly waited for the two champions to try their mettle. Sobrino and Marsilius, however, and the wiser heads who could see where harm and good lay, deprecated this combat and Agramant for assenting to it. / They insistently reminded him of the serious loss threatening the Saracen host, whether it were Ruggiero or the Tartar despot whose death harsh Fate prescribed. To oppose Charlemagne they would have far greater need of one of these two than of ten thousand of those remaining on hand—among whom it would be hard to find one stalwart. / Agramant recognized that they were right, but could not retract his promise. He adjured Mandricard and good Ruggiero to give him back what he had conceded, the more so in that their quarrel was over mere fiddlesticks and not worth submitting to armed combat. If they would not obey him in this, let them, he asked, at least postpone the battle. / Let them defer their singular conflict for five or six months, the time needed to drive Charlemagne from his realm, having stripped him of his sceptre, crown, and mantle. But, for all that they were anxious to obey their sovereign, both of them held aloof: each felt that to be the first to consent would be degrading. /

Now who entreated him more, even, than the king, more than any-one who expended words in vain to placate the Tartar, was fair Doralice, King Stordilan's daughter. With tears of grief she implored him to accede to the sovereign's request, to conform his wishes to those of the whole camp. She lamented and grieved that he kept her in a constant state of anxiety and trepidation. / 'Alas,' she cried, 'what am I to do to find peace of mind, if you keep hankering to pull on your armour and chain-mail to fight now one man, now another? Little chance I've had to congratulate myself that the battle came to naught that you undertook for me against your rival, since now no less a challenge has arisen! / Oh how little cause I had for pride that so excellent a king, so strong a champion was willing to risk his life for me in savage, perilous combat: for now I see you no less ready to run the same risk in so trivial a cause. What prompted you was your innate ferocity more than my love. / But if the love you are at pains to show me really has not changed, for its sake and for that of my poor tor-mented heart, I beg you not to concern yourself whether Ruggiero keeps the white bird on his escutcheon. I cannot see what difference

it makes to you whether he gives it up or retains it. / Little profit and
heavy loss may result from the battle which you are set on engaging.
Even if you wrest the eagle from Ruggiero, what a slender reward for
a mighty effort! But if Fortune turns her back to you (and you do not
hold her by the hair) you'll cause such loss that the very thought
makes my breast feel as though split with grief. / Even if you set less
store upon your life than upon a painted eagle, cherish it at least for
my life's sake—one of us won't die without the other. I'm not averse
to dying with you—I'm ready to follow you in life and in death: but
oh to escape the dissatisfaction of dying after your death!' /

With such words and many more besides, accompanied by sighs
and tears, she did not stop entreating her lover all night to withdraw
peacefully. He sucked her sweet tears from her moist eyes, and her soft
laments from her rose-red lips, and, weeping himself, thus replied: /
'Come, my love, for heaven's sake don't upset yourself for such a
trifle! If Charlemagne and the King of Africa and the entire armies of
the Moors and French here assembled raised their banners against me
alone, even then you'd have no cause to worry. How very little you
must think of me if a Ruggiero all by himself can make you anxious. /
You should remember that I alone, with the butt of a lance (I had
neither sword nor scimitar), drove through a great host of armed
knights. Gradasso, though he'll say so with shame and sorrow, will
confess to whoever asks him that he was my prisoner in a Syrian
castle—and he's in a different class to Ruggiero. / No more will King
Gradasso deny, and your Isolier knows it too, and Sacripant (yes
Sacripant, the Circassian king), and famous Grifon and Aquilant and
a hundred more besides, that they were captured there a few days
earlier—Mohammedans and Christians—and I freed them all that
same day. / They still have not recovered from their amazement at the
feat I performed that day—a greater feat than if I had been surrounded
by a hostile army of Moors and French together. Well then, is that
young sprig Ruggiero going to injure or worst me in single combat?
Now that I have Durindana and Hector's armour, is Ruggiero going
to instil fear into me? / Oh, why did I not go into the lists against
Rodomont, to show if I could win you in combat! I know I should
have displayed such prowess that already you would be foreseeing
Ruggiero's end. Dry your tears, for love of God, and don't take so
glum a view of my prospects. Don't mistake me: it is my honour,
not the white bird painted on the shield, which has impelled me to
this.' /

Thus he argued, but his woebegone lady replied to him in such
terms that she would not merely have changed his mind for him—
she would have shifted a pillar. Though he was in armour, she in a

dress, she was on the point of conquering him, and had induced him to say that if the king spoke to him again about a truce, he would be willing to content her. / And he would have, were it not that as soon as fair Aurora gave her hand, as usual, to the Sun, brave Ruggiero, eager to show that he wore the fine eagle-emblem as of right, and meaning to brook no further dilatory acts or words but to make the quarrel brief, sounded his horn and presented himself armed in the lists, which were all thronged about. / As soon as the proud Tartar heard the lofty sound challenging him to battle, he would not hear another word about a pact, but leapt from his bed and yelled for his arms. His face assumed so hard a look that Doralice herself dared not speak to him further of peace or truce. The battle had to take place. / He armed at once, scarcely delaying for the normal ministrations of his pages; then he sprang onto his good steed—Brigliador (once owned by Orlando, defender of Paris). Away he galloped to the arena chosen as the place in which to settle these mighty quarrels by arms. King Agramant and his court arrived at that moment, so the battle could start with little delay. /

The gleaming helmets were put on and fastened, the lances passed up; quick followed the trumpet's peal, which brought pallor to a thousand's cheeks. The knights placed their lances in rest, pricked their chargers' flanks and rushed at each other with such impetus that the sky seemed to fall, the earth to gape. / From either end the white bird could be seen coming, the one that carried Jupiter through the air (the same as was seen in Thessaly, though differently feathered). The boldness and courage of the warriors was clear from the way they wielded their massive lances, and even more at their blunt impact, when they resisted as towers to the winds, as rocks to the waves. / The splinters flew into the sky; Turpin writes, truthfully at this point, that two or three of them fell back incandescent, having reached the Sphere of Fire. Now the knights had drawn their swords and, like men who little fear each other, returned to the attack, each thrusting at the other's visor. / They made straight at each other's visors. They did not aim to topple each other by slaying the steeds: this would have been bad form, for the steed is innocent of the quarrel. Anyone who thinks that they might have agreed on such tactics knows nothing of ancient custom and is totally mistaken: unless otherwise agreed, the warrior who wounded a mount incurred disgrace, censure, and eternal blame. / They struck, then, at each other's visors: these were double-layered but even then scarcely resisted such an onslaught. Blow fell upon blow, raining thicker than hailstones which smash boughs and foliage, grain and stubble, dashing the hopes for the harvest. You know how Durindana and Balisard could cut, and what they could do in hands such as these. / But neither had yet unleashed a blow that did them full justice, so wary were they of each other.

Mandricard wrought the first damage, almost dispatching good Ruggiero: with one of those mighty strokes they knew how to deliver, his cruel sword sliced Ruggiero's shield down the middle, opened his breastplate and gashed his living flesh. / The cruel stroke chilled the hearts of the spectators, who feared for Ruggiero: most, if not all, of them were known to be on his side. Had Fortune effected the wish of the majority, Mandricard would already be dead or a captive. His blow, therefore, was generally frowned upon. / I believe some angel must have intervened to save Ruggiero who, now looking grimmer than ever, retaliated on the instant: he brought his sword down on the other's head, but in his surge of savage rage he hit too fast— if his blade did not cut truly I can scarcely blame him. / Had Balisard landed straight, Hector's helmet would have been enchanted in vain. Mandricard was so stunned by the blow that he dropped the reins; three times he looked like falling headlong while Brigliador (whose name you know, still rueing his change of rider) galloped round the arena. /

Never did a trodden snake or a wounded lion feel such stark fury as did the Tartar when he rallied from the blow which had knocked him senseless. If his wrath and arrogance swelled up, so much and greater was his access of strength and valour. He sent Brigliador leaping towards Ruggiero and swung up his sword. / He stood up in the stirrups and fetched him a blow at the helmet, confident that this time he would split him right down to the chest. But Ruggiero was too quick for him: before his arm fell to its dire effect he lunged, and his pointed sword made a gaping hole in his chain-mail where it protected his right armpit. / With Balisard he drew out the warm red blood also, and prevented fierce Durindana from striking to such dire effect. Even so, it made Ruggiero reel back against the horse's crupper and wince for pain. Had he worn a helmet less finely tempered, the blow would have left him an enduring memory. / Ruggiero did not falter, but spurred his steed and touched Mandricard on his right side. Here choicest metal and skilful tempering were of little avail against the sword which never fell in vain: if it was enchanted to any purpose, it was to make its blows irresistible to enchanted plate-armour and enchanted chain-mail. / All that it touched it gashed, leaving the Tartar with a wound in the side. He cursed heaven and fumed with such rage, the stormy sea was not more terrible. Now he prepared to engage his last ounce of strength: overcome with fury, he tossed far from him the shield with the white bird on the azure ground, and set both hands to his sword. / 'There now,' Ruggiero flung at him, 'you've amply shown that you don't deserve that emblem: you've just thrown it away, and earlier you slashed it—never more can you claim it as your due!'

Hearing these words, the Tartar was bound to lay into him with all the ferocity he could put behind Durindana—which he slammed down so hard upon the other's brow, a mountain would have fallen on it more lightly. / The blade split his visor down the middle—luckily for him, it was not flush against his face—then fell upon the saddle-bow, which was defenceless for all its double-thick armour plating, and passed through to the hip armour, rending the tasses like wax; it gave Ruggiero a bad thigh-wound, which was to take a long time to heal. / Both had their armour stained red with a double trickle of blood, so that opinions differed as to which was having the better of the fray. But Ruggiero was quick to remove the doubt with his all-chastising sword: he aimed a savage thrust right at the part left unprotected by the jettisoned shield. / It pierced the breastplate on the left side and found its way to the heart, for it penetrated more than a palm's width in from the side. So Mandricard had to forgo every claim to the white bird and to the famous sword—and to dear life itself, which he valued far more than sword and shield. /

The wretch did not die unvengeful: the very instant that he was struck his own sword (scarcely his own) flashed down and would have cleft Ruggiero's face had not Ruggiero earlier sapped his strength and drawn off much of his vigour—he had reduced his strength and vigour too much with the thrust beneath his right arm. / The instant Ruggiero took his life, Mandricard fetched him a blow that split the thick iron band and steel skull of his helmet. Durindana cut through skin and bone to penetrate two inches into Ruggiero's skull. Stunned, Ruggiero fell to the ground, his head streaming with blood. / Ruggiero was the first to fall, and the other after him, so that nearly everyone believed that Mandricard had won the honours of the battle. And Doralice, who shared the common illusion, after fluctuating many times between smiles and tears that day, raised her hands in thanks to God for giving such an end to the combat. /

But when the living showed clear signs of life, the dead of lifelessness, then sorrow and joy exchanged thrones in the hearts of the champions' supporters. The kings, lords, and leading knights went to congratulate and embrace Ruggiero, who had staggered to his feet, and accorded him no end of honour and glory. / Everyone congratulated Ruggiero and felt in their hearts what they spoke with their lips. Only Gradasso's thoughts differed sharply from what his tongue expressed: he displayed pleasure, but was gnawed by secret envy at the glorious victory. He cursed the Fate or Chance which had drawn

Ruggiero's name first from the urn. / What shall I say of the favours, what of the many sincere, affectionate blandishments lavished upon Ruggiero by King Agramant? Without Ruggiero he would never have trusted himself to unfurl his banners to the wind and set forth from Africa to venture against such a host. Now that Ruggiero had slain King Agrican's offspring, he prized him more than the rest of the world put together. / And it was not only the men who were thus disposed towards Ruggiero, but the women, too, who had come to France with the troops of Africa and Spain.

Doralice herself, who was bitterly weeping for her pale, white lover, might perhaps have joined the other women were she not inhibited by shame. / I say perhaps, not that I can prove it, but she might have done so easily enough, seeing Ruggiero's good looks, his qualities, and bearing. She was so ready to change her affections, as we have reason to know, she might well have given her heart to Ruggiero just not to see herself deprived of love. / Mandricard living was all very well—but what use was he to her, dead? For her needs she had to secure a man who was forceful and vigorous by night and day.

Meanwhile the most expert physician at court was prompt to come and look over Ruggiero's wounds; he pronounced that his life was in no danger. / With all diligence King Agramant had Ruggiero settled in his royal tent as he wanted to keep an eye on him night and day, such was his devotion to him, such his care. The king hung upon his bed the shield and all the other arms lately of Mandricard, all except Durindana, which was ceded to Gradasso. / With the arms, Mandricard's other possessions were given as spoils to Ruggiero, as also was Brigliador, the fine, handsome charger whom Orlando in his folly had abandoned. Ruggiero presented him to Agramant, realizing how much he would prize the gift.

Enough of this. We must return now to one who was vainly sighing and yearning for Ruggiero: / I shall tell you of the love-pangs endured by Bradamant as she waited. Hippalca returned to her at Montauban and brought her news of her beloved: she told her first about Rodomont and the steed Frontino; then about Ruggiero, whom she had found at the fountain with Richardet and the brothers of Agrismont. / She explained how she had left with Ruggiero in the hope of finding the Saracen and of punishing him for having stooped to wresting Frontino from a woman. And how this plan had miscarried because they took a different road. She also fully explained why Ruggiero had not come to Montauban, / and repeated word for word the explanation he had entrusted to her in his excuse; then she drew from her breast the letter he had given her to take to Bradamant.

She, looking no little perturbed, took the letter and read it: she would have appreciated it better had she not been expecting to see her beloved in person. / To see herself fobbed off with a letter, after expecting Ruggiero himself, clouded her lovely face with anxiety, sorrow, and pique. She kissed the letter ten and twenty times, her heart fixed on its writer; the tears she dropped on it prevented its catching fire from her burning sighs. / She read the letter four or six times, and wanted to have the oral message repeated as many times by Hippalca, who had brought her the one and the other. Still she wept, and I doubt that she would ever have been comforted were it not for the consoling prospect of seeing her Ruggiero soon: / Ruggiero had set a limit of fifteen or twenty days to his return, and this he had confirmed to Hippalca on oath—there was no danger of his defaulting.

'But who can reassure me about the unforeseen', lamented Bradamant, 'which can occur at any time, especially in time of war, to prevent him ever returning? / Alas, Ruggiero, who would have thought that, though I have loved you more than my own self, you should have been capable of loving your avowed enemies in preference to anyone else, even to me? You assist those you should be harrying; those whom you should help, you persecute. I don't know if you're ashamed or proud at your blindness in according help and punishment. / Your father was slain by Trojan (can you not realize this?—the very stones know it!). And you are at pains to see that Trojan's son, King Agramant, avoids ignominy and ruin. Is this your vengeance, Ruggiero, while your reward for those who have avenged your father is enough to make me die for grieving over their blood?' / These words the damsel addressed to her absent Ruggiero, and other tearful words besides, not once but many times.

Hippalca kept assuring her that Ruggiero would stick to his word and that she should await him, as she could do nothing else, until the day he had set for his return. / Hippalca's comforting and the hope which is the normal companion of lovers, allayed Bradamant's fear and sorrow, preventing her from weeping the whole time. She was persuaded to stay at Montauban and not to move from there until the limit promised on oath by Ruggiero—a limit he observed but poorly. / But if he defaulted on his pledge, he was in no way to blame. What with one thing and another he had no choice but to break his promise: he had to take to his bed and lie there for over a month, between life and death, so much did his pain increase after his combat with the Tartar. / The lovesick damsel waited for him all that time and longed for him in vain. She had no news of him beyond what she had heard from Hippalca and subsequently from her brother Richardet, who told her how Ruggiero had rescued him and freed Maugis and Vivian.

Though this news was gratifying, it was not an unmixed blessing, / for Richardet spoke also of Marfisa, her eminent valour and her beauty, and of how Ruggiero had left with her, saying he intended to join Agramant, who was precariously camped in a weak position. She applauded his going with so worthy a companion, but it gave her no cause for pleasure and congratulation. / She was oppressed by no slight suspicion: if Marfisa was as beautiful as she was reputed, and if she and Ruggiero had been together all this time, it would be a wonder if he were not in love with her. But she refused to believe it, so in hope and fear the poor damsel awaited the day that could make her happy or wretched. Sighing, she waited at Montauban, never leaving it. /

As she waited here, who should arrive one afternoon at the castle but the lord and master of the fair domain, the first of her brothers (I don't say in years but in honour, for two were born before him), the one who had illuminated them with glory and splendour as the sun the stars—Rinaldo. He arrived alone except for a page. / What brought him here was this: one day on his way back to Paris from Brava where, as I have said, he often went in search of Angelica's traces, he had heard the grim news about his cousins Vivian and Maugis about to be surrendered to Bertolai of Maganza; so he took the road to Agrismont. / Here he heard that they had since been rescued and their enemies exterminated, thanks to the intervention of Marfisa and Ruggiero, and that his brothers and cousins had all returned to Montauban. Suddenly he could not wait another second to be there with them and embrace them. / So Rinaldo came to Montauban, where he embraced his mother and his wife, his children, brothers, sister, and his cousins who had been captives. His arrival was like that of a swallow arriving with food in his beak for his hungry young. /

After a day or two there he left, taking others with him. Richard, Alard, Richardet, Guichard (the eldest of Aymon's sons), Maugis, and Vivian armed to follow the valiant paladin. Bradamant, awaiting the day which was coming too slowly for her liking, told her brothers that she was sick and would not join them. / And she spoke the truth: she was sick, though not of fever or bodily ill—it was her desire which blighted the spirit within her and made her distracted with love. Rinaldo delayed no longer at Montauban and led away the flower of his men. How he closed on Paris and what help he brought to the emperor the next canto shall relate.

THIRTY-FIRST CANTO

*1–7 Introductory. 8–41 Rinaldo crosses swords with Guidone
Selvaggio, who joins his party, as do Grifon, Aquilant, and
Samsonet. 42–48 Rinaldo learns from Fiordiligi of Orlando's
madness. 49–59 Rinaldo's night-attack on the Moorish camp.
59–78 Brandimart fights Rodomont on the bridge and is
captured by him. 79–89 The Moors routed and Agramant in
flight. 90–110 Gradasso and Rinaldo take up an old battle.*

WHAT sweeter, what more blissful state than that of being in love?
Whose life could be happier or more blessed than that of Love's
servant—were it not for the constant nagging of that dark suspicion,
that dread, that torment, frenzy, passion known as jealousy! / Instil
any other bitterness into this sweetest of pleasures and it will serve to
augment it, to perfect and refine it. Water tastes the better for thirst;
hunger adds relish to food; the man who has never known war cares
little for peace. / The eye may not see what the heart sees, but this can
be endured serenely. The reunion after an absence is all the more
comforting the longer the parting has been. To suffer merciless
bondage (so long as hope remains alive) can be endured: the reward
for faithful service will surely come, however much delayed. / All the
torments and pains of love, the tantrums, the rebuffs serve, by the mere
recollection of them, to heighten the rapture when it finally comes.
But should the infernal plague infect, contaminate, and poison a sick
mind, though happiness and jubilation should eventually ensue, they
will leave the lover indifferent. / A wicked, poisonous wound is
jealousy, against which lotions, poultices, incantations, wizard's
symbols are unavailing; useless, too, the constant study of benignant
stars or all magic ever learnt by its inventor, Zoroaster. It is a cruel
wound which steeps the victim in the very abyss of suffering and
brings him to despair and death. / O incurable wound, so easily
opened in a lover's heart, through false no less than through just
suspicions! So cruelly does it afflict a person, it clouds his reason and
changes him beyond recognition. O wicked jealousy, how false you
were to leave Bradamant all disconsolate! / I am speaking not of the
message with which her brother and Hippalca had embittered her
heart, but of the hard news brought to her a few days later: the
earlier news was nothing to what I shall tell you—but first, a digression: I must speak of Rinaldo as he approaches Paris with his troop. /

The next day towards evening they came upon a knight escorting a damsel; his shield and cloak were sable, slashed with a streak of white. Seeing that Richardet was riding ahead and looked like a bold warrior, the stranger challenged him to battle; and Richardet, never one to refuse, turned his steed and drew off to leave room to charge. / Without further words or further identifying themselves, they charged. Rinaldo and his group stopped to see the result of the impact. 'He's sure to hit the ground if our clash takes place my way, on solid footing.' Such was Richardet's thought, but what ensued was quite the reverse: / the stranger's lance caught him a blow beneath the visor which jerked him from the saddle and sent him sprawling two spears' lengths from his steed. Alard set off at once to avenge him—only to thud to the ground, dazed, and disabled: the impact had been so violent as to split his shield. / Guichard, seeing his two brothers prostrate, at once set his lance in rest. 'Wait! Wait!' Rinaldo cried, 'this third one is mine!'—but he had not yet fastened his helmet, so Guichard charged. He resisted no better than the others, and found himself floored at once. / Richard, Vivian, and Maugis each wanted to be next, but Rinaldo stepped in front of them fully armed, and put an end to their bickering: 'It is time to go to Paris,' he said. 'We should dally too long if I were prepared to wait for each of you to be felled in turn.' / This Rinaldo said to himself, so as not to be heard, as the others would have taken it amiss.

Meanwhile he and his adversary had drawn apart and come charging back at full tilt. Rinaldo was not left prostrate, for he could equal all the others combined. The lances shivered like glass, but at the impact the champions did not give an inch. / The two chargers collided so sharply, they both fell onto their cruppers. Bayard was up at once, scarcely pausing in his career—but the other steed took such a bad fall that he broke his shoulder and spine. His rider, seeing that he was dead, quit the stirrups and was on his feet at once. / Rinaldo had turned back and was approaching empty-handed when the stranger thus addressed him: 'Sir, the good steed you have taken from me was dear to me when he still lived; and I should be grossly failing in my duty to him were I to let him die thus unavenged. So come and see what you can do, for now we must fight.' / 'If the dead steed and nothing else is to bring us to blows,' replied Rinaldo, 'I shall give you one of mine, so take heart—I don't think he will be one whit inferior to yours.' 'If you think it's a horse I'm concerned about,' returned the other, 'you don't understand. As you don't grasp what it is I want, let me explain more clearly: / I mean that I should feel at fault were I not to try your swordsmanship and discover for myself whether in this skill too you match or surpass me. Dismount or stay mounted, as you please, only don't leave your hands at your sides—I'll gladly give you every advantage, so eager am I to cross swords with you.' / Rinaldo did not keep him waiting.

'You shall have your battle,' he promised; 'and my companions will go on ahead until I join them, so that you can fight boldly and without fear of them. Nobody will remain with me but a page to hold my horse.' So he bade his company to be on their way. / Rinaldo dismounted and gave Bayard's reins to his page while the stranger much commended his chivalry. When his standard had passed out of sight a long way off, he clasped his shield, brandished his sword and challenged the knight. /

Now started a combat the like of which was never seen for sheer ferocity. Each underestimated the other's prowess and endurance. When it was clear that they were evenly matched, and neither had reason either for pride or shame, they set aside all arrogance and rancour and applied all their skill to obtaining an advantage. / Their savage, ruthless blows could be heard resounding all about, a dreadful clangour, as the thick shields were bent in at the edges, armour prized apart, chain-mail cut open. They were less concerned to strike home than to parry, if they were to maintain a parity: their first slip could prove their last undoing. / The duel had lasted over an hour and a half, and the sun had sunk beneath the waves, and the veil of darkness had spread from one horizon to the other; but the warriors had not stopped for rest or paused in their exchange of furious blows, motivated not by rage or rancour but by thirst for honour. / All the while, Rinaldo pondered who the stranger could be, who was strong enough not merely to stand up to him, square and bold, but even to carry a frequent threat against his life: the knight had already cost him enough toil and sweat to leave him in grave doubt about the outcome. Were he able to do so honourably, he would gladly have broken off the battle. / On his side, the stranger, who equally had no indication that it was Rinaldo of Montauban—renowned throughout the army— whom he had brought to face him, sword in hand, with so little enmity, was sure that he could not have matched his valour against a more outstanding champion. / He would have forgone his undertaking to avenge his steed, and would have withdrawn from the perilous twosome were he able to do so without disgrace.

It had now turned so dark that almost every stroke went wide: they could scarcely hit and even less parry, for they could hardly see their swords in their hands. / Rinaldo was the first to suggest that they should not fight in the dark, but should defer the battle until lazy Arcturus had passed on. Meanwhile, he invited him to his own tent, where the guest would be no less safe than the host, and where he would be as amply waited on, honoured and esteemed as anywhere he had ever been. / Rinaldo hardly had to press the courteous knight to accept his invitation. Together they repaired to where the company from Montauban had assembled in a secure location. Rinaldo had his page give him a fine steed, beautifully caparisoned, fit for jousting and for swordplay, fit for anything, and presented him to his guest. /

The stranger learnt that his host was Rinaldo, for before reaching their destination he chanced to reveal his name. Now as they turned out to be brothers, they were touched with soft, affectionate feelings. Joy and fondness brought tears to their eyes. / This warrior was Guidone Selvaggio, who had earlier made a long journey by sea with Marfisa, Samsonet, Grifon, and Aquilant, as I described. The villain Pinabello had prevented him from seeing his kinsmen earlier, when he captured him and forced him to champion his wicked law. / Discovering that this was Rinaldo, the most renowned of eminent captains, whom he had wanted to see more ardently than a blind man longs for the vanished light, Guidone exclaimed delightedly: 'What fortune brought me to fight with you, sir, whom I have long loved and whom I crave to honour above all men? / Constance gave me birth on the furthest shores of the Black Sea. I am Guidone, conceived—like you—from the illustrious seed of noble Aymon. What has brought me here is my desire to see you and the rest of my kindred. And where my intention had been to honour you, I see I have come to do you injury. / But forgive me for so misusing you: I did not recognize you or the others. If I can make amends, tell me what I am to do, for to that end I shall refuse you nothing.' They embraced each other time and again, and, when they had finished, Rinaldo told him: 'Do not think of apologizing any further for our battle: / as proof that you are a true chip off the old block you could not produce better evidence than the dazzling valour which we have discovered in you. Had your conduct been more gentle and peaceable, we should scarcely have believed your claim. But the hind does not give birth to the lion, or the dove to the eagle or falcon.' /

They conversed as they rode on their way, neither activity precluding the other; so they came to the tented camp, where good Rinaldo told his troop that this was Guidone, whom earlier they had so looked forward to seeing. The news brought great pleasure to the men, who all felt he looked like his father. / I shall not describe the welcome accorded to him by Alard, Richardet, and his other two brothers, or by Vivian, Aldiger, and Maugis, his cousins, or by all the knights present, or what he said to them and they to him. To conclude, then, he was in favour with everybody. / I believe that Guidone would have had a warm welcome from his brothers at any time; but, given the need of the moment, he was still more welcome now than he would ever have been. When the new sun, crowned with luminous rays emerged from the sea, Guidone joined his brothers and kinsmen in rallying to their ensign. /

They journeyed all that day and the next till they reached the banks of the Seine, some ten miles from the besieged gates of Paris. Here, by a stroke of luck, they met Grifon and Aquilant, those two strongly-armed warriors—Grifon the White and Aquilant the Black, whom Gismonda had born to Oliver. / A damsel was conversing with them; she looked of no base origin, and was dressed in white silk edged with gold. She was graceful and fair of face, albeit tearful and distressed. From her face and gestures it was clear that she was talking of something most important. / Guidone recognized these knights, and they him, for they had been together a few days earlier. To Rinaldo he observed: 'Here are two whom not many can outdo in valour: if they come with us to Charlemagne's help, the Saracens will never hold their ground.' Rinaldo confirmed Guidone's assertion that the two were accomplished warriors. / He had recognized them equally well, for it was their custom to go about wearing as their colours one all black, the other all white. For their part, they recognized and greeted Guidone, Rinaldo, and their brothers. They embraced Rinaldo as a friend, eschewing their ancient enmity: / once upon a time they had been at odds over King Truffaldin—the story is too long to tell—but now they embraced with brotherly affection, all anger forgotten. Then Rinaldo turned to Samsonet, who had arrived a little earlier, and welcomed him with due honour, fully apprised of his great valour. /

The damsel recognized Rinaldo on a closer view, for she was acquainted with all the paladins, and she gave him news which distressed him: 'Your cousin, sir, to whom the Church and the mighty Empire are so indebted—Orlando, once so wise and respected—has lost his reason and roams the world. / I cannot explain the cause of this strange mischance. I saw his sword and other arms scattered abroad where he had thrown them down. And I saw a courteous knight gather them together devotedly, and adorn a tree with them by way of a trophy, enduing it with beauty and majesty. / But that very day the sword was removed by Mandricard: imagine what a loss to the Christians when Durindana passed once again into pagan hands. The pagan also seized Brigliador, who was wandering at large near the arms. / A few days ago I saw Orlando running about quite without shame, without his wits, without his clothes, uttering blood-curdling yells: to conclude, he is stark mad. Were it not that I could trust my eyes, I should never have believed anything so deplorable.' She went on to describe how she had seen him fall from the bridge clinging to Rodomont, and added: / 'I speak of this to anyone whom I take to be not unfriendly to Orlando, so that one of the many to whom I mention it may be moved to pity by his unfortunate plight and try to bring him to Paris or other friendly place to purge his brain. If Brandimart hears of it, I know he will do his utmost for him.' / The damsel was fairest Fiordiligi, whom Brandimart loved more than himself, and who was going to Paris to find him. She mentioned the sword, too: how it had sown discord and conflict and deep dissensions between Gradasso and Mandricard, and how, with the Tartar slain, it had passed to Gradasso. / Rinaldo felt no end of grief and distress over this strange misfortune, and his heart melted with tenderness, like ice in the sun. He was firmly resolved to search for Orlando wherever he might be, in the hope, once he had found him, of having him cured of his madness. /

But as he had assembled his contingent, whether by divine will or by chance, he wanted first to rout the Saracens and free the walls of Paris. He decided to defer the attack to dead of night, however (as this seemed advantageous)—to the third or fourth watch, when Sleep would have sprinkled the waters of Lethe. / He camped his men in the woods and rested them there all day. But when the Sun left the world in darkness and returned to his ancient nurse, and the sky was spangled with bears, goats, harmless snakes, and other beasts, who had been obscured by the greater light, Rinaldo moved his silent troop. / With Grifon and Aquilant, Vivian, Alard, Guidone, and Samsonet, he went forward a mile in front of the rest, with muffled steps and not a word spoken, till they came upon Agramant's outpost, sleeping: all were slain, none taken prisoner. Then, unseen and unheard, they reached the Moorish camp. /

Rinaldo's first contact with the Saracens was to leave their unwary sentries so badly mauled that not one of them was left alive. Their first line of defence thus smashed, the Saracens were no longer in the happiest state: still half-asleep, frightened, and unarmed, they could offer little resistance to warriors such as these. / To the greater terror of the Saracens, Rinaldo opened his attack to the shrill of trumpets and the war-cry of his name. He spurred Bayard, who was no sluggard but cleared the high palisades at a leap. Horsemen he overthrew, foot-soldiers he trampled, tents and pavilions he swept away. / Not one in the pagan host was so brave that his hair did not stand on end when he heard the grim watchwords 'Rinaldo' and 'Montauban' ring out. Africans and Spaniards turned tail without stopping to load their baggage: still smarting from having earlier sampled his fury, they were in no hurry to renew the experience. / Guidone followed him and did no less than he; no less did Grifon and Aquilant, Alard,

Richardet, and the other two; Samsonet carved a passage with his sword; Aldiger and Vivian demonstrated on others how ferocious they were in battle. Everyone who followed the Clairmont standard fought like hardy warriors. /

Rinaldo kept seven hundred retainers at Montauban and on the surrounding estates, all used to bearing arms in the cold as in the heat, and no less valiant than Achilles' Myrmidons. They were each one of them so stalwart in battle that a hundred of them together would not have fled before a thousand. Many among the pick of their number surpassed some of the famous champions. / And even though Rinaldo was not rich in cities and treasure, his treatment of them—in his words and attitude, and in constantly sharing with them what he possessed—was such that not one of their number was ever lured away with higher offers of gold. He never moved them from Montauban unless he required them elsewhere for urgent need. / But now, to help Charlemagne, he left his castle with but a small guard while this company of whose valour I speak drove into the African ranks. As they laid into them they might have been grim wolves among the woolly flocks on the Galeso, Phalantus' river, or lions among the goats along the Cyniphus, in Barbary. / Charles, who had received warning from Rinaldo that he was close to Paris and planned a night-assault upon the unexpecting camp, stood armed and ready, and, when the need arose, sallied forth to help with his paladins.

To their number he added Brandimart, the son of rich Monodant and faithful lover to Fiordiligi. / She had for many a day sought him throughout France in vain—a long journey. Now she recognized him from afar by his standard, and he, as soon as he saw her, left the carnage and became all gentleness again; he ran to embrace her. Brimful of love, he kissed her a thousand times (or very nearly). / In those far-off days men reposed great trust in all their womenfolk, leaving them to wander unescorted over hill and dale, in unknown parts, and still regarding them, on their return, as fair and virtuous, with no trace of suspicion between them. Fiordiligi now told her lover that Orlando had lost his reason. / Brandimart could scarcely have accepted another's word for so strange and terrible a story, but he believed fair Fiordiligi, whose word he had accepted for far greater things. It was not on mere hearsay, she told him: no, she had seen him with her own eyes. She was as capable as anyone of recognizing Orlando, and she told him where and when, / describing the perilous bridge which Rodomont held against all knights, where he was adorning a tomb, enhancing its majesty with the cloaks and arms of those he captured. She mentioned the horrifying, unbelievable feats she had seen the madman do here—hurling the pagan backwards into the river with the grave risk of never re-emerging. / Brandimart, who loved the count as much as one can love a comrade, a son, or brother, was disposed to search for him and (refusing no toil or danger) to see what he could do, by dint of medicine or magic, to infuse some sense into his mad mind.

Armed and mounted as he was, he set off there and then with his fair lady. / They set off for the place where the damsel had seen the count, and travelled by daily stages until they came to the bridge guarded by Rodomont. The watchman gave the signal to the pagan, and his pages were quick to bring out his arms and steed, so that he was all ready when Brandimart reached the bridge. / In a voice to match his wrath the Saracen yelled at him: 'Whoever you are whom Fate has brought here, whether you've lost your way or your head, dismount and strip off your arms! Make obeisance with them to the great tomb before I kill you and offer you as victim to the shades; for this I shall do, and you'll get no thanks from me!' /

Brandimart would give the braggart no answer but with his lance. He spurred his noble steed Batold to so dashing a charge that he showed that there was no one he could not equal for sheer spirit. Rodomont, his lance in rest, thudded full tilt across the narrow bridge. / His charger, who was well accustomed to the bridge and to making one opponent after the next fall from it, galloped confidently into the fray, while the other steed, perplexed by the unusual footing, moved with doubtful, timid, and tremulous step. The bridge, beyond being narrow and without parapets, was shaking, too, and seemed about to fall into the water. / The knights, both champion jousters, wielded lances the size of beams, no different from living tree-trunks, and exchanged blows none too gently. But the power and skill behind their savage, ponderous blows was of little service to their mounts: these both collapsed onto the bridge, and their riders with them, all of a heap. / In their zeal to be up again—which the spurs in their flanks insistently sharpened—they found the width of the bridge so restricted that there were no footholds to be had. An impartial fate therefore tipped them both into the water. A mighty thud resounded skywards, not unlike that heard from our own River Po when Phaeton, losing control of the Sun-chariot, plunged into it. / With the full weight of their riders, who remained firmly seated, the two steeds left the bridge to explore the bottom of the river and see if any fair nymph lurked down there. It was not the first, not even the second, time the pagan had leapt from the bridge into the water with his brave steed, so he knew the lie of the river-bed: / he knew where the footing was firm, where it yielded, where the shallows lay and the deeps. So, surging head and trunk from the river, he attacked Brandimart advantageously.

Brandimart, however, was being swirled in the current; his mount was stuck past recovery in the mud which glazed the river-bottom, so they both risked drowning there. / The current caught them up and overturned them, washing them into deeper water. Brandimart went under, with his horse on top of him, while from the bridge Fiordiligi, dismayed and horrified, entreated Rodomont with tears in her eyes: 'By her whose death you revere,' she prayed, 'do not be so cruel as to leave such a knight to drown! / Alas, kind sir, if ever you loved, have pity on me who love him. Be content to make him captive and adorn your monument with his ensign—no finer, no worthier spoils will you ever have brought to it.' Though the pagan was so barbarous, she found the words to move him. / He promptly rescued her lover who was kept buried under water by his steed and thought his last moment had come; though not thirsty, he had drunk a great deal. But he did not help him until he had relieved him of his sword, then of his helmet, after which he dragged him half-dead from the water and shut him with many others in his tower. /

When the damsel saw her lover taken prisoner her joy was at an end—though she would have been still less pleased to have seen him perish in the river. She wept on her own account, not on anyone else's, for she had been the cause of Brandimart's coming here: she had told him how she had recognized Orlando at the perilous bridge. / She left, determined to go and fetch Rinaldo, or Guidone, or Samsonet, or others from Charlemagne's court, accomplished warriors by land and water and capable of standing up to the Saracen. If they were no stronger than Brandimart, they might at least prove more fortunate than he. / Many days she travelled before she came upon any knight who looked up to the task of fighting the Saracen and freeing her lover. After searching a long time for someone apt for her purpose, she came upon a knight wearing a gorgeous, ornate cloak embroidered with cypress trunks. / Who he was I shall tell you later.

First I want to return to Paris and follow the great rout inflicted upon the Moors by Rinaldo and Maugis. I could never count the number of the fugitives nor of those who were dispatched to the Stygean waters. (Turpin had tried to count them all, but the coming of night had prevented him.) / Agramant had just fallen asleep in his tent when a knight awoke him and told him that he would be captured if he did not make off with all possible dispatch. The king looked round and saw the confusion of his men as they fled helter-skelter and unresisting, naked and defenceless, without time even to snatch up their shields. / Shocked and bewildered, he was being helped into his breastplate when Falsiron and his son Ferrau arrived, along with Grandonio, Balugant, and the rest of the clan. They explained to him the risk he ran of being killed or captured where he was: if he made good his escape, he could thank Fate for treating him kindly./ Marsilius and good Sobrino and the others all spoke in the same terms, urging that he stood as close to his undoing as he did to Rinaldo, who was approaching rapidly. If he waited for the paladin (a truly ferocious man) to arrive, and in such force, he would be bound to die, he and his friends, or to fall into the enemy's hands. / But he could withdraw to Arles or Narbonne with the small force he had on hand: both cities were strong and sound enough to keep the war going for many a day. With his royal person safeguarded, vengeance could be taken for this humiliation, and the army brought up to strength quickly in order finally to destroy Charlemagne. /

King Agramant took their advice, though it went against the grain, and set out for Arles—he chose the safest road that offered and seemed to fly along it. Of great assistance, beside his guides, was the fact of setting out by night. The troops from Africa and Spain who escaped Rinaldo's clutches numbered twenty thousand. / As for the numbers slaughtered by Rinaldo, and those slain by his brothers, and those by Grifon and Aquilant, and those who endured the cruel hostility of the seven hundred men at Rinaldo's beck, and those butchered by Samsonet, and those who fled to drown in the Seine: the man who could count them would be capable of counting the flowers strewn in April by Favonius and Flora. / It has been suggested that Maugis had a share in that night's victory, not that he sprinkled the land with blood or smashed any skulls, but that by magic spells he coaxed the infernal angels from the caverns of hell, with so many lances and banners that two Frances could not have assembled so many; / and that he provoked such an uproar of trumpets and drums and assorted noises, such whinnying of horses, such cries and clamour of footsoldiers that the plains, mountains, and valleys must have re-echoed for miles around. With this he gave the Moors such a fright that he routed them. / Agramant did not forget Ruggiero, who was still gravely ill from his wounds. He had him made as comfortable as possible on a horse with a smooth gait; and when they reached a point where the going was safer, he had him transferred to a boat and borne comfortably to Arles, where the troops were to assemble. / Those who turned their backs to Rinaldo and the emperor (almost a hundred thousand, I believe) took to the fields and woods, hills and valleys, trying to escape from the French; but most of them found their retreat cut off, so that what had been green or white was dyed red.

Not so did Gradasso, King of Sericana, whose tent was on the edge of the camp. / No, when he heard that their assailant was the lord of Montauban he so gloated with joy, he skipped about with glee: he praised and thanked his Creator for presenting him that night with the rare good fortune of being able to win Bayard, that matchless charger. / He had long nurtured two ambitions: to wear at his side the trusty sword Durindana (I think you will have read this elsewhere), and to ride this superlative courser. To this end he had armed and come to France with over a hundred thousand men. He had challenged Rinaldo to fierce battle for this horse, / and had come down to the sea-shore where their quarrel was to be determined. But Maugis interfered and upset the plan: he forced an unwilling departure upon his cousin, having embarked him on a ship at sea—a story that would be long in telling. From that time Gradasso had always dismissed the noble paladin as a craven coward. / Now when Gradasso learned that the assailant of their camp was Rinaldo he was overjoyed. He donned his armour, fetched his steed, and went in search of him through the inky darkness. All he met he floored: Africans and French he left equally indisposed, a jumbled heap of misery, for his good lance made no distinction between them. / He sought him here, he sought him there, frequently bellowing at the top of his voice and ever bearing towards where the corpses lay thickest, until he met him, sword against sword —for their lances had both shivered at once into a thousand splinters which flew right up to the starry chariot of Night. /

When Gradasso recognized the doughty paladin, not through sight of his emblem but by his fearsome blows and by Bayard who seemed alone to dominate the field, he was not slow to fling taunts at him for the poor show he had put up when he failed to appear for their duel on the agreed day and place. / 'Perhaps', he added, 'you hoped that if you could hide on that occasion we should never again come to blows in this world. Well, I've caught you up! Even if you go to the last pit of Hades or are assumed into heaven be sure that I shall follow you— be it to the blind-dark pit or to the supernal light—so long as you possess that steed. / If you haven't the courage to cross swords with me, and you recognize that you cannot stand up to me, and you prize your life above your honour, you can take the safe way out by abandon- ing your horse to me in peace. That way you can stay alive, if life is so dear to you: but live on foot, for you don't deserve a steed if you do so little credit to knighthood.' /

Richardet and Guidone were present at this speech, and they both whipped out their swords to show Gradasso how ill-advised it was. But Rinaldo intervened at once and would not suffer them to attack him. 'Am I incapable', he asked, 'of replying to a detractor without your help?' / Then, turning to the pagan, he said: 'Listen, Gradasso: I want to make it clear to you, if you pay attention, that I did come to the sea-shore to meet you, after which I shall maintain by force of

arms that I have told you the very truth, and that if you repeat that I
ever failed as a knight you shall lie. / But before we start to fight, I
do ask you to be very clear about my excuse, which is fully just and
true, so that you'll no more tax me without cause. Then my wish
shall be that we fight for Bayard on the terms agreed earlier, on foot
in single combat in an isolated spot, just as you stipulated.' / Like
any man of lofty spirit, the King of Sericana proved chivalrous and
was content to have the facts explained to him, as the paladin wanted,
by way of vindication. He accompanied him to the bank of the river,
where Rinaldo in simple words exposed the truth of the matter, calling
all heaven to witness. / Then he sent for Maugis, who was fully con-
versant with the facts, and who described his magic in detail, neither
adding nor suppressing. After this Rinaldo concluded: 'I mean my
arms to prove what this witness adduces: now or whenever you wish,
they will give you the truest proof.' /

King Gradasso, who did not want a second quarrel to interfere with
the first, placidly accepted Rinaldo's excuse, leaving open the question
of whether it was true or not. It was not on the soft shore of Barcelona
that they chose their battle-ground, as they had done before; they
agreed instead to meet in the morning at a spring close by. / Here
Rinaldo would bring his steed, to be placed in the middle, open to
claim. If the king slew Rinaldo or took him prisoner, he was to take
Bayard without more ado; but if Gradasso faltered, he was to be
fought to the death unless, incapable of going on, he surrendered—
in which case he would forfeit Durindana to Rinaldo. / With great
astonishment and greater sorrow (as I have said) Rinaldo had learnt
from fair Fiordiligi that his cousin had taken leave of his senses. He
had also heard about Durindana and about the battle over it, and how
Gradasso was now possessor of this sword which Orlando had embellished with a thousand palms. / Thus agreed, Gradasso returned
to his retinue, though Rinaldo invited him to be his guest.

When day broke the pagan king armed; so did Rinaldo, and they
both repaired to a spot near the spring, where they were to fight for
Bayard and Durindana. / Rinaldo's friends all seemed full of forebodings about the duel he was to fight with Gradasso, and were in
premature mourning: Gradasso was so valiant, strong, and skilful a
fighter and now that he had Orlando's sword at his side, everyone was
pale with fear for Rinaldo. / Who was more anxious and dubious than
any of them about this combat was Maugis; gladly would he have
interfered to make it miscarry, but he did not want to antagonize
Rinaldo any further—he had still not forgiven him for breaking up the
earlier fight by spiriting him onto the boat. / Leaving the others to
their doubts, their fears and gloom, Rinaldo set out happy and self-

assured, hoping now to clear himself of the blame which irked him even though it was unjustified. That would silence the folk from Ponthieu and Hautefeuille more than ever. He set forth in boundless confidence that he would win the honours and the triumph. / Their arrival at the limpid spring, each from his own side, was almost simultaneous. They greeted each other most warmly, showing each other such open friendliness, they might have been boon-companions, blood-brothers. But how they went on to strike each other I should like to relate another time.

THIRTY-SECOND CANTO

*1–9 With Agramant at Arles. 10–43 Bradamant vainly
awaits Ruggiero, and hears allegations of his infidelity.
44–110 Bradamant hears of the Queen of Iceland's embassy,
and has an adventure at Tristan's castle.*

I REMEMBER that I was to relate to you a suspicion (I did promise but then it slipped my mind) which had embittered fair Bradamant against Ruggiero: this suspicion, which had entered her breast to consume her heart, was more distasteful and cruel, its bite had more sting and venom, than that which she had derived from Richardet. / That was to be my song, but I started on another, for Rinaldo intruded, and then Guidone, who kept me busy as he held up Rinaldo's journey awhile. And so I went from one topic to another, quite oblivious of Bradamant. But now I have remembered, and I shall take up her story before continuing that of Rinaldo and Gradasso. /

But before I start I must first talk to you a little about Agramant. He had fallen back on Arles with the survivors of the great nocturnal conflagration, for the city was well-suited to rallying his scattered troops and bringing in reinforcements and provisions: it was situated on the coast, by the riverside; Africa lay opposite, Spain was close by. / Marsilius levied fresh troops throughout his kingdom, both mounted and on foot, regardless of quality. At Barcelona every vessel fit for service was made ready, by devoted (or constrained) efforts. Daily Agramant called a council and balked at no expense, at no exertion. Meanwhile frequent and heavy exactions were levied upon all the oppressed towns of Africa. / To obtain Rodomont's return (solicitation proving ineffective) he had the offer made to him of a royal cousin, daughter of Almont, with the kingdom of Oran for her dowry. But His Arrogance would not leave his bridge where he had collected so many arms and emptied so many saddles of those who had passed his way, and had covered his tomb with them. /

Marfisa, however, would not copy Rodomont, indeed not—when she heard that Agramant had been defeated by Charlemagne, his men slaughtered, captured, and robbed, and that he had retired to Arles with the small remnant, she set out thither without awaiting an invitation. She came to the support of his crown, offering him her worldly goods and her person. / With her she brought Brunello, and made a free gift of him to the king. She had held him ten days and ten nights, keeping him in constant fear of hanging, but had never laid a finger on him. Seeing that no one came forward to take up his cause, either by force or by intercession, she would not sully her proud hands in such despised blood, and let him go. / She forgave him all his past offences and brought him with her to Agramant at Arles. Imagine the king's delight at her coming to his assistance: as evidence of the store he set by it he appointed Brunello his witness—Marfisa had evinced a wish to hang him, so hanged he was forthwith. / He left the knave in a barren, deserted spot, food for the crows and vultures. Ruggiero, who had shielded him on an earlier occasion and might have saved his neck from the noose, was now ill and could not help him: such was the dispensation of divine justice. When he did hear of it, the deed was already done, so Brunello was left to his fate. /

Bradamant meanwhile was complaining at the length of those twenty days, the completion of which was to bring Ruggiero back to her and to the Faith. One who longs to return from prison or exile cannot wait for the day when he will recover his liberty or the blessed, longed-for sight of his beloved land. / The waiting was hard: Apollo's horses must be lame, she sometimes thought, or a wheel must have broken on the Sun-chariot, for it seemed unusually slow in its passage. To her each day seemed longer than the day when the Sun stopped in his course at the word of faithful Joshua; every night seemed longer than the night which had brought forth Hercules. / Oh how she envied the bears, the dormice, the somnolent badgers! How she would like to have slept through that whole period, never waking, hearing nothing until Ruggiero aroused her from torpid slumbers! But, far from being able to do this, she could not sleep one hour all night. / Now one cheek now the other she would press to her wearisome pillow without ever finding rest. Often she would open the window to see if Tithonus' bride was yet scattering her white lilies and red roses before the morning light. And once the day was dawned, she was no less anxious to see the sky decked with stars. /

When only five days or so remained, she stood in high hopes of a messenger arriving from one hour to the next to announce Ruggiero. She often climbed to a high tower which commanded a view over the dense woods and smiling countryside and over a stretch of the road leading to Montauban. / If she descried a flash of arms in the distance, or anything suggestive of a knight, she believed it must be her own Ruggiero, and her fair brow cleared. If it were an unarmed rider, or a man on foot, she grasped the hope that it might be a messenger from him—and even if this hope proved deceptive, she never stopped clutching at fresh ones. / Sometimes she would arm and ride down from the hill-top, confident of going out to meet him; but, not finding him, she expected that he would have arrived at Montauban by some other road, and the very desire which had lured her out of the castle sent her back inside on a fool's errand: she found him neither here nor there. /

Meanwhile the time-limit she had so yearned for expired. / It was one day over the limit; then two, three, six, eight, twenty days. Seeing no sign of her betrothed, hearing no news of him, she began to grieve in a way which would have moved to pity the snake-haired Furies in the realms of darkness. She vented her feelings upon her beautiful eyes, her white bosom, her golden curls. / 'Is it true then,' she cried, 'that I must seek for one who avoids and hides from me? Am I to prize one who disdains me, to entreat one who never answers me? Shall I suffer one who hates me to possess my heart, one who so esteems his lofty virtues that it would take an immortal goddess descending from heaven to kindle his heart to love? / He knows, the haughty man, that I love and adore him, but he will not have me for lover, nor for slave. He knows, the cruel man, how I am throbbing and dying for him, but he waits for my death before helping me. He hides from me for fear I may narrate to him my agony, which would be enough to bend his wayward will—like the asp, which, to protect its noxiousness, will not be lulled by song. / Oh stop him, Love, as he hastens away, free as the wind, and I run sluggishly after him; or restore me to the condition whence you took me, when I was subject neither to you nor to anyone. Alas, how vain and foolish are my hopes of ever winning you to pity by entreaties! You delight in drawing rivers of tears from people's eyes—this is meat and drink to you! / But on what can I put the blame if not on my own unreasoning desire? It wafts me up sky-high, so high that its wings get singed, so that they cannot sustain flight but leave me to tumble from the sky. But this is not the end of it: again my desire dons its wings, again they are scorched, so that I am in for ceaseless falls. /

'No, far more than on my desire, I should put the blame on myself for having admitted it to my breast: it has driven reason from its seat, and the best of my power can achieve less than my desire. It keeps transporting me from bad to worse, but I cannot rein it in for it has no rein.

And it assures me that it leads me to my death so that the expectation of it may augment my pain. / But why should I blame myself? What wrong, other than loving you, did I ever commit? What wonder if my frail, weak woman's senses were at once overwhelmed? Was I to resort to shielding myself lest I be struck by your superb looks, your noble presence, the shrewdness of your speech? Wretched indeed are those who avoid sight of the sun! / It was not only my fate which urged me on, but the trustworthy advice of others. Utter bliss was depicted to me as accruing from this love. Alas, if I was persuaded falsely, if the counsel that Merlin gave me was deceptive, I may well blame him—but I cannot withdraw my love from Ruggiero. / Merlin I can blame, and Melissa too, and so I shall for all time: they used infernal spirits to show me the fruit of my womb so as to enslave me with this false hope alone. I cannot see why they did it, unless perhaps they envied me my sweet, safe, blessed tranquillity.' /

She was so possessed by grief that no room was left in her for consolation. And yet, despite this, Hope would arrive and insist upon taking up residence in her breast, reviving memories of what Ruggiero told her at parting. Against the opinion of the other emotions, Hope would have her still expect his return. / A month past the time-limit, then, Hope was sustaining her, so that her spirits were less oppressed by grief than they would otherwise have been.

One day, though, as she was out on the road she often took in the hope of meeting Ruggiero, the poor damsel heard news which finally routed Hope as well. / She met a Gascon knight who had come straight from the African camp, where he had been held prisoner ever since the great battle before Paris. She engaged him in an intensive conversation, leading him to her prescribed goal when she asked after Ruggiero: on him she now dwelt to the exclusion of all else. / The knight gave a full account of him, for he knew the whole Saracen court. He described how Ruggiero had fought single-handed against stout Mandricard, and how he killed him only to lie wounded for a month, at death's door. Had his story ended here, he would have rightly exculpated Ruggiero. / But, as he added, there was a damsel in the camp named Marfisa, who was as beautiful as she was valiant, and no novice in the use of arms; Ruggiero loved her and she him, and they were seldom found outside each other's company—in the camp it was generally assumed that they had plighted their troth. / When Ruggiero was cured, he continued, the wedding was to be announced. This would highly delight every pagan king and prince: recognizing the superhuman valour attaching to them both, they expected the couple shortly to produce a race of warriors the likes of which were never known. /

The Gascon believed what he spoke, and not without cause, for it was the common opinion and belief throughout the Moorish camp, the topic on everyone's lips. What gave rise to these rumours were the many signs of goodwill that had passed between the pair. Rumour, be it good or bad, has only to issue from one person's lips for it to multiply endlessly. / The belief was established by her having come with him to the Moors' rescue, and never being seen except in his company; but what reinforced it was that, having quit the camp earlier, taking Brunello (as I described), she had returned, without any prior summons, purely to see Ruggiero. / She came into the camp not once but several times solely to visit him as he languished with his grievous wound. She would stay with him all day and leave in the evening. And she gave people all the more scope for gossip in that she had a reputation for haughtiness, deeming everyone contemptible: to Ruggiero alone did she offer kindness and respect. / As the Gascon affirmed the truth of his statement, Bradamant was a prey to so fierce an onslaught of anguish, it was all she could do not to collapse. Bursting with furious rage and jealousy she turned her steed without a word and, banishing all hope, turned homeward fuming. /

Still in her armour, she fell prone onto her bed, and, to avoid attracting attention to her cries, stuffed the bedclothes into her mouth. As she repeated what the knight had told her she plumbed such depths of sorrow that she could no longer endure it but had to vent her feelings, which she did in these words: / 'Ah me, whom shall I ever trust now? Every man must be faithless and cruel if you, my Ruggiero, are faithless and cruel, you whom I held to be so good and true. What cruelty, what base betrayal was ever heard mentioned in tragic laments but is not to be accounted less evil than yours, if you think of your indebtedness and my deserving! / As there lives no knight who is more dashing or more handsome than you, Ruggiero, none who is a patch on your valour, your breeding, or your nobility, why could you not have constancy ascribed to you along with your eminent, godlike qualities, and inviolable loyalty, to which all other virtues bow and yield? /

'Don't you know that neither valour nor nobility can be seen in its absence—just as no object (be it never so beautiful) can be seen where there is no light? It was easy for you to deceive a damsel whose lord and god, whose idol you were: you could have persuaded me that the sun was dark and cold. / What sin do you regret, cruel one, if you are not sorry for killing one who loves you? If you so make light of breaking your word, what is there that will burden your conscience? How do you treat your enemies if you torment me thus, who love you so? I shall avow that there is no justice in heaven if I am slow in seeing myself avenged. / If black ingratitude is the one sin that weighs heaviest on a man's soul—and for this Heaven's brightest angel was relegated to a place of cavernous darkness—and if a bad fault provokes a great scourge unless the heart be cleansed by proper amends: mind that a harsh scourge does not alight on you, thankless as you are and unwilling to atone. / You are greatly to blame also, cruel one, for theft, the worst of vices: not because you possess my heart—I would pardon you that—but because you have made yourself mine only to retrieve yourself from me against all reason. Give yourself back to me, wicked one: you well know that there is no saving one who keeps another's property. /

'You have left me, Ruggiero. I do not want to leave you, and even if I willed it, I should be unable to do so. But to escape from my wretchedness I can and want to end my days. My only regret is that I do not die in your good favour: had the gods allowed me to die when I was your beloved, death would never have been so blessed.' /

So saying, she jumped off the bed, disposed to die, and in a passion set her sword-point against her left side—until she noticed that she was in full armour. Now at this juncture her better spirit approached her and reasoned with her thus: 'O woman born of so exalted a stock, do you want to end your days so guiltily? / Would you not do better to go into battle where you might die with greater honour? If there you happened to fall to Ruggiero, he might yet regret your dying. But if you did die at his hands, who could possibly die happier than you? It is fitting that he should deprive you of life as he is the cause of your living in such sorrow. / It may happen that before you die you will avenge yourself on Marfisa who, by alienating Ruggiero with stratagems and guilty love, has been the death of you.' These thoughts seemed better to the damsel.

She at once made a device on her arms to betoken despair and the will to die. / Her surcoat was the colour to which the leaf turns as it fades once it is plucked from the tree, or when the tree's life-giving sap dries up. It was embroidered with trunks of the cypress, which never recovers its vigour once it has felt the hard axe. This garment was most suitable to her mournful state. / She took the horse which belonged to Astolfo, and the golden lance which tipped knights from the saddle at the lightest touch. Why Astolfo gave it to her, and where and when and from whom he himself had had it, I believe I need not repeat. She took it, then, but without knowing its incredible properties. / Without a page or any company she descended the hill and set out by the most direct route to Paris, where the Saracen camp had been—the news was not yet out that Rinaldo, helped by Charlemagne and Maugis, had raised the siege of Paris. /

She had left behind her the Quercy and Cahors, and the range from which the Dordogne River sprang into view, with Montferrant and Clermont, when she saw a woman coming along the same road; she had a pleasing look, and from her saddle a shield was slung. Three knights rode beside her. / More damsels and pages came too, in procession, some preceding, others following. Bradamant asked one of the men as he passed her who the woman was, and he replied: 'She has been sent as a messenger to the King of the French; she has come from beyond the Arctic Pole on a long sea-voyage from the Lost Island. / Some call it the Lost Island, others, Iceland, the land from where this shield you see is being sent to Charlemagne. Its sender is the island's queen, whose beauty is a very miracle—beauty such as Heaven has never before conceded to anyone. She has sent the shield subject to one express condition—the king is to give it to the knight who, in his opinion, is the world's paragon. / As she regards herself—and rightly so—as the most beautiful woman that ever lived, she wishes to find a knight who is unsurpassed for courage and strength. She is rooted and fixed in her intention (which is proof against a hundred thousand shocks), that none but the man who holds the primacy of honour in arms shall be her lover and her lord. / She hopes that in France, at the renowned court of Charlemagne, the knight may be discovered who will have furnished a thousand proofs that he is the mightiest and most courageous of all.

'The three accompanying the messenger are all kings and I shall tell you where from: one is from Sweden, one from Gothenburg, and one from Norway, and as warriors they have few, if any, peers. / These three, whose realms, though not close to, are less remote from the Lost Island (so called because its shores are known to few mariners), were and are lovers of the queen and rival suitors for her hand. To please her they have done feats which will be narrated as long as the heavens revolve. / But neither these will she accept, nor any other who is not, in her belief, the foremost champion of the world. "I am little impressed", she would tell them, "at feats you have wrought in our part of the world. And should one of you stand out from the other two as the sun among the stars, I shall think highly of him—and yet he will not seem to me to hold the distinction of being the best knight today bearing arms. / I propose to send to Charlemagne, whom I esteem and honour as the wisest sovereign in the world, a rich golden shield, on the condition that he award it to the knight who holds pride of place for valour among his warriors, whether that knight be his vassal or another's. The king's opinion shall, I propose, sharpen my judgement. / Once Charles has received the shield and presented it to the knight whose strength and courage he deems pre-eminent in any court— his own or another's—if one of you is able by sheer prowess to retrieve the shield for me, I will repose in that one all my love, all my desire, and will make him my consort and master." / These words have brought these three kings here from so remote a sea; they are resolved either to fetch back the shield or else to die at the hands of its new owner.'

Bradamant paid close attention to the page's explanation. He now pulled ahead of her and spurred his horse till he caught up with his companions. / She did not hasten after him at a gallop, but slowly pursued her way, pondering many thoughts and future prospects: she felt that this shield was bound to breed dissensions, quarrels, and immense antagonisms in France among the paladins and others, if Charles made to establish who was supreme champion and award it to him. / She was oppressed by this thought; but what oppressed her far more and caused her worse distress was her earlier thought, of Ruggiero who had withdrawn his love from her to bestow it upon Marfisa.

Her every sense was so steeped in this that she paid no attention to her road or thought where she was heading for or whether she would find comfortable quarters for the night. / As a boat, parted from the shore by the wind or other hazard, is carried adrift on the flood with no hand at the helm, so was the love-struck damsel, all wrapped up in thoughts of her Ruggiero, borne along as Rabican chose—her spirit, which should have minded the reins, was far, far away. / At last she raised her eyes and saw that the Sun had turned his back on the cities of Bochus, Mauretania's king, to plunge like a duck into the lap of his nurse, beyond Morocco. If her idea was to find accommodation out in the open in the brushwood, she was most unwise—a cold wind was blowing, and tonight she would be threatened with driving rain or snow. / She urged her horse to a faster pace, and in a little while saw a shepherd leaving the fields, driving his flock before him. She pressed him earnestly to tell her where she could find lodging, be it good or bad: however bad it might be, a night out in the rain would be worse. /

'I know of no place', replied the shepherd, 'that is less than some six leagues from here, except for one called Tristan's castle. But not everyone is able to put up there: the knight who means to stay there has first to acquire the right, lance in hand, and then to defend it. / If a knight finds room at the castle on his arrival, the lord of the castle will receive him, but on condition that the guest promises, if others arrive, to go out and joust with them. Should no one else turn up, there is no need for the guest to move; but if someone does arrive, he needs must re-arm himself and joust with him, and the one who comes off worse must give up his lodging and go out into the open air. / If two, three, four, or more warriors arrive there first all together, they can lodge there in peace, while whoever arrives alone after them is faced with a worse proposition: he has to joust with all of them together. Similarly, if a single traveller has arrived first, he will have to joust with the two, three, four, or more who arrive later. So if he has valour, he shall need every bit of it. / Similarly, if a woman or maid, whether accompanied or alone, arrives at this castle, and if, after her, another arrives, the more beautiful is accommodated while the lesser beauty has to stay outside.'

Bradamant asked where this place was, and the worthy shepherd replied not only in words but by pointing in the direction, some six miles away. / Although Rabican was a swift-footed steed, the damsel was unable to spur him along those roads, all muddy and pitted (the season being somewhat rainy), fast enough to arrive before sightless night had spread darkness on all sides. She found the gate shut, and informed the porter that she required lodging. / He replied that the place was occupied by ladies and knights who had arrived earlier and were now waiting round the fire for supper to be placed before them. 'I don't expect that the cook will have prepared it for *them*, if it is still there and they have not yet eaten it,' asserted Bradamant. 'Run along now. Here I am waiting for them—I know the rules, and mean to observe them.' /

The porter left and brought the message in to where the knights were taking their ease. They were none too pleased at the summons to go out and face the rigours of the cold. A heavy rain had started to fall. But they arose, sluggishly took up their arms, and in no great haste issued forth to where the damsel awaited them. The other guests remained within. / They were three knights whose attainments few men alive could surpass—and they were, furthermore, the very ones seen earlier that day with their ambassadress, the three who had boasted that they would fetch the golden shield from France back to Iceland. And because they had spurred their horses faster they had arrived ahead of Bradamant. / Few could outdo them in battle, but she would certainly be one of those few—she had no intention of spending the night out of doors, hungry and wet through. Those left within watched the joust from the windows and galleries by the light of the moon, which shone down despite the clouds and the driving rain. /

Imagine a lover, his passions aroused as he is about to gain admittance to enjoy some sweet thieving: he thrills when, after so much delay, he at last hears the bolt softly withdrawn. Similarly Bradamant, eager to try conclusions with the knights, rejoiced on hearing the gate opened, the bridge lowered, and on seeing them come forth. / The moment she saw the warriors come out across the drawbridge in close order, she turned to give herself room, then came charging back full tilt, resting her lance: this was the lance given her by her cousin Astolfo, which was never tilted in vain, but needs must tip out of the saddle every warrior it touches, were he Mars himself. / The King of Sweden was the first to charge, and the first to hit the ground, such was the impact of the lance (never lowered in vain) upon his helmet. Then in came the King of Gothenburg, only to find himself parted from his steed, head over heels. The third king landed upside-down, half-buried in a pool of slush. / As soon as with three strokes she had sent them all into headlong dives, she went up to the castle where she was to have shelter for the night. But before she entered, she was put under oath to go forth again in the event that she was called out to joust.

The lord of the castle, who had witnessed her high valour, paid her great respect. / So did the damsel who had arrived here this evening with the three kings, as I said, from the Lost Island, the ambassadress to the King of France. As Bradamant greeted her she politely rose (for she was gracious and affable) and, placidly taking her by the hand, led her to the fireside. / Now Bradamant started to disarm. She set down her shield and drew off her helmet, but a golden band with which she concealed and contained her long tresses came off with the helmet, so that her hair fell loosely over her shoulders, all at once revealing her for a maiden no less beautiful than fierce in battle. / As when the curtains part to reveal the scene—arcades, sumptuous buildings, statues, paintings, gilding everywhere, all lit with a thousand lamps; or when the Sun shows his face, clear and serene, through the clouds: so the damsel, lifting the helmet from her face, showed as it were a glimpse of paradise. / Her splendid tresses which the friar had cropped had now grown out again so that they could be gathered at the back of her head, though they were not the way they used to be. The lord of the castle was quite clear in his mind that this was Bradamant, whom he had seen on previous occasions, and now he made much of her and showed her respect even more than previously. / They sat beside the fire, regaling their ears with merry, honest conversation while other fare was being prepared to refresh the rest of the body.

Bradamant asked her host whether this system of obtaining lodging was newly devised or an old tradition, and when it was started, and by whom. He answered her thus: / 'In the reign of Fieramont, his son Clodion had a lady-love who was as dainty, beautiful, and refined as any lady in those days of old. He so loved her that he never took his eyes off her, any more than the shepherd Argus did off Io, so it is said, for his jealousy equalled his love. / He kept her here (for he had received this castle as a gift from his father) and seldom did he go out. With him he kept ten knights, among the best in France. While he was here, who should arrive but worthy Tristan, escorting a damsel whom he had rescued a few hours earlier; he was pulling along a fierce giant he had captured. / Tristan arrived when the Sun had already turned his back to the shores beyond Seville, and asked to be accommodated here, for there was no other lodging within ten miles. But Clodion, a man consumed with love and jealousy, decided that no stranger, whoever he be, should enter here while his fair lady was in residence. /

'After long and repeated entreaties had failed to secure him lodging, "Very well," he proposed, "what I cannot bring you to do by entreaties, I hope to make you do in spite of yourself." And he challenged Clodion and all ten of his retainers with a ringing cry, offering to prove, with lance and sword, that the prince was a discourteous boor. / His proposal was that if he unseated Clodion and his men while he himself firmly kept his saddle, he would stay in the castle all by himself and would lock him and his party out. Clodion, to avoid suffering this humiliation, risked meeting his death—a savage blow felled him to the ground, and the others likewise, and Tristan locked them out. / He entered the castle and found the lady I have mentioned, on whom Clodion doted; she was as beautiful as any other woman embellished with the gifts of Nature (no lavish giver). He conversed with her while her lover, outside the walls, was scorched and pummelled by the direst passion; he lost no time in sending pleas to Tristan not to refuse her to him. / Now although Tristan cared but little for her, and would never have been able to cherish any woman but Iseult (for the magic potion he had drunk prevented his according love or affection to any other woman), he wanted his revenge upon Clodion for his uncivil behaviour; so "I should deem it a great error", he replied, "for such a beauty to leave her residence. / If Clodion does not relish sleeping alone in the bushes but demands company, I have with me a fair, fresh young maid, though of less effulgent beauty. I am content for her to go out and obey him in all that he commands; but it seems to me right and proper that the fairest damsel should remain with the most stalwart among us." /

'Shut out as he was, unhappy Clodion roamed about all night long, fretting and fuming, as though on sentry-go for those sleeping comfortably within. Far more than at the cold and the wind he complained at the loss of his beloved's company. In the morning Tristan, feeling sorry for him, handed her over, putting paid to his torment, / for he told him, and made it absolutely clear, that he was returning her exactly as he had found her. Though he deserved every sort of penalty, he said, for his uncivil behaviour, he would rest satisfied with having kept him out of doors all night. He rejected the excuse that Love was to blame for so grave a fault: / Love should ennoble a base heart, not degrade a noble one. After Tristan's departure, Clodion lost no time in changing residence. But first he consigned the castle to a knight, a close friend, on the understanding that he, and whoever happened this way, should always follow this practice in the matter of lodging: / the stronger knight, the fairer lady was to be accommodated, while the vanquished party was to vacate the premises and sleep in the fields or anyway go to roost elsewhere. He had this laid down as a practice which, as you see, has lasted to our own day.'

While the host was relating this, the steward had had the supper laid / in the great hall (a more splendid one existed nowhere on earth), and from this hall he arrived with flaming sconces to lead in the fair damsels. As she entered, Bradamant looked about her, and so did the other maiden; they saw that the lofty walls were covered with the most noble of murals. / Such beautiful figures adorned the walls that, in gazing at them, they almost forgot about supper, even though they were fully ready for it, their bodies wearied from the day's exertions. The steward was dismayed, and so was the cook, that they were leaving the dishes to grow cold. 'You would do better to feed your bellies first,' it was suggested, 'and later your eyes.' /

They sat down, then, and were ready to set to when the host realized how wrong it was for him to harbour two women: one was to stay, the other had to be evicted—the more beautiful was to remain, the less to be banished to where the rain lashed and the wind howled. As they had not both arrived together, one had to leave, the other to stay. / He summoned two old men and some of his maid servants as proper judges in the matter. He scrutinized the two damsels and compared them to see which was the fairer. The ultimate conviction of all of them was that Bradamant was the fairer: she defeated the other damsel in beauty no less than she had defeated the warriors in valour. / To the damsel from Iceland, who was not a little uneasy about all this, the host said: 'You are not to see anything dishonourable in the observance of this custom. You must find yourself other lodging, for it is perfectly clear to all of us here that this damsel, though unadorned, surpasses you in beauty.' / As one may see a dark cloud rise in a few moments from a dank valley to obscure the face of the sun which has been so luminous: so at the hard sentence driving her forth into the rain and frost the damsel visibly changed, and no longer looked the gay, beautiful woman she had been up till then. / She paled and her face fell, for the sentence she heard was not to her liking.

But Bradamant, who pitied her and did not want her to leave, shrewdly remarked: 'It does not seem to me that any judgement can be regarded as mature and just unless an audience has first been given to the interested party, her denials and observations taken into account. / I, who am embracing her cause, affirm that, whether or not I am fairer than she, I did not gain admittance as a woman and I will not have my prospects determined as though I were one—who shall say, unless I take off all my clothes, whether or not I am of the same sex as she?

Well, what is not known should be left unspoken, especially when someone would suffer for it. / There are others who have hair as long as
mine, but this does not make them women. Whether I gained admittance as a knight or as a woman is evident enough: so why do you want
to attribute the female sex to me when all my actions have been a man's?
Your law requires that women should be ousted by women, not by
warriors. / And supposing I were a woman as you think (though I don't
admit it) but that my beauty were not up to this damsel's; I don't
imagine, even so, that you would want to deprive me of the reward of
my valour, even if I came second in comeliness. It does not seem to me
just to lose through inadequate beauty what I have won by valour at
arms. / And even if that were the rule, and the loser of the beauty-
contest had to leave, I should want to remain, whatever good or ill
might result from my obstinacy. From this you will surmise that the
contest between myself and this damsel is unequal: in a beauty-contest
she stands to lose a great deal, but could never prevail against me. / Now
where there is not an equal chance to win or lose, any contest must be
unfair; as a right, then, or as a special concession, let lodging not be
denied her. And if anyone dares maintain that my judgement is not
good and sound, I am ready to sustain it against him any time he
chooses—mine is right, his is wrong!' /

Moved to pity at the prospect of the gentle damsel being unjustly
driven out into the rain, where there was no roof for her, not so much
as an awning, Bradamant persuaded their host, with many arguments
and well-chosen words (but especially with her concluding remark) to
say no more but to accept her excuses. / Imagine a flower under the
most parching summer heat, when the grass is at its thirstiest: it is on
the point of exhausting the juices which keep it alive, when it feels the
beloved rain and is revivified. Similarly, seeing so challenging a defence mounted for her, the lady-messenger recovered all her lost gaiety
and beauty. / The supper, which had been placed before them some
while since but had remained untouched, was now enjoyed to the full
without any new knight-errant arriving to spoil the fun. The others
enjoyed it, but not Bradamant, still plunged in her gloomy sorrow—the
unjust fear and suspicion lodged in her heart spoiled her appetite. /
When she had finished—she would perhaps have taken longer were
it not for her desire to feast her eyes—she got up, and the other damsel
with her. And an attendant, at the host's signal, hastened off to light
plenty of candles, which spread light to every corner of the hall. What
followed I shall relate in the next canto.

THIRTY-THIRD CANTO

*1–5 Introductory. 5–58 French interventions in Italy foretold
in murals. 59–77 Bradamant discomfits the three kings, who
do penance. 78–95 Rinaldo's and Gradasso's fight interrupted,
to the latter's advantage. 96–128 In Nubia, Astolfo does
battle with the harpies.*

IN days of old there were painters like Timagoras, Parrhasius, Polignotus, Protogenes, Timantes, Apollodorus, Apelles (the most renowned
of these), and Zeuxis, artists whose fame (even though their bodies and
their works are extinct at Clotho's hands) will endure for ever, so long
as there are writers, and therefore reading and writing. / And in our
own day artists have lived, and still survive, such as Leonardo, Andrea
Mantegna, Giovanni Bellini, the two Dossis, and Michelangelo (who
equally as sculptor and painter is more divine than human), Sebastiano
del Piombo, Raphael, and Titian (the boast respectively of Venice,
Urbino, and Cadore), and others whose work is visibly of the same
eminence as is ascribed to the painters of old. / Now these painters
whose works we can see, and those who were in high regard thousands
of years ago used their brushes, either on panels or on walls, to depict
scenes which had happened. But you never hear of the ancients having
painted the future—nor is this evident in any contemporary work. And
yet scenes have been discovered that were depicted before they actually
took place. / But let no painter of old or of today boast that he can do
this: even art must yield here to simple magic which causes tremors to
the spirits in hell. Now this hall I mentioned in the last canto was
painted in a single night by demons summoned by Merlin with his
book—consecrated at Lake Avernus or else in the cave at Norcia. / This
magic art, with which our ancestors worked wonders, is extinct in our
own day.

But to return to the hall, where those who are to see the murals must
be waiting for me: as I said, at a signal a page lit the sconces and the
night, overwhelmed by the brightness, ebbed away, so that one would
not have seen better had it been broad daylight. / 'Up till today,' their
host explained to them, 'few of the wars here depicted have actually
taken place: they were painted before they happened, the artist having
divined them. You will be able to see depicted the occasions when
our troops will meet with victory in Italy, when with defeat. / In this

room Merlin the prophet disclosed the wars (successful or not) which
the French were to fight beyond the Alps from his day for the next
thousand years. He had been sent by the King of Britain to the Frankish
king who succeeded Marcomir—here is why he was sent and why he
had the work done. / After King Fieramont had occupied France—he
was the first to cross the Rhine into France with a Frankish army—
he conceived the idea of curbing proud Italy. This was because he saw
the Holy Roman Empire sinking further every day. And he wanted to
enlist Arthur, King of Britain, in his cause—for they were contempor-
aries. / But Arthur never embarked on any enterprise without first
consulting Merlin, a demon's son who could foresee a great deal of
the future. From him he discovered the dangers and the many trials
to which Fieramont would expose his men if he invaded the land divided by the Apennines and bounded by the Alps and the sea. All this
he imparted to the Frankish king. /

'Merlin showed him that nearly every king who was later to have the
sceptre of France would see his armies destroyed by the sword, or by
famine or plague; they would bring back from Italy fleeting happiness
and prolonged misery, little profit and endless harm—for there was no
warrant for the French Lilies taking root in Italian soil. / King Fieramont believed him, so much so that he determined on a different goal
for his army. And it is thought that Merlin, who could see what was to
come as though it were already past, had the full history magically
depicted in this hall at that king's request. The king had every future
action of the French divulged just as if it had already happened, / to
impress upon his successors that by taking up the defence of Italy
against all foreign aggression they could win victory and honour,
whereas whoever descended upon Italy to injure her, to place the yoke
upon her and tyrannize her was to be under no illusion but that beyond
the mountains he would find his grave yawning.' /

This said, he brought the ladies to the first of the paintings and
showed them Sigbert setting forth after being offered riches by the
Emperor Maurice. 'Here he is coming down from the Great St.
Bernard Pass into the plain formed by the Ambra and the Ticino. Here
is Autharis not merely repulsing the invader but routing him in a
shattering defeat. / Here is Clovis leading a force over a hundred
thousand strong over the mountains. Here the Duke of Benevento is
coming to confront him, outnumbered though he is. Here the duke is
pretending to leave his camp, and preparing an ambush; and here are
the French troops hastening to their abasement and death, lured by the
Lombard wine, like the carp rising to the bait. / See all the French
troops and captains dispatched to Italy by Childebert. But he no more
than Clovis can boast of having ravaged and conquered Lombardy: the

sword from heaven falls upon his army and wreaks such slaughter that every road is full of corpses, dead from the heat and from dysentery—not one in ten returns to safety.' / He showed Pepin, then Charlemagne descending on Italy, one after the other. For both the outcome was happy, for they had not come to harm her: Pepin had come to defend persecuted Pope Stephen; Charlemagne to defend first Adrian and then Leo. Pepin subdued Astolfo the Lombard, Charles defeated and captured his successor and restored the Pope's honour. / Next he showed them a younger Pepin whose forces appeared to extend solidly from the Po delta at Le Fornaci to the coast at Pelestrina. With great trouble and expense he builds a bridge from Malamocco extending to Rialto, and fights on it. Then he is shown fleeing, leaving his men to drown, for the wind and the sea has destroyed his bridge. /

'Here you can see Louis of Burgundy on his way to his defeat and capture. His captor makes him swear never more to take up arms against him, but here he is forswearing his oath, and here he is falling into a trap again. Here he is losing his eyes, and his men bring him back across the Alps, blind as a mole. / Here a certain Hugh of Arles is performing mighty deeds and expelling the Lombard Berengarii from Italy; two or three times he breaks their power after they have been restored, first by the Huns, then by the Bavarians. Finally he is overpowered and constrained to make a truce with the enemy, which he does not long survive. Neither does his heir outlive him long; he has to cede his entire kingdom to Berengarius. / Look at another Charles—of Anjou—setting Italy afire to assist the good Pastor; in two fierce battles he slays two kings: first Manfred, then Conradin. But now look at his forces oppressing the new kingdom with a thousand wrongs: here they are, scattered about among the cities and all killed as the bell tolls for Vespers.' / Then he showed them a French commander, the Count of Armagnac, coming down from the Alps to make war against the noble Viscontis (after an interval measured not in scores of years but of decades). The picture showed him investing Alessandria with French troops, mounted and on foot. But Visconti had placed a garrison inside the town and set an ambush a little outside it, / and the unwary French were skilfully lured into the trap, together with Armagnac, whose allies had drawn him into the unfortunate adventure. Their dead lay scattered about the fields while some of them were captured and brought into Alessandria. And the Tanaro, brimming with blood no less than with water, is shown dyeing the Po crimson. /

He next pointed out a certain Count della Marca and, each in turn, three Anjous: 'Look', he said, 'how they keep making trouble for the people who live in Calabria, Apulia, the Abruzzi, and Lecce. But no French or Italian help is enough to keep any of them on the throne—

see how Alfonso of Aragon, and then Ferdinand, drive them out as often as they return. / Look at Charles the Eighth coming down from the Alps with the pick of the French forces. He crosses the Liri and takes the whole kingdom of Naples without once resorting to lance or sword; the one exception is Ischia (the rock which straddles Typheus, pinioning his chest, belly, and arms) for he meets resistance from brave Inico del Vasto, of the noble blood of the Davalos.' /

After showing her Ischia, the lord of the castle, who was explaining the story to Bradamant, observed: 'Before I take you any further I shall tell you what my great-grandfather used to tell me when I was a child —something he said that he had heard from his own father, / who in turn had it from someone else (father or grandfather), and so on, one from another back to the one who had it directly from Merlin, who had these paintings you see executed without a brush in white, blue, and red. He had heard that when Merlin showed the king the castle I am now showing you on that high cliff, he explained to him what I shall now tell you. / In this castle, the king had been told, there was to be born at that time or shortly after—he was told the year and the day— a son to the valiant knight who defended it so courageously (he seemed to despise the fire raging on all sides and as far as the Faro). He would be a knight beside whom every man born hitherto would come second. / Nireus was not so handsome, Achilles not so outstanding for strength, Ulysses not so adventurous, Ladas not so swift, Nestor not so wise— though he knew so much and lived so long—Caesar not so clement and magnanimous (as he is reputed to have been), but their every boast weighed lightly against those of the knight to be born in Ischia. / And if ancient Crete gloried in being the birthplace of Jupiter, Caelus' grand-son; and if Thebes found joy as birthplace of Hercules and Bacchus; and if the boast of Delos was its twins, Apollo and Semele—then this island will not have to remain silent but soar to the skies in exaltation when it becomes the birthplace of the great marquis upon whom Heaven will lavish every grace. / Merlin told him, and told him often, that this birth was reserved for when the Holy Roman Empire was at its lowest ebb, so that he should be instrumental in restoring it to freedom. But as I am about to show you some of his feats, there is no need to describe them in advance.' With these words he returned to the murals at the point where Charles the Eighth's shining deeds were being depicted. /

'Here is Lodovico Sforza regretting having introduced Charles into Italy: he had called him in to harass his traditional rival, in Naples, not to drive him out. On his return, therefore, Charles discovers in Lodo-vico an enemy in league with the Venetians; he tries to capture the king, who courageously lowers his lance—as you see—and forces his passage willy nilly. / But those he has left behind to defend the new realm meet with quite a different fate: Ferdinand, assisted by the Marquis of Mantua, makes such a counter-attack that a few months later not one of them is left alive, on land or sea. However, the loss of a colleague treacherously slain seems to have marred his enjoyment of victory.' / With these words he pointed out Alfonso, Marquis of Pescara and went on: 'After a thousand enterprises shall have revealed in him a brilliance greater than a diamond's, he falls into a trap set for him by a double-dealing African villain: here he is, the finest knight of his day, falling, pierced through the neck by an arrow.' /

Next he showed them Louis the Twelfth crossing the mountains with Italian assistance; ousting Lodovico Sforza, he plants the fleur-de-lys in the fruitful Visconti territory. From here he sends troops in Charles' footsteps to bridge the Garigliano, but here they are broken and scattered, slaughtered or drowned in the river. / 'See the French army in Apulia enduring no less a carnage as it flees. And the man who has trapped them on two occasions is the Spaniard Consalvo Ferrante. But if Fortune frowns upon King Louis here, she smiles on him in the rich plain between the Alps and the Apennines which the Po divides as far as the surging Adriatic.' / This said, he reproached himself for overlooking what he should have mentioned earlier; and he turned back to point out a man selling the castle which his lord had entrusted to him. And he showed the treacherous Swiss capturing the man who had paid them to defend him. These two actions gave victory to the King of France with never a blow struck. /

Then he showed Caesar Borgia enhancing his position in Italy by this king's favour: every baron, every nobleman subject to Rome is shown being sent into exile. Next he showed the king removing from Bologna the Saw-emblem of the Bentivoglios and replacing it with the Della Rovere Acorns; then the rebellious Genoese being put to flight and their city subjugated. / 'See the countryside round Ghiaradadda strewn with corpses; every city opens its gates to the king and Venice barely escapes. And here is the king refusing to allow the Pope to cross the borders of Romagna and wrest Modena from the Duke of Ferrara— the Pope would not stop at that, but would have taken everything else from him too. / In his turn the king wrests Bologna from the Pope and restores the Bentivoglios. Look at the French troops retaking Brescia and sacking it. At almost the same time they relieve Bologna and rout the papal army. Then both sides, as you see, are betaking themselves to the low ground along the coastlands of Ravenna. / Here are the French; over there the Spaniards are swelling the ranks, and a mighty battle ensues. On either side troops are shown falling and dyeing the ground red—every ditch is shown brimming with human gore. Mars cannot decide to which side to award victory; finally it is an Alfonso who determines, by his courage, that France will stand firm while Spain yields, / and Ravenna is sacked.

'In his anguish the Pope chews his lip, and calls down a German tempest from the mountains which drives every Frenchman unresisting over the Alps. And in the garden from which he uproots the Golden Lilies he plants a seedling of the Sforzas. / Now here the French are back again. Here they are destroyed by the disloyal Swiss whom the young king has all too recklessly brought with him as auxiliaries—after they had captured and sold his father. Now look at the army preparing to avenge itself for the reverse it suffered at Novara when it fell beneath Fortune's wheel. /

'But now they have a new king: look at Francis, here, returning under happier auspices. See him out in front—he so blunts the aggressiveness of the Swiss, he practically annihilates them: never again shall the brutes pride themselves on their usurped titles of "tamers of princes" and "bulwark of the Church of Christ". / Here he is taking Milan in spite of the League, and making a pact with the young Sforza. Here is Bourbon defending the city for the King of France against the German attack. Here the city is being seized from the French king while he is away attending to other great matters, unaware of the arrogance and cruelty practised there by his troops. / Here is another Francis, who takes after his Sforza grandfather in courage and not merely in name; he drives out the French and reclaims his ancestral home with the sanction of the Church. Again the French return, but this time on a shorter tether, and not ranging about Italy so freely as previously, for the worthy Duke of Mantua cuts off their advance on the Ticino. / Frederick Gonzaga, the first flush of youth still in his cheeks, merits eternal glory for defending Pavia from the French and thwarting the designs of the Lion of St. Mark—all this by dint of his lance, but even more by virtue of diligence and skill.

'Now look at those two marquises, both of them a terror to our people, both of them glories of Italy, / both of the same blood, hatched in one nest. The first is son of Marquis Alfonso, the one who was entrapped by the negro, as you saw, and dyed the ground with his blood. See how often the French are driven from Italy by his counsel. The other, with the benign, serene expression, is Lord of the Vasto; his name is Alfonso. / He is the knight I spoke of when I showed you the island of Ischia, the one about whom Merlin had divulged many prophecies to Fieramont: his birth was to be deferred to a time when poor Italy, the Church, and the Empire would be in greater need than ever of help against the affronts of the barbarians. / See if the Swiss, and still more the French, obtain any joy at the battle of La Bicocca, thanks to

Alfonso here, and his cousin from Pescara, aided by Prospero Colonna. Here are the French preparing once more to retrieve their abortive enterprises: the king descends upon Lombardy with one army, sending another to take Naples. /

'But Fortune treats us like the dust that the wind catches up and swirls about, wafting it skywards and the next moment blowing it back to the ground from which it came; and she has the king believe that he has concentrated a hundred thousand troops round Pavia, for he looks only at his outlay in wages, not at whether his forces have in fact increased or dwindled. / The fault lies with his skinflint ministers, and with his own indulgence in having trusted them, if only a few rally to the standards when the call to arms is sounded in the night: for the king sees himself attacked inside his ramparts by the cunning Spaniards who, guided by the two Davalos, risk carving out a passage, be it in heaven or in hell. / Here see the flower of the French nobility obliterated in the field. See how many lances and swords hem in the brave king on every side. Look, his steed falls under him, but he still does not surrender or admit defeat, even though the enemy converges and concentrates on him alone and there is no one to help him. / The stalwart king defends himself on foot and steeps himself in his enemy's blood. But finally courage must yield to superior force: the king is taken, and here he is in Spain. And the foremost crowns of the defeated host and of the great captive king are presented, as you see, to the Marquis of Pescara and to the Marquis of Vasto, his constant companion. /

'While one army is destroyed at Pavia, the other, on its way to harass Naples, is shown as it were like a candle running out of wax, a lamp out of oil. Here is the king leaving his sons as prisoners of Spain and returning home. And here he is making war in Italy while others make war on him in his own land. / Look at the carnage and plunder which afflicts the length and breadth of Rome. See the arson and the rape—the sacred and profane fall victim equally. The forces of the League witness the devastation from close at hand, and hear the cries and laments, but instead of pressing forward they retreat, leaving the successor of Peter to be captured. / The king sends his general Lautrec with fresh troops, not this time to undertake anything in Lombardy but to rescue the Head and other members of the Church from thieving, sacrilegious hands—but he is so late that he arrives to find the Holy Father's liberty already restored. So he lays siege to Naples, the Syren's burial-place, and harries the whole kingdom. / Here the imperial fleet sets sail to the relief of the besieged city, but here is Doria who bars its way and sinks, burns and destroys it at sea. Look at how Fortune changes her mind, after having been so propitious to the French: fever now, not the lance, proves the death of them—not one in a thousand returns to France.' /

All this history and a great deal more, to describe all of which would take too long, was to be seen in the hall, painted in varying and beautiful colours. There was room enough for the whole series. The company perused them a second and third time and seemed quite unable to tear themselves away. And several times they re-read the legend inscribed in letters of gold beneath the beautiful pictures. /

The beautiful women and the rest of the company stayed on awhile to contemplate and converse until their host, who was well accustomed to doing the honours of the house, conducted his guests to their beds. When the others were all asleep, Bradamant finally betook herself to her bed where she tossed and turned but could not find sleep on either side. /

Towards daybreak she did close her eyes a little, and dreamed she saw Ruggiero who said to her: 'Why do you fret yourself and believe what is not true? You will see the rivers flow upstream before ever I turn my thoughts to any but you. If I did not love you, I should never love my heart, nor the pupils of my eyes.' / And he seemed to add: 'I have come to have myself baptized and do what I promised. And if I am late it is because I have been prostrated by a wound—but not one caused by Love.' At this point sleep evaporated, and the vision of Ruggiero with it. And Bradamant took up her lament, brooding thus within herself: / 'What soothed me was a deceitful dream; what torments me is, alas, a wakeful reality. What was good proved an evanescent dream; but my dire anguish is no dream at all. Why do my awakened senses not see and hear now what my imagination thought it heard and saw? Closed, my eyes see what is good; open, what is bad. Oh why? / Gentle sleep promised me peace, but bitter wakening plunges me back into turmoil; gentle sleep, for sure, has deceived me, but bitter wakening, alas, never lies. If truth is so troublesome, deception so agreeable, let me never more hear or see what is true! If sleep brings me bliss and wakefulness misery, let me never more wake from sleep. / O happy the animals lodged in a deep sleep for six months without ever opening their eyes! Never let me say that such a sleep resembles death, such a wakening, life: my own fate, unlike others', is to sense death in wakefulness, life in sleep. But if death resembles this sort of sleep, then come, good Death, close my eyes!' /

When the sun had tinged the horizon with red from end to end and the clouds had dispersed, it looked as though the new day would not be like the old. On waking, Bradamant put on her armour so as to resume her journey betimes, after thanking her host for the kind hospitality and the honours he had paid her. / She found that the ambassadress had left the castle with her train to join the three warriors awaiting her outside—the three whom the previous evening Bradamant had unhorsed with the golden lance, and who had endured a most uncomfortable, wet and windy night amid the hostile elements. / What made it worse was that they and their horses had gone without their supper, their teeth chattering as they squelched in the mire. But what vexed them almost more—and there would be no qualifying 'almost' about it once the messenger, along with her other reports, made it known to her queen—was that they had been overthrown by the very first lance to confront them on French soil. / So as soon as Bradamant had crossed the drawbridge and heaved into sight they challenged her to joust: they were ready to die or to have prompt vengeance for the insult they had suffered, so that the messenger—I never mentioned her name, Ullania—might withdraw the poor opinion she may, in her heart, have formed of them. / It never occurred to them that she could be a damsel—there was nothing feminine about her gestures. Bradamant refused, being in a hurry and not willing to stop. But they were so insistent that she could not refuse them without incurring blame; so she lowered her lance and at three strokes tipped them all onto the ground—and that was the end of the joust, / for, without a backward glance she turned away and vanished into the distance.

The warriors, who had come from such remote lands to win the golden shield, regained their feet without a word and seemed dumbstruck with amazement—she had floored them so brazenly. They dared not catch Ullania's eye, / for they had been all too boastful, many a time along the way, that there was not a knight nor a paladin who could stand up to the least of them. Ullania, therefore, to shame them even more and cure them of their vanity, informed them that it was a woman, not a paladin, who had unhorsed them. / 'Now that a woman has overthrown you,' she remarked, 'what must you think of Orlando or Rinaldo—is their fame unfounded? Should one of these two have the shield, tell me, will you acquit yourselves better against them than you have against a woman? I doubt it, and I expect you doubt it too. / Let this be sufficient for you—no need to establish clearer proof of your valour. Whichever of you is bold enough to want to try his mettle further in France is seeking to add injury to the insult he underwent yesterday and again today. Maybe he sets little store by utility and honour, but he may die at the hands of warriors such as these.' /

When Ullania had quite convinced the knights that it really was a damsel who had so besmirched their hitherto spotless reputations—and though one person would have sufficed, more than ten confirmed the truth of her assertion—they were on the point of turning their swords against themselves in an access of mortification and fury. / And in a rage they stripped off their armour, every piece of it, not excepting the swords at their sides, and flung it all into the castle moat. And they swore that, since they had been defeated by a woman who had knocked them all backwards to the ground, to expiate such a blunder they would go a whole year without ever wearing armour; / and they would go everywhere on foot, whether the going were level or hilly. And when the year was up, they still would not ride nor wear chain-mail unless they won themselves new armour, new steeds in combat. Disarmed, therefore, to purge their failure, they continued on foot while the others rode. /

That evening Bradamant came to a castle on the road to Paris; here she heard of Agramant's defeat at the hands of Charlemagne and of Rinaldo her brother. Good board and lodging was provided here, but none of these advantages profited her much: she ate little, slept little— far from finding rest, she could scarcely contain her emotions. /

But before I continue her story I want to revert to Rinaldo and Gradasso, who had of one accord tethered their steeds in the seclusion of the spring. Their battle, about which I want to tell you a little, was not to win lands or empires, but to secure for the stronger the sword Durindana and the charger Bayard. / No clarion or other signal told them when to move, no master of the lists rehearsed them in parrying and striking or fired their spirits with ardour, but each by agreement drew his sword and moved, agile, and dextrous, to the encounter. The blows began to sound, thick and heavy; tempers rose. / I know of no two other swords, tried and tested for solid durability, that would have stood up to three blows from their swords, whose virtues were limitless; they were of such perfect temper, proved in so many trials, that they could meet in a thousand clashes and more without breaking. / Rinaldo kept changing his stance as with great dexterity and skill he applied himself to eluding the devastation of Durindana, for he well knew how it could split and rend metal. Gradasso struck the mightier blows but most of them were borne away on the wind; if any did strike home, it was always at a point where the damage would be only light. / Rinaldo's aim was truer and frequently his blows stunned the pagan's arm. He would drive his sword now at his sides, now at the juncture of helmet and breastplate, but the armour appeared to be of adamant, and he could not break or tear a single mesh of it; the reason he found it so hard and strong was because it was enchanted. /

For a long time they were totally absorbed in their battle, never pausing to rest, each never allowing his eyes to leave the other's wrought-up face—until a second fracas distracted them and put paid to their furious onslaught. They both looked in the direction of the great shindy and saw Bayard in dire peril. / They saw Bayard fighting off a monster, bigger than himself, a bird. Its beak was over three yards long, its other features were bat-like; its feathers were inky-black, its great talons were sharp and sinister; it had fiery eyes, a cruel look, and wings large enough for a pair of sails. / It may have been a real bird, but I don't know where or when there ever was another like it; I have never seen such a beast, nor ever read of one—except in the pages of Turpin. This leads me to believe that the bird was an infernal spirit raised in that shape by Maugis in order to interrupt the battle. / Rinaldo believed as much, and later gave Maugis a piece of his mind. His cousin, however, would not confess to it but, to clear himself, swore by the Light which lights the sun that this was not to be imputed to him.

Be it bird or demon, the monster dropped on Bayard and grabbed him in its talons. / The steed, being powerful, at once snapped his reins and angrily set to against the bird with his hoofs and teeth. But the bird swiftly withdrew upwards, then returned and circled round him and struck at him with its pointed talons. Thus assailed and quite unprotected, Bayard fled. / He fled to the neighbouring wood and sought the densest foliage. The feathered monster followed him from above, keeping an eye trained on his quarry; but the good steed thrust far into the wood until at last he found concealment in a cave. Losing his traces, the winged beast returned skywards and searched for other game. /

Rinaldo and Gradasso, seeing the object of their battle depart, consented to postpone the fight until they had rescued Bayard from the talons which had sent him fleeing into the dark wood. They agreed that whichever of them found him would bring him back to this spring where they would then conclude their altercation. / They left the spring, following the newly trodden grass. Bayard was way ahead of them, for they had been slow in chasing after him. Gradasso, who had his steed close at hand, leapt onto him and dashed off through the wood, leaving Rinaldo far behind—and in a far from cheerful humour. / After a few steps he lost the traces of his steed, who followed a curious course, holding to the streams, rocks, and thickets, the thorniest wilds, in order to hide from those talons which dropped from the sky to assail him. After his vain effort, Rinaldo returned to the spring to await him, / in case Gradasso brought him back there, according to their pact. But seeing how fruitless this course was, he sadly regained the Christian camp on foot.

Now let us go back to the other, for whom events turned out quite differently: it was not justice but his good fortune if he heard the good steed neighing close by. / He found him in the cave, still so oppressed by his recent fright that he dared not leave his shelter, so the pagan had him at his mercy. He remembered their pact all right, about returning to the spring with him—but he was no longer disposed to observe it, and thus he argued to himself: / 'Let him who wants to pick a fight to win the steed do so—I prefer to win him peacefully. I came from one end of the world to the other only to make Bayard mine: now that I have laid hands on him, anyone who thinks I mean to let him go must be out of his mind. If Rinaldo wants him, what is wrong with his coming to the Indies, just as I have come here? / Let him take his chances in Sericana just as I have twice in France.' This said, he took the easiest road to Arles where he found the Moorish army. From here with Bayard and Durindana he left on board a well-pitched galley. But this is for another time—now I am leaving behind me Gradasso, Rinaldo, and all of France. /

I want to follow Astolfo, who saddled and bridled the hippogryph and rode him through the air like a palfrey, but at a pace to outstrip the eagle and falcon. When he had roamed France from sea to sea, from the Pyrenees to the Rhine, he turned Westward, to the mountains which divide France from Spain. / He crossed into Navarre and thence into Aragon, leaving all onlookers quite amazed. For a long while he kept Tarragona to his left, Biscay to his right; he came to Castille; he visited Galicia and the kingdom of Lisbon. Then he turned his course towards Cordova and Seville. Not a city, on the coast or inland, did he leave unvisited anywhere in Spain. / He saw Cadiz and the bourne set for the first sailors by invincible Hercules. Then he was disposed to roam about Africa from the Atlantic to the confines of Egypt. He saw the famous Balearics and Ibiza close to his route. Then he turned about and made for Moroccan Arzilla over the sea separating it from Spain. / He saw Morocco, Fez, Oran, Bône, Algiers, Bougie, all proud cities, all possessing the crowns of other cities—crowns of gold, not of leaves or grass. Then he spurred towards Bizerta and Tunis, visited Gabes and the island of Djerba; he saw Tripoli, Benghazi, Tolmeta, right to where the Nile crosses into Asia. / He saw the whole region between the coast and the wooded crests of the wild Atlas. Then he turned his back on the mountains of Carena and took his flight over those of Cyrenaica. He crossed the desert wastes and reached the confines of Nubia at Abyed, leaving behind him the tomb of Battus at Cyrene and the great temple of Ammon, now derelict. / From here he came to another Tremisen, where the rites of Mahomet are still followed.

Then he bent his flight towards the other Africans, the Ethiopians who live opposite these, across the Nile. He held his course towards the city of Nubia, a straight line between Dobaya and Cuoad—the former a Saracen town, the latter Christian, and they keep a constant armed watch at their border. / Senapo, Emperor of Ethiopia, wields the Cross instead of a sceptre. His realm, which teems with people and cities and wealth, stretches from here to the mouth of the Red Sea. He serves our Faith as his own, for it can save him from the Ultimate Banishment. It is here, if I am not mistaken, that fire is used in baptism. / At the great court in Nubia Astolfo dismounted and visited Senapo. The castle in which the Ethiopian sovereign resided was of an opulence far in excess of its strength: the chains on the drawbridges and gates, every hinge and bolt from top to bottom, indeed everything for which we use iron, here was made of gold. / Even though this finest metal was in such abundance, it was not disdained. The great loggias of the royal palace consisted of arcades in limpid crystal. Rubies, emeralds, sapphires, and topaz, spaced out proportionately, provided a glittering frieze of red and white, green, blue, and yellow beneath the fine ceilings. / The walls, ceilings, and floors were studded with pearls and rich gems. Balsam originated here—Jerusalem never had remotely such an abundance. From here derives the musk that we import, and from here too the amber, sent to be bartered on other shores. From here, in fact, come the very things which are so costly in our own lands. / It is said that the Sultan—the King of Egypt—pays tribute to this king and is subject to him because of the power he has to divert the Nile from its natural course and flow in a new bed, thus exposing Cairo and its neighbourhood to immediate famine. His subjects call him Senapo, while we call him Prester John. /

Of all the kings of Ethiopia there ever were he was the richest and the most powerful. But with all his power and all his riches he had suffered the loss of his eyes. And this was the least of his tribulations: what plagued and distressed him far worse was that, for all his reputed wealth, he was tortured by perpetual hunger. / Every time the poor unfortunate was driven by dire necessity to eat or drink, at once a swarm of infernal avengers would appear—those obnoxious brutes, the harpies. With their predator's snouts and talons they would scatter the dishes and snatch the food; and what their greedy bellies could not hold was left contaminated and befouled. / This was because, when he was still a green youth, seeing himself raised to such high honours—for beside his wealth he possessed more sinew than anyone else, and more courage—he became proud as Lucifer and planned war against his Creator. With his forces he took the road leading straight to the mountain from which Egypt's great river rises. / He had heard that on that craggy mountain which rose above the clouds and reached to the sky was situated the paradise known as terrestrial, where Adam and Eve once lived. With camels and elephants and an army on foot he arrogantly set forth: if people lived there, it was his great wish to subject them to his laws. / But God punished him for his rashness, dispatching an angel among his hordes: a hundred thousand of them died. Him he condemned to perpetual night, and from the caves of hell summoned to his table the horrible monsters which snatch and pollute his food and never leave him a taste of it. / A man had put him into a state of continuous despair with a prophecy that his meals would no longer be ravaged or befouled with stench once a knight was seen approaching through the air on a winged horse. As this seemed an impossibility, he lived all forlorn, bereft of hope. /

Now that, to their utter amazement, the people on every rampart, on every tower saw the knight's arrival, somebody ran at once to tell the king. The prophecy returned to his mind and in his joy he forgot to take up his faithful stick but, with his hands outstretched before him, groped his way towards the flying knight. / Astolfo described spacious circles to come down in the courtyard of the castle. The king, led before him, knelt down, extended his joined hands and cried: 'Angel of God, new Messiah, if I do not deserve pardon for so great offences, remember that it is our nature to sin often, yours ever to pardon those who repent. / Conscious of my transgression I do not ask—I dare not ask—for the eyes I used to have, though I should certainly believe that you could restore them, for you are one of the blessed spirits dear to God. Be satisfied with the great torment of not being able to see, without in addition that of perpetual famine. At least drive off the fetid harpies, to stop them from stealing my food. / And I promise to turn my lofty palace into a marble temple dedicated to you; its doors and roof will be of solid gold, and it will be adorned with jewels inside and out. It will be called by your holy name and sculpted with your miracle.' Thus said the king who could see nothing, as he vainly strove to kiss the duke's foot. /

'I am no angel of God, nor a second Messiah,' Astolfo replied; 'nor have I come from heaven: I too am a mortal man and a sinner, unworthy of the thanks you offer. I shall do my utmost to relieve your kingdom of the baneful monster by slaughter or rout. If I succeed, it is not me but God alone you must praise, by whose help I bend my flight hither. / Make these vows to God, to whom they are due; build to him your churches and altars.' As he spoke, they made their way amid the nobility up to the castle, where the king bade his servants prepare the banquet at once, hoping that this time the food would not be snatched from his grasp. / The banquet was duly prepared straight away in a splendid hall. Astolfo the duke sat down to it alone with Senapo, and the dishes arrived.

Now what came to their ears but a rush of wind all stirred up by those ghastly wings—and in flew those loathsome, those unspeakable harpies, lured from the sky by the smell of the food. / They were a swarm of seven, all with pale, wasted women's faces, emaciated and wizened by constant hunger, ghastlier than death's-heads. Their clumsy great wings were hideously deformed; they had rapacious hands, hooked claws, a swollen, fetid belly, and a long tail which curled in and out like a snake. / One moment they could be heard flying in; the next moment saw them all snatching the food off the table and upsetting the dishes. And they kept defecating so abundantly that one simply had to hold one's nose—the stench was insupportable. Astolfo flew into a rage and flourished his sword at the greedy birds. / One he caught on the neck, another on the rump, another in the chest, the next on the wing, but he might have been striking a bag of wadding—the blows were cushioned and ineffectual. The harpies left no plate or cup untouched, and did not clear off before they had ravaged or sullied and contaminated the lordly banquet. /

The king had been relying upon the duke to drive away the harpies for him; and now that he saw no more reason to hope, he sighed and moaned in despair. But Astolfo now thought of his horn, which had always helped him at critical passes, and he reached the conclusion that here was the best way to be rid of the monsters. / First he made the king and his barons block their ears with hot wax so that when he sounded his horn they would not have to flee out of the city. Then he took the hippogryph's bridle, jumped into the saddle and grasped his marvellous horn. Finally he signalled to the steward to re-lay the table and bring on more food. / So the table was set in a loggia and fresh food was brought on for another meal. In flew the harpies as usual, and Astolfo at once reached for his horn. The birds, who had not closed their ears, could not abide the noise when they heard it, but fled in terror, oblivious of the food and of all else. / At once the paladin spurred after them. The hippogryph flew out of the loggia and, leaving the castle and the great city, soared through the air in pursuit of the monsters. Astolfo kept blowing his horn, and the harpies fled towards the torrid zone, till they reached the towering mountain where the Nile rises—if it rises anywhere. /

Almost at the base of the mountain a deep cave penetrates below ground—it is said to be undoubtedly the gateway for a descent into hell. It was for this, as for a safe shelter, that the swarm of predators made, and dropped down to the banks of Cocytus and even beyond, to put themselves out of earshot. / At the dark, nebulous hole which gives access to those who abandon the light, the illustrious duke stopped his horrible noise and made his steed fold his wings. But before I take him any further, so as not to depart from my custom, my page being quite filled up, I mean to end this canto and rest.

THIRTY-FOURTH CANTO

*1–3 Introductory. 4–43 Astolfo visits hell and hears Lydia's
story. 44–67 Astolfo visits the Earthly Paradise and meets
St. John. 68–92 With St. John he visits the moon to recover
Orlando's wits.*

O RAVENOUS, baneful harpies! How ruthlessly you wreak divine
vengeance at every table in purblind, wayward Italy, to punish her
(maybe) for faults of old. Innocent children and devoted mothers
succumb to starvation as they watch these evil monsters make one meal
of everything on which they have expected to live. / That man perpetrated the worst of crimes who opened the cave which had been closed
for many a year: out came the stench and gluttony to pervade Italy and
corrupt her. Happy days were at an end, and peace driven out. Ever
since has Italy been steeped in wars, in poverty, and trouble—so to
remain for years to come, / until the day she takes her feckless children
by their curls and shakes them, and drives them from forgetful Lethe,
shouting: 'Is there no one here to emulate the courage of Calais and
Zetes, to rid our tables of the grasping talons and the stink, to restore
them to joy and cleanliness as they did for Phineus, and Astolfo for the
King of Ethiopia?' /

The paladin with his horrible noise drove the foul harpies in headlong
flight until he drew rein at the base of a mountain where there was a
cave into which they had vanished. He listened carefully at the entrance
and heard the air rent with shrieks and reverberating with sobs and
endless wailing—a clear sign that this must be hell. / He decided to go
in and look at those who had lost the light of day, and penetrate to the
heart of the place and inspect the ravines of hell. 'What should I fear if
I enter?' he asked himself. 'I can always use my horn to help me. I shall
rout Pluto and Satan; and the three-headed dog?—I shall shift him out
of my path.' / At once he dismounted from his winged steed and left
him tethered to a bush.

Then he descended into the cave, first taking the horn in which he
placed all his trust. He did not go far before his nostrils and eyes were
assailed by a black, noisome smoke, heavier than smoke off pitch or
sulphur. This, however, did not deter him from pressing on. / But
the further he went, the denser grew the smoky darkness, until he saw
that he could not continue but would be forced to turn back. Now he

saw something, he could not tell what, which moved in the vault above him, the way a hanged man's corpse sways in the wind after it has been out in the rain and the sun for days on end. / On his smoke-darkened path the light was so scanty that he could not make out what it could be, hovering in the air like that. By way of experiment, he let fly at it with his sword a couple of times—only to conclude that it must be a spirit, for he might have been striking the empty air. /

Then he heard a sad voice speak: 'Please,' it said, 'go on down without harming others. The black smoke which billows up from the infernal flames is quite bad enough.' Puzzled, Astolfo stopped and addressed the shade: 'May it please God to clip the smoke's wings so that it no longer rises up to you—pray, tell me about yourself. / And if you would have me bring news of you to the world above, I am ready to do this for you.' The shade replied: 'If it is but in my reputation that I return up to the lovely light of day, such a gift appeals to me so strongly it drags the words out of me and constrains me to tell you my name and my circumstances, though to speak is irksome and tiring. /

'I am Lydia,' she began, 'daughter of the King of Lydia and born to eminence, but condemned to this eternal smoke by the supreme justice of God for having been obnoxious and spiteful to my faithful suitor while I lived. This cave is full to infinity of women like myself, put to the same torture for the same offence. / Further down where the smoke is thicker and the torment worse, is cruel Anaxaretes. Her body, on earth, was turned to stone and her soul came down here to suffer, since she could endure to watch her poor afflicted lover hang himself for her. Near me is Daphne, who now realizes her error in making Apollo run after her so. / It would take an age to tell you one by one of the wretched souls of the hard-hearted women down here: they are so many, they are legion. To tell you about the men who have suffered for their ingratitude would take even longer: they are punished in a worse place, blinded by smoke and roasted by fire. / For as women are more gullible, those who deceive them deserve a worse punishment. Theseus knows this, and so does Jason, Aeneas (invader of Latinus' realm), and Amnon, too, against whom his brother Absalom unleashed his bloody fury on Tamar's account. And yet others, men and women—there is no end to those who have deserted wife or husband. /

'But now to tell you of myself in particular, and to confess the fault which landed me here. In former life I was beautiful, but so vain that I know of no one to equal me: which of the two I possessed in greater degree—pride or beauty—I cannot say, though my arrogance and pretensions sprang from my beauty, a delight to everyone's eyes. / At that time there was living in Thrace a warrior who was held to be the foremost champion in the world. He had heard my singular beauty praised by more than one credible witness, and he was moved to dedicate to me all his love, believing that, in recognition of his valour, I should cherish him in my heart. / He came to Lydia, where he was captivated in yet stronger toils once he had set eyes on me. With the other warriors he enlisted in my father's service, where his fame increased. His high valour and the multifarious exploits he accomplished would take too long to recall—and his countless merits, had he only served a man readier to acknowledge them. / My father conquered Pamphylia, Caria, and Cilicia by this warrior's efforts, never moving his forces against the enemy except at his direction.

'Now the Thracian, deeming that the services he had rendered entitled him to do so, one day took it upon himself to ask the king for my hand in marriage in reward for all the conquests he had brought to him. / The king rejected him; he entertained more grandiose plans for his daughter's marriage—a soldier of fortune possesses nothing but his valour. My father was all too devoted to gain and avarice, the seed-bed of all vice; he had as much use for grace and courage as a donkey has for a harp. / Alcestes (to give the warrior his name), seeing himself rejected by the very man who was under the greatest obligation to gratify him, took his leave. He left my father with the threat that he would make him sorry for having refused him his daughter. Then he went to the King of Lydia's long-standing rival, the King of Armenia, a mortal enemy, / and so worked upon him that he incited him to take up arms and make war upon my father. Renowned for his exploits, Alcestes was appointed commander of the Armenian forces. All the spoils of the conquest, he promised, would go to the king, with one exception: all he wanted for himself as fruit of his labours, once he had swept the board, was me, with my graceful, delicate limbs. /

'I could never describe to you the damage Alcestes did to my father in that war: he shattered four of his armies, and in less than a year he deprived him of all his domains, all but one castle fortified by tall cliffs. Here the king shut himself with the pick of his household and with all the treasures he could amass in a hurry. / And here Alcestes besieged him, reducing him in a short while to such straits that he would have been more than content had he been able, by handing me over as wife, nay, servant, with half his kingdom thrown in, to ward off all further inroads. He could see himself otherwise soon being deprived of the little he had left, and dying a prisoner. / He was disposed to try every possible remedy before it came to that; so he sent me, as the cause of all the trouble, out to Alcestes.

'I went to him intending to surrender myself as his prey and to beg

him to take what share he wanted of our realm and abate his wrath. /
When Alcestes heard that I was on my way to him, he came to meet me.
He was pale and trembling—to look at him, he might have been a
vanquished prisoner, not a conqueror. Realizing how he burned for
me, I did not speak to him the way I had originally intended; seeing the
opportunity, I hit upon a new idea in keeping with the condition in
which I found him. /

'I began by disparaging his love for me and complaining bitterly at
his cruelty, at his iniquitous treatment of my father and his attempts to
have me by force. He would, I told him, have succeeded by a softer approach sustained only a few days longer, had he been able to persevere
in the behaviour which had found favour with the king and with all of
us. / If my father at first had refused his honest suit (for he was somewhat wayward by temperament and never acceded to an initial request),
he still had no call to refuse further service, or to be so quick to take
offence. No, by doing ever better, he could have been certain of arriving quickly at the desired reward. / And even if my father had persisted
in his refusal, I should so have entreated him that he would have made
my suitor my husband. But supposing I had found him obstinate? I
should so have worked on him on the sly that Alcestes would have been
no little pleased with me. But as he chose to try this other approach, I
had made up my mind that I should never love him. / And though I
had come to him out of pity for my father, he was not to delude himself
—he would derive little joy from the pleasure I would all unwillingly
afford him: for the moment I had satisfied his depraved lust with this,
my violated body, I would stain the ground red with my blood. / These
and similar words I uttered when I realized the hold I had over him;
and I made him more penitent than any desert hermit. He fell at
my feet and begged me to avenge myself on him for so great a fault
with the dagger which he took from its sheath and pressed into my
hand. /

'Finding him in the state he was, I decided to press my advantage to
the limit. I held out to him the hope of still being able to enjoy me if he
merited this by mending his ways and seeing to the restitution of my
father's ancient realm—and if he consented, in days to come, to win
me by love and service, never more by arms. / This he promised to
do, and sent me back to the castle intact, just as I had come, not hazarding so much as a kiss on my lips. You see how firmly I had set the yoke
upon his neck! How effective Cupid had been, feathering all those
arrows on my behalf! Alcestes went to the King of Armenia, to the
beneficiary, according to their pact, of whatever was captured; / and
using his best powers of persuasion, begged him to leave my father
in possession of his kingdom, whose lands he had plundered and des-

poiled, and to content himself with his own Armenia. But the king flushed scarlet with anger and told Alcestes not even to think of it: he did not propose to abandon this campaign so long as my father was still left with an inch of land. / And if Alcestes' mind were changed by a mere slip of a woman, so much the worse for him: he, the king, did not propose to forfeit, at his request, everything that he had toiled a whole year to acquire. Alcestes entreated him again, only to complain that his prayers made no impression. In the end he lost his temper and threatened to have his way by force if not by free consent. / Their tempers rose to the point of angry recriminations, then to angrier deeds: Alcestes drew his sword against the king, and, despite the thousand retainers flocking to him, slew him on the spot. That very day he routed the Armenians with the help of the Cilicians and Thracians in his pay, and of other followers he commanded. /

'Pursuing his victory, he restored to my father the whole of his kingdom in less than a month, and entirely at his own expense. Further to compensate him for the damage done, in addition to other spoils, he wrested for him a part of neighbouring Armenia and Cappadocia, extorting from another part a heavy tribute, and ravaged Hyrcania right to the sea. / Instead of a triumph at his return, we considered putting him to death, but desisted for fear of being worsted, seeing how strongly supported he was by his friends. I pretended to love him, and each day I increased his hope of my becoming his wife. But first, as I told him, I wanted him to display his strength against our other enemies. / I would send him off, sometimes alone, sometimes with a few men, upon bizarre, dangerous missions, enough to kill any number of others but not him—everything succeeded for him, and he would come back victorious, though often he was faced with horrifying monsters, at grips with giants and cannibals which infested our land. / Hercules was set to work by Eurystheus and by his step-mother Juno in Lerna, Nemea, Thrace, Erymantus, the valleys of Aetolia, in Numidia, on the Tiber, on the Ebro, and elsewhere: but this was nothing to the tasks imposed by me on my lover with deceitful prayers and murderous intent as I sought to be rid of him. /

'Unable to compass my first intention, I achieved another no less effective: I made him insult all those whom I believed were attached to him, and turned them all against him. He felt no greater happiness than in obeying me unreservedly; in his readiness to do my bidding he was no respecter of persons. / Once it seemed to me that this method had spelled extinction for all my father's enemies, and that I had conquered Alcestes by his own hand, for he had left himself friendless on our account, I now told him roundly what I had hitherto concealed from him behind a mask of deception: that I cordially detested him and was seeking every way to have him killed. / But then considering that this course would expose me to public censure—my debt to him was common knowledge, and I should be known ever after for cruelty—I decided it would be enough if I simply forbade him ever more to come into my presence: I never wanted to see or speak to him again, or listen to a message or accept a letter from him. / So tormented was he by my ingratitude that in the end sorrow mastered him and, after long pleading for mercy, he fell ill and died. In punishment for my wickedness, my eyes constantly water and my face is smudged with black smoke. So shall I remain for all time—in hell there is no redemption.' /

When unhappy Lydia had finished, Astolfo went on to see if anyone else were lodged here; but the dense smoke which punished ingratitude so swelled before him that it prevented him from making another step forward—indeed he had to turn back and beat a hasty retreat, if the smoke were not to be the death of him. / The close cadence of his footfalls had all the appearances of a gallop, not of an amble or even a trot. He kept gaining ground in his upward climb until he saw the entrance to the cave; and light started to filter through the murky gloom. Labouring heavily as he toiled onwards, he finally emerged from the cave and left the smoke behind. / And in order to cut off the return of those greedy-guts, the harpies, he assembled boulders and cut down several trees (for ginger and pepper trees grew there) and as best he could fenced off the mouth of the cave. This work proved so successful that the harpies were never to reappear. / While he was in the dismal cave, the black smoke from the black pitch not only tainted and sullied his exposed skin but also penetrated beneath his clothing, so he was induced to go in search of water. Eventually he saw a spring issuing from a rock in the forest, and here he washed himself from top to toe. / Then he mounted his flying horse and rose into the air to reach the summit of the mountain, for it was generally believed that the orb of the moon stood not far from its highest peak. His urge to explore directed his aspirations heavenwards, spurning the earth. More and more height he gained until he reached the summit. /

The flowers which the breeze had painted on these smiling slopes looked like so many coloured gems—sapphires, rubies, gold, topaz, and pearls, diamonds, chrysolites, and jacinth. And the grass was so green that were it to grow down here it would outdo emeralds. No less beautiful were the boughs of the trees, permanently in fruit and in blossom. / In the branches lovely little birds sang; they were of many hues, white, blue and green, red and yellow. The murmuring brooks and quiet lakes were more limpid than crystal. A soft breeze, which seemed never to falter or fail, kept the air constantly astir so as to temper the heat of the day. / And as it blew, it ravished each blossom, fruit, and leaf of its particular odour, blending them all into a sweetness which nourished the spirit. In the middle of the plain stood a palace which seemed to be ablaze with a living flame, it radiated such splendour and light, beyond all mortal experience. / The palace had a perimeter of over thirty miles. Astolfo on his steed ambled slowly towards it, admiring the beautiful scene on every side. As he compared what he saw with this rank world we live in, he dismissed our world as ugly and evil and loathed by Heaven and nature in comparison with the sweetness, light, and happiness up there. /

When he was close to the gleaming edifice he was stunned with amazement: its smooth wall was fashioned from a single stone which shone redder than a carbuncle. What a stupendous work, what ingenious architect! What structure in our world resembles it? Let him be silent who proposes any of our Seven Wonders for such glory. / In the luminous vestibule of that house of bliss Astolfo was approached by an old man in a carmine robe and milk-white cloak. He was white-haired and a thick white beard mantled his chin and fell to his chest. His face was so venerable, he looked like one of the elect of Paradise. / With a cheerful smile he addressed the paladin, who had respectfully dismounted: 'O baron', he said, 'who by God's will have ascended to the earthly paradise: as the cause of your journey and the object of your desire are equally hidden from you, your arrival here from the Northern hemisphere is, believe me, not without highly-placed help. / It is to discover how you are to help Charlemagne and rescue the Holy Faith from peril that you have made so long a journey to come, all unawares, to consult me. You are not to attribute your coming here to your intelligence or courage, my son: neither your horn nor the winged horse would be of any use to you had not God given them to you. / Later we shall converse at greater leisure and I shall tell you how you are to proceed. But first come in and restore yourself—you must feel by now you have fasted long enough.'

The old man had more to say, and much surprised Astolfo when he revealed himself as the Evangelist: / it was John, beloved of the Redeemer, on whose account the word went around the disciples that he was destined not to end his years in death. The Son of God was induced, therefore, to tell Peter: 'If I have him remain thus till I come, what is it to you?' Now although he did not say, 'he is not to die', it is clear that this is what he meant. / John, upon his assumption here, found company, for the patriarch Enoch had arrived already, and also the great prophet Elias: they were yet to see their last evening, and they are to enjoy eternal spring outside the foul, pestilential air until the angels' trumpets give the signal that Christ is returning on the white clouds. /

The saints gave the knight a good welcome and allotted him a room. In another his steed was provided with good forage a-plenty. They gave Astolfo some of the fruits of paradise; in view of their flavour he was inclined to think that Man's first parents might well have been excused if this is what made them fail in obedience. / The adventurous duke had partaken of food and sleep enough to give Nature her due, for every conceivable amenity was here available, and Aurora had left her aged consort (of whom she never tired, for all his years) when he too left his bed—to find that the disciple so beloved of God had come to fetch him. / He took him by the hand and told him many things which need to remain unspoken.

Then he said: 'Perhaps you don't know what is happening in France, my son, though you've come from there. Your Orlando has misappropriated the standards committed to him, and God is punishing him —for He is harshest against those He most loves, when they offend Him. / At his birth God endowed him with strength and courage to the highest degree and—what was quite abnormal—made him invulnerable to steel of any sort, in order thus to constitute him defender of His holy Faith, just as He made Samson defender of the Hebrews against the Philistines. / But your Orlando has given his Lord a poor return for such great benefits: for the greater duty he had to foster the Faithful the worse has been his desertion of them; so blinded has he been by his lustful passion for a pagan woman, the Faithful have suffered twice and more from his ruthless attempts to slay Rinaldo, his faithful cousin. / Therefore God has sent him mad, to go about with bared chest and belly, and has so clouded his reason that he cannot recognize anyone, still less himself. We read that in this fashion God also punished Nebuchadnezzar, driving him to folly for seven years, when he cropped grass and hay like an ox. / But since the paladin's wrongdoing has been far less serious than Nebuchadnezzar's, the divine will has imposed a period of only three months to purge his sin. And if our Redeemer has permitted you to arrive up here after so long a journey, it is quite simply so that you may learn from us the way to bring Orlando to his senses. / You shall, in fact, have to make a further journey with me and leave the earth altogether: I have to take you the orb of the moon, this being the planet that travels closest to us, for the medicine to restore Orlando's sanity is kept there. Tonight when the moon arrives over us we shall set out.' /

The apostle discoursed about this and that for the rest of the day. But when the sun had plunged into the sea and the sickle-moon had risen above them, a chariot was made ready, designed for travelling about those skies—it had once lifted Elias from mortal gaze in the mountains of Judaea. / The holy Evangelist harnessed four horses (of the most fiery red) to the shafts, and when he and Astolfo were settled in the chariot he took the reins and urged the steeds skywards. The chariot made a circle before lifting into the air, and soon arrived in the midst of the eternal fire, but the old man wrought a miracle whereby it gave no heat. / They crossed the whole sphere of fire and thence continued to the realm of the moon, which looked to them for the most part like untarnished steel. They found it equal in size (or nearly) to this ultimate sphere of ours, the earth, including the ocean that girdles it. /

Here Astolfo had a double surprise: what a big place the moon was from close up, when to us, who look at it from down here, it seems but a little sphere! And how he had to screw up his eyes if from up there he wanted to descry the earth and the sea spread over it; the earth being unilluminated, its features can span but a short distance. / The rivers, lakes, and fields up there were not as they are down here. The plains, valleys, mountains, cities, and castles were different, and there were houses the like of which for sheer size the paladin had never seen before or since. And there were spacious, empty forests where nymphs were forever hunting game. /

Astolfo did not stop to explore everything, for that was not the object of his coming. He was led by the holy apostle into a valley shut in between two hills, where everything that is lost on earth (be the fault ours or that of time or fate) fetches up miraculously. What is lost here collects up there. / I do not mean only dominion and wealth, subject to the vagaries of fickle Fortune. I mean also what is beyond Fortune's power to give or take: there is many a reputation up there which, little by little, time has consumed down here like a moth. There, too, are countless prayers and vows made to God by us sinners. / The tears and sighs of lovers, the useless time lost in gaming, the chronic idleness of ignorant men, the empty plans which know no rest, the vain desires are in such numbers that they clutter almost the whole place. In short, no matter what you ever lost here you would find if you went up there. /

As Astolfo passed among these mounds he asked his guide about various of them. Noticing a lofty pile of tumid bladders from which seemed to emanate a hubbub of cries, he was told that these were the ancient crowns of the Assyrians and of Lydia, of the Persians and Greeks—once so illustrious, now forgotten almost to their very names. / Next he saw a heap of gold and silver hooks: gifts made in hope of reward to kings, to greedy princes, to patrons. He asked about garlands he saw which concealed a noose: all flattery, he was told. Verses written in praise of patrons wore the guise of exploded crickets. / Love affairs pursued to little purpose had the shape of gilded bonds, jewel-studded shackles. There were eagles' talons—and these were, I am told, the authority which lords vest in their servants. The bellows littering the hillside all around denoted the praise given by princes and the favours conferred upon their favourites, all wafted away with the flower of their years. /

Cities and castles and immense treasures lay here in a confused jumble of ruins. They were treaties, he was told, and ill-concealed plots. He saw snakes with maiden's faces: the works of coiners and thieves. Then he noticed an assortment of broken phials: service as wretched courtiers. / He came upon a great mess of pottage and asked his mentor about it. 'That', he explained, 'is the charity left by a person after his death.' Then he skirted a great mound of sundry flowers once sweet-smelling but now reeking. This (begging your pardons) was the Donation of Constantine to good Sylvester. / He saw great quantities of bird-lime for ensnaring: your charms, good ladies. It would take an age if I were to describe in verse each thing that was pointed out to him—after countless thousands I should still not be finished, for every one of our needs is to be found up there. Folly, however, whatever its degree, is missing from there: it stays down here and never leaves us. / Astolfo had some lost days and other oddments of his own to look for; without his guide, he would never have recognized them in their different transformations.

Next he came upon the substance which, it seems, is so innate in us that never were prayers offered to God for its possession: I mean brains. There was a mountain of them here, only a far bigger one than of anything previously mentioned. / They took the form of a soft, tenuous liquid, apt to vaporize if not kept tightly sealed. It could be seen collected in various phials of greater or lesser size adapted for this purpose. The one containing the mighty brain of mad Orlando was the biggest of them all. It was also distinguished from the others by the inscription upon it: 'The wits of Orlando'. / All the rest were similarly inscribed with the name of the person to whom the wits belonged. The valiant duke discovered a good portion of his own; but what surprised him far more was how many belonged to people he had credited with having all their wits about them—there was abundant evidence of how witless they really were, to judge by the amount that was here to hand. / Some lose their wits in loving, some in seeking honours, some in scouring the seas in search of wealth, some in hopes placed in princes, some in cultivating magical baubles; some lose them over jewels, some over paintings, and some over other objects which they value above all else. Here the wits of sophists, astrologers, and poets abound. /

Astolfo collected his, for the author of the mysterious Apocalypse permitted him. He held to his nose the phial containing his wits and they just seemed to make their way back into place. Turpin asserts, it seems, that from there on Astolfo lived sensibly for a long time, until a subsequent caprice of his lost him his wits a second time. / Astolfo took the fullest, most capacious phial which contained the where-withal to restore Orlando to his senses. It was not as light as he had imagined when it lay on the pile with the others.

Before he returned down to the lower spheres from this radiant one, he was led by the holy apostle into a palace built beside a river. / Each room was full of lengths of spun flax, silk, cotton, and wool, dyed in various colours, some pleasing, others hideous. In the first courtyard a white-haired woman was winding them onto reels—the way in summer one sees peasant women drawing the moist cocoons off the silkworms as they harvest the new silk. / When one skein was finished, another was brought in its place, the first taken away; another woman would sort out the attractive from the ugly threads which the first left all in confusion. 'What is going on here? I can't make it out,' asked Astolfo. 'The old women are the Fates,' replied John; 'with these threads they spin lives for you mortals. / As long as one of these threads is spun out, so long does a human life last, and not a moment longer. Here Death and Nature keep watch to know the hour when a person is to die. The other Fate is responsible for selecting the beautiful strands to be woven into an adornment for paradise; out of the ugliest ones tough bonds are fashioned for the damned.' / The skeins already wound and requisitioned for further use were all given little plaques stamped with the relevant name, some in iron, others in silver or gold. / Then they were disposed in thick piles from which a tireless old man was seen taking them away with never a moment's pause, always returning for more. / The old man was so swift and expeditious, he seemed to have been born to run. He kept leaving that hillside with a load of these name-plates gathered in his lap. Where he went and why he did this will be explained to you in the next canto, if you signify with your usual kind attention that this would be agreeable to you.

THIRTY-FIFTH CANTO

*1–2 Introductory. 3–9 In praise of Hippolytus of Este. 10–30
Poets praised as preservers from oblivion: the allegory of the
birds of Lethe. 31–51 Bradamant overthrows Rodomont to
rescue Fiordiligi's beloved. 52–80 Bradamant overthrows
three Saracens and challenges Ruggiero.*

WHO will ascend to heaven, mistress mine, to fetch me back my lost
wits? They have been ebbing away ever since my heart was transfixed
by the arrows shot from your fair eyes—not that I complain of my
misfortune so long as it grows no worse than it is now: I fear that any
further depletion of my wits shall reduce me to the very condition I
have described in Orlando. / I do not imagine, however, that there is
any need for me to take flight through the air to the orb of the moon
or into paradise in order to recover my wits. I don't believe they inhabit those heights. Their haunts are your beautiful eyes, your radiant
face, your ivory breasts, those alabastrine hillocks; and I shall sip them
up with my lips if that proves the way to recover them. /

Astolfo went through the spacious palace gazing at all those lives-to-
be, after seeing those already spun reeled onto the fateful spools. And
he noticed one life-thread which seemed to glitter more than fine gold.
If jewels could be skilfully powdered and then spun out in a thread, such
a thread would not be remotely as splendid as this one. / The gorgeous
thread delighted him beyond measure—it was unique—and there came
to him a strong desire to know when this life was to be lived and whose
it was to be. The Evangelist made no secret of it: its first year was to be
twenty years before the ciphers M and D marked the interval since the
birth of the Word Incarnate. / And as this thread was resplendent and
beautiful beyond compare, so also would be the uniquely fortunate era
which was then to begin: it would derive as a perpetual and unfailing
inheritance every one of those rare and eminent graces which man
acquires by Nature's or Fortune's kindness, or by his own efforts. /

'Between the mighty branches of the king of rivers', he continued,
'there now nestles a humble little village; before it flows the Po; behind it spreads a misty vortex of deep marsh. I see it becoming, with
the passage of time, the fairest of all the cities of Italy, not only for its
walls and great regal piles, but also for the quality of its learning and
manners. / Such high and sudden eminence will not result from ran-

dom chance: Heaven has ordained it, so that the city may be a fitting birthplace for the man of whom I speak. A branch is grafted, and its growth carefully fostered when it is expected to fruit; and the jeweller refines his gold if he intends it as a setting for precious gems. / No soul in the realm of Earth was ever clothed in such beauty. Rare has been—and shall be—the spirit descending from these higher spheres who can match the excellence that the Eternal Mind intends to bestow upon Hippolytus of Este. Hippolytus of Este is the name of the one whom God has chosen to inherit so rich a gift. / Those accomplishments which, shared among many, would shed sufficient lustre on them all, will be all concentrated upon the adornment of the man of whom you have asked me to speak. He shall foster the pursuit of every virtue. Were I to give a full description of his eminent merits, I should be carried so far that Orlando would wait in vain for his lost wits.' /

Thus did Christ's imitator talk to Astolfo. And when they had seen every room in the great building from which human lives emanated, they emerged beside the river, whose sand-clouded waters ran turbid and repellent. Here they found the old man who kept coming to the river-bank with the name-plates. / I don't know if you remember—the old man we left at the end of the last canto (old in his features, that is, but so sprightly in his movements that he was faster than any deer). He kept endlessly reducing the pile of name-plates, filling his lap with them and dropping—or rather dispersing—his precious burden into the river, known as Lethe. / When the old prodigal came to the river-bank, he shook out his brimming lap and tipped all his plaques into the turbid waters. A countless number sank to the bottom without any use being derived from them; and of the myriad sunk in the sand of the river-bed, scarcely one was preserved. / Crows of every species, greedy vultures and various other birds wheeled and scudded along that river in a strident discord of cries. They all fell on this plentiful bounty when they saw it being scattered; some grasped the plaques in their beaks, others in their hooked talons, but they carried them no distance: / when they tried to take wing, they lacked the strength to lift their burden, so that these magnificent names, too, were robbed by Lethe of their renown. Among so many birds there was but a pair of swans, as white, my Lord, as your device; they, with serene assurance, brought back in their beaks the plaques which fell to them. / In this way those beneficent creatures recovered a few despite the evil designs of the mischievous old man, who would have consigned them all to the river; oblivion consumed the rest. Now swimming, now winging their way through the air, the sacred swans reached a hill beside the cruel river, and on the hill-top, a shrine. / The place was sacred to Immortality. Here a beautiful nymph came down from the hill to the shore of

Lethe's stream and took the names from the swans' beaks. And she affixed the names round a statue set upon a pillar in the middle of the shrine. Here she consecrated them and took such care of them that they remained on view for all time. /

Who was the old man, and why did he so fruitlessly impart all those fine names to the river? And what of the birds, and the holy shrine from which the fair nymph came down to the river's edge? Astolfo wanted to know the latent meaning, to penetrate the mystery of all these things. He asked the man of God about them, and here was his reply: / 'Understand that not a bough moves down on earth but its motion is remarked up here. There must be a correspondence, albeit under differing guise, between every effect on earth and in heaven. The old man, whose beard flows down his chest and who is so swift-footed that nothing ever stops him, achieves up here the same effects, the same work, that Time does on earth. / When the threads are fully wound upon the reel, human life comes to an end, down below. Down there fame would persist, up here the echo of it—immortality and divinity subsisting in both spheres—were it not for the bearded one here, and down there for Time constantly at work, ravaging. Our old man, as you can see, throws the names into the river; Time immerses them in eternal oblivion. / And just as up here the crows of various sorts, the vultures and other kinds of birds all strive to pick out of the water the names which catch their eye, so down on earth the same is done by the panders, sycophants, buffoons, pretty-boys, tale-bearers, those who infest the courts and are better welcomed there than men of integrity and worth, / those who are reputed gentlemen at court because they can emulate the donkey, the scavenging hog. Now when just Fate (or rather Venus and Bacchus) have wound up their master's life-thread, all these folk I mention, supine cravens that they are, born only to feed their bellies, carry his name on their lips for a day or two, only to let the burden fall into oblivion. / But as the swans with their glad song convey the plaques safely to the shrine, so it is that men of worth are rescued from oblivion—crueller than death—by poets. O shrewd and sagacious princes, if you follow Caesar's example and make writers your friends you need have no fear of Lethe's waters! /

'Poets too are rare as swans—poets worthy of the name—partly because God will not permit too many men of eminence to reign at a time, and partly through the fault of niggardly lords who leave the heaven-sent geniuses to beg. Suppressing good and exalting evil, they banish the fair arts. / Believe me, God has robbed these simpletons of their wits and clouded their judgement, making them shun Poetry so that death should consume them whole and entire. They would otherwise emerge living from the grave even if their lives had been a disgrace: had they only known how to cultivate her friendship, they would give off a fragrance better than spikenard or myrrh. / Aeneas was not as devoted, nor Achilles as strong, nor Hector as ferocious as their reputations suggest. There have existed men in their thousands who could claim preference over them. What has brought them their sublime renown have been the writers honoured with gifts of palaces and great estates donated by these heroes' descendants. / Augustus was not as august and beneficent as Virgil makes him out in clarion tones—but his good taste in poetry compensates for the evil of his proscriptions. And no one would know whether Nero had been wicked—he might even, for all his enemies on earth and in heaven, have left a better name—had he known how to keep friendly with writers. / Homer made Agamemnon appear the victor and the Trojans mere poltroons; he made Penelope faithful to her husband, and victim of a thousand slights from her suitors. But if you want to know what really happened, invert the story: Greece was vanquished, Troy triumphant, and Penelope a whore. / Listen on the other hand to what reputation Dido left behind, whose heart was so chaste: she was reputed a strumpet purely because Virgil was no friend of hers.

'Don't be surprised if this embitters me and if I talk about it at some length—I like writers and am doing my duty by them, for in your world I was a writer too. / And I, above all others, acquired something which neither Time nor Death can take from me: I praised Christ and merited from Him the reward of so great a good fortune. I am sorry for those who live in an evil day when Courtesy has shut her door: pallid, lean, and wizened, they beat at it day and night in vain. / So, as I was saying, poets and scholars are few and far between. Where they are offered neither board nor lodging even the wild beasts desert the place.' As the saintly old man said this his eyes blazed like two flames. Then he turned to Astolfo with a gentle smile and his over-wrought face became once more serene. /

But let us leave Astolfo with the Gospel-maker, for I want to leap the distance between heaven and earth—my wings can no longer support me at such heights. I am returning to Bradamant, the damsel who had suffered a cruel attack from Jealousy wielding a heavy spear. When I left her, she had after a brief combat floored three kings in succession. / That evening she had arrived at a castle on the road to Paris, where she had learnt of Agramant's retreat to Arles after his defeat by her brother, Rinaldo. Convinced that Ruggiero must be with Agramant, as soon as the new light showed in the sky she took the road to Provence, hearing that Charlemagne was in pursuit thither. / On her way towards Provence by the most direct road, she met a damsel, fair of face and agreeable of manner, though tearful and distressed.

This was gentle, love-smitten Fiordiligi, who had left her beloved Brandimart at the bridge, a captive of Rodomont. / She was going in search of a knight habituated to battling in water and on land equally well, like an otter, and ferocious enough to be set against the pagan. Ruggiero's disconsolate lover courteously greeted this other disconsolate damsel as they met, and asked her the reason for her sorrows. /

Fiordiligi, looking at her, thought she saw a knight suitable to her purpose; and she started to tell her about the bridge where the King of Algiers barred the way, and how he had wrested her lover from her, not by dint of greater strength but because he was astute enough to derive advantage from the narrow bridge and the river. / 'If', she said, 'you are as brave and chivalrous as your appearance suggests, for God's sake avenge me on the man who has robbed me of my lord and brought such sorrow upon me. Or at least advise me where to go to find one who can stand up to him and who is sufficiently skilled in arms and fighting to discount any advantage the pagan may gain from the river and the bridge. / Not only will you be fulfilling the part of a chivalrous man and a knight errant, you shall also be calling up your valour in aid of the most faithful of all faithful lovers. On his other virtues it is not for me to discourse—they are so many that whoever has not heard about them can be said to be bereft of sight and hearing.' / The noble-hearted damsel, always drawn to feats which could earn her a glorious name, decided at once to go to the bridge—all the more readily now that she was desperate and could be going to her death: believing herself miserable in the loss of her Ruggiero, she had no love of life. /

'For what I'm worth, love-smitten lass,' replied Bradamant, 'I'll offer to undertake this difficult, dangerous exploit, and this for a number of reasons I shall pass over, but chiefly for one: because you ascribe to your lover a quality ascribed, I think, to only few men: that he is faithful in love. I swear to you I believed that in this all men were forsworn.' / She ended these words with a sigh, a sigh straight from the heart. Then, 'Let's go,' she said. And the next day they arrived at the river, at the perilous pass.

When they were sighted by the sentinel who always alerted his lord with a trumpet blast, Rodomont armed and took his station, as usual, by the river-bank at the bridge. / When Bradamant presented herself, he threatened to put her straight to death unless he made an oblation of her arms and steed to the great tomb. Bradamant, fully apprised of how Isabel had died at his hands, for Fiordiligi had told her, retorted to the proud Saracen as follows: / 'Why do you make the innocent do penance for your crime, you brute? It is with your own blood that you should placate her: you killed her and the whole world knows it. Far more acceptable to her, then, as oblation and victim than all the arms and trappings of those you have unhorsed is that I should avenge her by killing you. / And the offering will please her all the more from my hand, since I am a woman as she was. I have come here to no other purpose than to avenge her, and this is my sole wish. But before we match our valour it would be as well to make a pact: if I am defeated, you will do with me as you have done with your other captives. / But if I defeat you (as I hope and expect) I want your horse and your arms, and those alone I shall offer at the tomb; all the rest I shall remove from the marble walls. And I shall have you release to me all your warriors.'

'What you suggest seems fair to me,' replied the other. 'But I could not give you the prisoners for I do not have them here: / I have sent them to my kingdom in Africa. But I promise you on my honour that if by some quirk of Fate you remain mounted while I'm left on foot, I shall see to having them all set free in the time it takes to send a quick messenger on the errand you require of me if I lose. / But if you are the one to succumb—which is more plausible and is bound to happen—I would not have you surrender your arms or leave your name to be inscribed among the vanquished. I should offer up my victory to your comely face, lovely eyes, and tresses, all redolent of love and gracefulness. It is enough if you dispose yourself to love me where before you hated me. / Such is my valour, such my strength that you should feel no disgrace at losing.' He smiled slightly—a wry smile betraying anger more than anything else. The damsel made no reply to the arrogant Moor, but returned to the foot of the wooden bridge, spurred her steed and charged at him with her golden lance. /

Rodomont prepared for the joust. He charged at full tilt, hooves clattering across the bridge—a noise to deafen many an ear at quite a distance. The golden lance worked its accustomed magic: the pagan, hitherto a champion jouster, was lifted from his saddle, poised in mid-air, then dropped headfirst onto the bridge. / As she passed, she scarcely found room to slip by on her horse, and was in great peril of tumbling into the river—it was a close-run thing. But Rabican, who was conceived by wind and fire, was so quick and agile that he found a footing on the very brink—he would have walked along a sword's edge. / She turned and went back to the prostrate pagan. 'Now can you see who has lost', she teased, 'and which one of us must submit?' The pagan remained dumb with amazement that a woman should have unseated him. He could not, or would not, answer—he was as one crazed, stupefied. / Silent and glum he picked himself up, took five or six steps, then pulled off his shield, his helmet and all the rest of his armour and threw them against a rock. Then he vanished alone and on foot, not omitting first to instruct one of his pages to go and carry out the promise about the captives, according to his word. /

He left, and nothing more was heard of him except that he was living in a dark cave. Bradamant meanwhile had hung up his arms on the high tomb, and had had the arms removed of every knight who, she could tell by the inscription, belonged to the court of Charlemagne. The rest she did not remove, nor let anyone else remove. / Beside those of Brandimart there were those of Samsonet and of Oliver, who had taken the most direct road hither in order to find Orlando. Here they were captured, and a day earlier had been sent away by the proud Saracen. Bradamant had their arms removed from the high mausoleum and locked inside the tower. / All the other arms, stripped from the pagan warriors, she left hanging from the walls.

These included the arms of a king who, for the sake of his steed Frontalact, had bent his steps in vain: I mean those of Sacripant, King of Circassia. After much wandering over hill and dale he fetched up here where he lost his other horse, to continue on his way disarmed and unencumbered. / He had left the perilous bridge disarmed and on foot, the concession accorded by Rodomont to those of his faith. But he had no heart to return to the camp: he lacked the nerve to do so—after the boasts he had made, it would be too shaming to return in this reduced state. / He was seized, now, by a fresh urge to resume his search for Angelica, who alone was rooted in his heart. As chance would have it, he soon learnt (I could not say from whom) that she was on her way back to her own country. Pricked and spurred by Cupid, he set off at once, therefore, in her traces. /

But I want to return to Bradamant, Aymon's daughter. In a fresh inscription she set forth how she had freed the pass. Then she turned to Fiordiligi, who was sore at heart and whose face was downcast and tearful, and gently asked her where she would like to go from here. 'I should like to go to the Saracen camp at Arles,' she replied, / 'where I hope to find a ship and good company to cross to the African shore. I shall never stop until I come to my lord and husband. To shorten his captivity I mean to try a number of ways, so that if Rodomont's promise to you should miscarry I may have one or two other recourses.' / 'Let me offer you my company for a stretch of the way', said Bradamant, 'until you find Arles before you. Here, as a favour to me, I would have you seek out King Agramant's champion, Ruggiero, whose name is on everyone's lips and return to him this good steed off whom I have thrown the haughty Saracen. / I should like you to speak to him in precisely these words: "A knight who is confident of proving clearly before all the world that you have broken faith with him gave me this steed to give you so that you should be readily prepared. He said that you are to put on your armour and chain-mail and await his coming to do battle with you." / Say this to him and nothing else; and if he asks you who I am, say that you don't know.' Gentle as ever, Fiordiligi replied: 'After what you have done for me I shall never tire of spending in your service not merely words but life itself.' Bradamant thanked her and passed Frontino to her by the bridle. / The two fair travellers proceeded together along the river, many a long day's journey, until they came in sight of Arles and could hear the sea thundering on the nearby shore.

Bradamant stopped by the outposts at the approaches to the city-walls to give Fiordiligi time enough to deliver the steed to Ruggiero. / Fiordiligi, after passing through the wicket, across the bridge and in through the gate, found a guide to conduct her to where Ruggiero lived. Here she stopped and gave her message to his page, as instructed, and entrusted Frontino to him. Expecting no reply, she then pursued her way, the quicker to fulfil her own ambition. / Ruggiero was left bewildered and mystified: he could not begin to imagine who it was who was challenging him, who it was who had sent a messenger to insult him and to confer a kindness on him. He could not conceive or imagine how such a man—or anyone else for that matter—could call him a pledge-breaker. And the last person he would have suspected was Bradamant. / His suspicions fastened more readily upon Rodomont than upon anyone else; he pondered why he should hear such a charge from Rodomont, but the reason escaped him. Apart from him, he knew of no one in the whole world with whom he had a quarrel. Meanwhile Bradamant sought battle and loudly blew her horn. /

The news came to Marsilius and Agramant that a knight had come seeking battle. Now Serpentine happened to be with them, and he asked to be allowed to don armour and chain-mail, promising to capture this presumptuous fellow. The people crowded to the ramparts: not a child, not a dotard was backward in coming to watch who would win. / In gorgeous surcoat and fine array Serpentine da la Stella entered the lists, only to fall flat on the first impact. His steed seemed to have wings to flee with, but the damsel galloped after him and courteously fetched him back. 'Mount,' she bade the Saracen as she handed the bridle to him, 'and have your master send me a better champion.' / The African king, who was up on the ramparts overlooking the lists with a large retinue, was no little surprised at the courtesy the damsel had shown to Serpentine: she was entitled to take him prisoner but she did not, as he remarked in the hearing of the Saracens. Serpentine returned and, as bidden, asked the king to send her a better champion. /

Grandonio of Volterna, the haughtiest warrior in Spain, fumed and implored until he was second into the fray. He set out uttering menaces: 'Much good may your courtesy do you: if you fall to me, I shall take you, a prisoner, to my liege—but you shall die here if I am up to the mark.' 'I should not want your boorishness to impair my courtesy', returned the damsel, 'or prevent me from warning you to turn back before the hard ground makes your bones ache. Go back, and tell your liege from me that I haven't come forward for the likes of you: I have come here to seek battle with a warrior worthy of the challenge.' / At these pungent, biting words the pagan flared up in a passion: incapable of verbal reply, and seething with rage, he turned his steed. Bradamant turned too, and impelled Rabican—and her golden lance—against the braggart. As the magic lance touched his shield, it sent him spinning head over heels. / Magnanimously the warrior-damsel caught his steed for him and observed: 'Did I not tell you that you would have done better to carry my message than to be so eager to joust with me? Now please ask your king to choose from among his host a warrior who can match me; let him not waste my energy against the rest of you, who have little experience in arms.' / Those on the ramparts, who could not imagine who the warrior could be who kept his saddle so firmly, repeated the names of the legendary champions—names which made them shiver on the warmest days. Many said that it must be Brandimart; the majority agreed on Rinaldo, though several would have favoured Orlando did they not know of his pitiful condition. /

Ferrau sought the third bout, explaining that it was not as though he expected to win, but the warriors who had fallen before him would have a better excuse if he fell too. Then he equipped himself with all that was needed for the joust, and out of the hundred chargers he had in his stables he selected one who was eminently sure-footed and swift. / He set out towards the damsel to joust with her; but first he saluted her and she him. She asked: 'If I am allowed to know, pray tell me who are you?' Ferrau told her—he seldom concealed his identity. 'I shall not refuse you,' she said, 'though I should rather it had been another.' / 'Who?' asked Ferrau. 'Ruggiero . . .' she replied; and she could scarcely proffer the word—as she spoke it her beautiful face flushed pink as a rose. She added: '. . . whose famous feats have induced me to come for this trial. I crave nothing else, nothing else matters to me but to sample for myself what he can do as a jouster.' / She uttered the words in all simplicity, words which perhaps some evil minds may have taken in another sense. Ferrau answered: 'First let us see which of the two of us has the greater skill at arms. If I go the way of the many before me, the noble knight whom you are clearly so keen to invite to joust will come to make amends for my poor showing.' / Bradamant kept her visor raised as these words were exchanged. Gazing at her beautiful face, Ferrau felt himself already half-vanquished. 'This one seems to me an angel from heaven,' he mused. 'Even if she does not touch me with her lance, I am already conquered by her fair eyes.' / They drew apart; then, as with the others, Ferrau was knocked clean out of the saddle. Bradamant held his steed and said: 'Be off and do as you promised.'

Shamefaced, Ferrau went to Ruggiero, who was with King Agramant, and told him that the knight was asking to joust with him. / Ruggiero, still unaware who it was who was challenging him to battle, was delighted, confident of victory. He called for his armour and coat of mail; his courage was no whit jarred at having witnessed the hard knocks which felled the others. How he armed and how he set forth and what happened next I shall keep for the next canto.

THIRTY-SIXTH CANTO

1–10 Introductory. 11–58 The abortive fight of Marfisa and Bradamant, with Ruggiero's intervention. 58–84 Atlas reveals the kinship of Ruggiero and Marfisa, and what follows from it.

A NOBLE heart, wherever it be found, will always be gracious—it cannot be otherwise: it has derived from nature and habit a quality which it is then powerless to alter. Similarly a base heart, wherever it be found, will clearly show itself for what it is: Nature inclines to evil, a garb that proves difficult to change. /

Among the warriors of old, examples of chivalrous and noble conduct were frequently to be seen, but seldom in our own day: aye, wicked practices a-plenty were to be seen or marked, Hippolytus, during the war in which you adorned the churches with captured standards and towed the enemy ships, laden with booty, to your father's shores! / Every cruel, inhuman deed ever practised by Tartar, Turk, or Moor was perpetrated, if not indeed by will of the Venetians (for they have always been of exemplary justice), by the criminal hand of their mercenaries. I say nothing of all the fires they started, which burned down our farms and country retreats— / though this was indeed an ugly vengeance, especially against yourself: when you were in the emperor's camp at the siege of Padua, it was well known that you on more than one occasion forbade the firing of churches and villages, and had the fires put out once started, for thus it pleased your innate chivalry. /

I speak not of this, or of so many other villainous deeds of cruelty, but of one alone, the mere mention of which could draw tears from a stone: that day, my Lord, when you sent your household guard ahead of you against the fort to which the enemy had inauspiciously withdrawn from their ships. / They rode full into the sea, as when Hector and Aeneas sallied forth to burn the Greek galleys. I saw Ercole Cantelmo and Alessandro Ferruffino, drawn on by excessive boldness, spur their steeds and together outstrip the rest of us to harry the enemy right within their defences. They thrust so far that the latter had an awkward passage back while the former's was cut off: / Alessandro did escape, Ercole was caught. What must have been your feelings, then, O Duke of Sora, when you saw your valiant son's helmet drawn off amid a thousand swords, and watched him led to a ship's boat and there beheaded. I am surprised that the mere sight did not kill you just as the sword killed your son. / Cruel Slavonians, where did you learn your soldiering? In what Scythian land is it understood that a man should be killed after he has been caught, after he has surrendered and no longer defends himself? You killed him for defending his native soil. O cruel age of ours—the sun ought not to shine on you, for you teem with men the like of Tieste, Tantalus, and Atreus! / Cruel barbarians, there was no more valorous youth in his day from one pole to the other, from the furthest coasts of the Indies to the sun-set shores, but you had to take his head off! His youth and comeliness could have evoked pity in an anthropophagus, in Polyphemus, but not in you, for you are more wicked and brutal, far, than any Cyclops, any Lestrigon. / I do not believe that a similar example exists among the warriors of old—they studied courtesy and gallantry and were not cruel as victors. And Bradamant, far from harming those whom she had evicted from their saddles at a touch of her lance to their shields, even caught their horses for them and had them remount. /

I told you earlier how this valiant and beautiful damsel had unhorsed Serpentine da la Stella, Grandonio of Volterna, and Ferrau, and then left each of them to remount; and how she sent the third, Ferrau, to Agramant (who took her for a knight) to convey her challenge to Ruggiero. / Ruggiero was delighted to accept the invitation and called for his arms. While he was arming himself in the king's presence, the other courtiers reverted to discussing who this remarkable knight could be who was such a practised hand with a lance; and they asked Ferrau whether he recognized the knight, having spoken with him. / 'Make no mistake,' Ferrau assured them, 'it is none of those you have named. I had plain sight of the face, and it looked to me like that of Rinaldo's younger brother—but now that I have experienced this knight's great prowess and realize that Richardet could never have measured up to it, I believe it must be his sister who, from what I hear, looks very much like him. / She has a reputation for being as strong as Rinaldo—as any paladin—though from what I have seen today, I should imagine she outdoes her brother, and Orlando her cousin.' Hearing her mentioned, Ruggiero blushed the colour of the morning sky; his heart fluttered, he was quite distracted. / At this mention he felt the stab, the stimulus of Cupid's dart; he felt a blaze within and at the same time an icy touch of apprehension in his bones—a fear that some sort of pique had gnawed away the burning love for him which had once possessed her. Bewildered by this, he could not decide whether to go out to fight her or to stay where he was. /

Now Marfisa was here and felt a strong urge to enter the lists; she was ready armed (you would seldom have found her otherwise, night or day) and, hearing that Ruggiero was arming, she realized that to let him go first would be to deprive herself of the victory. So she decided to forestall him, expecting to reap the rewards. / She leapt onto her steed and charged away to where Bradamant waited with beating heart for Ruggiero, anxious to make him her captive, and concentrating on where to aim her lance so as to do him the least injury. Marfisa emerged from the gate; the crest on her helmet was a phoenix, which she wore either out of pride, / to denote that she was unique for martial prowess, or else to celebrate her chaste intention of living single for ever.

Bradamant scrutinized her and, not recognizing the features of her beloved, asked to know her name, and learnt that she was the one who enjoyed his love; / or rather, the one whom she believed to be enjoying his love, the one whom she detested so passionately she saw herself dying if she did not requite her grief in vengeance upon her. She turned her horse and charged ferociously, meaning not to unseat her but to run the lance clean through her breast and be free of all further jealousy. / One thrust, and Marfisa had to test for herself the hardness of the ground—a thing so much outside her experience that it drove her almost wild with rage. She had scarcely hit the ground when she drew her sword, meaning to be avenged of her fall. But Bradamant, no whit less fiery, cried: 'What's this? You're my prisoner! / I may have shown courtesy to the others, Marfisa, but I shan't to you: there's little good in you, I hear, and plenty of insolence.' These words evoked from Marfisa a roar like a sea-wind against a cliff. Speechless with fury, she could give no utterance to her reply except as a screech. / She flashed her sword, striking wildly, both at Bradamant and at her steed, in the chest and belly; but Bradamant made him spring aside with a jerk of the reins, meanwhile thrusting her lance in a fit of anger. A mere touch of the weapon sent Marfisa sprawling in the dust, / but she was on her feet at once, trying to wreak mischief with her sword; again Bradamant darted her lance, again Marfisa was knocked flat. (Bradamant was no weakling, true, but she was not so superior to Marfisa that she could have knocked her down at each stroke—this was the virtue residing in the magic lance.) /

Now a few knights from our side had arrived where the joust was progressing in a space between the two camps (not half a league apart), having seen the prowess shown by their champion—whom they could not recognize, beyond identifying her with the Christian side. / Seeing these knights approach his walls, Agramant, King Trojan's noble son, whom no contingency, no peril was going to catch unawares, gave the call to arms, sending many troops on a foray from the walls. Among these was Ruggiero, who had been forestalled into the lists by hasty Marfisa. / The love-struck young man watched the outcome of the duel, all palpitating in fear for his beloved bride, for he knew how Marfisa could fight. I say he feared for her at the start, when the two made their ferocious charge. But, seeing how the combat developed, he was struck with amazement; / and as this duel did not end with the first encounter, as the previous duels had done, he was deeply anxious lest some sort of mischief result: he was concerned for both of them, for he loved them both, not that his love was the same for each—for the one it was fire and passion, for the other, affection rather than love. / He would gladly have parted the combatants, had this been possible honourably. But his comrades were leaping into the fray, meaning to influence it, lest Charlemagne's champion win, for he appeared to be the stronger. On their side, the Christian knights pressed forward, ready to engage. /

Here, there, the call to arms was heard—now an almost daily occurrence. Those on foot: to horse! Those unarmed: to arms! Every man to his standard! More than one trumpeter scurried about giving the signal, the shrill paean of war; while these roused the cavalry, the drums and tabors roused the foot-soldiers. / The skirmish was engaged, as violent and bloody as can be imagined. Valiant Bradamant, burdened with exceptional regret that she had not succeeded in killing Marfisa— her dearest wish that day—turned this way and that to catch sight of Ruggiero for whom she pined. /

Then she recognized him, by the silver eagle on his azure shield, and stopped to concentrate her gaze, and thoughts, upon his shoulders, his chest, the gracefulness of his physique and bearing—until, imagining that another woman was being favoured by it all, in an access of fury she broke out: / 'What! Is another woman to kiss those lovely, sweet lips if I am not to? Ah, let it never be that you should belong to another: if you are not mine you must be no one's! Sooner than die alone of passion I will have you die with me at my hands: though I lose you here, at least hell will restore you to me and you shall be with me in eternity. / If you slay me, you should in justice also afford me the consolation of being avenged, for every law provides that he who slays another shall forfeit his own life. Even so, your loss would not equal mine, for you would die of right, I, wrongly. I shall kill one who wants me dead, alas; but you, cruel man, will slay one who loves and adores you. / Good hand of mine, what makes you fear to open my enemy's heart with the sword? He has so many times stabbed me to death under the pledge of love and peace, and now he can consent to take my life, with no pity for my grief. Come, heart, be bold against this ruthless one; kill to avenge my thousand deaths.' / Thus saying, she spurred against him, but first, 'Beware, false Ruggiero,' she cried, 'you shall not, if I can help it, parade the rich trophy of a damsel's heart!'

When Ruggiero heard this, he thought it must be his betrothed, as in fact it was, whose voice he so clearly remembered that he could have recognized it among a thousand. / He well realized what underlay her words: she was accusing him of breaking the compact they had made. In order to explain, therefore, he signalled his wish to speak with her. But she, driven by grief and anger, was already charging, visor shut, to unseat him—and perhaps where there was no sand. / Seeing her so incensed, Ruggiero braced himself in his armour and in the saddle and set his lance in rest; but he held it poised and deflected in such a way that it would not hurt her. The damsel, who was closing to strike and injure him, her mind hardened against pity, could not bring herself, once she was near, to throw him to the ground and do him intended harm. / So their lances proved ineffectual at this encounter; and sufficient it was for Love to joust with both of them, striking at their hearts with an amorous lance.

Unable to bring herself to harm Ruggiero, the damsel turned elsewhere the passion blazing within her, and wrought feats which were to remain famous as long as the heavens revolved. / In no time she threw to the ground three hundred and more with that golden lance. She won the battle that day single-handed, alone she routed the Moorish host. Ruggiero roamed in all directions until he could approach her and say: 'I'll die if I do not speak with you. Alas, what have I done to you that you must shun me? Listen, for love of God!' / As at the warm breath of the mild South Wind blowing off the sea the snows melt, and the icy glaciers which had been so hard; so at this prayer, at this brief lament Bradamant's heart, which anger threatened to make harder than marble, at once turned soft and compassionate. / She would not or could not answer him other than by spurring Rabican across his path and beckoning to him as she sped off as far from the rest as she could. She betook herself to a secluded valley far from the crowd; here there was a patch of level ground in the middle of which stood a small plantation of cypresses which seemed all to bear the same stamp. / In that little wood a high tomb of white marble had recently been erected; a brief inscription identified who lay within for anyone who cared to know. Bradamant reached this spot but (I believe) paid no heed to the inscription. Ruggiero spurred after the damsel hot-foot until he caught up with her in the wood. /

But let us return to Marfisa. She had remounted her steed and was coming to find the warrior-damsel who had floored her at first encounter. She saw Bradamant leave the throng with Ruggiero in pursuit, and never dreamt that he could be following her out of love: she assumed it was to settle a quarrel with arms. / She spurred her steed and followed their traces, to reach the wood almost when they did. How welcome her arrival was to the couple any lover will gauge without my describing it. But Bradamant took it the harder, seeing the damsel on whom she blamed her own misery. Who could dissuade her from believing that Marfisa had been spurred hither by her love for Ruggiero? / And once more she called Ruggiero false: 'Was it not enough for you, false one, that I should know your perfidy by hearsay, but you must also flaunt the woman before me? I see how you long to drive me away from you; and to satisfy your pernicious desire I want to die—but I shall first see that the cause of my death die with me.' /

This said, angry as a viper, she sprang at Marfisa, striking that damsel's shield such a blow of her lance as to spin her backwards out of the saddle, to land with her helmet half buried in the ground. It could not be said that Marfisa was taken unawares: no, she braced herself as best she could, but still she hit the ground headfirst. / Bradamant, who wanted to die or to slay Marfisa, was in such a passion that she never thought to strike her again with the lance, so as to floor her again, but straightway to sever her bust from her head half stuck in the sand. She threw aside her golden lance, drew her sword and at once dismounted. / But she was too late: she found herself face to face with Marfisa, who was brimming with rage after seeing herself so easily thrown to the sand at the second encounter. Ruggiero was much distressed at this, but useless it was for him to yell and entreat: hate and fury so blinded the damsels that they grappled in a frenzy. / Straight off they were at half-sword length; and in their blazing indignation they pressed forward, each advancing beneath the other's sword-arm so that they perforce had to come into a clinch. They dropped their swords, no longer serviceable, and groped for other weapons. Ruggiero begged and besought them both, but his words were fruitless. /

Seeing that his entreaties were worthless, he made to part them by force: he wrested from each one her dagger and dropped them at the foot of a cypress. Now that they no longer had a weapon with which to harm each other, he interposed himself with prayers and threats, but all in vain—having nothing else to fight with, they continued their battle with punches and kicks. / But Ruggiero did not give up: he grasped now one, now the other, by the hand, by the arm and tugged them each away. His result was to kindle Marfisa into a blaze of anger against him. Detached from Bradamant, Marfisa, who scorned all mankind, overlooked Ruggiero's friendship and fell upon him with her sword. /

'You unmannerly boor, Ruggiero, to disturb our fight! I shall make you rue it, though—this hand will be enough to beat you both together!' Ruggiero tried with gentle words to placate Marfisa, but found her in such a temper against him that his words were wasted on her. / In the end Ruggiero, flushing with anger, drew his own sword. I do believe that neither Athens, nor Rome nor any other place ever offered a spectacle to bring such pleasure to the onlookers as this one ravished and delighted jealous Bradamant, banishing as it did her every suspicion. / She had picked up her sword and drawn aside to watch. Ruggiero's strength and skill made him seem, in her eyes, the God of War; and if he looked like Mars, Marfisa looked like a Fury unleashed. True it is that for a while the young champion took care to hold back— / he knew the capability of his sword from long experience of using it: where Balisard fell, no enchantment could resist it—spells became powerless and inoperative. Therefore he took care to present neither the edge nor the point of his sword when he struck but always the flat of it. For a long time he was careful of this, but the moment came when he lost patience: / Marfisa landed him a fearful blow to split his skull; he raised his shield to ward off the blow, which smashed against his eagle emblem. A magic charm prevented the shield from splitting, but did not prevent his arm from being numbed. Had his armour been other than Hector's, the fierce blow might have taken off his arm / and then descended upon his head which the enraged damsel meant to strike.

Ruggiero could scarcely move his left arm, scarcely sustain his fair eagle. So he eschewed all pity: in his eyes a spark seemed to ignite and he lunged as hard as he could: Marfisa, alas for you, had you been hit! / I cannot quite tell how it happened, but the sword drove into a cypress tree, embedding itself a palm's width and more in the trunk. (The place was thickly planted.)

At that moment a great earthquake shook the mountain and the valley floor, and from the tomb in the midst of the wood a voice could be heard issuing, louder than any human voice. / 'Let there be no fight between you,' cried the dreadful voice, 'it is wrong and inhuman for a

437

brother to slay his sister, for a sister to slay her brother. You, my Ruggiero, and you, my Marfisa, believe my words—they are not vain: in one womb from one seed you were conceived, and you came together into the world. / You were conceived by Ruggiero the Second; Galaciella was your mother; having dispatched your unhappy father from this life, her brothers, all heedless that she was heavy with the weight of you, that you both come from their own stock, abandoned her at sea in a frail craft to drown. / But Fortune, who had already chosen you for glorious deeds though you were still unborn, made the boat run safely aground on the uninhabited coast of the Syrtes. Here Galaciella gave you birth, after which her elected soul ascended to paradise. As God willed, and it was your destiny, I happened to be near. / I gave your mother as decent a burial as was possible in so desert a place; you two babes I wrapped in my cloak and took up with me to the mountains of Carena. There I made a lioness tamely leave the jungle and her young, and took great care to have her suckle you for ten months and another ten. /

'One day when I had to leave home and go on a journey, a band of Arabs happened by—you may remember. They took you away, Marfisa, but could not catch you, Ruggiero: you ran faster. I grieved at your loss, and watched over Ruggiero the more diligently. / Ruggiero, you know how your mentor Atlas protected you while he lived. I had heard the fixed stars' prediction that you were to die, betrayed, in the Christian camp, and to avert the evil influence, I tried to keep you away. But, unable in the end to oppose your will, I fell sick and died of grief. / Before dying, though, I had these heavy slabs assembled with infernal help to make my tomb on this spot, where I foresaw that you would fight with Marfisa. And of Charon I loudly demanded: "When I am dead, you are not to take my spirit from this wood until Ruggiero arrives here with his sister to fight." / So my spirit has awaited your coming these many days in this pleasant shade, so that you, Bradamant, who love our Ruggiero, be no more possessed by jealousy. But now it is time for me to abandon the light and take myself off to the cloister of darkness.' Here he fell silent, leaving Marfisa, Bradamant, and Ruggiero lost in wonder. /

With great joy Ruggiero recognized Marfisa as his sister, and she him. They embraced each other without distress to Bradamant, who burned for Ruggiero. And as they recollected details of their early years—things done and said and experienced—they discovered with greater certainty that all that the spirit had told them was true. / Ruggiero did not conceal from his sister how deeply Bradamant was rooted in his heart, and he chose fond words to describe the many debts he owed to her. He would not rest until he had composed the

quarrel they had pursued hitherto, and made them, in token of reconciliation, embrace each other most tenderly. / Marfisa reverted to asking who their father was and of what family; and who had slain him and
how, whether in narrow confines or on the field of battle, and who had
committed their poor mother to be killed by the cruel sea. For if she
had heard about it as a child, she now retained little or no memory of
it. / Ruggiero set about explaining to her their descent from the Trojans by Hector's line; how Hector saved Astyanax from Ulysses' hands
and the besetting snares, leaving in his place one of his children of
similar age, and escaped from Troy; and how, after a long sea-voyage,
he arrived in Sicily and ruled over Messina. /

'His descendants, leaving Messina's lighthouse beyond the Straits,
ruled over parts of Calabria, but after many successions they moved to
Rome. From their blood was sprung more than one illustrious emperor
and king, in Rome and elsewhere, starting with Constantius and
Constantine up till Charlemagne, son of Pepin. / Ruggiero the First
was of this stock, and so was John the Baron, Buovo, Rambald
and, finally, Ruggiero the Second, who got our mother pregnant, as you
heard Atlas say. The shining deeds of our descendants will be celebrated
in history throughout the world, you shall see.' He went on to describe
how King Agolant arrived with his sons Almont and Trojan (Agramant's
father); / and how he brought with him a damsel—a daughter of his—
of such prowess that she unhorsed many a paladin; and how she ultimately fell in love with Ruggiero and, for love of him, defied her father
and received baptism and married him. He described how the traitor
Bertram burned with incestuous love for his sister-in-law, / and how
he betrayed his country, his father, and two brothers, hoping thus to
gain possession of her: he opened Reggio to the enemy—who disposed
of them all hideously. And he described how Agolant and his cruel,
evil sons put Galaciella, six months pregnant, in a boat adrift in the
sea during the storms in the depth of winter. /

Serenely Marfisa attended to her brother's words. She rejoiced to be
issued from a spring fed by streams so bright—Mongrana on the one
side, Clairmont on the other, as she knew, both without compare for
men of eminence, the splendour of the world for years without end. /
But when her brother came to the treacherous murder of their father
by Agramant's father, grandfather, and uncle, and to the ordeal inflicted upon their mother, Marfisa could no longer listen to him.
'Brother, with respect', she broke in, 'you have been all too remiss not
to have avenged our murdered father. / If you could not steep yourself
in the blood of Almont and Trojan, who died too soon, you should have
taken vengeance upon the sons. Why, as you live, is Agramant alive?
Here is a mark on your face which you never remove: far from putting

this king to death after such great crimes, you even live at his court, and in his pay. / I swear to God that I mean to adore Christ as true God, just as my father did, and not to take off this armour till I have avenged him and my mother. And you shall cause me displeasure—you do already—if I see you any more in the ranks of King Agramant or of any other Moorish prince, unless with your sword drawn to their detriment.' /

Oh how these words elated fair Bradamant and rejoiced her! She encouraged Ruggiero to do as Marfisa admonished him. He should come and present himself to Charlemagne, she said, who paid such honour, adulation, and respect to the bright name of his father, Ruggiero, and even now called him a peerless champion. / Ruggiero was quick to aver that this indeed is what he should have done at the outset; but that, not having well understood the facts as he afterwards did, he had left it too late: as it was Agramant who had buckled on his sword, it would be a crime to slay him, and he would be a traitor, for he had accepted him as his liege lord. / But as he had already promised Bradamant, so he promised Marfisa that he would try every way to bring about an occasion whereby he could secede without dishonour. If he had not yet done so, he was not to blame but Mandricard, who had left him in the state everyone knew of as a result of their combat: / to this, Marfisa, coming daily to his bedside, was as good a witness as any. After much discussion by the two renowned warrior-damsels, it was ultimately concluded that Ruggiero should return to the standards of his liege until the occasion fell to him to transfer with justice to Charlemagne. / Let him go,' said Marfisa to Bradamant. 'Have no fear: in a few days I shall see to it that Agramant be no longer his lord.' So said she, without specifying exactly what she had in mind to do.

Ruggiero finally took leave of them and turned his horse to return to his liege, / when sobs could be heard from the nearby valley, which made them all attentive. They all bent their ears to listen to what sounded like a woman's weeping. But here I want to end this canto; humour me, for I promise to narrate to you better things if you come to listen to me in the next canto.

THIRTY-SEVENTH CANTO

1-24 On Woman and Fame. 25-122 Ruggiero, Bradamant and Marfisa hear of wicked Marganor, the woman-hater, and take vengeance upon him.

IF those accomplished ladies who have striven night and day with the most diligent application to acquire some gift that Nature bestows only upon the industrious—and some brilliant work will have been the happy product—if those ladies, I say, had devoted themselves instead to those studies which confer immortality upon mortal virtues, / and had been able by themselves to achieve undying reputation without having to beg it from authors, their fame would soar to heights perhaps beyond the reach of any of the male sex. Male writers are so eaten to the heart with malice and envy that they often pass in silence over the good they might have mentioned, while promulgating all the evil they know. /

For many men are not satisfied with titivating each others' reputations: they must also take it upon themselves to disclose any blemishes in woman. They—the men of old, I mean—would never allow women the upper hand, but did their utmost to keep them down, as though the fair sex's honour would cloud their own, as mist obscures the sun. / But there was never a hand set to paper, nor a tongue forming words, which possessed the power (though it employed every skill to inflate evil and belittle good) to extinguish woman's glory to the point where none survives: some does, but not the full tally—not by a long streak! / There is no denying, though, the existence of Harpalice or Tomiris, or of Camilla and Pentesilea, helpmates of Turnus and Hector, or of Dido, who made a long sea-voyage to settle in Libya, followed by the men of Sidon and Tyre, or of Zenobia, or of Semiramis who victoriously conquered the Assyrians, Persians, and Indians: these women and a few others were not alone in deserving immortal fame for their armed achievements. / Faithful, chaste, virtuous, and constant women have existed not only in Greece and Rome but in every region where the Sun spreads his rays between the Indies and the Garden of the Hesperides. Their virtues are lost to fame, though: out of a thousand names barely one is mentioned. This is because the writers of their day were deceitful, envious, and mean. /

You ladies who incline to meritorious deeds, do persist in following your bent; do not be deflected from your high calling by the fear of not being paid the honour due to you. Just as there is no good which lasts forever, so it is with the bad: if hitherto paper and ink have not favoured you, we have now arrived in our own day. / First, Marullo and Pontano are for you; and two Strozzis, father and son; there is Bembo, and Capello, and Castiglione who, like him, has formed courtiers in his own image; there is Luigi Alamanni. There are two Gonzagas, beloved equally by Mars and the Muses, both of the family that rules Mantua, the city divided by the Mincio which surrounds it with deep ponds. / One of these two, beside being inclined by his own instinct to honour and revere you ladies, and to make Parnassus and Cynthus echo with your praises, exalting you to the skies, has made a total surrender to you thanks to the love, the fidelity, the sturdy spirit shown by his Isabella, undaunted by threats of reprisal and ruin. / He can never tire, therefore, of paying you honour in living verse. And if other men speak ill of you, there is no man readier than he to take up arms in your cause, no knight in the world more reckless of his life in defence of what is good. While providing matter for the pen of others, by his own pen he quickens others' glory. / And if a woman so richly endowed with all the virtues to be found in the fair sex never wavers in her constancy but supports him as a very pillar, despising every blow of fate—truly he deserves such a woman. He deserves her and she him: never was a couple better assorted. / He leaves fresh trophies on the banks of the Oglio, disseminating—amid the swords and flames, the ships and carriage-wheels—pages so well indited that the nearby stream could well envy him.

Then there is Ercole Bentivoglio whose limpid notes add lustre to your glory; there is Renato Trivulzio, too, and my Guidetto, and Molza, called by Apollo to write of you. / There is Ercole, Duke of Chartres, son of my lord Alfonso; he spreads his wings like a melodious swan and as he flies he sings, making your name heard in the heavens. There is my lord the Marquis of Vasto; not only do his deeds furnish matter enough for the scribes of a thousand Athens, a thousand Romes, but also it is clear he means to immortalize you with his pen. /

And beside these and other men who have brought and still bring you glory, you can bring it upon yourselves: many of you have left, and are leaving, your needles and fabrics to visit the Muses at the source of Hippocrene, there to slake your thirst; and you are so transformed on your return that we have more need of your labours than you of ours. / If I am to give a proper account of each one of these ladies, identifying them and paying them their due, I shall have to rule more than one sheet of paper and speak of nothing else in my canto today. And if I choose five or six to praise, I may offend and provoke the rest. What, then, shall I do? Must I pass over them all, or single out but one from so many? /

I shall choose one—and shall so choose as to confound envy, for no woman will have cause for umbrage if I pass over the rest to praise this one alone. This one woman has not only made herself immortal with a style, a sweetness I have never heard bettered; but she can draw from the grave and immortalize whomsoever she speaks or writes about. / Just as Phoebus confers more radiance upon his white sister the Moon, and attends to her more than to Venus or Mercury or any other star which moves with the heavens or gyrates on its own; so he breathes more fluency, more sweetness upon the one I speak of than upon the others, and gives such power to her lofty words that in our day he has adorned the heavens with another sun. / Victoria is her name—appropriate for one born amid victories, one who, wherever she goes, is preceded or followed by Victory, her constant companion, and is ever adorned with triumphal trophies. She is another Artemisia, who was praised for devotion to her Mausolus: indeed, she is so much the greater in that to rescue a man from the grave is a feat so much more splendid than to bury him. / If Laodamia, if Portia, Brutus' wife, if Arria, Argia, Evadne, and many other women deserved praise for having claimed burial with their deceased husbands, how much more honour is due to Victoria who, despite the Fates and Death, has drawn her consort out from Lethe and from the Styx, the river which nine times encircles the infernal shades! / If Alexander envied proud Achilles the glorious clarion of Homer, how much more, were he alive today, would he envy you, invincible Francesco of Pescara, that a wife so chaste, so dear to you, should sing the eternal honour due to you, and that she has brought such resonance to your name that you need crave no shriller trumpet. /

If I proposed to set down on paper all that could be said about this lady, or all that I could wish to say, I should go on and on and still leave a great deal unspoken. And the pleasant tale of Marfisa and her companions, which I promised I should pursue if you came to hear me in this canto, would be neglected. / Now since you are here to listen to me and I to fulfil my pledge, I shall reserve till greater leisure my efforts to give full expression to her praises—not that I imagine she needs my poems who produces her own so plentifully, but I need to satisfy this desire of mine to applaud and honour her. / To conclude, ladies, every age has produced many a woman meriting a legend, but the envy of writers has deprived you of posthumous renown. This will no longer be true now that you see to assuring your own immortality. Had the two sisters-in-law been capable of this, their excellent deeds would all be better known: / I mean Bradamant and Marfisa, whose eminent victories I attempt to restore to the light, though nine out of ten of them have slipped me by; those that I do know I most willingly describe, for every good action that lies hidden ought to be revealed, and besides, I crave to please you, ladies, whom I love and respect. /

Ruggiero had taken his leave, as I said, and was about to go. He had pulled his sword out from the tree-trunk, this time unimpeded, when a loud wailing not far off made him pause, and with the damsels he set off in that direction, to bring help if needed. / As they pressed on, the sound grew more distinct and the words more recognizable. They came to a hollow where they found three damsels uttering these laments, and they were most strangely attired: their dresses had been cut off below the navel by some person of scant courtesy, and, not knowing how better to conceal themselves, they were sitting on the ground and dared not rise. / Like Erichthonius, Vulcan's son, who was fashioned out of the dust without a mother—Pallas had him raised under the earnest care of Aglauros, the damsel whose gaze was overbold: just as he would hide his deformed feet by remaining seated in the chariot he was first to devise, so did those three damsels keep their secret parts concealed by sitting. / This monstrous, unseemly spectacle turned noble Marfisa and Bradamant the colour of a spring rose in the gardens of Paestum. Bradamant noticed at once that one of them was Ullania, who had come to France as ambassadress from the Lost Island. / She recognized the other two damsels equally, for she had seen them before in her company; but she addressed her words to the one whom she most respected. She asked her who was the wicked man, so estranged from law and custom as to disclose to the public eye those secrets which Nature evidently made a point of hiding. /

Ullania, who, by Bradamant's speech as much as by her emblem, recognized her as the one who a few days earlier had unseated the three warriors, told how some evil folk, closed to pity, had in a castle nearby not only insulted her by shortening her clothes, but had beaten her and done her other wrong. / She could not tell what had become of the shield or of the three kings who had kept them company so long through so many countries. She did not know whether they were dead or captives. She had taken this road, she said, though she found travel on foot most fatiguing, to complain to Charlemagne of the outrage, hoping that he would not tolerate it. / The warrior-damsels and Ruggiero being as compassionate as they were brave and bold, their handsome faces darkened when they heard and, worse, beheld such grave wrongs. And, forgetful of all else, without awaiting a plea or summons to vengeance from the distressed damsel, they hastened off towards that castle. / They most considerately decided, by common consent, to leave off their cloaks, which provided ample cover for the pudenda of those unfortunates. Bradamant would not let Ullania retrace on foot the road she had already trodden, so she pulled her up behind; Marfisa and good Ruggiero did likewise with the other two. / Ullania showed Bradamant, who was carrying her, the shortest way to the castle, and Bradamant, for her part, encouraged her with the promise that she would avenge her on her persecutors.

They left the valley by a long road which zigzagged up a hill. The sun was hidden in the sea before they rested on their journey, / when they came to a hamlet set on the summit of the steep hill—a hard climb. Here they found good lodging and fare such as that neighbourhood could afford them. Looking about, they noticed that the place was full of women, young and old; in such a throng not a single man's face was to be seen. / If Jason and his Argonauts were amazed at the women of Lemnos, who slew their husbands, sons, fathers, and brothers, so that their whole island could not boast two male faces, no less amazed were Ruggiero and his companions when they reached their night's lodging. / That evening the two damsels provided Ullania and her maidens with three gowns which, if somewhat rustic, were at least entire.

Ruggiero summoned one of the women living here and asked her where the menfolk were, for he could see not one. She replied as follows: / 'This may be a surprise to you—so many women without men—but to us, who live here as unhappy exiles, it is a heavy penalty, past enduring. And, to make our hard banishment the more intolerable, the fathers, sons, and husbands we so love are harshly segregated from us: our cruel tyrant will have it so. / After subjecting us to a thousand slights, the barbarous brute has banished us hither from his lands, some two leagues off, where we were born. And if our menfolk come to us, or if he hears that we have welcomed their coming, he has threatened them and us unfortunates with death and every torment. / He is so hostile to our name that he will have us no closer to him than I said, nor let any of our menfolk come to us, as though he feared contagion from the smell of woman. Already twice the trees have laid aside and resumed the glory of their tresses since the evil tyrant became possessed of this folly, and there is no one to set him to rights. / For the people fear him worse than death itself: he is spiteful and, what is more, Nature has endowed him with super-human strength: he has the build of a giant and the force of a hundred men. And it is not just his subjects whom he oppresses—his behaviour to alien women is even worse. /

'If you care for your honour and for these three damsels here, you will find it safer, better and more sensible not to continue but to take another road. This one leads to the castle of the man of whom I speak, where you may sample for yourselves the brutal methods he has established, to the injury and degradation of ladies and knights who venture there. / Marganor is the name of the tyrant of this place. Neither Nero nor any other who had a reputation for savagery was more evil or sinister; he thirsts after human blood, especially female, more than the wolf after the lamb's. He drives out ignominiously all women whose dire fate has brought them to his castle.' /

Ruggiero and the damsels wished to know what had driven the wicked man to this. They asked the woman kindly to continue, or rather to embark upon the complete story. 'The lord of the castle', she began, 'was a cruel, inhuman savage from the start, but to begin with he concealed his evil bent and did not disclose his true nature. / For his two sons, while they were alive, behaved quite differently from their father: they welcomed visitors and avoided doing anything cruel or degrading. Here all was courtesy, elegance, refinement, for their father, for all his avarice, never thwarted their desires. / The ladies and knights who happened this way were made so welcome that they would leave with a very warm regard for the eminent courtesy of the two brothers, both of whom had assumed the sacred order of knighthood. One of them was called Cilander, the other Tanacre; they were brave champions and of royal mien. / Truly they merited all praise and honour, and would have continued to do so had they not abandoned themselves to that urge which we call Love. This led them astray from the right path into the labyrinth of error. And all the good they had ever done was all at once contaminated and defiled. /

'There arrived here a knight from the court of the Greek emperor, accompanied by his lady, a well-bred damsel, and beautiful beyond one's wildest dreams. Cilander fell so deeply in love with her that he thought he would die if he did not possess her. At her departure, he felt, he would have to take leave of his life. / Now since prayers would have been unavailing he decided to take her by force. He armed and silently hid where they were to pass, near the castle. His natural impulsiveness and his burning love inhibited any mature reflection: seeing the knight approaching, he charged out to attack him, lance to lance. / At the first impact he expected to unseat him and carry off the victory and the lady; but his adversary, a champion at arms, shattered his breastplate as though it were glass. The news reached Cilander's father at the castle; he had him brought back on a stretcher and, finding him dead, buried him with many tears in the ancestral tomb. /

'There was no variation, however, in the extent of the hospitality afforded to all comers, for Tanacre possessed all of his brother's courtesy and grace. That same year a baron came with his wife to the castle from a distant land; he was amazingly stalwart, while her beauty was indescribably exquisite. / She deserved praise for her virtue and solid worth, no less than for her beauty. As for the baron, he was of noble stock, and valiant to a degree seldom ascribed to others: it well became a man of his merits to enjoy a treasure of such value and excellence as he possessed. His name was Olinder of Longueville; his lady, Drusilla. / Young Tanacre burned for her no less than his brother for the earlier lady; the evil desire he entertained for her brought a bitter taste to his mouth. No less than his brother, he chose to break every rule of sacred hospitality rather than to suffer his obdurate, new-formed desire to prove the death of him. / But as he had before his eyes the lesson of his brother and how he had died, he considered taking her in such a way as not to fear Olinder's vengeance. All at once the virtue on which he used to repose did not merely dwindle but altogether died in him—for he was not normally sunk in the waters of vice, at the bottom of which his father lay. /

'In deep silence that night he assembled twenty armed men and placed an ambush in some caves along the road some distance from the castle. Here next day he barred Olinder's way and blocked all his escape routes; though the baron put up a stout defence, he was in the end robbed of his life and of his consort. / Olinder slain, he led away the beauty captive, and so distressed that she had no wish to remain alive but begged to be dispatched as a kindness. To kill herself she leapt off the edge of a ravine, but die she could not, though she was all battered and bruised, her skull cracked. / Tanacre had to bring her home on a stretcher; he was quick to have her attended by a physician, for he did not want to lose so cherished a prey. And while he was having her cured he made preparations for their wedding: a woman so beautiful and chaste deserved the name of wife, not of mistress. / Tanacre thought of nothing else, desired nothing else, cared about nothing else, spoke of nothing else. Aware that he had wronged her, he admitted his guilt and did what he could to make amends, but all in vain: the more he loved her and the harder he tried to appease her, the more she loathed him, and the more resolute her determination to kill him. /

'But this hatred by no means blunted her wits: she recognized that if she were to carry out her intention she would have to dissemble, to lay hidden snares; she would have to give an exterior show of desiring the opposite of her true goal (Tanacre's destruction); she had to show herself detached from her first love and fully surrendered to him. / Her face affected peace, but her heart cried out for vengeance and studied nothing else. She turned over many possibilities: some she accepted, some rejected, leaving others undecided. She felt that she would realize her ambition by compassing her own death—here she would attain her end; and where and how better to die than in avenging her dear husband? / So she displayed gladness and pretended to yearn for this wedding above all else. Far from showing any reluctance, she forced aside whatever might delay it. She adorned and painted herself more than the other women: she seemed to have totally forgotten Olinder—her only desire being for the wedding to take place according to the custom of her own country. / Not that there was any truth in her assertion about the custom of her country—but her mind was concentrated exclusively on the one end she intended, so she invented a lie which brought her the hope of slaying her husband's murderer.

'She said, then, that she wanted the wedding to be in her native tradition, and went on to explain: / the widow who remarries must, before acceding to her new husband, placate the spirit of the deceased one whom she has offended, by having offices and masses celebrated in the church in which his bones are laid, in remission of his sins. When the sacrifice is finished, the new bridegroom must give his bride the ring. / Meanwhile the priest is to say suitably devout prayers over the wine, brought for this purpose, and bless it. Then he pours it from the flagon into a chalice and gives it to the couple—but it is to be presented first to the bride who must be the first to set her lips to it. / Tanacre, unaware of what lay behind her wanting the marriage to take place according to her custom, told her to do as she pleased so long as this shortened the time for their union. Little did the wretched fellow realize that she was thus compassing her vengeance for Olinder's death, and that her desires were fixed so intensely upon this one object that she thought of nothing else. /

'Now Drusilla had an old serving woman who was captured with her and had remained with her. She summoned her and whispered in her ear so that none of the household could hear: "Prepare me a quick-acting poison, as I know you can, and bottle it for me—I have found a way to kill the treacherous son of Marganor. / Yes, and I know a way to save myself, and you too, but I shall tell you later, at greater leisure." The old woman left and prepared the poison, bottled it and returned to the palace, where she found a full flask of sweet Candian wine in which to put the baneful juice; here she kept it for the wedding-day, all delays now being removed. /

'On the appointed day Drusilla came to the church decked in jewels and gracefully attired. Here she had had Olinder's tomb suitably elevated on two pillars. Here the office was solemnly intoned, and everyone, man and woman, came to listen. Marganor himself, more jovial than usual, came with his son and friends. / As soon as the holy obsequies were done and the poisoned wine had been blessed, the priest poured it into a golden chalice as Drusilla had instructed. She drank as much as was seemly, enough to produce its effect; then, with a happy smile, she presented the cup to her bridegroom, who drained it to the bottom. / He returned the cup to the priest and cheerfully opened his arms to embrace Drusilla. But now her sweet docility, her equable temper changed. She thrust him back forbiddingly, her eyes, her whole countenance ablaze.

' "Stand back, traitor!" she cried out in a dreadful passion. / "Am I to be your pleasure, your happiness while all I have from you is tears, sorrow, and anguish? No—I must have you die at my hands: this has been poisoned, do you realize? I only wish you had a baser executioner, that your death were not so light and easy a matter—I know of no torments, no executioner drastic enough to equal your heinous crime. / Alas that the manner of your death is not the perfect oblation I envisaged: had I been able to accomplish it as I wanted, it would have been without defect. (Sweet consort, pardon me for this; consider my good intentions and accept my sacrifice.) You, I have killed you as best I could, unable to do so as I should have wished. / But the penalty I cannot exact here as I want, I hope to see your soul suffer it in the next world, and I shall be there to watch." Then, raising to heaven her radiant face and clouded eyes, she added, "Accept this victim, Olinder, with the love of your avenging wife. / And beg Our Lord's grace for me that I may join you today in paradise. If He says to you that no soul accedes to His Kingdom without merits, tell Him I have merits: I bring to His holy temple the rich spoils of this evil, wicked monster. What merits can be more deserving than to expunge so hideous and foul a plague?" /

'Speech and life died in her at once; but, dead, the smile still lingered on her face, happy to have punished the cruelty of the man who had wrested her dear husband from her. I do not know whether she was preceded or followed by the departing spirit of Tanacre— preceded, I suspect, the poison acting more quickly upon him as he had drunk deeper. /

'Seeing his son collapse and die in his arms, Marganor was ready to die too, overwhelmed by the grief which struck him so unexpectedly. Two sons he had had; now he was alone. Two women had brought him to this pass; one was the cause of the first one's death, the other slew the second by her own hand. / Love, pity, indignation, pain, anger, a wish to die, vengefulness—these emotions all crowded in upon the unhappy, bereaved father; he seethed like the wind-whipped sea. Vengefully he approached Drusilla to ascertain whether her life had fully ebbed away and, goaded by burning hatred, he sought to vent his feelings on the insentient corpse. / As a snake, pinioned to the sand by a stick, vainly attacks it with his fangs; or as a mastiff dashes after a stone tossed at him by a wayfarer, and vainly gnaws at it in his rage, refusing to let it be until he has vented his spite upon it: so it was with Marganor, far more savage than any snake or mastiff, as he savaged the lifeless body. / And since the villain's feelings were not assuaged by rending and battering the corpse, he strode into the crowd of women in the church, and indiscriminately set to mowing us down with his cruel, pitiless sword, the way a peasant scythes his hay. There was no stopping him but he slew thirty in an instant, and wounded a good hundred. / He is so feared by his people that not a soul dared thwart him. The women and all the humble folk fled from the church—no one stayed behind who could escape. His raging blood-lust was finally restrained by his friends with entreaties and main force. He left tears everywhere behind him as he was coaxed back into his hill-top castle. /

'But his anger was not spent, and he decided that all the women must leave; only the entreaties of his friends and of the whole people prevented his slaughtering us all. That same day he issued an edict for our total expulsion. Here is where he chose to set our confines, and woe to the woman who ever again approaches the castle! / So husbands were separated from their wives, sons from their mothers; and woe to the man who risked coming to us if it came to the knowledge of any who would report him to Marganor: for he has punished many a man with heavy fines, and put many another to a cruel death. And he has imposed a rule in his castle, worse than any you have ever heard or read of: / any woman discovered in the valley—some do find their way there—is to be beaten across the shoulders with a willow-rod and then ejected; but first her dress is to be shortened to expose that which Nature and modesty conceals. And if any woman happens there escorted by an armed knight, she is to be slain. / Aye, those escorted by knights, our tyrant (no friend to mercy) drags off to the tombs of his dead sons and personally slits their throats, as sacrificial victims. Their escorts are ignominiously deprived of their arms and steeds and thrown into prison. This he can do, for night and day he keeps more than a thousand men standing by. / I must add that if he does release any knight, he first makes him swear on the Sacred Host that he shall hate the female sex so long as he lives. So if you wish to bring destruction upon these ladies and yourselves with them, go and look at those walls which shelter the villain, and see for yourselves whether strength or cruelty predominates in him.' /

With these words the woman moved the warrior-damsels first to pity, then to such indignation that, had it not been night-time but day, they would have made off to the castle at once. But they stopped where they were until, as soon as dawn indicated that every star was now to yield place to the sun, they armed and remounted. /

On the point of setting out, they heard on the road behind them an extended trample of hooves which made them all turn to look down the hill. About a stone's throw away they saw a band of some twenty armed men, some mounted, some on foot, taking a narrow path. / They were leading, mounted on a horse, a woman whose face betrayed her advanced age, the way a person is led who has been condemned for some crime to the stake, the block, or the gallows. In spite of the distance, the village women recognized her, by her face and clothing, as Drusilla's servant, / who had been captured along with her mistress by the predator, Tanacre, as I have said, and who later was entrusted with preparing the poison of dire effect. She had not gone into the church with the other women, anticipating what in fact ensued. Instead she had fled away to where she hoped for safety. / But Marganor got wind of her flight to Austria, and never relaxed his efforts to lay hands on her in order to burn or hang her. Eventually base greed, excited by gifts and lavish promises, induced a baron, who was holding her on his domain, to release her to Marganor. / He had sent her on her way as far as Constance, loaded onto a pack-horse like so much merchandise, tightly bound and gagged, and shut inside a chest. And now this posse had brought her here at the instance of the ruthless tyrant who had banished all pity from himself, so that he could vent his rage upon her. /

As the mighty Po, which rises on Mount Viso, grows in majesty and power in measure as it nears the sea, receiving on its journey the waters of the Ambra, Ticino, Adda, and other tributaries: so it was with Ruggiero and the two damsels—the more they heard of Marganor's crimes the more ferocious their wrath as they set forth against him. / The warrior-damsels were so incensed with hatred and anger against the brutal man for his misdeeds that they decided to punish him in spite of all the men he could muster. But they deemed a quick dispatch too kind a punishment, and not consistent with offences such as his; it was better to make him aware of death by prolonging it with torments. /

But the right thing to do was first to free the old woman before she was led to her death by those ruffians. The swift chargers covered the distance fast, their reins abandoned, their flanks well spurred. Never did those attacked endure a rougher, more savage assault: they were lucky to escape naked, abandoning shields, woman, and arms. / As the wolf, returning all unwary to his lair with his prey, finds his road barred by the huntsman and his hounds, and drops his burden and darts into the dark undergrowth where he sees it is thinner: similarly the fugitives were no less quick at escaping than their assailants at attacking them. / They abandoned not only the woman and their arms but also a good number of horses, for they felt freer in their movements thus

as they hurled themselves into ravines and over precipices. For Bradamant, Marfisa, and Ruggiero this was a godsend: they helped themselves to three horses to carry the three damsels who had made the
horses sweat the previous day, riding mounted behind. /

With greater dispatch they now pursued their way towards the
castle of evil repute. They wished to bring the old woman with them to
witness Drusilla's revenge, but she, fearing the worst, vainly refused,
with tears, cries, and shrieks. So Ruggiero forcibly pulled her up
behind on good Frontino and galloped off with her. / Finally they
reached a point from where they could look down upon a large, opulent
town consisting of many houses; it was open on all sides, for no wall
nor moat surrounded it. In the middle a rock rose above it, supporting
a lofty castle. They made boldly for this, knowing it to be Marganor's
lair. / Once they were within the town, some soldiers guarding the
entrance closed a barrier behind them, while they could see that the
further exit was also barred. Now Marganor appeared with a band of
armed men, mounted and on foot. In a few insolent words he revealed
the wicked custom of his domain. /

For all reply Marfisa, who had concerted her action first with
Bradamant and Ruggiero, charged at him and, strong and valiant as she
was, never setting her lance or drawing her famous sword, caught him
such a blow on the helmet with her fist that he slumped down senseless
in the saddle. / At the same time, Bradamant sprang forward and so
did Ruggiero, who tilted so valiantly, that, without taking his lance
out of rest, he slew six men, one struck in the belly, two in the chest,
one in the neck, one on the head; on the sixth man the lance broke as he
fled—after penetrating his back to emerge through his chest. / Bradamant floored whomever she touched with her golden lance; she might
have been a thunderbolt flung from the burning sky to shatter and
prostrate all that it hits. The people cleared off, some up into the castle,
others out to the open ground; others shut themselves into the churches
or into their homes. Not a man remained in the street—none but
corpses. / Marfisa meanwhile had bound Marganor's hands behind
his back and entrusted him to Drusilla's woman, now happy and
tranquil enough. They then discussed whether to set fire to the town
if it did not repent of its crimes, abrogating Marganor's evil law and
accepting the one which Marfisa would impose. /

There was no difficulty in obtaining the townspeople's consent:
not only were they afraid that Marfisa, with her talk of wholesale
slaughter and arson, might go beyond her threats, but also they were
totally hostile to Marganor and his preposterous law. In fact they had
behaved as most people do, obeying most readily those they hate the
worst. / So they all distrusted each other, no one daring to betray his

secret wish, but leaving one man to be banished, another slain, this one to forfeit his possessions, that one his honour. And yet the heart, which was silent here, cried out to Heaven until it called forth vengeance from God and the saints: and vengeance, if it was slow in coming, later made up for its delay with massive punishment. /

Now the townsfolk, bursting with anger and hate, sought their revenge in actions and in tale-bearing—as in the proverb, everyone hastens to chop the storm-felled tree for firewood. Let Marganor be an example to rulers, that he who commits evil will ultimately be overtaken by evil. Great and small rejoiced to see him punished for his wicked crimes. / Many men whose wives, sisters, daughters, or mothers had been slain by Marganor, no longer concealing their rebellion, ran to kill him with their own hands. The noble warrior-damsels and stalwart Ruggiero were hard put to defend him, for they meant him to die of suffering, privation, and torment. / They committed him naked and so tightly bound that to jerk loose would be no easy matter, into the hands of the old woman who loathed him as much as a woman can detest an enemy; and she assuaged her misery by bloodying his body with a sharp goad which a peasant bystander gave her. / Nor did the ambassadress and her two handmaids, who would never forget the humiliation they had suffered, have to stand idly by or do less than the crone by way of vengeance: so great was their urge to attack him that their strength deserted them before they had fully vented their passion; but they struck him with stones, they clawed and bit him, they pricked him with needles. / A torrent swollen by prolonged rains or melting snow will go on a rampage, hurling trees and rocks down the hillside, carrying down meadows and crops; but in time its arrogant mien relaxes and its strength is so sapped that a child, a woman can cross it at any point, often dry-shod; / so it was with Marganor, who once caused shudders wherever his name was mentioned; but strangers had arrived to beat him to his knees and so subdue his might that mere children could slight him, some tweaking his beard, others pulling his hair.

Now Ruggiero and the damsels turned their steps to the castle on the rock. / Those within handed it over to them without demur, as also its opulent contents, part of which were ransacked, and the rest given to Ullania and her ill-used companions. The golden shield was discovered here, and also the three kings, captives of the tyrant—they had come here on foot and unarmed, as I believe I have mentioned: / from the day when they were unseated by Bradamant, they had gone everywhere unarmed and on foot, escorting the damsel who had come from such distant shores. I cannot say whether or not it was to her advantage that they were unarmed: she might have fared the better for their defence, but far the worse had they tried resistance and failed. /

For she, like every woman who arrived there with armed escorts, would have been taken to the tomb of the two brothers and there wretchedly slain in sacrifice. To exhibit one's unseemly parts is, after all, more endurable than to die; furthermore, this and all other disgraces are attenuated if one can say that they were forcibly imposed. /

Before the warrior-damsels left they imposed a pledge on the inhabitants—that the husbands would make over to their wives the administration of the territory and all else. Any man who dared defy this rule would be severely punished. In fact, what elsewhere appertains to the husband was here to fall to the wife. / Then they extracted a promise that whoever happened this way, be he knight or page, would be offered no welcome, would be forbidden entry beneath any roof unless he swore by God and the saints (or by any oath more binding) that he would ever be Woman's friend, and enemy to her enemies. / If they already had a wife, or if sooner or later they were to acquire one, they were ever to be subject to her and obedient to her every fancy. Marfisa would be back, she said, before the year was out and the trees had shed their leaves; and if she found the law being flouted, the town could expect fire and destruction. /

Before they left they had Drusilla's remains removed from their present defiled resting-place and laid with her husband's in as sumptuous a tomb as the place could provide. Meanwhile the old woman was making Marganor's back red with pricks; she was only sorry to have to discontinue her torture for lack of stamina. / The brave warrior-damsels noticed a column standing beside a church; on it the impious tyrant had inscribed his cruel, insane law. Now they attached the shield, breastplate and helmet of Marganor to it after the manner of a trophy, and had their own law there inscribed. / Here they stopped long enough for Marfisa to have the column inscribed with her law, which contradicted the one already engraved there to the death and ignominy of womankind. The damsel from Iceland now left the company to repair her costume, for she deemed it a disgrace to appear at court unless attired and adorned as before. / Here Ullania remained, and Marganor remained in her power, until one day, lest he somehow slip free and again molest damsels, she made him leap off a tower— never until that day had he made a bigger jump.

No more of her or her escorts; let us follow the group returning towards Arles. / All that day and the next until mid-morning they journeyed until they came to the parting of the ways, one leading to the Christian camp, the other to the walls of Arles; here the lovers embraced again and took a long leave-taking, always so hard and bitter. Finally the damsels proceeded to the camp, Ruggiero to Arles; and here I end my canto.

THIRTY-EIGHTH CANTO

*1–6 Introductory. 7–23 Bradamant and Marfisa welcomed
by Charlemagne. 23–35 Astolfo, back from the moon, leads
a Nubian army to invade Agramant's kingdom. 35–64
Agramant holds a council and is persuaded by Sobrino to
end the war by a duel of champions. 65–90 The preparations
and start of the duel between Ruggiero and Rinaldo.*

You gentle ladies who have been kind enough to listen to my verse,
I see from your faces that you take amiss this sudden parting of
Ruggiero from his true love, and that it grieves you scarcely less than
it grieved her. And you argue from it that Love's fire must burn but
faintly in him. / Now were there any other reason for his leaving her
against her wishes, though he had hopes of greater wealth than that
which Crassus and Croesus amassed between them, I should share
your opinion that the arrow which struck him did not strike to the
heart: for neither silver nor gold could purchase such rapture, such
contentment. / But if it was to protect his honour, he deserves not
merely pardon but indeed praise—for protecting, that is, what would
redound to his shame and discredit were he to leave it unguarded.
And had Bradamant stubbornly insisted on his staying with her, she
would have given clear evidence either of paltry love or of scant wisdom. /
For if a damsel in love ought to cherish her beloved's life as much as,
or more than, her own (I am speaking of a damsel stricken by a good
strong dart which has penetrated her to the core), then she ought to
value his honour above his pleasure in the same degree as honour is of
greater value than life—which is preferred to all other pleasures. /

Ruggiero did his duty by following his liege, whom he could only
desert to his shame, for lack of any sufficient excuse. If Almont had
murdered Ruggiero's father, Agramant could not bear the blame; he
had in many ways since then made amends to Ruggiero for his forbears' sins. / Ruggiero, then, would do his duty by returning to his
liege; and Bradamant did hers by not obliging him to stay with her as
she could have done by constant entreaties. If he did not satisfy her
now, he would be able to another time; but the man whose honour
falters for a moment will not be able to satisfy it in a hundred years, not
in two hundred. /

So Ruggiero returned to Arles where Agramant had withdrawn with his remnant. Bradamant and Marfisa, firm friends now that they were related, went together to where Charlemagne, hoping to rid France (by battle or siege) of so persistent a nuisance, had offered the greatest proof of his power. / Once she was recognized in the Christian camp, Bradamant occasioned great joy and celebration; everyone revered and saluted her and she responded with a nod. Rinaldo, hearing of her arrival, came to greet her, while Richard, Richardet, and her other kinsmen did not lag behind—they were all happy to welcome her. /

When it was discovered that her companion was Marfisa, the renowned champion who gloried in a thousand lustrous palms from Cathay to the limits of Spain, there was not a man, rich or poor, who stayed in his tent: the eager crowd gathered from all parts, jostling, shoving and craning for a sight of so fine a pair together. / Reverently they came into the emperor's presence. This was the first occasion (writes Turpin) that Marfisa was ever seen to kneel: of all the emperors and kings she had ever seen, Saracen and Christian, who were distinguished for valour or wealth, only Charlemagne seemed to her worthy of this honour. / Charlemagne came out from his pavilion to meet her and welcomed her cordially. He had her sit next to him, elevated above every king, prince, and baron. Those who did not take their leave were dismissed, so that soon there remained only the pick of the gathering—the paladins and the foremost lords—while the despised rabble was excluded. /

'High and mighty lord, glorious and august!' Marfisa suavely began. 'You command respect for your white cross from the Indian Ocean to the Pillars of Hercules, from snowy Scythia to parched Ethiopia: no wiser, no juster monarch reigns than you. Your fame, which is unbounded, has drawn me hither from the ends of the earth. / And, truth to tell, my sole motive has been envy: I came only to make war on you—for there was to be no king, however mighty, but must hold to the law I held. To this end I have dyed the fields red with Christian blood; and I was all prepared to manifest further tokens of my cruel hostility had I not fallen in with one who has made me your friend. / When I was most intent on devastating your ranks I learnt (how, I shall explain at greater leisure) that good Ruggiero of Reggio was my father, a man unjustly betrayed by his wicked brother. I was carried across the sea in my poor mother's womb and was born in sorry circumstances. A sorcerer brought me up until my seventh year, when some Arabs stole me from him. / They sold me in Persia as slave to a king. When I grew up, I killed him, for he tried to take my virginity. I slew all his courtiers, too, drove out his depraved offspring and seized his kingdom. And so it befell me that, when but a month or two past eighteen, I had taken seven kingdoms. / And, envious of your renown (as I have said), I was determined to abase it from its eminence.

'Perhaps I should have succeeded, perhaps it was folly; but now that I am here I have discovered something to subdue this ambition and clip the wings of my passion: I am related to you. / And as my father was kinsman and vassal to you, so am I your vassal and kinswoman. And the jealousy, the insolent hatred I felt against you I now put by—or rather I reserve it all for Agramant and for those who were kindred to his father and uncle, those who were guilty of my parents' death.' / She wished to become a Christian, she continued. Then, after dispatching Agramant, she proposed, if Charlemagne agreed, to go back to her Eastern kingdom and baptize it. This done, she would make war against any part of the world where Mahomet and Trivigant were worshipped: her every conquest, she promised, would be a gain for the Holy Roman Empire and for the Christian Faith. /

The emperor's eloquence matched his wisdom and valour: he spoke highly of the excellent damsel, her father and her forbears, replying with consistent courtesy which gave clear evidence of his nobility of heart. He ended by accepting her for kinswoman and daughter. / Now he arose and embraced her again, and kissed her on the forehead as his daughter, whereupon those from the clan of Mongrana and of Clairmont came up to her delightedly. It would take too long to describe the honours paid her by Rinaldo, who had several times experienced her fabled prowess during the siege of Albracca. / It would take too long to describe how young Guidone rejoiced to see Marfisa, as also did Aquilant, Grifon, and Samsonet, who were with her in the cruel city of the killer-women; and Maugis, Vivian, and Richardet, for whom she had proved so trusty a companion at the slaughter of the wicked Maganzas and those evil traffickers from Spain. / Charlemagne personally saw to preparing a place sumptuously adorned for Marfisa's baptism on the following day. He sent for the bishops and higher clergy, well versed in the laws of Christianity, in order to instruct Marfisa fully about the holy faith. / Archbishop Turpin arrived in his sacred pontifical attire and baptized her; then Charlemagne, with suitable ceremony, helped her out of the sanctifying font.

But now it is time to bring help to the vacant starveling brain of Orlando with the phial which Astolfo the duke fetched down from the nether heavens in Elias' chariot. / Once possessed of this excellent phial which was to heal the mind of our great warrior-champion, Astolfo had descended from the luminous sphere to alight on the earth's highest point. Here John showed him a herb of outstanding virtue, with which he bade him, on his return, touch the King of Nubia's eyes and heal them / so that, for this and his earlier

benefaction, the king should give him men with whom to attack Bizerta.
How he was to arm and train these raw folk for combat, and how
unscathed to cross the dazzling sand-wastes the holy old man instructed him point by point. / Then he bade him remount the winged
steed (once Ruggiero's and, before his, Atlas'). Dismissed by John, the
paladin left the sacred territory and, hugging the course of the Nile,
soon came in sight of Nubia. He landed in the capital city and found
Senapo again. / Great was the joy which his return brought to the
king, who well recalled how his visitor had rid him of the unsufferable
harpies. But when Astolfo dissipated the moisture congealed upon his
eyes which robbed him of light, and restored his vision to him, Senapo
adored and worshipped him, and exalted him as a god. / Therefore
he gave him not only the men he requested for his invasion of Bizerta,
but fully a hundred thousand more, and offered his own services into
the bargain. The host could scarcely be contained in the open country
—they were all on foot, there being a shortage of horses, though plenty
of elephants and camels. /

The night before the Nubian army was to set out, Astolfo mounted
the hippogryph and hastened South until he reached the mountain
native to Auster, the South Wind that blows towards the Bears. He
found the cave whence the impetuous wind, when aroused, would dart
out through a narrow cleft. / Now, as advised by his mentor, he had
brought with him an empty wineskin which he applied deftly and
quietly against the fissure while the fierce wind slept, exhausted, in the
dark mountain cave. The trap so escaped Auster's notice that, when he
thought to leave in the morning, he was caught and secured inside the
skin. / Delighted to have caught so great a prize, the paladin returned
to Nubia and the same morning set out at the head of his swarthy
troops and his baggage-train. The glorious commander safely crossed
the fine sands with his whole army, untroubled by fear of the wind's
mischief, as he made for the Atlas mountains. /

Once across the range, he reached a spot from which the coastal
plain and the sea could be descried. Here he picked the cream of his
troops, those most highly disciplined, and stationed them at intervals
at the foot of a hill. Leaving them here, he climbed to the hill-top with
the air of a man with important matters to attend to. / After kneeling
to invoke his holy patron, confident that his prayer was heard, he sent a
great quantity of rocks a-rolling down the hill. Ah, what shall be denied
to the man who truly believes in Christ! The stones could be seen
growing, for no natural cause, as they rolled down, to form belly and
legs, neck, and muzzle; / they went bounding down the slopes with
ringing neighs and, on reaching the plain, shook their cruppers—they
were horses now, some bay, others roan, or dappled. The troops

waiting at the bottom grabbed them as they came. Thus in a few hours they were all mounted—for the horses were born already saddled and bridled. / Eighty thousand one hundred and two was the number of foot-soldiers mounted by Astolfo in one day. With this force he scoured Africa, pillaging, burning, and taking prisoners.

To guard his realm until his return, Agramant had left behind the Kings of Fers and Algaziers and King Branzardo. These set out against Astolfo, / after having dispatched a slender galley, impelled by oars and sail as though in flight, to bring word to Agramant that his kingdom was suffering havoc and depredation at the hands of the King of Nubia. Keeping constant course day and night, the ship reached the Provençal coast to find the king no little beset at Arles, for Charlemagne's camp was but a mile away. /

When King Agramant heard of the danger in which he had left his own realm in order to win Charlemagne's, he called a council of the Saracen kings and princes. After turning once or twice from Marsilius to King Sobrino, the eldest and wisest of those present, he spoke thus: / 'Aware as I am how unsuitable it is for a commander to admit: "I never thought of that", I shall confess it nonetheless. For when a disaster occurs which is quite remote from normal human providence, then such an error seems sufficiently excusable. This is precisely my case— I was wrong to leave Africa bereft of troops if it was to be invaded by the Nubians. / But who would have imagined, other than God alone from whom no prospect is hidden, that so great a horde of folk from so far a land should come to harry us? Between them and us lie the shifting sands ever drifted by the winds. And yet they have come to lay siege to Bizerta; they have laid waste a great part of Africa. / Now I seek your advice on this question, whether to leave having accomplished nothing, or to pursue our enterprise until I have captured Charlemagne. How am I both to save our own realm and also leave this empire in ruins? If any of you knows the answer, pray divulge it so that we may hit upon the best plan and so proceed.' /

Thus spoke Agramant. And he turned his eyes to the King of Spain seated beside him, as though to request of him an answer to the question he had posed. So Marsilius, after rising from his respectful genuflection and bowing to him, settled himself in his throne of honour and gave tongue as follows: / 'Whether Rumour brings us good or evil news, my liege, she tends always to exaggerate. Far be it from me, then, to be immoderately depressed by the bad or encouraged by the good which comes to pass—I shall always nurture the fear, or the hope, that the event is of less importance than has been stated, and not exactly as I hear it from so many tongues. / All the less credit will I give a story the more it defies belief. Now we can see how believable it is for a king of so remote a region to have set foot in embattled Africa with so large a host, crossing the sand-wastes to which Cambyses committed his troops with such unfortunate results. / I can well believe that it is Arabs who have come down from the mountains to sack and pillage, to kill and capture, having met with scant resistance. And that Branzardo, who has remained there as lieutenant and viceroy, has written thousands in place of tens so that his excuse may seem more plausible. /

'Still, let us concede that they are Nubians—perhaps rained down from the sky miraculously, or perhaps arriving concealed in the clouds, for they were not remarked along the way. Do you fear that folk such as these will ravage Africa unless with the aid of allies? Your garrison would be a sad lot indeed if they were frightened by so unwarlike a people! / Were you to send but a few ships merely to display your standards, they will have fled back to their borders, be they Nubians or paltry Arabs, before even our mooring-lines have been cast off. It is only your presence here with us, separated from your kingdom by the sea, which has given them the courage to make war on you. / Now, while Charlemagne is without his nephew, now is your chance to retaliate—in the absence of Orlando none of the enemy can resist you. If from blindness or neglect you forgo the victory which awaits you, the goddess, who now smiles, will turn her back upon you, to our injury and enduring shame.' / With these and other words the Spaniard craftily sought to persuade the council that the Saracens should not leave France until Charles had been driven out.

But King Sobrino, who clearly saw the drift of King Marsilius' advice, which promoted his own advantage rather than the common good, thus replied: / 'When I urged you to remain at peace, my liege, would that I had proved a false prophet. Or, if I indeed spoke truly, would that you had trusted your loyal Sobrino instead of bold Rodomont, and Marbalust, Alzirdo, and Martasin: I wish I had them now before me, especially Rodomont, / to taunt him for his boast that he would shatter France like brittle glass and follow your lance—nay, surpass it indeed—in heaven and hell! Now, in time of need, he sits scratching his belly, sunk in repulsive, dismal idleness. And I, who was called a coward for having warned you of the truth, am still with you— / and so shall remain until I reach the end of this my life, which, though burdened with years, is daily at risk for you in battle with the most famed champions of France. Nor will any man soever dare tax me with wrongful conduct. And many who have boasted their superiority have achieved no more than I, nor even as much. /

'I speak thus to show that what I said before, and what I must tell you now, springs neither from cowardice nor from evil will but from true love and faithful service. I urge you to return to your ancestral homeland as soon as you can. The man who loses his own possessions in order to acquire another's must be accounted a fool. / Reckon up the gain: thirty-two vassal kings of yours set sail with you. Were I to make a fresh count, scarcely one third of us would be found remaining, all the rest being dead. May it please Almighty God that no more of us fall: but if you must continue, I fear that soon not a quarter, not a fifth of us will remain, and your wretched people will be quite obliterated. / Orlando's absence is a help—we are a remnant whereas we might have been none at all. But this does not remove the danger, though it prolongs our agony. There is Rinaldo, who has given ample evidence that he is no lesser man than Orlando; and there are his kinsmen, and all the paladins, eternal threats to our Saracens. / Then they have that second Mars (reluctant though I am to praise the enemy), valiant Brandimart, a stout champion no less than Orlando. I have sampled his prowess myself, and have also discovered it at others' expense. Besides, it is many days since Orlando has been gone, but we have counted more losses than gains. /

'If we have lost hitherto, I fear that henceforth our losses will be yet more serious. Our side has lost Mandricard; Gradasso has withdrawn his help; Marfisa has deserted us in our extremity, and so has Rodomont, of whom I must say that if his loyalty matched his force, we could well spare Gradasso and Mandricard. / While we are deprived of the help of these, and so many thousands of our troops are dead, and those due to come have now arrived, and no further ship is expected bringing more, Charlemagne has acquired four men reputed no less mighty than Orlando and Rinaldo—and with reason, for you would not easily find another such foursome between here and Bactria. / I do not know whether you realize who Guidone Selvaggio is, and Samsonet, and Oliver's twin sons, Grifon and Aquilant: I respect and fear them more than any other captain or knight arrived from Germany or other country of foreign speech to confront us in the Empire's cause—though the new folk arrived in their camp to our detriment are by no means to be underrated. / As often as you go into battle you will have the worst of it and be routed. If Africa and Spain often lost the day when we were sixteen against eight, how shall it be when Italy and Germany are united to France, as also the English and Scots, and we shall be six against twelve—what are we to expect but disgrace and disaster? / If you stubbornly persist in this enterprise you shall lose both your army here and your realm at home. But if you change your plan and return home, you will save your remnant and also your kingdom. To forsake Marsilius would be unworthy of you and everyone would think the worse of you for doing so. But there is a remedy: to make peace with Charles—which must suit him if it suits you. /

'If, however, you feel that, being the first victim of war, you can derive scant honour from suing for peace; and if you are more concerned to continue the fight—you can see how it has gone hitherto!— at least make sure of victory. This you may perhaps achieve if you take my advice: confer upon one champion alone the prosecution of your quarrel, and let that one be Ruggiero. / You know as well as I that in single combat, weapon in hand, Ruggiero is no whit inferior to Orlando, to Rinaldo, or to any other Christian champion. But if you insist on a total military confrontation, then for all that Ruggiero's valour is superhuman, he will never be more than one single man, and against an entire host he will meet his match. / The right course seems to me, if you agree, to send to the Christian sovereign and tell him this: to end the dispute and prevent your shedding more of his men's blood (and he of yours beyond number), you ask him to put into the field against a warrior of yours one of the boldest of his. And let these two assume the whole of the fighting until one is victor, the other vanquished. / The pact would be that the loser's sovereign would have to pay tribute to the victor's. I do not believe that Charlemagne will object to this condition, even though he now holds the advantage. I rely so much upon the strength in Ruggiero's arm to achieve victory, and right is so much on our side that he must win, though he were confronted with Mars.' /

With these and other more telling arguments Sobrino prevailed upon Agramant. Interpreters were chosen the same day, and the same day an embassy was sent to Charlemagne. He, blessed with so many excellent champions, regarded the battle as virtually won. He entrusted the enterprise to good Rinaldo, in whom, after Orlando, he placed the greatest reliance. / Both armies were equally delighted with this pact: all were weary in body and spirit, all were reluctant for more. Everyone had plans to rest for the remainder of his days. Everyone cursed the wrath, the passions which had provoked him to rivalry and broils. /

Rinaldo, seeing the eminence to which he was raised, for Charlemagne had placed far greater trust in him than in all the rest for so crucial an enterprise, happily prepared for the honourable task. He disdained Ruggiero: Ruggiero, he assumed, would prove quite defenceless against him. He would never consider him a match even though he had slain Mandricard in combat. /

Ruggiero, on the other hand, though greatly flattered that his sovereign should have chosen him as the pick of his champions to whom to entrust so vital a matter, nonetheless evinced deep gloom and sadness. It was not as though fear disturbed his breast—he did not fear Rinaldo, not even had Orlando fought beside him— / but he was aware that

Rinaldo's sister was his dear and most faithful consort, who was forever jabbing and cudgelling him with letters betraying a dire sense of
grievance. Now if to the erstwhile complaints be added that of his
taking the field and putting her brother to death, he would transform
her love to such detestation that he would be at a loss ever to placate
her again. /

If Ruggiero grieved and lamented in silence over the battle which
he would unwillingly undertake, his dear bride sobbed and wept on
learning the news a few hours later. She beat her lovely breast, tore her
golden tresses, bedewed and rent her innocent cheeks, and bitterly
accused Ruggiero of thanklessness, her fate of cruelty. / However
the duel ended, it could afford her nothing but distress. She could not
face the thought of Ruggiero dying in this encounter—the idea was
unthinkable. But if Christ meant to punish repeated faults by destroying
France, then her brother would die, and an evil yet more disastrous
would befall her: / to make a public return to her betrothed had been
uppermost in her thoughts night and day, her constant dream—but in
this event she would never be able to do so without incurring censure,
ignominy, and her people's hostility. Such was the pledge uniting
them, there was little to be gained by withdrawing or by second
thoughts. / There was, however, a certain person who would not
endure to listen to Bradamant's tears, her cries of distress: I mean
Melissa, the sorceress who was accustomed to bringing faithful help
in her times of trial. She arrived to comfort her and, when the time
came, brought her powerful help; she would disrupt the forthcoming
combat which caused her such tears and anxiety. /

Meanwhile Rinaldo and illustrious Ruggiero prepared their arms
for the combat, the initiative in which devolved upon the champion of
the Holy Roman Empire. And since he always went on foot, ever since
losing his good steed Bayard, he chose to fight on foot, sheathed in
plate-armour and chain-mail, with battle-axe and dagger. / Whether it
was by chance, or whether due to the recollection of Rinaldo's provident and shrewd cousin Maugis, who knew how keenly Balisard,
Ruggiero's sword, could ravage armour, both champions agreed to
fight without swords, as I have said. They agreed on a site, too, in a
broad plain near the walls of ancient Arles. / Scarcely had watchful
Aurora put her head out of Tithonus' bower to initiate the day and
hour fixed for the battle when from either side the seconds came
forth; they rigged up a pavilion at either end of the lists, and next to
each erected an altar. / A short while later the pagan host could be
seen marching out in orderly ranks. In their midst rode the African
king, armed and sumptuously arrayed in barbaric splendour. Riding
with him on a footing of equality came Ruggiero, mounted on a bay

charger with black mane, white forehead, and two white fetlocks. Marsilius did not disdain to act as his squire. / The helmet which earlier he had so toiled to wrest from the head of Mandricard—the helmet, celebrated in a greater poem, which Trojan Hector wore a thousand years before—now King Marsilius carried for him, riding beside him. Other princes and noblemen had shared out between them the rest of the arms, well gilded and rich with jewels. /

On the other side, Charlemagne issued from the great ramparts with his soldiery; he proceeded in the same fashion as if he were setting out to give battle. His renowned peers surrounded him, and Rinaldo accompanied him, fully armed except for the helmet, once King Mambrino's, which was borne by the paladin Ogier the Dane. / Duke Namo carried one of the battle-axes, Solomon, King of Brittany the other. Charles assembled his host at one end of the field, at the other end were the troops of Africa and Spain; no one at all appeared in the middle—a great tract of land remained empty, for, by common edict, anyone who set foot there, other than the two warriors, would be executed. / The pagan champion was given the second choice of weapons; then two priests stepped forth, one from either sect, book in hand. The book our priest held contained the unblemished life of Christ; the other's book was the Koran. With the priest of the Gospel stepped forward the emperor; with the other, King Agramant. / Reaching the altar which had been erected for him, Charles raised his palms to Heaven and prayed: 'O God, who suffered death to redeem our souls from death! O Lady, so highly favoured that God took from you his human body and spent nine months in your holy womb while still preserving your virginal flower! / Be my witnesses that I bind myself and all my successors to give to King Agramant, and to whomever shall be chosen to succeed him in the governance of his realm, twenty measures of pure gold each year if today my champion is defeated. And I promise an immediate truce which will endure forever. / And if I default in this, may your dreadful wrath blaze up at once to strike me alone and my children, but no one else who is with us here, so that in the shortest time men may realize what it means to break a pledge to you.' As he spoke, Charles kept his hand on the Gospel and his eyes raised heavenwards. /

Then the pagans arose and went to the altar which they had richly adorned; here Agramant swore that he would recross the sea with his host, and would pay the same tribute to the emperor, if Ruggiero were defeated today. And there would be a perpetual truce between them on the conditions already propounded by Charlemagne. / Similarly, calling Mahomet to witness in no uncertain voice, he promised on the book held by his Imam to observe all he had said. Then the two sovereigns quickly strode off the field and rejoined each his own ranks. Hereupon the two champions came out to swear their oath, which was as follows: / Ruggiero promised that if his king came—or sent someone—to interrupt the combat, he would no longer be his champion nor his vassal but would devote himself to Charlemagne. And Rinaldo swore that if his sovereign caused him to forsake the battle before either he or Ruggiero were defeated, he would become Agramant's champion. /

The ceremonies concluded, each returned to his own side. Here they did not tarry long before the clear trumpets gave them the signal for the fierce assault. Now the courageous champions advanced upon each other, choosing their steps with wary skill. Now battle was joined in a clash of steel, a whirl of weapons, high and low. / As each feinted at the other's head or foot by turns, advancing now the stock of his battle-axe, now the axe-head reversed, they displayed such swift dexterity that to describe it would surpass belief. Unhappy Ruggiero, fighting the brother of the lady who possessed his heart, struck at Rinaldo with such restraint that he was considered the less valiant. / He was more intent on parrying than on striking, and did not know his own mind: he would not have rejoiced to kill Rinaldo, but had no wish to die himself. Now I seem to have reached the point where I must defer my story; you shall hear the rest in the next canto if you will join me there to hear it.

THIRTY-NINTH CANTO

1–18 Agramant, deceived by a spell, breaks the truce and renews the war. 19–35 Astolfo frees Rodomont's captives, who join him in besieging Bizerta. 35–65 Astolfo and his friends subdue Orlando and restore his wits. 66–86 Agramant deserted, his army routed, he embarks for Africa, but his fleet is set upon by Astolfo's.

RUGGIERO'S distress was truly bitter and bore harshly upon him, racking his body, and still more his mind, for two deaths confronted him without escape: he would die at Rinaldo's hand if he succumbed to him; but if he overcame him, then at Bradamant's—for if he slew her brother, he was bound to incur her hatred, more abhorrent to him than death. / Rinaldo harboured no such thoughts; victory was his only concern. He wielded his battle-axe with rabid fury, aiming now at the other's arm, now at his head. Good Ruggiero swung about to parry the blows with his axe; he swerved this way and that, and, if he struck, aimed at a spot where he would inflict the least injury. / Most of the pagan chiefs felt that this combat was all too one-sided: Ruggiero was too reluctant to lay about him, Rinaldo was having too much the better of it. The King of the Africans watched the battle in dismay. He fretted and fumed, blaming the whole blunder on Sobrino, whose ill-conceived idea this had been. /

Meanwhile Melissa, a well-spring of magical arts, had transformed her features, assuming the likeness of Rodomont: in her face and gestures she resembled the Algerian king. Now she appeared, armed in the dragon-hide; and the shield, and the sword at her side were the very ones he bore, no less. / She spurred her steed—a demon in disguise—and, coming before the dejected sovereign, addressed him with furrowed brow in a booming voice: 'My liege, how can you be so mistaken as to expose a callow youth to the risks of combat against so mighty and renowned a Frenchman, in a challenge so vital that the realm and honour of Africa depends upon its outcome? / Forbid this battle to continue—it would prove too disastrous. Think nothing of violating the truce, breaking the oath—on Rodomont's head be it. Let each man show how his sword cuts—with me present, each one of you is worth a hundred men!' These words worked so powerfully upon Agramant that without another thought he darted forward. / The conviction of having Rodomont beside him led him to disdain the truce: he would not have set so much store by a thousand other warriors come to his assistance. In a trice, then, you could see lances lowered, steeds spurred on each side. Melissa, having ignited battle with her phantoms, disappeared.. /

Seeing their combat interrupted in violation of every oath and contract, the two champions stopped belabouring each other; indeed, all blows forgotten, each gave his word not to molest the other until it was established who had been the first to break the truce, old Charlemagne or young Agramant. / They renewed their oath to be enemies to whoever first broke faith. Everybody hurried and scurried, some advancing, others turning back; one and the same action could tell the cowards from the brave—all ran in equal haste, but while the latter pressed forward, the former retreated. / Imagine a greyhound eyeing the timid hare as it scuttles about him in circles, but unable to join the other hounds, for the huntsman is restraining him: he howls and groans in sheer frustration, yelps in vain, tugs and jerks at the leash. Thus had proud Marfisa and Bradamant been so far today. / Many a rich prize had they already noticed on the broad plain; how they had sighed for sheer sorrow and regret, unable as they were to go after their plunder, all on account of the truce!

Now that they saw the truce broken, however, they joyfully leapt upon the Africans. / Marfisa drove her lance through the chest of her first opponent, and it emerged a yard through his back. Then she drew her sword and shattered four helmets like glass in less time than I have told it. Bradamant proved no less effective, though her golden lance worked on another principle: all whom it touched it floored—twice as many, they were—but it slew none of them. / They kept so close together in this that each was the other's witness. Then they separated and gave themselves to harrying the Moors wherever their passion drew them. Who could reckon up the number of warriors sent sprawling by that golden lance, or of heads severed from trunks or split by Marfisa's terrifying sword? / As in the season of the winds, when the new grass can be seen on the Apennine ridges, two boisterous torrents rise close by, to take each a different path as they fall; they rip up boulders and tall trees along their steep banks, and flush cornfields and meadows down to the valley-floor; they almost vie with each other to wreak the greater damage on their way: / so it was with the two noble warrior-damsels as they scoured the battle-field, each on her own, wreaking destruction in the African ranks, the one with her lance, the other with her sword.

Agramant was hard put to rally his men to their standards and keep them from flight. Vainly he questioned and glanced about him—he could discover no trace of Rodomont. / It was at his instigation, he remarked, that he had broken the truce which he had solemnly pledged, calling the gods to witness; then he had vanished so suddenly. Nor could he see Sobrino: Sobrino had withdrawn into Arles, proclaiming his innocence and expecting harsh vengeance to overtake Agramant today for his breach of faith. / Marsilius too had fled into the city, utterly aghast. So Agramant was hard put to stand against the hosts of Italy, Germany, and England led by Charles—valiant men every one, with the paladins dispersed among them like the jewels in a golden embroidery. / Beside the paladins there were some warriors as accomplished as any in the world: there was the intrepid Guidone Selvaggio; there were Grifon and Aquilant—to make no further mention of the spirited pair of damsels already alluded to. These all killed so many Saracens that they are beyond counting. /

But, deferring this battle a little, I want to cross the sea without a ship. My concern with the French is not such as to preclude my reverting to Astolfo. I have already told you of the blessings conferred on him by John the Apostle, and I believe I have told you that King Branzardo and the King of the Algaziers had put all their troops into the field against him. / These troops were all that Africa could furnish in a hurry: men infirm with age as well as those of sound years—they may as well have recruited women. Agramant, stubbornly pursuing his vengeance, had twice emptied Africa; only a small remnant was left, and these made a timorous, unwarlike army— / in evidence of which, scarcely had they sighted the enemy in the distance than they all ran away. Astolfo and his more seasoned troops drove them ahead like sheep and left them strewed about the countryside.

A few escaped to Bizerta, but stout Bucifar was taken prisoner. King Branzardo escaped into the city, / but was far more distressed at the loss of Bucifar than if he had lost all else: Bizerta was a large city and would take a great deal of defending, no simple task on his own. He would dearly have loved to ransom Bucifar. Now, while he brooded over this in glum dismay, it occurred to him that he had for many months been holding prisoner the paladin Dudone. / Rodomont had captured Dudone, son of Ogier the Dane, beneath the walls of Monaco, on the coast, during his initial incursion, and had held him prisoner ever since. Branzardo decided to exchange him for Bucifar, and sent a message to the commander of the Nubians, since he had heard from a reliable source that this was Astolfo of England: / Astolfo, being himself a paladin, would, he judged, be eager to free a paladin. Indeed the good duke, hearing the facts, proved to be of one mind with Branzardo. Dudone, once liberated, thanked Astolfo and joined him in conducting the war, by sea as by land. /

As Astolfo had a countless horde which seven Africas together could not have withstood, recalling the holy apostle's injunction to undertake the recapture of Aiguesmortes and Provence from the Saracen invaders, he made a further selection of a large company of men who seemed to him the least inept for sea-going duty. / Then he gathered as many leaves as he could hold in both hands, plucked off various branches—laurel, cedar, olive, and palm—and, going to the water's edge, threw them into the sea. O fortunate souls, beloved of Heaven! O bounty seldom conferred by God upon mortals! O sublime miracle produced on those leaves when they were in the water! / They grew in number beyond counting; they grew curved and thick, long and heavy; the veins crossing them turned into hard ribs, into thick planks; they retained a point at the fore-end and all at once they were boats of as many different kinds as were the trees from which they had been plucked. / It was a miracle to see the scattered leaves producing caravels, galleys, and tall galleons, and equally so in that they were as well equipped with sails, rigging, and oars as any ship. Nor was the duke short of crews to man the vessels in the raging winds: from nearby Sardinia and Corsica he had helmsmen and captains, quartermasters, and pilots. / Those who took to the sea numbered twenty-six thousand, men of every sort. Dudone sailed as their commander—he was a shrewd warrior and stout, by land and sea.

The fleet was still waiting off the Moorish coast for a more favourable wind when a ship put in there, laden with captive warriors. / It was carrying those whom bold Rodomont had captured at the perilous bridge where the tilting-ground was so restricted, as I have several times mentioned earlier. Among these were Oliver (brother of Orlando's wife), loyal Brandimart, Samsonet, and others whom I need not name—Germans, Italians, and Gascons. / Here the master, unaware of the enemy's presence, brought in his galley, leaving the port of Algiers, his intended goal, many miles astern, for a strong wind had got up and driven him beyond it. Now he imagined he was putting into a safe refuge, like Procne returning to her twittering nest. / But when he noticed the Imperial Eagle, the Golden Lilies, and the Leopards close by, he blanched like a man suddenly aware that his incautious foot has trodden upon a horrid poisonous snake which has been slumbering torpidly in the grass: he recoils in a fright and flees from the angry, venomous reptile. / But the master could not escape, nor conceal his prisoners. With Brandimart, Oliver, Samsonet, and many others he was brought before Astolfo and Dudone, who showed delight on seeing their friends. These requested that their warder, to requite him for bringing them here, be condemned to the galley-benches. / The Christian knights, as I said, were welcomed by Astolfo, in whose pavilion a banquet was given in their honour, and they were provided with arms and all else of which they stood in need. For their sakes Dudone postponed his departure: no less was to be gained, he felt, from conversing with barons such as these than from setting out a day or two earlier. / He received reliable information about France and Charlemagne—how they were faring—and about where a landing would be safest and most effective.

While he was listening to them, they became aware of a growing pandemonium, and the alarm was raised so frantically that they all fell to wondering. / Astolfo and his goodly company, all in a group conversing, were armed and mounted in a trice and hastened towards the centre of the commotion, questioning everyone along the way. And they reached a spot where they beheld a man so ferocious that, though naked and alone, he was ravaging the whole army. / He had a wooden staff which he swung before him, and it was so solid and heavy and so firmly clenched that at every swing a man fell to the ground in not the best of health. Already he had dispatched more than a hundred, and no one any longer tried to resist him unless by shooting arrows from a distance—certainly no one ventured to await his approach. /

Dudone, Astolfo, and Brandimart and Oliver, who had hastened towards the noise, were still marvelling at the savage's great strength and remarkable spirit when they saw a damsel dressed in black come galloping up on a palfrey; she greeted Brandimart and threw her arms about his neck. /

It was Fiordiligi, who was so inflamed with love for Brandimart that, when she left him captive at the narrow bridge, she almost went crazy with sorrow. She had crossed the sea after learning from Rodomont, his captor, that he had been sent prisoner to Algiers with many knights. / On the point of embarking at Marseilles, she had found a Levantine ship which had brought an old retainer of King Monodant, Brandimart's father. He had scoured many a province, wandering over land and sea in search of Brandimart; on the way he had received news that he was to be found in France. / Now she recognized him for Bardino, the man who had abducted Brandimart as a little boy from his father and taken him to be brought up at Rocca Silvana. When she learned the reason for his journey, she had induced him to set sail with her, telling him how Brandimart had come to cross over to Africa. / On landing, they heard that Bizerta was besieged by Astolfo, and it was rumoured that Brandimart was with him. At sight of him, Fiordiligi sped towards him, giving clear evidence of the joy which was all the greater for the sorrows that had preceded it. / The courteous knight was no less pleased to see his loyal true-love whom he adored above all else; he embraced and hugged her in a gentle welcome, and the first kiss did not sate his inflamed desire, nor did the second or third.

He looked up, however, and noticed Bardino, her companion. / He reached out, meaning to embrace him and ask what brought him here, but there was no time: the army was fleeing in disorder before the staff with which the naked madman was clearing himself a path. Fiordiligi scrutinized the naked man's face and cried to Brandimart, 'It's the count!' / At the same time Astolfo, who was present, recognized him for Orlando by certain signs he had been advised of by the holy ancients in the Earthly Paradise. Otherwise they should none of them have recognized in him the noble baron: after so long disdaining his own body, in his folly, his face resembled a beast's more than a man's. / Stabbed to the heart with pity, Astolfo turned, weeping, to Dudone, who stood beside him, and then to Oliver: 'Look!' he cried. 'That's Orlando!' And they all gazed at him intently, wide-eyed; to find him thus reduced filled them with wonder and compassion. / Most of those lords were moved to tears of distress.

'Now is the time to discover the art of healing him,' observed Astolfo, 'not to weep over him.' With this he jumped from his horse, and so did Brandimart, Samsonet, Oliver, and saintly Dudone, and all

together they fell upon Charlemagne's nephew, to capture him. /
Seeing himself encircled, Orlando swung his staff in frantic desperation, and taught Dudone the serious consequences of his rashness
when he tried to venture within arm's length, his head protected by
his shield. Were it not for Oliver absorbing part of the blow with his
sword, Orlando's injudicious staff would have shattered Dudone's
shield, helmet, head, and torso. / It broke only his shield, though
landing such a thump on his helmet that he fell to the ground.

Meanwhile Samsonet swung his sword with such vigour that it
caught the staff two arms' lengths from the top and cut it clean in two,
while Brandimart grabbed him from behind, clinching him with both
arms as tightly as he could, and Astolfo seized him round the legs. /
Orlando gave a jerk which sent Astolfo flying off to land on his back
ten feet away. But Brandimart, who had a tighter hold, he could not
shake off. Oliver ventured too close and received a clout so severe that
it felled him: he turned ashy pale and the blood gushed from his nose
and eyes. / Had his helmet been less than perfect, Oliver would have
been killed by that clout; as it was, he fell like one who has rendered
up his soul to paradise. Back on their feet, Astolfo, Dudone (the latter's
face swollen), and Samsonet, who had delivered the deft stroke, all
jumped on Orlando together. / Dudone clasped him forcefully from
behind and tried tripping him up. Astolfo and the rest clung onto his
arms, but even so, their combined efforts could not hold him. Anyone
who has seen a bull being baited—savage jaws snap at his ears, and as
he runs off, bellowing, he drags the hounds along with him but cannot
shake free of them— / may imagine Orlando dragging all those warriors
with him.

At this point Oliver got up from the ground where the great blow
had felled him; and seeing that this was no way to achieve what
Astolfo intended, he hit upon a plan to bring down Orlando, and put it
into effect—successfully. / He called for ropes, quickly made a slip-
knot in one end of each, had some of them secured to the Count's
arms and legs, the rest round his body. Then he distributed the other
rope-ends to those present, and thus brought down Orlando, the way a
farrier will bring down a horse or ox. / Once down, they were all on top
of him, and bound his hands and feet yet more securely. Orlando
jerked this way and that, but his efforts were all in vain. Astolfo now
ordered him to be removed, saying that he was going to heal him.
Dudone, a giant, loaded him onto his back and carried him down the
beach to the water's edge. / Astolfo had him washed seven times, and
seven times had him plunged beneath the water so as to cleanse his
face and brutish limbs of the unsightly layers of grime. Then, with
certain herbs gathered to this end, he had his mouth sealed, as it

puffed and huffed, for he was not to draw breath other than through his nose. / Astolfo had prepared the phial which contained Orlando's wits. This he applied to the count's nose to such effect that, as he inhaled, he sucked it dry.

O wonder of wonders! He recovered his wits in their pristine condition—and intellect, brighter and more lucid than ever, once more informed his graceful speech. / As one who, in a heavy, oppressive sleep, has been seeing horrible shapes of monsters who do not and cannot exist, or has dreamt of having committed some gross enormity, lingers in wonderment when sleep is ended and he is once more master of his senses: so Orlando, recovered from his ravings, remained bemused and stupefied. / He stared at Brandimart, at Oliver (fair Aude's brother), and at Astolfo who had restored his senses to him; and, as he looked at them in utter silence, he mused on how and since when he came to be here. He turned his gaze this way and that but could not conceive where he was. He wondered at finding himself naked, and bound with so many ropes from shoulders to feet. / Then, choosing the words uttered by sobered Silenus to those who had trussed him up in the cave, 'Solvite me', he said; and his face was so serene, his eyes so much less crazy than before, that he was untied; and they supplied him with clothing which they had sent for. Bitterly he regretted his aberration, and they all consoled him. /

His old self once more, a paragon of wisdom and manliness, Orlando also found himself cured of love: the damsel who had seemed hitherto so beautiful and good in his eyes, and whom he had so adored, he now dismissed as utterly worthless. His only concern, his only wish now was to recover all that Love had stolen from him. /

Meanwhile Bardino told Brandimart that his father Monodant was dead and that he had come at the instance, first of his brother Ziliant, then of all the folk who inhabit the islands scattered over the sea furthest to the East—and there was not another realm in the world so wealthy, populous, and happy—to call him to the throne. / He adduced, among other things, the attractions of the homeland: should he be disposed to taste its sweetness, he would have no further appetite for foreign travel. Brandimart replied that he wanted to serve Charlemagne and Orlando for the duration of the war. If he could see the end of it, then he would give further thought to his own affairs. /

The next day Dudone the Dane set sail with his army for Provence. Orlando closeted himself with Astolfo and was told how the war stood. Then he laid all Bizerta under siege, giving the credit, however, for every victory to the English duke—who, for his part, did everything under the count's supervision. / What dispositions did they make?

How did they lay siege to the great city? From which side did they attack, and when? How come it fell at the first assault? Who shared the honours with Orlando? If I neglect to pursue these questions now, do not fret—I am leaving them only for a brief interval. Be pleased to learn, meanwhile, how the French were harrying the Moors. /

King Agramant was almost deserted in his greatest peril of the whole war: many of the pagans, Marsilius and Sobrino among them, had retired inside the walls of Arles—and these kings had then betaken themselves to the fleet, doubtful of their safety on land. Many a Moorish warrior, many a Moorish captain, had followed their example. / Agramant pursued the fight until he could do so no longer, whereupon he turned tail and fled for the city gates, not far away. Rabican galloped swiftly after him, goaded and flogged by Bradamant, who was longing to slay him, for he had so many times deprived her of Ruggiero. / Marfisa nursed the same desire, in order to wreak belated vengeance for her murdered father, and used her spurs to impress upon her steed that she was in a hurry. But neither damsel arrived in time to cut off the king's retreat into the fortified city and thence to the safety of his fleet. / As a brace of handsome, noble hunting-leopards, unleashed at the same moment, see themselves foiled in their pursuit of deer or hardy goat, and turn back almost shame-faced, piqued, and bashful for being too late, so did the two damsels turn back, sighing, when they saw the pagan escaped. / They did not draw rein, though, but plunged into the throng of fugitives, and at each sword stroke felled several never to rise again.

The routed troops were in a sorry plight, for even in flight there was no safety: Agramant, for his own protection, had given orders to shut the gates giving onto the battlefield, / and to cut all the bridges across the Rhône. Alas, unfortunate populace: where the monarch's needs are at stake, you are always accounted as no better than sheep or goats! Some drowned in the river, some in the sea; others stained the earth with their blood. Many were slain, few taken prisoner, few being worth a ransom. / Where the Rhône stagnates, near Arles, the countryside is full of tombs, as can be seen to this day: here lie the great multitude slain on either side in this latest battle—though the slain were not evenly divided, far more of the Saracens being dispatched to the shades by the hands of Bradamant and Marfisa. / Meanwhile King Agramant had ordered his heavier ships to make sail, and put out to sea, leaving a few lighter vessels to take off those who sought safety on board. He stood off the coast two days, to assemble the fugitives, and also because the winds were contrary. On the third day he hoisted sail again, intending to return to Africa. /

473

King Marsilius was in great dread lest his Spain were made to pay the price, lest the lowering storm broke at last upon his own fields. He had himself set ashore at Valencia, and took great pains to repair castles and forts and prepare for the war which was to prove his ruin and that of his friends. /

Agramant, then, set sail for Africa in his ill-equipped vessels which were half-empty: empty of men, but laden with rebellion, for three men out of four had been left behind in France. Some called the king overbearing, others cruel, others stupid; and, as usually happened in such cases, everyone hated him in secret, but kept silent out of fear. / Among two or three friends who trusted each other, lips would be unsealed, though, to vent their anger and resentment. And unhappy Agramant still deluded himself that everybody loved and pitied him. This was because he never saw any but feigning faces, never heard anything but flattery, guile, and untruths. / The king had planned not to put into Bizerta, in view of the definite tidings he had that the Nubians held the coast. He intended to continue and make shore well beyond, to avoid the harsh obstacles of an opposed landing; once ashore, he would make straight for his hard-pressed people to bring them help. /

But his unkind destiny was at variance with this wise and provident plan: it dictated that the fleet brought miraculously into being from the leaves on the beach and now furrowing the waves *en route* for France was to encounter his own by night—a dark, overcast, inclement night, furthermore, so that he should be at all the greater disadvantage. / Agramant had received no hint of Astolfo dispatching so vast a fleet; nor would he have believed the assertion that one little branch could make a hundred ships. So he sailed in the confidence that he would meet no one bold enough to attack him; he posted no look-outs in the crow's nests to give him warning if they descried anything. / Therefore the ships Astolfo had entrusted to Dudone, with their complement of armed warriors, having espied the Saracen fleet at nightfall and altered course towards it, caught the enemy off guard; having established by their speech that they had encountered Moors, their enemies, the Christians dropped anchor and linked themselves with chains. /

Seconded by the wind, the great ships bore down upon the Saracen fleet with such force that they sent several vessels to the bottom. The Christians then set to work, hand and brain allied, to raise a tempest of missiles, fire-brands, and slung boulders such that no sea-storm could ever have matched it. / Dudone's troops, blessed with abnormal strength and courage from on high (the time having come to punish the Saracens for more than one offence), proved so effective at inflicting damage, both in close combat and from a distance, that Agramant could find no shelter. A cloud of arrows descended upon him; he was hemmed in with swords and grapnels, pikes, and axes. / He felt the crash of great millstones as they dropped, hurled from mechanical catapults to shatter ships, prow and stern, opening broad gashes for the sea to enter. The dreaded fires caused worse damage yet: they were quick to ignite, slow to burn out.

The luckless rabble tried to escape from the dire peril but only ran further into the thick of it. / Some, hunted by the sword and the enemy, dived overboard to finish drowned in the sea. Others, ready of hand and quick-footed, slipped away to safety in the first available ship's boat: but here they would be repulsed, the boat already overladen, and the hand which was too determined to gain a hold was left grasping the bulwarks while its parent-body slid back to bloody the waters. / Others who sought refuge, or at least a kinder death, in the water, found swimming of no avail and, feeling their breath and spirit deserting them, would be lured back by fear of drowning towards the greedy flames they had been fleeing: they would cling onto a burning hulk and, seeking to shun two deaths, would incur both. / Yet others made for the water in dread of spear or axe they saw approaching, but in vain: a stone or arrow would catch them from behind and stop their straying too far. But I might perhaps find it wise and expedient to end my poem here, while it still pleases, rather than continue to a point where you begin to weary of it.

FORTIETH CANTO

1–5 Introductory. 5–9 Agramant and Sobrino flee from the naval battle. 9–35 The storming of Bizerta by the Christians under Orlando. 36–61 Agramant meets Gradasso on an island and they issue a challenge to Orlando. 61–82 Ruggiero clashes with Dudone.

WERE I to describe that naval battle in detail I should have a long task; and to describe it to you, noble Hippolytus, invincible son of Ercole, would be like bringing vases to Samos or owls to Athens, as they say (or crocodiles to Egypt): for whatever I tell you from hearsay, my Lord, you have witnessed for yourself and led others to witness. / What a prolonged spectacle you offered your loyal people, that night and day when they watched, as at the theatre, the enemy fleet trapped in the Po betwixt fire and the sword! What cries, what laments were to be heard, what a flood of water to be seen dyed with human gore! You saw—and demonstrated to many—how many ways there are of dying in such a battle. / I did not witness it myself, for six days earlier I had been travelling in all haste, changing horses at every post, to sue for help at the holy feet of the Great Shepherd. Neither horse nor foot-auxiliaries proved necessary, however: you had so crushed the Golden Lion of Venice, tooth and claw, that from that day I have never felt his menace. / But Alfonsin Trotto, who was present, and Annibal and Pier Moro, and Afranio and Alberto, and three of my kinsmen, and Lodovico da Bagno, and Francesco Zerbinato—they all told me enough to convince me. Then the quantities of banners I saw donated in church were finally conclusive, as also the fifteen captured galleys I saw on our shores along with a thousand smaller vessels. / Whoever saw those ships afire and sinking, and witnessed the various forms of carnage inflicted to avenge the burning of our villas, till every vessel was captured, will be able to visualize the deaths and torments suffered by the wretched Africans with King Agramant amid the salt waves that dark night when Dudone attacked them. /

When fierce battle was joined it was night and no light was visible. But once the sulphur, pitch, and bitumen had been copiously poured out to set prows and bulwarks ablaze, and the greedy flames burned and devoured the ill-defended galleys, everyone could see as clearly as if night had been turned into day. / Now Agramant had underrated the enemy when it was still dark, never doubting but that any challenge he encountered would be ultimately overcome by his resistance; once the darkness lifted, though, and he saw what he would not earlier believe—that the enemy fleet was twice the strength he had imagined —he changed his tactics. / With a handful of men he transferred to a lighter craft in which he had stowed his cherished possessions, including Brigliador. Silently he slipped away between one vessel and the next until he reached a safer stretch of water, remote from his hard-pressed fleet which Dudone was reducing to so pitiful a state—devoured by flames, engulfed by the seas, stricken by the sword, while he, the cause of it all, was making good his escape. / Agramant fled; with him was Sobrino, to whom he regretted not having listened when he divined the future and forewarned him of the evils which had now overtaken him.

But let us return to Orlando the paladin. He advised Astolfo to raze Bizerta before it was reinforced, so that it could never again make war on France. / Orders, thus, were issued for the host to marshall for battle three days hence. To this end, Astolfo had kept back many ships—Dudone did not take them all—and these he placed under the command of Samsonet, as fine a warrior at sea as on dry land. Sam-

sonet invested Bizerta from the sea, his fleet riding at anchor a mile
outside the harbour. / As true Christians who never affronted danger
without God's aid, Astolfo and Orlando gave orders that all hands
should turn to prayer and fasting. Three days hence, at the given
signal, everyone must be ready to storm Bizerta, which, once captured, was to be given up to fire and pillage. / Once the fasts and
prayers had been devoutly performed, relatives, friends, and acquain-
tances started entertaining each other to meals: they offered each
other refreshment for their drained, exhausted bodies and embraced
each other tearfully, their behaviour and speech such as dearest
friends adopt on leave-taking. / In Bizerta the holy priests prayed
with their grieving flock, beating their breasts and sobbing as they
invoked their Mahomet, who hears nothing. What vigils, what
promises, what gifts were not pledged in private! What shrines,
statues, altars, in public—eternal monument to their sorry plight!/
The Imam blessed the people, after which they took up arms and
repaired to the ramparts.

Fair Aurora still lay abed with her spouse Tithonus, and the sky
was still dark when Astolfo stood to arms from the landward side,
Samsonet from the sea. On hearing Orlando's signal, they launched a
violent attack upon Bizerta. / The city was sea-girt on two sides while
the other two stood on dry land. Its walls had been constructed with
singular perfection in days of old; beyond this, however, it had little
in the way of defences, for from the moment when King Branzardo
had taken refuge here he had been short of masons—and of time—to
fortify the place. / To Senapo, the Nubian king, Astolfo entrusted
the task of so raking the battlements with firebrands, sling-stones, and
arrows that no one would dare show his face at them. Thus soldiers,
mounted and on foot, laden with boulders and beams, axes and other
materials, would be enabled to advance in safety right up to the walls. /
The previous day the water to the moat had been cut off, exposing the
muddy bottom in several places. Now this and that was thrown into the
moat, after passing from hand to hand; soon it was filled up and
choked so as to extend the level plain right to the city walls, which
Astolfo, Orlando, and Oliver now enabled the infantry to scale. / The
Nubians, impatient of all delay and lured by the hope of booty, dis-
regarded the imminent dangers and, covered by their shields in
tortoise-shell formation, hastened to advance upon the city with their
battering-rams and other instruments for breaching towers and
smashing gates. But they did not find the Saracens unprepared:/
metal missiles, fire, merlons, ponderous roofs came raining down to
shatter the planks and beams assembled for their siege-engines. In
the pre-dawn darkness, at the ill-starred opening of the battle the

baptized heads suffered grave damage; but when the Sun issued from his radiant palace, Fortune turned her back upon the Saracens. /

Orlando had the assault redoubled on all sides, by sea and land. Samsonet, whose fleet had stood offshore, now closed the land and launched a fierce attack from the sea with slings and arrows and various siege-engines. At the same time he assembled lances and ladders and the full arsenal of naval warfare. / Oliver, Orlando, Brandimart, and Astolfo himself (that stalwart flyer) engaged battle with stark ferocity, attacking from the landward side. The army had been divided into four contingents, each one led by one of these. Whether attacking the walls, the gates, or elsewhere, they all gave a dazzling display of valour, / which could be the better discerned individually than if they had all attacked pell-mell; those deserving rewards or citations were apparent to a thousand watchful eyes. Wooden towers on wheels were dragged up, while others were carried forward on the backs of elephants trained for the task: the towers they bore quite overtopped the battlements. /

Brandimart placed a ladder against the wall and climbed, inciting others to do likewise. Many followed him, dauntless and confident, for his men derived courage from him: not a man stopped to consider if the ladder could bear so much weight. Brandimart thought only of the enemy; he fought his way up until he grasped a merlon. / Here he gained a handhold, then a foothold, and leapt onto the battlements to show his mettle to the full, brandishing his sword as he knocked the foe off their feet and slashed and speared and swatted them. But suddenly the ladder gave under the excess weight: one and all, Brandimart excepted, plunged head over heels into the emptied moat, one atop another. / He did not falter, though, or consider retreating, even though he could see none of his men behind him and realized he was a target for the entire city. Many besought him to turn back, but he would not listen. He pressed on: yes, he leapt down into the city from the ramparts, a good thirty feet high. / He hit the hard ground without hurt, as though cushioned by feathers or straw, and lay into those within reach—he pounded, stabbed, and ripped them as if they had been so many pieces of cloth. He charged into one group and another: one group and another took to their heels. /

Those outside the walls, meanwhile, who had witnessed his leap, thought he must be beyond rescuing. The news spread through the attacking host by word of mouth, murmured and whispered until it grew and grew on its rounds, enhancing the peril as it did so. The winged rumour reached Orlando, then Astolfo, then Oliver (the attack being conducted at several points), never pausing in its swift flight. / Hearing that too long a delay would entail the loss of so illustrious a comrade, these warriors who loved Brandimart and esteemed him (Orlando especially), snatched up ladders and clambered up them each at a different point; they vied with each other to display heroic courage; their very mien was so bold and dashing that a glance was enough to daunt the enemy. / Imagine a ship rashly ventured onto a storm-lashed sea. The waves assault it; first at the prow, then along the bulwarks they seethe angrily as they seek an entry. Wanly the captain sighs and groans: something must be done but he has neither wit nor nerve to do it. Finally one wave swamps the vessel and, where it has breached, the whole sea pours in. / Similarly, once these three had stormed the ramparts, they created so wide a breach that their men could follow them in safety up a thousand ladders now placed against the walls. Meanwhile the solid battering-rams had broken through so thunderously in so many places that doughty Brandimart could be assisted from not one but several points. / It was as when the Po, proud king of rivers, goes on the rampage: he breaks his banks, forces his passage into the fields of Ocnus where he carries away in his flood the fertile ploughland and fruitful crops, entire flocks complete with their sheep-folds, herdsmen and sheep-dogs all pell-mell; amid the elm-tree tops the fishes dart where earlier the birds had fluttered. /

Such was the violence of the impetuous host as it surged through the gaps in the walls into the city to destroy the ill-captained Saracens with fire and the sword. Murder, robbery, and violence done to life and property hastened the downfall of the rich, triumphant city which had been queen of all Africa. / The dead lay all about. Countless bloody gashes had produced a swamp darker and more foul than the one which rings Hades. A trail of fire spreading from house to house burnt down palaces, arcades, and mosques. The empty, ransacked houses echoed with cries and shrieks and the thud of beaten breasts. / The victors could be seen emerging from the doorways of the ill-fated homes laden with rich spoils: some carried fine vases, others costly garments, others silverware stolen from the ancient household gods. Some men dragged out the children, others the grieving mothers; rape and a thousand other crimes were committed, which Orlando and Astolfo in great part knew of but were unable to prevent. / Bucifar of the Algaziers was slain by a stroke of doughty Oliver; King Branzardo, losing heart and hope, took his own life; and Folvo was captured by Astolfo with three wounds from which he shortly died. These had been the three left by Agramant to guard the realm in his absence. /

Agramant, who meanwhile had deserted his fleet and escaped with Sobrino, wept and lamented over Bizerta from a distance, seeing so great a conflagration on the shore. On closer approach he learnt exactly what had befallen his city, and thought to slay himself. Indeed he would have done so had not Sobrino stopped him. / 'What happier victory for your enemy, my liege,' he said, 'than to hear of your death, which would leave him to the peaceful enjoyment of his conquest! Your remaining alive forbids him this satisfaction—he will always have cause to fear. He well knows that Africa cannot long be his except by your death. / If you die, you deprive all your subjects of hope, their sole remaining asset. I hope that you shall live to redeem them, to rescue them from their misery, and restore them to happiness. I know that if you die your subjects will be forever prisoners and Africa forever a wretched tributary. If you will not live for your own sake, my liege, live to avoid harm to your people. / You can count upon your neighbour, the Sultan of Egypt, for money and troops: he will be reluctant to see Charlemagne establishing such power in Africa. Your kinsman Norandin will make every effort to restore you to your kingdom. Armenians, Turks, Persians, Arabs, and Medes—you'll have help from all of them for the asking.' /

With these and similar words the shrewd old man tried to restore his liege's hope of soon recovering Africa. Perhaps, though, he secretly feared the reverse: he well recognized the sorry straits reached by whoever lets his kingdom be wrested from him and has recourse to barbarians for help, and how such a man will often sigh and moan in vain. / Hannibal, Jugurtha, and other men of old gave sound witness to this. So, in our own day, did Louis the Moor who subjected himself to another Louis. Your brother Alfonso learnt from their example, my Lord: he has always regarded it as sheer folly to rely more on others than on himself. / When an angry Pontiff made war upon him, neither threats nor promises could induce him to commit his realm to alien hands—and this although he could place little reliance on his own defective powers, yes, and though his would-be champion, the King of France, had been driven from Italy, while his enemy, the King of Spain, had invaded his realm. /

King Agramant had set course Eastwards and made for the open sea when a wicked storm off the land crossed their path—a savage onslaught. The master, who was at the helm, looked at the sky and exclaimed: 'I can see so violent a storm getting up that the ship will make no headway against it. / If you mark my advice, my lords, we should run for an island close by to port, until the tempest has subsided.' The king consented and thus escaped danger, the vessel running onto the beach to port which lies (a seaman's refuge) between the African shore and Etna, Vulcan's furnace. / The little island was uninhabited except by the lowly myrtle and juniper. It provided pleasant isolation and solitude for deer, roebuck, and hares. It was little known except to fishermen: often they hung their damp nets to dry on branches hacked clean for this—while the fish could sleep in tranquil waters. / Here they came upon another vessel, driven this way earlier by Fate, and bringing Gradasso, the great champion who governs Sericana, after he left Arles. On dry land, the two kings embraced each other with suitable dignity and reverence: they were friends, and shortly before this had been comrades-in-arms under the walls of Paris. / Gradasso was profoundly sorry to learn of Agramant's reverses. He consoled him and, being a chivalrous king, offered his own services. But he would not hear of Agramant's going to the untrustworthy Egyptians for help.

'Pompey should be a warning to fugitives of the dangers of resorting to Egypt,' he observed. / 'Now that you have told me how Astolfo has come to wrest Africa from you with the aid of the Ethiopians, Senapo's subjects, and how he has burnt down your capital city; and that Orlando is with him, whose brain was till recently addled— I think I have hit upon an excellent plan to recoup your fortunes. / I shall for your sake undertake to engage Orlando in single combat; against me he will, of course, be quite helpless—and would be even if he were made of solid iron or copper. Once he is dead, the Christian Church may be accounted as so many lambs for a hungry wolf. Furthermore I have thought of a way to rid Africa of the Nubians in a trice—for me it will be child's play. / I shall prevail upon the other Nubians, those this side of the Nile, who obey a different law, and the Arabs (rich in horses), and the populous Macrobians (rich in gold), the Persians, and Chaldeans, all of whom—among so many others— obey my rule: I shall make them invade Nubia. Your Nubians will not incline to linger in your land!' /

Gradasso's second offer struck Agramant as excellently conceived, and he felt himself indebted to Fortune for bringing him to this desert island. But on no account would he accept Gradasso's undertaking battle on his account, if he thought thereby to recover Bizerta: it was more than his own honour could stand. / 'If anyone is to challenge Orlando, such a combat is my due,' he replied. 'And I am ready for it. Let God dispose of me as He will, for better or worse.' 'Come, let us do it my way,' cried Gradasso, 'a way which has just occurred to me: let us both assume this combat against Orlando, with another on his side.' / 'So long as I am not excluded I shall not complain,' remarked Agramant. 'Whether I am first or second, I know that I could not find in the whole wide world a better comrade-in-arms than you.' 'Then what about me?' asked Sobrino. 'I may seem to you old, but I must be more experienced than you; in danger it is good to have sound judgement as well as strength.' / Sobrino was a robust old man in sound health, and well tried in arms; he said that he felt as vigorous in his old age as he had done when a stripling.

His request was accepted as just, and a messenger was at once dispatched to the African shore to convey their challenge to Count Orlando, / who was summoned to present himself in Lipadusa with an equal number of armoured knights. Lipadusa was an island set in the same sea which now surrounded them. The messenger pressed on under oar and sail, as one on urgent business, until he reached Bizerta. Here he found Orlando distributing the spoils and the captives among his troops. / The challenge issued by Gradasso, Agramant, and Sobrino was proclaimed in public, and so rejoiced Orlando that he had the messenger honoured with copious gifts. He had already learnt from his comrades that King Gradasso was wearing his sword Durindana; to recover it he had been meaning to go to India, / assuming, once he learnt of his departure from France, that he would not find Gradasso elsewhere. Now he was offered a closer meeting-place where he could hope to regain his possession. The fine horn of Almont was another motive for accepting the challenge so eagerly, and Brigliador no less so—for he knew that they had passed to Agramant. /

As comrades-in-arms he chose trusty Brandimart and his brother-in-law Oliver, knowing from experience what they were worth, and recognizing how devoted to him they both were. He looked everywhere for a good steed, good breastplate, coat of mail, swords, and lances for himself and his companions—I think you know that none of them possessed his usual arms. / Orlando, as I have several times mentioned, strewed his all over the place in his madness. Rodomont had seized the others' which were now locked in the high tower by the river's edge. Not much was to be found in Africa: King Agramant had taken all that was any good to France for his war—not that Africa had much in any case. / Orlando called in whatever could be found, however rusty and tarnished. Meanwhile he went for a walk along the beach with his companions and discussed the imminent combat. When they were more than three miles from camp he happened to look seaward and notice a ship running into shore under full sail. / The ship came skimming on, all sails set, with no helmsman or crew, as the wind and its fate drove it, until it ran ashore.

But before telling more of this, my love for Ruggiero recalls me to his story and bids me speak of him and of Rinaldo. / I told how these two warriors withdrew from their combat when they saw the pacts and agreements broken and every squadron and legion in a ferment. They tried to discover from those who passed exactly who it was who had first broken the pledges and occasioned such a calamity, whether Emperor Charles or King Agramant. / Meanwhile one of Ruggiero's pages, a loyal, practical, astute man who had never lost sight of his master during the savage skirmish between the two camps, came to bring him his sword and steed so that he could help his side. Ruggiero mounted and grasped his sword, but would not engage in the broil. / He left this place, but not before renewing his agreement with Rinaldo that if Agramant were found to be the truce-breaker, he would forsake him and his guilty band. Ruggiero did not want to engage in further combat that day, but only concerned himself with stopping one man and the next to ask whether Agramant or Charles had been the first to break the truce. / From everyone he heard that Agramant's side had been the first. Ruggiero loved Agramant, and if he deserted him over this, it was because he deemed it no trifling fault. The Africans had been broken and scattered, as I have said, and from the top of Fortune's fickle wheel had dropped to the bottom: so it pleased the Lady who keeps the world a-spinning. /

Ruggiero debated within himself whether to stay or to follow his liege. The love of his lady acted as a bridle, preventing his crossing again to Africa: it turned him round completely and spurred him off on the opposite course, with threats of punishment if he did not stand firmly by the pact sworn with Rinaldo. / On the other hand he was no less needled and nagged by his restless concern that if he abandoned Agramant in these circumstances he would be regarded as a timorous coward. If many were able to justify his remaining here, many others would find his reasons unacceptable: an oath unjustly and wrongfully sworn, they would maintain, should not be observed. / All that day and the following night he remained alone, and the next day too, cudgelling his perplexed brain as to whether to follow Agramant or stay behind. In the end he decided to follow his liege back to Africa: conjugal love had great influence over him—but fealty and honour even greater. / He turned back towards Arles, hoping to find the fleet still there to carry him back to Africa; but he saw no ship on the sea nor in the river, nor any Saracens, except dead ones. Agramant had left, taking with him every available vessel; the rest he fired in port. /

This plan failing, then, he set out along the seashore towards Marseilles. He meant to board some ship and persuade it, by prayers or by force, to carry him to the further shore. Meanwhile Dudone, son of Ogier the Dane, had arrived with the captured barbarian fleet. It would not have been possible to throw a grain of wheat into the water, so thickly covered was it with the swarms of ships laden with victors and vanquished. / All the pagan ships remaining after the fires and wrecks of that night (except for a few which had escaped) were brought into Marseilles by Dudone. Here now were seven of the

kings who had ruled in Africa: they were tearful and glumly silent—
seeing their people vanquished, they had surrendered with seven
ships. /

Dudone had descended onto the beach, meaning to see Charlemagne that day. He had arranged an elaborate triumph over the
captives and a trophy of their spoils; the captives extended all along
the shore, surrounded by the jubilant Nubian victors who made the
whole place echo with Dudone's name. / From a distance Ruggiero
was led to hope that this might be Agramant's fleet; to know for sure
he spurred his steed. But on approaching, he recognized among the
prisoners the King of the Nasamons, Baliverzo, Agricalt, Farurant,
Manilard, Clarindo, and Rimedon, all weeping with bowed heads. /
Fond of them as he was, he could not endure their remaining in the
abject state in which he found them. Arriving here empty-handed,
however, he realized that prayers unaccompanied by force would serve
little purpose; so he lowered his lance and attacked their captors, giving
the usual proof of his valour. He grasped his sword and in no time
more than a hundred lay on the ground. /

Dudone heard the uproar and witnessed the slaughter, but did not
recognize its perpetrator. He saw his own men fleeing in terror,
crying out in anguish. Promptly he called for his steed, helmet, and
shield—his chest, arms, and thighs being already armoured—leapt
into the saddle and reached for his lance, mindful that he was a paladin
of France. / He bade everyone stand aside and set spurs to his horse.
Ruggiero meanwhile had killed a further hundred, raising the prisoners' hopes. Seeing the saintly Dudone coming alone and mounted,
every one else being on foot, he reckoned that this must be their leader,
and charged at him eagerly. / Dudone was already charging when he
noticed that Ruggiero was coming at him without a lance; so he flung
his own far from him, scorning to attack with such an advantage.
Seeing this chivalrous act, Ruggiero said to himself, 'This man cannot
conceal that he is one of those consummate warriors known as the
paladins of France. / If I can persuade him, I should like him to reveal
his name to me before matters go further.' So he asked him, and learnt
that he was Dudone, son of Ogier the Dane. Dudone imposed the
same burden on Ruggiero and found him equally obliging. Having
divulged their names, they challenged each other and came to grips. /

Dudone had the iron club which brought him eternal honour in a
thousand feats; with it he gave clear proof that he stemmed from
Ogier, the valiant Dane. Ruggiero drew the sword which opens every
helmet, every breastplate, the like of which never existed, and offered
Dudone a sample of his prowess. / But as his constant concern was to
harm his lady as little as possible, and he was sure to hurt her if he

bespattered the ground with Dudone's blood—well versed in the French genealogies, he knew that Dudone's mother Armellina was sister to Beatrice, Bradamant's mother— / he never attacked with his sword-point and rarely with its edge, but protected himself whenever the club descended, sometimes by parrying, other times by stepping aside. Turpin believes that Ruggiero could at will have slain Dudone in only a few blows; but, however often Dudone left an opening, he would never strike except with the flat of his sword. / Ruggiero could use the flat of his sword as well as the edge, for it was of solid temper; with it he dealt out such ringing blows as to make Dudone see stars— so much so that he could barely keep his saddle. But I shall defer my story to another time so as to make it more agreeable to my listeners.

FORTY-FIRST CANTO

1–3 Introductory. 4–22 Ruggiero vanquishes Dudone, sets sail with his freed prisoners and meets with shipwreck. 22–46 Orlando, Brandimart, and Oliver, having equipped themselves with such arms as Fortune brought them, go to their battle with Agramant, Gradasso, and Sobrino. 46–67 Ruggiero survives shipwreck to receive baptism from a holy hermit on a sea-girt rock. 68–102 The great battle of the three Christian and three pagan champions.

IF the fragrance clinging to a well-groomed head of hair or beard, or to the dainty attire of dapper youth or maiden (often Cupid's tears release it), if it still lingers pervasively after several days, that in itself affords ample proof of the native virtue inherent in it. / The heavenly liquor which Icarus, to his own undoing, dispensed to his harvesters, and which is said to have tempted Celtic tribes to cross the Alps without hardship, must clearly, to remain so good at the year's end, have been delicious from the outset. The tree which does not shed a leaf during the stormy season must obviously have been green in the springtime. / Similarly, the glorious house of Este, whose effulgent chivalry has endured from age to age and seems ever to gain lustre, offers the firmest grounds for the presumption that the man who engendered the illustrious family must have shone, as the sun among the stars, with every mark of honour that can raise a mortal to heaven. /

Just as in all his actions Ruggiero used to give shining proof of the highest valour and courtesy and to enhance his nobility, so now he revealed himself to Dudone, disguising his true strength (as I told you) out of reluctance to slay him. / Dudone had clearly recognized Ruggiero's reluctance to dispatch him—for now he was too weak and exhausted to protect himself. When it was obvious to him that Ruggiero was holding back and respecting his life, even though Dudone could not match his strength and stamina, at least he was not going to yield to him in chivalry. / 'Let us make peace, sir,' he cried, 'for I can no longer win. I can no longer win, for already I must concede defeat: I am prisoner of your chivalry.' 'I am no less eager than you to make peace,' replied Ruggiero, 'but on this condition: that you release to me these seven captive kings'— / and he pointed out those seven kings I mentioned, all fettered and bowed down. Nor, he added, was he to be stopped from leaving with them for Africa. So the kings were set free, as Dudone conceded, and Ruggiero was also given the choice of any vessel he wished; so he set sail for Africa. /

He cast off, hoisted the sail, and abandoned himself to the treacherous wind, which at first reassured the helmsman by filling the sails to blow the ship on course. The coast receded fast and soon was hidden, giving to the sea an illusion of boundlessness. It was at dusk that the wind revealed its perfidy: / from following astern it veered to cross their bows, then blew head-on, then shifted again. Blowing now from aft, now from the fore, now from the beam, it turned the ship off course and confounded the sailors. The waves surged up, proud and threatening, and the white flocks seethed across the sea. The travellers feared as many deaths as there were waves to assail them. / One wind came from astern, driving them on, a second from the bows, forcing them back; another raked across the ship, and each wind threatened to capsize them. The man at the helm paled with dread and heaved deep sighs; in vain he cried out, in vain he signalled for the yard to be swung over or dropped. / But the signal and the shout were unavailing: the rainy night reduced vision, while the voice rose unheard into the air, into the air already more than resonant with the unison cries of the sailors and the thunder of clashing waves. Neither at stem nor at stern, neither to port nor to starboard could a command make itself heard. /

The raging wind howled through the rigging, a fearsome sound; the sky was lit by frequent lightning-flashes, dreadful thunder rolled in the heavens. One man ran to the helm, others to the oars, each went automatically to the post to which he had been trained. Some strained to untie, others to make fast; yet others bailed, returning the sea to whence it came. / Now the fearful gale, roused by the sudden anger of the North Wind, shrieked as it set the sail flogging against the mast. The seas reached up almost to touch the heavens. The oars smashed and, as the tempest's wrath achieved a paroxysm, the prow veered off and the unprotected vessel broached to. / The starboard side dipped under water and the keel threatened to swing upright. Everyone cried out, commending themselves to God, convinced that now they would go to the bottom. Fate sent blow upon blow—one passed, the next followed: overwhelmed at many points, the vessel let the hostile waves flood in. /

From all sides the tempest mounted a cruel, frightening assault. At one moment they saw the sea rear up so high it seemed to reach the heavens; at the next, they were themselves lifted so high upon a crest that to look down seemed like a glance into hell. They had little or no hope to comfort them; inevitable death faced them. / All night they drifted across the changing sea as the wind drove them, the fierce wind which should have dropped as day broke but only increased in violence. A barren rock appeared before them: they tried to avoid it but lacked the means and the cruel wind, the dire tempest bore them towards it willy nilly. / Time and again the pale-cheeked helmsman struggled to force the tiller round and steer a safer course, but the rudder broke and the seas carried it away, and the ferocious wind so filled the sail that there was no reefing nor lowering it. They had no time for new measures or fresh counsel, for the mortal peril was too imminent. /

Once it was realized that the ship was doomed and beyond rescue, each man saw to his own safety: there was a race to leap into the ship's boat—which at once became so overladen it was almost gunwales under. / Seeing the master, the bo'sun, and all the rest hastily abandon ship, Ruggiero, who was in his tunic but not in his armour, decided also to seek safety in the boat; but he found it so laden with people, as yet more piled in, that the water lapped over the sides and it sank to the bottom under its load. / It sank to the bottom, carrying down all those who relied on it to abandon ship. Anguished cries to heaven for help could now be heard, but the voices did not endure for long: the seething waters surged in spitefully to occupy every orifice from which the tearful cries issued. / Some remained submerged, never to reappear; others rose to break the surface. Here a swimmer's head emerged, there an arm or a bare leg. Ruggiero, nothing daunted by the storm's menace, struggled to the surface. He noticed the barren rock not far off, the one which he and his companions had avoided in vain. / He hoped, by striking out with his arms and legs, to reach dry land here, so he kept blowing the all-pervasive brine from his face.

Meanwhile the storm-wind drove on the empty ship, deserted by those poor souls who (alas for them) were enticed to their death by their very urge to survive. / How fallible are men's expectations! The vessel abandoned to her fate survived after her master and crew had left her with no hand on the helm. It seemed as though the wind had changed its mind when it saw all the men make off: it brought the ship onto a better course, and instead of striking rocks she ploughed a safe furrow. / And where she had held an uncertain course under the helmsman's command, once she was free of him, she made straight for Africa, fetching up two or three miles from Bizerta, on the Egyptian side. Here she stopped, for lack of wind and water, lodged in the barren desert sand.

Here it was that Orlando came upon her in the course of a walk, as I related earlier. / Now, curious to discover whether or not the ship were deserted, he made his way to her with Brandimart and Oliver in a light skiff. Going below deck, he found it quite deserted. All he found was good Frontino, Ruggiero's steed, and also his arms and sword— / Ruggiero had been so pressed to escape that he had had no time to grab his sword. Orlando recognized Balisard, as the sword was called: it had once been his own. You will of course have read the whole tale of how Orlando seized it off Falerina (that time when he destroyed her beautiful garden, too) and how Brunello stole it from him / and made a gift of it to Ruggiero at the foot of Mount Carena. Orlando already had ample experience of its fine edge and solid temper. So he was in raptures and thanked God, believing—as he was later often to assert—that the Almighty had sent it to him for so great a task: / his confrontation with Gradasso of Sericana. Gradasso's valour was tremendous and, furthermore, he was known to possess Bayard and Durindana. Not recognizing the rest of Ruggiero's arms, he did not value them as highly as if he had tried them for himself; he imagined they were good, but more for display than for endurance. / As he had little need, then, for the suit of armour (which was in fact enchanted and impenetrable), he was content to assign it to Oliver. Not the sword, however—this he buckled on. To Brandimart he allotted the steed, thus fulfilling his wish to ensure that each of his companions should have an equal part of the booty. /

Each champion strove to have sumptuous new apparel ready for the day of battle. For his emblem Orlando had embroidered the tower of Babel struck by lightning. Oliver wanted for his a hound couchant argent, its leash laid on its back, and the motto 'Till he come'. His cloak was to be of gold, as befitted him. / For love of his father and his own honour's sake Brandimart proposed to wear on the day of battle only dark, sombre attire. Fiordiligi made him a surcoat as handsome and elegant as could be, adorned with a hem studded with rich jewels; for the rest, the garment was an austere black. / Fiordiligi herself made the surcoat, to be draped over the knight's breastplate and over his steed's crupper, chest, and mane. It deserved to set off a finer suit of armour. From the day she embarked on her task, however, until the day she completed it, and still afterwards, the damsel could never summon up a smile nor hint of laughter. / She was in constant dread that her Brandimart would be torn from her. She had seen him embroiled in a hundred perilous combats in a hundred places before this, but never had she been so frozen with terror, nor looked so pale as on this occasion. The very novelty of her fear heightened her anxiety and made her tremble. / When their arms and equipment were all ready, the three knights hoisted sail, leaving Astolfo and Samsonet in charge of the army of the Faithful. Fiordiligi, her heart stabbed with fear, filled the heavens with her prayers and laments as she followed the sail out on the sea as far as her sight would take her. / Astolfo and Samsonet had great difficulty in distracting her from gazing out to sea. They brought her back to the palace and left her lying on her bed, prostrate and trembling.

Meanwhile a following breeze bore on the three chosen warriors, whose ship made straight for the island where so great a combat was to be fought. / Orlando went ashore with his brother-in-law Oliver and Brandimart. They chose the Eastern end to set up their pavilion—perhaps no casual choice. Agramant arrived the same day and took the opposite station. As the day was far advanced, they deferred the combat till the next morning. / Until the new day dawned, armed guards stood watch on either side.

In the evening Brandimart, with his lord's permission, betook himself to the Saracen quarters and spoke with the African king: they had once been friends, indeed Brandimart had crossed to France under the standards of King Agramant. / After greeting one another and joining hands, the Christian knight propounded many a friendly argument to the pagan king to induce him to call off this combat. He offered, with Orlando's approval, to restore to him every city between the Nile and the Pillars of Hercules if he were willing to believe in the Son of Mary. /

'As I love you greatly and always have done, my lord, I offer you this advice,' he said. 'Believe me, I regard it as sound advice, for I myself have taken it. I knew Christ for God, Mahomet for a dupe, and I long to set you on the path I have taken—I long, my lord, to see you with me in the way of salvation, you and all those I love. / Herein lies your good, and no other counsel will profit you, least of all that of doing battle with Orlando. Your gain, if you win, can never measure up to what you set at risk by losing; you have little to gain by winning, but more than a little to lose if you are defeated. / What if you do slay Orlando and the two of us who have come to conquer or to die with him? I cannot see how this would restore to you your lost dominions: you need not hope that our decease would so change the situation as to leave Charles short of men here to garrison every last keep.' /

Thus spoke Brandimart, who would have continued had not Agramant, with anger in his voice, scorn in his eyes, broken in: 'What a rash fool you are, as is anyone who sets out to proffer his advice unasked, whatever it is worth! / In truth, I find it hard to believe your assertion that your advice proceeds from the love you still bear me, seeing you now as I do in Orlando's company. I more readily believe that, having fallen prey to the monster who devours the soul, you aim to drag all men with you into the perpetual pains of hell. / Whether I am to win or lose, whether I am to recover my ancestral kingdom or be forever banished from it—the decision is known to God, whose thoughts neither I nor you nor Orlando can search. Come what may, base terror shall never reduce me to any act unworthy of a king. Were I certain to die, I should sooner die than disparage my own blood. / Go back now—and if tomorrow you do not acquit yourself better on the field of battle than you seem to have today as an orator, Orlando will be poorly seconded.' These last words Agramant flung out in a passion. Now each turned back and retired to bed until dawn rose out of the sea. / As the new day brightened they were armed and mounted in a trice. They exchanged but few words and, with but the briefest delay, set their lances in rest.

But would it not be unpardonable, my Lord, if in my urge to pursue their story, I left Ruggiero in the sea so long that he drowned? / The young man struck out through the formidable swell with his arms and legs. If there was menace in the wind and sea, he suffered worse anxiety from his conscience. He feared that Christ was taking vengeance upon him: he had made so light about obtaining baptism in clean water when the occasion offered, and now he was being baptized in this bitter, salt water. / He recalled the promises so often made to his lady, and the oath he had sworn before fighting Rinaldo, none of which he had honoured. Penitently he asked God time and again not to punish him now, and swore faithfully from the bottom of his heart to become a Christian if he set foot on shore, / and never more to take up sword or lance for the Moors against the Christians. He would return straight to France and render due honours to Charlemagne; he would no longer dally with Bradamant but would achieve the honourable consummation of his love. By a miracle, as he made his vow he felt an increase of strength and swam more buoyantly. / He gathered strength and, his spirit unflagging, he struck the waves and swept them aside. The waves followed hard upon each other; one raised him up, the next carried him forward. Thus, bobbing up and down, he struggled to the shore and finally emerged from the water, soaked through, at a point where the rock sloped most gently into the sea. /

All the others who had abandoned ship were overwhelmed by the waves and remained in the water; Ruggiero, however, climbed out onto the lone rock, as it pleased God in His great goodness. Once he was safe from the sea on the stark, barren rock, though, a new fear possessed him of being exiled within such narrow confines and of meeting his death here from privations. / Still, with indomitable heart and ready to endure whatever Heaven sent him, he set out boldly to climb the hard rock, making straight for the top of the cliff.

He had not gone a hundred steps when he saw a man ravaged by years and abstinence; his dress and manner proclaimed him a hermit worthy of all deference and respect. / When Ruggiero was close by the hermit called out to him, 'Saul, Saul, why do you persecute my Faith?', just as the Lord had spoken to Saint Paul when he struck him down, to his redemption. 'You expected to cross the sea without paying your passage, and to defraud another of his due. See, God has a long reach and grasps you when you think you are furthest from Him!' / The holy man had that night been sent a vision by God of how with His help Ruggiero was to reach this rock. God had given him a complete revelation of Ruggiero: all his past life, his future, his atrocious death, his sons, and grandsons, too, and all his posterity. / The hermit went on first to upbraid Ruggiero, then to console him. He chided him for having delayed placing his neck in the gentle yoke, for doing grudgingly, when he saw Christ threaten him with a whip, what he should have done when he was under no compulsion and Christ had called him with entreaties. / Then he consoled him, saying that whether early or late, God does not deny Christ to those who seek Him; he told him the Gospel parable of the labourers in the vineyard who all received the same wage.

With charity and devoted zeal the hermit instructed Ruggiero in the Faith as they walked slowly towards his cell, which was cut out of the hard rock. / Above the holy cell stood a chapel facing East; it was beautiful and convenient. Below it a wood stretched down to the water's edge, planted with laurel, juniper, myrtle, and fruitful palms; it was forever watered by a murmuring spring which cascaded down from the summit. / It was almost forty years since the hermit had come to this rock, a place chosen for him by the Lord as suitable for leading the holy life of a solitary. He lived off the fruit of one tree and another and off pure water. Now he had reached his eightieth year— a healthy, robust existence free of worries. / The old man lit a fire in the cell, and loaded the table with an assortment of fruit, so that Ruggiero could restore himself a little once he had dried his clothes and hair. He learned here at greater leisure all the great mysteries of our Faith and the next day the old man baptized him in the pure spring. / Ruggiero was most content to stay in this place, for the good servant of God declared his intention of sending him back in a few days to where he most wanted to go. Meanwhile they talked of many things— the kingdom of God, Ruggiero's own affairs, his posterity. /

The Lord, who knows and sees all, had revealed to the holy hermit that Ruggiero would live for seven years, no more, from the day he received the faith; the slaying of Pinabello by his lady Bradamant would be laid at his door, as well as Bertolai's death at his hands; and he would be killed by those evil Maganzas, a ruthless clan. / This treachery would remain so hidden that no news of it would leak out, for he would be buried at the very spot where he was killed by the wicked men. Therefore he would not be at once avenged by his sister and his faithful wife who would, while heavy with child, make a long journey in search of him. /

Here, between the Adige and the Brenta, at the foot of the hills which so enchanted the Trojan Antenor—with their sulphur springs and gentle brooks, their smiling ploughlands and pleasant meadows —that he gladly chose them in preference to his own Mount Ida, his lamented Lake Ascanius and beloved River Xanthus: here in the forest, not far from Phrygian Ateste, she was to bear her child. / Her child, also called Ruggiero, would grow up handsome and valorous. Those Trojans would recognize him as of Trojan blood and elect him their lord. Then Charlemagne, whom he, as a young man, would help against the Lombards, would give him the right to rule over this fair land, and the honourable title of Marquis. / And as Charles, in making this award, would say to him in Latin, 'Este Signori qui', the land would, as a good omen, be known to future ages as Este: the first two letters of the earlier name Ateste would be dropped. God had also predicted to His servant the harsh vengeance obtained for Ruggiero. / A little before daybreak he would appear to his faithful wife in a dream and tell her who it was who had slain him, and show her the place where he lay. So she with her redoubtable sister-in-law Marfisa would destroy Ponthieu by fire and the sword; nor would the Maganzas suffer any less injury from her son Ruggiero, when he was old enough. / The holy old man spoke to Ruggiero about many an Azzo, Alberto and Obice and their fine posterity up to Niccolò, Leonello, and Borso, Ercole and Alfonso, Hippolytus and Isabel; he restrained his tongue, however, and divulged less than he knew—he told Ruggiero what it was suitable to disclose and suppressed what required suppressing. /

Meanwhile Orlando, Brandimart, and Oliver, their lances lowered, were closing with Gradasso (the Saracen Mars he might be called) and the other two—Agramant and Sobrino—who from the opposite end had spurred their good steeds to a gallop. At their charge, the shore and nearby sea resounded. / At the impact every lance flew skywards in splinters and the sea visibly swelled at the great noise, which could be heard all the way to France. Gradasso and Orlando clashed; they would have been evenly weighted were it not that Bayard seemed to give Gradasso the advantage over his opponent. / Bayard struck the less powerful steed Orlando was riding with so incredible an impact as to make him stagger from side to side, then measured his length on the ground. Orlando tried three or four times to pull him to his feet, tugging and spurring, but when this proved impossible, he dismounted, grasped his shield and drew Balisard. / Oliver and Agramant clashed—with equal honours. Brandimart unhorsed Sobrino, but it was questionable whether the fault were the rider's or his mount's: Sobrino was unaccustomed to being unseated. Whosoever the fault, Sobrino found himself on the ground. / Now Brandimart, seeing King Sobrino floored, did not press his advantage but assailed Gradasso, who had equally floored Orlando. Between Oliver and Agramant the combat continued as it had begun: having broken their lances on each other's shields, they had returned to grapple with naked blades. /

Seeing that Gradasso showed little interest in pressing his advantage either—not that Brandimart's harrying left him much scope to do so—Orlando looked round and saw that Sobrino was also on foot and unengaged. So he threw himself at him, and the heavens trembled at his ferocious mien as he moved. / Seeing the onslaught of a man such as he, Sobrino braced himself in a posture of defence, the way a helmsman turns the ship's prow into the threatening wave as it comes piling in with a roar: when he sees the waves mounting that high, he wishes himself on dry land. Sobrino raised his shield against the devastation of Balisard (the sword fashioned by Falerina), / but so finely tempered was Balisard that armour could scarce resist it; moreover, in the hands of a man of Orlando's unique power, it cleft the shield. It may have been rimmed with steel, but this did nothing to slow the sword-stroke—it cleft the shield and split it from crown to base and attained Sobrino's shoulder behind it. / It struck his shoulder, which was protected by a double thickness of plate-armour and a coat of mail, but little did this profit him—the sword left a gaping gash. Sobrino struck back, but vainly did he try to wound Orlando: the Creator of the Heavens and stars had endowed him with a skin which could never be pierced. / Valiant Orlando redoubled his blows and thought to strike Sobrino's head from his shoulders. Recognizing Orlando's prowess and the inefficacy of fending him off with his shield,

Sobrino stepped back, but not enough to prevent Balisard fetching him a blow on the forehead. It was with the flat of the blade, but so mighty a blow as to dent his helmet and leave him dazed. / The savage blow floored Sobrino, who lay prostrate for a long time.

Orlando thought he was out of the battle and lay dead, so turned to attack Gradasso before he overcame Brandimart, for the pagan's armour, sword, and steed (and possibly his strength) gave him the advantage over his opponent. / Bold Brandimart, however, mounted as he was on Frontino (the good steed formerly of Ruggiero), measured so well up to the Saracen, that he did not appear to be at any great disadvantage. Had he had as good a breastplate as Gradasso, he would have stood up to him even better; but, feeling himself poorly armoured, he often had to side-step. / No horse understood Brandimart's commands better than Frontino: he seemed to have the knack of always evading Durindana's blows as they fell. Elsewhere, Agramant and Oliver were locked in hideous battle; they had to be accounted two champions of equal skill and of virtually equal strength. /

Orlando had left Sobrino on the ground, as I said. Now, anxious to help Brandimart, he strode rapidly towards Gradasso, on foot as he was, and would have attacked him, but he noticed Sobrino's mount wandering at large on the battlefield, and lost no time in grabbing him. / He seized the horse, unopposed, and with one leap was in the saddle. He brandished his sword in one hand while the other held the gorgeous bridle. Gradasso noticed Orlando advancing, yelling his name, but remained unconcerned—he expected to bring night upon him, and upon Brandimart and Oliver, before it was yet dusk. / Relinquishing Brandimart, he turned upon Orlando and lunged at his gorget. His sword went clean through but stopped at the skin—to pierce that he would have laboured in vain. Meanwhile Orlando swung down Balisard: where it cut, all enchantments failed. It sliced through all it met in its descent, helmet, shield, breastplate, and cuisse, / and left Gradasso with gashes to his face, chest, and thigh. Never since he possessed Durindana had blood been drawn from him; it seemed to him unaccountable, indeed it filled him with fury and distress that this sword, which was not Durindana, should cut him so. Had the stroke been longer or delivered closer, it would have cloven him from head to belly. / He could no longer rely on his weapon as before, that was now clear. He fought with greater caution and care than hitherto and took a more defensive posture. Brandimart, seeing that Orlando had relieved him of the combat with Gradasso, took up his station between the two duels so as to assist wherever the need first arose. /

The battle being thus advanced, Sobrino, after lying prostrate a long time, returned to his senses and got up. His face and shoulder ached badly. He looked about him and, seeing his liege, he moved in long, silent strides towards him, unobserved, to give him help. / He came up behind Oliver, who was wholly concentrating on Agramant, and delivered so wicked a slash at his mount's hamstrings that the beast collapsed at once. Oliver fell with him and, taken unawares as he was, his left foot remained trapped in its stirrup beneath the horse. / Sobrino redoubled his blows and expected to slice off his head with a side-swipe, but he was prevented by the burnished steel of the armour, once Hector's, fashioned by Vulcan. Brandimart saw the danger and charged full tilt at Sobrino, knocking him over and striking him on the head. The fierce old man was quickly on his feet again, though, / and returned to dispatch Oliver and send him post haste into the next world—or at least to prevent his extricating himself from his horse. But Oliver had his better arm uppermost and could use his sword to defend himself; he so slashed and thrust that he kept Sobrino at sword's length. / He hoped, if he could ward him off for a little, shortly to be free of his predicament. He saw that Sobrino was all wet and stained with blood, and that he was shedding so much onto the dust that he must shortly succumb; he was so weak he could scarcely stand. Oliver made repeated efforts to get up but the horse would not roll over. /

Brandimart had now reached Agramant and started assailing him; one moment he was beside him, the next, in front—Frontino spun about as smoothly as a lathe. Brandimart had a good steed; but Agramant's was no whit inferior—he had Brigliador, a gift from Ruggiero who had taken him from proud Mandricard. / As for the king's armour, it gave him a decided advantage: it was tried and tested and utterly flawless, whereas Brandimart's was simply whatever he had been able to lay his hands on in a hurry; but he relied upon his own valour to exchange it shortly for a better suit, for all that the African had bloodied his right shoulder with a savage blow, / and Gradasso had scarred his side with a wound that was no laughing matter. The doughty warrior watched for his moment and managed to drive his sword home. The blow slashed Agramant's shield, wounded him in the left arm and grazed his right hand. But this was no more than child's play compared with the exchanges between Orlando and Gradasso. /

Gradasso had half-disarmed Orlando: he had smashed his helmet—top and sides—swiped his shield to the ground, pierced his breastplate and chain-mail behind it. Orlando remained unscathed—he was enchanted. But the paladin had done him worse damage, wounding him in the face, in the throat, full in the chest, beside the wounds already mentioned. / Gradasso despaired at the sight of himself all hideously smeared with his own blood while Orlando, after so many blows delivered, was still bone dry from head to foot. So he raised his sword two-handed, expecting to split him from crown to belly and all, and brought it down at half blade-length, as intended, on the fierce count's forehead. / With anyone but Orlando he would have succeeded, he would have split him down to the saddle; but the sword rebounded, bright and unsullied, as though from a flat-sided blow. Orlando saw a star or two as he looked down, dazed; he dropped the reins and would have dropped his sword were it not tied to his wrist by a chain. / The steed ridden by Orlando was so frightened by the sound of the blow that he dashed off along the dusty plain, showing his paces as a racer. Stunned by the blow, the count had no strength to curb him. Gradasso pursued and would soon have reached him, had he spurred Bayard a little more. / But as he turned he caught sight of Agramant in desperate straits: Brandimart had grasped his helmet with his left hand and loosened the fastenings in front, meaning to try conclusions with his dagger. The king could offer little resistance, Brandimart having wrested his sword from him. /

Gradasso broke off his pursuit of Orlando and galloped towards Agramant. Now Brandimart little dreamed that Orlando would let Gradasso evade him; he had neither eye nor mind for him but, all unwary, was bent upon plunging his knife into the pagan's throat. Gradasso reached him and brought his sword down two-handed with all his might on his helmet. /

Father of Heaven, make room among your chosen spirits for your faithful martyr who has reached the end of his stormy travels and now furls his sails in harbour. Ah Durindana, how can you be so cruel to your lord Orlando, slaying before his eyes the best and most loyal comrade he had in all the world! / An iron band two inches thick encircled the helmet, which was lined with a steel mesh; the ponderous blow snapped the one and the other. Ashy-faced, Brandimart pitched straight out of the saddle; blood streamed from his head to flow into the dust. / Orlando recovered his senses and, looking back, saw his Brandimart on the ground; and from Gradasso's posture over him he inferred that the pagan had slain him. I know not whether rage or grief prevailed in him; but he had so little time for tears that grief was checked and rage flared up more promptly. But now it is time to end this canto.

FORTY-SECOND CANTO

1–6 Introductory. 7–23 Orlando's combat concluded. 23–28
Bradamant reproaches absent Ruggiero. 28–67 Rinaldo con-
cludes his search for Angelica. 68–104 Rinaldo, guest in an
opulent palace, is offered the chance to prove his wife's fidelity.

WHERE is the sturdy rein, the steely knot, the chain of adamant (if such can exist) that will hold Anger within Reason's bounds and prevent him from overstepping the mark when you see someone whose heart is riveted to yours in constant love enduring shame or mortal injury through violence or deceit? / And should this passion occasionally turn the mind to acts of cruelty, that is excusable, for at such times it is not under the protective rule of Reason. When Achilles saw Patroclus staining the ground with his blood under his borrowed helmet, he was not satisfied with slaying his friend's slayer but had perforce to lacerate the corpse, dragging it about. /

A similar rage fired your troops, all-conquering Alfonso, the day when you were struck on the brow by a great stone which so injured you that they all believed your soul had taken flight. This goaded them to such fury that ramparts, walls, and ditches provided no defence to your foes but they were all slain, leaving none to tell the tale. / The sight of your fall provoked the pain which stung your men to pitiless fury; had you remained standing, their swords perhaps would have enjoyed less licence. As it was, it sufficed to restore the Bastia to your hands in fewer hours than the number of days the Cordovans and Granadans took to wrest it from you. / Perhaps the avenging Deity permitted you to be thus disabled at that point, so that the outrage perpetrated earlier by the Spaniards be punished: for when poor Vestidello, keeper of the castle, had surrendered to them, all wounded and exhausted as he was, those troops, for the most part circumcized Mohammedans, had fallen upon the defenceless man with a hundred swords. / To conclude, there is no anger to equal that which you feel on seeing your lord, your kinsman or boon-companion injured before your eyes. So Orlando was surely right to be cut to the quick, to flare up on so dear a friend's account, seeing Brandimart lying dead from the fearsome blow dealt him by King Gradasso. /

As the Numidian shepherd will grasp his stick with frantic rage, seeing the horrible snake slither away once its poisonous fangs have slain his child playing in the sand: so did Orlando rabidly grasp his sword which was unmatched for sharpness. The first man he came upon was King Agramant; / bleeding, swordless, with but half a shield and unfastened helmet, and wounded in more places than I can say, he had dragged himself out of Brandimart's clutches like a half-dead falcon from the clutches of the hawk and of the hunter who, whether from spite or folly, has set the bird after him. Orlando rushed at him and with a neat blow struck him where head and trunk join. / The helmet unfastened, the neck was unprotected, so Orlando sliced it clean off like a reed. Agramant fell; the heavy trunk of Africa's monarch gave one last shudder in the sand. His spirit fled to the waters from which Charon hooked it into his boat. The count did not linger over him but went after Gradasso with Balisard. / When Gradasso saw Agramant fall, trunk parted from head, he quailed, he blanched—a thing he had never done before. As Orlando reached him he seemed quite overcome, as though foreknowing his doom. He made no attempt to protect himself as the mortal blow descended. / Orlando stabbed him in the right side beneath the lowest rib; Balisard plunged into his belly to re-emerge a palm's width from his left side, steeped in blood to the hilt. Without a doubt here was the hand of the world's best and bravest champion dealing a blow which sent to his death a prince unmatched for strength in all the pagan realm. /

Not all that elated by his victory, the paladin leapt from his saddle to run, weeping and distraught, to his beloved Brandimart. He noticed how gory was the ground where he lay, while his helmet looked as if split open with an axe—for all the protection it had offered him, it might have been made of brittle bark. / Orlando drew the helmet off his head to find his brow cleft down to the nose. Even so, Brandimart had enough life in him yet to ask pardon for his sins from the King of Paradise before his day waned; and to encourage the count, whose cheeks were bathed in tears, to bear up. /

'Orlando,' he asked, 'remember me in your prayers to God. No less do I commend to you my Fiordi . . .' but before he could say 'ligi' he was finished. And the music and harmonious voices of angels could be heard in the air, for his spirit, freed of its bodily vesture, took flight to heaven amid sweet melody. / Orlando should have rejoiced at so devout an end: he knew for certain that Brandimart had ascended to the empyrean, for he saw the heavens open to him. He was only human, though, his will conditioned by the frail senses, and he found it hard to suffer the loss of one who was more to him than a brother without the tears bedewing his face. /

Sobrino had lost a great deal of blood—it flowed down his side and down his cheeks. He had fallen supine some time earlier; by now his veins must have been empty. Oliver still lay unable to release his foot: nor could he retrieve it except in a dislocated and half-crushed condition after his steed had been lying on it so long. / Had his brother-in-law not come to his help (all sad and tearful though he was) he would never have been able to free his foot by himself. It gave him such acute pain that, when it was released, he could neither walk nor stand upon it. His leg, too, was so deadened, that he could not move it unaided. / Orlando had little joy of his victory: the sight of Brandimart dead was beyond enduring, and he was not wholly reassured about his brother-in-law. Sobrino still survived, but the shadows were creeping in upon him—with his loss of blood, his life would soon have drained out. / The count had him removed, all bleeding as he was, and entrusted him to the care of physicians. He spoke to him words of comfort, as though he were a kinsman—the action finished, he was purged of all malice, he was all clemency. The arms and horses of the dead he had removed, leaving all else to the disposal of their retainers. /

Here Federigo Fregoso has thrown some doubt on the truth of my tale: after scouring every nook and cranny of the Barbary coast with his fleet he arrived at this spot, which he found so rugged, precipitous and wild that there is not a place, he maintains, in the whole weird island where the foot may be set down flat. / He thinks it unlikely that six knights, the flower of the world's chivalry, could have conducted their mounted combat on this craggy rock. To which objection here is my reply: in those days there was at the foot of the rock an area suitable as a tilting ground, but subsequently an earthquake dislodged a great pinnacle which crashed down to obliterate it. / Therefore, O brightest splendour of the Fregoso house, O serene, undying light, if ever you rebuked me over this, perhaps in the very presence of your brother, the triumphant duke who has brought peace to your land: dismiss all rancour, let love prevail in all things, and, I pray you, be not backwards in assuring him of the possibility that even here I am telling the truth. /

At this point Orlando, glancing out to sea, noticed a light craft approaching under full sail; it appeared to be making for the island. I do not wish to tell you yet whose it was, for more than one of my characters is awaiting my attention.

Let us turn to France to see whether, now that the Saracens have been expelled, all is going well or ill. / Let us see what the much-abused Bradamant is up to, the faithful lover who has seen her happiness withdrawn to such a distance. She has seen how empty was the oath Ruggiero had sworn a few days earlier, after listening to the two sides. As here too he had not kept his word, there remained nothing upon which she could hang her hopes. / She resorted to the tears and laments with which she was now all too familiar, and reverted to taxing Ruggiero with cruelty (as so often before) and her fate with ruthlessness. Unfurling her sails to the blasts of woe, she called heaven unjust, impotent, and feeble, for had it not condoned such falsehood and given no evident sign of disapproval? / She set to accusing Melissa and to cursing the oracle in the cave: it was at their deceptive bidding that she had plunged into the sea of love in which she was left to perish. Then she complained to Marfisa that her brother had broken his troth; as she wept, she unburdened herself upon her, tearfully begging for her help and commending herself to her. / Marfisa was a little off-handed: she comforted Bradamant, which was all she could do, but did not believe that Ruggiero would sink so low: she expected him shortly to return to his bride. Should he not return to her, she gave Bradamant her word that she would never brook so grave an injury: either she would challenge her brother to battle, or make him observe his pledge. / In this way Marfisa somewhat stemmed her grief: being able to vent it made it more endurable.

Now that we have seen Bradamant grieving and calling Ruggiero a wicked arrogant traitor, let us see whether her brother Rinaldo was faring better—there was not a pulse or sinew, bone or marrow in his body which did not feel inflamed with love. / Yes, Rinaldo who, as you know, was so enamoured of fair Angelica; he had been caught in Cupid's net not so much by her beauty as by magic. The other paladins were enjoying peace now that the strength of the Moors was broken: among the victors Rinaldo alone had remained ensnared and re-pining for love. / He had sent out a hundred messengers to seek for news of her. He sought for news himself.

Finally he betook himself to Maugis, who had often helped him in his need. Blushing with embarrassment, he confessed his love and besought him to reveal where Angelica, for whom he yearned, was to be found. / Maugis was no little surprised by so strange a turn of affairs: he knew that Rinaldo could have had Angelica to bed a hundred times and more had he so wished. Maugis himself had gone to great lengths, in deed and word, using prayers and threats to move him in her favour and persuade him of her passion, but he had never suc-ceeded in prevailing upon him, / for all that Rinaldo could, by relent-ing, have rescued him from captivity. It had to be now, when there was less reason for it—and no advantage to Maugis—that Rinaldo was spontaneously drawn to Angelica! Maugis begged his cousin to recollect the wrong he had done him on this score for no good reason, and how he had almost let him perish in a dark dungeon simply for having crossed him. / But the more persistent Rinaldo seemed in his pleas, the clearer proof this afforded Maugis of the strength of his cousin's passion. Rinaldo's prayers were not lost upon him; they had the effect of sinking the past injuries in the ocean of oblivion. So he made ready to help. / He promised an answer within a given interval, and gave him to hope that it would be favourable and that he would be able to tell him what path Angelica had taken, whether in France or elsewhere.

Then he betook himself to the inaccessible cave up in the mountains where he normally conjured up the spirits; he opened his book and summoned them in droves. / Then he selected one who was familiar with love-matters, and asked him how it was that Rinaldo, so hard-hearted once upon a time, was now so impressionable. He discovered about the two springs, the one instilling love's fire, the other abating it, and how there was no recourse against the evil wrought by the one except in the water of its counterpart. / He learnt how Rinaldo, after drinking from the spring which banishes love, showed himself so stubbornly hostile to fair Angelica's prolonged entreaties. And how his evil star then led him to imbibe love's heat from the other spring, by virtue of whose waters he changed over to loving her to whom he had previously taken an excessive dislike. / It was indeed his evil star and harsh fate that had led him to draw fire from that icy spring, for almost at the same moment Angelica happened to drink from the other spring, devoid of sweetness, which left her heart so drained of love that from thenceforth she fled him more hastily than a serpent. He loved her, and his love found for its mark one filled with loathing for him. / The demon gave Maugis a full account of Rinaldo's unusual case, and told him about Angelica too, how she had given herself totally to a young African, and how she had left Europe altogether, setting sail from the Spanish shore across the restless sea to India in a galley of the venturesome Catalans. /

When Rinaldo came to his cousin for an answer, Maugis sought to dissuade him from loving Angelica, who had become enthralled with a barbarian of the lowest sort. Now she was so far from France that it would not be easy to follow her traces—she was already more than half-way on her journey home with Medor. / Angelica's departure would not have greatly depressed the impassioned lover, nor would the thought of returning to the East have dismayed him or robbed him of his sleep. But the news that a Saracen had forestalled him in gathering the first-fruits of his love left him feeling such anger and misery that never in his life had he been in such agony. / There was nothing he could say. His heart fluttered, his lips trembled, he was utterly tongue-tied; there was a bitter taste in his mouth, as though from poison. He dashed away from Maugis and, after a spell of weeping and self-pity, decided upon a return to the Orient, driven by his passionate jealousy. / He sought leave from Charlemagne, with the excuse that he was honour-bound to search for his steed Bayard, whom Gradasso the Saracen had abducted against the code of chivalry. He intended to prevent the deceitful pagan from ever boasting that he had seized him from a French paladin with lance or sword. / Charles gave him leave to go; he and all of France was sorry to do so, but he could not deny what appeared so honourable a request. Dudone and Guidone wanted to accompany him, but Rinaldo refused them both.

Sighing and lovesick, then, he left Paris all by himself. / What he was unable to forget was that he could have possessed her a thousand times, and a thousand times in his obstinate folly he had refused the gift of so rare a beauty. What a time of bliss and rapture he had lost by his refusal! Now he would accept to die could he enjoy but one brief day of it. / What he could never escape was the thought of how a poor simple soldier could have displaced in her breast the entire merits, the full ardour of all her previous suitors. His heart torn by thoughts such as these, Rinaldo journeyed Eastwards, making straight for the Rhine and Basle, until he reached the great forest of the Ardennes. /

The venturesome paladin had penetrated several miles into the woods, far from all human habitation, where the going was roughest and most dangerous, when all at once he saw the sky lower, the sun disappear, and out from a dark cave there issued a strange monster in the shape of a woman. / Her head possessed a thousand lidless eyes which she could never shut—I believe she never slept—and an equal profusion of ears. Instead of hair she had a great tangle of snakes. This terrifying shape emerged from the shadow of hell. Her tail was a larger, savage snake which coiled and knotted itself about her torso. / The sight of this monster making to attack him sent terror, such as perhaps no one had ever experienced, coursing through Rinaldo's veins. This was something which had never, in the course of a thousand exploits, ever happened to him before. However, he put on a bold front and shakily grasped his sword. / It was clear from the monster's fierce attitude of attack that she was a champion fighter. The poisonous snake was brandished overhead before being darted at Rinaldo. It lunged at him from one side and the other while he vainly groped after it, swinging his sword in a succession of swipes but never reaching his mark. / The monster darted her serpent now at his chest, to bring a chill to the heart beneath his armour, now at his visor to creep over his face and down his neck. Rinaldo broke away from the combat and spurred his steed for all he was worth—but Hell's Fury was no cripple: she sprang up behind him with one leap. /

Wherever he went, plunging and wheeling, the cursed monster stuck to him. However much his steed bucked, Rinaldo could find no way to be rid of her. His heart trembled like a leaf, not so much lest the serpent molest him further as because it inspired in him such horror and revulsion. He cried out, he groaned, he wished he were dead. / He sped along the worst paths, where the going was hardest, the woods thickest, the slopes steepest, the valleys thorniest, the gloom deepest, in the hope of shaking off the horrible, poisonous monster—hideous, loathsome thing. And he would perhaps have met a sorry end were it not that help soon arrived. /

But help did arrive in time in the shape of a knight in shining armour; his crest was a broken yoke, his escutcheon, Or, flames of fire gules: the same emblem was embroidered on his majestic attire and on his steed's caparison. He was holding his lance, while his sword was at his side, and the club hanging at his saddle threw out flames. / The club flamed, perpetually incandescent but never consumed. Against it there was no protection, neither excellence of shield nor temper of breastplate nor thickness of helmet: wherever they found it, knights had to give way to the ever-flaming torch. Nothing less would suffice to deliver our Rinaldo from the cruel monster. / Being of stout heart, the knight galloped in the direction of the noise until he saw Rinaldo pinioned in a thousand knots by the monster with her ghastly snake; he was feeling hot and cold all over, for he had no way of unseating her. The knight approached and struck the monster in the side, knocking her off to the left. / Hardly had she touched the ground than she was up, her snake-tail coiling tautly; the knight did not provoke her further with his lance but resorted to his fire-brand. He grasped it and rained down a storm of blows on the writhing serpent, leaving the horrid beast no time to aim one back, whether straight or wide. / While he kept the monster at bay and drove her back, and belaboured her, in requital for unnumbered wrongs, he advised the paladin to be off, taking the road which climbed uphill. Rinaldo did as bidden and without a backward glance rode hard till he was lost to sight, though the hill was a steep one to climb. / The knight drove the fiendish monster back to her dark hole, there to gnaw at herself and weep eternally with her thousand eyes. Then he rode up behind Rinaldo, to serve him as leader and guide; he followed him to the topmost ridge and accompanied him to deliver him from that place of deep gloom. /

Finding him returned, Rinaldo expressed infinite thanks. He was, he said, in his debt, to place his own life at his service no matter where. Then he asked him his name, so as to know who it was who had saved him, and so that he could forever praise his great kindness in front of his fellows and before Charlemagne. / 'Take it not amiss if I choose not to reveal my name yet', replied the other.

'I shall tell you before the shade creeps on a step, only a short while hence.'

They continued together and came to a fresh spring whose murmur enticed shepherds and travellers to its limpid waters, there to drink of Love's oblivion. / These, my Lord, were the ice-cold waters which dowse Love's flames. Angelica drank from this spring, which gave rise to the hatred Rinaldo inspired in her ever after. And if earlier she had quite failed to attract him, if she had found in him only a rooted antipathy, the cause, my Lord, need be sought no further than here: he had drunk from these waters. / When he noticed that they had reached the limpid stream, the knight accompanying Rinaldo, hot from his exertions, reined in his steed and asked: 'Do you mind if we stop here?' 'By no means,' replied Rinaldo. 'The mid-day heat is oppressive and, what is more, the hideous monster has so harried me that a rest would be most agreeable.' / They both dismounted and let their horses browse in the forest, while they drew off their helmets in the green meadow dotted with red and yellow flowers. The heat and a tormenting thirst sent Rinaldo running to the crystal spring, where a gulp of the cool liquid banished both thirst and passion from his overheated breast. / When the other knight saw him raise his lips all moist from the water and repent his capricious love, dismissing all desire for it, he drew himself up and, with a lofty air, divulged what he would not tell before: 'Rinaldo, my name is Wrath. I am here only to free you from your shameful yoke.' /

Thus saying, he vanished, and his steed vanished with him. To Rinaldo it seemed quite miraculous: he looked about him, wondering where the knight was. He did not know whether it was a question of enchanted spirits, be it one of Maugis' minions sent to break the chains which had so long oppressed him, / or an angel sent by God from His exalted throne, in His ineffable goodness, to dissipate his blindness, as once He had sent one to Tobias. But whether it were a good or evil spirit, or whatever else it was that had restored his freedom, he offered thanks and praise. By that spirit alone he recognized that his heart was cured of its lovesickness. / He reverted to his original hatred for Angelica; now she did not seem worth pursuing a mile, let alone for so long a journey. Nonetheless he still proposed to continue towards India and Sericana so as to recover Bayard: his honour obliged him to and, besides, he had already proposed this to Charlemagne. /

The next day he reached Basle where news had already arrived of Count Orlando's imminent combat with Gradasso and Agramant. This news had not been notified by Orlando himself—someone had arrived hot-foot from Sicily bringing a reliable account of it. / Rinaldo wished to join Orlando in this combat, but realized how far he had to go. At a gallop, plying whip and spurs, changing mount and guide every ten miles, he crossed the Rhine at Constance, sailed over the Alps, reached Italy, passed Verona, passed Mantua, reached the Po, and hastened to cross it. /

The sun was declining towards nightfall and the first star was appearing in the sky when, as Rinaldo stood by the river-bank debating whether to change horses again or wait here until night's darkness were dispersed by the bright new dawn, he saw a knight approaching. He appeared courteous in his mien and bearing. / The knight greeted him affably and enquired whether he had taken a wife. Rinaldo affirmed that he had, but the question surprised him. 'I am glad to hear it,' remarked the other, and added, so as to clarify the reason for his question, 'Be so good, I pray you, as to be my guest tonight; / I shall show you something which a married man should be only too happy to see.' Rinaldo, weary from his pace of travel and ready for a rest, accepted the knight's offer and took a different road with him— besides, he had an innate urge to witness or hear of any new adventure. /

They turned off the road the distance of an arrow's flight and found themselves before a great palace. Pages came swarming out to light their way with blazing torches. Rinaldo went in and looked about him. The place he saw was an unusual sight: massive in construction, beautiful in plan and execution—a place unsuited to a man of private means. / The gateway was gorgeously framed in hard slabs of serpentine and porphyry; the doors themselves were of bronze, carved with figures which seemed to breathe, to look about them. This gave onto an archway where fine mosaic-work played tricks upon the eyes; and this in turn led into a courtyard framed by porticoes each one a hundred yards long. / Each portico had its own gateway preceded by an arch; these were all of equal size, but each was copiously adorned in a different fashion. A stairway led off each archway, sloping up so gently that a laden donkey could climb it; each stairway terminated in another arch giving onto a room. / The upper archways were of a width to straddle the lower gateways. Each one was supported on two pillars, one of bronze, the other of marble. It would take too long to sketch in detail the ornate galleries round the courtyard; and beside what showed on the surface, what delights the architect had concealed below ground-level! / The tall pillars with gilded capitals supporting the gem-encrusted galleries, the precious marbles sculpted into various shapes by skilful hands, the paintings, reliefs and profusion of works of art (though night obscured most of them) gave evidence that the combined wealth of two kings would not have sufficed for so great an edifice. /

Supreme among the objects of wealth and beauty with which the prosperous place abounded was a fountain which dispensed fresh water a-plenty through a number of outlets. Here it was, at the centre of the courtyard, that the servants laid the tables; the fountain commanded a view of—and was overlooked by—the four gates of the majestic house. / The fountain had been fashioned with endless subtlety and care by a diligent and skilful craftsman. It was shaped like a pavilion or loggia consisting of eight distinct arches. It was roofed with a gilt enamelled sky. Eight white marble statues supported the sky left-handed. / The ingenious sculptor had carved cornucopias which each one held in her right hand; from these the water fell with a pleasant murmur into an alabaster basin. With greatest craft he had reduced the eight pillars to the shape of women, more than life-sized, each one different in dress and face, though all equally fair and graceful. / The feet of each one of these statues rested on a pair of beautifully carved figures depicted open-mouthed, as though happily indulging in melodious song. Their appearance, as they sang, seemed to convey a total dedication to their task of praising the fair ladies poised upon their shoulders—they resembled their models to the life. / The sculptures in this lower range held in their hands long and capacious scrolls on which were inscribed in terms of highest praise the names of the worthier figures above them; adjacently their own names were also inscribed in clear letters. Rinaldo examined the knights and ladies one by one by candlelight. /

The first inscription to meet his eyes named Lucretia Borgia with every honour: Rome, her native city, should exalt her beauty and virtue above that of the Lucretia of old. The two figures shown wanting to assume so excellent and glorious a burden were inscribed as Antonio Tebaldeo and Ercole Strozzi—Linus and Orpheus of their day. / The next statue was no less pleasing or beautiful and was thus inscribed: 'This is Isabel, daughter of Ercole. Ferrara shall prosper from being her birth-place far more than from any other advantage: as the years unfold, she will confer upon her city blessings and good fortune.' /

The two who evinced a fervent desire to give a perpetual resonance to her glory were both named Gian Jacobi, one Calandra, the other Bardelone. Occupying the third and fourth stations through which the water issued from the pavilion in a narrow stream were two women alike in honour, beauty, and merit, alike too in nation and blood. / One was called Elizabeth, the other, Leonora; and, as the inscription proclaimed, they would confer such renown upon Mantua that the city would be no prouder of Virgil, who brings such glory to her. The two figures below Elizabeth's venerated hem were Giacomo Sadoleto and Pietro Bembo. / Castiglione and Muzio Arelio, men of refinement and culture, supported Leonora; their names, then unknown, now so famous and respected, were inscribed upon the marble. Next was one upon whom, by divine indulgence, Fortune (who will both smile and frown) was to lavish as much excellence as ever would reign, or in the past had reigned, in a human breast. / The gilded letters identified her as Lucretia Bentivoglio, and among the counts on which she was praised was this: that the Duke of Ferrara was pleased and happy to be her father. Singing of her in a sweet, limpid voice was Camillo, to whom Bologna and the Reno listened with all the rapt wonder with which the Amphrysus once listened to its shepherd. / With Camillo was one on whose account Pesaro (where the Isauro mixes its fresh waters with the broad salt reaches) was to spread her fame from the Indus to Mauretania and from the lands of the South Wind to those of the North, far more than from the weighing of Roman gold whereby she acquired her name. I mean Guido Postumo, awarded a double crown, on this side by Pallas, on that, by Phoebus. /

The next in order was Diana. 'Observe not the pride in her mien,' read the inscription. 'She shall prove no less clement in heart than fair of face.' The learned Celio Calcagnini shall trumpet her glory and good name far and wide, in Monese's Persian kingdom, in Juba's Africa, in India, and Spain; / and so shall Marco Cavallo—he shall create in Ancona a spring of poetry such as the winged horse set a-flowing from Mount Parnassus (or was it Helicon?). Next to her proudly stands Beatrice, whose inscription reads thus: 'Beatrice, living, rejoices her consort: her death leaves him forlorn— / as indeed it leaves all Italy which, victorious with her aid, is enslaved without it.' Shown writing and singing her praises with high eloquence was Niccolò of Correggio together with Timothy, pride of the Bendideis, both of them destined to halt the flow of the river between its banks at the sound of their lyres—I mean the Po where of old the nymphs wept amber. /

Between this and the Borgia column (already described) there stood the eighth of these more-than-life-sized women. She was formed out of alabaster; her appearance was so overwhelming and sublime that, though she was veiled and simply clad in black, with neither gold nor jewels, she looked no whit less beautiful among her more embellished sisters than does Venus among her sister-planets. / Not even a close contemplation of her face could decide whether grace or beauty were predominant there, whether it spoke more of majesty or wit or virtue. 'Whoever will speak of her to the full,' proclaimed the inscription, 'will surely assume the worthiest of tasks—but one never to be fulfilled.' / Her pedestal-man was beautifully carved, gentle, and graceful; but for all that, she seemed offended that one so uncouth should presume to sing her praises with his humble song; her support was but one alone, with no companion (I know not why). The names of all the others were inscribed: only their two had been left blank by the sculptor. / The statues delimited a circular basin floored with dry coral, blissfully cool with the crystal-clear water collected there before being channelled into a canal which irrigated the green meadow, dotted with blues, whites, and yellows; it branched into several streams —balm to the soft grasses and tender shrubs. /

As Rinaldo conversed over supper with his courteous host, he frequently reminded him to fulfil his promise without further postponement. Glancing at him from time to time, Rinaldo noticed that his heart was burdened down with some pressing sorrow; and never a minute would pass but a burning sigh issued from his lips. / Frequently, impelled by curiosity, Rinaldo was on the point of opening his mouth to question him, but the words, restrained by tact, never came out. When supper was over, a page appointed to that task placed on the table a fine golden chalice, bejewelled on the outside, and brimful of wine. / Now the master of the house looked up at Rinaldo and sketched a smile, though a careful observer could see that he was closer to tears than to laughter.

'I think the time has come to satisfy you', he said, 'about that of which you keep reminding me. I shall show you an example which anyone who has a wife ought to appreciate seeing. / Every husband, in my view, should always watch to see if his wife loves him, to know whether he is deriving honour or shame from her, whether he is to be called beast or man on her account. The wearing of horns is the lightest burden in the world, even though it so degrades a man— almost everyone else sees them while the man wearing them never notices he has them. / If you know your wife to be faithful, you have better reason to love and respect her than does the man who knows his to be guilty or who is beside himself with suspicions about her. Many husbands are wrongly jealous of wives who are good and chaste; many feel assured of their wives even while they are being cuckolded. / Should you wish to know whether your wife is chaste, as I believe you think her, and so you ought (for it would be hard to convince you she were not unless you already had clear evidence), you can see for yourself without relying on another's word if you drink from this cup: it is placed here for no other purpose but to show you what I have promised. / Drink from it and you shall witness a notable effect: if you belong to the Order of Cuckoldry, the wine will spill all over your chest, and not a drop will reach your lips; but if your wife is faithful, you shall drink it straight off. Now set to and see how you are fated.' Thus saying he watched to see if the wine spilled onto Rinaldo's chest. /

Almost persuaded to seek for what perhaps he would rather not have found, Rinaldo reached out, grasped the chalice and made to undergo the test. But then he considered the danger he might be incurring by setting it to his lips. Permit me, however, to rest, my Lord; then I shall tell you what the paladin replied.

FORTY-THIRD CANTO

1–5 Introductory. 6–46 Rinaldo hears the Mantuan knight's tale of the cup which betrays infidelity. 47–144 Continuing his journey, Rinaldo hears the boatman's tale of the magic dog. 145–199 Brandimart's funeral, and the reunion of Christian champions on the hermit's rock.

O DETESTABLE avarice! O greed for gain! If you so easily entrap base souls, already filthy from other stains, that comes as no surprise: but what if you bind with the same rope, gaff with the same hook one who, could he have avoided you, would have deserved all honour for his nobility of spirit? / Some there are who can measure earth, sea, and sky, disclose the origins of all Nature's works, and rise so high as to fix their eyes on God; and yet, stung with your lethal poison, they find their one overriding priority is to amass wealth—this alone concerns them, in this they repose all their well-being, all their hope. / Others there are who destroy armies, who will be seen ever the first to force the gates of embattled cities, the last to retreat in perilous combat: but they have no defence against your shutting them till death in your black dungeon. Others, industrious in the pursuit of knowledge and skills, would achieve distinction, but you leave them in obscurity. / And what shall I say of certain eminent and beautiful ladies who show themselves more solidly rooted than pillars to resist the good looks, the qualities, the perseverance of their faithful suitors? But here comes Avarice to cast, it seems, an instant spell over them: in one day she bestows them, incredibly, upon some unloved, monstrous old dotard. / If I lay a complaint against Greed, it is not without reason—let those who can understand be as clear as me about this. I am not digressing or losing my thread, but my words are to be applied no less to what I am about to say than to what I have already said. Now let us return to Rinaldo, who was on the point of drinking from the goblet. /

I was saying that he wanted to think a little before setting the cup to his lips. He thought, then said: 'He would be an utter fool who sought for what he had no wish to find. My wife is a woman, and every woman is pliant. Let my faith remain undisturbed: it has stood me in good stead hitherto—what am I to gain by putting it to the test? / Little good and much harm could result, for sometimes God objects to being tested. Whether in this I am being wise or foolish I know not, but I desire no further knowledge than is suitable. Have this wine removed: I do not, and prefer not to, thirst for it. God has proscribed this kind of certainty even more than he proscribed the Tree of Life to our first father. / For just as Adam, after tasting the apple which God had with His own lips forbidden him, fell from happiness to tears, and lived in affliction for ever after; so if a man wants to know everything his wife has said and done, he falls from bliss to tears and despondency, and out of this he can never drag himself.' / As good Rinaldo spoke thus and pushed away the hateful chalice, he saw tears welling from the eyes of his host who cried, once he had calmed down a little, 'A curse on the woman who persuaded me to make the trial which deprived me, alas, of my sweet consort! / Why did I not know you ten years sooner, so as to have sought your advice before the onset of my misery, my constant weeping which has well-nigh blinded me? But let me lift the curtain on the scene to reveal to you my sorrows, so that you may weep with me. I shall give you a full account of my incomparable affliction, right from the beginning. /

'You passed, not far from here, a city surrounded by a clear river, as by a lake, which flows from Lake Garda and extends to run into our Po. The city was built at the time when Thebes fell to ruin—the city of Agenor and the men born of a serpent's teeth. Here I was born, a Mantuan of good family, but poorly housed and in humble circumstances. / If Fortune did not see fit to make me wealthy at birth, Nature made up for her parsimony, giving me beauty above my peers. Because of my good looks, more than one of the fair sex fell in love with me in my youth, and (though it is unseemly for a man to boast) I knew how to play the gallant. /

'In our city there lived a learned man, incredibly knowledgeable on every subject. When he finally closed his eyes to the day he was aged one hundred and twenty-eight. He lived alone and unwedded all his life except towards the end, when Love induced him to purchase a handsome woman by whom he secretly had a girl. / To prevent his daughter taking after her mother, who for a price sold her chastity, which alone is worth more than all the gold in the world, he banished her from society: he chose the remotest spot to build this immense, gorgeous palace, the labour of demons under a spell. / He had his daughter raised here by chaste old women, and she grew into a great beauty. At that age, he forbade her to see or hear mention of another man. And to give her an example to follow, he had the likeness carved or painted here of every chaste woman who ever held the gate shut against illicit amours. / Not only those of Virtue's friends who embellished the world in its infancy, and whose fame, thanks to the ancient chronicles, will never see its last day; but other chaste women, too, who are yet to adorn the whole of Italy: these also he had portrayed here exactly as they were to look, like the eight you see on this fountain. /

'When the old sage believed that the damsel was ripe enough for a man to harvest her, I (as good or ill luck would have it) was the one deemed worthy of her. As his daughter's dowry he bestowed upon me the broad acres beyond the palace walls, reaching twenty miles in every direction—both the dry land and the waters stocked with fish. / For sheer beauty and good breeding one could not have wished for better. At needlework and embroidery she was as deft as Athena. To see her move, to hear her play music and sing she seemed divine, not mortal. And she had so applied herself to the humanities that she knew them as well as her father, or very nearly. / Beside great intelligence and equal beauty (which would have captivated the very stones) she had a loving, gentle disposition the mere thought of which sends me into transports. There was nothing she enjoyed or craved more than to be with me wherever I went. We lived a long time with never a quarrel, until finally one arose through my fault. / Five years after I had submitted to the conjugal yoke my wife's father died, and shortly afterwards the troubles began from which I still am suffering, and I shall tell you how: while I was enveloped by the love of this lady I praise, as by wings, a noblewoman of the city conceived the deepest possible passion for me. /

'She was as skilled in sorcery and spells as any enchantress could be: she could turn night into day, day into night, arrest the sun, set the earth in motion. What she could not do, however, was to prevail upon me to heal her love-struck heart with the one remedy which I could impart only at my wife's expense. / For all her charm and beauty, for all the love I knew she bore me, for all the generous gifts and promises which she would insistently lavish upon me, never could she persuade me to retrieve the smallest flame from my first love and bestow it on her. What prevented me was the awareness of my wife's fidelity. / The hope, the belief, the certainty I nurtured of my wife's fidelity would have made me spurn young Helen of Troy at her most beautiful— indeed all the wisdom and wealth offered to the shepherd Paris on Mount Ida. But my repulses did not succeed in ridding me of her. /

'One day when the sorceress (called Melissa) caught me away from the palace and was able to talk to me at leisure, she found a means to disturb my peace, using dark jealousy as a spur to drive out my rooted confidence. She began by commending my intention of rewarding fidelity with fidelity. / "But you cannot assert that she is faithful to you unless you first see proof of her fidelity. If she does not fall when she might have fallen, then believe that she is faithful and chaste. But if you never let her go anywhere without you, if you never leave her free to see another man, what makes you so confident in affirming her chastity? / Leave home for a while, let it be known in the towns and villages that you have left and that she is still here. Give suitors and messengers a chance: if pleas and presents do not induce her to insult her wedding-bed (believing all the while that her lapse is a secret), then you may declare that she is faithful." /

'With these and similar words the enchantress persisted until she had persuaded me to put my wife to the test and look for clear evidence of her fidelity. "But supposing", I asked, "that she is not what I take her to be? How am I to know whether she merits punishment or reward?" / "I shall give you a goblet", replied Melissa, "which has rare and remarkable properties; it was made by Morgana to acquaint her brother, King Arthur, with his wife Guinevere's lapse. The man whose wife is chaste may drink from it, but not the man whose wife is adulterous: then the wine he expects to drink spills out to splash his chest. / Before you leave, try it: I expect that you shall not spill a drop, for I believe your wife is still untainted, as you shall see. But if on your return you try the experiment again, I cannot vouch for your chest—if you do not splash yourself but drink the whole draught, you shall be the happiest of married men." /

'I accepted her offer; she gave me the goblet, I tried it, and all went well—I found my dear wife, as I hoped, good and chaste at that point. "Now leave her a little," suggested Melissa; "stay away from her for a month or two, then come back and try the cup again, to see if you drink it or spill it down your chest." / It seemed to me a hard thing to go away, though, not because I doubted her fidelity but because I could not bear to be without her for two days, not even for one hour. Said Melissa, "I shall bring you to the truth by a different path: change your speech and dress and present yourself to her in another's likeness." /

'There is a city close by, sir, protected between the horns of the Po, full of menace. Its jurisdiction reaches from here to where the sea washes back and forth across the shore. This city, Ferrara, yields to its neighbours in antiquity, but not in wealth or beauty. It was founded by the survivors of Troy who escaped Attila's scourge. / The reins of power are manipulated there by a rich, young, handsome knight, who chanced to enter my house one day when out a-hawking. Setting eyes upon my wife, he was at once so struck with her that she left her seal on his heart. Subsequently he tried many devices in order to incline her to his wishes, / but she repulsed him so often that eventually he gave up trying, though he never forgot her beauty, for Love etched it in his memory. Now Melissa so wheedled and cajoled me that she persuaded me to assume his likeness—she altered my whole appearance (I cannot tell how), face, speech, eyes, and hair. /

'Having given my wife to believe that I had left for the East, I made my return transformed into the young suitor—his very gait, speech, dress, and appearance. Melissa was with me in the likeness of a page; with her she brought jewels as rich as ever came out of the Indies or Ethiopia. / Knowing the way about my palace, I walked straight in, and Melissa with me. I found my wife in an ideal situation, for no footman or lady's maid attended her. I made my prayer to her, then brought out the baneful stimulus to evil—rubies, diamonds and emeralds which would have moved the firmest heart— / and told her that this gift was trifling next to what she might expect from me. I mentioned, too, the opportunity of her husband's absence. I reminded her of the length of time I had been her suitor, as she knew, and suggested that so faithful a service deserved some reward in the end. / At first she frowned not a little, blushed, refused to listen. But the sight of the beautiful jewels sparkling like fire quite mollified her. In a few faint words (the mere thought of which is death to me) she replied that she would gratify me if she could be sure that no one would ever find out. / I felt this answer like a poisoned shaft piercing my soul. Coldness stole through my veins and marrow; my voice stuck in my throat.

'Then Melissa lifted her spell and restored me to my own shape. Imagine the colour my wife became, seeing herself induced into such error by me. / We both turned the colour of death; we both remained mute, with downcast eyes. I scarcely had voice enough to cry out: "Would you betray me, wife, with one who would purchase my honour?" For all answer she could only furrow her cheeks with tears. / Great was her shame, but greater still her indignation at the way I had abused her; she worked herself up into a full-blooded rage, a bleak hatred. At once she decided to escape from me, and, at the hour when the Sun dismounts from his chariot, she hurried to the river and had herself conveyed downstream in a boat of hers, a fast night-journey. / In the morning she presented herself to the knight who had once loved her, the one behind whose face and likeness I had tempted her—to the detriment of my honour. No doubt her arrival brought pleasure to the man who had been and still was in love with her. Thence she sent to me to bid me abandon hope that she would ever more love me or be mine. /

'Alas, she has been living with him ever since in sheer delight, and mocks at me, while still I languish from the pain I brought upon myself, and can find no relief from it. My hurt becomes worse all the time, and it is right that I should die of it. Little time now remains to me. I do believe I should have died in the first year were I not supported by one consolation: / among all the men who have been under my roof these last ten years (and I have set this cup before all of them), I have not found one who has failed to spill it down his chest. To have so many companions in my own position gives me some solace amid so much wretchedness. You among countless men have alone been wise enough to refuse the perilous test. / The result of my urge to explore beyond the limit permissible in investigating one's wife has been that I shall never know another hour's peace in my life, whatever its duration. At first Melissa was glad of this, but her frivolous glee was short-lived: as she had been the cause of my trouble, I hated her so, I could not bear the sight of her. / Unable to stand the hatred of the one whom she claimed to love more than her life, and whose mistress she had expected to become the moment her rival was gone, she took herself off without further delay so as to avoid having the cause of her pain so much before her. She made so complete a departure that I never heard of her again.' /

That was the sad knight's story. When he came to the end of it, Rinaldo was moved to pity; he mused for a while, then observed: 'Melissa did indeed advise you badly to go stirring up the hornets' nest. And you were most ill-considered to go in search of that which you wished not to find. / If your wife was induced by greed to betray you, do not be surprised: she is not the first woman to succumb in so great a struggle, nor the fifth. Spirits far sturdier have been driven to worse iniquities for less. How many men have you heard mentioned who have betrayed master or comrades for gold? / If you were anxious to see her resist, you should not have assailed her with such brutal weapons. Do you not realize that neither marble nor the hardest steel will stand up to gold? I think you behaved worse in tempting her than she did in succumbing so soon. Had she put as great inducements in your way, I know not whether you would have proved any stronger.' /

This said, Rinaldo rose from the table and asked to go to bed—he hoped to take a little rest, then set out an hour or two before dawn. He had little time, and that little he dispensed with great parsimony, letting none go to waste. The master of the house told him that, if he wished, he could retire to bed, / for the room and bed were ready; but that if he were to take his advice, he could enjoy a pleasant night's sleep and still cover a few miles as he slept: 'I shall have a boat made ready; you can be wafted along in it and travel in safety all night as you sleep, completing a day's journey along your way.' / Rinaldo was glad to accept the offer and much thanked his kind host, after which he was quick to go down to the river, where the boatmen awaited him. In the boat he lay down at his ease to rest. Impelled by six oars, it was borne, light and swift, upon the current and glided like a bird on the wing. / The French knight dozed off the moment he laid down his head, after first giving instructions for his awakening as they approached Ferrara. They passed Melara on the left bank, Sermide on the right, then Figarolo and Stellata, where the Po branches in two—a menacing pair of horns. / The helmsman chose the right-hand branch, leaving the left-hand one flowing towards Venice. They passed Bondeno, and already in the East the night-blue sky could be seen fading as Aurora, scattering her entire basketful of flowers, tinged it with scarlet and white. When the two forts of Tealdo appeared in the distance, Rinaldo raised his head. /

'O most fortunate of cities!' he exclaimed. 'My cousin Maugis predicted of you, after contemplating the fixed and the moving stars and coercing some prophetic demon—I was making this journey with him at the time—that your glory was to reach such heights that you would be the prize and boast of all Italy!' / As he spoke, he was gliding swiftly down the King of Rivers in the boat which seemed to have wings, and he came to Belvedere, the little island next to Ferrara. And though it was then deserted and neglected, he rejoiced at seeing it nonetheless, and gave it a hearty greeting, for he knew how beautiful it was to be made in the course of time. / On a previous journey this way which he had made with Maugis, he had heard him predict that when the Fourth Sphere had run his course in the Ram seven hundred times, this would become the happiest island of any which is bounded by sea, lake, or river: no one, after seeing it, would any more sing the praises of Nausicaa's island. / He learnt that for splendid structures it would outdo Capri, the island so beloved by Tiberius; the Hesperides would yield to this lovely spot for the plants of every species, however rare, which would grow here; it would boast as many kinds of animal as exist, more than Circe ever had in sheepfold or stable; and Venus would take up her abode here with the Graces and Cupid, forsaking Cyprus and Cnidus. / All this, he learnt, would be owed to the diligent efforts of one who, combining knowledge and power with purpose, would so endow the city with dykes and walls that it would stand secure against the world without invoking outside help. The lord who was to effect this would be Alfonso, son of Ercole and father of Ercole. /

Thus Rinaldo recollected what his cousin had told him earlier as he predicted the future, for they often discussed these things together. As he gazed upon the humble town he observed: 'How can it be that these marshes shall one day blossom with every humane study? / How shall a city so extensive and so beautiful grow out of so modest a village? How shall all this surrounding swamp-land become cheerful, opulent fields? Fair city, henceforth I shall employ myself in paying honour to the love, the chivalry, and nobility of your masters, to the eminent virtues of your knights and illustrious citizens. / May Our Redeemer in His ineffable goodness, may your princes in their wisdom and justice keep you forever in abundance and happiness, in peace and charity. May He defend you against every attack of your enemies and betray their wiles. May your neighbours chafe at your happiness before ever you feel envy towards any of them.' / While Rinaldo thus spoke, the slender skiff clove the water so swiftly that a falcon is not swifter to heed his master's cry and descend to the lure. The helmsman took the right-hand branch off the right-hand branch; San Giorgio's houses and walls were lost to view behind them, and the towers of La Fossa and Gaibana receded in turn. /

As one thought leads to another and that to yet another, Rinaldo happened to reflect upon the knight in whose palace he had supped the night before. He felt that the knight had, in truth, good cause to grieve on account of this city. He thought of the goblet which divulges to a man his wife's misdeeds, / and he remembered the trial which the knight mentioned having carried out—that among all he had put to the test, not one had drunk without spilling the wine down his chest. Initially regretful, he went on to reflect: 'I did well to refuse the test. Had it proved successful, I should have proved my belief; but where would failure have left me? / My belief in my wife amounts to a certainty—I could add little to it. Therefore, had I succeeded in the test, I should have derived little advantage from it; but I should have done myself no little harm, had I discovered in my Clarice that which I had rather not. It would have been a wager of one thousand to one, with a great deal to lose and little to gain.' /

As Rinaldo thus brooded, head bowed, he was closely observed by one of the boatmen who sat facing him. The boatman, divining the thought which so preoccupied him, and being an articulate and self-assured man, induced him to strike up a conversation, / which brought them to conclude that the man who had put his wife to the ultimate test was indeed a fool. For the woman who is armoured with chastity to ward off the promise of gold and silver would far more easily defend herself against a thousand swords and fiery flames. / 'You were right to reprove him for offering her such lavish gifts,' pursued the boatman;

'not everyone has what it takes to withstand these bludgeon-blows. I do not know if you heard about a young woman (you may have heard talk of it in your part of the world) who saw her husband make the same mistake—and as a result he condemned her to death. / My master must have been aware that gold and other prizes bend the most inflexible. But this slipped his mind at the crucial moment, and he compassed his own ruin. He knew the moral tale as well as I do (it happened in his and my homeland, a city near here, surrounded by the lake and marsh of the dammed-up Mincio): / I mean the tale of Adonio the Mantuan, who presented a judge's wife with the choice gift of a dog.' 'The story has been confined to this neighbourhood,' replied the paladin, 'and has not crossed the Alps. I have never heard it mentioned either in France or in the foreign parts where I have travelled. So do tell it to me, if you please, for I would hear it most willingly.' /

'There once was a man from these parts called Anselmo. He was of good family, and spent his youth in a long gown learning juris-prudence, the science of Ulpian. He looked for a beautiful, virtuous wife of noble birth, one who befitted his own station; and he found one, of transcendent beauty, in a neighbouring city. / She so abounded in beauty and grace, she seemed made of love and delicacy—too much so, perhaps, for his peace of mind, being the man he was: as soon as she was his, he became the most jealous man that ever lived, not that she gave him any cause, beyond her uncommon brains and beauty. / In the same city there lived a knight of ancient and honoured stock: he was descended from the proud line sprung from the same serpent's teeth which gave birth also to Manto and to those who with her founded Mantua, my homeland. The knight was called Adonio, and he fell in love with the beautiful lady. / To win her he started to lavish his money with a free hand, on clothes, on banquets, on self-aggran-dizement to the limits for a man of his station. The treasury of the Emperor Tiberius would not have afforded such extravagance, and I do believe it was not two winters before he had run through his entire fortune. / His house, which had been crowded with friends from morning to night, was now deserted, once there were no more par-tridges, pheasants, and quails; and he, who had been the life and soul of the party, was cast aside and almost fell to beggary. Having been reduced to poverty, he decided to leave for some place where he was unknown. /

'With this intention he left town one morning, without a word to anyone, and, sighing and weeping, walked along the lake which washes its walls. For all his present distress he did not forget the lady who was queen of his heart. Now a great chance came to him which carried him from the depths to the heights: / he saw a peasant beating about some brushwood with a large stick. Adonio stopped and asked him the reason for such exertions, and the rustic explained that in the undergrowth he had espied a very old snake, the like of which for length and girth he had not seen in all his days, nor ever expected to see again. / He did not propose to leave until he had found and killed it. Adonio heard him out with but scant patience, for he always championed snakes: the family-emblem was a serpent, to commemorate the serpent's teeth, sown in the ground, from which his forbears had issued. / His words and gestures to the rustic were enough to make him reluctantly abandon his quest. The snake, therefore, was not slain, nor hunted any longer, nor otherwise molested. Adonio now continued to where it was plain that his antecedents were less well known. He lived outside his homeland, in penury and distress, for seven years. / Never did he check his thoughts from roving after his beloved, never did he cease to love, regardless of the distance interposed and the straitness of his circumstances: his heart was so addicted to love that it was forever afire, forever bleeding. Finally he was constrained to return to the beauty upon whom he so longed to set eyes once more. Bearded, woe-begone, his clothes in rags, he set out on his return journey. /

'At this time my city had to send an ambassador to the Holy Father, to wait upon His Holiness for a length of time unspecified. Lots were cast and they fell upon the judge—woe the day which was to occasion him tears forever after! To avoid having to go he made excuses, pleaded, offered gifts, made promises, but was forced in the end to concede. / Had he seen his side ripped open and a hand reach in to pluck out his heart, he would have found that no harder to bear than his present agony. Pale and wan with jealous fear for his wife during his absence, he begged and entreated her, in such manner as he thought would help him, not to be unfaithful to him. / Neither beauty nor birth nor fortune, he told her, is enough to set a woman on the very pinnacle of honour if she is not chaste in reputation and in deed; and this virtue is all the more to be prized when it triumphs in the face of temptation: now, in his absence, she would have ample occasion to make trial of her chastity. / With these and many other such words he tried to persuade her to remain faithful to him. She grieved at their painful separation; oh how she wept and lamented! She swore that she would see the sun grow dark before ever she were so cruel to him as to break faith: she would sooner die than ever entertain such an idea. /

'Although he believed what she promised and swore and was somewhat appeased he tried nonetheless to discover more—and accrued further reason for tears. He had a friend who was past master in the art of predicting the future; he knew practically all there was to know about magic and spells. / He begged him to assume the task of discovering whether or not his wife (named Argia) would be faithful and chaste during his absence. Persuaded by his entreaties, the friend took his dividers and marked out the heavens as they then appeared. Anselmo left him to his task, returning the next day for an answer. / The astrologer kept his lips sealed rather than give the judge painful tidings. He tried many excuses to remain silent until, in face of his friend's ambition to inflict injury upon himself, he told him that his wife would betray him the moment he set foot out of doors: neither beauty nor entreaties would sway her, but greed for gain would corrupt her. / If you are familiar with the ways of Love, I leave you to imagine how this threat from higher spheres, compounded with his existing doubts and anxieties, must have weighed upon him. The worst element of the oppressive misery afflicting him was the realization that even her chastity had its price. /

'Now, to take what measures he could to prevent her from falling into this trap (for Want will sometimes drive us even to rob a sanctuary), he placed in her keeping all the jewels and money he possessed (which was plenty); all his worldly goods, all the income deriving therefrom he placed in her hands. / "Feel free to enjoy it and spend it not simply for your necessities but indeed for any purpose you wish," he told her. "Squander it, lavish it, give it away, sell it. I shall require no accounting from you later so long as you restore yourself to me just as I leave you now: so long as you keep yourself exactly as you now are, do as you will, though I find neither estate nor home left on my return." / He begged her not to stay in town unless she heard that he was there, but to remove to the country, where she could live in greater comfort, away from society. This he said in the belief that the humble folk he employed among the flocks and in the fields would not be able to contaminate his wife's chaste intentions. / Argia all this while clasped her fair arms round her timorous husband's neck, and bathed his face in the tears streaming from her eyes: she was dismayed that he should deem her guilty just as though she had already betrayed him. His mistrust arose, she felt, because he placed no reliance on her fidelity. /

'It would take too long to rehearse everything they said to each other on parting. "I recommend my honour to you," were his final words. He took his leave and departed, feeling, as he turned his steed, that in truth his heart was leaving his breast. She followed him as far as she could with her eyes, which bathed her cheeks with tears. /

'Meanwhile Adonio, wretched and down-at-heel, pale and unshaven, as I said, had set out on his homeward journey, hoping to avoid recognition. He reached the lake beside the city, at the spot where he had saved the snake which had been harried in the thick scrub by the peasant who aimed to kill it. / It was daybreak as he reached this spot, and a few stars still shone in the sky, when he saw a damsel approaching along the shore. She was elegantly dressed for travel and looked well-born, though no page or handmaid appeared in her company. /

'She greeted him affably and addressed him in these words: "Although you do not recognize me, sir knight, I am your kinswoman, and deeply in your debt. We are related because we both trace our proud ancestry back to mighty Cadmus. I am Manto the sorceress. I laid the foundation stone for this city, and, as perhaps you have heard, I called it Mantua after myself. / I am a sorceress: let me explain to you exactly what this means. We sorceresses were all born at our appointed times, for we are susceptible to whatever may befall us, save only to dying. But there is attached to our immortality a condition which is no more agreeable than death: on every seventh day each one of us can rely upon being transformed into a snake. / How repulsive to see oneself slithering about, covered with ugly scales! There is no affliction in the world to match it, and we all regard life as a curse. To come to the debt I owe you (for I should like to tell you how it originated): you will realize how, being as we are on those days, we run the risk of untold injuries. / No creature on earth is so loathed as the snake; we, therefore, who assume their likeness, are preyed upon and hunted by one and all, for whoever sees us chases and beats us. If we cannot escape underground we feel the weight of our pursuers' arms; were we able to die we should fare better than to have to linger under the blows, all battered and maimed. /

' "My great debt to you goes back to the time when you were passing by this pleasant shady stretch and you rescued me from the peasant who had been tormenting me: had you not come, I should not have escaped a fractured skull and back. I should have been left crippled and maimed, even though I could not be killed, / for on the days when we drag ourselves along the ground, wrapped in a serpent's hide, the heavens, which at other times are subject to us, refuse to obey us, and we are powerless. At other times a word of ours will stop the sun and dim its radiance, will make the stable earth revolve and change its station, will kindle ice and freeze fire. / I am here to reward you now for the good turn you did me that time. Now that I am free of my viper's mantle, there is no favour of which I am incapable. I shall make you now three times as rich as you were from your paternal inheritance, and I shall see that you are never poor again: the more you spend, the greater your wealth shall grow. / And as I know that you still are in the bonds in which Love originally tied you, I mean to show you exactly how to proceed in order to assuage your appetite. Now that I hear that her husband is away, you are to try my advice without delay—go and visit the lady, who is living in her country villa, and I shall come with you." /

'She went on to tell him in what guise he was to present himself to his beloved, how to dress, precisely what to say to her, how to entreat and tempt her. She also devised the form she herself would assume, for, outside the day when she roamed with the reptiles, she could assume any likeness in the world she chose. / She put him into the habit of a pilgrim who begs alms for the love of God from door to door. Herself she changed into a dog, the smallest in creation, with long hair, whiter than ermine—a dog pleasing to behold and remarkable for its abilities. Thus transformed, they set off for the house of fair Argia. /

'The young man stopped first at the labourers' huts, where he began to play a set of pipes he had: at their sound, the dog reared up and danced. Word of this was brought to the lady of the house, who came out to watch, then summoned the pilgrim into her presence—just as her learned consort's fate would have it. / Here, in obedience to Adonio's commands, the dog began performing dances, both native and foreign, stepping and posturing in his own fashion. Altogether he carried out his master's instructions so attentively, just as a human would, that the onlookers gazed wide-eyed and scarcely drew breath. / The charming little dog provoked Argia's amazement, then her cupidity. Through her nurse she offered the canny pilgrim a not inconsiderable sum. "If I were given more money than was required to satisfy even a woman's greed," he replied, "it would not pay for one foot of my dog." /

'And to corroborate his words, he drew the nurse into a corner and bade the dog be good enough to give her a gold mark. The dog shook itself and there was the coin. Adonio told the nurse to pick it up, adding "Does that seem to you the right price for me to part with a dog of such beauty and utility? / No matter what I ask of it, I never finish empty-handed; sometimes it shakes out pearls, other times rings, or the finest, most costly garments. But tell your mistress that it will be hers to command, not for gold—for gold will not buy it—but on her agreeing to sleep one night with me, she may keep the dog to do her bidding." / Thus saying, he gave her a new-hatched jewel to present to her mistress. The nurse estimated that there must be greater profit in this token than in a remittance of ten or even twenty ducats. She returned with the message to her mistress, and encouraged her to buy the marvellous dog, for it would cost her nothing to part with the price of its purchase. / Fair Argia was at first reluctant, partly because she did not wish to be unfaithful, and partly because she was not

convinced of all the claims made for the dog. The nurse reminded
her that such a fortune would seldom come her way, and nagged her
persistently until she prevailed upon her to take the opportunity to see
the dog another day with fewer witnesses. /

'This next assignation with Adonio proved the mortal ruin of the
judge: Adonio brought forth doubloons by the score, strings of pearls,
jewels of all sorts, and subdued proud Argia, who was all the less
ready to resist when she discovered that the man before her was the
knight her suitor. / The encouragement of her shameless nurse, the
entreaties, the mere presence of her lover, the sight of the wealth he
was bringing her, the unfortunate judge's absence, the hope that no
one would ever report her: these factors all did such violence to her
notions of chastity that she accepted the dog and in payment abandoned herself into her lover's arms. / Adonio long culled the fruits of his
beautiful lady; the sorceress endowed her with a rich love, and
Argia, in her turn so loved her that she would never be parted from her.

'The sun passed through all the signs before the judge was given
leave to go. Finally he returned, but in a state of deep suspicion on
account of what the astrologer had told him. / Arrived back in his
homeland, he went straight to the astrologer's to ask him whether his
wife had deceived him or whether she had preserved her love and
fidelity. The astrologer located the site of the pole and worked out the
position of all the planets; then he replied that what he had feared had
happened, as predicted. / Seduced by enormous gifts, his wife had
bestowed herself upon another. This came as such a blow to the judge,
a lance- or dagger-thrust could not have injured him worse. To be
even surer, though he was all too ready to believe the soothsayer, he
sought out the nurse and, taking her aside, tried artfully to elicit the
truth. / In a most round-about way he attempted various approaches
to pick up a trace. At first he found nothing, for all his diligence: the
nurse, nobody's fool, simply denied everything, stony-faced, and
had the cunning to keep her master suspended between doubt and
certainty for over a month. / If he ever considered the pain which certainty would cause him, how he ought to have cherished his doubts!
After vainly trying with prayers and gifts to obtain the truth from the
nurse, but always applying the wrong key to the lock, being a shrewd
man, he waited for the first quarrel—for where you have women you
have quarrels and strife. /

'Now just what he expected happened: the next time that nurse
and mistress fell out, the nurse came to him with no prompting on
his part, and told him all, concealing nothing. It would take too long
to describe the unfortunate judge's feelings; his gloom was so oppressive it nearly drove him out of his mind. / In an access of rage he

decided to slay himself—but his wife first: a blade steeped in the blood of both would free her from guilt, himself from anguish. Impelled by this blind fury, he returned to town, whence he sent one of his trusted henchmen to the villa with instructions as to what to do. / He was to go to his wife Argia at their villa and tell her that her husband was so badly stricken with fever that she would be hard put to it to find him still alive. Without awaiting further escort, therefore—the message went—if she cared for him she was to set out with his servant. She would come without a word: he was sure of that. On the way the man was to cut her throat. /

'The servant went to summon his mistress, to do to her as his master had commanded him. She picked up her dog, mounted her horse, and set out. The dog had warned her of the danger but bade her to go nonetheless: it had already made plans to bring her aid in her great need. / The henchman left the high road and took various lonely by-ways until he came out, as intended, at a stream which runs into this river from the Apennines. Here there was a dark wood, far from all human habitation, a quiet place, suitable, he felt, to the cruel deed required of him. / He drew his sword and told his mistress what his master had ordered so that, before dying, she could seek God's pardon for all her guilty deeds. As the man prepared to strike her she hid herself—exactly how, I cannot tell. That was the last he saw of her; he sought her everywhere but ended as the dupe. /

'Returning to his master all shame-faced and crestfallen and thoroughly mystified, he told him of the extraordinary occurrence, quite at a loss to explain how it came about. The judge did not know that his wife had the services of Manto the sorceress, for the nurse, who had told him all else, had withheld this, I know not why. / He did not know what to do. He had not avenged the mortal insult; he had not assuaged his torment. What had been a mote was now a beam, so burdensome had it become. The fault hitherto known to few would now be so open that, he feared, it must soon come out. He might have hidden the earlier fault; this new one would soon be public knowledge. / The wretched husband well realized, now that he had divulged his felonious intentions, that she would avoid returning under his subjection by entrusting herself to the keeping of some powerful lord, to his own disgrace and humiliation. She might even fall into the hands of a man who would prove to be both adulterer and procurer. / To forestall this, he hastily dispatched letters and sent messengers to search for and enquire after her throughout Lombardy, omitting no town. Then he went in person; there was no place but he either visited it himself or sent someone there to make enquiries. But he never succeeded in picking up the smallest clue leading to news of her. /

'Finally he called the henchman to whom he had entrusted the cruel, but abortive, deed, and had himself taken to the spot where Argia had vanished, as he had described. Perhaps she remained hidden in a thicket during the day, to take refuge in a house by night. The man led him to the spot: but instead of the dense woodland he expected to find, he came upon a great palace. / Fair Argia had caused her sorceress to build this enchanted palace, an instant creation wrought in alabaster. It was sheathed in gold, within and without. No tongue can express, no mind can conceive how beautiful it was outside, how sumptuous within. Next to it, my master's palace, which last night seemed to you so gorgeous, would be a peasant's hovel. / Not only the public rooms, the galleries, and bedrooms but even the stables and cellars were hung with finest-quality draperies, richly woven in various fabrics. There were endless gold and silver vessels, precious stones, blue, green, and russet, cut and adapted to the creation of dishes, chalices, and goblets. Silks and cloth of gold abounded. / The judge, as I said, stumbled upon this palace where he never expected even a hut, but only empty woods. He was so astonished, he thought he must have gone out of his mind. He did not know whether he were drunk or dreaming, or whether his wits had taken flight. /

'Before the gate he saw an Ethiopian with broad nose and thick lips. Never before or since, he was convinced, had he set eyes upon so hideously repulsive a face. For the rest, he shared the deformities attributed to Aesop—enough to depress a saint in paradise. He was greasy, dirty, dressed like a beggar, and I have gone but half-way towards describing his ugliness. / Seeing no one else there from whom to enquire who owned the palace, Anselmo approached and asked him. "This palace is mine," replied the man. The judge assumed that the fellow was fooling him and telling a lie, but the negro swore that it was his and no one else's. / He offered to let the judge go in, if he wished, and explore it; and if he found there anything he fancied, whether for himself or for his friends, he was welcome to take it. Anselmo gave his horse to his servant to hold and, crossing the threshold, was conducted through the public rooms and bedchambers; he saw all there was between cellar and attic. / As he contemplated the design of the palace, its situation, its sumptuous finish, the majesty of its decorations, he kept repeating, "Not all the gold under the sun could purchase this extraordinary palace." To this the ugly Moor replied, "Even this has its price: if not with gold or silver, nonetheless it may be bought with what costs you least." / And he made the same request to the judge that Adonio had made to his wife. This loathsome, disgraceful request made Anselmo consider the negro a brute and insane. The negro, however, was not put off by the third and fourth repulse, but tried to persuade him one way and another, each time offering him the palace. In the end the judge acceded to his depraved desire. /

'All this while, his wife Argia had been hidden close by; as soon as she saw him fall, she leapt out and cried, "Aha! A fine thing for a man reputed a learned Doctor to do!" Caught out in the depth of depravity, he was struck speechless and blushed, as you may imagine. Oh would that the earth had opened to the centre so that he could have jumped into it! / Argia relieved her feelings by shaming Anselmo and heaping abuse upon him. "What should be your punishment for what I saw you do with so contemptible a man", she cried, "if you kill me for following a natural instinct, seduced by the prayers of my lover? He was handsome and noble, and, next to the gift he made to me, this palace is worth nothing. / If you thought I deserved to die, know this: you deserve a hundred deaths! Now although I can dispose of you here at will, such is my power, I do not mean to exact a worse vengeance for your misdeed. Let us give and receive equally, husband: as I pardon you, so do you pardon me. / Let us make peace and concord, every past error forgotten. May I never, in word or deed, remind you of your lapse, nor you of mine." The husband felt that he was being offered favourable terms and showed no disinclination to forgive. So they reverted to peace and harmony and cherished each other ever after.' /

Thus said the boatman, and the end of his story made Rinaldo laugh—though shame for the judge made him blush. He greatly praised Argia, who had the wit to snare her bird in the same trap into which she herself had fallen in guilty circumstances. /

When the sun had travelled higher, the paladin had a meal made ready which the previous night the hospitable Mantuan had provided on a most lavish scale. Meanwhile the beautiful countryside slid by on the left, the immense swamp on the right. Argenta with its walls came and went, as did the reach into which the Santerno flows. / I believe that the Bastia was not there yet, about which the Spaniards could not afford to boast though they raised their standard over it—not that it offered the men from Romagna less reason for sorrow. Hence they made for Filo, on the right bank, and their boat seemed to be flying. After this they turned into a dead-end which brought them close to Ravenna by noon. / Though Rinaldo was often short of money, this time he had sufficient to dispense it freely to the boatmen before taking his leave of them.

Now with frequent changes of horse and groom he passed Rimini that evening, and without awaiting the dawn at Montefiore, he pressed on to reach Urbino almost as the sun did. / No Frederick lived there yet, nor Elizabeth; Guido was not there, nor Francesco Maria, nor Leonora, who with tactful courtesy would have constrained so eminent a warrior to spend at least one night with them—as they have done for many a year and still do today to ladies and knights who pass their way. / As nobody held his bridle here, Rinaldo continued straight on down to Cagli. He crossed the Apennines where they are cloven by the Metaurus and the Gauno; thus they were no longer on his right. He crossed Umbria and Etruria, descended on Rome, thence continued to Ostia from where he crossed the sea to Trapani (the city to which, in filial devotion, Aeneas committed Anchises' bones). / Here he changed ship and had himself quickly conveyed to Lipadusa, the island chosen by the combatants, where they had already foregathered. Rinaldo urged the sailors to press on with all speed by oar and sail; but the winds were contrary and too feeble for his needs, so that he arrived just too late. /

He arrived just as Orlando had completed his glorious and beneficial exploit, slaying Gradasso and Agramant, though the victory was bloody and hard-won. Brandimart had died there, and Oliver lay on the sand where he languished from the weight of a dangerous blow, while his damaged foot tortured him with pain. / The count could not check his tears when he embraced Rinaldo and told him how his Brandimart had been killed, who bore him such fidelity and love; neither could Rinaldo remain dry-eyed when he looked upon his friend's cloven skull. Then Rinaldo went to embrace Oliver who was sitting with his foot broken. / He consoled them as best he could, though he could find no comfort for himself, seeing that he had arrived in time for the dessert, or, rather, when the table had been already cleared. Gradasso's and Agramant's retainers took their lords' bones to Bizerta, the ravaged city, where they buried them, and brought news of the combat. /

Astolfo and Samsonet rejoiced greatly over Orlando's victory, though not to the same degree as if Brandimart still enjoyed the light of day. His death diminished their joy and clouded their features. Which of them now was going to bear the painful tidings to Fiordiligi? / The preceding night, Fiordiligi had dreamed that the garment she had woven and embroidered with her own hand to send off Brandimart suitably clad was bespattered all over with red drops. It appeared that she herself had embroidered it thus, and she regretted it. / She observed, in her dream, 'But my lord bade me make it all black. How have I come, then, to embroider it in so strange a manner, contrary to his wishes?' From this dream she drew a bad premonition. That evening the news came—though Astolfo kept it from her when he went with Samsonet to see her. /

As soon as they entered and she noticed in their faces the absence of joy at such a victory, without any further intimation she knew that her Brandimart no longer lived. Her heart was so overwhelmed by this, her vision so dimmed, her other senses so diminished, that she slid to the ground like one dead. / When she revived, she thrust her hands into her hair and wrought havoc upon her fair cheeks, vainly repeating her beloved's name. She tore at her hair and scattered it; she shrieked like a woman possessed, like the Maenads (we are told), who dashed and spun about to the sound of horns. / She begged now one now the other to bring her a dagger so that she could stab herself to the heart. Then she wanted to rush to the ship which had arrived in port with the two dead pagans, so as to attack their corpses and wreak harsh vengeance upon them. Then she wanted to cross the water to seek out her lord and die beside him. /

'Alas, Brandimart,' she cried, 'why did I let you go without me on such an exploit? Never before did your Fiordiligi see you leave without following you. How I should have helped you, had I come! I should have kept my eyes fixed upon you, and had Gradasso come up behind you, I should have saved you with a single cry. / Or perhaps I could have been fast enough to come between you and avert the blow: I should have shielded you from it with my head, for my death would have been no grave a loss. I shall die at all events, but my unhappy death will be quite profitless, whereas, if I had died in your defence, I could not have spent my life better. / If the hard Fates and all Heaven had forbidden my helping you, I should at least have given you a last kiss, I should at least have bedewed your face with my tears. And before your soul returned with the holy angels to its Maker I should have said to it, "Go in peace and there await me: wherever you are, I shall hasten to follow you." / Is this, Brandimart, the kingdom of which you were to wield the sceptre? Is this how I was to enter Dammogir with you? Is this how you were to receive me on your royal throne? Ah, cruel Fortune, what great plans you have destroyed, what hopes dispelled for me today! Alas, after losing my sovereign good, why should I defer losing all else?' /

As she uttered these and other words, so violent a passion surged through her anew that she tore at her fair tresses again, as though they were wholly to blame. She wrung her hands and bit them, she dug her nails into her breast and lips.

But, leaving her to languish in tears, I shall return to Orlando and his companions. / He set course towards Etna, the mountain which lights the darkness with its fire, darkens the day with its smoke. He had with him his brother-in-law Oliver, who was in no little need of a physician; he wanted, equally, to give Brandimart burial in a suitable

place. The wind was favourable, and the shore lay not far to their right. /
It was as day waned, with the cool breeze favouring them, that they
cast off, the Moon, silent goddess, pointing their way with her bright
crescent. The next day they put into the pleasant shore of Agrigento.
Here Orlando made arrangements for a ceremonial funeral for the
following evening. /

After seeing his orders obeyed, Orlando returned to where they
had left the corpse of the man whom he had loved loyally in life and
in death; the light of the sun was now almost spent. With him were
much of the local nobility who, at his invitation, had hastened into
Agrigento, illuminating the shore with flaming torches and making it
echo with their cries and laments. / Here Bardino, burdened with
years, was weeping by the bier; after all the weeping he had done on
board ship, he should by now have wept out his eyes. He called the
Heavens cruel, the stars evil; and roared like a fevered lion while he
attacked his white hair and wrinkled skin. / At the paladin's return the
cries rose louder, the weeping redoubled. Orlando approached the
corpse and gazed silently at it for a while, looking as wan as a morning-
gathered privet-flower or soft acanthus would do by evening.

He sighed deeply, his gaze rooted to the corpse, then addressed it
thus: / 'Dear, loyal comrade, Brandimart the strong: here you are,
dead. I know you are alive in paradise, having won a life which neither
heat nor cold may ever again wrest from you. Forgive me if you see me
weeping: it is because I have remained here and am not with you in so
great a joy, not because you are not with me here below. / Without
you, I am alone; without you, there is nothing on earth I can any
longer possess to enjoy. If I was with you in tempest and battle, why
not then also in repose and fair weather? How great is my failing if it
prevents my escape from my imprisoning clay to follow in your traces.
If I was with you in adversity, why do I not now share in your reward? / Yours is the gain, mine the loss. You are alone in your gain, I
not alone in my loss: Italy, France, Germany share my sorrow. Oh,
what grief it must be for my liege and uncle, for the paladins, what
grief for the Empire and the Christian Church, who have lost their
foremost bulwark! / How greatly shall your enemies' terror be allayed
by your death! How much shall the pagan world be strengthened, how
greatly shall its courage, its morale be enhanced! Alas, how must it be
for your lady! Even here I can see her weeping, hear her cries. I
know that she blames me; perhaps she hates me, since on my account
all her hope lies dead. / But, Fiordiligi, one consolation at least remains to us who are deprived of Brandimart: every warrior alive must
envy him the glory of his death. The Decii, Curtius, the Roman
swallowed up in the Forum, Codros, the boast of the Argives—they

did not sacrifice their lives with greater profit to others or honour to themselves.' /

These and other words spoke Orlando. Meanwhile the friars, grey, white, and black, and all the other clergy filed past, two by two, in a long procession, praying God for the soul of the deceased, that He would grant him rest among the blessed. The myriad lights appeared to have turned night into day. / The bier was lifted up, and counts and knights took it in turns to carry it. It was covered in purple silk picked out with gold and large pearls in a recurring motif. The splendid, jewel-studded cushions were no less beautifully or majestically worked. Here lay the knight, clad in material of the same colour and weave. / Ahead of these had passed three hundred mourners picked from among the poorest in the land, all of them identically dressed in black attire reaching to the ground. There followed a hundred squires mounted on great chargers, all good war-horses; horses and squires wore mourning attire which brushed the ground. / Preceding and following the hearse were many fluttering banners painted with different emblems. These had been seized from countless defeated hosts and won for Caesar and Peter by the might of the champion now lying dead. Many a shield there was, too, bearing the emblem of the eminent warriors from whom they had been captured. / Many a hundred others came to fulfil various functions at the funeral; like the rest, they all carried flaming torches and were dressed or, rather, enveloped in black. Then came Orlando, his red, sorrowful eyes suffused with tears; and Rinaldo, no happier than he. Oliver was absent with his broken foot. /

It would take too long to describe in verse all the ceremonies, the sable garments distributed to the mourners, the torches burning down. Everyone converged upon the cathedral; there was not a dry eye anywhere: a man so handsome, so good, so youthful excited pity in everybody regardless of sex, rank, or age. / He was brought into the church, and after the superfluous effusions of the weeping women, and after the priests' eleisons and the rest of the prayers recited over him, he was laid in a tomb set upon two pillars and covered, at Orlando's bidding, with a rich cloth of gold until he could be moved to a more sumptuous tomb. / Before leaving Sicily, Orlando sent for porphyry and alabaster. He had a tomb designed and for its execution he engaged the best craftsmen at great price.

It was Fiordiligi, on her arrival, who had the great slabs and pilasters set in place—she had them fetched over from the African coast after Orlando's departure. / Since her tears were inexhaustible, her sighs unquenchable, and since she was quite unable to find emotional satisfaction in all the offices and masses she had said, Fiordiligi conceived the wish never to leave this spot until her soul left with her last breath. So in the tomb she had a cell built, in which she closeted herself for life. / Beside sending her messengers and letters, Orlando went in person to fetch her away. If she returned to France, he meant to attach her to the suite of Empress Galerana with a handsome pension. Should she ask to return to her father, he would escort her to Laodicea. Should she wish to serve God, he would build her a convent. / But she remained in the tomb, where, exhausted by penance and by days and nights of prayer, she lived only a short while before Fate cut her life-thread.

The three French champions had already left the island where of old the Cyclops had their caves. They were sad and distressed to have left behind their fourth companion. / They had not wanted to leave until a physician had attended to Oliver: as they had been unable to obtain medical care at the outset, treatment would now be altogether more difficult. Listening to him agonize, they were all afraid for him. As they discussed this among themselves, a suggestion occurred to the shipmaster which won their approval: / not far from there, he said, there lived a hermit on an isolated rock. No one ever had recourse to him in voin, be it for advice or assistance. He could achieve miracles: he could give sight to the blind, raise the dead to life, stop the wind with a sign of the cross, calm the sea at its angriest. / They were not to doubt but that, if they visited this man so beloved of God, he would give a clear sign of his powers and restore Oliver to them, cured.

This advice pleased Orlando so much that they laid their course for the holy place and, never permitting the vessel to sheer off, sighted the rock at daybreak. / Skilled seamen conning the ship, they safely closed the rock, where, with the sailors' and attendants' help, they lowered Oliver into the ship's boat, to be taken over the foaming waves to the solid rock and thence up to the holy cell—to that of the same old man who had baptized Ruggiero. /

The servant of the Heavenly King welcomed Orlando and his companions, cheerfully blessed them, then asked them about themselves—even though he had received foreknowledge of their coming from those who had won beatitude. Orlando told him that he had come to obtain help for his comrade Oliver, / who, while fighting for the Christian cause, had come to a perilous pass. The holy man relieved him of all anxiety and promised a total cure. He possessed no ointments or other medicines in common use, but he went into his oratory and prayed to Our Saviour. Thence he emerged in buoyant confidence / to give Oliver his blessing in the name of the three Eternal Persons, Father, Son, and Holy Spirit. Oh, the power Christ gives to those who believe in Him! He cured the knight of all pain and so restored his foot that it was even sounder than before. /

Now Sobrino was present at this. He felt his condition worsening daily, such was the state of his wounds. On seeing the clearly miraculous cure wrought by the holy man, he decided to renounce Mahomet and confess Christ, living and powerful. His heart touched with faith, he asked to be initiated in our sacred rite, / so the man of God baptized him and, with a prayer, also restored his health to him. Orlando and the other knights were no less happy to see this conversion than to see Oliver delivered from his dangerous plight.

Ruggiero rejoiced even more than the rest; his faith and devotion greatly increased. / He had been on this rock ever since the day when he reached it by swimming. The devout old hermit was a gentle presence among those warriors; he prayed and encouraged them to avoid contamination but to aim to pass unspotted through this mortal vale known as life, in which fools so delight, but to keep their eyes steadfastly on the paths to heaven. / Orlando sent a servant to the ship to fetch bread, good wine, cheese, and ham; they prevailed upon the man of God to be good enough to eat flesh and drink wine as they did, though he had forgotten the taste of delicacies, accustomed as he was to fruit. When they had refreshed themselves at table, they fell to discussing many topics among themselves. /

And as often happens in conversation, one thing leading to another, Ruggiero was finally recognized by Rinaldo, Oliver, and Orlando as the same Ruggiero who was so eminent a champion, the one whose valour everyone concurred in praising. Rinaldo had not recognized him for the warrior he had stood against in the lists. / King Sobrino had identified him rightly enough the moment he saw him appear with the hermit; but he chose to stay quiet rather than risk a mistake. Once it was borne in upon the others that this was Ruggiero, world-famous for his bravery, chivalry, and high valour, / and knowing him to be now a Christian, they all approached him with beaming faces. Some took his hand, others kissed him, or hugged and embraced him. Rinaldo of Montauban gave him a particularly cordial and respectful welcome: why he more than the others, I shall explain in the next canto, if you would like to listen.

FORTY-FOURTH CANTO

*1–3 Introductory. 4–34 The triumphal return to Charle-
magne's court; Astolfo dismisses his helpers. 35–75 Bradamant's parents thwart Rinaldo's promise of her to Ruggiero.
76–104 Ruggiero goes to the Orient to slay his rival, Leo.*

THE bond of friendship tends to be better secured in the homes of the
poor, and where there is misfortune and hardship, than it is amid the
invidious wealth and luxury of royal courts and splendid palaces, full
of snares and mistrust, where charity is extinct and friendship not to be
found, other than counterfeit. / This explains why pacts and agreements among princes and rulers are so fragile. Kings, popes, and emperors make alliances today: tomorrow they will be mortal enemies,
because their outward semblance is not in keeping with their hearts—
heedless of right and wrong, they pursue only their own advantage. /
Little capable though such men are of friendship (for this will not
subsist where all discussion, be it light-hearted or grave, is artificial),
if hostile Fortune sweep them all down to a humbler berth, they
learn soon enough what friendship is, though they never learnt
before. /

In his cell the saintly old hermit was more successful at uniting his
guests in a strong bond of genuine love than others would have been in
a royal court. This bond was so durable that till death it never worked
loose. In all of them the old man found kindness—their hearts were
whiter than swan's down. / In all of them he found warmth and courtesy, with none of the wickedness I have described in those who never
come into the open but always hide behind false pretences. They totally forgot every injury they had ever inflicted upon each other; had they
all been sprung from the same seed and the same womb they could not
have shown greater mutual charity. /

Rinaldo, in particular, showed his friendship and respect for Ruggiero. For one thing, he had sampled his courage and ferocity in armed
combat; for another, he found in him as charming and gentle a knight
as ever existed; but, most of all, he recognized the debt he owed him on
many a score. / He knew that Ruggiero had saved Richardet from
mortal peril when the King of Spain had him caught in bed with his
daughter; and that he had rescued Maugis and Vivian, Buovo's two
sons (as I related) from the hands of the Saracens and of the wicked

men who accompanied Bertolai of Maganza. / This debt, Rinaldo felt, obliged him to love and respect him. And he was only too sorry and regretful that he had not been able to do so earlier, when Ruggiero was in the African court and Rinaldo in Charlemagne's service. Now that he found Ruggiero here, a convert to Christianity, he was able to make good his earlier omission. / The courteous paladin made much of Ruggiero; he paid him honour and plied him with promises.

As he witnessed this benevolence, the wise hermit took occasion to suggest: 'All that remains, now that friendship has sprung up between you, is for affinity to be contracted—and I hope to obtain this without demur. / Thus from your two illustrious stocks which have no equal for nobility in all the world a new stock will be born, of greater splendour than the radiant sun through all its revolutions. As the years and decades pass it will grow in beauty and endure—let me not hide what God imparts to me—so long as the heavens maintain their accustomed course.' / The old man continued in this vein so as to persuade Rinaldo to give his sister Bradamant to Ruggiero—not that either of them needed much pressing. Oliver and Orlando applauded this union and hoped that Aymon and Charlemagne would endorse it and that all France would commend it. /

They spoke thus, unaware that Aymon, with Charles' approval, had just declared his intention of awarding her to the Greek Emperor Constantine, who had requested her on behalf of Leo, his son and heir to his mighty throne. The young man had become enamoured of her without having set eyes on her, simply on the strength of the tales of her valour. / Aymon's reply to the request had been that he would make no disposition of her before he had discussed it with his son Rinaldo, then absent from court. He believed that his son would be prompt to agree, would indeed be delighted to acquire so magnificent a kinsman; out of the great respect he bore his son, however, he would not reach a decision without him. / Now Rinaldo, far from his father and quite ignorant of the emperor's proposals, promised his sister to Ruggiero on his own word and on that of Orlando and those others present in the hermit's cell, the hermit himself being the most insistent. He truly believed that Aymon would be pleased to contract such a kinship. /

That day and night and a great part of the next day they remained with the holy monk, almost forgetting to return to their ship in spite of the favouring wind. But their crew, reluctant to prolong their stay further, sent message after message which finally succeeded in detaching them from the hermit. / Ruggiero, who had been so long an exile confined to the island, bade farewell to his holy master who had taught him the true faith. Orlando buckled onto him his sword Balisard, and restored to him the armour of Hector and his good steed Frontino, both as a clear token of affection and in the knowledge that they had all belonged to him earlier. / And even though Orlando had a better claim to the enchanted sword, which he had wrested from the terrifying garden by dint of a painful struggle, than did Ruggiero, who had it as a gift from a thief (who also gave him Frontino), nonetheless he willingly gave it to him with the rest of the arms as soon as Ruggiero requested them. / The devout old man blessed them and they returned on board ship. The oars were committed to the water, the sails to the South Wind, and the weather so smiled upon them that they had no need of prayers or vows to enter the harbour of Marseilles.

But let them stay here until I bring Astolfo, the glorious duke, to join them. / When Astolfo learned of the bloody and scarcely joyful victory at Lipadusa, seeing that France would now be safe from attack by the Africans, he decided to send the King of Nubia home with his troops by the same route along which he had travelled to Bizerta. / Dudone, Ogier's son, had already sent back to Africa the fleet which had defeated the pagans at sea. By a further miracle, as soon as the swarthy crews had left the ships, their bulwarks, prows, and sterns reverted once more to leaves: Astolfo restored them to their original condition. Then the wind got up, whisked them into the air like feathers, and dispersed them in an instant. / The Nubians, then, all left Barbary, some on foot, others mounted, but not before Astolfo had confessed his debt of infinite, unfailing gratitude to King Senapo for having come in person to his aid with all the power at his disposal. The duke gave them the turbid and violent South Wind to carry imprisoned in a wineskin. / Aye, he delivered it to them shut in a wineskin, this wind which comes out of the South with such impetus that it sweeps the dry sand into waves, scooping it up and whirling it heavenwards. This way, however, they would carry it for their own convenience and avoid suffering from it on their journey. Once arrived home, they were to release it from captivity. / Turpin writes that as they crossed the high Atlas passes, their horses all of a sudden reverted to boulders, so the troops returned as they had come.

But it is time for Astolfo to cross to France; so, having pacified the principal cities of the Moors, he made the hippogryph take wing. / In a wing-beat he flew to Sardinia, thence to Corsica. Now he held his course over the sea, pulling the bridle slightly leftwards until he checked his weightless flight over the rich coastlands of Provence. Here he fulfilled Saint John's instructions: / the holy Evangelist had bidden him spur the hippogryph no further, once he reached Provence, and offer no further restraint with saddle and rein to his spirited flight, but restore him to liberty. The nether heaven (that of the Moon), which always acquires what we lose, had already sequestered the sound from his horn: the moment it was brought into the holy precincts, its voice not merely failed but vanished. /

Astolfo reached Marseilles the very day on which Orlando arrived with Oliver, Rinaldo, good Sobrino, and right excellent Ruggiero. The memory of their dead comrade prevented the paladins from celebrating their reunion as they should otherwise have done after so great a victory. / Charlemagne had received news from Sicily of the two kings slain and Sobrino captured, and of Brandimart's death. Then he had learnt about Ruggiero. In heart and face he was infused with joy on shedding an intolerable burden which had weighed so heavily upon his shoulders that it was to take him a while to make a complete recovery. / To honour these knights who were the prop, the chief pillar of the holy empire, Charlemagne sent the nobility of his realm to meet them at the Saône. Then he himself issued forth from the walls with the flower of his household guard of kings and dukes, with his empress and her train of beautiful, noble damsels in all their finery. / The emperor, smiling and serene, and his paladins gave the clearest demonstration of love to Count Orlando and his comrades, as did also their friends and kinsmen, the nobility and the commons. Cries of 'Mongrana' and 'Clairmont' could be heard.

Once they had all embraced, Rinaldo, Orlando, and Oliver presented Ruggiero to their liege. / They told him that he was son of Ruggiero of Reggio, his father's equal in valour. Our own battalions would testify to his courage and strength and to the skill behind his blows. At this point Bradamant and Marfisa (noble brace of beauties) stepped forward; Ruggiero's sister embraced him—the other damsel observed greater propriety. / The emperor bade Ruggiero remount (for out of reverence he had dismounted) and proceed beside him on a footing of equality; to do him honour he paid him every attention, overlooking nothing. He knew of Ruggiero's return to the Faith, for the warriors had reported everything to him the moment they stepped ashore. /

They returned into the city in triumphal pomp. All was festivity: sprays of green, garlands everywhere; the streets strewn with garments. A pervasive cloud of fronds and flowers descended on and around the victors, scattered open-handedly from balconies and windows by fair matrons and maids. / As they turned the corner at various points they found hastily constructed arches and trophies which depicted Bizerta ruined and in flames and other creditable subjects. Elsewhere there were stages built for various games and spectacles, mimes and re-enactments. Everywhere there were inscriptions, aptly enough: 'To the saviours of the Empire'. / To the braying of trumpets, the melody of pipes and every kind of music, amid smiles and cheers, amid the jubilation of the fervent crowd which the space could barely contain, the great emperor dismounted at his palace. Here for several days the company attended to its pleasure, with masques and tournaments, farces, balls, and banquets. /

One day Rinaldo informed his father Aymon that he wanted to give his sister to Ruggiero: in the presence of Orlando and Oliver he had promised her to him as wife. These two shared his opinion that the family could not have contracted as good a kinship—let alone a better —for nobility of blood and for valour. / Aymon listened to his son with indignation that he should dare to marry off his daughter without consulting him: he proposed to make her the bride of Constantine's son, not of Ruggiero who, far from possessing a realm, had nothing on earth which he could call his own. Ruggiero did not realize that nobility was worth little, and valour less, unless allied to wealth. / More even than Aymon, Beatrice reproved her son and taxed him with arrogance. In public and private she opposed Bradamant's betrothal to Ruggiero: she meant to do all in her power to make her daughter Empress of the East. But Rinaldo remained obstinate: he was not going to retract his word, not a jot of it. / The mother, imagining that her noble-hearted daughter seconded her ambitions, encouraged her to say she would sooner die than ever be wife of a penniless knight. If Bradamant acquiesced to this slight from her brother, Beatrice would never more own her for daughter. She was to oppose a flat refusal and remain obstinate, for Rinaldo would never succeed in forcing her. /

Bradamant remained silent, not daring to contradict her mother, whom she so worshipped and respected that the thought of disobeying her would never have entered her head. On the other hand she would have felt greatly at fault if she were prepared to give verbal assent to what she was not prepared to do. She would not for she could not, Love having robbed her of what little powers of self-disposal she possessed. / She dared not refuse nor make a show of approval; she merely sighed and made no answer. Then, when she was out of earshot, her eyes spilt a flood of tears. Part of the grief tormenting her she imparted to her breast, to her blonde tresses, striking the one, rending the other, and as she wept alone, thus she spoke: /

'Shall I pit my desires against those of one who ought to have greater command over my will than I have? Shall I make so light of my mother's wishes as to defer them to my own? Ah, what sin can be so grave for a damsel, what fault so heinous? How should it be if I were to take a husband against the wishes of one whom I must always obey? / Ah me! Shall filial duty, then, prevail upon me to abandon you, my Ruggiero, and embrace a new hope, a new desire, a new love? Or shall I set aside the reverence and duty which good children owe to good parents, and respect only my own good, my happiness, my pleasure? /

I know what I ought to do: I know my duty as a virtuous daughter. I know it, but what good is that? If Reason is so impotent, why have not the senses greater power when Love expels Reason and makes her stand aside—when he forbids even the mere thought of my disposing of myself other than at his pleasure, when he makes me speak and act only at his dictation? /

'I am daughter of Aymon and Beatrice, and I am, alas, slave of Love. If I sin I look to my parents for pardon and pity; but if I offend Love, who shall be sufficient to avert his wrath from me with prayers and make him listen to but one of my excuses rather than put me to instant death? / What a long, stubborn effort have I devoted to bringing Ruggiero to the Faith, and at last I have done so: but what use has this been to me if my well-doing turns to another's advantage? In this way the bee renews her honey each year, but not for her own use or possession. I will die, though, sooner than take a husband other than Ruggiero. / If I am not obedient to my father and mother, I shall be to my brother, who is far shrewder than they and whose brain has not been addled by surplus years. Orlando also approves Rinaldo's wish; I have them both on my side, a pair whom the world honours and respects more than all the rest of our house put together. / If everyone regards these two as the flower, the glory and splendour of the house of Clairmont; if everyone sets them above the rest and exalts them higher than the brow is above the foot, why should I wish to be given away by Aymon rather than by Rinaldo and Orlando? I should not wish it, all the less since I was not committed to the Greek while I was promised to Ruggiero.' /

If Bradamant fretted and grieved, Ruggiero was no more serene, for although the Greek proposal was not yet common gossip, it was no secret to him. In his heart he blamed Fortune for preventing him from enjoying his prize, all because she had not endowed him with riches and realms when she had so lavished them upon thousands who deserved nothing. / Of all the other gifts which Nature bestows or which can be acquired by effort he realized that he had as large and well-chosen a share as any had ever enjoyed: there was none as handsome as he, seldom could anyone resist his strength, and no one could better claim the prize for nobility and majesty of temper. / But honours are in the arbitrary gift of the common throng, to give and take back as they think fit—and 'common throng' is a description I apply to everyone, excepting only the wise: the tiara, sceptre, or crown does not rescue pope, king, or emperor from this designation, but only prudence and sound judgement, gifts conferred by Heaven on but few. / The commons, as I say, respect only wealth; there is nothing on earth they admire more; those who lack it they ignore and despise, however well endowed they may be with beauty, courage, physical strength, and agility, virtue, wisdom, and goodness—especially in the circumstances I am here discussing. /

'Even if Aymon does intend to make his daughter an empress,' observed Ruggiero, 'may he not be too quick to conclude the nuptials with Leo: let him but give me a year's grace, and I hope in that interval to depose both Leo and his father. Once I have seized their crowns, I should make a creditable son-in-law to Aymon. / But suppose he does make her daughter-in-law to Constantine without delay as he has said; suppose he does disregard the promise made to me by Rinaldo and his cousin Orlando in the presence of the holy hermit, of Oliver and Sobrino, what then? Shall I sustain so grave an injury? Or should I die sooner than submit to it? / Oh what shall I do? Shall I avenge my wrong upon her father? Setting aside the objection that it would take time to accomplish it, and the question of whether it would be wise or foolish to attempt it at all, supposing I did slay the old reprobate and all his line, that would not make me happy—indeed it would run counter to my aim, / which ever has been (and still is) that fair Bradamant should love me and not hate me. But if I slay Aymon, if I do or attempt anything to her brother's detriment or that of her other kinsfolk, do I not give her just grounds to call me an enemy and no longer wish to be my wife? What am I to do, then? Am I to endure it? Ah no, better to die! / Or rather no, not to die, but that imperial Leo die with better reason, for having ventured to sully my happiness. I mean to make away with him and his wicked father. Fair Helen made Paris, her Trojan lover, pay less dearly (and, earlier, Proserpina cost Pirithous less) than I shall make father and son pay for my grief. /

'Can it be, my love, that you are not sorry to leave your Ruggiero for this Greek? Can your father force the Greek upon you even though your brothers are on your side? But I fear that you are readier to conciliate Aymon than me, and that a Caesar looks to you a far better match than a mere private citizen. / Is it possible that the lofty spirit, the great valour and eminent virtues of my Bradamant could ever be corrupted by a royal name, the glory and pomp of an imperial title, and bring her to spurn her pledged word and break her vows? Or would she choose to antagonize Aymon rather than retract her constant pledge to me?' /

Ruggiero said this and much else as he communed with himself; and often his utterances were picked up by whoever happened to be with him, so that on more than two occasions his torment was related to the very one on whose account he suffered it. Bradamant was no less pained to hear him thus lament than she was by her own sorrows. / But of all the sorrows reported to her as tormenting Ruggiero the one which grieved her most was the fear afflicting him that she might forsake him in preference for the Greek. To hearten him and dislodge this erroneous notion from his breast, she had one of her trusted handmaids one day bring him this message: /

'I mean to remain till death just as I have ever been, Ruggiero, and more so, if possible. Whether Love prove kind or harsh to me, whether Fortune spins me high or low upon her wheel, I am an immovable rock of true fidelity, though buffeted all about by wind and sea. Never did I shift for storm or fair weather, and never will I do so. / You will sooner see a diamond cut and shaped by a lead chisel or file before my constant heart be broken by any stroke of Fortune or by Love's anger. You will sooner see a turbid brook babble its way back towards the Alpine peaks before new accidents, whether good or bad, turn my thoughts into new channels. / I have submitted myself, Ruggiero, to your dominion, perhaps more even than others would believe. I know that greater fealty than this was never sworn to a new prince; that no king or emperor in the world possesses his realm more securely than you. You have no need to construct moats or towers for fear that another may come to seize your throne. / You have no need to engage help, for you shall meet no assault that cannot be resisted. There is no wealth sufficient to vanquish me—nor will so paltry a prize as lucre win a noble heart. In my eyes, there is no majesty, no crowned eminence (which so dazzles the ignorant), no beauty (which so persuades the frivolous) that I should ever prefer to yours. /

'Do not fear that my heart may ever again be cut to a new shape: your image is sculpted there beyond defacing. Beyond a doubt my heart is not of wax: if Love gave it one tap he gave it a hundred before he set to chipping it to your image. / Ivory, gems, any hard rock which best stands up to the chisel may be broken—but not so as to assume a different shape to that which it took before. My heart is no different in nature from marble or other stone which contends with steel: Love may shatter it to pieces, but never can he carve other beauties upon it.' /

To these words she added many more, full of love, fidelity, and comfort, enough to restore him to life a thousand times if he had died a thousand deaths. But when they were most convinced that their hopes were in harbour and safe from storms, they were driven out to sea, far from the shore, by another black, blustering gale. /

Bradamant, who wished to achieve far more than she promised, summoned up her natural boldness and, throwing caution to the winds, one day approached the emperor. 'Sire,' she said to him, 'if ever I did anything to win Your Majesty's approval, be content to grant me a boon. / And before I name my request, promise me on your royal word

to accede to it; then I will have you see how just and rightful it was.'
'Your valour merits that you be granted what you ask, my dear,' replied Charlemagne, 'and I promise to satisfy you though you ask for a share of my kingdom.' / 'Here is the boon I crave, Your Majesty,' requested the damsel. 'Permit no husband to be bestowed upon me until he has demonstrated greater prowess at arms than I possess. I must make trial of whoever would have me, either with lance or sword: let the first man to defeat me win me; let the defeated seek other brides.' / The emperor cheerfully observed that the request did her credit; she was not to worry—he would do exactly as she asked.

Now this conversation was not held in secret so as to remain confidential. That very day, therefore, it came to the ears of her elderly parents, Aymon and Beatrice, / both of whom were equally incensed and indignant with their daughter: it was clear to them from her request that she preferred Ruggiero to Leo. To forestall her in her intention, they promptly removed her from court by a trick and took her off with them to Roccaforte. / This was a most important castle on the sea-shore between Perpignan and Carcassonne which Charlemagne had given to Aymon a few days earlier. Here they held her prisoner, meaning to send her one day to the East so that, willy nilly, she would have to forsake Ruggiero and accept Leo. / If the damsel was spirited and valiant, she was also submissive, and even though she was not under guard but could come and go as she pleased, she still remained obedient to her father's curb. But she was determined to suffer captivity, death, any torment and cruelty sooner than to forsake Ruggiero. / Rinaldo saw his sister taken from him by Aymon's guile; she was no longer at his disposal and his promise to Ruggiero proved empty; he complained of his father, therefore, and denounced him, quite eschewing filial respect. But Aymon little heeded his words and meant to dispose of his daughter as he pleased. /

Discovering this, Ruggiero feared that if Leo lived much longer he would obtain Bradamant by force or by consent while he himself remained deprived of his lady. Without a word to anyone, he devised the intention to slay him, to translate His August Majesty to divine honours. If not deceived in his hope, father and son would lose to him both life and throne at once. / He donned again the armour which was once Trojan Hector's and later Mandricard's, and he had good Frontino saddled. He altered his crest, escutcheon, and surcoat: for this exploit he did not want to display the white eagle on the azure ground; what he wanted on his shield was a lily-white unicorn on a scarlet ground. / He chose the most faithful of his pages and required no other company than his; he bade him never to reveal anywhere that he was Ruggiero. After crossing the Moselle and the Rhine, he traversed Austria into

Hungary. He rode along the right bank of the Danube until he reached Belgrade. /

Where the Sava flows into the Danube and with it turns towards the Black Sea he saw a great host assembled in tents and pavilions under the imperial ensigns: Constantine was aiming to recover Belgrade, which the Bulgars had wrested from him. Constantine was there in person, and with him was his son and all that the Greek Empire could muster. / Within Belgrade and outside, covering the entire hill-slope right down to where the river lapped its foot, the Bulgarian army faced him. Both armies descended to the Sava to drink. When Ruggiero arrived, Greek and Bulgar were at the river, arrayed for combat, the one to bridge the river, the other to prevent this. He found a fierce battle engaged. / The Greeks were four against one. They had pon- toons ready for launching and showed a fierce determination to force a crossing to the left bank. Meanwhile Leo played a quiet trick: he drew away from the river, made a wide detour and, where he rejoined it, threw a bridge across and hastened over it. / With a great host, all of twenty thousand men, some mounted, some on foot, he rode along the bank and made a savage flank-attack upon the enemy. The moment the emperor saw his son heave in sight on the left bank, he launched boat after boat to bridge the river and crossed it with all available forces. /

The Bulgar chief, King Vatran, a brave, astute, and skilled warrior, strove in vain to fend off so fierce an onslaught, but Leo caught his steed and wrenched it to the ground bare-handed. As Vatran would not surrender, he was slashed dead amid a thousand swords. / The Bulgars had resisted till this point; but seeing the loss of their leader and the storm rising all about them, they turned to face the enemy with their backs. Ruggiero had arrived among the Greeks; when he saw this defeat, he decided without a second thought to help the Bulgars, for he hated Constantine, and Leo even more. /

He spurred Frontino, who resembled the wind as he galloped, and overtook all the cavalry to outstrip the troops who were forsaking the plain and fleeing in terror to the hills. He stopped many of them and made them turn to face the enemy; then he lowered his lance and charged, looking so formidable that even Mars and Jupiter in heaven quailed. / Out in front he noticed a knight on whose scarlet cloak was embroidered, in silk and gold, an ear of millet on its stalk—or so it looked. He was Constantine's nephew through his sister, but no less dear to him than his own son. Ruggiero smashed his shield and breast- plate like glass and drove his lance through to protrude a palm's width from his back. / Leaving him dead, he brandished Balisard and ad- vanced upon the cluster he saw nearest to him. He assailed one man after the next, splitting here a torso, there a skull. He steeped his sword here in a chest, there in a flank or a throat. He slashed chests and hips, legs, hands, and shoulders, and the blood flowed away like a river. / In view of these strokes, no one was any longer ready to withstand him, such was the general dismay. So the face of the battle changed at once: the Bulgars recovered their courage and turned to give chase to the Greeks, where earlier they had fled from them. In a trice you could see every rank dissolved, every standard routed. /

Seeing his troops flee, Leo had withdrawn to a high hill. From this eminence he could see everything, and he was glumly bewildered to realize that the destruction of his army was solely the work of this one knight who was slaughtering so many men. For all the damage done to himself, Leo perforce had to commend the knight and award him the palm for prowess at arms. / From the knight's emblem and surcoat, the shining armour richly gilt, he realized that although he helped the enemy, he was not of their number. In a daze he watched his superhuman exploits and fostered the notion that he must be some angel descended from the heavenly choir to punish the Greeks for their many offences against God. / Many another man would have detested Ruggiero, but Leo, large-hearted to a sublime degree, was conquered by his valour and would not have wished to see any harm done to him. Had his losses been six times as great, had he lost part of his kingdom as well, he would have minded less than to have seen so worthy a knight slain. / Even if a child is beaten and sent away in anger by the mother he loves, he will not run to his sister or father but return to his mother and hug her tenderly. So it was with Leo: though Ruggiero had slaughtered his front squadrons and was threatening the rest, he could not hate him, for he was more inclined to love him for his valour than to hate him for the harm done. /

But if Leo felt love and admiration for Ruggiero, I fear that he was poorly requited, for Ruggiero hated him and craved nothing better than to kill him by his own hand. He sought him with his eyes and kept asking people to point him out, but by luck and caution the astute Greek avoided a confrontation. / To prevent the rest of his troops being killed, he sounded the retreat, and sent a swift messenger to his father, the emperor, praying him to turn back and recross the river: he would be quite content if his retreat were not cut off. He himself with the few he rallied turned back towards the bridge by which he had crossed. / Many remained in the power of the Bulgars, their corpses littering the hill-slopes to the river's edge; and they all would have ended their days there had not the river soon afforded them a rampart. Many fell from the pontoon bridge and drowned, while many more pressed on without looking back until they found the ford, and many were led captive into Belgrade. /

The day's battle was over—with the death of their leader almost a humiliating defeat for the Bulgars, had it not been for the champion who had saved the day for them, the knight of the scarlet shield with the white unicorn. They all crowded round him in high spirits, owing their victory to him. / One man saluted him, the next one knelt to him, others kissed his hand or foot; everyone drew as close as possible; happy the man who had a close look at him, happier still the one who touched him, believing that what he touched was nothing less than celestial. Their acclamations rose to the sky as they all prayed him to be their king, their captain, their chief. / Ruggiero told them that he would be their king and captain and whatever else they pleased, but that he would not lay hand on rod or sceptre nor today enter Belgrade: before imperial Leo retreated further, before he recrossed the river, he meant to follow him and dog his traces until he caught him and put him to death, / for he had come a thousand miles and more for this purpose and for no other.

So without delay he left the army and took the path indicated to him, the one by which Leo was fleeing towards the bridge, fearing, perhaps, that he might be intercepted. Ruggiero set off after him so promptly that he did not summon his page or stop for him. / Leo had such an advantage in his flight (it should certainly be called a flight, not a withdrawal) that he found his river-crossing open and free. Then he destroyed the bridge and fired the ships. Ruggiero did not arrive there until the sun's rays were hidden. He did not know where to lodge. He rode on in the moonlight without finding any castle or house. / Not knowing where to stop, he rode on all night without ever dismounting.

At sunrise he noticed a city nearby to his left. Here he decided to pass the day, thus permitting his steed Frontino to recuperate after being made to walk so many miles that night: not once had Ruggiero rested him or removed his bridle. / Ungiardo ruled in this city; he was a very dear vassal of Constantine, and had supplied many troops, mounted and on foot, for his war. Strangers were not refused entry here, so in went Ruggiero, who was made so welcome that he had no need to go further to find better or more generous accommodation. / That evening a new guest came to the inn—a Roumanian knight who had been in the fierce battle in which Ruggiero had come to the aid of the Bulgars; he had barely escaped his hands and had been terrified out of his wits—he was still shaking as he imagined that the knight of the unicorn was chasing him. / One look at Ruggiero's shield told him that the knight who carried this emblem was the same who had routed the Greeks and brought death upon so many. He ran to the palace and sought an audience to break the pressing news to Ungiardo. He was admitted at once and reported what I shall reserve for the next canto.

FORTY-FIFTH CANTO

1-4 Introductory. 5-21 Ruggiero, thrown into a dark dungeon, awaits death. 22-81 Ruggiero, rescued by Leo, is sent in Leo's guise to win Bradamant in combat. 82-117 While Ruggiero and Bradamant mope at their mutual loss, Marfisa obtains that Leo should still fight Ruggiero for his prize.

THERE is no stability to Fortune's Wheel: the higher a poor devil rises on it, the sooner you will see him plunge down, head over heels. Take Polycrates, for instance, or Croesus, King of Lydia, or Dionysus and others I could mention: in one day they plummeted to the depths from the pinnacle of glory. / On the other hand, the lower a man has dropped on the Wheel, the closer he is to the point of rising if the Wheel keeps turning. Some have almost had their neck on the block one day and ruled the world the next. Instances of this are Servius, Marius, and Ventidius of old, and in our own day, Louis. / I mean King Louis, father of my lord Alfonso's son's wife. He was defeated at Saint-Aubin, fell into his enemies' clutches and was about to lose his head, while not much earlier the great Mattia Corvino stood in even worse danger: then, past the crucial point, Louis was placed on the throne of France, Mattia on that of Hungary. / History, ancient and modern, is full of examples to show that good and evil, glory and shame follow hard upon each other, each putting a period to the other. They show the folly of trusting in man, in his wealth, his dominion, his conquests, or of despairing when Fortune frowns, for she keeps her Wheel forever turning. /

With the victory he had won over Leo and his father, the emperor, Ruggiero had become so confident in his good fortune and great valour that he was convinced of his ability to slay father and son all by himself though scores of cavalry and infantry opposed him. / But Fortune, who refuses to play any man's game, showed him in a few days how quick she was to raise only to drop, how quick to turn hostile, then friendly. She taught him the lesson by means of a man who soon brought hardship and ignominy upon him—the knight who had barely escaped his hands in the fierce battle. / He told Ungiardo that the warrior who had broken Constantine's forces and cowed them for years to come had been here today and here would spend the night. If Ungiardo seized Fortune by the locks, without further toil on his part she would

544

permit his liege to place the yoke upon the Bulgars, once this knight was made captive. / From the folk who had fled the battle and withdrawn hither—they arrived endlessly in batches, for they could not all cross the bridge—Ungiardo had learnt about the carnage which had dispatched half the Greeks; he knew it was a solitary knight who had broken one army and saved the other. / He was amazed that the warrior should have come on his own, unpursued, to place his head in the noose, and his smiling face, his cheerful words, and gestures bore witness to his delight.

He waited till Ruggiero lay asleep, then sent his guards silently to seize him in bed, all unsuspecting. / Accused by his own shield, he was held in Novengrad, a prisoner of Ungiardo, the cruellest man alive, who now was cock-a-hoop. What could Ruggiero do? He was naked and already bound when he awoke. Ungiardo sent a messenger hot-foot to bear the news to Constantine. /

In the night Constantine had withdrawn all his forces from the Sava and retired with them to Beletinec. This town belonged to his brother-in-law Androphilos, father of the knight whose armour had been pierced and ruptured as though made of wax at the first impact of the doughty warrior now in fierce Ungiardo's hands. / The emperor had the town walls strengthened, the gates repaired, for he was afraid that the Bulgars, with so mighty a champion for leader, might not stop at giving him a fright—they might kill off the rest of his troops. Hearing, therefore, of his capture, he no longer feared them now, not even if the whole world banded together with them. / He was beside himself with joy, he basked in a sea of milk. 'Now the Bulgars are truly beaten,' he observed with cheerful confidence—on hearing of the warrior's capture he was as sure of victory as any fighter would be who had lopped off both his opponent's arms. / The son had no less cause to rejoice than the father: beside hoping to recapture Belgrade and conquer every Bulgar stronghold, he also proposed to win the warrior's friendship by kindness, and to enlist his support. With a comrade such as this, he would have no cause to envy Charlemagne for Rinaldo and Orlando. /

Quite different was the ambition nurtured by Theodora, the emperor's sister, whose son Ruggiero slew when he drove his lance through the young man's chest to protrude a palm's width from his back. She threw herself at Constantine's feet and moved him to pity with the copious tears which fell onto her breast. / 'I shall lie at your feet, my lord,' she said, 'until you grant me vengeance upon the villain who murdered my son, now that he is captured. Beside being your nephew, think how much he loved you, think how much he did for you, and think how wrong you would be not to wreak vengeance upon his slayer. / Look at how God, in pity at our plight, has removed this cruel man from the field and made him fly like a bird into the snare, so that my son should not have long to wait unavenged by the banks of the Styx. Give this man to me, my lord, and allow me to assuage my torment by procuring his.' /

Her words, her tears and lamentations proved so effective—and she refused to rise though the emperor tried three or four times to pull and persuade her to her feet—that he was finally forced to yield and order the knight's surrender to her. / This was done without delay: the next day the knight of the unicorn had been handed over to cruel Theodora. To have him quartered alive, to subject him to a degrading public execution seemed to her too slight a punishment; she studied the question of inventing some novel and appalling death. / Meanwhile the cruel woman had him shackled, hands, feet, and neck, and thrown into a dark dungeon cell where Apollo's rays never penetrated. She kept him starved of food except for a little mouldy bread, and even this was stopped for two days now and then. And she entrusted him to the keeping of a gaoler even readier than she was to ill-treat him. /

Oh if fair Bradamant, Aymon's valiant daughter, if great-hearted Marfisa had learnt how Ruggiero was repining thus in prison, they would both have risked death to rescue him; to bring him aid Bradamant would have slighted her parents. /

Meanwhile Charlemagne, who had given Bradamant a tacit promise to forbid her becoming wife to any man who in single combat proved her inferior in courage and strength, had his decision trumpeted about, not only at court but also throughout his dominions. The news spread rapidly. / Here was his proclamation: every claimant to the hand of Aymon's daughter had to undertake armed combat with her from sunrise to sunset. If he lasted thus far and was not defeated, no more was to be said: the damsel was to concede him victory and raise no objection to his taking her. / She would concede the choice of weapons, regardless of who made the request: this concession she could well afford, adept as she was with every weapon, whether she were mounted or on foot. Aymon, who could not and would not thwart the emperor, was finally forced to yield; after much argument he decided to return with his daughter to court. / However furious Beatrice was with her daughter, she still looked to her honour, and had her richly fitted out with beautiful clothes in various styles and colours.

Bradamant went to court with her father, but when she did not find her true love there it no longer appeared to her the same court which had formerly been so alluring in her eyes. / Imagine a person who has seen a garden in April or May, all green leaves and beautiful flowers, and then sees it when the Sun slants his rays Southwards and affords but a short day: he will find it quite bare, squalid, and dreary.

Thus did the court appear to Bradamant on her return after Ruggiero's departure: it was not as she had left it. / She dared not enquire after him for fear of attracting greater suspicion, but she kept an ear open and sought to hear word of him without actually asking. His departure was known, but nobody knew what road he had taken, for he mentioned his departure to no one except to the page he took with him. /

Oh what sighs, what alarm! She feared he had virtually fled. She feared most of all that he had gone away to forget her: seeing Aymon opposed to him and all hope lost of ever being her spouse, he may have put distance between them in the hope, perhaps, of freeing himself from his love. / Or he might have decided, the quicker to rid his heart of her, to go from one country to the next in search of a woman who would make him forget his earlier love—as one nail drives out the other, so 'tis said. But this notion was succeeded by another which depicted Ruggiero as staunchly loyal, / and she would reproach herself for heeding so unkind, so foolish a suspicion. One thought, then, would defend Ruggiero, the next accuse him, and she would listen to both, inclining now to the one, now to the other, never resolving upon either. But she would generally incline towards the more cheering thought and recoil from the other. /

Whenever she remembered Ruggiero's repeated assurances, she was heartily sorry for her grave fault in harbouring jealousy and suspicion, and she chided herself and beat her breast just as though she were in his presence, saying, 'I have done wrong I admit, but the culprit has done still worse wrongs. / The culprit is Love, who has imprinted you as a lovely, graceful shape upon my heart, infusing into it your daring, your brilliance, your manliness which is a by-word. I cannot conceive that any woman, married or single, can be offered a glimpse of you and not catch fire, and not use every device to free you of my love and bind you each to her own. / Alas, would that Love had etched in me your thoughts as he has etched your face: I know I should find them as obvious as they now seem obscure. And I should be so free of Jealousy that it would never more provoke me; instead of my barely holding her at bay, I would kill her dead, let alone defeat her. /

'I am like the miser so intent upon his buried treasure; he cannot stop fearing that it will be stolen from him. Now that I cannot see and hear you, Ruggiero, fear works more strongly in me than hope; though fear is vain and deceitful I know, I cannot but surrender to it. / Trust as I might, I know not which part of the world conceals you, my Ruggiero; but once the blissful radiance of your face lightens my eyes, this deceitful fear shall be ousted and crushed by true hope. Ah come back, Ruggiero, and strengthen the hope which fear has almost killed in me! / When the sun sets, the shadows increase and give rise to vain

547

fears; when his splendour returns, the shadows wane and the timid find new courage; thus without Ruggiero I am afraid, but once I see him, my fear is ended. Ah come back, Ruggiero, return before fear has quite conquered hope! / At night every star is a living light that dies at the dawn of day; thus when my Sun removes his presence from me, dire fear raises its horns only to flee the moment the Sun shows above the horizon and hope returns. Ah come back, come back, dear light, and banish the wicked fear which devours me! / If the Sun draws away to leave the days shortened, all the beauty that the earth possesses goes into concealment. The winds rage, bringing snow and ice; no bird sings, no flower or green bough is to be seen. Thus when you take your sparkling eyes off me, my gorgeous Sun, a thousand baneful fears produce in me several harsh winters in a single year. / Ah come back, my Sun, come and restore the sweet spring I long for; sweep away the ice and snow and bring peace to my heart, so clouded now and bleak.'

As Procne or Philomena grieved after leaving in search of food for their little ones and returning to find an empty nest; or as the turtle-dove grieves who has lost her love, / so did Bradamant grieve, fearing that her Ruggiero had been taken from her. How often she bedewed her face in tears, though as furtively as she could. But how much more heart-broken would she have been had she known what she did not know: that her beloved was languishing in prison, condemned to a cruel death. /

Now as the All-Holy One would have it, the cruelty practised by the vicious old woman upon the worthy knight she held captive, as she devised novel tortures with which to slay him, came to the ears of Leo, the emperor's gallant son. The Lord inspired him to rescue the captive and thus prevent a man of such eminent virtue from perishing. / The chivalrous prince, though ignorant of Ruggiero's identity, was devoted to him, stirred as he was by valour which appeared to him unique, nay superhuman. So he pondered, he plotted and planned until finally he decided how to rescue him in a manner to prevent his cruel aunt from laying the blame at his door. / He spoke secretly to the gaoler who held the keys to the prison and told him of his wish to see the knight before the grave sentence passed against him was enacted. At nightfall he summoned one of his henchmen, a tough, resolute fellow to have in a brawl, and sent for the gaoler to open to him without the word getting out that he was Leo. /

The gaoler came unescorted and secretly led Leo and his companion to the tower in which he kept the knight reserved for the extreme penalty. Once inside, while the gaoler had his back turned to open the cell-door, they threw a noose round his neck and promptly gave him his quietus. / They pulled open the trap-door and Leo, grasping a flaming torch, lowered himself on a rope suspended there for that purpose down to where Ruggiero was hidden from the sun. He found the prisoner bound hand and foot and extended upon a grating, barely a palm's width above water-level. Here in his cell a month or less would have seen the end of him with no need for outside intervention. /

Leo gave Ruggiero a compassionate embrace and said: 'Your prowess at arms, sir knight, binds me to you indissolubly in willing servitude forever. It compels me to place your good before my own, to ignore my own safety for the sake of yours, and to prefer your friendship to that of my father and all my kindred. / I am Leo, you see, son of Constantine, and I have come in person to rescue you. If ever my father discovers, I risk being banished or at any rate incurring his eternal displeasure: he hates you on account of all his men you routed and killed at Belgrade.' /

As he strove to untie the captive he addressed more words to him calculated to revive him. Said Ruggiero: 'I am infinitely beholden to you, and I propose to sacrifice the life you restore to me at whatever moment you claim it, should it ever prove necessary to lay it down for you.' / Ruggiero was removed from that place of darkness and the dead gaoler was left in his stead. Neither he nor the others were recognized leaving. Leo took Ruggiero to his quarters and persuaded him to stay there four days or so in safe concealment. Meanwhile he meant to recover his guest's arms and noble steed which Ungiardo had taken. / The next day Ruggiero's flight was discovered; the prison was found open, the gaoler strangled. Various culprits were suggested, everyone discussed the question but no one guessed the truth. Leo was the last person anyone would have suspected: it was generally held that he had good reason to make away with him but certainly not to help him. /

Ruggiero was astounded and abashed by chivalry such as this, which so jogged him out of the frame of mind in which he had travelled all these miles hither that his second thoughts bore no resemblance to those they replaced: if his mind had first been filled with hatred, anger, and venom, it was now all love and devotion. / His exclusive concern now, his sole desire night and day, was to hit upon the means to discharge his enormous obligation with an equal and greater courtesy. Were he to devote the rest of his life, whatever its duration, to serving Leo, were he to risk certain death a thousand times, he could not, he felt, do as much for him as he deserved. /

News had arrived meanwhile of Charlemagne's edict whereby suitors for Bradamant's hand were to try their might against her with sword and lance. These tidings brought little joy to Leo—indeed they caused him to pale visibly. Having no illusions about his prowess, he knew that he could never match her in armed combat. / He pondered the matter and realized that his wits would have to supply the deficiencies of his strength: he would have this warrior, whose name he did not yet know, appear with his ensign. He judged that the force and courage of his champion would make him the match of any French knight, and was confident that if he entrusted the task to him, he would defeat Bradamant and win her. / Two tasks faced him, though: first, to dispose the knight to acceptance; second, to put him into the field in his own place in such a way as to arouse no suspicions. He sent for him, explained the problem and with effective words prayed him to undertake this combat in another's name, under a false ensign. /

The Greek's eloquence had its effect, but even more did the great debt Ruggiero owed him, a debt from which he would never feel discharged. Therefore however hard, however close to impossible it seemed to him, nonetheless, with a smile on his face if not in his heart, he replied that he would do it. / Although he felt a fierce stab of pain the moment he had said this, a pain which constantly molested him night and day, although his death was now apparent to him, he was never to confess that he regretted his word. He would have died not once but a thousand times sooner than disobey Leo. / Indeed he was certain to die, for if he relinquished the damsel he would also forsake his life: either grief would break his heart, or, if it did not, he would with his own hands tear open the wrapping which enveloped his soul and draw it out. Anything would be easier for him than to see her belong to another. / He was prepared to die but he could not yet say in which manner. Sometimes he thought of disguising his true strength in the combat and exposing his side to the damsel, for no death could be more blessed than to expire at her hands. But then he recognized that if, through his failing, Leo did not have her to wife, he would not have discharged his obligation, / for he had promised to undertake the single combat against Bradamant, not merely to simulate it and go through the motions, procuring Leo little profit. Therefore he would stand by his pledge, and though one idea after another came to him, he banished them all and submitted only to the one enjoining him not to break his word. /

Leo, with his father's consent, had made ready arms, horses, and a retinue of suitable size, and had set out accompanied by Ruggiero, to whom he had restored his fine arms and Frontino. Day after day they travelled until they reached France, then Paris. / The prince would not enter the city but pitched his pavilion in the fields outside. The same day, he sent to the French king to apprise him of his arrival. Charlemagne was pleased, and repeatedly showed his hospitality by means of visits and gifts. Leo explained his business and asked him to help expedite it, / summoning into the field the damsel who would not accept a husband whose might fell short of hers: he had come to ensure that she either became his wife or put him to death. Charles accepted his commission and had Bradamant appear the next day outside the gates in the lists, which were hastily erected that night beneath the high walls. /

The night preceding the day set for the combat Ruggiero felt like a man condemned to die in the morning. Anxious not to be recognized, he had chosen to fight in full armour. He would not employ lance or steed or any weapon other than a sword. / He eschewed the lance, not because he feared the golden lance which had been Argalia's, and later Astolfo's, the lance which made every opponent quit the saddle. (Apart from King Galafron, who had had the lance made for his son, nobody knew of its powers or that it was made by sorcery. / Indeed Astolfo and Bradamant, to whom it succeeded, both believed that if triumph always attended their jousting it was not due to any magic but simply to their own prowess: they would achieve the same results, they reckoned, with any other lance they chanced to use.) The only reason that Ruggiero did not joust was so as not to exhibit Frontino: / if his lady set eyes on the steed she could easily recognize him, for she had long had charge of him and ridden him at Montauban. Ruggiero, whose one concern was to avoid recognition, would not use Frontino nor anything which could betray his identity. / For this engagement he wanted another sword, knowing that Balisard would find any breast-plate soft as dough: no temper was sufficient to withstand its onslaught. Even his new sword he blunted with a hammer to make it less effective. Thus armed, as day first streaked the horizon, Ruggiero entered the lists. / To pass for Leo he donned Leo's surcoat and adopted his escut-cheon—gules, an eagle displayed with two heads Or. The deception was easily compassed for they were of identical build. The one stepped forth; the other eluded all eyes. /

The damsel's ambition was very different from Ruggiero's: if he hammered his sword blunt so that it would not cut or pierce, Brada-mant sharpened hers and willed it to penetrate his armour and pierce his living flesh; she wanted each cut and thrust to be so well delivered as to attain his heart. / The spirited damsel behaved like those impe-tuous Barbary steeds one has seen awaiting the signal to charge: they dance about, nostrils flared, ears spread. Never dreaming that her op-ponent was Ruggiero, she seemed to have fire in her veins as she awaited the trumpet, and could scarcely control herself. / Sometimes a thunder-clap is followed by a fearsome gust of wind which churns the billowing seas and scoops up the black dust to spin it skywards; the wild beasts take flight, flocks and shepherds flee, the air dissolves into hail and rain: such was the damsel when, on hearing the signal, she grasped her sword and assailed Ruggiero. / But Ruggiero was secure in the armour which Vulcan had given to Trojan Hector, and he no more yielded to the vicious attack hurled against his chest, his sides, his head than a mature oak or thick, solidly-planted tower would yield to the North Wind, or a hard rock to the angry seas which pound it night and day. /

Cut and thrust, the damsel kept attempting to drive her sword through the joints in the armour-plating so as to relieve her wrath. She laid into him from one side then the other, all fretful and aggrieved that her efforts were fruitless. / A commander investing a city solidly defended with stout walls will assault it repeatedly, trying now to beat down the gates, now the high towers, or else to fill in the moat: in vain will he drive his men to death without finding a way in. Thus did Bradamant toil and strive without success to prize open armour-plating or chain-mail. / She struck sparks off his shield, off his fine helmet, off his breastplate as she rained down blows by the thousand, fore- and back-handed, upon his arms, head, and chest: they fell more thickly than hailstones clanging on a farm roof. Ruggiero stood on his guard and defended himself adroitly, but never attacked her. / Now he would stand firm, now pivot or withdraw, hand and foot acting in concert. Now he would advance his shield, now turn his sword to deflect his opponent's hand. He never struck her, or, if he did, took care to strike where he reckoned to do least damage.

The damsel longed to bring an end to the combat before the day waned. / She recalled the edict and remembered her danger if she were not quick: if within the day she did not capture or slay her claimant, she would be the captive. Phoebus was already preparing to plunge into the sea by the Pillars of Hercules when she began to doubt her own strength and lose hope. / The more hopeless she became the more enraged she grew and she redoubled her blows, still meaning to rupture the armour which had remained undamaged all day. She was like an artisan who has been slow at his allotted task and sees that it is night: in vain he hastens on his work and efforts until strength and daylight forsake him both at once. / O unhappy damsel, if you recognized this man whom you want to slay, if you realized he was Ruggiero from whom your own life-thread depends, I know that you would sooner kill yourself than him, for I know that you love him more than yourself; and when you learn that he is Ruggiero, I know that you will regret these blows you have struck. /

Now Charlemagne and many of his company who believed the challenger to be Leo, not Ruggiero, observing how robust and deft he was as he confronted Bradamant and how skilful at protecting himself without injuring her, changed their minds and remarked: 'They are well suited to each other—he is truly worthy of her, she of him.' /

When Phoebus was quite hidden in the sea Charles stopped the battle and declared that Bradamant should take Leo for husband without further ado. Ruggiero did not stop to rest or to remove his helmet or chain-mail, but returned at once on a little cob to the pavilion where Leo awaited him. / Twice and more Leo threw his arms round Ruggiero's neck in a brotherly embrace, then, drawing off his helmet, kissed him most affectionately on both cheeks. 'You are always to dispose of me at your good pleasure,' said the prince. 'Draw freely upon me and upon my state: you will never exhaust your credit. / I know of no reward that could ever relieve me of my obligation to you, not even if I took the crown off my head and placed it on yours.'

Ruggiero, heart-sick and disgusted with life, made little reply. He returned Leo's ensigns, resumed his unicorn-emblem, / and, visibly fatigued and listless, took his leave as soon as he could and returned to his quarters, it being now midnight. He armed himself completely, saddled his steed and, without farewells, mounted and set off unperceived, leaving the choice of path to Frontino. / Taking highways and by-ways, crossing woods and fields, all night long Frontino carried his master who never stopped weeping. He invoked death, the only release from his obstinate grief; in death he took comfort; beside death he could see nothing to put an end to his unbearable torment. /

'Who am I to blame, alas,' he cried, 'for robbing me at one stroke of all my good? If I am not to suffer unavenged, whom shall I turn upon? No one has harmed me and brought me to this pass but I alone, I can see. It is therefore on myself that I must avenge myself for bringing all this woe upon myself. / Were I alone the injured party I could perhaps forgive myself, though not without difficulty (nay, but I would not wish to). How much less should I forgive myself, though, if Bradamant is injured as much as I am? Even were I to forgive myself, it would not be right for me to leave her unavenged. / To avenge her, therefore, I ought to die—indeed I want to, for I know of nothing but death to save me from my pain, so this is no problem. I am only sorry that I did not die sooner, before I had done her wrong. Oh what happiness if I had died while cruel Theodora's prisoner! / Even if she had slain me after torturing me as her savage whim directed, I could at least have looked to Bradamant for pity at my plight. But when she discovers that I have preferred Leo to her, that I have knowingly deprived myself of her in his favour, she will be right to hate me, alive and dead.' /

These and many other words he uttered, accompanied by sobs and sighs. Daybreak found him amid dark woods, weird and wild. In his desperate state he was eager to die; wishing to do this as secretly as possible, he felt that this place offered good concealment and was right for his purpose. / He thrust into the thick of the woods, where the shady boughs looked most closely intertwined. First, though, he freed Frontino and sent him well on his way. 'O my Frontino,' he said, 'if I were able to reward you as you deserve, you would have little cause to envy Pegasus, who has flown to heaven and lives among the stars. / I know that neither Cyllarus nor Arion, nor any other horse mentioned by Greek or Latin authors ever surpassed you or deserved more praise. If in all things else they equalled you, I know that in one respect none of them can take pleasure in boasting of a distinction, an honour conferred on you alone: / you were so beloved by one who is the most beautiful, noble, valiant damsel who ever lived that she herself looked after you, she herself saddled and bridled you. My lady cherished you! Ah, but why do I call her mine any longer if she is no longer mine, if I have given her to another? Why should I delay turning this sword against myself?' /

If Ruggiero miserably moped here and moved the birds and beasts to pity (there being no one else to hear his cries or witness the tears streaming onto his breast), do not imagine that Bradamant was any happier in Paris, now that she had no pretext to save her or defer her accepting Leo. / Sooner than accept a consort other than her own Ruggiero there was nothing she would not try—break her word, antagonize Charles and his court, her relations and friends, or, all else failing, take her life with poison or the sword: she thought it far preferable to terminate her existence than to live deprived of Ruggiero. /

'Alas, my Ruggiero,' she cried, 'where have you gone? Can it be that you are so far away that you alone of all men did not hear of the edict? Had you heard of it, I know that no one would have answered the challenge sooner. Alas, what conclusion am I to reach but the very worst? / How can it be, Ruggiero, that you alone have not heard what is known to all the world? If you have heard but have not come at once, what reason can there be but that you are dead or captive? The truth, if we knew it, must be that this son of Constantine has laid a trap for you: the miscreant must have blocked your path to prevent your arriving here before him. / I begged Charlemagne as a favour that I should not be awarded to any man my inferior in strength, believing as I did that you would be the one I should fail to resist in armed combat. Apart from you I disdained all others; but God has requited my rashness and now this man has won me who never undertook a feat of honour in his life. / But if I am overborne through not having been able to kill or capture him—how unjust this seems to me!—I shall not abide by the emperor's award. True, I shall be called flighty if I now deny what I said earlier—but I shall be neither the first nor the last to prove inconstant. / If I prove firmer than any rock in keeping faith with my lover, if in this I surpass every woman that ever lived, that is

enough for me. If in all things else I be called inconstant I do not care
—so long as I gain by my inconstancy. So long as I be not obliged
to accept this man, let them call me wayward as a leaf.' /

These and other words interspersed with many a sigh and tear she
repeated all through the night which succeeded that unhappy day. But
when Night had retired with her shadows to the Cimmerian caves,
Heaven, which had vowed her to Ruggiero from the beginning, came
to her help / in the form of Marfisa: the haughty damsel went in the
morning to Charlemagne and stated that her brother Ruggiero was
being gravely wronged. She refused, she said, to countenance his being
robbed of his wife without so much as a word. Yes, she would undertake to prove against all comers that Bradamant was Ruggiero's wife. /
First of all she would prove to Bradamant herself—if she dared deny it
—that in her very presence she had pronounced to Ruggiero the words
spoken by one contracting matrimony. The accustomed ceremony had
been enacted so that they were no longer free to dispose of themselves
or to leave each other to contract new engagements. / Whether Marfisa spoke the truth or not, I have no doubt but that the intention
behind her words was, rightly or wrongly, to obstruct Leo regardless
of the truth. Also, that she acted with the consent of Bradamant who,
to recover Ruggiero and discard Leo, could see no way more honourable or direct than this. /

Greatly perturbed by this, the king sent at once for Bradamant and
informed her, in Aymon's presence, of what Marfisa undertook to
prove. Bradamant hung her head, abashed, neither confirming nor
denying, so that it was easy enough to surmise that Marfisa had spoken
the truth. / The news delighted Rinaldo and Orlando, for it should
have scotched the marriage which Leo imagined was virtually contracted. In spite of Aymon's obstinacy, Ruggiero would have fair
Bradamant, and they could give her to him without a quarrel, without
tearing her forcibly from her father's hands. / For if they supported
Marfisa's assertion, her story would be proof against discrediting; thus
they would more honourably and without further strife achieve what
they had promised.

But Aymon observed: 'This is a plot hatched against me; you have
made a mistake, though—even if what you have concocted were the
very truth, you have not done with me yet. / What if she really was
foolish enough to betroth herself to Ruggiero, and he to her as you
profess (not that I yet admit or believe it), when and where did this
happen? I mean to obtain the facts clearly, explicitly, and openly. It
certainly never happened if not before Ruggiero's baptism. / But if
it happened before Ruggiero became a Christian, then what is it to me!
—the wedding, of course, was invalid, she being a Christian, he a

pagan. Besides, Leo should not have been put to the risk of combat to no purpose; and I doubt whether our emperor will be prepared to retract his word for this. / What you tell me now you should have mentioned before the question was ever broached and the emperor, at her request, had issued the challenge which brought Leo here to battle.'

Thus Aymon confuted Rinaldo and Orlando so as to break the compact between the two lovers. Charlemagne listened but would not take sides. / As you hear the leaves rustle in the tall trees when Auster or Boreas blows, or as the waves hiss over the shore if Aeolus rages against Neptune: so did France seethe with this debate, which so concentrated all discussion, captured all ears that all other topics were scanted. / Some spoke for Ruggiero, some for Leo, though most sided with the former, ranging themselves about ten to one against Aymon. The emperor inclined neither way but encouraged debate and referred the question to his parliament.

Now in stepped Marfisa, as the betrothal was to be deferred, and made a fresh proposal: / 'Since Bradamant cannot belong to another man while my brother is still alive, if Leo truly wants her, let him rely upon his courage and strength to wrest his life from him. Let the one who dispatches his opponent to the shades achieve his goal without further rivalry.' Charlemagne at once put this to Leo as he had informed him of everything earlier. /

Leo, who was confident of defeating Ruggiero, indeed of meeting any challenge without difficulty so long as he could rely upon the knight of the unicorn, made the wrong decision and accepted. He did not realize that his champion had withdrawn in bleak sorrow to the dark lonely wood; he imagined that Ruggiero had wandered off a mile or two and would come straight back. / He regretted this soon enough, for the champion on whom he placed undue reliance did not reappear that day nor the next two, and left no news of himself. Now without his champion Leo did not feel ready to undertake this combat against Ruggiero. To avoid ignominious disaster, then, he sent away to find the knight of the unicorn. / He sent his searchers to towns, villages, and farms, near and far, and, not content with this, mounted horse himself and set off to search. But neither he nor Charles' men would ever have obtained news of him were it not for Melissa's intervention—which I shall relate to you in the next canto.

FORTY-SIXTH CANTO

*1–19 The Poet's friends await him at his journey's end.
19–72 Leo, discovering Ruggiero's identity, withdraws his
claim to Bradamant and presents him at Charlemagne's
court as the damsel's rightful spouse. 73–100 The wedding
of Bradamant and Ruggiero, with a description of the nuptial
pavilion. 101–140 Ruggiero slays Rodomont in single combat.*

NOW if my chart tells me true, the harbour will soon be in sight and I
may hope to fulfil my vow ashore to One who has accompanied me on
so long a voyage. Oh, how I had paled at the prospect of returning
with but a crippled ship, or perhaps of wandering forever! But I
think I see . . . yes, I do see land, I see the welcoming shore. / I can
hear a thunder of rejoicing—the air quivers, the sea rumbles with it; I
hear a shrill of trumpets drowned by the mighty roar of the crowd.
Now I begin to discern who these people are who fill both shores of
the harbour. They all seem delighted that I have reached the end of so
long a voyage. /
   Oh what fair, what virtuous ladies, what excellent knights I see
gracing the shore, and what good friends, too! I shall be forever
indebted to them for the happiness they feel at my return. I can see
'Mamma' Beatrice out on the tip of the pier with Ginevra and other
ladies from Correggio. With them is Veronica Gambara, the darling of
Phoebus and the choir of Muses. / I can see another Ginevra from the
same family, and Julia with her. I see Ippolita Sforza and my lady
Domitilla Trivulzio, who was raised in the Muses' sacred grotto. I can
see you, Emilia Pia, and you, Margherita, in company with Angela
Borgia and Graziosa. Fair Bianca and Diana d'Este are there with
Ricciarda and their other sisters. / There is fair (but even more wise
and virtuous) Barbara Turca and her friend Laura; from the Indus to
the furthest coasts of Mauretania the Sun does not behold a more
kindly pair than these two. Over there is Ginevra, whose merits add
such golden, jewelled lustre to the Malatesta clan that no imperial
palace ever possessed more highly respected or well deserved em-
bellishments. / Had she been at Rimini at the time when Caesar,
puffed up by his conquest of Gaul, was debating whether to cross the
Rubicon and antagonize Rome, I do believe that he would have furled
all his banners, divested himself of his rich burden of trophies and

accepted laws and covenants at her insistence; and he might never have turned oppressor of freedom. /

There is the wife of my lord of Bozolo with his mother, his sisters and other ladies—his cousins; also the ladies from the houses of Torelli, Bentivoglio, Visconti, and Pallavicini. Here is Julia Gonzaga: for grace and beauty she surpasses all women alive today and all those whose fame has survived from the days of the Greeks, Romans, and Barbarians. / Wherever she turns, wherever she looks with those serene eyes of hers, all other women yield to her in beauty—more, they admire her as a goddess descended from heaven. With her is her sister-in-law, Isabella Colonna, who never broke her troth for all that angry Fortune harried her for a long while. There is Anne of Aragon, star of the Vastos; / beautiful, noble, courteous, and wise, she is a temple of chastity, love, and loyalty. With her is her sister Joan, whose radiant beauty is enough to tarnish all other women's looks. Here is Vittoria Colonna, who has rescued her triumphant spouse from the dark shore of the Styx to make him gleam in the firmament (despite the Fates and Death) in a unique fashion. / Here are my ladies of Ferrara; here too, those from the court of Urbino; and I recognize the Mantuan ladies and as many beauties as Lombardy and Tuscany possess. If my vision is not ruined by the dazzle of all those beautiful faces, the knight in their company (and to whom they are showing such respect) is the great Aretine luminary, Accolti the Unique. /

I can see his nephew Benedetto with his purple hat and mantle; with him are Ercole Gonzaga and Lorenzo Campeggi, Cardinals of Mantua and Bologna, the boast of the Sacred College. On their faces and in their gestures I read (if I'm not dreaming) such pleasure at my return that I see I shall never find an easy way to discharge my debt to them. / With them are Lattanzio, Claudio Tolomei, Paulo Pansa, Trissino, and Juvenal the Latinist, I think; also my friends the Capilupis, Sasso, Molza, and Florian Montino. There too is Julio Camillo, who shows us an easy and shorter route to Ascra's banks. I believe I can also descry Marc' Antonio Flaminio, Sanga, and Berni. / There is my lord Alessandro Farnese, and what a learned company surrounds him: Fedro, Capella, Porzio, Filippo of Bologna, Maffei of Volterra, Maddaleni, Blosio, Pierio, the ever-mellifluous Vida of Cremona, Lascari, Musuro, Navagero, Andrea Marone, and the monk Severo. /

There are two more Alessandros in that group—degli Orologi and Guarino. There is Mario da Alvito, and the divine Pietro Aretino, scourge of princes. I can see two Girolamos—Verità and Cittadini. I can see Mainardi, Leoniceno, Pannizzato, Calcagnini and Teocreno. / I can see Bernardo Cappello—and Pietro Bembo, who rescued the purity of our gentle idiom from the drabness of common usage and gave us an example of how it ought to sound. Behind him is Guasparro degli Obizi admiring the sight of ink spent to such good purpose. I see Fracastoro, Bevazano, Trifon Gabriele and, further off, Bernardo Tasso. / I can see Niccolò Tiepoli and Niccolò Amanio looking at me. There is Antonio Fregoso, evidently happy and surprised to see me reaching land. My friend Valerio is there: he has drawn away from the ladies—perhaps he is discussing with his companion, Barignano, how to avoid forever falling for them when they always wound him. / I can see Pico and Pio, sublime, godlike geniuses connected by ties of affection and of blood. The man in their company to whom all the worthiest are showing such respect is a person I have never met; but if I have been given a true description, he must be the man I have so longed to meet—Jacopo Sannazaro, who obliges the Muses to quit the hills and reside on the sandy shore. /

There is the learned, faithful, diligent Secretary Pistofilo; with my good Angiaro and the Acciaiuolis he is delighted no longer to have to fear the sea on my account. I can see my kinsman Annibal Malaguzzo with Adoardo, in whom I place great hope that he will spread the fame of my native town from Gibraltar to the Indies. / Vittor Fausto and Tancredi rejoice to see me back, as do a hundred others: every one of them, man and woman, look pleased at my return.

So let me not delay completing the short passage that still remains, for the wind is favourable. Let us return to Melissa and describe how she helped to save Ruggiero's life. / Melissa (as I know I have told you many times) was most anxious to see Bradamant and Ruggiero united in the bonds of matrimony. She was so concerned with the fortunes of both that she wanted hourly news of them; therefore she always kept in touch with them by means of spirit-messengers: as one spirit returned another was dispatched. / She saw that Ruggiero had fallen prey to relentless grief. He stayed in the shadowy darkness where he proposed to kill himself by starvation, for on no account would he taste food again. But she was quick to save him: leaving home, she took a path which brought her face to face with Leo. / After sending page after page to scour the vicinity for the knight of the unicorn, he had also set out to find him. The wise enchantress, then, who was riding a spirit which she had saddled and bridled that day and turned into a palfrey, came upon Constantine's son. /

'Sir, if you truly are as noble as your face suggests,' she said to him, 'if your outward appearance is a true reflection of your chivalry and kindness, do come to the support and aid of the best knight of our day: he is on the point of dying unless he soon receives aid and comfort. / He is the best knight who ever wore a sword at his side, a shield on his arm, the most handsome and noble of any, living or dead, and he is on the verge of death (if no one comes to his support) simply because of a signal courtesy he has performed. Come, sir, for love of God; do see if any counsel will serve to save him.' / It at once came to Leo that the knight she spoke of must be the same one whom he was seeking and for whom he had sent his men searching the countryside. Therefore he spurred in haste after Melissa who had urged him on so merciful an errand. She led him only a short distance to where Ruggiero lay at death's door. /

When they found him he had been fasting for three days; he had so far surrendered to melancholy that he could barely have stood up—and then only to fall down again without a push. He lay on the ground fully armed and helmeted, his sword buckled on. He had made a pillow of the shield on which the white unicorn was painted. / Here he lay brooding on the injury he had done to his lady, on how thankless, how thoughtless he had been, and if he wept he also raged. In his passion he chewed his hands and his lips, and bedewed his cheeks with continuous tears. So wrapt up in her was he that he did not hear Melissa's and Leo's arrival, / nor did he break off his lament, his sighs and tears. Leo stopped; he strained to listen, then dismounted, and approached him. He recognized that Love was the cause of his agony, but did not know exactly who the lady was on whose account he underwent such misery, for Ruggiero had not let slip her name. / Leo drew closer and closer until they were face to face; he greeted him with brotherly affection, bending down and embracing him. I do not know how pleased Ruggiero was at Leo's unexpected arrival: he feared that Leo would disturb and vex him and want to prevent his suicide. /

With the gentlest, softest words that came to mind, with all the love he could show, Leo addressed him: 'Do not be reluctant to disclose to me the cause of your sorrow. Few evils in this life are so bad but one may struggle free of them if their cause be known; so long as there's life there's hope. / How it grieves me that you should have wished to hide from me, knowing as you do that I am your true friend—and not simply from the moment I became inextricably bound to you, but ever since the day when I had reason to be your mortal enemy forever. Now I would have you rely upon me to place my substance, my friends, my life at your disposal. / Do not hesitate to confide your sorrow to me: let me see whether you cannot be delivered from it by force or by blandishments, by lavish expense, by astuteness or guile. If my efforts should prove unavailing, then let death come to your relief—but do not invoke death before all has been done that may be done.' /

He persisted with such effective entreaties, with such kindly words that Ruggiero could not but be moved, his heart not being made of iron or of flint. If he refused to reply he would be guilty, he realized, of an ungracious attitude. So he replied, but the words stuck two or three times in his throat before he could begin: /

'When you learn who I am, my lord—as I am about to tell you—I am sure that you will be no less eager for my death than I am, possibly more so. I am the man you hate: I am Ruggiero. I hated you too, and it was with the intention of slaying you that I left court many days ago. / I could not see Bradamant taken from me for your sake, when I heard that Aymon favoured you. But if man proposes, God disposes: the great favour you conferred upon me in the plight in which I landed made me alter my opinion of you. Not only, then, did I eschew the hatred I had earlier borne you, but also I determined to be yours forever. / Not realizing that I was Ruggiero, you begged me to win you the damsel: you might as well have asked me for the heart out of my breast, or for my very soul. My choice, as I showed you, was to satisfy your desire rather than my own. Bradamant has become yours. / Possess her in peace—I far prefer your good to mine. But if I have deprived myself of her, suffer me also to rob myself of life: it would be easier for me to continue living without a soul than without Bradamant. Besides, she can never be legitimately yours while I live: we have already contracted marriage, and she cannot have two husbands at once.' /

On learning that this knight was none other than Ruggiero, Leo was so aghast that he was struck motionless as a statue: dumb, rooted, unblinking, he looked less like a man than like a statue donated to a shrine by a votary. This, he felt, was gallantry the like of which had never been known before or since. / Now that he knew him for Ruggiero, his earlier affection for him did not diminish: it positively increased to a point where Ruggiero's anguish pained him no less than its victim. This being so, and also to demonstrate his title to be an emperor's son, he would not suffer Ruggiero to outdo him in chivalry though he might surpass him in all else. /

'That day when you ravaged my army with your incredible valour,' he said, 'had I known that you were Ruggiero as I know now, for all that I hated you, your valour would have captivated me just as in fact it did without my knowing your identity; and hate would still have given place to my present love, just the way it did. / I shall not deny that I loathed the name of Ruggiero before I knew that you were he; but dismiss the notion that my erstwhile hatred has increased. Had I known at the time when I rescued you from prison what I know now, I would still have done for you what I now mean to do. / And if I would have done it willingly before, when I was under no obligation to you as I now am, how much more should I do so now when I would be the most thankless of men were I to decline to do so? You denied yourself, deprived yourself of all your good to bequeath it to me; but I restore your gift, and with greater pleasure than I derived from receiving it. / How much more fitting that you rather than I should have the lady: I love her for her virtues, but there is no question of *my* cutting off my life-threads if she became another's. Your death might enable me to take her as lawful wife once the matrimonial bonds between you have been undone—but I would not consent. / I would sooner lose not merely Bradamant but all my wordly goods, and my life to boot, than have it said that I ever occasioned pain to a knight such as you. Truly I regret your diffidence: you could dispose of me as fully as of your own self, but you preferred to die of sorrow than to look to me for help.' /

These words he said and many more which it would take too long to relate. He kept rebutting Ruggiero's arguments until the latter cried: 'I concede and am content not to die. But when shall I ever discharge my obligation to you, for now you have twice restored me to life?' /

Melissa had savoury dishes and precious wine brought in a trice, and encouraged Ruggiero—he was practically beyond help unless he took himself in hand. Meanwhile Frontino had caught the sound of horses here and galloped back; Leo had his pages catch and saddle him and return him to Ruggiero. / Only with great effort and Leo's assistance did Ruggiero succeed in mounting, so far had his strength diminished, which a few days earlier was enough to defeat an entire army, then to achieve in combat what he went on to achieve under false insignia. They left this spot and had not travelled half a league before they came to a monastery / where they rested for the remainder of the day, and for the one following and the one after that, so much so that the knight of the unicorn recovered his pristine strength.

Then, with Melissa and Leo, Ruggiero returned to royal Paris. Here he found that an embassy from the Bulgars had arrived the previous evening. / For this people, who had elected Ruggiero their king, had sent this embassy to fetch him, it being supposed that he was in France at Charlemagne's court. They wanted to swear fealty to him, to give him dominion over themselves and crown him. Ruggiero's page, who was with them, had brought tidings of him. / He spoke of the battle he had fought at Belgrade in the Bulgars' cause, where he defeated Leo and his father the emperor, slaughtering and routing their troops. Therefore they had made him their sovereign in preference to every man of their own nation. He spoke of how Ruggiero had then been captured by Ungiardo at Novengrad and handed over to Theodora. / And how a reliable report had reached them that his gaoler had been found slain, the prisoner escaped, the cell open—but what then became of him nobody knew.

Ruggiero entered the city surreptitiously and no one caught sight of him. The next day he and his companion Leo went to Charlemagne. / Ruggiero presented himself with the golden two-headed bird on the red ground; as agreed between them, he wore the same insignia and cloak as he had in the battle—it was all slashed, holed, and battered so that he was recognized at once as the knight who had fought Bradamant. / Leo arrived with him in sumptuous royal attire, unarmed, and surrounded by an honourable retinue. He bowed to Charlemagne, who had already risen to welcome him.

Then, holding by the hand Ruggiero, focus of all eyes, thus he spoke: / 'This is the worthy knight who defended himself from dawn till the day's ending; and since Bradamant did not slay or capture him or drive him from the lists, he is certainly the victor, noble Sire, if he has correctly understood your edict, and has earned her for wife. He has come therefore to claim her. / Beside his entitlement by virtue of the edict, there is no other man with a claim as strong as his. If it takes valour to merit her, what knight deserves her better than he does? If she is to go to the man who loves her best, there is no man to surpass or match him in this. Here he is ready to defend his right with arms against any who would oppose him.' / Charles and all the court were astonished to hear this, for they had thought it was Leo who had fought the battle, not this unknown knight.

Now Marfisa, who had been listening to Leo with the rest, but who had scarcely been able to hear him out in silence, stepped forward and cried: / 'Ruggiero is not here to decide the issue between himself and this claimant to Bradamant's hand; therefore, to prevent her being taken from him hugger-mugger for lack of any vindication on his part, I, who am his sister, undertake his cause against whoever claims a right to Bradamant or claims to surpass Ruggiero.' /

So bitter was her anger as she pronounced these words that many feared she would carry them into effect without awaiting Charlemagne's leave. Now Leo, seeing no further purpose in Ruggiero's incognito, removed his helmet and turned to Marfisa saying: 'Here he is, ready to give you a good account of himself.' / Imagine how whitehaired Aegeus felt at the horrible banquet where he recognized his son in the man whom, at his wife's insistence, he had offered poison—any further delay in recognizing him by his sword, and the old man would have killed him. Thus was Marfisa on discovering that the knight she had hated was Ruggiero. /

She now hastened at once to embrace him and could only cling to his neck. Rinaldo, Orlando—but first Charlemagne—kissed him fondly on either cheek. Dudone, Oliver, Sobrino, none of them evidently could show him too much attention, none of the paladins or barons neglected the occasion to greet him. /

When the embraces were over, Leo, a gifted speaker, set out to tell Charlemagne and all those present of Ruggiero's robust valour, which he had witnessed at Belgrade (to the detriment of his own troops), and how in his eyes it had quite eclipsed the wrong inflicted. / Therefore, when Ruggiero was captured and handed over to Theodora, who would have practised every kind of torture on him, he personally delivered the captive from prison, in spite of all his kinsfolk. He related how Ruggiero, to requite Leo for having rescued him, conceded him a favour the like of which never was nor will be known. / He went on to describe in detail what Ruggiero undertook for him, and how afterwards, seared by the pain of having to relinquish his bride, he had made ready to die—and dead he would be now, had help not come. He told his tale with such sweetness that there was not a dry eye in the audience. / Then he addressed himself to stubborn Aymon with such effective entreaties that not only did he sway him and move him to change his mind, he even persuaded him to go in person to beg Ruggiero's forgiveness, asking to be accepted as father-in-law, and promising Bradamant to him. /

More than one messenger it was who hurried off jubilantly to bring the glad news to her in the solitude of her room where she bewailed her sad plight and her life hung in the balance. If the blood had drained from her heart, drawn out by Pity, when Grief first gnawed her, at this news it ebbed out again, so much so that the damsel almost died of joy. / Forceful and spirited as you know her to be, she was now so sapped of vigour that she could no longer keep to her feet. A man condemned to the block, to the noose or wheel or other grisly death, and who already has the black bandage over his eyes, would not cry out for greater joy on hearing of his reprieve. /

Mongrana and Clairmont rejoiced at the new bond uniting the two branches. No less, however, did Ganelon deplore it, with Count Anselm, Falcone, Gini and Ginami: but they concealed their envious squalid thoughts behind a different façade while they awaited vengeance as the fox lies in wait for the hare. / Not only had Rinaldo and Orlando killed many of their evil clan on various occasions (though the reciprocal injuries were wisely silenced by the king), but also the more recent deaths of Pinabello and Bertolai had brought them little cause for joy. Still, they kept their malice concealed, pretending to be uncertain whom to blame. /

The Bulgarian ambassadors, who had come to Charlemagne's court (as I have said) in the hope of finding the doughty knight of the unicorn, their elected king, blessed their good fortune for fulfilling their hope when they heard that he was here. Reverently they cast themselves at his feet and prayed him to return to Bulgaria. / The sceptre and royal crown awaited him at Adrianople, they told him, and they begged him to come back and defend the realm, for Constantine was said to have raised a large army to molest them and was returning in person. But if the Bulgars could have their king back with them, they hoped to wrest Constantine's empire from him. / Ruggiero did not deny their request but accepted the crown and promised to be in Bulgaria three months hence, Fortune permitting. When Leo heard this he encouraged Ruggiero to stand by his word: once he held sway over the Bulgars there would be peace between them and Constantine. / He had, furthermore, no need to hasten his departure from France to take command of his troops, for Leo would see that his father surrendered all the territory he had overrun. As for Bradamant's ambitious mother, she found none of the virtues ascribed to Ruggiero as powerful a motive for cherishing her son-in-law as the title of King by which he was now called. /

The wedding was of suitably regal splendour, for it was the emperor himself who took charge of the preparations—for all the world as if he were marrying off his own daughter. The merits of the damsel (to say nothing of her family's) were such that if he had spent half his kingdom upon her it would not have seemed to him excessive. / He proclaimed open court, where all were welcome in safety; and he conceded the freedom of the lists for nine days to anyone who had a quarrel to settle. He had the fields decked with wreaths and gay flowers, and so brightened them with silks and gold that the world never knew a happier spot. / Paris could not have contained the numberless visitors, rich and poor, of every degree—Greeks and Romans, Goths and Vandals, everyone was there. There was no end to the delegations, to the notables sent from all over the world. They were all most comfortably housed in pavilions, tents, and arbours. / The previous night Melissa the sorceress had made ready the nuptial chamber, adorned with unique excellence. How long had the prophetess awaited this moment, how long had she looked forward to this union, foreseeing the fruit which their plant was to yield! /

She had placed the fertile bridal bed in the middle of a great capacious pavilion: no more sumptuous, ornate, or delightful tent was ever erected anywhere, in peace or war, before or since. She had brought it from the coast of Thrace—lifting it just as it was sheltering Constantine during a visit to the sea-side. / Melissa had the pavilion wafted to Paris from Constantinople by demon-bearers. She did it with Leo's consent, or rather so as to impress him with a display of her consummate skill which could bridle the worm of hell and make him do her bidding (with all the rest of the wicked tribe of rebel-angels). / She lifted it in full daylight from over Constantine, sovereign of Greece, together with its guy-ropes, tent-pole, and every fitting within and without. She had it borne through the air to make of it an ornate chamber for Ruggiero. Then, when the nuptials were done, she miraculously returned it whence it came. /

The gorgeous pavilion was embroidered almost two thousand years earlier. A Trojan damsel with a prophetic gift, named Cassandra, had devoted long vigils to making it all with her own hand. It was a splendid gift from her to Hector, her illustrious brother. / Using various silks and thread of gold she had gaily embroidered the cloth with her own hand, portraying upon it the most gallant knight who was ever to issue from her brother's stock, even though she knew that he was to be several branches removed from the stem. While he lived, Hector treasured the gift, partly for its fine workmanship, partly because it was his sister who had made it. / But when he was treacherously done to death and the Trojans suffered at the hands of the Greeks—false Sinon having opened the gates to them—and worse befell them than was ever recorded, the pavilion passed by lot to Menelaus. He took it with him to Egypt where he ceded it to King Proteus in exchange for his wife whom that tyrant had stolen from him. / Helen was the woman's name on whose account he gave the pavilion to Proteus. It passed from one Ptolemy to the next until it was bequeathed to Cleopatra, from whom Agrippa's troops seized it along with other spoils at sea off Leucas. So it came into the hands of Augustus and Tiberius and remained in Rome until Constantine's day— / Constantine, whom fair Italy was to rue as long as the heavens revolved. Constantine, sick of the Tiber, took the precious tent to Byzantium. Melissa took it from a different Constantine. Its ropes were of gold, its pole of ivory; it was embroidered all over with beautiful figures, better than any from the brush of Apelles. /

Here the Graces, gaily attired, are attending a queen in child-bed. A babe is born, of such beauty the like of which the world has never seen from the First Age to the Fourth. Jupiter, eloquent Mercury, Venus, and Mars are there: with a generous hand they scatter over him celestial flowers, sweet ambrosia and heavenly perfumes. / 'Hippolytus', reads an inscription in minute characters on the swaddling-bands. Grown a little stronger, he is taken in hand by Adventure, while Virtue leads the way. New arrivals are portrayed, wearing long hair and garments: they have come on Corvino's behalf to ask the tender lad's father for him. / Next he is shown taking respectful leave of his father and mother, Ercole and Eleonora, and arriving at the Danube, where the people flock to see him and worship him as a god. Corvino, the wise King of Hungary, admires and honours him for his maturity in his tender childhood years, and praises him above all his barons. / Here the sceptre of Strigonia is being placed in his hand while still in his tenderest youth. The child is portrayed forever at his uncle's side, whether in the palace or the camp—if the powerful king makes expeditions against the Turks or against the Germans, Hippolytus is always beside him, intent on performing noble feats and learning valour. /

Here he is shown spending the best of his early years under a scholar's discipline—Fusco is here to expose to him the hidden meaning in the classics. 'This you must avoid, this pursue if you are to achieve glory and immortality,' he appears to be saying, so well has the artist portrayed their gestures. / Next he is seen as a cardinal sitting in the consistory at the Vatican while still a youth; he reveals his wisdom with a fluency which excites the wonder of the whole assembly. 'What shall he be like when he reaches maturity?' they seem to be asking each other in amazement. 'Oh if ever the mantle of Peter falls to him, what a fortunate, what a holy age it shall be!' /

Elsewhere the illustrious boy is shown at play. Here he confronts bears up in the craggy peaks, here, boars down in the swampy valleys. Here he is riding a jennet which appears to outstrip the wind as he chases a roebuck or veteran deer—which is shown overtaken to be felled at a single stroke, the sword splitting it in two equal halves. / Elsewhere he is depicted in a venerable group of poets and philosophers: he has one of them describing for him the course of the planets, another scrutinizing the earth, another, the heavens. One poet composes mournful elegies, the others, bright idylls or heroic poems or graceful odes. Elsewhere he is listening to sundry musicians; and his dancing is motion at its most graceful. /

The first part of the embroidery depicted the boyhood of the glorious youth. The rest of it was decorated by Cassandra with instances of his prudence, justice, fortitude, and temperance, and of the fifth virtue closely associated with these: munificence. He radiates all these virtues. / This part shows the young man with Lodovico Sforza, unhappy Duke of Milan: during peace he sits with him in council, at war he joins him behind the Viper standards. In good times and bad he is shown of constant loyalty. He follows the duke in his flight, comforts him in adversity, escorts him in danger. / Elsewhere he is seen deeply concerned for the safety of Alfonso and of Ferrara. By a novel contrivance he brings to light the conspiracy plotted against their most just brother by his closest kinsmen and gives him clearest proof of it—thus inheriting the name conferred upon Cicero by Rome, the city he saved. /

Next we see him in shining armour hastening to rescue the Church; with a mutinous handful of troops he confronts a trained army, but his mere presence there affords such help to the priests that the fire is dowsed before it catches. (It might be said of him that he came, he saw, he conquered.) / Elsewhere he is on his native shore fighting against the strongest fleet that the Venetians ever dispatched against the Turks or Greeks. He utterly routs it and presents it, with all the captured booty, to his brother, keeping, as you see, nothing for himself other than the honour—which he cannot give away. /

The ladies and knights scrutinized the embroideries without understanding them, for they had no one to explain to them that they represented what lay in the future; but they took pleasure in admiring the beautifully-wrought faces and in reading the inscriptions. Alone Bradamant rejoiced in secret: instructed by Melissa, she knew their full history. / Although Ruggiero was not as well-versed as Bradamant, he still recalled how frequently Atlas had commended this Hippolytus among his descendants.

Who could recite in full the many courtesies bestowed by Charlemagne upon everyone? There was a constant variety of festive games, and the table was always laden with food. / Here it became evident who were the champion warriors, for each day a thousand lances were broken. Combats were fought, mounted and on foot, some paired off, others in a *mêlée*. Ruggiero showed greater prowess than the rest; he jousted day and night, and always won. In dancing, in wrestling, in everything he always emerged the honoured victor. /

On the final day, at the opening of the solemn festive banquet, while Charlemagne was sitting with Bradamant and Ruggiero on his right and left, a knight in armour appeared out of the landscape, riding full tilt towards the banqueters. Like his steed, the knight was all in black; he was of giant build and arrogant mien. / He was Rodomont, King of Algiers. After the humiliation inflicted on him at his bridge by Bradamant, he had sworn not to wear armour, hold sword or sit saddle until he had spent a year, a month and a day in a cell as a hermit. (Thus knights in those days used to punish themselves for such lapses.) / Although in this interval he heard of all that had happened to Charlemagne and to his own liege, Agramant, so as not to deny his oath, he still would not take up arms, as though none of this concerned him. But once he had seen out the year, the month, and the day, here he came to the French court with new arms, new steed, sword and lance. /

He did not dismount or bow or make any gesture of respect: he displayed only contempt for Charles and his paladins and the mighty lords here present. All were astonished that he took such liberties; they pushed aside their food, broke off their conversations and listened to what the warrior had to say. /

When he stood opposite Charles and Ruggiero he loftily cried out: 'I am Rodomont, King of Sarthia, and I challenge you, Ruggiero, to battle. Before the sun sets I mean to prove to you that you have been disloyal to your liege and that, as a traitor, you deserve no place of honour amid these knights. / Although your treason is transparent because, being a Christian, you cannot deny it, to make it clearer still I have come to prove it in these lists. If anyone here offers to fight for you, I shall accept him; and if one does not suffice, I shall accept half a dozen—to all I shall maintain what I have said to you.' /

At these words Ruggiero stood up and, with Charlemagne's leave, retorted that he lied, as did anyone who called him a traitor. His behaviour towards his liege had always been such that no accusation could rightfully be made against him. He was ready to maintain that he had always done his duty to him. / He was capable of defending his cause, he affirmed, without invoking anybody's help: indeed, he expected to show Rodomont that a single opponent would be as much as—and possibly more than—he could handle. Rinaldo, Orlando, the Marquis Oliver, his sons Grifon the White and Aquilant the Black, Dudone, Marfisa, all rushed to defend Ruggiero against the fierce pagan / on the grounds that a new bridegroom should not upset his honeymoon. To all Ruggiero replied: 'Stop fussing—these excuses are ignoble!'

The armour (once Mandricard the Tartar's) was fetched and all delays were curtailed. Count Orlando fitted Ruggiero's spurs, Charlemagne slung the sword at his side, / Bradamant and Marfisa put on his breastplate and other armour. Astolfo held his thoroughbred, Dudone son of Ogier held his stirrup, Rinaldo, Namo, and Oliver promptly cleared the lists, driving everyone out of the arena kept ever-ready for combats. /

Matrons and maids blanched with fear for Ruggiero, who seemed to them no match for the ferocious pagan. They were like doves driven from the cornfields back to their nests by raging winds in a storm of thunder and lightning, while the inky sky threatens rain and hail to cause havoc among the crops. / The common people and most of the knights and barons read the odds no differently, for they had not yet forgotten what the pagan had done to Paris: all alone he had destroyed a great part of it by fire and the sword—the evidence still remained and would for many a day. Nowhere else did the realm suffer greater damage. /

Bradamant's heart trembled more than any other's, not that she imputed to Rodomont the greater strength or the greater courage; not that she believed that Justice was on the pagan's side (She often commits the honours of battle to her allies). But she could not avoid being afraid, for anxiety is a natural product of love. / Oh how willingly would she have taken that uncertain battle upon herself, even had she been more than certain of losing her life in it! She would have chosen to die any number of deaths (if death may be endured more than once) rather than permit her spouse to run the risk. / But she could find no way of persuading him to leave the combat to her; all she could do was glumly to watch the battle, her heart in her mouth.

Ruggiero and the pagan hurtled towards each other, lances lowered. At the impact the lances seemed to turn into icicles, their shafts into birds which flew into the sky. / The pagan's lance struck Ruggiero's shield full in the middle, but to little effect, so perfect was the steel which Vulcan had tempered for glorious Hector. Ruggiero equally attained the other's shield, but he pierced it through, for all that it was bone, plated inside and out with steel and five inches thick. / Ruggiero's lance could not withstand the heavy impact and failed him at the first assault, breaking into splinters which seemed to wing their way sky-high; were it not for this, it would in its savage onset have pierced the breastplate, even had it been coated with adamant, and the battle would have been over. But the lance broke, and both horses sank back onto their cruppers. /

With bridle and spur the knights forced the steeds back onto their feet; and, tossing aside their lances, they seized their swords and returned to strike each other with cruel savagery. With masterly skill they turned their spirited mounts (aptly light-footed) this way and that as they applied their pointed swords to testing each other's armour for flaws. / Today Rodomont did not have the tough dragon's-hide breastplate on his chest, nor did he have Nembrot's sharp sword nor his usual helmet on his head: when he lost to Bradamant on the bridge, he left his usual arms appended to the shrine-wall, as I believe I related to you earlier. / He had other arms of highest quality but not as perfect as his usual ones—not that either the old nor the present arms, nor even stronger ones would have resisted Balisard, for no enchantment or spell, no steel however choice or finely tempered could withstand it. Ruggiero strove to such good effect that he pierced the pagan's armour in a number of places. /

Now the pagan, seeing his armour bloodied at so many points, and aware that he could not prevent most of the sword-strokes reaching his flesh, was goaded to a greater fury than the sea in a winter storm. He threw away his shield and with all his might brought his sword down two-handed on Ruggiero's helmet. / He put all his weight (and

no weight was heavier) behind his two-handed blow as he struck
Ruggiero: the force of it was similar to that of the pile-driver on twin
pontoons in the Po which, after being raised by men with winches,
drops onto the pointed stakes. The enchanted helmet saved Ruggiero—
without it, the blow would have cleft rider and steed in two. / Twice he
sagged; he slackened his arms and legs to fall. Before he had a chance
to recover the Saracen repeated his savage blow. Then he made to
strike a third time, but the fine sword could not withstand so intense a
hammering—it flew into splinters, leaving the cruel pagan disarmed. /
This did not stop Rodomont, who flung himself on his dazed opponent
while his head was so benumbed, his brain so clouded. The Saracen
shook him awake all right: he threw a powerful arm round his neck and
put him in so tight a clinch as to root him out of the saddle, then
flung him to the ground. /

The moment he hit the ground he was on his feet, more ashamed,
even, than angry, for he glanced at Bradamant and saw the dismay
on her lovely face: his fall had filled her with well-nigh mortal anxiety.
Quickly to amend this disgrace, Ruggiero seized his sword and faced
the pagan. / Rodomont drove his steed at him, but Ruggiero skilfully
avoided him, stepping back, and as he passed, grabbed the horse's
bridle in his left hand and slewed him round, while with his right he
sought to wound the other in the side or the belly or chest. He hurt him
in two places—in the flank and thigh. / Now Rodomont, who still held
the pommel and hilt of his broken sword, struck Ruggiero such a blow
on the helmet that one more would have knocked him senseless. But
Ruggiero, to whom victory justly belonged, grasped him by the arm
and, using both hands, tugged so hard that he finally dragged him from
the saddle. /

Whether it was his strength or his agility, the pagan landed in such a
way as to retain an equal footing with Ruggiero: he landed, that is, on
his feet. Otherwise it was felt that Ruggiero, with his sword, was in the
stronger position. Ruggiero tried to hold off the pagan and avoid a
close grapple: he had no interest in permitting so large and thick-set a
man to fall upon him. / Meanwhile he observed how the Saracen was
bleeding from his side and thigh and other wounds: he hoped that he
would weaken little by little until he had to concede victory. Rodomont,
though, still held the sword-hilt and pommel and, gathering all his
strength, he hurled it at Ruggiero. The impact stunned him worse than
ever— / it struck him on his helmeted cheek and on the shoulder, and
the blow made him reel and stagger and almost collapse. The pagan
now made for him, but his foot betrayed him, weak as he was from his
thigh-wound: trying to move faster than he could, he fell onto one
knee. /

Ruggiero was quick to strike him violently in the chest and face; he hammered him and, clasping him tightly, wrestled him to the ground. With an effort the pagan regained his feet and hugged Ruggiero in a body-clinch. Together they turned and shook and strained, uniting skill with extreme force. / Rodomont, however, had been drained of much of his strength through his opened thigh and flank, while Ruggiero, with his agility, skill, and experience as a wrestler, felt he possessed the advantage and meant to retain it. Where he saw the pagan's blood flowing most freely, where his wounds were the worst he attacked him, using his chest as also both hands and feet. / In a passion of rage, the pagan seized Ruggiero by the neck and shoulders; he tugged and heaved, he levered him off the ground on his chest, he spun him this way and that, clinched him, and strove to make him fall. But Ruggiero remained self-possessed and called upon all his prudence and valour in order to maintain the upper hand. /

After trying several different holds, the doughty champion put a lock on his opponent, heaved his chest over to the left and bent all his might to holding him there; at the same time he advanced his right leg, thrust it between the other's knees and strained: this lifted Rodomont clear of the ground. He flung him down on his head. / Rodomont dented the ground with his head and shoulders; such was the impact that a gush of blood from his wounds spurted high to dye the earth red. To prevent the Saracen from rising again, Ruggiero, who had Fortune by the mane, held a dagger over his eyes with one hand while the other clutched his throat as he knelt on his belly. / In the gold-mines of Hungary or Spain it sometimes happens that the roof suddenly caves in upon the miners lured in by base cupidity, and they are crushed to a point where they can scarcely draw breath; the Saracen, once he was floored, found the victor no less oppressive. /

Ruggiero had drawn his dagger and brandished it over Rodomont's visor as he tried with menaces to make him surrender, offering to spare his life in exchange. But Rodomont, less appalled by death than by the betrayal of the smallest sign of cowardice, jerked and twisted and applied all his strength to rolling on top of Ruggiero: but he answered not a word. / Imagine a mastiff beneath a ferocious wolf-hound which has clamped its teeth on his throat: with blazing eye and frothing mouth the mastiff strives in vain to free himself of the predator's grip, but the latter surpasses him in strength if not in fury. Similarly any thought the pagan had of escaping from beneath victorious Ruggiero proved ineffectual. / He twisted and struggled nonetheless until he brought his right arm back into play; in his hand he clasped a dagger which he too had drawn in the fray, and now he tried to stab Ruggiero beneath his back-plate. The young man realized the trap into which he might fall if he delayed dispatching the impious Saracen; / so two or three times he raised his arm to its full height and plunged the dagger to the hilt in Rodomont's forehead, thus assuring his own safety.

Released from its body, now ice-cold, the angry spirit which, among the living, had been so proud and insolent, fled cursing down to the dismal shores of Acheron.

ANNOTATED INDEX

Absalon, *see* Amnon

Abyed, on Nubia's western frontier, Muslim town on left bank of Nile: 33.100

Acciaiuoli, Jacopo, secretary to Ercole I; **Pier Antonio**, retainer of Alfonso; **Giovan Battista**, secretary to Alfonso; all Florentines: 46.18

Accolti, Francesco, nicknamed the Unique, Aretine poet and lady's man: 46.10

Acheron, one of the rivers of Hades, it could never be recrossed by the dead: 46.140

Achilles, Greek (Thessalian) champion against the Trojans: 26.81, 95; 29.19 invulnerable (except for his heel); 31.56; 33.28; 35.25; 37.20; 42.2

Acorns, Golden, emblem of the Della Rovere Pope, Julius II: 14.4

Acroceraunus, mountain range in Epirus terminating in dangerous sea-cliffs: 21.16

Acteon, huntsman who surprised chaste Diana bathing naked and was changed into a stag: 11.58

Adam: 33.110; 43.8

Adda, tributary of Po, site of disastrous Venetian defeat by Louis XII of France at Ghiara (1509): 17.4; 37.92

Adige, river flowing south of Este, north-east Italy: 41.63

Adoardo, poet from Reggio Emilia, Ariosto's native town: 46.18

Adonio, the Mantuan lover of Argia, in the boatman's tale: 43.71

Adonis, beautiful youth loved by Venus: 7.57

Adria, town east of Rovigo, an Este domain: 3.40

Adrian I, Pope, helped by Charlemagne against Desiderio the Lombard: 33.16

Adrianople, Bulgar capital, near Black Sea: 46.70

Aegeus, King of Athens, father of Theseus: 46.59 Theseus arrived home unrecognized, except by his step-mother Medea, who persuaded Aegeus to poison him as an enemy, but Aegeus at the last moment recognized his son by the sword he used for cutting his meat at table.

Aegistus, Clytemnestra's lover who killed her husband Agamemnon but was killed by Orestes: 21.57

Aeneas, Trojan hero, lover of Dido before leaving her to found Rome: 19.35; 34.14 deserter of Dido; 35.25; 36.6; 43.149

Aeolus, the Wind-god, son of Jupiter: 10.70; 45.112

Aesop, Greek story-teller reputed to have been an ugly hunchback: 43.135

Afranio, Count of Pavia, musician and luminary at Este court: 40.4

Africa (Africans), also known as Barbary; the reference is in practice to the Mediterranean littoral, from the Atlantic to Cyrenaica. (Cf. Egypt, Nubia): 1.1, 6; 2.25; 9.2; 13.83; 14.1; 15.21; 17.76; 18.24, 46; 20.26; 30.12; 32.3; 33.98; 39.20; 40.37

Agamemnon, King of Mycenae, brother of Menelaus, commanded Greeks against Troy: 35.27

Agenor, father of Cadmus who founded Thebes: 43.11

Aglauros, *see* Erichthonius

Agolant, an African king, father of Almont, Trojan and Galaciella (a daughter who married Ruggiero II of Reggio and gave birth to Ruggiero and Marfisa), and invader of Charlemagne's realm in Calabria: 2.32; 12.43; 17.14; 36.72

Agramant, King of Africa, son of Trojan, grandson of Agolant and supreme commander of the Saracen expedition against Charlemagne: 1.1, 6; 2.32; 3.69; 8.69; 11.5; 12.70 calls a muster of troops before last attack on Paris; 13.81; 14.10 musters his troops before Paris; 14.98 prepares to storm Paris; 15.6 attacks one of the gates; 16.17 thwarted by Rinaldo's reinforcements; 18.26; 18.40; 18.157 in a hard battle thrown back from the walls of Paris; 24.110 recalls Rodomont and Mandricard to his camp; 25.2; 26.107; 27.33 his champions hurl Christians back inside Paris; 27.40 tries to sort out quarrels among all his champions; 30.19 sorts out precedence of Mandricard's quarrels; 30.70 prizes Ruggiero, slayer of Mandricard, who gives him Brigliador; 31.80 surprised by Rinaldo's night-attack, has to retreat to Arles; 32.3 consolidates position at Arles; 35.66 Bradamant's challenge conveyed to him; 36.25 calls troops into skirmish outside Arles; 36.77 blood-feud against him urged on Ruggiero by Marfisa; 38.5 served by Ruggiero despite blood-feud between their families; 38.37 calls council on hearing of Astolfo's invasion, and decides on duel of champions; 38.85 presides at duel of champions; 39.3 misled into interrupting the duel, leading to rout of Saracens; 39.66 retreats to Africa but fleet attacked by Dudone; 40.5 escapes with Sobrino from ravaged fleet; 40.36 avoids Bizerta, meets Gradasso and issues challenge to Orlando; 41.36 arrived at Lipadusa, rejects Brandimart's advances; 41.68–42.9 the battle at Lipadusa, is killed by Orlando

Agricalt, African King of Amon: 14.22; 16.81; 40.73

Agrican, King of Tartary, father of Mandricard; to win Angelica's hand he invaded Cathay but was killed by Orlando: 1.80; 8.43, 62; 14.30; 19.32; 23.79; 30.70

Agrigento, south-west Sicily, where Brandimart was buried: 43.166

Agrippa, Octavian's admiral who defeated Antony and Cleopatra off Actium, a Greek promontory near Leucas: 46.83

Agrismont, castle of Buovo: 25.71; 26.55, 90; 30.76 the brothers are Aldiger, Maugis and Vivian; 30.91

Aiguesmortes, French Mediterranean port: 2.63; 27.128; 28.92; 39.25

Alamanni, Luigi, Florentine poet, he conveyed to Ariosto Machiavelli's congratulations on first edition of the *Orlando*: 37.8

Alard, Rinaldo and Bradamant's eldest brother: 23.22; 30.94; 31.10, 35, 51

Albany, Scottish duchy, first Polynex's, later Ariodant's: 5.7; 6.15; 10.86; 16.55

Albertazzo I d'Este, vassal of Otto I: 3.26

Albertazzo II d'Este, here alleged to have married Countess Matilda, granddaughter of Emperor Henry I: 3.29

Alberto d'Este, (1) Uberto's successor, probably legendary: 3.25

Alberto d'Este, (2) Niccolò II's successor: 3.40

Alberto Cestarelli, cleric in Hippolytus' service: 40.4

Albion, name of England because of white (*albus*) cliffs of Dover: 9.16

Albracca, fortress in Cathay in which Angelica locked herself to avoid the suit of King Agrican of Tartary; all the princes who sought her hand repaired thither to dazzle her with their feats: 1.75, 80; 11.3; 27.72; 38.20

Albret, Duke of, serving with Charlemagne: 18.179

Alcabrun, Scottish chief: 10.85

Alcestes, Thracian champion who died from ill-treatment by Princess Lydia: 34.16

Alcina, sorceress, sister of Morgana and Logistilla, ensnares Astolfo, then Ruggiero on her island until Melissa destroys her charms: 6.35–8.16; 10.36; 10.48 her pursuit of Ruggiero thwarted; 10.70 her quarrel with Logistilla; 10.108; 12.21; 13.46; 15.10

Alda of Saxony, daughter of Otto I, wife of Albertazzo I of Este: 3.27; 13.73

Aldiger of Clairmont, bastard son of Buovo, half-brother of Maugis and Vivian, raises alarm on their behalf and guides rescue party: 25.4, 72, 94; 26.3, 68, 75; 31.35, 55

Aldobrandino d'Este, (1) to help Innocent III against Otto IV he raised a large sum from Florentine bankers, leaving his brother Azzo as a pledge; he wrested his city of Ancona back from the Celanos but they had him poisoned: 3.35

Aldobrandino d'Este, (2) son of Obizzo III: 3.40

Aleria, favourite wife of Guidone Selvaggio, escapes with him to France: 20.74, 80, 95, 102; 31.8

Alessandria, Piedmont, where the Viscontis defeated the Florentines and French mercenaries under Count of Armagnac: 33.21

Alexander the Great: 7.59; 19.74 faced with disentangling a knot of rope with no observable ends, he sliced it through with his sword; 26.47; 37.20

Alexandra, daughter of Queen Orontea, beloved of Elbanio: 20.37

Alexandretta, Levantine sea-port near Syrian–Turkish border: 18.74; 19.54 site of the city of warrior-women from whom Marfisa, Astolfo, Guidone and their party barely escape; 22.5

Alfonso of Aragon, King of Sicily, drove René d'Anjou off throne of Naples: 33.23

Alfonso d'Avalos, Marquis of Pescara, *see* Avalos, d'

Alfonso d'Avalos, Marquis of Vasto, *see* Avalos, d'

Alfonso, King of Biscay, the one Spanish king to remain a Christian: 24.25

Alfonso d'Este, son of Ercole I and Eleonora of Aragon, father of Ercole II, brother of Hippolytus and Ariosto's patron: 3.50, 58; 3.60 the two Estes not named here were two brothers, Ferrante and Giulio, who conspired to kill Alfonso in a vendetta but were caught out by Hippolytus; 7.62; 14.2; 25.14; 33.40; 40.41 refers to his participation in the League of Cambrai against the Venetians, then his alliance with the French against the Holy League of Julius II and subsequent popes; 41.67; 42.3 at the recapture of La Bastia, where Alfonso was stunned by a fragment from the battlements; 43.59; 46.95 see this heading, above, under 3.60

Alfonso and **Alfonsino d'Este,** two bastard sons of Alfonso by Laura Dianti: 3.59

Algarve, Portuguese troops led by Grandonio: 14.12

Algaziers, the, African people whose king was Bucifar: 38.35; 39.19

Algiers, ruled by Rodomont: 14.25; 17.11; 28.92; 29.39; 33.99; 39.31

Almansillans, a Numidian tribe led by Caico: 14.23

Almeria, Spanish Mediterranean city, normally ruled by Follicon: 14.16; 16.67

Almon, Scotsman, retainer of Zerbin: 13.22; 24.19, 45

Almont, son of Agolant the African king, he instigated his father's invasion of Charlemagne's province of Calabria; Orlando killed him in Aspromont and took his helmet and sword Durindana; with his brother Trojan he killed Ruggiero's father and tried to kill his mother: 1.28; 8.91; 12.31; 14.43; 17.14; 18.49; 20.5; 24.49; 27.54; 32.5; 36.60, 72; 38.5

Alpheus, physician and astrologer at Charlemagne's court: 18.174

Alps, the: 14.6; 24.54; 26.44 alludes to vengeance for French defeat by Austrians at Novara (1513); 27.101

Altaripa, a castle of Count Anselm of the Maganza clan, near Ponthieu in France: 2.58; 22.47; 23.3, 44

Alteo, Saracen killed by Lurcanio: 18.54

Alvaracks, or the Fortunate Isles, supposedly the Canaries: 14.27; 15.74

Alvito, Mario da, learned historian, secretary to Isabella d'Este: 46.14

Alzirdo, King of Tremisen, killed by Orlando as he leads his troops against Paris: 12.69, 74; 14.29; 23.71; 38.49

Amanio, Niccolò, man of learning and of letters, friend of Bandello the *novelliere*: 46.16

Amaryllis, shepherdess beloved by Tityrus, in Virgil's *Eclogues*: 11.12

Amazons, legendary tribe of warrior-women, fierce fighters ruled by Hippolyta: 7.6; 19.71; 27.52

Ambalde, a Parisian: 14.125

Ambra and Ticino, tributaries of Po, rivers forming Lombard plain: 33.13; 37.92

Amirante, Spaniard in Marsilius' court: 14.16

Ammon, god identified with Jupiter, worshipped in Libya and Egypt: 29.59; 33.100

Amnon, son of King David and brother of Tamar, he violated her then had her banished, but his brother Absalon avenged her, taking his life: 34.14

Amon, south of Cyrenaica, site of temple of Jupiter: 14.22

Amostant, Saracen slain by Orlando: 8.85

Amphrysus, river in Thessaly, where Apollo was condemned to herd King Admetus' flocks: 42.88

Analard, Count of Barcelona: 14.16

Anatolia, Asia Minor: 22.6

Anaxaretes, damsel turned to stone for ingratitude to lover: 34.12

Anchises, father of Aeneas, escaped with son from Troy and was buried at Trapani, Sicily: 43.149

Ancona: 3.31, 37; 42.91

Andria, in the domain of Bari: 3.39

Andronica, symbol of Fortitude, lady attendant on Logistilla: 10.52; 15.11, 18

Androphilos, Leo's uncle: 45.11

Andropono, Greek priest in French army; Ariosto carelessly kills him twice: 14.124; 18.177

Angelica, daughter of Galafron, Emperor of Cathay, sister of Argalia; a ravishing beauty, she is sent to Charlemagne's court to destroy it, captivating Orlando, Rinaldo, Maugis, as also many Saracen princes: 1.5; 1.7 sequestrated by Charlemagne; 1.10 escapes from Namo, flees from Rinaldo and Ferrau; 1.33 reveals herself to Sacripant; 1.77 her hatred of Rinaldo explained; 2.11 eludes her lovers and meets a hermit; 8.30 endures the hermit, then is seized by the pirates of Ebuda and offered as sacrifice to the orc; 9.3; 10.92–11.12 rescued from orc by Ruggiero but has to elude his subsequent advances; 11.76; 12.3 Atlas borrows her features to lure Orlando into enchanted palace; 12.23 visits enchanted palace and with her ring releases Orlando, Ferrau and Sacripant, then eludes their pursuit, and breaks up fight between Orlando and Ferrau by stealing Orlando's helmet; 19.17 happens on wounded Medor, heals him but falls enamoured of him and marries him; 19.40 sets out with him for Spain; 22.25; 23.102 her love for Medor discovered by Orlando; 24.48; 27.8; 29.58 narrow escape from mad Orlando on beach in Tarragona; 30.16 returns to Cathay; 39.61 Orlando cured of her; 42.29 pursued by Rinaldo who is soon cured of her

Angeliero of Gascony, a champion of Charlemagne: 16.17; 18.10

Angelino of Bordeaux and **Angelino of Bellande,** paladins: 15.8; 16.17; 18.10

Angiaro, friend of Ariosto at the Este court, identity disputed: 46.18

Anglant, title of Orlando's father, Milo, and, by extension, Orlando's own: 1.57; 11.61; 12.49, 66; 27.11

Angus, fief of Lurcanio: 10.86

Anne of Aragon, daughter of Ferdinand I of Aragon, wife of Alfonso d'Avalos, Marquis of Vasto: 46.9

Anne of Brittany, wife of Louis XII of France: 13.72

Anjous, three: Louis III, Duke of Calabria, King of Naples for ten years; René his brother, king for seven years until deposed by Alfonso of Aragon; René's son John, pretender to the throne: 33.23

Annibal Collenuccio, courtier of Hippolytus: 40.4

Anselm, (1) of Altaripa, Count of Maganza, father of Pinabello : 2.58; 22.47; 23.4, 45, 57; 46.67

Anselm, (2) of Flanders: 14.123

Anselm, (3) of Stanford, killed by Dardinel: 18.47

Anselmo, Mantuan judge, husband of Argia, in boatman's tale: 43.72

Antenor, Trojan sage who escaped during the sack of Troy and took refuge in the Euganean Hills, west of Venice: 41.63

Anteus, a giant, son of Neptune and Ge, the Earth-goddess, he could not be overthrown while his feet touched mother-earth; Hercules beat him by lifting him clear and throttling him: 9.77; 18.24; 23.85

Antioch, Syrian city, home of Martano, Orrigilla's lover: 15.102; 16.5; 17.60, 86, 124; 18.71, 76

Antony, Mark, Roman Triumvir: 3.33; 15.33

Anubis, Egyptian jackal-headed god, son of Isis and Osiris, worshipped at Canopus: 15.58

Apelles, famous Greek painter in age of Alexander the Great: 28.4; 33.1; 46.84

Apennines, the: 3.37; 4.11; 14.99; 43.149

Apollo (Phoebus), the Sun-god, drives the sun-chariot; also god of poetry:

3.2; 3.34 reference to Ferrara and the Po, into which Phoebus' son Phaeton plunged with the sun-chariot, whereupon Phaeton's sisters' tears evoked tears of amber from the poplars; 8.38; 12.68; 25.44; 26.50; 27.102; 32.11; 33.29; 34.12; 37.12; 42.88

Apollodorus, ancient Athenian painter, said to have invented the paint-brush: 33.1

Apulia, province on the Adriatic: 3.47; 7.4; 15.34; 20.21; 33.35 French defeat by Spaniards at Cerignola

Aquilant the Black, twin brother of Grifon the White, sons of Oliver: 15.67 battles with robber Orrilo then leaves for Jerusalem with Astolfo; 18.70 surprises Orrigilla and Martano and sees to Grifon's revenge; 18.116 joins forces with Astolfo, Samsonet and Marfisa and sails for West, but runs into storm; 19.43 driven ashore in land of killer-women, Alexandretta; 20.69 escapes with his friends; 20.102 captured by Pinabello and made to serve as his champion for a year and a month; 22.48, 85 jousts with Ruggiero but is floored by magic shield; 30.40; 31.37; 31.51 joins Rinaldo's relief expedition; 38.21, 58; 39.18 attacks Saracens; 46.108

Aquilo, the North Wind: 8.81

Aquitania, South-western France: 10.66; 14.3

Arabia, Arabs: 9.5; 14.92; 15.22; 38.44; 40.39, 50

Arabia Felix, Northern Arabia: 15.39

Arachne, who was taught weaving by the goddess Pallas Athene but, getting above herself, had her handiwork turned into a spider's web: 7.23

Aragon, Spanish dynasty ruling in Naples: 13.68; 14.5 refers to the house of Ferdinand from which Emperor Charles V stemmed; 15.23; 27.51

Aragon, Louis of, Cardinal, cousin of Alfonso d'Este: 26.49

Arbante, son of King Cimosco of Frisia, briefly husband to reluctant Olympia: 9.25

Archidant, Spanish Count of Saguntum: 14.16

Archites, disciple of Pythagoras: 14.88

Arcturus, the northern star: 31.26 lazy because it shines while men sleep

Ardennes, forest between the Meuse and the Rhine, location of springs of Love and Hate: 1.78; 22.7; 27.101; 42.45

Arelio, Muzio, or Giovanni Muzzarelli, Mantuan man of letters at court of Leo X: 42.87

Arethusa, nymph transformed into a spring as she escaped her suitor, the river Alpheus; by a subterranean course she came out on the island of Ortigia in Syracuse harbour, where her waters and Alpheus' mixed: 6.19

Aretino, Pietro, Venetian comic playwright whose scabrous pen gave him an exaggerated influence over men of eminence in his day, hence his self-appropriated nickname 'Scourge of princes': 46.14

Argalia, Angelica's brother, came with her to use his enchanted weapons against Charlemagne, but was killed by Saracen Ferrau: 1.25; 8.17, 42; 11.4; 12.31; 15.41; 23.15

Argalifa, King of the Libyans of Libicana: 14.18

Arganio, King of Libya in place of Dudrinas: 14.18

Argenta, an Este domain some twenty miles from Ferrara: 3.41; 43.145

Argeus, husband and victim of Gabrina: 21.14

Argia, (1) daughter of Adrastus, wife of Polynices who died at Thebes fighting his brother Eteocles; captured while trying to bury him despite

Creon's ban, and though rescued by Theseus, bewept her spouse all her remaining days: 37.19

Argia, (2) wife of Mantuan judge, in boatman's tale: 43.72

Argilon of Melibea, knight killed by Guidone: 20.7, 61

Argo, ship of the Argonauts who, piloted by Tiphys, sailed to Colchis to capture the Golden Fleece: 13.61; 15.21; 37.36

Argos, renowned for cruelty because of Danaos' daughters who killed their husbands: 5.4

Argosto, deceased King of Marmonda: 14.18

Argus, legendary prince with a hundred eyes, fifty always open, whom Juno appointed to keep watch on Io (*q.v.*): 14.107; 32.83

Ariodant, Italian knight at court of Scotland, brother of Lurcanio and lover of Guinevere; Ariosto's invention: 5.16–6.15; 10.86; 16.55, 64, 78; 18.56, 155

Ariosto, Ludovico, wry allusions to himself by the poet: 1.2; 2.1; 3.3, 56; 9.2; 14.108; 16.1; 22.2; 24.3, 66; 27.123; 28.2, 102; 29.2; 30.1; 35.1; 40.3 his mission to Pope Julius II; 40.4 his three kinsmen may have been his cousin Alfonso and his brothers Alessandro and Carlo; 42.95 unnamed pedestal-man praising his beloved Alessandra; 46.1

Arles, in Provence, on the Rhône, whither the Africans retreat after their defeat outside Paris, and whence they are driven back to Africa: 12.71; 27.101 refers to the Mediterranean coast; 31.83; 32.3; 35.62; 37.121; 39.72; 40.46

Armagnac, Count Jean d', hired by the Florentines to fight Gian Galeazzo Visconti, his attempt to take Alessandria failed, he was caught in a trap and killed: 33.21

Armellina, mother of Dudone and sister of Beatrice, which made her Bradamant's aunt: 40.80

Armenia: 17.82; 18.128; 22.5; 34.20 King of Armenia in Lydia's tale; 40.39

Arnold of Toulouse: 14.125

Arnulph, Rhenish duke: 14.122

Arria, wife of Cecina Paetus, a conspirator against Emperor Claudius; on his condemnation, she stabbed herself mortally then gave him the dagger to do likewise: 37.19

Artalic, Saracen soldier: 16.65

Artemia, warrior-woman of Alexandretta: 20.54

Artemisia, Queen of Caria, who built the Mausoleum, one of the Seven Wonders of the World, to entomb her deceased husband Mausolus: 37.18

Arthur, King, instituted the Round Table: 4.52; 26.39; 33.8; 43.28

Arundel, Earl of: 10.80

Arzilla, Moroccan city south of Tangiers, ruled by Bambirago: 14.23; 25.32; 33.98

Ascanius, lake in Phrygia, Asia Minor: 41.63

Ascra, river in Boeotia, Greece, associated with poet Hesiod who is said to have achieved poetic inspiration by drinking its waters: 46.12

Aspromont, in Calabria, where King Agolant of Africa invaded Charlemagne's realm; much of the traditional Carolingian epic centres on the war in Aspromont: 1.30; 12.43; 17.14; 27.54

Assuan, in Southern Egypt: 29.59

Astolfo, an English paladin, son of King Otho of England, cousin of Orlando and Rinaldo: 6.33 transformed into a myrtle by Alcina, warns Ruggiero against her; 7.17; 8.16 released by Melissa; 10.64 reaches Logistilla's; 11.4; 15.10 his adventures with Caligorant and Orrilo, Grifon and Aquilant; 18.70 goes to Damascus with Samsonet and Marfisa, then sails for West and runs into storm; 19.43 driven ashore on land of killer-women, Alexandretta; 20.65 uses magic horn to effect his party's escape from killer-women, but is himself left behind; 22.4 returns to France, liberates Atlas' captives with his book and horn, and takes hippogryph; 23.9 entrusts Rabican and magic lance to Bradamant, then flies away on hippogryph; 33.96 his aerial voyage to Nubia, kingdom of Senapo; 33.119 drives harpies back to hell; 34.3 penetrates hell and hears Lydia's tale; 34.48 flies up to Earthly Paradise and meets Saint John; 34.68 by chariot to the moon with Saint John, where he collects Orlando's lost wits; 35.3 still on moon; 38.23 recruits Nubian army and invades Agramant's kingdom; 39.19 besieges Bizerta; 39.38 captures Orlando and restores his wits; 40.9 leads storming of Bizerta; 41.34; 43.154 learns of Brandimart's death; 44.18 dismisses Nubian allies, returns to France, dismisses hippogryph; 45.66 his vanity; 46.110

Astolfo, King of the Lombards defeated by Pepin: 28.4 in the tale told to Rodomont; 33.16 his successor was Desiderio

Astorga, or Asturia, in Northern Spain, belonging, with Salamanca, Placencia, Palencia, Zamora and Avila to old kingdom of Leon, west of Old Castille: 14.14

Astrea, goddess of Justice: 3.51; 15.25

Astyanax, son of Hector, rescued from burning Troy, forefather of Este line: 36.70

Ateste, ancient name of Este, northern Italy; Phrygian because founded by Trojan Antenor: 41.63

Athena, see Pallas

Athens: 40.1 Athens' goddess, Pallas, had an owl for her symbol

Athol, Earl of: 10.85; 18.51

Atlas, sorcerer who brought up Ruggiero and the infant Marfisa, and, knowing Ruggiero vowed to an early death by treachery, endeavours to keep him out of harm's way: 2.37 his abductions to his castle, riding a hippogryph; 2.47 he fights Ruggiero and Gradasso; 4.4; 4.16 worsted by Bradamant; 7.39; 7.43 has put Ruggiero under Alcina's spell; 11.16 disguises himself as Bradamant to lure Ruggiero into his enchanted palace; 12.4 disguises himself as Angelica to lure Orlando into his enchanted palace, but is thwarted by Angelica herself, whose magic ring is proof against all spells; 13.49 Melissa warns Bradamant against him; 20.111; 22.17 his palace destroyed by Astolfo whom he has lured there; 22.22 routed; 23.9; 24.55; 27.14; 36.59 his spirit tells Ruggiero and Marfisa of their kinship

Atlas mountains, North-west Africa: 33.100; 38.31; 44.23

Attila, who led the Huns to conquer Rome: 17.3; 43.32

Atys, youth beloved by the goddess Cybele, Saturn's wife: 7.57

Aude, sister of Oliver, betrothed to Orlando: 38.59

Augustus (Octavius, then Octavian), the emperor, patron of Virgil: 3.18, 56; 15.24, 33; 35.22, 26; 46.83

Aurora, or Dawn, young wife of ancient Tithonus: 10.20; 11.32; 12.68; 13.43; 15.57; 18.103; 23.52; 30.44; 32.13; 34.61; 38.76; 40.14; 43.54

Auster, the South Wind: 8.81; 38.29; 45.112

Autharis, Lombard king who repulsed the Franks under Childebert: 33.13

Avalos, d', illustrious Spanish family at court of Ferdinand I of Aragon, King of Naples: 26.54; 33.24; 33.51 the cousins Alfonso and Francesco

Avalos, Alfonso d', Marquis of Pescara, brother of Inico and father of Francesco del Vasto; while secretly negotiating with a Moor who promised to surrender a citadel, said Moor treacherously killed him: 33.33, 47

Avalos, Alfonso d', Marquis of Vasto, son of Inico and cousin of Francesco, he was one of Charles V' scommanders against the French at the age of twenty-six; he received Ariosto as envoy from Alfonso d'Este and gave the poet a pension; Ariosto gave him one of the first three copies of his poem: 15.28; 26.52; 33.27, 47, 49, 53; 37.13

Avalos, Francesco d', Marquis of Pescara, son of Alfonso of Pescara and husband of Vittoria Colonna, also cousin of Alfonso del Vasto; he was one of Charles V's commanders against the French: 15.28; 26.52; 33.47, 49, 53; 37.20

Avalos, Inico d', Marquis of Vasto, brother of Alfonso of Pescara and father of Alfonso, Marquis of Vasto, he held Ischia for Ferdinand of Aragon against Charles VIII of France: 33.24; 33.27 his son was Alfonso d'Avalos (see above)

Avernus, lake near Naples regarded in *Aeneid* as entrance to Hades: 19.84; 33.4

Avino, Avolio, Otho, and **Berenger**, paladins always listed together: 15.8; 16.17; 17.16; 18.8

Aymon, Duke of Dordogne, married to Beatrice of Bavaria, father of many champions including Rinaldo, Bradamant, and Richardet: 1.12; 2.31; 16.45; 20.6, 65; 30.94; 31.31; 44.12, 35; 45.24, 108; 46.35, 64

Azumara, region of Africa corresponding to Azemmour, South of Casablanca, ruled by Dardinel: 14.27, 48

Azzo d'Este, I Hugo's brother and successor in 969: 3.26

Azzo d'Este, II succeeded in 1039: 3.29

Azzo d'Este, III ruled Verona and Ancona: 3.31

Azzo d'Este, V is in fact VII, defeated Frederick II at Parma in 1243 and killed the tyrant Ezzelino in 1250: 3.32

Azzo d'Este, VI is in fact VIII, brother of Aldobrandino I, married Beatrice, daughter of Charles II of Anjou: 3.37, 39

Babel, where Nembrot built a tower by which to assault God: 14.71, 118; 26.121; 41.30

Baccano, village between Orvieto and Perugia: 28.19

Bacchus, the Roman Wine-god: 28.92; 33.29; 35.21

Bactria, Persia, east of the Caspian :38.57

Bagno, Lodovico da, in Este court, godfather to Ariosto's son Virginio: 40.4

Balastro, African King of Djerba: 14.22; 16.83; 18.45

Balinfron, African King of Mulga, replaces Cardoran as King of Cosca: 14.23, 113

Balinverne, Spaniard, one of Marsilius' leaders: 14.15

Balisard, Ruggiero's enchanted sword, originally made by the sorceress Falerina in order to kill Orlando, who seized it from her only to have it stolen from him by Brunello who gave it to Ruggiero: 7.76; 25.15; 26.21, 105, 126; 27.72; 30.51; 36.55; 38.75; 41.26 found by Orlando in abandoned ship, he keeps it for forthcoming battle; 41.70; 42.11; 44.16 Orlando returns it to Ruggiero; 44.87; 45.68; 46.120

Baliverzo, African king: 14.24; 15.6; 16.75; 40.73

Balugant, a Spaniard, one of Marsilius' leaders, placed in command of the troops from Leon: 14.12, 107; 18.42; 31.81

Bambirago, African King of Arzilla: 14.23; 15.6; 16.75, 81

Barbary, Agramant's North African realm: 18.46; 31.58

Barcelona: 16.60; 19.41; 32.4

Barco, or Park of Ferrara where the besieging Venetians camped: 3.46

Bardelone, Gian Jacobi, Mantuan poet: 42.85

Bardino, faithful servant of King Monodant, he abducted the king's son Brandimart and later had his succession recognized: 39.40, 62; 43.168

Baricondo, King of Majorca: 14.13; 16.67

Barignano, Pietro, poet and academician at court of Leo X: 46.16

Bastia, Este fortress seized by Julius II's Spaniards, who killed Vestidello, its defender, then recaptured, 1513, by Alfonso d'Este: 3.54; 42.4; 43.146

Bath, Bishop of: 10.81

Batold, Brandimart's steed: 31.67

Battus, founder of Cyrene, where he was honoured with splendid tomb: 33.100

Bavarte, Spaniard in Marsilius' court: 14.16

Bayard, Rinaldo's charger, endowed with human intelligence: 1.12 eludes Rinaldo; 1.32, 72; 2.3, 6, 19; 4.53; 5.82; 9.60; 16.43, 84; 18.146; 23.26; 31.14, 53, 90; 31.104 Gradasso fights Rinaldo for him; 33.78; Gradasso makes off with him; 38.74; 41.28, 69; 42.42, 67

Bayona, on the Galician coast south of Vigo: 13.6

Bayonne, South-west France, fief of Bertolai: 25.74

Bear, the Great Bear, figuratively for the North: 3.17; 38.29

Beatrice, mother of Rinaldo, Bradamant and many of Charlemagne's champions, wife of Aymon: 2.31; 23.24; 30.93; 40.80; 44.37; 45.25; 46.72

Beatrice d'Este, daughter of Ercole I, sister of Alfonso and Hippolytus, married to Ludovico Sforza (il Moro): 13.62; 42.91

Beatrice d'Este, daughter of Aldobrandino, wife of Andrew of Hungary: 13.64

Beatrice d'Este, daughter of Azzo VI, became a nun, 13.64 was beatified

Beatrice, 'Mamma', daughter of Niccolò da Correggio, wife of Niccolò Quirico Sanvitale: 46.3

Beelzebub, prince of devils: 9.91

Beletinec, north of Zagreb: 45.11

Belgrade, at the junction of the Sava with the Danube: 44.78

Bellamarina, North African region adjacent to Morocco: 14.25

Bellini, Giovanni, praised by Ariosto among the greatest contemporary painters, patronized by Alfonso d'Este: 33.2

Bellona, Roman War-goddess: 26.24

Belvedere, Ferrara's pleasure-garden island in Po, celebrated by Celio Calcagnini: 43.56

Bembo, Pietro, Venetian man of letters, secretary to Leo X, close friend of Ariosto and supervisor of his son Virginio's studies at Padua; author of *Gli Asolani*: 37.8; 42.86; 46.15

Bendidei, Timothy, Ferrarese poet and courtier: 42.92

Benedetto Accolti, nephew of Francesco Accolti, he was Cardinal of Ravenna and secretary to Clement VII: 46.11

Benedict, Saint, founder of Western monasticism: 14.88

Benevento, Grimoald, Duke of, defeater of Clovis the Frank: 33.14

Bentivoglio, ruling family of Bologna: 46.7

Bentivoglio, Ercole, Ferrarese poet, nephew of Alfonso I, friend of Ariosto, wrote six satires: 37.12

Bentivoglio, Lucretia, bastard daughter of Ercole d'Este, wife of Annibale Bentivoglio of Bologna: 42.88

Berengarius, father and son of same name; the father, constantly fighting for his Lombard throne, was killed in 924; the son, after defeating Hugh of Arles and his son Lothair, was deposed by Otto I in 964 and imprisoned in Bamberg, Saxony: 3.26; 33.19

Berkeley, Marquis of: 10.80

Bernard, *see* Bibbiena

Berni, Francesco, Florentine poet and satirist who rewrote Boiardo's *Orlando Innamorato* in pure Tuscan Italian; he was a canon of Florence cathedral and secretary to Cardinal di Bibbiena: 46.12

Bertolai of Bayonne, of the Maganza clan, traditionally feuding with the house of Clairmont; he tried to acquire the captive Vivian and Maugis from Ferrau's mother: 25.74, 94; 26.12, 69; 30.91

Bertold of Este, defeated troops of Emperor Henry II; 3.29

Bertram, brother of Ruggiero II of Reggio, betrayed the city to the Africans under Agolant, with result that Ruggiero II and his wife Galaciella, parents of the hero Ruggiero, died: 36.73; 38.14

Berwick on Tweed, Rinaldo's port for Scotland: 4.53; 8..25

Bevazano, Agostino, Venetian man of letters, friend of Bembo: 46.15

Bianca Maria of Catalonia, daughter of Alfonso of Aragon, wife of Leonello d'Este: 13.73

Bianchardin, Spanish, commander of the Asturians: 14.14

Bibbiena, Bernard Divizi di, Cardinal, private secretary to Leo X, eminent man of letters: 26.48

Bicocca, La, outside Milan, where Alfonso and Francesco d'Avalos and Prospero Colonna beat the French and Swiss under Lautrec: 33.49

Bireno, Duke of Zeeland, married Olympia, then abandoned her on desert island; Ariosto's invention: 9.22–10.32; 11.56, 63, 76

Biscay, refers to a Spanish port on Bay of Biscay as well as to the Bay itself: 9.23, 38; 33.97

Bithynia, region east of Hellespont: 22.6

Bizerta in Tunis, Agramant's capital: 18.158; 33.99; 38.25; 39.21, 42; 40.9; 43.153

Blaye at mouth of Gironde, here stands for Biscay coast: 27.101

Blosio Palladio, from Sabina, Latinist at papal court, secretary to Clement VII and Paul III: 46.13

Bochus, King of Mauretania (who betrayed his son-in-law Jugurtha to the Romans): 32.63

Bogio da Vergalle, killed by Dardinel: 18.53

Bolga, unidentified region of Africa: 14.24

Bologna, Louis XII wrests this from the Bentivoglios and gives it to Pope Julius II, then restores it to the Bentivoglios: 33.37, 39; 42.88

Bondeno, close to Stellata, where the Panaro joins the Po: 43.54

Bone, Algerian port, formerly Hippo: 33.99

Bordeaux, where Charlemagne was defeated: 3.75; 8.73

Boreas, the North Wind: 5.57; 45.112

Borgia, Angela, relative of Lucretia and in her suite, she influenced rivalry between brothers Hippolytus and Giulio d'Este which led to abortive plot against Alfonso and Hippolytus: 46.4

Borgia, Cesare, son of Pope Alexander VI, recaptured lost papal dominions with French help: 33.37

Borgia, Lucretia, daughter of Pope Alexander VI, wife of Alfonso d'Este, mother of Ercole II and highly praised by Ariosto: 13.69; 42.83; 42.93 unnamed statues next to Lucretia Borgia's are, probably, of Ariosto's beloved Alessandra Benucci and, certainly, of the poet himself

Borso d'Este, first duke, succeeded his brother Leonello in 1450: 3.45; 41.67

Bougie, Algerian sea-port city, ruled by King Branzardo: 33.99

Bourbon, Charles de, viceroy to Francis I in Milan: 33.44

Bozolo, on the left bank of Oglio; its lord was Federico Gonzaga, his wife was Giovanna di Lodovico Orsini, his mother Antonia del Balzo: 46.7

Brabant, region round Brussels: 22.7

Bradamant of Clairmont, daughter of Aymon and Beatrice and sister of Rinaldo, destined to marry Ruggiero and give birth to the Este line; a Christian warrior-damsel: 1.60 overthrows Sacripant; 2.30 meets Pinabello who tricks her; 3.4 in Merlin's cave Melissa reveals her glorious posterity; 4.3 guided to Atlas' castle by Brunello; 4.15 defeats Atlas, frees Ruggiero only to lose him at once; 7.34 gives magic ring to Melissa to rescue Ruggiero from Alcina; 10.72, 108; 11.2; 11.19 Atlas borrows her shape to lure Ruggiero into his enchanted palace; 12.17 sought there by Ruggiero; 13.44 Melissa directs her to Ruggiero in Atlas' palace, where she is imprisoned; 20.102; 22.20 released by Astolfo; 22.30; 22.31 reunited with Ruggiero, she meets and pursues Pinabello to death, losing Ruggiero again in the process; 23.2 meets Astolfo and at his request takes Rabican home to Montauban; 23.25 sends Frontino to Ruggiero by a messenger; 24.55; 25.9 Ruggiero mistakes Richardet for her; 26.2; 30.76 at Montauban pines for Ruggiero's return; 31.6, 78; 32.10 pining for Ruggiero at Montauban, hears news which fills her with jealousy; 32.49 leaves to find Ruggiero at Arles; 32.65 obtains lodging at Tristan's castle by unhorsing three Scandinavian champions; 33.5 the prophetic murals in Tristan's castle explained to her; 33.59 after restless night and after once again unhorsing the Scandinavians, continues towards meeting Ruggiero; 35.31 at Fiordiligi's invitation, unhorses Rodomont on his bridge to release his captives; 35.57 to Arles with Fiordiligi who conveys challenge to Ruggiero; 35.66 floors Serpentine, Grandonio and Ferrau as she waits to fight Ruggiero; 36.11 her abortive fight with Ruggiero in the mêlée outside

Arles; 36.43 fights Marfisa; 36.59 learns from Atlas of Ruggiero's and Marfisa's kinship and is reconciled with both; 37.24 with Ruggiero and Marfisa overthrows misogynist Marganor; 38.7 returns to Charlemagne's standards at Arles; 38.70 distraught over duel of champions; 39.10; 39.67 slaughters Saracens after interruption of duel; 41.63 birth of Ruggiero's son foretold; 42.24; 44.12 promised by Aymon to Greek Prince Leo; 44.35 torn between love and filial duty; 44.68 proposes trial by combat with her suitors; 45.22; 45.66 her vanity; 45.70 fights Ruggiero, taking him for Leo, and loses; 46.35 Leo withdraws his claim; 46.65; 46.73 her wedding to Ruggiero; 46.110 at Ruggiero's duel with Rodomont

Brandimart, Christian knight, a convert of Orlando's and now Orlando's most faithful friend; is also faithful lover of Fiordiligi: 8.86 leaves Paris in Orlando's traces; 12.11 imprisoned by Atlas in his enchanted palace; 22.20 released by Astolfo; 24.54, 55; 27.33 defends Charlemagne outside Paris in absence of other Christian champions; 29.43; 31.46; 31.59 told by Fiordiligi of Orlando's plight, leaves Paris and goes to fight Rodomont; 31.67 defeated by Rodomont but, at Fiordiligi's intercession, imprisoned instead of killed; 35.53; 38.55; 39.30 freed by Astolfo; 39.38 reunited to Fiordiligi, meets Bardino and helps Astolfo restore Orlando's wits; 39.62 invited to succeed to his father Monodant's throne; 40.21 first over wall at storming of Bizerta; 40.58 chosen by Orlando as comrade-in-arms on Lipadusa; 41.25 allotted steed Frontino by Orlando; 41.37 diplomatic mission on Lipadusa to Agramant; 41.68–42.19 the battle at Lipadusa, where he is killed by Gradasso; 43.165 buried at Agrigento by Orlando

Branzardo, King of Bougie, one of Agramant's three lieutenants in Bizerta: 38.35; 39.19; 40.15, 35

Brava, domain of Orlando: 18.99; 27.11; 30.91

Brehus, distinguished in the legends of the Round Table for his spite towards women: 29.30

Brenta, river flowing north of Este, North-east Italy: 41.63

Brescia, north Italian city sacked by French troops of Louis XII: 14.10; 33.39

Briareus, giant with a hundred arms, fought in the titans' rebellion against the gods: 6.66

Brigliador, Orlando's steed: 8.84; 9.60; 11.80; 12.7; 23.26, 115; 24.49; 24.115 seized by Mandricard; 26.125, 132; 30.46, 55; 30.75 falls to Ruggiero who gives him to Agramant; 31.44; 40.8, 57; 41.91

Britain, 'or England, as it was later called': 2.26; 8.28; 18.18; 27.29; 33.7 king is Arthur

Brittany, (Bretons): 9.6, 8, 60; 10.113; 13.72

Brunello, a thief in the service of Agramant who, in exchange for the theft of Angelica's ring, gave him the throne of Tangiers: 3.69; 3.76–4.15 leads Bradamant to Atlas' castle where she robs him of magic ring; 10.108; 11.3; 14.19 at Agramant's muster before Paris, but in disgrace for loss of ring; 18.109 thief of Marfisa's sword; 19.18; 27.72 his thefts at Albracca; 27.86 seized by Marfisa, who takes him away to hang him; 32.7 pardoned by Marfisa but hanged by Agramant; 41.26

Brutus, Marcus, one of Caesar's assassins: 37.19

Buchan, Earl of: 10.86

Bucifar, King of the Algaziers, one of Agramant's three lieutenants in Bizerta: 38.35; 39.21; 40.35

Buckingham, duchy of Godfrey: 10.82

Budrio, or Molinella, where Ercole d'Este was wounded by a bullet while achieving victory for the Venetians, who later invaded his own realm: 3.46

Bulgars, who offer crown to Ruggiero on death of their King Vatran: 44.79; 45.12; 46.48, 69

Buovo, (1) of Agrismont, brother of Aymon, father of Maugis and Vivian, also of Aldiger (out of wedlock): 25.72

Buovo, (2) descendant of Ruggiero I of Reggio, ancestor of Buovo d'Antona from whom sprang the houses of Mongrana and Clairmont: 36.72

Buraldo, African king placed in charge of the Garamants: 14.18, 113

Burgundy, fief of Oliver, father of Grifon and Aquilant: 22.80

Bursia, in Bithynia, east of Hellespont: 22.6

Cadiz: 14.12; 33.98

Cadmus, Phoenician who founded Thebes in Boeotia, killing a serpent and raising an army by sowing its teeth in the ground: 43.97

Caelus, father of Saturn, grandfather of Jupiter: 33.29; 46.5

Caesar, Augustus, symbol of the Empire: 35.22; 43.178

Caesar, Julius: 7.59; 15.33; 26.47; 33.28; 35.22 here refers to Caesar Augustus; 46.6

Cagli, south of Urbino on the Candigliano, tributary of the Metaurus; 43.149

Caico, African King of the Almansillans: 14.23

Cairo, Egyptian capital, visited by Astolfo: 15.61, 90; 33.106

Calabria, the toe of Italy: 3.47; 33.23 Calabria, Apulia, Abruzzi, Lecce, for Kingdom of Naples; 36.71

Calabrun, late King of Aragon, killed by Orlando: 16.60

Calais: 2.27; 8.27; 22.8

Calais and Zetes, Argonauts, sons of Boreas, delivered Phineus from the harpies in Thrace: 34.3

Calandra, Gian Jacobi, Mantuan poet, secretary to the Marchesa di Mantova: 42.85

Calamidor of Barcelona: 16.60

Calaon, feudal domain near Padua granted to Ruggiero's son by Charlemagne: 3.25

Calatrava, city of New Castille: 14.14

Calcagnini, Celio, eminent Ferrarese man of letters and physicist, friend of Ariosto: 42.90; 46.14

Caligorant, robber giant of the Nile whom Astolfo captures: 15.43, 94

Caligula, Roman emperor of evil repute: 3.33; 17.1

Callitrephia, Bradamant's nurse and mother of Hippalca: 23.28

Camaldoli, monastery on Mount Falterona, in the Apennines: 4.11

Cambyses, King of Persia, tried to attack temple of Ammon in African desert but was defeated by sandstorm: 38.43

Camilla, Volscian princess and huntress, she fought with Turnus against Aeneas: 20.1; 25.32; 37.5

Camillo, Julio, from Friuli, wrote verse in Latin and Italian: 46.12

Camillo Paleotti, poet from Bologna: 42.88

Campeggi, Lorenzo, of Bologna, Cardinal and diplomat; Ariosto applied to him for legitimization of his son Virginio: 46.11

Canaries, the, islands off West Africa, whence troops led by Finadurro: 14.22; 18.48

Cancer, constellation of the Crab; here the reference is to the direction of the West Indies: 4.50

Cannae, where Hannibal defeated a Roman army: 17.4

Canopus, Anubis' temple, at the mouth of a western branch of the Nile fifteen miles from Alexandria: 15.58

Cantelmo, Ercole, son of Sigismondo, Duke of Sora, died in assault by Alfonso d'Este against Venetian fort on the Po: 36.6

Capella, Bernardino, Roman poet at court of Leo X: 46.13

Capello, Bernardo, Venetian man of letters, friend of Ariosto and Bembo: 37.8; 46.15

Capilupi, five men of letters from Mantua, close friends of Ariosto: 46.12

Capri, the island retreat of Emperor Tiberius: 43.58

Capricorn, sign of Zodiac for December/January: 14.26; 15.22

Carena, mountains of, the northern ridge of the Atlas: 33.100; 36.62; 41.27

Carpathian channel, between Rhodes and Karpathos: 17.27

Casimir, Spanish soldier: 16.65

Cassandra, Trojan princess, sister of Hector and prophetess, she embroidered nuptial tent: 46.80

Castiglione, Baldessare, Mantuan who lived at court of Urbino, and in service of Clement VII as ambassador to Charles V at Madrid; author of The Courtier: 37.8; 42.87

Castille, region of Spain; Old Castille (capital, Burgos) in the north, New Castille (capital, Toledo) in the centre: 2.63; 12.4; 14.5, 12; 27.51, 55; 33.97

Catalans, troops led by Doriphoebus: 14.11

Catalonian king, who fought a duel with Ercole d'Este, is probably Ferdinand of Aragon: 3.47

Cathay, broadly the extreme Orient bordering on Tartary and Sericana; more specifically, between India and Tartary; Cathay and India often used as synonymous terms; homeland of Angelica: 1.54; 8.72; 10.71; 18.101 Albracca; 19.37

Caucasian Gates, the Dariel Pass in the Caucasus: 8.62

Cavallo, Marco, poet from Ancona, he wrote in Latin: 42.91

Celano, Counts of, at war with Aldobrandino d'Este: 3.36; 13.73 Countess, wife of Azzo VI of Este, whose son Aldobrandino was poisoned by a Count of Celano

Celts, claimed by Livy to have crossed the Alps for the Italian wine: 41.2

Ceres, goddess, daughter of Cybele who resided on Mount Ida, and mother of Proserpina who was abducted to hell by Pluto, god of the Underworld: 12.1; 28.92 Ceres is goddess of the harvest

Ceuta, opposite Gibraltar, ruled by Dorilon: 14.22, 113; 18.48; 30.15

Ceylon: 15.17

Chaldeans, in Babylon: 40.50

Charlemagne, King and Emperor of France and Holy Roman Emperor;

focus of the Carolingian epics: 1.1; 1.7 sequestrates Angelica; 2.24 in Paris prepares for siege and sends Rinaldo to England; 8.22, 70; 8.87 angered at Orlando's furtive departure from Paris; 10.74; 13.12; 14.68 orders prayers to save Paris; 14.103 prepares to resist assault on Paris; 15.8 guards gate against Agramant; 16.17 defends Paris; 17.6 confronts Rodomont; 18.8 drives him out of Paris; 18.97, 155; 18.163 besieges Saracen camp; 23.98; 24.108; 25.5; 27.7; 27.20 his blockade of the Saracen camp lifted by arrival of Saracen champions; 27.33 blockaded in Paris again; 30.28; 31.39 recruits arrive to help him; 31.59 breaks out from Paris in conjunction with Rinaldo's night attack; 32.6; 32.60 Queen of Iceland's demand upon him; 33.16 historically, invaded Italy in 773 to help Pope Adrian I against Desiderio the Lombard, then again in 799 to restore Pope Leo III to throne; 36.71, 79; 38.11 welcomes Marfisa into his service; 38.65 invited by Agramant to settle war by duel, and appoints Rinaldo his champion; 38.79 presides at duel; 39.17 attacks Saracens; 41.64; 42.42; 44.26 welcomes Orlando and his companions, and Astolfo, and Ruggiero; 44.69 agrees to Bradamant's trial by combat with her suitors; 45.22 publishes edict about Bradamant's challenge; 46.73 supervises wedding of Bradamant to Ruggiero; 46.109

Charles V, King of Spain, born in Ghent, son of Philip of Austria and Joan of Aragon, Holy Roman Emperor in 1519: 15.23 predicts his conquests in the East and West Indies and his successes against the French in Italy; 26.34 hunts the allegorical beast

Charles VIII, King of France, son of Louis XI, invaded Italy at Lodovico il Moro's invitation, and conquered all kingdom of Naples except Ischia: 33.24, 31

Charles of Anjou, brother of Louis IX of France, invaded Italy to help Clement IV against the Swabians; beat Manfred at Benevento and Conradin at Tagliacozzo; later his troops were slaughtered in the Sicilian Vespers uprising: 33.20

Charon, ferryman of departed souls across River Styx into the Underworld: 36.65; 42.9

Chelindo and Mosco, bastard sons of King Calabrun of Aragon: 16.60

Chersonnese, Golden, Malacca Peninsula: 15.17

Childebert II, Frankish king, invaded Lombardy at Emperor Maurice's instigation but was stopped by Autharis: 33.15

Chiron, a centaur who, in Dante's *Inferno*, guards the murderers in the river of blood: 13.36

Christ, Jesus: 14.8, 102; 15.92; 17.73; 28.82; 34.58; 35.29; 36.78; 38.81; 41.38, 47; 43.193

Christians, usually as the side in battle opposed to the Saracens: 1.10; 8.69; 13.10; 14.74, 110; 15.64 refers to the Mamelukes; 17.6; 24.110; 27.18; 29.39; 39.81; 40.11; 41.49

Church, Holy, Church of Rome: 3.25, 30, 36; 9.1; 14.71; 15.91; 16.38; 26.45; 33.45; 40.49; 46.96

Cicero, Roman orator and statesman who scotched Catiline's conspiracy against Rome, earning for himself the title *pater patriae*: 46.95

Cilander, son of Marganor, killed while trying to seduce guest's wife: 37.46

Cimmerian Caves, in bleak Scythia, the abode of Sleep: 45.102

Cimosco, King of Frisia, invades Holland to marry his son to Olympia, but is slain by Orlando: 9.25; 11.21

589

Circassia, realm of Sacripant, in the northern Caucasus, bordering the Black Sea: 1.45; 12.27, 51; 19.31

Circe, who kept so many animals, including Ulysses' companions, changed into pigs: 43.58

Cittadini, Girolamo, a Lombard Latin poet who was in Ippolito Sforza's service and lived at Ferrara: 46.14

Clairmont, the family to which Orlando and his cousin Rinaldo belong, their fathers Milo and Aymon being brothers; the clan's traditional enemies are the Maganzas: 2.67; 16.29; 20.5; 23.57; 26.9 Richardet and Aldiger; 36.75; 38.20; 44.29; 46.67

Clarence, Henry, Duke of: 10.78; 16.67

Clarice, sister of Yvon, King of Gascony, wife of Rinaldo: 30.93; 43.66

Clariel, knight killed by Rinaldo: 20.6

Clarindo, African King of Bolga: 14.24, 113; 40.73

Claude of Tours: 14.125

Cleopatra, Queen of Egypt, hostess to Caesar, later to Mark Antony, poisoned herself with an asp on Antony's forsaking her: 7.20; 10.56; 46.83

Clodion, son of Fieramont, King of the Franks, and originator of law prevailing at Tristan's castle: 32.83

Cloridan, African soldier in Dardinel's service, helps Medor try to bury their king's corpse, but is killed; Ariosto's invention: 12.65; 18.165–19.15

Cloris, the goddess Flora, beloved of Zephyr, pursued by Mercury: 15.57

Clotho, one of the three Fates, who spins the human life-thread: 10.56; 33.1

Clovis, Frankish king, confused here with his son Clotharius III who invaded Italy while Grimoald, Duke of Benevento, was otherwise engaged; Grimoald, outnumbered, defeated the Franks by inducing them to get drunk, then slaughtering them: 33.14

Clytemnestra, wife and murderer of Agamemnon: 20.13; 21.57

Cnidus, on coast of Asia Minor, principal shrine of Aphrodite (Venus), with famous statue by Praxiteles: 43.58

Cochin, sea-port north-west of Cape Comorin: 15.17

Cocytus, one of the rivers of Hades: 33.127

Codros, King of Attica, saved Athens from the Dorians by plunging, disguised, into the enemy ranks: 43.174

Colonna, Fabrizio, Roman prince, father of Vittoria Colonna, he fought with the Spaniards against the French at Pavia, where Alfonso d'Este prevented his falling into French hands: 14.5

Colonna, Isabella, daughter of Vespasiano Colonna, wife of Luigi Gonzaga da Gazzolo despite opposition of Pope Clement VII: 37.9; 46.8

Colonna, Prospero, Roman prince, Fabrizio's brother, one of Charles V's commanders against the French: 15.28; 33.49

Colonna, Vittoria, daughter of Roman Prince Fabrizio Colonna, wife of Marquis Francesco d'Avalos of Pescara, she was an eminent poetess and friend of artists including Michelangelo: 37.16; 46.9

Comacchio, Po-delta town, an Este domain: 3.41

Comorin, Cape, Hindustan: 15.17

Compostella in Gallicia, north-west Spain, shrine of Saint James: 19.48

Conrad, German in Charlemagne's army: 18.177

Conradin, tried to recapture his Italian possessions from Charles of Anjou but was defeated at Tagliacozzo, then beheaded: 33.20

Constance, Dacian woman, mother of Guidone Selvaggio by Aymon: 31.31

Constantine, Roman emperor who ill-advisedly gave lands to the Church, thus initiating the Church's Temporal Power, and who transferred his capital from Rome to Constantinople: 17.78; 34.80; 36.71; 46.84

Constantine, Greek emperor who claims Bradamant as wife for his son Leo, and whose war with the Bulgars is thwarted by Ruggiero: 44.12, 79; 45.5; 46.22, 70, 77

Constantine, Tunisian city, ruled by Libanio: 14.21

Constantine, marsh at mouth of Pedia in Cyprus, on site of ancient Salamis: 18.136

Constantinople, seat of Greek emperor: 15.102; 17.75

Constantius Clorus, father of Roman Emperor Constantine: 36.71

Cordova: 14.12; 33.97; 42.4

Coreb of Bilbao, friend of Odoric but loyal to Zerbin: 13.24; 24.19

Corineo, African king, succeeds Balinfron to throne of Mulga: 14.23; 15.7

Corinna, Greek poetess from Boeotia, sixth-century B.C.: 20.1

Correggio, Niccolò da, courtier of Alfonso d'Este, poet, friend of Ariosto: 42.92

Corsica: 27.130; 39.28; 44.24

Cortez, Hernando, conquered Mexico for Spain under Charles V: 15.27

Corvino, Mattia, prince of Hungary, victor against the Turks, husband of Beatrice of Aragon, whose sister was Leonora, wife of Ercole I d'Este; thus he was uncle to Hippolytus whom he summoned to his court: 45.3 refers to his being imprisoned by King Ladislas, but released on the king's death and raised to the throne: 46.86

Cosca, African region not identified, ruled by Balinfron: 14.23, 113

Crassus, M. Licinius, Triumvir with Caesar and Pompey, killed fighting the Parthians, but not before amassing proverbial wealth in the eastern provinces: 38.2

Creon, tyrant of Thebes, who forbade burial to Eteocles and Polynices, his predecessors, and condemned to death the latter's wife and sister for violating his ban: 17.2; 19.12

Crete, (Cretans): 20.14; 33.29

Croesus, King of Lydia, of proverbial wealth until defeated by Cyrus of Persia: 38.2; 45.1

Crotona, in Magna Graecia (Southern Italy), with its temple of Juno: 11.71

Cumaean sibyl, prophetess who lived a thousand years: 7.73; 19.66; 20.120

Curtius, to placate the wrath of the gods, rode into an abyss opened in the Forum in Rome: 43.174

Cyclops, one-eyed giant living in Sicily: 43.185

Cygnus, grieving for his friend Phaeton, he was turned into a swan: 3.34; 29.19 (invulnerable)

Cyllarus and Arion, legendary horses of antiquity, the former a gift of Neptune to Juno, from her to Pollux, and the latter belonging to King Adrastus: 45.93

Cyniphus, Libyan river noted by Virgil for its goats: 31.58

Cynthus, in Delos, mountain birthplace of Apollo and Semele, and sacred to the Muses: 37.9

Cyprus, island sacred to Venus: 17.26, 66; 18.74; 18.136 first port is Famagusta; 19.48 specific shrine uncertain; 20.10; 43.58

Cyrenaica, Cyrene, west of Egypt: 33.100

Daedalus, noted for his technical ingenuity, he invented human flight and contrived the Cretan labyrinth: 25.37

Dalinda, lady-in-waiting to Guinevere the Scottish princess: 4.69; 5.4–6.16

Damascus, capital of Syrian King Norandin: 16.5; 17.17; 18.7, 59

Damietta, in the Nile delta, lair of Orrilo: 15.64, 90

Dammogir, capital of Monodant's kingdom, the Far Islands: 43.163

Danube, river flowing into Black Sea, figuratively as northern limit of the world: 3.17; 20.6; 22.6; 44.78; 46.87

Daphne, nymph who escaped Apollo's pursuit by having her river-god father turn her into a tree: 34.12

Dardinel, son of Almont, commander of the troops from Azumara, killed outside Paris by Rinaldo while defending his emblem, and buried by Medor and Angelica: 12.65; 14.27, 108; 16.54, 83; 18.47, 146, 165

Davalo, *see* Avalos, d'

Dawn, *see* Aurora

Decii, the, Publius Decius Mus (and later his son), in obedience to a dream, rode into the enemy ranks to be cut down in order to secure victory for Rome: 43.174

Delos, Greek island, birthplace of Apollo and Semele: 33.29

Demosthenes, persuasive Greek orator: 17.90

Denis of Tours: 14.125

Derby, Earl of: 10.81

Desiderio, King of the Lombards, Charlemagne's enemy, slain by Ruggiero's son: 3.25

Desmond, Earl of: 10.87

Devil, my Lord's, name of cannon built for Alfonso d'Este: 25.14

Devon, fief of Raymond: 10.81

Diana, the chaste huntress of Antiquity: 1.52; 11.58

Diana: 42.90 *see* Este

Dicilla, symbol of Justice, lady attendant on Logistilla: 10.52

Dictea, Cretan town: 20.14

Dido, Queen of Carthage celebrated by Virgil, who killed herself when Aeneas forsook her: 10.56; 19.35; 35.28; 37.5

Dionysus, tyrant of Syracuse, won several victories against Carthage but was finally killed: 45.1

Discord, fetched by Michael to set the Saracen champions at loggerheads: 14.76; 18.26, 34; 24.114; 26.122; 27.35, 37, 100

Djebel, North Levantine sea-port: 18.74

Djerba, island off Tunisia, ruled by Balastro: 14.22; 18.46, 49; 33.99

Dobaya and Cuoad, towns of uncertain location on Nubian border: 33.101

Domitian, Roman emperor of evil repute: 17.2

Doralice, daughter of Stordilan, King of Granada, betrothed to Rodomont:

14.40; 14.50 seized by Mandricard on her way to her fiancé Rodomont, but soon consents to him; 14.114; 18.28; 23.38; 23.71 witnesses Mandricard's duel with Orlando over the sword Durindana; 24.71 stops duel between Mandricard and Zerbin; 24.95 witnesses duel between Mandricard and Rodomont; 24.110–25.4 stops duel; 26.68 at Merlin's fountain; 26.128 borne off on possessed horse, thus stopping fight at Merlin's fountain; 27.5 borne back to father in Agramant's camp, pursued by lovers; 27.51; 27.102 invited to choose between her lovers, chooses Mandricard; 29.3; 30.17; 30.31 begs Mandricard not to fight Ruggiero; 30.67; 30.71 an inconstant lover

Dorchin, Saracen killed by Lurcanio: 18.54

Dordogne river, range from which it rises is Massif Central: 32.50

Doria, Andrea, Genoese admiral who switched sides from the French to the Spaniards; also famous for his war against pirates: 15.30; 26.51

Doria, Filippino, defeated Charles V's fleet off Naples: 33.57

Doricon, Spaniard in Marsilius' court: 14.16

Dorilon, African King of Ceuta: 14.22, 113

Doriphoebus, King of the Catalans: 14.11

Dorset, Earl of: 10.80

Dossi, Dosso, and **Giambattista**, Ferrarese painters; Dosso painted portrait of Ariosto and of Alfonso and Ercole d'Este, and an illustration from *Orlando Furioso*: 33.2

Dragontina, sorceress who imprisoned Orlando and companions till Angelica freed him with her magic ring, proof against all spells: 11.4

Drusilla, captured by Tanacre, she poisoned herself and him during their wedding: 37.52

Dudone, paladin, son of Ogier the Dane, a saintly giant who fought with a club; 6.41; 39.22 delivered from prison by Astolfo; 39.29 admiral of Astolfo's fleet dispatched to Provence; 39.38 helps Astolfo restore Orlando's wits; 39.64; 39.80 sails for Provence and attacks Agramant's fleet; 40.5 destroys the fleet; 40.70–41.7 landed in France with his prisoners, has to fight Ruggiero and loses to him his prisoner-kings; 42.43; 44.20 dismisses Nubian fleet; 46.60 welcomes Ruggiero to court; 46.110

Dudrinas, deceased King of Libya: 14.19

Durindana, the sword of Orlando, originally Trojan Hector's, passed to Almont from whom Orlando won it in Aspromont: 9.3; 11.50; 12.46, 79; 14.43; 23.60, 78; 24.50 thrown away by Orlando, found by Zerbin; 24.58 Mandricard takes it; 24.61, 106; 26.105; 27.54; 30.19, 41, 51, 61, 66; 30.74 passes to Gradasso; 31.44, 91, 104; 33.78; 40.56; 41.28, 80, 100

Durrance, river flowing into Rhône near Avignon: 20.106

Ebuda, island west of Scotland, assumed to be in Hebrides group, scene of Angelica's and Olympia's sacrifice to the sea-monster: 8.51, 64; 9.11, 58, 91; 10.93; 11.28; 19.39

Edward, Earl of Shrewsbury: 10.82; 16.30, 85; 18.10

Egypt: 15.39, 90; 17.66; 20.26; 33.98, 106; 40.39

Elbanio, knight who captures love of Queen Orontea's daughter Alexandra: 20.36

Eleonora, daughter of Ferdinand of Aragon, King of Naples, wife of Ercole I d'Este, mother of Alfonso, Hippolytus, Beatrice and Isabel: 13.68; 46.85

Eleusinian goddess, Ceres, who was worshipped in Attican town of Eleusis: 12.3

Elias, the Old Testament prophet: 14.88; 34.59; 34.68 borne to heaven in fiery chariot; 38.23

Elizabeth and Leonora: 42.86; 43.148 *see* Gonzaga

Emilia Pia, wife of Antonio da Montefeltro of Urbino, was friend of Bembo and Castiglione: 46.4

Encelades, giant struck by Jupiter's thunderbolt and buried under Etna: 12.1

Endymion, shepherd beloved by the Moon-goddess Selene: 18.185

England (English): 2.26; 6.33; 8.25; 9.16, 93; 10.72; 11.79; 14.66; 16.28, 40; 18.146; 22.7; 27.29; 38.59

Enoch, son of Cain, carried up to God in his lifetime: 34.59

Ercole I d'Este, son of Niccolò III, succeeded Borso in 1471, died in 1505; married to Eleonora of Aragon; father of Hippolytus, the poet's patron, and of Alfonso, the reigning duke: 1.3; 3.46; 26.51; 41.67; 42.88; 46.87

Ercole II d'Este, Duke of Chartres, son of Alfonso d'Este and Lucretia Borgia, married Renée of France: 3.58; 13.71; 26.51; 37.13

Erichthonius, son of Vulcan, whose seed fell on the ground as he tried to make love to Pallas Athena; the child's feet were misformed into serpents; Pallas gave him in a basket to the keeping of Cecrops' daughters of whom one, Aglauros, disobediently looked inside and was turned to stone; Erichthonius made himself a four-horse chariot in which he disguised his nether half: 37.27

Erifilla, symbol of Avarice, worsted by Ruggiero: 6.12–7.7

Eritreans, on the African shore of the Red Sea: 15.12; 17.21

Errol, Earl of: 10.87

Essex, Earl of: 10.79

Este, the ducal house ruling Ferrara, patrons and employers of Ariosto (and later of Tasso): 3.2, 25; 7.60; 13.57; 41.3, 65

Este, Bianca d', daughter of Sigismondo d'Este, wife of Alberigo Sanseverino: 46.4

Este, Diana d', daughter of Sigismondo, cousin of Alfonso and Hippolytus: 42.90; 46.4

Este, Ricciarda d', about whom nothing is known: 46.4

Etearch, Spanish soldier: 16.65

Ethiopia, or Nubia, ruled by Senapo: 11.44; 13.82; 15.19; 15.58 the source of the Nile; 20.5; 33.101 here for Nubians

Etna, Mount: 5.18; 12.1; 40.44; 43.165

Etruscans (Etruria), neighbours and, under Mezentius, allies of the Romans: 17.2; 43.149

Ettinus, the Virgin of, pilgrimage shrine now unidentifiable: 19.48

Eurystheus, King of Mycenae, imposed twelve impossible labours on Hercules in hope of getting rid of him: 34.39

Evadne, wife of Capaneus, one of the seven kings who attacked Thebes; when he was struck by thunderbolt, she chose to die on his funeral pyre: 37.19

Eve, the first woman, the first victim of Satan: 11.22; 27.13; 33.110

Ezzelino da Romano, tyrannized Verona, Treviso and Padua, was killed by Azzo V d'Este: 3.32; 17.3

Faenza, Este domain by purchase: 3.40; 14.9 surrendered to troops of French invader Louis XII rather than be sacked like Ravenna

Falcone, Gini and **Ginami,** of the Maganza clan in the conspiracy against Ruggiero: 46.68

Falerina, sorceress who made the sword Balisard: 25.15; 41.26

Falsiron, brother of Marsilius, father of Ferrau, commander of troops of Old Castille: 14.12, 107; 18.42; 27.49; 31.81

Famagusta, Cypriot port: 18.136

Farnese, Alessandro, Roman man of letters, the future Pope Paul III, great patron of the arts, had the Vatican's Greek manuscripts printed: 46.13

Faro, Messina lighthouse: 33.27

Farurant, African King of Mauretania: 14.21; 16.75; 40.73

Fates, three divinities presiding over human life; Clotho assigned the life-thread, Lachesis spun it, Atropos cut it: 34.89; 37.19; 43.162, 185; 46.9

Fausto, Vittor, successor to Mussuro as professor of Greek at Venice; also Superintendent of the Galleys at the Arsenal: 46.18

Favonius and **Flora,** Roman deities who foster the growth of flowers and orchard crops: 31.85

Fedro, Tommaso Inghiranni, known as, from Volterra, Prefect of Vatican Library: 46.13

Ferdinand, King of Naples, bastard son of Alfonso of Aragon: 33.23

Ferdinand, II of Naples, drives out French: 33.32

Ferrante, Consalvo, of Cordoba, Great Captain of King of Spain, Viceroy of Naples, twice victor over French in Italy: 26.53; 33.35

Ferrante Gonzaga, son of Francesco II and Isabel of Este, brother of Ercole Gonzaga; became Charles V's Viceroy in Sicily: 26.51

Ferrara, domain of the Estes: 26.49 refers to Alfonso; 33.38; 35.6; 42.84; 43.32, 55; 46.95

Ferrau, a Spanish champion, nephew of Marsilius, in love with Angelica, whose brother Argalia he has killed: 1.14 fights Rinaldo; 1.24 reproved by Argalia's ghost; 12.11 imprisoned in Atlas' enchanted palace; 12.29 released by Angelica, who eludes him while he fights Orlando for his helmet; 12.59 Angelica having absconded with the helmet, Ferrau finds and keeps it; 12.48; 14.15 commands Saragossan troops and Marsilius' household guard; 14.107 rearguard in assault on Paris; 16.71 at battle of Paris; 18.42 rallies fugitives before Paris; 19.32; 24.55; 25.75 Maugis and Vivian were his captives; 27.31 to Agramant's rescue outside Paris; 27.49, 69; 27.80 acts as Rodomont's squire in duel with Mandricard; 31.81; 35.74 unhorsed by Bradamant outside Arles; 36.13 alerts Ruggiero that unknown challenger is Bradamant

Ferruffino, Alessandro, captain in service of the Estes, narrowly escaped capture in assault on Venetian fort on Po: 36.6

Fers, in Agramant's African dominions, ruled by King Folvo: 38.35

Fez, south of Tripolitania, ruled by Malabuferso: 14.22; 16.76; 33.99

Fiammetta, protagonist in tale told to Rodomont: 28.52

Fieramont, (1) Duke of York: 10.78; 16.67

Fieramont, (2) King of the Franks, son of Marcomir, first king to cross to left bank of Rhine: 32.83; 33.8

Fieschi, Ottobono and **Sinibaldo,** Genoese brothers: 26.50

Figarolo, island in Po above Ferrara: 43.53

Filippo Beroaldi of Bologna, Vatican Librarian, published first five books of Tacitus: 46.13

Filo, seven miles below Argenta on Po di Primaro: 43.146

Finadurro, African king, leads troops of Canaries and Morocco: 14.22, 113; 18.45

Fiordiligi, faithful lover, then wife, of Brandimart, converted to Christianity by Rinaldo: 8.89 sets out in Brandimart's traces; 24.53; 24.73 witnesses Zerbin's duel with Mandricard for the sword Durindana; 29.43 witnesses Orlando's tussle on bridge with Rodomont; 31.38 tells Rinaldo of Orlando's plight; 31.59 reunited to Brandimart, tells him of Orlando's plight and guides him to Rodomont's bridge; 31.73 persuades Rodomont to spare defeated Brandimart's life; 35.33 persuades Bradamant to defeat Rodomont on his bridge and release his captives; 35.57 to Arles with Bradamant on whose behalf she delivers Frontino and a challenge to Ruggiero; 39.39 recovers Brandimart outside Bizerta; 41.31 prepares Brandimart's attire for battle of champions; 43.154 learns of Brandimart's death; 43.182 builds cell in Brandimart's tomb and there ends her days

Fiordispina, daughter of Spanish King Marsilius, loves Bradamant, mistaking her for a male, but Richardet rectifies error: 22.39; 25.27

Flaminio, Marcantonio, from Treviso, writer of elegant Latin verse: 46.12

Flanders, now Belgium: 9.38, 48; 10.31; 14.123; 18.180; 22.7; 26.27

Florentines: 3.35; 11.74; 26.45

Foix, Gaston of, nephew of Louis XII of France, won battle of Ravenna in 1512 but was killed while pursuing the enemy: 14.6

Folco d'Este, son of Albertazzo and Alda of Saxony, resided in Saxony, leaving the Italian possessions to his brother Hugo: 3.28

Follicon of Almeria, bastard son of Marsilius: 14.16; 16.67 referred to as of Granada

Folvirant, King of Navarre killed by Rinaldo: 14.11

Folvo, King of Fers, one of Agramant's three lieutenants in Bizerta: 38.35; 40.35

Forbes, fief of Herman: 10.87

Fornaci, Le, now Fossone, the southernmost of the Po's mouths: 33.17

Fortunate Isles, *see* Alvaracks

Fossa, La, on Po outside Ferrara, but the tower no longer extant: 43.63

Fracastoro, Girolamo, Veronese poet, physician and astronomer: 46.15

France (French): 1.1; 2.14; 3.49, 55; 8.17; 11.77; 12.4; 13.60; 14.1; 15.92; 17.73; 18.133; 27.29; 33.6 French incursions into Italy rehearsed; 45.3

Francesco Maria della Rovere, Duke of Urbino, nephew of Guidobaldo di Montefeltro and husband of Leonora Gonzaga; Ariosto attended his court in 1507: 43.148

Francesco d'Este, son of Alfonso and of Lucretia Borgia: 3.59

Francis I of France, cousin and son-in-law of Louis XII: 26.34 the Allegorical Beast he hunts is compounded of ignorance, greed, pride and guile; 26.43 his triumph at Melegnano to avenge defeat at Novara; 26.45 the castle is the fortress of Milan; 33.43 avenges defeat at Novara; 33.53 captured at Pavia by Spaniards

Francis: 33.45 *see* Sforza, Francesco

Francolino, estate ten kilometres from Ferrara, on the Po: 15.2

Franconia, now North-west Bavaria: 22.6

Fraud, tells Michael where to find Silence: 14.86

Frederick of Montefeltro, Duke of Urbino, father of Guidobaldo: 26.50; 43.148

Frederick Barbarossa, German emperor thwarted by Rinaldo d'Este in fight with Church: 3.30

Frederick II, German emperor defeated in 1243 by Azzo V d'Este: 3.33

Fregoso, Antonio, poet, courtier of Lodovico il Moro: 46.16

Fregoso, Federigo, Genoese naval commander, friend of Ariosto; he eventually took Holy Orders and became Cardinal Archbishop of Salerno: 42.20; 42.22 his brother Ottaviano, Duke (or Doge) of Genoa

Frisia, Holland north of Rhine, ruled by Cimosco: 9.25, 82; 10.16, 32; 11.79; 18.180

Fronesia, symbol of Prudence, lady attendant on Logistilla: 10.52

Frontalact: 27.71, *and see* Frontino

Frontino, Ruggiero's steed, originally Sacripant's, who called him Frontalact, till Brunello stole him at Albracca and gave him to Ruggiero: 4.46, 48; 23.26 passes to Rodomont; 26.55, 58, 92, 132; 27.16, 70, 113; 28.86; 35.54 recovered by Bradamant; 35.61; 37.97; 41.25 passes to Brandimart; 41.79; 44.16 restored to Ruggiero; 44.77, 101; 45.61, 92; 46.46

Furies, the, three infernal snake-haired monsters who harry mortals who have wrought a crime: 18.125; 21.47, 57; 32.17; 36.54

Fusberta, the sword of Rinaldo: 2.10; 16.49, 82

Fusco, Tommaso, tutor then secretary to Hippolytus of Este: 46.89

Gabes, Tunisian port: 33.99

Gabriele, Trifon, Venetian nobleman, a leading humanist and patron of the arts: 46.15

Gabrina, an evil crone: 12.92; 13.3 guards Isabel for the bandits till Orlando drives her away; 13.42; 20.106 picked up by Marfisa who constrains Zerbin to become the crone's escort; 21.3 the story of her wicked seduction of Philander told to Zerbin; 22.1, 50; 23.39 has Zerbin condemned to death for Pinabello's death; 23.92 her horse's bridle stolen by Mandricard who sends her on her way out of control; 24.36 falls into Zerbin's clutches and is sent off with Odoric for enforced escort; 24.45 hanged by Odoric; 26.8

Gaetulians, nomadic tribe of Libyan hinterland, led by Rimedon: 14.23

Gaibana, tower six miles from Ferrara on the Po di Primaro, no longer extant: 43.63

Galaciella, daughter of the Saracen Agolant, married the Christian Ruggiero II of Reggio, and was abandoned at sea by her brothers Almont and Trojan, and died, but not before giving birth to the champions Ruggiero and Marfisa: 2.32; 36.60, 73

Galafron, Great Khan of Cathay, who sent his son Argalia and daughter Angelica to destroy Charlemagne's realm: 8.43; 12.35; 45.65

Galahad, knight of Round Table: 4.52

Galatea, shepherdess beloved by Tityrus and Meliboeus, in Virgil's *Eclogues*: 11.12

Galerana, Marsilius' sister, Charlemagne's wife: 43.184; 44.28

Galeso, river noted by Horace for its sheep; it flows to east of Taranto, city founded by Phalantus: 31.58

Galicia, in North-west Spain, the home of Isabel: 13.4; 14.13; 33.97

Gambara, Veronica, wife of Count Giberto X di Correggio, a distinguished poetess, and regent in her son's minority: 46.3

Ganelon of Ponthieu or **Maganza**, traditionally the traitor of Roncesvalles where Roland (Orlando) was ambushed, and later to be murderer of Ruggiero; one of Charlemagne's paladins: 15.8; 18.10; 46.67

Ganges, River, often for eastern confines of the world: 15.17; 16.23; 19.106

Ganymede, a beautiful youth abducted from Mount Ida by an eagle in order to serve Jupiter as cup-bearer: 4.47; 7.20; 26.100

Garamants, Sudanese tribe south of the Syrtes: 14.17; 29.59

Garbo, region of Barbary Africa, ruled by King Sobrino: 14.66

Garda, Lake, out of which the Mincio flows, passing through Mantua on its way to the Po: 43.11

Gardo, Saracen killed by Lurcanio: 18.54

Garigliano, or **Liri**, river-boundary of Papal States and Kingdom of Naples: 33.34 Louis XII's defeat in 1503

Garonne, River: 3.75; 27.101

Gascony: 9.6; 12.71; 14.18; 27.19

Gauno, another name for the Candigliano, tributary of the Metaurus: 43.149

Gawain, principal Knight of the Round Table: 4.52

Gazzolo, Luigi da, or **Luigi II Gonzaga**, soldier and poet, friend of Ariosto: 26.50; 37.8 married to Isabel, daughter of Vespasiano Colonna

Genoa, city of Andrea Doria; 15.32; 33.37 subdued by Louis XII

George, Saint, slayer of dragon: 15.98

Gerard of Roussillon, brother of Buovo and, according to some authorities rejected by Ariosto, father of Aldiger: 25.72

Germany (Germans): 1.6; 3.28, 36, 55; 10.72; 11.23; 12.4; 17.74; 27.29; 33.41 the German tempest are the Swiss who beat the French at Novara and restored Francesco Sforza to Milan; 46.88

Ghiaradadda, between rivers Adda and Oglio, where Louis XII beat the Venetians: 33.38

Ghibellines, the Imperial faction in the wars between Pope and Emperor: 3.35

Gibraltar: 15.31; 16.37; 30.10

Ginevra, wife of Giangaleazzo the son of Niccolò di Correggio: 46.3

Ginevra, daughter of Giberto di Correggio and Veronica Gambara, and wife of Paolo Fregoso: 46.4

Gismonda, mother of Grifon and Aquilant; according to an early tradition, not followed by Boiardo or Ariosto, her two sons were by Richardet and were snatched, the one by a griffin, the other by an eagle, and were loved, the one by a white-dressed fairy, the other by a black-dressed one, whose colours they adopted; the fairies tried to keep them from a predicted death in France: 15.73; 31.37

Giuliano de' Medici, son of Lorenzo il Magnifico, brother of Leo X, father of Ippolito de' Medici: 26.51

Gloucester, Oldrade, Duke of: 10.78; 16.67

God, and His interventions on Christian side: 10.5; 11.28; 14.75, 95; 15.24, 92; 16.32; 17.1; 23.2, 53; 24.84; 34.56; 41.27; 42.66; 43.7; 45.41

Godfrey, Duke of Buckingham: 10.82

Gonzaga, Elizabeth, sister of Marquis Francesco II, wife of Guidobaldo I di Montefeltro, Duke of Urbino; she features as presiding genius in Castiglione's *The Courtier*: 42.86; 43.148

Gonzaga, Ercole, son of Francesco II and Isabel of Este, brother of Frederick, a Cardinal, presided over Council of Trent: 26.51; 46.11

Gonzaga, Francesco II, married to Isabel of Este: 13.60; 26.49 his brother-in-law of Ferrara is Alfonso d'Este, his son-in-law of Urbino is Francesco Maria della Rovere, Duke of Urbino; 33.32 helps Ferdinand II of Naples to oust French

Gonzaga, Frederick, son of Francesco II Gonzaga and Isabel of Este, took Pavia in 1523: 26.49; 33.45

Gonzaga, Julia, daughter of Prospero, wife of Vespasiano Colonna: 46.7

Gonzaga, Leonora, daughter of Marquis Francesco II, married Francesco Maria della Rovere, Duke of Urbino: 42.86; 43.148

Gonzaga, Luigi, (1) *see* Gazzolo, Luigi da

Gonzaga, Luigi, (2) a second Gonzaga of this name, praised as soldier and poet, has not been definitely identified: 37.8

Gonzaga, Margherita: 46.4 may refer to a brilliant lady of this name in the suite of Elisabetta di Montefeltro, Duchess of Urbino; or it may refer to the wife of Federico II, Duke of Mantua, recipient of an advance copy of the *Furioso*

Gonzaga, Sigismondo, Cardinal under Julius II, patron of the arts, friend of Ariosto: 26.49

Gothenburg, Southern Sweden; its king a suitor for Queen of Iceland's hand: 32.54, 76; 33.66; 37.112

Graces, Greek divinities, a threesome symbolizing seductive beauty: 28.97; 43.58; 46.85 the queen they attend is Eleonora of Aragon

Gradasso, King of Sericana, allied to Agramant; he invaded France to win Orlando's sword Durindana and Rinaldo's steed Bayard: 2.45 fights Atlas; 4.40 liberated by Bradamant; 12.11 imprisoned by Atlas in his enchanted palace; 17.62; 22.20 released by Astolfo; 24.55; 27.7; 27.14 to Agramant's rescue; 27.49 quarrels with Mandricard over sword Durindana; 30.18 forced to entrust his quarrel with Mandricard to Ruggiero; 30.39; 30.74 Ruggiero wins him Durindana; 31.89 challenges Rinaldo for Bayard; 33.78 fight with Rinaldo interrupted, but purloins Bayard; 38.56; 40.45 meets fleeing Agramant and Sobrino and decides them on challenge to Orlando; 41.28; 41.68–42.11 battle at Lipadusa, where he kills Brandimart and is killed by Orlando

Granada, Moorish kingdom of Stordilan: 14.13, 40; 27.51; 42.4

Grandonio of Volterra, a Spanish leader, placed in command of troops of Algarve: 14.12, 107; 18.42; 27.80; 31.81; 35.69

Graziosa Maggi, noble lady of the Este court, a gifted musician: 46.4

Grecian queen, Helen of Troy: 10.3

Greece (Greeks): 3.55; 15.100; 17.77; 18.71; 20.10; 27.130; 35.27; 44.80

Greek, the, protagonist in tale told to Rodomont: 28.56

Grifon the White, twin brother of Aquilant the Black, sons of Oliver: 15.67 battles with robber Orrilo, then leaves for Jerusalem with Astolfo;

15.101 his love for Orrigilla; 16.4 she and Martano fool him; 17.17 arrives at Damascus for tournament, hears story of Norandin; 17.69 triumphs at Norandin's tournament, then suffers shame and captivity through Orrigilla's treachery; 18.3 savages Damascan mob; 18.59 reconciled with Norandin and avenged, thanks to Aquilant, on his betrayers; 18.116 joins forces with Astolfo, Samsonet and Marfisa and sails for West but runs into storm; 19.43 driven ashore in land of killer-women, Alexandretta; 20.69 escapes with his friends; 20.102 captured by Pinabello and made to serve as his champion for a year and a month; 22.48; 22.84 jousts with Ruggiero but is floored by magic shield; 30.40; 31.37; 31.51 joins Rinaldo's relief expedition; 38.21, 58; 39.18 attacks Saracens; 46.108

Grillo, Christian drunkard: 18.176

Guadalquivir, river in realm of Madarasso: 14.12

Guadiana, river in Estremadura, Spain: 14.14

Gualciotto, late King of Bellamarina, North Africa: 14.25

Guarino, Alessandro, secretary to Alfonso d'Este and professor at Ferrara: 46.14

Guelph of Este, two of this name mentioned by Melissa, probably dukes of the Bavarian/Saxon branch: 3.32

Guichard, the third (not the first, as Ariosto asserts) of Aymon's sons: 30.94; 31.11

Guidetto, Francesco Guidetti, Florentine man of letters, friend of Ariosto: 37.12

Guido of Bourgogne and Guido of Montfort, paladins: 15.8; 16.17; 18.10, 155

Guidobaldo, son of Frederick of Montefeltro, Duke of Urbino and husband of Elizabeth Gonzaga: 26.50; 43.148

Guidone Selvaggio, son of Aymon by Constance, a Dacian woman, so half-brother to Rinaldo: 19.79 a prisoner of the warrior-women of Alexandretta, he has to fight Marfisa in the lists, then falls into collusion with her and her party; 20.4 tells tale of warrior-women, then contrives escape with his new-found friends; 20.102 captured by Pinabello and made to serve as his champion for a year and a month; 22.48; 22.85 jousts with Ruggiero but is floored by magic shield; 31.8 with his wife Aleria on Paris road, meets Rinaldo and brothers and fights with them, then joins them; 31.51 in night attack on Saracen camp; 31.98; 38.21, 58; 39.18 attacks Saracens; 42.43

Guinevere, daughter of King of Scotland, sister of Zerbin: 4.57; 5.7–6.15

Guinevere, wife of King Arthur and lover of Sir Lancelot: 43.28

Hades, the subterranean hell of ancient mythology: 2.42; 9.91; 14.82; 16.83; 18.144; 19.84; 24.79; 40.33 swamp ringing it is the Styx

Hadrian, Roman emperor whose mausoleum by the Tiber is now the Castel Sant' Angelo: 29.33

Halcyons, little sea-birds, originally a human couple, the husband dying in a shipwreck, the wife for sorrow throwing herself off cliff: 10.20

Hampton, Earl of: 10.80

Hannibal, Carthaginian who defeated Rome in several battles: 18.24; 26.47; 40.41 defeated by Scipio, he took refuge with Prusias, King of Bithynia, who feared to protect him from the Romans, so he took his own life

Haramon of Cornwall, killed by Dardinel: 18.52

Harpalice, Thracian princess and Amazon praised in *Aeneid*: 20.1; 37.5

Harpies, in Roman mythology three (here seven) monstrous vultures with women's faces, which plunder food off tables: 33.108; 34.1, 46

Harriman, Duke of Somerset: 10.81; 16.30, 85; 18.10

Hautefeuille, seat of Anselm's branch of the Maganza clan: 31.109

Hector, Trojan hero, whose arms, made by Vulcan, were conquered by Mandricard, except for the sword, won by Orlando: 14.31; 18.64; 19.66 his mother Hecuba; 23.78; 24.60, 104; 26.99; 30.41; 35.25; 36.6; 36.70 Ruggiero's and Estes' forbear; 37.5; 41.88; 45.73; 46.80

Hecuba, widow of Priam of Troy, mother bereaved of fifty children: 7.73; 10.34; 19.66

Helen of Troy, sparked off war between Greeks and Trojans when Trojan prince Paris abducted her from her husband, King Menelaus of Sparta: 10.3; 11.70; 43.20; 44.56 alludes to the sack of Troy; 46.83

Heliogabalus, last of the Antonine family of Roman emperors, and renowned for evil: 17.2

Henry VIII of England, praised for hunting the Allegorical Beast (*see under* Francis I): 26.34

Henry II, German emperor, defeated at Parma by Bertold d'Este: 3.29

Henry, Duke of Clarence: 10.78; 16.67

Henry, Earl of Salisbury: 10.82

Heraclion, Emperor of the Greeks, in Hermonides' story: 21.13

Hercules (and Pillars of, straits of Gibraltar as Western limit of world): 4.61; 6.17; 15.22; 16.37; 17.113; 23.85; 27.51; 32.11 Jupiter lengthened the night during which he begot Hercules out of Alcmena; 33.29, 98; 34.39 some of the labours imposed by Eurystheus and Juno here referred to are the slaying of the Lernaean hydra, strangling of Nemean lion, slaying of Diomedes, King of Thrace's horses, capture of boar of Erimanthus, battle with river-god Achelous in Aetolia, with giant Anteus in Numidia, with giant Cacus on the Tiber, and with Geryon in Spain

Herman of Forbes: 10.87

Herman of Monmouth: 10.82

Hermit,
    (1) sorcerer-hermit met by Angelica: 2.12; 8.30, 67; 10.94
    (2) who warns Astolfo against giant Caligorant: 15.42
    (3) who escorts Isabel with Zerbin's body to Provence: 24.87; 28.95–29.7
    (4) on desert island, who baptizes Ruggiero and Sobrino, heals Oliver, and propounds Ruggiero–Bradamant nuptials: 41.52; 41.56 the parable is in *Matthew 20*; 43.187; 44.4

Hermonides of Holland, wounded by Gabrina's champion, Zerbin, while attempting justifiable vengeance upon her: 20.144; 21.5

Hermophylus and Carmond, at Norandin's tournament: 17.99

Hermus, river of Asia Minor which receives the Pactolus and equally famed for gold-bearing deposits: 17.78

Herod, King of Judaea, tried to kill the Infant Jesus but was foiled by the Wise Men who had originally alerted him: 10.69

Heroes, Land of the, near Gulf of Suez, in Egypt according to Ptolemy's atlas: 15.39

Hesperia, Cape Verde (Senegal), troops led by Soridan: 14.22

Hesperides, the legendary garden with the golden apples taken by Hercules, but, figuratively, the lands of the setting sun: 1.7; 37.6; 43.58

Hibernia, or Ireland, whose King is Hubert: 9.11, 92; 10.92; 11.30

Hilarion, first hermit of Palestine, a model of sanctity: 8.45

Hill, Eli, and **Delphin,** killed by Dardinel: 18.47

Himavian range, the Himalayas, extending north to the Altai: 10.71

Hippalca, servant and confidante of Bradamant, sent by her to Ruggiero with his steed Frontino: 23.28; 26.55, 88; 30.76; 31.7

Hippocrene, spring flowing from Mount Helicon (Boeotia) where winged horse Pegasus struck a rock with his hoof; consecrated to the Muses: 37.14

Hippogryph, winged steed with griffin's head, chest and feathers, captured and tamed by Atlas; Ariosto's invention: Atlas rides him 2.37, 49; 4.4, 18; Ruggiero rides him 4.42; 6.18, 57; 7.78; 8.18; 10.66, 91; 11.8, 13; Astolfo rides him 22.24; 23.9; 33.96; 34.48; 38.26; 44.23

Hippolyta, Queen of the Amazons: 25.32; 27.52

Hippolytus of Este, son of Ercole I, brother of Alfonso, born in 1479, made a Cardinal at fourteen, died in 1520; the poet's patron: 1.3 poem dedicated to him; 3.50, 56; 3.57 refers to his victory over the Venetians in 1510 at La Polesella where he destroyed their ships; 7.62; 15.2 also refers to La Polesella; 18.1 praised as careful judge; 26.51 pursues Allegorical Beast; 35.8 his golden life-thread; 36.2 refers to Emperor Maximilian's war with Venice, when the Estes fought on Maximilian's side and restrained the hand of vengeance against Padua; 40.1 his victory over the Venetians at La Polesella; 41.67; 46.85 lavishly praised

Hippolytus II of Este, son of Alfonso and of Lucretia Borgia, nephew of Hippolytus I and like him a Cardinal: 3.58; 26.51

Holland, roughly south of Rhine, invaded by Cimosco of Frisia, restored to Olympia: 9.22, 59; 10.16, 30; 11.73, 79

Homer, his allegations about the Greeks and Trojans: 35.27; 37.20

Honorius II, Pope, conferred Ancona on Azzo III d'Este: 3.31

Horatius, Roman hero who alone held the bridge against the Etruscans: 18.65

Hubert, King of Hibernia, ravages isle of Ebuda, marries Olympia whom Orlando had rescued from the orc, and restores her to her throne: 9.11; 11.30, 59

Hubert of Mirford, killed by Dardinel: 18.47

Hubert of Tours: 14.125

Hugh of Arles, warred extensively in Italy against Berengarius I and II, but ultimately was driven out, leaving behind his son Lothair II who was killed by Berengarius II: 33.19

Hugh of Dordogne, baron in Charlemagne's suite: 18.10, 12

Hugo I d'Este, won Milan (and the Viper-emblem) from King Berengarius: 3.26

Hugo II d'Este, rescued Otto III and Pope Gregory V from Crescenzio's rising in Rome (997): 3.27

Hugo of Tours: 14.125

Hungary (Hungarians): 10.72; 13.64; 22.6; 44.78; 45.3; 46.136

Huns, Goths, and **Lombards,** invaders of Italy who brought the downfall of the Roman Empire: 17.2

Hyperborean lands, the extreme north: 10.71

Hypermnestra, the only one of Danaos' fifty daughters to disobey their father's command to kill their husbands: 22.2

Hyrcania, northern province of Persian empire, on the Caspian: 10.71 Hyrcanian Sea, the Caspian; 16.23

Icarus, (1) son of Daedalus, used wings made by his father to fly (but the wax melted when he flew too near the sun): 27.32

Icarus, (2) son of Ebalus, King of the Laconians, gave wine to his harvesters who, thinking it poison, killed him: 41.2

Iceland, or the Lost Island: 10.88; 32.51

Ida, (1) mountain near Troy, scene of Paris' judgement: 11.70; 41.63; 43.23

Ida, (2) mountain in Crete, residence of Venus and Cybele: 12.1; 26.100

Idomeneus, King of Crete who, to fulfil a vow to Neptune, killed his own son: 20.14

India, Indies, usually means the whole of Asia: 1.5; 46; 3.69; 7.39; 8.62; 10.70, 108; 15.12, 18, 22; 19.21; 30.16; 37.6; 40.56; 42.67

Indus, the Indian river, figuratively as eastern limit of the world: 3.17; 4.61; 7.36; 13.63; 18.177

Ino, for sorrow at the death of her son Learchus, she flung herself into the sea with her other son Melicertus and was changed into a sea-nymph: 11.45

Io, nymph beloved by Jupiter who changed her into a heifer; Juno made Argus keep watch on her: 32.83

Ireland, (Irish): 5.59; 8.51; 9.93; 10.87; 11.52, 77; 16.40, 76

Iroldo, Christian knight captured by Atlas: 4.40; 22.20

Isabel, Princess of Galicia, lover of Zerbin; Ariosto's invention: 12.91; 13.2 tells Orlando of her abortive elopement with Zerbin, Odoric's attempt to rape her, and her capture by brigands, and is rescued by Orlando; 14.64; 18.40; 20.134; 23.54 reunited with Zerbin by Orlando; 24.15 sees justice done to Odoric by Zerbin; 24.47 helps Zerbin collect Orlando's arms, then witnesses Zerbin's duel with Mandricard over the sword Durindana; 24.71 intercedes with Doralice to suspend duel, but Zerbin dies of wounds; 24.86 with a hermit's help she takes Zerbin's body to Provence; 28.95 is courted by Rodomont; 29.3 eludes Rodomont by having him kill her; 30.17

Isabel of Este, daughter of Ercole I, sister of Alfonso and Hippolytus, wife of Francesco II Gonzaga of Mantua: 13.59, 68; 41.67; 42.84

Isabella: 37.9 *see* Colonna

Isauro River, now the Foglia, delimits northern boundary of March of Ancona: 3.37; 42.89

Ischia, island in Bay of Naples, surmounted by Epomeo, extinct volcano crushing giant Typheus; here Alfonso d'Avalos, Marquis del Vasto, resisted fleet of French King Charles VIII: 33.24

Iseult, beloved by Tristan: 32.89

Isoliero, from Pamplona, brother of Ferrau, he was freed by Mandricard from a Syrian sorceress and, coming to France, was put in command of the troops from Navarre: 14.11, 20, 107; 16.54; 27.80; 30.40

Israel, avenged by Red Sea drowning Pharaoh's Egyptians as these pursued the fugitives under Moses: 15.39

Italy: 3.16, 25, 33, 49, 55; 7.61; 12.4; 13.60; 14.9; 15.32; 17.2, 76, 79; 27.29; 33.6 French incursions into Italy rehearsed; 34.2 harpies (French under Charles VIII) called into Italy by Lodovico il Moro

Ivo, baron in Charlemagne's suite: 18.10

Jaffa, Syrian port: 15.98; 18.74

Jason, leader of the Argonauts, condemned to hell for betraying Medea: 34.14; 37.36

Jativa, or San Filippo di Jativa, south of Valencia: 28.54

Jealousy, ally to Discord: 18.28; 35.31; 42.46; 45.33

Jerusalem, regented for Charlemagne by Samsonet: 15.93; 16.5; 17.18, 75; 18.70, 134; 21.35; 33.105

Jews, the Apostle who betrayed his master to them is Judas Iscariot, betrayer of Christ: 22.2

Joan of Aragon, sister of Anne and wife of Ascanio Colonna: 46.9

Job, Old Testament patriarch, byword for pious resignation: 26.92

Jocondo, protagonist in tale told to Rodomont: 28.7

John the Apostle and Evangelist, Saint: 16.13; 22.2; 34.54; 34.58 Jesus' prophecy about him; 35.4, 28; 38.24; 39.19; 44.24

John the Baron, descendant of Ruggiero I of Reggio: 36.72

John and Denis, Saints, invoked by Charlemagne as patrons of Paris: 27.30

Joshua, Israelite leader who ordered the sun to stand still while he achieved a victory: 32.11

Jove, also Jupiter, King of the gods in Latin mythology: 2.8; 3.3; 7.20; 14.7 here for Pope Julius II

Juba, King of Mauretania: 42.90

Judas, in the depths of (Dante's) hell for his betrayal of Christ: 11.28

Jugurtha, King of Numidia, defeated by Rome, he was surrendered to them by Bocchus, his father-in-law: 40.41

Julia di Correggio: 46.4

Julius II, Pope, author of the Holy League against the French and their Este allies: 3.55; 14.4, 7

Juno, goddess, wife of Jupiter, step-mother of Hercules: 11.71; 34.39

Jupiter, known also as Jove: 9.78; 30.48 featured as bestriding an eagle; 33.29; 44.85; 46.85

Juvenal the Latinist, from Parma, man of letters and antiquary: 46.12

Kent, Duke of: 10.79

Kildare, Earl of: 10.87

Ladas, Alexander the Great's dispatch-runner: 33.28

Lady of the Lake, from the Arthurian legends; induced the wizard Merlin to enter his tomb alive only to find himself unable to escape from it, so he remained there incarcerated body and soul: 3.10

Lancaster, duchy of Lionet: 10.77; 16.40, 66

Lancelot, knight of Round Table, lover of Arthur's Guinevere: 4.52

Lanfusa, mother of Ferrau and wardress of his prisoners: 1.30; 25.74; 26.69

Langhiran, Spaniard in Marsilius' court: 14.16

Languedoc, southern France west of the Rhône: 13.45

Laodamia, wife of Protesilaos, first Greek to die at Hector's hands outside Troy; she chose to die with him: 37.19

Laodicea, North Levantine sea-port: 18.74; 43.184; 17.94 Baron of, in Norandin's tournament

Larbin, King of Portugal, killed by Rinaldo: 14.13

Largalifa, Spaniard in Marsilius' court: 14.16; 18.44

Larissa, Syrian city between Antioch and Damascus: 18.77

La Rochelle: 13.16, 22; 20.135

Lascari, Giovanni, a Greek from Constantinople, he served Lorenzo de' Medici, became Louis XII's ambassador to Venice, took service under Leo X at Rome, promoted Greek scholarship in Italy: 46.13

Latini, Fausto, courtier of Astolfo, King of the Lombards: 28.6

Latinus, King of Latium, attacked by Aeneas: 34.14

Lattanzio, Sienese man of letters: 46.12

Laura, probably the third wife of Alfonso d'Este, a commoner by birth but highly cultivated: 46.5

Lautrec, General, Francis I's commander in Italy, reached Rome too late in 1527 to help Pope Clement VII against Charles V's Germans and Spaniards: 33.56

League, the: 33.44 coalition of states including Spain formed by Leo X to check Francis I of France; 33.55 coalition formed against Charles V of Spain after Battle of Pavia by defeated King Francis I of France, Pope Clement VII and numerous Italian states; the League was powerless to prevent Charles' sack of Rome (1527)

Lemnos, Aegean island between Mount Athos and Hellespont, on path of Argonauts, it was inhabited by the Amazons: 37.36

Leo, son of Emperor Constantine of Greece, Ruggiero's rival for Bradamant: 44.12, 36, 79; 45.5, 41, 115; 46.21, 51, 72

Leo III, restored to Papal throne by Charlemagne: 33.16

Leo X, Pope, Giovanni de' Medici: 17.79; 26.34

Leon, in Spain, whose troops are led by Balugant: 14.12

Leonardo da Vinci, praised among Ariosto's greatest contemporary painters: 33.2

Leonello d'Este, bastard of Niccolò II, seized power in 1441: 3.45; 41.67

Leoniceno, Niccolò, physician and man of letters from Vicenza, served under Ercole I and Alfonso d'Este: 46.14

Leopards, in emblem of English sovereign: 39.32

Lestrigons, legendary cannibals, mentioned in *The Odyssey*: 36.10

Lethe, river in Elysian fields, land of the virtuous dead, whose waters afford oblivion: 25.93; 31.49; 34.3; 35.11; 37.19

Levanter, the East Wind: 8.81

Libanio, African King of Constantine: 14.21

Libya, Agramant's kingdom, the full Mediterranean littoral as far as Egypt: 12.4; 13.82; 14.19 Arganio's Libyans, formerly led by Dudrinas, come from Libicana, part of Libya; 29.59; 37.5 for Carthage

Licaon, whose daughter Callisto was loved by Jupiter who turned her into the constellation of the Bear, or Plough: 20.82

Lilies, Golden, on French royal ensign: 1.47; 13.81; 14.4; 15.28; 23.98; 24.108; 26.34 refers to Francis I of France, Emperor Charles V (in the original edition the Lilies here were actually ascribed to Charles of Burgundy), and Henry VIII of England (who still had French possessions); 33.10, 41; 39.32

Limasol, Cypriot sea-port: 19.46

Linus and Orpheus, legendary poet and musician respectively of Greek antiquity: 42.83

Lion, Winged or Golden, Venice: 3.49; 15.2; 40.3

Lion, 24.34 *see* Leo X

Lionet, Duke of Lancaster, King Otho's nephew, leader of English troops relieving siege of Paris: 10.77; 16.40, 66; 18.155

Lipadusa, Lampedusa, island midway between Sicily and Tripoli, where the battle of the six champions took place: 40.55; 41.36; 42.20; 43.150

Lippa of Bologna, second wife of Obizzo III d'Este: 13.73

Liri, or **Garigliano,** river-boundary between Papal States and Kingdom of Naples: 33.24

Lodovico il Moro, Sforza Duke of Milan, married to Beatrice d'Este, invited Charles VIII then Louis XII into Italy, to his cost: 13.62; 33.31; 33.34 French kings oust him, throwing him into arms of Venice; 40.41 his soliciting help from Louis XII of France, who captured him; 46.94

Logistilla, good sorceress, daughter of Love, victimized by her evil sisters Alcina and Morgana: 6.43; 7.79; 8.15, 19; 10.43, 46, 70; 15.10

Lombards, warlike tribe of Northern Italy: 3.25; 28.4; 41.64

Lombardy, into which the Sforzas invited the French, who stayed: 13.63; 17.77; 26.45 Francis I's victory over Swiss, Papal troops, Spaniards and Florentines in Battle of Melegnano, 1515; 33.49 French defeat at Pavia

London, visited by Rinaldo in quest of troops, and by Ruggiero on the hippogryph: 8.26; 10.73; 22.7

Louis the Moor, *see* Lodovico il Moro

Louis XII of France, invader of Italy, his daughter Renée married Ercole II, Alfonso d'Este's son: 13.72; 14.8; 33.34 invades Italy with Trivulzio, is defeated at the Garigliano and in Apulia, but wins Milan with aid of a traitor within the gates and of Swiss duplicity; 33.42 defeated at Novara; 40.41; 45.2 after beheading of his father, the Duke of Orleans, who had been defeated at Saint-Aubin near Rennes, Louis was imprisoned by the victor, Charles VIII, but ultimately came to the throne

Louis of Burgundy, invaded Italy to attack Berengarius I and was crowned at Pavia, but Berengarius drove him out; on his second invasion and defeat by Berengarius, the latter had him blinded: 33.18

Louis from Provence: 14.125

Low Head, unidentified cape of Western Scotland: 5.59

Lucania, province of Southern Italy: 3.47

Lucina, daughter of King of Cyprus, bride of King Norandin of Syria, suffers at hands of Orcus: 17.26; 18.93, 140

Lucretia, Roman heroine who killed herself after being raped by a son of King Tarquin: 29.28; 42.83

Lugo, city in the Romagna, an Este domain: 3.41

Luna, possibly ancient Tuscan town of Luni near Sarzana, more likely the Roman name for La Spezia: 18.135; 20.101

Lurcanio, Italian knight, brother of Ariodant, at the Scottish court; Ariosto's invention: 4.57; 5.17; 5.44–6.15; 10.86; 16.64, 78; 18.40, 53

Lydia, daughter of King of Lydia, she was condemned to hell for her spite towards Alceste: 34.11

Lydia, in Asia Minor: 17.78; 18.77; 34.11 King of Lydia in Lydia's tale

Macrobians, Ethiopians on the Upper Nile, deemed to be Asiatics rather than Africans, subjects of Gradasso: 40.50

Madarasso, King of Andalusia: 14.12; 18.157

Maddaleni, Fausto, Latin poet at court of Rome: 46.13

Maenads, the, women in hysterical trance during feasts of Bacchus: 43.158

Maffei of Volterra, either Mario or Raffaele, both erudite Romans: 46.13

Maganza, a clan in bitter enmity with the house of Clairmont; Ganelon, betrayer of Orlando in the Carolingian legends belongs to this house; so does Pinabello: 2.58, 67; 14.123; 23.57; 26.10; 38.21; 41.61, 66

Magi, Gulf named by, bay of Bahrein (Ptolemy's *Magorum Sinus*) in Persian Gulf: 15.37

Magic,
  book, Astolfo's: 15.13, 79; 22.16
  horn, Astolfo's: 15.14, 38, 53; 20.88; 22.10, 20; 33.125; 44.25
  lance, golden, Astolfo's: 8.17; 11.4; 18.118; 23.15; 32.48, 75; 33.69; 35.48; 36.10, 23; 37.102; 39.12; 45.65
  ring, Angelica's: 3.69; 7.35, 47, 65; 8.16; 10.107; 11.3; 12.23, 29, 34; 13.46; 14.19; 19.18; 27.72; 29.64
  shield, Atlas': 2.55; 3.67; 4.17; 6.67; 7.76; 8.10; 10.49, 107; 11.8; 22.67, 92
  springs of Love and Hate: 1.78; 42.35, 61

Mahomet, worshipped by the Infidels: 12.59; 18.55; 25.44; 33.101; 38.18, 86; 40.13; 41.39; 43.193

Mainardi, Giovanni, Ferrarese physician at Hippolytus' court, helped Ariosto in his last illness: 46.14

Majorca, kingdom of Baricondo: 14.13

Malabuferso, African King of Fez: 14.22; 15.7; 16.76

Malaga: 14.12; 30.9

Malagur, Spaniard in Marsilius' court: 14.16

Malaguzzo, Annibal, from Reggio Emilia, Ariosto's birthplace, he was cousin and close friend of the poet: 46.18

Malamocco, island protecting Venice's lagoon from the Adriatic, west of the Lido: 33.17

Malatesta, Ginevra, possibly Ercole II d'Este's sister and wife of Sigismondo Malatesta of Rimini, possibly a Malatesta wife of Obizi di Ferrara: 46.5

Malea, Cape, south-eastern promontory of Peloponnese, noted for storms: 20.100

Malgarin, Spaniard, one of Marsilius' leaders: 14.15

Malindo and Ardalic of Flanders, serving with Charlemagne: 18.180

Mallea, marsh on left bank of Po di Volano, near Ferrara, where wild boar abound: 14.120

Malzarise, Spaniard, one of Marsilius' leaders: 14.15

Mambrino, a knight who had seized Rinaldo's betrothed; Rinaldo killed him and took his helmet: 1.28; 18.151; 20.6

Mamuga, unidentified town north of Aleppo, Syria: 18.77

Mandricard, son of Agrican and King of the Tartars, one of the fiercest Saracen champions; he sought Orlando to avenge Agrican's death at his hands, also to wrest from him the sword Durindana, the only item of Hector's arms which he had not laid hands on when he overcame a Syrian sorceress: 14.30 from Agramant's camp, sets off to find conqueror of Alzirdo and Manilard, not realizing this was Orlando: 14.38 seizes Doralice on her way to her fiancé Rodomont; 14.115; 17.62; 18.29; 23.38; 23.71 fights Orlando for the sword Durindana; 24.58 fights and kills Zerbin for the sword Durindana; 24.93–25.4 duel with Rodomont over Doralice; 26.67 tries to capture Marfisa as gift to Rodomont in place of Doralice; 26.98 fights Ruggiero over the eagle-emblem; 26.131 lured away with Rodomont in pursuit of Doralice; 27.6 pursues Doralice to Agramant's camp and raises Charlemagne's blockade; 27.40 his duel with Rodomont over Doralice forestalled by quarrel with Gradasso over sword Durindana; 27.107 preferred to Rodomont by Doralice; 30.17 is killed by Ruggiero in duel over eagle-emblem; 31.44; 38.56

Manfred, son of Frederick II, killed at Benevento while trying to recover his possessions from Charles of Anjou: 33.20

Mangiana, vast region south of Cathay described by Marco Polo: 10.71

Manilard, King of Norizia, unhorsed by Orlando as he leads his troops against Paris: 12.69, 82; 14.29; 23.71; 40.73

Mantegna, Andrea, praised among Ariosto's greatest contemporary painters: 33.2

Manto, Theban sorceress, mother of Ocnus who founded Mantua: 13.59; 43.74, 96

Mantua, Melissa's city, also that of Isabel of Este, who married Marquis of Gonzaga; it was founded by Ocnus, son of Manto the sorceress, who arrived there after the destruction of Thebes: 13.59; 33.32 the Marquis of Mantua who helped Ferdinand II of Naples drive out the French, notably in siege of Atella, was Francesco Gonzaga; 33.45 Duke of Mantua is Frederick Gonzaga; 37.8; 42.69, 86; 43.11, 70

Marbalust, King of Oran: 14.17, 108; 16. 47; 38.49

Marca, Jacques de Bourbon, Count della, married Queen Joan II of Naples and usurped her throne but was deposed: 33.23

March, Earl of: 10.80

Marcomir, supposedly first King of the Franks, succeeded by Fieramont: 33.7

Marcus Aurelius, Roman Emperor: 15.26

Marfisa, Saracen warrior-damsel, sister (as it turns out) of Ruggiero: 13.42; 18.99 joins Astolfo and Samsonet on road to Damascus, where she disrupts Norandin's tournament by seizing the prize-armour as hers; 18.133 sails with her friends for the West but runs into storm; 19.43 driven ashore in land of killer-women, challenges ten knights to save her party and defeats all but one; 20.4 escapes from land of killer-women; 20.103 leaves her friends at Marseilles, and has encounters with Gabrina, Pinabello and Zerbin; 21.5; 22.49; 25.4, 97; 26.3 joins Ruggiero, Richardet and Aldiger in rescue of Maugis and Vivian and is struck by Ruggiero's valour; 26.68 resists Mandricard's bid to make a present of her to Rodomont; 26.87

608

agrees to fight for Agramant against Charlemagne; 26.136 leaves for Agramant's camp with Ruggiero; 27.15 to Agramant's rescue; 27.40 bids to fight Mandricard; 27.85 seizes Brunello and leaves Saracen camp vowing to hang him; 30.88; 32.5 in Agramant's withdrawal to Arles; 32.30 reported to be Ruggiero's lover; 36.16 unhorsed by Bradamant and pursues her outside Arles; 36.43 fights with Bradamant and Ruggiero; 36.59 learns from Atlas of her kinship with Ruggiero and is reconciled with Bradamant; 37.24 with Ruggiero and Bradamant overthrows misogynist Marganor; 38.7 enrols behind Charlemagne's standards at Arles and is baptized; 38.56; 39.10; 39.68 slaughters Saracens after interruption of duel of champions; 41.66; 42.26; 44.30 welcomes Ruggiero to Charlemagne's court; 45.103 Ruggiero's champion for Bradamant's hand; 46.56, 110

Margan, Saracen soldier: 16.65

Marganor, tyrant rendered misogynist by death of his sons owing to women; overthrown by Marfisa and companions: 37.38, 121

Margherita: 46.4 *see* Gonzaga

Maricold, King of Galicia killed by Orlando: 14.13

Marius, Roman general and dictator: 3.33; 17.1; 45.2 banished from Rome, he returned to assume supreme power

Mark and Matthew of Mont Saint Michel, in Charlemagne's guard against Rodomont: 18.10

Mark, Lion of Saint, Venice: 15.2; 33.46

Marmonda, probably area east of Cyrenaica, capital Tobruk: 14.18

Marone, Andrea, poet at court of Hippolytus: 46.13

Mars, god of War: 3.45, 66; 9.79; 15.56; 16.45; 17.113; 26.24, 50, 80; 27.62; 32.75; 33.40; 36.54; 37.8; 38.55, 64; 41.68; 44.85; 46.85

Marseilles, which Bradamant holds from Charlemagne: 2.63; 13.45; 20.102; 24.92; 26.58; 39.40; 40.69; 44.18, 26

Marsilius, King of Spain, brother of Galerana, Charlemagne's wife, and his former ally, but has now sided with Agramant in the invasion of France: 1.6; 2.37; 12.71; 14.10 musters his troops before Paris; 14.15, 33, 66; 14.107 rearguard in assault on Paris; 18.41; 18.156 finally retreats outside Paris; 22.39 father of Fiordispina; 24.110; 25.7; 25.70 catches Richardet in daughter's bed; 27.67; 27.81 helps Agramant sort out quarrels between Saracen champions; 30.19, 27; 31.82 urges Agramant to withdraw to Arles; 32.4; 35.66; 38.41 advises Agramant to attack Charlemagne; 38.78 Ruggiero's squire in duel of champions; 39.17 withdraws into Arles; 39.74 retreats to fortify Spain against counter-invasion

Martano of Antioch, Orrigilla's lover, causes humiliation to Grifon, his rival: 15.102; 16.6; 17.17, 71, 109; 18.71

Martasin, African King of the Garamants killed by Bradamant: 14.17; 38.49

Marullo, Michele, Greek man of letters who wrote in Greek and Latin and lived in Tuscany: 37.8

Massilia, otherwise Numidia, North Africa: 18.22

Matalista, Spaniard commanding troops of Calatrava: 14.14; 16.67 referred to as of Almeria

Matilda, Countess of Tuscany, grand-daughter of Emperor Henry I, she received Pope Gregory VII at Canossa: 3.29

Maugis, son of Buovo, brother of Vivian, cousin of Rinaldo, a sorcerer: 11.4; 25.4, 72; 25.96 with Vivian prisoner of Ferrau, about to be bartered to the Maganzas, traditional enemies; 26.3 rescued by Ruggiero and others;

26.38 explains Merlin's Allegory of the Beast; 26.54, 68; 26.74 in scuffle with Mandricard and Rodomont; 26.127 breaks up fight by putting devil into Doralice's horse; 27.2; 30.87; 30.94 to Paris with Rinaldo; 31.12 makes to fight Guidone; 31.35, 79; 31.86 helps Rinaldo rout Saracens by night; 31.92; 33.85 suspected of interrupting Rinaldo/Gradasso duel; 38.21, 75; 42.30 helps Rinaldo seek Angelica despite past incident when Rinaldo hated her and would not yield to her love even though this would have procured Maugis' release from her captivity, for she had promised Maugis his freedom if he persuaded Rinaldo in her favour; 43.55

Mauretania, whose troops are led by Farurant: 14.21; 18.48; 32.63

Maurice, late sixth-century Emperor of Constantinople: 33.13

Maximilian I, Archduke of Austria, then Holy Roman Emperor, took part in League of Cambrai against Venice, then in the Holy League against France; he is the knight here alluded to: 26.34

Maximinus, Roman emperor of evil repute, elected by acclamation from the army: 17.2

Mecca, Muslim Holy City, near which Samsonet first met Orlando: 15.95

Medea, killed her two sons by Jason when he forsook her: 3.52 compared for cruelty to Pope Julius II and his successors in trying to drive the Estes from their realms; 20.42; 21.56

Media, land south of the Caspian Sea: 1.5; 40.39

Medici, Ippolito de', Cardinal, son of Giuliano, nephew of Leo X: 26.51

Medor, young African soldier in service of King Dardinel, whose corpse he seeks to bury with his friend Cloridan's help; wounded by a Scots knight, he is saved by Angelica, who falls in love with and marries him; Ariosto's invention: 12.65; 18.165–19.42; 23.102; 29.58; 30.16

Melara, on left bank of Po, near Ostiglia: 43.53

Meliboeus, shepherd in love with Galatea: 11.12

Melicertes, son of Ino, who flung herself into the sea for sorrow on death of other son; he was turned into a sea-sprite: 11.45

Melissa, Mantuan sorceress; Ariosto's invention: 2.72 in Merlin's cave; 3.8 shows Bradamant her glorious posterity; 7.38–8.19 rescues Ruggiero from Alcina's spell; 10.64, 108; 13.46 tells Bradamant of her female posterity, and warns her how to rescue Ruggiero from Atlas' palace; 32.25; 38.73; 39.4 procures interruption of duel between Rinaldo and Ruggiero; 42.26; 43.20 her infatuation for a Mantuan knight; 46.19 reconciles Ruggiero to life, with Leo's aid; 46.76 sends for nuptial pavilion

Mella, tributary of Po close to Brescia, a city sacked by the French: 17.4

Memphis in Egypt, on the Nile: 15.61

Menelaus, King of Sparta, who lost his wife Helen to Paris of Troy: 11.70; 46.82

Mercury, thieving god of commerce, Jupiter's winged messenger: 15.57; 37.17 refers to the planet Mercury—Maia (Mercury's mother) in the Italian; 46.85

Merlin, British sorcerer and prophet from the Arthurian legends: 3.9, 16, 64; 7.37; 11.4; 13.58; 22.72; 26.30, 39; 32.24; 33.4, 9

Metaurus, river flowing into the Adriatic south of Fano: 43.149

Mezentius, Etruscan king, Turnus' ally against Aeneas who killed him: 17.2

Michael, Archangel, sent by God to bring Silence and Discord to Charlemagne's aid: 14.75; 15.48; 18.26; 27.34, 100

Michelangelo Buonarotti, praised by Ariosto among the greatest contemporary painters: 33.2

Milan: 3.26; 33.44

Mincio, river flowing out of Lake Garda to join the Po beyond Mantua: 13.59; 37.8; 43.70

Minerva, or **Pallas Athena**, goddess of wisdom, renowned as an embroiderer: 11.75

Minos, King of Crete, appointed Judge in the Underworld: 20.25; 26.129 his angels are devils

Mirabald, ex-King of Bolga in Africa: 14.24

Mirra, incestuous with her father: 25.36

Mistral, a north wind: 13.15

Modena, an Este domain: 3.38; 33.38 Louis XII stops Julius II from seizing it

Molza, Francesco Maria, from Modena, author of much love poetry, friend of Ariosto: 37.12; 46.12

Monese, Persian Satrap who defeated a Roman army: 42.90

Monferrato, William of, ruled duchy of Monferrato (Piedmont) and was related to the Gonzagas of Mantua: 26.53

Mongia, possibly Mugia, village north-west of Santiago, near Cape Finisterre: 13.15

Mongrana, family founded by Sinibaldo, son of Buovo d'Antona; among his descendants was Oliver whose sister, Alda (Aude) married Orlando: 36.75; 38.20; 44.29; 46.67

Monmouth, fief of Herman: 10.82

Monodant, King of the Far Islands, father of Brandimart and Ziliant: 19:38; 31.59; 39.40, 62

Montauban, castle built by Rinaldo and his clan on the Dordogne, in Gascony, it is the only fortress to stand out against the Saracen invasion from Spain: 1.12; 23.14, 20; 25.46; 26.88; 30.76, 93; 31.56, 90; 45.67

Montefiore, or **Montefiorito**, province of Forli: 43.147

Montferrant and **Clermont**, in Auvergne, now united as Clermont-Ferrant: 32.50

Montino, Florian, friend of Ariosto, identification questioned: 46.12

Montpellier, French Mediterranean town: 2.63; 28.94

Moon-goddess, known in Greek mythology under name of Selene in heaven, Artemis (Diana) on earth, Hecate in the Underworld: 18.184

Moors, invaders from Africa: 1.1; 9.5, 23; 14.65; 15.99; 16.18; 17.6; 18.156; 31.79; 41.49

Morando, a Greek, instrument in Gabrina's hands in Hermonides' tale: 21.36

Morath, leader of the Scandinavian troops relieving siege of Paris: 10.89

Moravians and **Bohemians**, lands now in Czechoslovakia: 22.6

Moray, Trason, Duke of: 10.85; 16.55

Morea, the Greek Peloponnese: 20.100

Morgan, Spaniard, one of Marsilius' leaders (perhaps same man as Pulci's comic giant): 14.15

Morgana, sorceress, sister of Alcina and Logistilla, supposed also sister of King Arthur: 6.38, 43; 19.38; 43.28 alludes to incident when Guinevere, King Arthur's wife, is Morgana's rival in love with Sir Lancelot, and she betrays the wife to the husband by means of an enchanted goblet

Moro, Pier, courtier of Hippolytus, later of Alfonso d'Este: 40.4

Morocco, here a city as well as a country, its king is Finadurro: 14.22, 113; 18.46, 48; 32.63; 33.99

Moschino, defender of Paris, but also name of celebrated toper at Ercole I's court: 14.124

Moselle, tributary of the Rhine: 44.78

Mulga, in Algeria, its king is Corineo: 14.23

Muses, nine mythological sisters who presided over the liberal arts: 20.1; 37.8, 14; 46.3, 17

Mussuro, Marco, Greek from Candia, pupil of Lascari, taught Greek grammar at Padua, became an archbishop, admired by Erasmus: 46.13

Mycenae, renowned for cruelty because of Atreus serving up to Tieste his son Pelops, and of Clytemnestra killing her husband Agamemnon: 5.4

Mygdonia, Phrygia in Asia Minor: 17.78

Myrmidons, armed retinue of Achilles: 31.56

Nabateans, a tribe of Arabia Petraia: 1.55; 15.12

Namo, Duke of Bavaria, Charlemagne's childhood companion, now his most trusted adviser: 1.8; 8.73; 15.8; 17.16; 18.8; 38.80; 46.110

Naples, the city and the kingdom: 3.38; 13.60; 33.24, 49, 56

Narbonne, French Mediterranean town in Saracen hands: 2.63; 31.83

Nasamons, North African tribe between Cyrene and Benghazi, led by Pulian: 14.22; 40.73

Nausicaa, her island, where Ulysses was shipwrecked and enjoyed an idyll, is Corfu: 43.57

Navagero, Andrea, Venetian man of letters and diplomat, disciple of Mussuro: 46.13

Navarre, Franco-Spanish kingdom on both sides of Pyrenees: 14.5, 11; 16.55; 33.97

Nebuchadnezzar, King of Babylon: 34.65

Neiera, shepherdess featuring in Virgil's *Eclogues*: 11.12

Nembrot, builder of Tower of Babel wherefrom to assault God, and ancestor of Rodomont: 14.118; 26.121; 27.69; 46.119

Neptune, god of the sea: 8.54; 11.44; 15.19; 45.112

Nereids, sea-nymphs, daughters of Nereus: 11.45

Nero, Roman emperor of evil repute: 3.33; 17.1; 35.26; 37.43

Nestor, oldest and wisest of Agamemnon's counsellors in war against Troy: 7.44; 33.28

Niccolò d'Este II, Aldobrandino's brother: 3.40

Niccolò d'Este III, succeeded his father Alberto, foiled the attempt on his throne by Azzo, son of the outlawed Francesco d'Este and worsted Ottobuono III, tyrant of Parma and Reggio: 3.42; 41.67

Nicosia, on Cyprus: 16.11; 17.66; 18.140

Nile, African river, figuratively as southern limit of the world; it also divides Christian from Muslim Nubia: 3.17; 10.56 the Queen of the Nile is Cleopatra; 15.31, 41, 58; 16.56; 29.59; 33.99 Blue Nile deemed by the ancients to rise in Asia; 38.26; 40.50

Ninus, King of Assyria, husband of Semiramis; who sat next upon his throne was the debauched Sardanapalos: 7.20; 25.36 alludes to allegation that Semiramis was Ninus' mother as well as wife

Nireus, after Achilles the most handsome of the Greeks at the siege of Troy: 33.28

Norandin, King of Syria, whose bride Lucina almost succumbs to monstrous Orcus, and who foolishly slights first Grifon, then Marfisa: 16.8; 17.23; 18.3, 59, 126; 19.77; 40.39

Norcia, cave at, on Mount Vittore near the lake; the Sibyl is said to have withdrawn to the cave, and books of magic were consecrated in the lake's devil-ridden waters: 33.4

Norfolk, Duke of: 10.79

Norizia, African kingdom ruled by Manilard: 12.69; 14.28; 23.73

Normandy (Normans): 9.8; 14.3, 123; 15.34 their Apulian territory was realm of Melfi

Northumberland, Earl of: 10.79

Norway, and King of: 4.52; 10.88; 32.54; 32.76 its king a suitor for the Queen of Iceland's hand; 33.66; 37.112

Novara, in Piedmont, where in 1513 French were defeated: 33.42

Novengrad, or Novigrad, town north-west of Zagreb, between the Sava and the Drava: 44.101; 45.10

Nubia (Nubians), region, and city, corresponding to Ethiopia, between the upper Nile and the Red Sea, ruled by Christian Emperor Senapo; on the left bank of Nile is Muslim Nubia: 33.100; 38.26; 40.18, 50; 44.21

Numa Pompilius, legendary King of Rome: 3.18

Numidia, North Africa: 18.22

Obizi, Guasparro degli, prominent Paduan who gave Ariosto hospitality during an illness: 46.15

Obizzo d'Este I, vassal of Frederick Barbarossa and his son Henry; mentioned with his son Folco and other heirs: 3.32

Obizzo d'Este II, son of Rinaldo II, succeeded Azzo Novello in 1264: 3.39

Obizzo d'Este III, son of Aldobrandino I, purchased Faenza for the Estes: 3.40

Ocnus, Theban, son of Manto and founder of Mantua: 13.59; 40.31 the plain surrounding Mantua

Ocricoli, now Otricoli on the Via Flaminia near Rome, but exact site of loop in Tiber no longer verifiable: 14.38

Octavius, Triumvir who defeated Antony and, as Augustus, founded Roman Empire: 15.33

Odo, a Parisian: 14.125

Odoric of Biscay, friend and dependant of Zerbin, he betrays his lord's trust in the matter of abducting Isabel, and, though pardoned, is ultimately hanged: 13.11; 24.16, 45

Ogier the Dane, father of Dudone and a paladin, though formerly a Saracen: 15.8; 17.16; 18.8, 155; 27.32; 38.79; 40.79

Oglio, tributary of the Po, flows past Gazzolo (Sabbioneta), estate of Luigi Gonzaga da Gazzolo: 37.12 the nearby stream is the Mincio, celebrated by Virgil

Oldrade, (1) Duke of Gloucester: 10.78; 16.67

Oldrade, (2) of Flanders: 14.123

Olimpio dalla Serra, Spanish soldier: 16.71

Olinder of Longueville, husband of Drusilla whom Tanacre tried to ravish: 37.51

Oliver, a paladin, traditionally Orlando's boon companion, brother of Aude, Orlando's fiancé, and father of Grifon and Aquilant; his title is Marquis of Vienne or Burgundy: 15.67; 17.16 with Charlemagne confronts Rodomont; 18.8, 155; 22.80; 27.32 wounded outside Paris; 31.37; 35.53 prisoner of Rodomont; 39.30 freed by Astolfo; 39.38; 39.53 helps Astolfo restore Orlando's wits; 40.17 at storming of Bizerta; 40.58 chosen by Orlando as comrade-in-arms at Lipadusa; 41.25 allotted Hector's armour by Orlando; 41.68–42.19 the battle at Lipadusa, is gravely wounded; 43.165 taken by Orlando to the hermit on the island to be healed; 44.11 favours Ruggiero/Bradamant nuptials; 46.60 welcomes Ruggiero to court; 46.110

Olympia, daughter of Count of Holland, victim of Cimosco, then of Bireno, then of the pirates of Ebuda, twice rescued by Orlando, finally married Hubert, King of Hibernia; Ariosto's invention: 9.19–10.34; 11.33, 70

Olympus, Mount, seat of the gods: 7.20

Ombruno, challenger in Norandin's tournament: 17.87

Oran, Algerian sea-port and kingdom, ruled by Marbalust: 14.17, 108; 16.41, 47; 32.5; 33.99

Orc, the, sea-monster with an appetite for fair damsels, unleashed by Proteus on Ebuda: 8.51, 65; 9.58; 10.94, 100; 11.28, 34; 19.39

Orcus, blind monster akin to Polyphemus, who ravaged Norandin's bridal-party: 17.29; 18.140

Orestes, son of Agamemnon, killed his mother Clytemnestra and her lover Aegistus who had murdered his father; he was then hounded by the Furies: 21.57

Orgagna, sorceress of the enchanted garden: 25.15

Orghetto of Maganza: 14.123

Orlando, principal hero of the Carolingian legends; nephew and chief support and paladin of Charlemagne in his war against the Saracens; betrothed to Alda (Aude) but in love with Angelica: 1.2, 28; 1.55 praised by Angelica; 2.16; 6.33; 8.63; 8.71 dreams of Angelica in danger and leaves besieged Paris to seek her; 9.1 seeking for Angelica, he is driven off course to Holland; 9.21 hears Olympia's tale of woe and takes vengeance on Cimosco, before pursuing his course; 11.21 seeking Angelica on Ebuda, finds Olympia and rescues her from the orc which he kills; 12.3 deluded by Atlas into seeking Angelica in the enchanted palace; 12.24 pursues Angelica in rivalry with Sacripant and Ferrau; 12.38 Ferrau fights him for his helmet, which Angelica makes off with; 12.66 defeats troops of Saracen kings Manilard and Alzirdo; 13.2 hears Isabel's tale and rescues her from the brigands; 14.33; 15.95; 18.97, 147; 19.18, 31, 37, 42; 20.5, 107; 23.53 rescues Zerbin from Anselm of Altaripa and reunites him to Isabel; 23.71 fights Mandricard who claims the sword Durindana from him; 23.100 comes upon evidence of Angelica's love for Medor, and loses his reason; 24.2 Orlando naked and berserk; 24.55; 24.58 his arms gathered up by Zerbin, his sword taken by Mandricard; 25.15; 27.8 absent in Charlemagne's great need; 27.54; 29.39 grapples with Rodomont on bridge, both of them ending in river; 29.49 further excesses, and his chase after Angelica along a beach; 30.4 devastates Malaga, then swims across sea to Ceuta in

Africa; 31.42 his plight divulged to Rinaldo by Fiordiligi; 34.62 punished with loss of his wits for deserting Christian standards; 34.64 allusion to fights with Rinaldo featured in Boiardo; 38.54; 39.36 starts to massacre Nubian camp but is captured by Astolfo and his friends and his wits are restored to him; 39.61 cured of Angelica; 40.9 supervises and participates in storming of Bizerta; 40.56 accepts Agramant's challenge on Lipadusa and chooses Brandimart and Oliver as comrades; 41.24 coming upon Ruggiero's abandoned arms and steed, shares them with his comrades, keeping sword Balisard; 41.68–42.19 the battle at Lipadusa, where he slays Gradasso and Agramant; 42.12 grieves over Brandimart; 43.165 buries Brandimart at Agrigento, then takes Oliver and his companions to the hermit's island; 44.11 favours Ruggiero/Bradamant nuptials; 46.60 welcomes Ruggiero to court; 46.109

Ormida, African king placed in charge of troops from Marmonda: 14.18, 64, 113

Orologi, Alessandro degli, Paduan nobleman and *letterato*: 46.14

Orontea, Cretan, founder of realm of killer-women: 20.24, 47

Orontes, Syrian river on which Antioch stands: 18.75

Orrigilla, a perfidious beauty who, in league with Martano, leads her lover Grifon into trouble: 15.101; 16.4; 17.17, 71, 109; 18.71

Orrilo, Egyptian brigand of the charmed life, ultimately killed by Astolfo: 15.65; 18.122

Ostia, at mouth of Tiber, formerly port of Rome: 43.149

Otho, King of England, Charlemagne's ally, Astolfo's father: 6.33; 8.27; 10.77; 22.8

Otto I, German emperor who defeated Berengarius with Este help: 3.27

Otto III, Ottobuono, tyrant of Reggio and Parma, lost his life trying to oust Niccolò III d'Este: 3.43

Otto III, German emperor, grandson of Otto I: 3.27

Otto IV, German emperor, conferred Ancona on Azzo III d'Este: 3.31, 35

Oxford, Earl of: 10.81

Pactolus, river of Asia Minor, now the Sarabut, famed by Virgil and Horace for gold deposits: 17.78

Padua: 16.27 refers to artillery of Hippolytus and Alfonso d'Este used in vain effort to help Emperor Maximilian and League of Cambrai to stop Venetians retrieving Padua; 36.4

Paestum, near Naples, ancient Roman town famous for gardens: 37.28

Paleotti, Camillo, poet from Bologna: 42.88

Palestine: 18.70, 96

Palidon of Moncalieri, Piedmontese killed by Cloridan: 18.175

Pallas Athena, or Minerva, goddess of wisdom, and deft at embroidery: 3.66; 11.75; 37.27; 42.89; 43.18

Pallavicini, princely house of Milan: 46.7

Pannizzato, Niccolò Ferrarese man of letters, supposedly taught Ariosto: 46.14

Pansa, Paulo, Genoese Latin scholar: 46.12

Paphos, on Cyprus, principal shrine of Venus: 18.137

Paris, the Trojan (or Phrygian) shepherd-prince, whose judgement of the three goddesses, Venus, Juno and Minerva, resulted in the war with

Greece, Venus having awarded Helen, Spartan Menelaus' wife, to him as a bribe: 11.70; 43.23; 44.56

Paris, besieged by the Moors: 2.16; 8.27, 69; 12.61, 68, 70; 14.65, 104; 16.16, 26; 17.7; 18.13, 185; 22.8; 27.8; 31.7, 59; 32.49; 45.61; 46.48, 75

Parma: 3.29, 43; 27.47 castle on road to Borgo San Donnino (Fidenza) is Castelguelfo

Parnassus, Pindus and **Helicon**, mountains in Greece sacred to Apollo and the Muses: 29.29; 37.9; 42.91 the winged horse is Pegasus (*and see* Hippocrene)

Parrhasius, late fifth-century B.C. Greek painter from Ephesus: 33.1

Pasiphae, wife of Minos of Crete, coupled with a bull and produced the Minotaur: 25.36

Patrick, Saint; reference to his well, supposedly giving access to Purgatory: 10.92

Patroclus, Achilles' friend who borrowed the hero's armour in which to fight Hector, but was killed: 42.2

Paul, first hermit in Egypt, model of sanctity: 8.45

Pavia, on the Ticino, where Francis I was defeated by the Spaniards: 33.46, 50

Pegasus, winged horse ridden by Perseus, later by Bellerophon, he opened the Muses' spring of Hippocrene by striking a rock on Mount Helicon with his hoof: 42.91; 45.92 also a constellation

Pelestrina, at the mouth of the Bacchiglione, between Chioggia and Venice: 33.17

Pembroke, Earl of: 10.79

Penelope, wife of Ulysses, who resisted all suitors during his long absence: 13.60; 35.27

Pentesilea, daughter of Mars, Queen of the Amazons, killed fighting for the Trojans against Achilles: 26.81; 37.5

Pepin, Frankish king, son of Charles Martel, father of Charlemagne, invaded Italy to help Pope Stephen III against Astolfo, Lombard king: 33.16; 36.71

Pepin, King of Italy, son of Charlemagne, made unsuccessful attempt to capture Venice: 33.17

Persians: 15.12, 22; 40.39, 50

Pesaro: 3.37; 42.89 on River Foglia, formerly the Isauro, its Latin name was Pisauro = weigh-gold

Pescara, Francesco, Marquis of, *see* Avalos, d'

Peter, Saint: 22.2; 33.55 successor here is Clement VII; 34.58; 43.178 symbol of the Roman Church

Phaeton, son of Apollo, tried to drive the sun-chariot but crashed into the Po: 3.34; 31.70

Phalantus, Greek soldier of fortune, bastard son of Queen Clytemnestra, legendary founder of Taranto: 20.14; 31.58

Pharaoh, who tried to stop Israelites escaping through parted waters of Red Sea: 15.39

Phidias, great Athenian sculptor, fifth-century B.C.: 11.69

Philander, brother of Hermonides, seduced then killed by Gabrina: 21.13

Philistines, slaughter by Samson using jawbone of an ass: 14.45

Philomena, the nightingale, into which the maiden, sister of Procne, was transformed to evade the wrath of Tereus after slaying his son as a vengeance: 10.113; 45.39

Phineus, a Thracian king endowed with prophetic gift, he incautiously disclosed Jupiter's counsels for which he was blinded, and he killed the children of his first marriage for which he was afflicted by the harpies, who plundered and soiled his table: 34.3

Phoebus, another name for Apollo, the Sun-god, *q.v.*

Phryxus, the modest beast carrying him was the ram of the golden fleece, who bore him off to Colchis, dropping his sister Helle into the Hellespont en route: 11.82

Phyllis, shepherdess featuring in Virgil's *Eclogues*: 11.12

Picardy: 9.6; 14.3, 75, 96; 16.30

Piceni, inhabitants of Ancona region: 3.35

Pico della Mirandola, Gianfrancesco, learned nephew of the famous humanist Giovanni, he studied at Ferrara: 46.17

Pierio, Giampietro Valeriani, from Belluno, historian, poet, professor of Rhetoric, luminary of Papal court: 46.13

Pinabello of Maganza, son of Anselm of Altaripa and one of Charlemagne's crooked vassals; 2.34–3.6 leads Bradamant into a trap; 20.105; 20.111 unhorsed and humiliated by Marfisa; 22.4; 22.47 having forced Aquilant, Grifon, Samsonet and Guidone to be his champions, watches them confront Ruggiero, but is recognized by Bradamant who pursues and kills him; 23.2, 38; 31.29

Pinadoro, King of Constantine killed by Ruggiero: 14.21

Pio, Alberto, Lord of Carpi, poet, Ariosto's fellow-pupil under Gregory of Spoleto: 46.17

Piombo, Sebastiano del, Venetian, praised by Ariosto among the greatest contemporary painters: 33.2

Pirithous, King of the Lapiths, accompanied Theseus to the Underworld to seize Proserpina from Pluto, but was chained to a rock in punishment: 44.56

Pistofilo, Bonaventura, notary and chancellor to Alfonso d'Este, he helped Ariosto enter the duke's service after leaving that of Hippolytus: 46.18

Pluto, King of the Underworld, brother of Jupiter, married to Proserpina: 34.5 the three-headed dog is Cerberus, who guards the entrance to Hades

Po, known as the King of Rivers: 3.41; 53; 31.70; 33.17, 22; 35.6 the village is the infant Ferrara; 37.92; 40.2 refers to Venetian defeat at La Polesella; 40.31; 42.69; 42.92 refers to incident noted under Apollo 3.34; 43.11; 43.32 the city is Ferrara, the lowered horns of the Po pointing east towards Francolino and south towards Ferrara: 46.122

Polignotus, Athenian painter, fifth-century B.C.: 33.1

Polycrates, tyrant of Samos who built up a fortune but was finally murdered: 45.1

Polynex, Duke of Albany, the King of Scotland's Lord High Constable: 5.7–6.3

Polyphemus, man-eating cyclops (one-eyed pastoral giant) in *The Odyssey*: 36.9

Pomerania, Upper Saxony: 10.71

Pompey, Roman Triumvir and admiral: 15.31; 40.47 defeated by Caesar at Pharsalus, he sought refuge in Egypt but Ptolemy had him murdered

Pontano, Giovanni, Umbrian poet, secretary to Ferdinand I of Aragon: 37.8

Ponthieu, *see* Pontieri

Pontieri, or **Ponthieu,** of uncertain location in Western France, seat of Ganelon's branch of the Maganza clan, murderers of Ruggiero: 3.24; 7.38; 22.47; 23.3; 31.109 Maganzas who spread slander about Rinaldo; 41.66

Pontus, Asia Minor south of Black Sea: 20.5

Portia, daughter of Cato of Utica, wife of Brutus the conspirator, took her life when he was killed: 37.19

Porzio, Camillo de' Porcari, known as, Roman bishop and professor of Rhetoric: 46.13

Postumo, Guido, poet and physician from Pesaro, courtier of Hippolytus: 42.89

Prando the Norman: 14.123

Prasildo, Christian knight captured by Atlas: 4.40; 22.20

Prester John, fabled Khan of Tartary or Negus of Abyssinia according to medieval lore: 33.106; *and see* Senapo

Pride, ally of Discord: 18.27, 34; 24.114; 26.122; 27.100

Procne, to avenge her husband King Tereus' cruelty to her sister Philomena, she killed their infant son and had him served up to its father: 3.52; 21.56; 39.31 she was turned into a swallow; 45.39

Proserpina, daughter of Ceres, carried down to Underworld by Pluto, god of the Underworld: 12.1; 44.56

Proteus, (1) old marine deity, shepherd of Neptune's sea-flocks: 8.51; 11.44

Proteus, (2) King of Egypt, who seized Helen from Paris on his way to Troy and only released her to Menelaus in exchange for booty: 46.82

Protogenes, fourth-century B.C. Greek painter from Caria: 33.1

Provence, where there were still Christian strongholds against the Moors: 7.49; 9.6; 13.45; 14.125; 24.92; 27.127; 28.96; 39.25; 44.24

Prusion, African King of the Alvaracks: 14.27; 15.7; 16.75, 81

Ptolemais, now Tolmeta, Cyrenaica: 18.165

Ptolemy, here Egyptian royal dynasty in general: 46.83

Pulian, African King of the Nasamons: 14.22, 108; 16.44; 40.73

Pyrenees, the: 1.5; 4.7, 11; 19.40; 24.54; 28.91; 29.50

Pythagoras, Greek philosopher whose disciples had to practise silence: 14.88

Pytho, dragon killed by Apollo: 26.41

Quercy and Cahors, region and capital in South-west France: 32.50

Quinsai, great city described by Marco Polo, in Mangiana, supposedly modern Hangchow: 10.71

Rabican, Astolfo's wind-swift steed, formerly Argalia's: 7.77; 8.3; 15.40; 18.118; 22.10, 22, 29; 23.9; 32.48, 69; 35.49; 36.40; 39.67

Rama, probably Ramla, on way from Jerusalem to Jaffa: 16.5

Rambald, son of Buovo, father of Ruggiero II of Reggio: 36.72

Ranier, baron in Charlemagne's suite: 18.10

Raphael Sanzio, of Urbino, praised by Ariosto among the greatest contemporary painters; he portrayed Ariosto in his *Parnaso* in the Vatican Stanze, and painted scenery for Ariosto's comedy *I Suppositi* in Rome: 33.2

Ravenna, where in 1512 Alfonso d'Este, allied to the French, defeated Pope Julius II's German and Spanish mercenaries: 3.53, 55; 14.2, 9; 33.39; 43.146

Raymond, Earl of Devon: 10.81

Raymond and Pinamont, Londoners killed by Dardinel: 18.47

Reggio in Lombardy, Ariosto's birthplace, an Este domain, rebelled under Otto III: 3.39, 43

Reggio in Calabria, realm of Ruggiero's forefathers: 36.74

Renée of France, daughter of Louis XII and of Anne of Brittany, wife of Ercole II d'Este, Lucretia Borgia's son: 13.72; 45.3

Reno, river flowing west of Bologna: 42.88

Rhine, River: 14.122; 15.25; 22.6; 27.101; 33.8; 42.45; 44.78

Rhodes: 17.66; 20.100

Rhône, river flowing through Arles: 2.64; 12.71; 20.106; 27.101; 28.91; 39.71

Rialto, at centre of Venice's island-complex, last refuge against attack: 33.17

Ricciarda, daughter of the Marquis of Saluzzo, married Niccolò III d'Este; her sons Ercole and Sigismondo were exiled to Naples, but on Borso d'Este's death she saw the legitimate line restored: 13.67

Richard, Earl of Warwick: 10.78; 16.67; 18.10

Richard, son of Aymon, a younger brother of Rinaldo: 30.94; 31.12; 38.8

Richardet, twin brother of Bradamant, and lover of Fiordispina: 22.38; 25.4; 25.8 rescued from pyre by Ruggiero and tells him of his romance with Fiordispina; 25.71 with Ruggiero and Aldiger sets out to rescue Maugis and Vivian; 26.3 the rescue of Maugis and Vivian; 26.55; 26.68, 77; 26.119 in scuffle with Mandricard and Rodomont; 27.2; 30.87; 30.94 joins Rinaldo to rescue Charlemagne; 31.7; 31.8 unhorsed by Guidone Selvaggio; 31.35; 31.55 in night attack on Saracen camp; 31.98; 38.8 welcomes Bradamant and Marfisa at Arles

Richmond, Earl of: 10.80

Rifean Hills, located in Arctic Scythia, possibly the Urals: 4.18

Rimedon, African King of the Gaetulians in place of Grifaldo: 14.23; 40.73

Rimini, on Adriatic, governed by the Malatestas, it surrendered to troops of French invader, Louis XII, rather than be sacked like Ravenna: 14.9; 43.147; 46.6

Rinaldo, son of Aymon and Beatrice, pillar of the house of Clairmont and, with his cousin Orlando, chief prop and paladin of Charlemagne; Orlando's rival in pursuit of Angelica: 1.8; 1.11 pursues Angelica, fights with Ferrau; 1.28; 1.77 his love of Angelica explained; 1.80–2.3 fights with Sacripant; 2.26 sent to Britain by Charlemagne; 4.51 in Scotland hears of a worthy enterprise; 5.4–6.16 hears Dalinda's story of Guinevere wronged and wreaks appropriate vengeance; 6.33, 41; 8.22 raises fresh troops in England; 10.74; 14.95; 16.28 launches his reinforcements against Moors besieging Paris; 18.40 harries Africans; 18.146 kills Dardinel; 19.19; 20.6; 25.76; 27.8 hunting for Angelica; 30.90 stops at Montauban to collect brothers for fresh assault on Saracens; 30.93 his wife is Clarice; 31.7 crosses swords with Guidone Selvaggio, who joins his party; 31.51 with his force, falls upon sleeping Saracen camp in night attack; **31.90** challenged by Gradasso for Bayard; **33.78** fight with Gradasso interrupted, but loses Bayard; **38.8** welcomes Bradamant and Marfisa at Arles; **38.54**; **38.65** appointed champion by Charlemagne for duel of champions; **39.1** his duel with Ruggiero interrupted; **40.61**; **42.28** put onto Angelica's tracks by Maugis, sets out in search of her, but encounters in the Ardennes cure him of her; **42.46** the monster is Jealousy; **42.67** reaching the Po on his way to join Orlando on Lipadusa, he receives hospitality from a rich but forlorn knight; **43.6** refuses to test wife's fidelity, and hears sad knight's tale; proceeding down the Po, hears boatman's tale of Argia and the magic dog; **43.145** travels on to Lipadusa in time only to re-embark with Orlando for Brandimart's burial in Sicily; **43.185** continues with companions to hermit's island; **44.6** befriends Ruggiero; **44.35** quarrels with his father over Bradamant's betrothal; **46.60** welcomes Ruggiero to court; **46.110**

Rinaldo d'Este, (1) supposedly originator of the Este emblem (azure, eagle argent), he helped Pope Alexander III in his war against Frederick Barbarossa, enforcing peace on the latter: **3.30**

Rinaldo d'Este, (2) son of Azzo Novello, Duke of Spoleto, held hostage at Naples by Frederick II in 1231 and poisoned by him: **3.38**

Roccaforte, Aymon's castle between Perpignan and Carcassone, impossible to locate: **44.72**

Rocca Silvana, where Brandimart met Fiordiligi when they were both in bondage to the count: **39.41**

Rodomont, African King of Sarthia and Algiers, a descendant of Nembrot and foremost champion of the Saracens: **14.25** at the muster of troops before Paris; **14.40** betrothed to Doralice; **14.65**; **14.108–15.9** storms the walls of Paris; **16.19** ravages the city single-handed; **17.6** takes his toll in Paris; **18.8** overwhelmed by Charlemagne's superior numbers and withdraws; **18.32** learns of Mandricard's seduction of Doralice and sets out in pursuit; **23.33** seizes Frontino as horse is being led to Ruggiero; **24.93**; **24.94–25.4** duel with Mandricard over Doralice; **26.55**; **26.67** at Merlin's fountain meets Marfisa and her friends, then Ruggiero, but refuses all challenges to battle; **25.131** lured away with Mandricard in pursuit of Doralice; **27.6** pursues Doralice to Agramant's camp and raises Charlemagne's blockade; **27.40** duel with Mandricard over Doralice forestalled by quarrel with Sacripant over steed Frontino; **27.107** spurned by Doralice, he leaves the Saracen camp for home, but stops in Provence; **28.3** hears misogynist tale; **28.85** in Provence meets and succumbs to Isabel; **29.1** eluded by Isabel whom he inadvertently kills; **29.39** thrown into river by Orlando; **31.45**; **31.66** defeats and captures Brandimart; **32.5** wooed vainly by Agramant; **35.40** unhorsed on bridge by Bradamant and forced to order release of prisoners, he vows to eschew arms for a year and more; **38.49, 56**; **39.4** Melissa borrows his features to induce Agramant to interrupt duel of champions; **46.101** killed by Ruggiero in a duel

Rodonna, a city of imprecise—and disputed—location, said to correspond to Ptolemy's Rhodumna, south of the Loire: **2.37**

Romagna: **3.53, 55** refers to Ravenna, *q.v.*; **33.38** the Pope here referred to is Julius II; **43.146** men of Romagna grieved over death of Vestidello and wounding of Alfonso d'Este at La Bastia

Rome (Romans): **3.27**; **14.65**; **17.78**; **19.48**; **26.32** court of; **33.55**; **36.71**

Ronco, river flowing near Ravenna, a city sacked by the French: **17.4**

Ross, duchy of Zerbin: 10.84

Rouen, near mouth of Seine: 22.10; 27.101 here stands for Channel coast

Rovigo, named after the rose (the Greek *rhodos*), an Este domain: 3.41

Rubicon, boundary-stream between Rome and Cisalpine Gaul near Rimini, to cross which was to open hostilities with Rome; Julius Caesar returning from conquest of Gaul crossed it in his bid for supreme power: 46.6

Ruggiero, (1) descendant of Trojan Astyanax, ruler of Calabria: 36.72

Ruggiero, (2) of Reggio, father of the hero Ruggiero and of Marfisa, and vassal of Charlemagne, he was betrayed by his brother Bertram and murdered by Almont and Trojan, his wife's brothers: 2.32; 36.60, 72; 38.14; 44.30

Ruggiero, (3) descendant of Hector of Troy, ancestor of the House of Este, son of Ruggiero II of Reggio; a Saracen champion, he is in love with the Christian heroine Bradamant: 1.4; 2.32; 2.45 fights Atlas, his guardian whom he resents; 4.40 rescued from Atlas' castle by Bradamant only to be abducted on the hippogryph; 6.16–8.21 his enslavement by Alcina and rescue by Melissa; 10.35 evading Alcina's pursuit, reaches Logistilla's domain and she sends him back to Europe on the hippogryph; 10.74 witnesses review of British troops; 10.92–11.15 rescues Angelica from the orc but she finds cause to elude him; 11.16 lured into Atlas' enchanted palace by 'Bradamant'; 12.17 seeks for Bradamant in the palace; 13.75 Atlas borrows his shape to lure Bradamant into his palace; 22.20 released by Astolfo; 22.31 reunited with Bradamant, he sets out on an errand of mercy only to have to fight Pinabello's four champions first; 23.5 Bradamant grieves at being parted from him; 23.35 his steed Frontino stolen by Rodomont; 24.55; 25.4 rescues Richardet from the pyre and hears of his romance with Fiordispina; 25.71 with Richardet and Aldiger sets out to rescue Maugis and Vivian, having first written letter for Bradamant; 26.2 helps rout Maganzas and Saracens about to barter the lives of Maugis and Vivian; 26.55; 26.62 leaves with Hippalca to find Rodomont and steed Frontino; 26.88 fights Rodomont for Frontino and Mandricard for the eagle-emblem; 26.137 leaves for Agramant's camp with Marfisa; 27.15 to Agramant's rescue; 27.40 draws lot to fight Mandricard over eagle-emblem once Mandricard has fought Rodomont; 27.112 lets Rodomont leave on Frontino; 29.73 cursed by Ariosto for giving magic ring to Angelica; 30.18 kills Mandricard in duel over eagle-emblem, but is gravely wounded; 30.73 Agramant has him tended; 31.88 carried to Arles in Agramant's retreat; 32.10 a false report to Bradamant makes her jealous of him on account of Marfisa; 35.63 from Fiordiligi receives Bradamant's challenge and the return of Frontino; 36.11 avoids fighting Bradamant in the mêlée outside Arles; 36.50 fights Marfisa; 36.59 learns from Atlas of his kinship with Marfisa and is reconciled with Bradamant; 37.24 with Bradamant and Marfisa overthrows misogynist Marganor; 38.5 returns to his sovereign Agramant at Arles; 38.61 proposed by Sobrino as Saracen champion in duel of champions; 39.1 his duel with Rinaldo interrupted; 40.61–41.7 attempting to rejoin Agramant in Africa, fights duel with Dudone and obtains release of his prisoner-kings; 41.8 sails for Africa but is shipwrecked on desert island; 41.27; 41.47 baptized by hermit; 43.194 joined here by Orlando and his companions; 44.6 befriended by Rinaldo and urged by hermit to marry Bradamant; 44.76 thwarted by rival suitor Leo, sets out for Greece to kill him, and at Belgrade helps Bulgars defeat his army; 45.5 captured, imprisoned by Leo's aunt, rescued by Leo; 45.56

undertakes to fight Bradamant to win her for Leo; 45.84 this deed accomplished, he rides away, death in his heart; 46.21 reconciled to life by Melissa and Leo, who withdraws his claim to Bradamant, he returns to Charlemagne's court; 46.73 his wedding to Bradamant; 46.101 kills Rodomont in a duel

Ruggiero, (4) son of Ruggiero and Bradamant, avenger of his father's death; Charlemagne will make him first Marquis of Este: 3.24; 41.64

Rumour: 14.95; 18.96; 22.93; 32.32; 38.41

Sacripant, Saracen champion, King of Circassia, in love with Angelica: 1.38 vouchsafed sight of his beloved; 1.60 overthrown by Bradamant; 1.80–2.3 fights with Rinaldo; 2.62; 4.40 freed from Atlas' castle by Bradamant; 8.63; 12.11 imprisoned in Atlas' enchanted palace; 12.24; 12.28 released by Angelica, who at once eludes him; 19.18, 31; 27.7; 27.14 to Agramant's rescue; 27.49; 27.69 quarrels with Rodomont over steed Frontino, previously his own as Frontalact; 27.113 leaves camp in pursuit of Rodomont; 30.40; 35.54 prisoner of Rodomont

Sadoleto, Giacomo, from Modena, man of letters and Cardinal: 42.86

Saffet, Levantine sea-port: 18.74

Safi, Moroccan sea-port: 18.46

Sagittarius, sign of Zodiac for November/December: 14.26

Saguntum, Spanish town ruled by Archidant: 14.16

Saint Andrews, in Eastern Scotland, seat of Scottish king: 5.76

Saint Malo, deemed to be located where in fact Avranches is: 9.15

Salintern, Norandin's champion at the tournament of Damascus: 17.97

Salisbury, fief of Henry: 10.82

Salviati, Giovanni, Cardinal, nephew of Leo X and Bishop of Ferrara: 26.49

Samos, Greek island famous for its pottery: 40.1

Samson, champion of the Hebrews, who slaughtered the Philistines using the jawbone of an ass: 14.45; 34.63

Samsonet, son of King of Persia, converted to Christianity by Orlando when he followed him to France; now Charlemagne's Regent in Jerusalem: 15.95 welcomes Astolfo, Grifon and Aquilant; 18.96 to Damascus with Astolfo and Marfisa, then sails for West but runs into storm; 19.43 driven ashore in land of killer-women, Alexandretta; 20.69 escapes with his friends; 20.102 captured by Pinabello and made to serve as his champion for a year and a month; 22.48; 22.64 jousts with Ruggiero and is unhorsed; 31.41; 31.51 recruited to Rinaldo's relief force; 35.53 prisoner of Rodomont, shipped off to Algiers; 38.21 but welcomes Marfisa to Charlemagne's camp (Ariosto's lapse); 38.58; 39.30 freed by Astolfo; 39.47 helps Astolfo restore Orlando's wits; 40.10 storms Bizerta from the sea; 41.34; 43.154 learns of Brandimart's death

Sanga, Giovan Battista, Roman Latin poet, secretary to Clement VII: 46.12

San Giorgio, village outside Ferrara, formerly an island between two branches of the Po: 43.63

Sannazaro, Jacopo, eminent Neapolitan poet at court of Frederick of Aragon, he wrote *Arcadia*: 46.17

Santa Marta, west of Bayona on the Galician coast: 13.11

Santerno, river flowing past Imola to join the Reno near La Bastia: 3.53; 43.145

Saône, river joining the Rhône at Lyons: 20.106; 27.101, 127; 28.87; 44.28

Sappho, Lesbian poetess, fourth-century B.C.: 20.1

Saracens, North African Muslim invaders of France: 7.34; 13.10, 81; 14.1; 18.146; 24.110; 25.5; 27.18; 31.52; 39.82

Saragossa, capital of Spanish King Marsilius: 14.15; 25.49

Sardinia: 39.28; 44.24

Sarmatia, Asian to the east of the Caspian, European to the west: 10.71

Sarthia, unidentified African region adjacent to Algiers, ruled by Rodomont: 14.25, 40

Sasso, Panfilo, of Modena, wrote verse in Italian and Latin: 46.12

Satallone, a Parisian: 14.125

Sataly, or Antalya, on Turkish coast facing Cyprus: 17.65; 19.46

Saul of Tarsus, converted by Christ on road to Damascus and known thereafter as Paul the Apostle: 41.53

Sava, river flowing into the Danube by Belgrade: 44.79; 45.11

Saxony, ducal house passed by marriage to Folco d'Este: 3.28; 13.73

Scheldt, troops from, who fought at Ravenna: 14.3

Scipio, Roman general who defeated Hannibal: 7.59

Scotland (Scots): 4.51; 8.22; 10.16, 83; 11.79; 16.28, 40, 79; 19.8; 38.59

Scythia, region north of the Black Sea, subject to Agrican, King of Tartary: 8.62; 10.71; 15.12

Seine, Paris's river: 14.104, 108; 16.29; 18.21, 159; 27.32, 114; 31.37

Seleucia in Syria, whose lord fights in Norandin's tournament: 17.87, 100

Semele, twin of Apollo: 33.29

Semiramis, legendary Queen of Assyria and Babylon, victorious in war: 25.36; 37.5

Senapo, legendary Emperor of Nubia (or Ethiopia), a Christian, also known as Prester John; Astolfo's ally against Agramant: 33.102; 38.24; 40.16; 44.21

Septimius Severus, Roman Emperor: 15.26

Sericana, Gradasso's Chinese kingdom: 1.55; 10.71; 31.101; 33.95; 40.46; 42.67

Sermide, on right bank of Po, east of Ostiglia: 43.53

Serpentine de la Stella, commander of the Galicians: 14.13, 107; 16.82; 18.42; 27.80; 35.66

Servius Tullius, son of a slave-woman, he became King of Rome: 45.2

Severo, Don, a learned monk from Firenzuola in Lombardy, he frequented the court of Rome until the conspiracy against Leo X: 46.13

Seville: 14.12; 27.51; 33.97

Sforza, ducal family which ruled Milan: 13.63 and see Lodovico il Moro; 33.41 seedling is Francesco Sforza

Sforza, Francesco, son of Lodovico il Moro: 26.51; 33.36 betrayed to Louis XII; 33.41 restored to Milan by Swiss mercenaries; 33.44 makes pact with Francis I of France; 33.45 takes after homonymous grandfather

Sforza, Ippolita, Milanese, wife of Alessandro Bentivoglio of Ferrara, friend of Bandello the *novelliere*: 46.4

Shrewsbury, fief of Edward: 10.82

Sicily: 13.73 the King of Sicily is Charles II, whose daughter Beatrice married Azzo VIII; 20.100

Sidon, Baron of, in Norandin's tournament: 17.93

Sigbert, Frankish king; in fact none of the three Sigberts reigned at time of Maurice or Autharis, or crossed into Italy: 33.13

Sigismondi, the two: brother and son respectively to Ercole I d'Este: 3.58

Silence, fetched by Michael to cloak arrival of English reinforcements: 14.76, 94; 16.42

Silenus, father of the satyrs, he brought up Bacchus; once found in drunken sleep in cave by shepherds who tied him up and dyed his face with blackberry: 39.60

Sinagon, King of Calatrava, killed by Oliver: 14.14

Sinai, Mount, in Arabia, shrine of Saint Catherine of Alexandria: 19.48

Sinibaldo, see Fieschi

Sinon, Greek who misled the Trojans into accepting the wooden horse and thus opening their gates to be conquered: 46.82

Slavonian sea, the Adriatic: 4.11; 36.8 Slavonians in Venetian service

Sobrino, African King of Garbo, Agramant's trustiest and wisest counsellor: 14.24 leads his troops at muster before Paris; 14.66, 108; 16.41 at battle of Paris; 18.40; 18.159 feats outside Paris; 27.96 prevents Agramant challenging Marfisa; 30.27; 31.82 urges Agramant to withdraw to Arles; 38.48 advises duel of champions to settle war with Charlemagne; 39.3; 39.16 withdraws into Arles; 40.9 escapes from shattered fleet with Agramant; 40.36 advises him against suicide, then joins him and Gradasso in challenge to Orlando; 41.68–42.19 the battle at Lipadusa, where he is wounded; 43.193 brought to island-hermit by Orlando, is healed and baptized; 44.26; 46.60 welcomes Ruggiero at Charlemagne's court

Solomon, King of Brittany, a paladin: 15.8; 18.10, 155; 38.80

Somerset, duchy of Harriman: 10.81

Sophrosina, symbol of Temperance, lady attendant on Logistilla: 10.52; 15.11

Sora, Sigismondo, Duke of, bereaved father of Ercole Cantelmo: 36.7

Soridan, African King of Hesperia: 14.22, 113; 16.75, 81

Spain (Spaniards), realm of the Saracen King Marsilius—and, more recently, of Ferdinand and of Charles V: 1.6; 3.54; 9.2, 6; 10.70; 12.61; 13.82; 14.1, 106; 16.41; 17.74; 26.45; 29.57; 32.3; 46.136

Sparta, whose queen, Helen, Paris abducted when he was visiting King Menelaus: 11.70

Spineloccio the Norman: 14.123

Stellata, on right bank of Po above Ferrara: 43.53

Stephen III, Pope, helped against Lombards by Pepin the Frank: 33.16

Stordilan, King of Granada, father of Doralice: 14.13, 40; 18.157; 24.110; 27.5, 50, 102: 30.31

Strafford, Duke of: 10.86

Strigonia, Hungarian archbishopric conferred on Hippolytus of Este, aged seven, by his uncle Corvino: 46.88

Strozzi, Ercole, Ferrarese poet and playwright, son of Tito Vespasiano, friend of Ariosto: 37.8; 42.83

Strozzi, Tito Vespasiano, Ferrarese poet at court of Ercole I d'Este and of Alfonso, friend of Boiardo and Ariosto; wrote in Latin: 37.8

Styx (Stygian), one of the rivers of Hades in classical mythology; the gods swore their binding oaths by its waters: 2.42; 23.73; 29.28; 31.79; 37.19; 45.17; 46.9

Suffolk, Duke of: 10.79

Sulla, Roman dictator: 3.33; 17.1

Sweden, and king of: 10.88; 32.54; 32.76 its king a suitor for Queen of Iceland's hand; 33.66; 37.112

Swiss, mercenaries in the wars fought in Italy: 17.74; 26.45 their defeat at Melegnano (1515); 27.19; 33.36 Swiss mercenaries of Francesco Sforza betray him to Louis XII; 33.42 Swiss fight against and defeat French at Novara; 33.43 defeat by Francis I at Melegnano; 33.49 defeat at La Bicocca

Sylvester I, Pope, recipient of Donation of Constantine: 34.80

Syria: 16.5; 17.23; 18.96; 19.54

Syrian Sorceress from whom Mandricard wrested Hector's arms and freed Gradasso, Sacripant, Isoliero, Grifon and Aquilant: 14.31

Syrtes, African coast near Tripoli: 36.61

Tagus, Portuguese river, figuratively as western limit of the world: 3.17

Tamar, daughter of King David, violated by her brother Amnon, avenged by her brother Absalon: 34.14

Tanacre, son of Marganor, killed by his reluctant bride: 37.46

Tanaro, flows past Alessandria into Po: 33.22

Tancredi, Angelo, professor at University of Padua: 46.18

Tanfirion, formerly African King of the Almansillans: 14.23

Tangiers, ruled by Brunello the thief: 14.19; 27.87

Tardocco, deceased King of Djerba: 14.22; 18.46

Taro, tributary of the Po, site of Battle of Fornovo won by Charles VIII of France: 13.60; 17.4

Tarquin, last King of Rome, evicted after a son of his caused the suicide of Lucretia: 29.28

Tarragona, Catalogna in Eastern Spain: 29.57; 33.97

Tartary, land to west of Cathay; 'the Tartar' is normally Mandricard, King of Tartary: 1.5; 14.30

Tartus, Levantine sea-port north of Tripoli: 18.74

Tasso, Bernardo, poet from Bergamo, he was secretary to Renata d'Este and later at court of Cardinal Luigi d'Este; Torquato Tasso, poet of *Jerusalem Delivered*, was his son: 46.15

Tealdo, immediately west of Ferrara, on left bank of Po, where two forts were built by the Estes: 43.54

Tears, Isle of, Ebuda, *q.v.*: 10.93

Tebaldeo, Antonio, Ferrarese poet, tutor of Isabel of Este, secretary to Lucretia Borgia: 42.83

Teocreno, Benedetto Tagliacarne, known as, from Sarzana, near La Spezia, tutor to the Fregosos of Genoa, later to sons of Francis I of France: 46.14

Tesira, King of Portugal: 14.13; 18.157

Thames, River: 8.26; 10.73; 22.8

Thebes, Greek city founded by Cadmus, son of Agenor, with aid of companions born of dragon's teeth; city renowned for cruelty on account of Creon and the Oedipus story: 5.5; 17.2; 33.29; 43.11

Theodora, aunt of Leo, Ruggiero's captor: 45.15

Thermodont, River, flows through land of the Amazons and into Black Sea: 27.52

Theseus, King of Athens, condemned to hell for having deserted Ariadne, his helper against the Minotaur: 34.14

Thessaly, northern Greece, where Caesar fought Pompey at Pharsalus, then Antony and Octavius fought Brutus and Cassius at Philippi—though the Roman eagles were gilt, not argent: 30.48

Thomas the Apostle, land of; Malabar coast, round Madras, but here is confused with another Malabar, on Cambodian peninsula: 15.16

Thrace, north-eastern Greece: 22.6; 46.77

Thule, legendary island of Northern Seas: 10.88

Tiber, River: 14.38; 29.33

Tiberius, (1) Roman emperor of evil repute, who spent his declining years on Capri: 17.1; 43.58; 46.83

Tiberius, (2) sixth-century Roman Emperor of Constantinople, who amassed enormous wealth from his conquests: 43.75

Ticino, River, tributary of the Po: 33.45 refers to French defeat at Pavia, on the Ticino: 37.92

Tidaeus, outlaw who joined Polynices in war against his brother Eteocles, King of Thebes; here refers to Azzo d'Este who tried to oust Niccolò III (*q.v.*): 3.41

Tiepoli, Niccolò, Venetian nobleman, elegant Latin poet, awarded doctorate by Julius II in person for his skill in debate: 46.16

Tieste, Tantalus, and Atreus; Atreus killed Tantalus, son of his brother Tieste and served the boy up to his father; another son of Tieste killed Atreus; the same son killed Agamemnon, Atreus' son: 36.8

Timagoras, fifth-century B.C. painter from Chalcidia: 33.1

Timantes, ancient Greek painter from Sikion, contemporary of Parrhasius and Zeuxis: 33.1

Tiphys, helmsman of the *Argo*, ship of the Argonauts: 13.61; 15.21

Tirse and Corimbo of Apamea, in Phrygia, at Norandin's tournament: 17.96

Titans, race of giants who made unsuccessful assault on Jupiter's throne: 3.3

Tithonus, spouse of goddess Aurora, by marrying whom he obtained immortality but not eternal youth: 8.86; 11.32; 18.103; 32.13; 34.61; 38.76; 40.14

Titian Vecellio, from Pieve di Cadore, praised by Ariosto among the greatest contemporary painters; he painted a portrait of Ariosto reproduced in the 1532 edition of *Orlando Furioso*: 33.2

Tityrus, shepherd in love with Amaryllis: 11.12

Tobias, Israelite cured of blindness by his son under guidance of archangel Raphael: 42.66

Toledo, capital of New Castille: 14.14

Tolmeta, ancient Ptolemais in Cyrenaica: 18.165; 33.99

Tolomei, Claudio, Sienese poet and philologist: 46.12

Tomiris, Queen of the Massagetes who killed Cyrus the Great, the Persian king, in a revenge expedition: 37.5

Torelli, princely family of Bologna: 46.7

Trajan, Roman emperor: 15.26; 15.40 Trajan's canal, connecting the Gulf of Suez with the Nile delta

Trapani, western Sicily: 43.149

Trasimene, Lake, where Hannibal defeated a Roman army: 17.4; 26.47

Trason, Duke of Moray: 10.85; 16.55, 64

Trebbia, River, where Hannibal defeated a Roman army: 17.4; 26.47

Tremisen, Algerian kingdom of Alzirdo: 12.69; 14.28; 23.73

Tremisen, Muslim city on left bank of middle Nile, bordering Christian Nubia: 33.101

Tripoli, North Africa: 9.5; 33.99

Tripoli, Syria: 18.134; 19.46

Trissino, Gian Giorgio, from Vicenza, erudite poet and playwright: 46.12

Tristan, the legendary knight, lover of Isolde: 4.52; 32.65 the castle named after him; 32.84 his quarrel with Clodion

Tritons, mounts ridden by the sea-sprites, they are half-man, half-fish and they blow on conch-shells: 11.45

Trivigant, idol worshipped by the Infidels: 12.59; 38.18

Trivulzio, Domitilla, highly cultivated Milanese lady, wife of Count Francesco Torello: 46.4

Trivulzio, Gian Giacomo, Milanese commander appointed Marshal by Louis XII of France; while French governor of Milan in 1500 he had had to flee and make way for Lodovico Sforza, having roused the hostility of the citizens by his exactions—a lesson the French ought to have taken to heart: 14.9

Trivulzio, Renato, Milanese poet: 37.12

Trojan, father of Agramant; with his father Agolant and his brother Almont he killed Ruggiero's father; he himself was slain by Orlando in Provence: 1.1; 12.31; 17.14; 30.83; 36.60, 72

Tronto, River, delimits southern boundary of March of Ancona: 3.37

Trotto, Alfonsin, bailiff to Alfonso d'Este: 40.4

Troy (Trojans), ancestral birthplace of the House of Este and city of Hector: 3.17; 5.18; 14.31; 20.10; 26.81, 99; 35.27

Truffaldin, King of Baghdad, who betrayed the fortress of Albracca to Agrican; Grifon and Aquilant were forced to champion him against Rinaldo but Rinaldo finally killed him: 31.40

Turca, Barbara, probably from the illustrious Turchi family of Ferrara: 46.5

Turkey (Turks), a threat to sixteenth-century Christendom in Greece, Italy and Hungary: 17.6, 66, 75; 40.39; 46.88

Turnus, King of Latium who resisted Aeneas: 37.5

Turpin, legendary Archbishop of Rheims, said to have accompanied Charlemagne in his march on Spain and died at Roncesvalles; a *Life of Charlemagne* is ascribed to him, and Ariosto, like Boiardo before him, hides behind his authority whenever he doubts his own facts: 13.40; 18.10, 155, 175; 23.38, 62; 24.44; 26.23; 28.2; 29.56; 30.49; 31.79; 33.85; 34.86; 38.10, 23; 40.81; 44.23

Tuscan sea, the Tyrrhenian: 4.11

Tyndarean swan-god, Jupiter; Leda, wife of Tyndareus, bore one son, Pollux, by Jupiter who had assumed the form of a swan; by her husband she bore another son, Castor; thus one half-brother was an immortal, the other a mortal, but they preferred to take turns in Olympus and Hades; here refers to mutual love of Alfonso and Hippolytus of Este: 3.50

Typheus, giant whose feet consisted of serpents, and who led assault against Jupiter; the mountain which crushes him is island of Ischia in Bay of Naples: 16.23; 26.52 Ischia in the emblem of the d'Avalos; 33.24

Tyre, Levantine sea-port: 18.74

Uberto d'Este, grandson of Ruggiero and Bradamant, probably legendary: 3.25

Ullania, ambassadress from Queen of Iceland, accompanied by three Scandinavian kings bringing golden shield to Charlemagne: 32.50, 78; 33.66; 37.28, 121

Ulpian, Domitius, Roman legal expert, counsellor to Emperor Septimius Severus: 43.72

Ulysses, hero of *Odyssey*, who was long away from his wife Penelope, first at the Trojan war, then on his voyage home to Ithaca: 13.60; 33.28; 36.70 Astyanax smuggled out of Troy in spite of him

Umbria: 3.32, 35; 43.149

Ungiardo, governor of Novengrad for Emperor Constantine: 44.102; 45.7

Urbino, Central Italy, seat of the Della Roveres: 26.49 refers to Francesco Maria della Rovere: 43.148

Valencia, Southern Spain, here a byword for effeminacy: 7.55; 19.41; 39.74

Valerio, Gian Francesco, Venetian priest, friend of Ariosto, purveyor of the misogynist tale told to Rodomont: 27.137; 28.78; 46.16

Vallombrosa, French monastery invented by Ariosto: 22.36; 23.17; 25.84

Var, river flowing into Mediterranean east of the Rhône: 2.64

Vasto, Marquis Alfonso del, *see* Avalos, d'

Vasto, Marquis Inico del, *see* Avalos, d'

Vatran, King of the Bulgars: 44.83

Venice (Venetians): 3.46, 52; 33.31, 38; 36.3; 46.97 refers to their defeat at La Polesella

Ventidius, brought to Rome as a prisoner, he later became a senator and friend of Caesar: 45.2

Venus, Latin goddess of Beauty and Love: 1.52; 11.70; 15.56; 18.136; 35.21; 37.17; 42.93; 43.58; 46.85

Verità, Girolamo, Veronese friend of Ariosto, unidentified: 46.14

Verona: 3.31; 42.69

Vestidello Pagano, commander of garrison at Este fort of La Bastia, surrendered after valiant defence and was murdered by the Spaniards: 3.54; 42.5

Vesuvius, Mount: 5.18

Vida, Girolamo, from Cremona, Bishop of Vercelli, poet, close friend of Ariosto: 46.13

Vienne, in Burgundy, fief of Oliver: 27.32; 28.91

Virgil, Latin poet, born in Mantua, whose *Aeneid* celebrated Emperor Augustus' antecedents, just as Ariosto celebrated those of the Estes: 3.56; 35.26, 28; 42.86

Visconti, ducal family that ruled Milan; it had close ties with the Estes: 13.63; 33.21 specifically Gian Galeazzo

Viso, Mount, in Piedmontese Alps, source of the Po: 37.92

Vivian, son of Buovo, brother of Maugis, cousin of Rinaldo; with Maugis he is prisoner of Ferrau about to be bartered to traditional enemy, the Maganzas, but rescued by Ruggiero and others: 25.4, 72, 96; 26.3, 54, 68, 73, 119; 30.87, 94; 31.12, 35, 51; 38.21

Volana, in the Po delta, where fish is plentiful: 9.65

Vulcan, Latin god of Fire, blacksmith of the gods, his furnace was in Mount Etna, where he forged Jove's thunderbolts and made Hector's arms: 2.8; 3.51; 11.75; 12.2; 15.56; 26.100; 37.27; 40.44; 41.88; 45.73

Wales, Prince of, regent in the English king's absence: 8.27

Walter, a Parisian: 14.125

Warwick, fief of Richard: 10.78

William of Burnich, killed by Dardinel: 18.52

Wise Men, or **Magi** (*q.v.*), who came from the East to worship the Infant Jesus, and avoided Herod on their return journey so as not to betray the child's location: 10.69

Wood, Claude, killed by Dardinel: 18.47

Worcester, Earl of: 10.81

Wrath, rescues Rinaldo from Jealousy: 42.53, 64

Xanthus or **Scamander**, river flowing across plain of Troy: 41.63

Xenocrates, disciple of Plato, noted for his austerity: 11.2

Xerxes, King of Persia who led an army and fleet to invade Greece: 20.73

York, Fieramont, Duke of: 10.78; 16.67

Zamora, unidentified Barbary town: 18.46

Zamora, in Spanish Leon: 14.14

Zanniolo, stream which, with the Po and the Santerno, delimits the battleground of Alfonso d'Este against the Germans and Spaniards: 3.53

Zeeland, a Danish island whose duke is Bireno: 9.23, 61, 82, 87; 10.15; 11.79

Zeeland, islands off south Holland coast: 9.59

Zenobia, third-century A.D. Queen of Palmyra, revolted against the Romans and set up empire including Egypt and Asia Minor, but was conquered by Emperor Aurelian: 37.5

Zephyr: the mild West Wind: 11.82

Zerbin, a Christian knight, son of King of Scotland, brother of Guinevere, lover of Isabel; Ariosto's invention: 5.69 unable to rescue his sister; 8.24; 10.83 leads Scottish troops relieving siege of Paris; 13.6 Isabel tells of his attempts to fetch her back to Scotland; 13.44; 14.64; 16.40 at the relief of Paris; 18.40; 18.155 feats outside Paris; 18.188–19.16 corners Cloridan and Medor, leaving the former dead; 20.117 unhorsed by Marfisa who makes him Gabrina's escort; 21.3 wounds Hermonides who tells him story of

Gabrina's wickedness; **22**.3 finds Pinabello's corpse; **23**.39 arrested by
Pinabello's father, at Gabrina's instigation, and led to his execution; **23**.53
rescued by Orlando who reunites him with Isabel; **24**.15 metes out justice
to Odoric and to Gabrina; **24**.46 gathers up Orlando's arms, fights Mandricard who claims the sword Durindana, and is killed; **26**.8; **29**.11

Zerbinato, Francesco, courtier of Hippolytus, friend of Ariosto: **40**.4

Zeuxis, great Greek painter, fourth-century B.C.: **11**.71; **28**.4; **33**.1

Ziliant, son of King Monodant and brother of Brandimart, was freed by
Orlando from the sorceress Morgana who was enamoured of him: **19**.38;
39.62

Zoroaster, first of the sorcerers: **31**.5